Academic Libraries: Achieving Excellence

in Higher Education

Proceedings of the Sixth National Conference of the
Association of College and Research Libraries
Salt Lake City, Utah April 12-14, 1992

Edited by

Thomas Kirk, Director
Hutchins Library
Berea College
Berea, Kentucky

Copy Preparation by

Donna Lakes
Hutchins Library
Berea College
Berea, Kentucky

Association of College and Research Libraries
A Division of the American Library Association
Chicago, 1992

Published by the Association of College and Research Libraries, a division of the American Library Association, 50 East Huron Street, Chicago, IL 60611-2795

ISBN: 0-8389-7622-0

This publication is printed on acid-free paper.

Printed in the United States of America.

Contents

Theme papers

Contributed Papers

I. Academic Librarianship

V. General Administration

VI. Readers Services

VII. Technology

Program Sessions

VIII. Administration

IX. Bibliographic Instruction

X.   Buildings

Introduction

I am pleased to present to you the *Proceedings* of ACRL's Sixth National Conference, "Academic Libraries Achieving Excellence in Higher Education," held in Salt Lake City . I am pleased because there are a couple of firsts included in this volumes. One first is the inclusion of the theme addresses. Thanks to the graciousness of Catherine Stimpson, Julian Bond, Paul Saffo and David Penniman we were able to obtain copies of their papers and to present them to you. As I edited these papers a number of weeks after the conference it was exciting to sense again the vibrance of their messages and clarity of their well chosen words. In addition to providing a record of those stimulating talks, the printed text gives us the benefit of their scholarship. Where appropriate references to the literature which shaped the ideas presented at the conference are included in these proceedings.

The second 'first' is a fuller reporting of the 'program' sessions. Thanks to the efforts of those responsible for the program sessions these proceedings include summaries of the programs or texts of the brief talks given by panel members. More is said about the program sessions at the beginning of that section of the *Proceedings*. I am delighted we could include these in a fuller report of the Sixth National Conference.

The program content of this conference and the preparation of these proceedings could not have happened without the many hours devoted to writing, editing, reviewing and finally preparing this final copy. Stella Bentley, of the University of California, Santa Barbara coordinated the solicitation and review of the contributed papers. Thanks to her for the very smooth flow of the papers and related written communications. To the reviewers of the contributed papers thanks. Without their help the refereeing process that has become an important element of the national conferences would not be possible. Mary Ellen Elsbernd, Northern Kentucky University, and her committee did the same for the program sessions and presented the conference attendees with the largest set of program sessions at an ACRL National Conference. Sherrie S. Bergman, Wheaton College, Massachusetts, and Clarence E. Chisholm, Pennsylvania State University, along with the Executive Committee selected the theme speakers and Sherrie and Clarence handled the details of the speakers' participation.

Thanks are due to the contributors for their remarkable consistency in meeting deadlines and following through on endnote corrections, rephrasing of text and correcting all the other little glitches which develop in the preparation of a document like these proceedings.

The person most responsible for the delivery to you of this physical volume is Donna Lakes, computer operator *par excellence*. I have puzzled over the years at the lack of an adequate title to describe a person with Donna's talents. Much more than just the operator of a microcomputer, Donna's role was to oversee the conversion of files from a number of formats and word processing programs into one program, make all of the editorial corrections which this fussy editor required, and then prepare the final format by fully exercising the muscle of a page layout program. * I still do not have a title for Donna's work but I know it is quality work. To Donna thanks for an extraordinary accomplishment.

To the staff of ACRL, particularly Cathleen Bourdon, thanks for all the behind the scenes work needed to carry on such a conference. I congratulate you on a terrific job.

Finally a thanks to Berea College and my family for giving me the time needed to edit the manuscripts. I appreciate their patience when my editing work took me away from the other things I was supposed to be doing.

I have taken certain liberties with the authors' text in order to better ensure clarity as well as consistency in the presentation of the *Proceedings*. Because of the tight time frame, authors have not seen the revised manuscripts. I trust they will be pleased with my work and that I have not done any serious injustice to their text.

I have enjoyed this project and hope that conference attendees will find this a fitting published record of the 1992 ACRL National Conference. For readers who could not attend I hope the *Proceedings* are a useful record of the ideas discussed at the conference.

Thomas G. Kirk,
Berea College
Berea, Kentucky

July 10, 1992

*The camera ready copy was prepared on a Macintosh using Microsoft's Word 3.01 and PageMaker version 4.0.

Reviewers of Contributed Papers

Mignon Adams
Ellen Altman
Donna Arrowood
Martha Bailey
Barry Baker
Betsy Baker
Lizabeth Bishoff
Martha Bowman
Jennie Boyarski
Patricia Breivik
Sharon Bullard
Charles Bunge
Micholas Burkel
Dwight Burlingame
Janice Burrows
Susan Cady
Jennifer Cargill
Allen Cohen
James Comes
Barbara Dewey

Connie Dowell
Carolyn Dusenbury
Evan Farber
Karen Feeney
Janice Fennell
Barbara Ford
Beverlee French
Mary George
Joan Giesecke
William Gosling
Gary Handman
W. Lee Hisle
Irene Hoadley
Bill Hubbard
Phyllis Hughes
Cecily Johns
Michael Kathman
Lyn Korenic
Susan Kroll
Mary Larsgaard

Gary Lawrence
Beverly Lynch
Mary Jo Lynch
Nancy Magnuson
Leslie Manning
Deanna Marcum
Charles Martell
Eleanor Mathews
Charles McClure
Gary Menges
Tamara Miller
William Miler
Gerald Munoff
Brian O'Connor
Maureen Pastine
Ling-Yuh Pattie
Gary Peete
Sara Penhale
Ruth Person
Linda Piele

Maxine Reneker
James Rettig
Anne RImmer
Iene Rockman
Ralph Russell
Michael Ryan
Jordan Scepanski
Jasper Schad
Judith Serebnick
Pamela Snelson
Helen Spalding
Virginia Steel
Carla Stoffle
Katina Strauch
Roberto Trujillo
David Walch
Patrick Wilkinson
Paul Willis
Betsy Wilson
Barbara Wittkopf

Moderators

Mignon Adams
Martha Bailey
Detrice Bankhead
Stella Bentley
Joseph A. Boisse
Sharon Bullard
Nicholas Burckel
Sandy Dolnick
Carolyn Dusenbury
Janice Fennell
Stephen Foote
Mary George
Patricia M. Kelley

Richard Meyer
Gerald Munoff
Diane Parker
Maureen Pastine
Linda Piele
Michael Ryan
Jordon Scepanski
Jasper Schad
R.N. Sharma
Helen Spalding
Carla Stoffle
John Tyson
Charles Willett

National Conference Execective Committee

Joseph A. Boisse, Conference Chair
Stella Bentley, Contributed Papers Co-Chair
Thomas Kirk, Contributed Papers Co-Chair
Sherrie S. Bergman, Speakers Co-Chair
Clarence E. Chisholm, Speakers Co-Chair
Mary Ellen Elsbernd, Program Chair
Roger K. Hanson, Local Arrangements Chair
Jean E. DeLauche, Poster Session Co-Chair
Mara Pinckard, Poster Sessions Cso-Chair
Cathleen Bourdon, Conference Manager
Sandy Donnelly, Exhibits Manager

ACRL Board of Directors
1991–1992

Anne K. Beaubien
Jacquelyn M. McCoy
Barbara J. Ford
Karin E. Begg
Eileen Dubin
Evan Ira Farber
Ray E. Metz
Linda L. Phillips
Shelley E. Phipps
Barbara J. Wittkopf
Rochelle Sager
Leslie A. Manning
Althea H. Jenkins

THEME
PAPERS

Civil Rights, Then and Now

Julian Bond
Washington, D. C.

It is a great pleasure to be here.

I am the son of a college president and a university librarian. My mother is a reference librarian at the Clark/Atlanta University Library serving the Atlanta University Center Complex.

Although their children started their school lives in segregated, country schools, they tried to insure that we got the best education we possibly could.

Thus long before I heard the word diversity or multiculturism applied to education or the workplace, I knew a black man invented the machine that made the shoe industry possible and another had designed the city of Washington, another had invented the traffic light and another had discovered blood plasma. Long before I ever dreamed the nation would celebrate a black man's birthday—indeed long before I had heard of or even met that man before he became my teacher— my teachers in rural one-room schools with outhouses made sure I knew who I was and where I came from and what contribution my people had made.

We also learned how to think.

We didn't learn that Columbus had discovered America, but that Columbus discovered America *for Europe;* those who met him didn't need discovering; they already knew they were here.

We knew the textbooks which described the Civil War as "a war of Northern aggression" or said the war was fought over states' rights were just plain wrong. The war was fought over whether our great-grandfathers and mothers would be someone else's property. And when years later, we were told that the war in Vietnam was "a war of Northern aggression", we knew we had heard that phrase somewhere before.

We've come a long way since I was a schoolboy. Our common national understanding of our past and present is generally greater now than it was then, even if all the details aren't crystal clear. And our under- standing of history is clearer, even though we still argue over what that history means.

One part of the history we know more about is the history of the mid-century movement for civil rights. Whether called that, or the black struggle or the free- dom fight, we know more about it now than ever before.

In a few years, for example, we will have a pretty clear understanding of what Martin Luther King did and said and thought and where he was nearly every week of his life between the beginning of the Mont- gomery Bus Boycott in 1955 until his murder in Memphis in 1968.

This increase in our knowledge about one of the 20th Century's most notable figures has come about, at least in part, because of the continued and increased interest among Americans in King, in the movement associ- ated with him, and the times which produced him and other notable figures in our common past.

The film-maker Oliver Stone has cleverly capitalized on this interest, in his new movie JFK. Both those Americans who can remember where they were when Kennedy was killed and those who knew of the mur- dered President only second hand are drawn to exam- ine what happened in Dallas that November day, to wonder who did it and why.

For the last several years I have been a history teacher, telling college students about the great movement for civil rights that swelled to prominence in the 1950s and 1960s. Some of my students confuse George Wallace, the governor of Alabama in the 1960s, with Mike Wallace, the television newsman then and now. Others confuse Montgomery NAACP leader E. D. Nixon with former President Richard Nixon. What and how I teach reflects a great shift in historiography, a rethinking of by whom and how the civil rights movement was made.

Looking at that movement from today, we see a

3

different view of the events and personalities of that period. Instead of the towering figures of Kings and Kennedys standing alone, we now see an army of women and men. Instead of famous speeches made to multitudes, we now see the planning and work that preceded the speech. Instead of a series of well publicized marches and protests, we see long organizing campaigns and brave and lonely soldiers often working in near solitude. And instead of a sudden upsurge in activism in Montgomery in 1955, we see a long and unceasing history of challenges to white supremacy that began in slavery. When we look back at our times from the 21st Century, what will we see?

If we look at today—at the 1980s and early 1990s—through the same lens we used to use to examine the 1950s and 1960s, we may well see only the electoral and ideological victories of Ronald Reagan and George Bush. In that narrow view, Ronald Reagan discovered a cultural and electoral backlash against the 1960s and rode it to power. Once in office, he and his successor institutionalized their revolution, discrediting and then weakening the government's efforts to help the poor and powerless, strengthening the effort to reward the rich and powerful. But Ronald Reagan and George Bush did not create the politics that gave them power, however skillful they became at exploiting racial fears and selfishness. Instead, they should be seen as the natural descendants and heirs of two centuries of racial politics, modern-day proponents of an ancient series of arguments against equality.

More than 35 years ago, for example, racist whites in Montgomery used arguments against integrating the busses that were the same as those employed against the civil rights bill of last year. Giving in to black demands would give blacks a special status over white people they do not deserve. Having a court order integrate the busses would make blacks wards of the state. Insistence on integration robbed blacks of racial pride. And most importantly, upsetting traditional patterns of white supremacy and black inferiority would alienate whites, destroying an imaginary conception of racial harmony that existed in the segregated world. It isn't hard to recall hearing versions of those arguments on the floor of the United States Senate and in the White House last year. We don't have to go back to Montgomery 37 years ago. In 1962 a United States Senator from Connecticut named Prescott Bush ended his Senate service by introducing a civil rights bill stronger than proposals made earlier by President John F. Kennedy. A year later, and two weeks after Martin

Luther King's famous "I Have A Dream" speech at the March on Washington, his son George Herbert Walker Bush kicked off his first race for public office by opposing Kennedy's civil rights bill. He was "emphatically" against the section that would force hotels and restaurants to admit blacks, he told Texas newspapers.[1]

Young George Bush was no stranger to the argument that equality for blacks hurt whites. Bush told Texas voters he would work to develop job opportunities for those "displaced from jobs . . . by the new civil rights act."[2] "The new civil rights act was passed to protect 14% of the people," candidate Bush said. "I'm also worried about the other 86%"[3] Recycling old arguments against justice comes naturally in a society that has long embraced the ideal but not the reality of equality. If there has been a frightening consistency to the arguments made by freedom's opponents, the supporters of justice have been consistent too. For all of this century, the movement for civil and human rights has followed the program put forth by W.E.B. Dubois in 1905:

We must complain. Yes plain, blunt complaint, ceaseless agitation, unfailing exposure of dishonesty and wrong—this is the ancient unerring way to liberty, and we must follow it.

Next, we propose to work. These are the things that we as Black men must try to do. To press the matter of stopping the curtailment of our political rights; to urge Negroes to vote honestly and effectively; to push the matter of civil rights; to organize business cooperation; to build schoolhouses and increase the interest in education; to bring Negroes and labor unions into mutual understanding; to study Negro History; to attack crime among us . . . to do all in our power by word and by deed to increase the efficiency of our race, the enjoyment of its manhood rights, and the performance of its just duties. This is a large program. It cannot be realized in a short time. . . (But) this is the critical time."[4]

DuBois correctly predicted then that the struggle of the 20th Century would be the struggle of the color line.

From before DuBois' time until today, black Americans have generally followed his prescription for action, pursuing civil rights, economic justice, and entrance into the mainstream of American life.

The years since then saw gains won at lunch counters and movie theaters and polling places, and the fabric of legal segregation was destroyed. What had begun as a movement for elemental civil rights has now become largely a political and an economic movement, and black men and women hold office and weld power in numbers we never dreamed of before.

Despite impressive increases in the number of black people holding public office, and despite our ability to sit and eat and ride and vote in places which used to bar black faces, in some ways non-white Americans are worse off in the present than in the recent years that went before.

Four years ago, when the final phase of the 1988 presidential campaign formally began, both George Bush and Michael Dukakis saw an America many Americans never see. For both candidates, America was a land of happy families and successful suburbs, where every child waves an American flag and every day is the Fourth of July. But there was then and is now another America, a shadow America neither candidate dared to show or tell.

As the 1980s began, the nation chose a president whose terms could hold awful parallels with the end of Reconstruction almost exactly 100 years before. Then and now, a president, desperate for power, entered into an illicit arrangement, not just with the unreconstructed South, but with the national unreconstructed mentality which believed then as it does now that private profit and public arrogance could be pursued at the expense of those living on the economic edge.

The 1980 election was won by an amiable incompetent whose sole intent was removing the government from every aspect of American life. He intended to take the government out of the business of enforcing equal opportunity. He intended to eliminate affirmative action for women and minorities. He intended to erase the laws and programs written in blood and sweat in the quarter century since Martin Luther King became the premier figure in the freedom movement and an American majority became single-minded in pursuit of human freedom.

For the Reaganites, conflict of interest became a precondition for employment in government. A band of financial and ideological profiteers descended on Washington like a crazed swarm of right-wing locusts bent on destroying the rules and laws which protected our people from poisoned air and water, and from greed. But nowhere was their assault on the rule of law so great as in their attempt to subvert, ignore, defy and destroy the laws which require an America that is bias free.

A constituency of the comfortable, the callous and the smug was recruited to form solid ranks against the forgotten. They enforced the national nullification of the needs of the needy, the gratuitous gratification of the gross and the greedy and practiced the politics of impropriety, prevarication, pious platitudes and self-righteous swinishness. They forced a form of triage economics upon us, producing the first increase in infant mortality rates in twenty years and pushing thousands of poor and working poor Americans deeper into poverty. By mid-term, the Census Bureau reported that the number of people living in poverty had increased over the previous four years by more than nine million, the biggest increase since these statistics were first collected over two decades ago. Today the poorest two-fifths of our population receives a smaller share of the national income and the richest two-fifths a larger share than at any time since 1947. If we are to believe with Thomas Jefferson that "the common man is the most precious resource of the state," that precious resource is in real danger of economic extinction today.

They increased American interference in the lives of our neighbors in this hemisphere and in other countries around the globe. These are the legacies of the Reagan years, the decade of the dominance of greed.

Those years were a festive party, thrown for America's rich. The middle class got by on two paychecks, median family income was stagnant, and the percentage of young families who own their own homes went down for the first time since the depression. The poorest tenth of the population saw their income fall by 10%. Young men between 25 and 34 saw their wages drop a dollar an hour. Savings and investment were down in the Reagan years. More Americans were working longer hours at lower pay.

Despite low numbers of Americans unemployed, the percentage living in poverty remained the same, higher than in any years since the 1970s. Over the last year and a half, total employment in America dropped by more than 3 million jobs.

And for those Americans whose skins are black or brown, the poverty rate went up while median family

5

income went down. For children of any color, the numbers living in poverty doubled by 1987. Poverty for black and Hispanic senior citizens went up, poorer children got poorer, and the gap between rich and poor grew wider.

After a twenty year decline, infant mortality rates for blacks went up.

By 1986, the wealth of the average white family was twelve times the wealth of the average black family. In 1969, three fourths of all black men were working; by the 80s end, only 57% had a job. For these families, it was never morning in America. The only shining points of light they see are daylight through the cracks in their walls.

Permit me to speak as we go with two voices—first as a contemporary fellow passenger on what promises to be a tough and frustrating trip from the present toward the twenty-first century, and second, as a witness and participant on an earlier leg of that journey, a trip whose stops included Selma and Saigon, Jackson and Johannesburg, a trip which will take us from Ole Miss to U. Mass.; from Bull Connor's dogs to Ronald Reagan's judges; from the Ku Klux Klan to Neo-Nazis, the Ayran Nation and the Posse Comitatus; from Brown v. Board of Education to Ward's Cove Packing Co. v. Antonio; from James Earl Ray to Bernard Goetz and David Duke; from bombs in Birmingham to bigotry in Boston and a beating in Los Angeles.

In many ways, the Southern freedom movement was a second Reconstruction, whose ripples were felt far beyond the southern states and whose victories benefited more than blacks.

Like the first, almost exactly 100 years before, it focused on making the civil rights protections of America's half citizens more secure. Like the first Reconstruction, the second saw gains for blacks extended to protections for others. Like the first Reconstruction, the second gave new life to movements of other disadvantaged Americans, and like the first Reconstruction, the second ended when the national purpose wavered and reaction swept the land.

Before it ended, it was our democracy's finest hour. A voteless people voted with their bodies and their feet, and showed the way for other social protest. The anti-war movement drew its earliest soldiers from the southern freedom army; the movement for women's

rights took many of its cues, and its momentum, from the southern movement for civil rights.

These three impediments to democracy' success— gender, race and abusive power— were all weakened by the movement's drive, and we are all better for it today.

Important steps in the movement came in the summer of 1954. In April 1954, Martin Luther King, Jr., preached his first sermon as pastor of Dexter Avenue Baptist Church. He was twenty-five years old. He could not have known that in nine years, he would be the most famous black American, speaking at the March on Washington to the largest gathering of civil rights supporters in American History. And he could not have known that in 14 years he would be dead.

Ten days after the first sermon, the French forces in a faraway garrison called Dien Ben Phu were overcome. None of us imagined then that 55,000 American men would die in Vietnam.

Ten days after the French fell, legal segregation began to fall as well; the United States Supreme Court ruled on May 17, 1954, that segregated public schools were against the law. The Court's ruling destroyed segregation's legality, and an army of nonviolent protesters quickly arose to challenge its morality as well.

The southern movement for civil rights—like the war in Vietnam—showed Americans at our best and worst. At our best we were and are a caring people, heroic and brave. At our worst we were and are a narrow and selfish people, devoted to skin privilege, to economic advantage for only a few.

And here, at home, in the American South, a decades-long struggle against great odds did win real victories, not just for southern blacks, but for American ideals as well.

A year and a half after Martin Luther King arrived in Montgomery, another black woman was arrested for refusing to give her seat to a white man on a city bus. One year and five days after Rosa Parks' arrest, a young lawyer named Nelson Mandela was arrested in South Africa. Mrs. Parks' arrest in Montgomery triggered a year-long bus boycott that broke the back of segregation in Montgomery, and the inspiration of the Montgomery movement set nonviolent fires in towns and cities across the south.

In 1960, college students adopted the Montgomery technique of nonviolent resistance, and thousands accepted jail without bail by sitting down to stand up for their rights. The next year, they attacked segregated interstate travel with their bodies and segregated ballot boxes across the South as well. There were lives lost along the way, and laws passed; by 1965 Jim Crow was legally dead.

After the successes of the 1960s, the movement for civil rights faltered in the 1970s and has been in stages of advance and retreat ever since.

Today we see a very different picture, a population largely indifferent to the poverty around them, a people more concerned about trapped whales in Alaska than babies trapped in poverty in Alabama.

But the current threat to civil rights comes not from southern sheriffs or bombs, but from the national government and the White House itself.

In 1968, the Kerner Commission concluded that "white racism" was the single most important cause of continued racial inequality in income, housing, employment, education and life chances between blacks and whites.

But by the middle 1970s, the growing numbers of blacks and women and other minorities, pressing for entry into and power in the academy, the media, business, government and over traditionally white institutions, created a backlash in the discourse about race.

Opinion leaders—in government and private life A— began to redefine and reformulate the terms of the discussion. No longer was the Kerner Commission's formulation acceptable. The indictment of white America could be abandoned. Instead, black behavior became the reason why blacks and whites live in separate worlds. Racism retreated and pathology advanced, and the burden of racial problem solving shifted from the creators of racism to its victims.

The color-blind society that was the 1960s ideal became today's imagined reality. The failure of the lesser breeds to enjoy its fruits became their fault alone. Thus pressure for additional, stronger civil rights laws became special pleading. America's most privileged population, white men, suddenly became a victim class. Aggressive blacks and pushy women were responsible for America's demise.

All this occurred despite almost daily incidents of racial attack, and a series of public opinion surveys which demonstrates most white Americans believe racial minorities are less than equal human beings, lacking in thrift, morality, industriousness and patriotism.[5] In the opinion of our fellow citizens, Willie Horton and Bill Cosby are the same man, equally undesirable as neighbor, schoolmate, co-worker, or defender of our common soil.

Ronald Reagan had never seen a civil rights law he liked; his appointees to the federal courts and the Department of Justice were determined to destroy or disobey every civil rights law they read. They made dangerous, precipitous and radical shifts toward contravening the Constitution and the law of the land.

The ultimate result of such policy was contempt for the rule of law itself. Had they prevailed, our constitutional rights would have been protected only when they were popularly agreed to, or when a person who supports them was elected President of the United States.

For the past and present Administrations, the Constitution is a document of infinite elasticity, to be tailored and snipped to fit the passions of the moment.

The human costs of these actions are beyond measure. When the government becomes the aggressor against the civil rights of its people, it becomes the promoter of prejudice and makes common cause with the stain of white supremacy that has persisted throughout our History.

Despite this dreary record, there were successes, and the bipartisan Congressional majority on civil rights remained intact. In one sense, the movement has succeeded beyond its original sponsors' wildest dreams or fears.

Today, through administrative order, court decisions and legislative act, the protected classes extend to a majority of all Americans, including white ethnics, the aged, short people, the chemically dependent, the left-handed, the obese, all religions. We ought to examine how the road to equal rights became so crowded and what the consequences are.

Obviously, something is wrong when the claims of the descendants of property sold in the African slave trade are held equal with the claims of short, chemi-

7

cally dependent, left-handed white men.

Many ethnic, racial, religious, and other groups have legitimate grievances. The central moral dilemma of this nation, however, is how it treats the one group whose members it enslaved. The law has a special obligation to blacks—as the sole beneficiaries of the Thirteenth Amendment—when it comes to defining and remedying discrimination. When a limited number of awards is demanded by a limitless number of claimants, then civil rights are as threatened today as they were by Bull Connor 25 years ago.

A second front against racial justice was opened in the 1980s and has gained strength ever since. Led by scholars and academicians, funded by corporate America, this movement of neoconservatives aimed its efforts at removing government regulation from every aspect of our lives, and found a handy hated target in civil rights. While professing strong support for equal rights, these neo-Bourbons opposed every tool devised to achieve that goal. They discredited affirmative action, not only because it threatened ancient skin privilege, but because it served as an easy symbol of despised government intervention. For these new racists, equal opportunity is a burden society cannot afford to bear. Their less than subtle message is that including blacks and women excludes quality.

The truth is that true equality requires an increase in unwanted competition these new States' Righters cannot stand; their old-boy networks, in academia or in industry, cannot tolerate federal imposition of equal rights. They argue that the civil rights laws of the 1960s eliminated all discrimination, that the playing field is now level, that every contestant stands equal at the starting line. That some contestants have no shoes, that others find their legs gripped by heavy baggage from the past, and that an advantaged few begin the race at the finish line is of no consequence to these champions of the new order.

The movement today suffers not from its imagined excesses, but from the lies and distortions of its opponents.

They tell us discrimination against minorities is not a problem; society must protect itself from discrimination against the majority instead. They tell us school teachers and unemployed mothers are "special interests." They tell us civil rights remedies produce civil wrongs.

Yesterday's movement has been criticized—in the perfect hindsight of today—for winning gains for middle class blacks alone, but middle class blacks in Montgomery did not ride the city's busses, and college professors and bankers in Greensboro did not eat their lunch at the five and ten.

Someone needs to disabuse the modern world of the notion that the beneficiaries of race-centered affirmative action are somehow "profiting" from it, as if the movement's goals were an investment shared by a greedy few—a subtribe of ebony Ivan Boeskys trading up life's ladder. There is no "profit" in receiving right treatment. Receiving rights others already enjoy is no special benefit or badge of privilege; it is the natural order of things in a democratic society.

The continuing disparity between black and white life-chances is a result of epidemic racism and an economic system dependent on class division.

Abundant scholarship notwithstanding, there is no other possible explanation—not family breakdown, not lack of middle class values, not lack of education or skills, not absence of role models. These are symptoms. Racism is the cause; its elimination is the cure. The last item on the civil rights agenda—economic justice—remains unfulfilled and unaddressed.

Martin Luther King lost his life supporting a garbage workers' strike in Memphis; the right to decent work at decent pay is as important as the right to vote. "Negroes," King said in 1961, "are almost entirely a working people. There are pitifully few Negro millionaires and few Negro employers."[6]

That there are more Black millionaires today is a tribute to the movement King lead; that there are proportionately fewer blacks working today is an indictment of our times and our economic system, a reflection of our failure to keep the movement coming on.

The first 4 years of the kinder, gentler administration only reminds us how much things remain the same. The names have changed, but not the actions and the assault on racial equity continues with just as much determination as before. The President began by choosing as the nation's chief civil rights lawyer a man most Americans would not choose to represent them in People's Court; he continues a performance that is loud in rhetoric but lacks execution through his

8

dismaying attitude toward the Civil Rights Act of 1991 and his nomination of Clarence Thomas to the Supreme Court.

If the 1990s promise expanded freedoms in Eastern Europe and South Africa, we have a right to ask what we can expect at home. We were right to celebrate the death of totalitarianism overseas, but the clear signs of economic collapse here at home may mean we cannot crown capitalism king just yet.

Twice before in the twentieth century we saw the private economy unable to cope with the challenges it faced. In the 1930s we embraced an aggressive, interventionist government when the private economy proved unable to beat back the depression and put wages into people's pockets once again. We embraced an activist government again when it became clear that the capitalist system had failed to moderate or restrain the privation which afflicted one in every five Americans just three decades ago.

Government's efforts worked then; they reduced poverty by more than half and relieved some of poverty's grimmest conditions—malnutrition, poor housing, ill health. They provided successful job training, raising the economic level of thousands of Americans. They provided early education for low-income children, increasing their chances for success in life. They increased visits by the poor to doctors, and they cut our substandard housing stock in half.

The message from the Congress and the White House is not encouraging. The President's last State of the Union speech continued the reverse Robin Hood traditions of the Reagan years; squeezing the needy to fatten the greedy. Between Bush and Reagan, there's not a new paradigm's worth of difference. The Democrats have forgotten how to be an opposition. They read the President's lips too, but seem unable to form words or programs of their own. There is no courage on Capitol Hill; coalitions of the comfortable have replaced the notion that our society could be organized in a kinder, gentler way.

Today black Americans face conditions as daunting as the fire hoses and billy clubs of thirty years ago. An Urban League report tells us that blacks lost, not gained ground in the 1980s. And on the streets and sidewalks where black America lives, crime and violence rule. Homicide is the leading cause of death for 15 to 34-year-old black men and women, and 95% of the mur-

ders are black-on-black crimes. These are not drive-by shootings or strangers killing strangers; in most of these deaths the killer and victim knew each other. These are friend shooting friend.

In life chances, life expectancy, years of education completed, median income—in all the standards by which life is measured, black Americans see a deep and widening gulf between the American dream and the reality of their lives.

For the past decade, an often indifferent and sometimes hostile federal government helped to widen the gap; today the neo-segregationist majority on the Supreme Court denies minorities and women relief in the federal courts. Court decisions and presidential indifference send a signal to the rest of America; to business and labor and education. For nearly all of the last twenty years, the old interracial coalition that championed civil rights at Selma's bridge and in Congress' halls has been in retreat.

We knew we had lost a champion with the death of Martin King; we never imagined support for equal rights would die as well. Martin Luther King isn't the only soldier missing from the freedom fight; he was part of an interracial army that numbered tens of thousands. We look back on the King years with some nostalgia, for those were the years when we were truly able to overcome. Our inability to do so today is conditioned, at least partially, by the way we recall Martin Luther King.

For most of us, Martin Luther King is an image seen in grainy, black and white television film taken in Washington a quarter of a century ago, the gifted preacher who had a dream. But Martin Luther King was more than that, and the movement more than Martin Luther King. King did more than tell the nation of his dream at the March on Washington. In the years before and after he addressed the human condition, the larger world beyond America's shores.

In some ways, we have become King-dependent, summoning his memory as a substitute for action. But we forget that he stood at the head of thousands, the people who made that mighty movement what it was. From Jamestown's slave pens to Montgomery's boycotted busses, these ordinary men and women labored in obscurity, and from Montgomery forward they provided the soldiers of the freedom army. They walked to work in dignity, rather than ride in shame. They faced mobs in Birmingham and death in Mississippi. They sat at lunch counters, and they stood and marched and organized.

Martin Luther King didn't march from Selma to Montgomery by himself. He didn't speak to an empty field at the March on Washington. There were thousands marching with him, and before him, and thousands more who one by one and two by two did the dirty work that preceded the triumphal march. Black Americans didn't just march to freedom; they worked their way toward civil rights through the difficult business of organizing. Knocking on doors, one by one. Registering voters, one by one. Developing a community effort, block by block. Creating an effective organization, town by town. Creating coalitions, nationwide.

Today we look to others to lead and direct us; yesterday we told the leaders where the people were, what the people wanted leaders to do.

There is an enormous opportunity for service available to each of us, wherever and whoever we may happen to be. From the block club to the Girl Scouts and Boys', Clubs to the PTA and the local political club, from the NAACP to political campaigns—there's nowhere willing hands and minds aren't welcome, nowhere they will be turned away.

Most of us here are or will be successful in our lives. Many went before us to smooth our way, and our job is to smooth the way for those who come behind us.

During the decade of the 1960s, a great social movement fought to win a place at the table for those citizens previously consigned to eating in the kitchen if indeed they ate at all.

Now that the legal and extralegal barriers have been largely removed, the battle for the remainder of the twentieth century is to close the widening gap. None of us has much difficulty envisioning the world we want or the programs, which if adopted, would ring the new dawn in. We want a society whose single aim is the democratic satisfaction of the needs of its people.

We want to guarantee all Americans an equal opportunity to participate in the organization of society, and in the shaping of public and private decisions which affect their lives. We want to guarantee that no one goes without the basic necessities—food, shelter, health care, a healthy environment, personal safety and an adequate income.

Instead, the hopes and dreams of generations that each succeeding year would be the year in which the land of the slave finally becomes the home of the free have been set aside in favor of defense spending, balanced budgets and corporate domination of the economy.

In spite of the progress made so far, many real problems remain to be solved. We are second from last among industrialized nations in the money we spend on our children's schools. We've let our infrastructure, our streets and roads and bridges, fall apart. For many in the middle class, only mom's paycheck keeps them out of the poorhouse. Most Americans can't afford to be sick, can't pay the doctor when they are. Yet we seem to find more than enough to feed the military machine. In just three years in the 1980s we spent more than $1 trillion dollars on military expenditures.

To understand how much one trillion can buy, use six of America's midwestern states as an illustration. We could build a $75,000 house, place it on $5,000 worth of land, furnish it with $10,000 worth of furniture, put a $10,000 car in the garage—and give this to each and every family in Kansas, Missouri, Nebraska, Oklahoma, Colorado and Iowa.

We'd have enough left over to build a $10 million hospital and a $10 million library for 250 cities in those six states.

There would still be some money left. After giving every family a furnished house and car, and each town a library and a hospital, we would have enough left over to equip two armies. We'd have enough left from our trillion dollars to put aside, at 10% interest, enough money to pay a salary of $25,000 dollars for an army of 10,000 nurses and $25,000 dollars for an army of 10,000 teachers.

And those families with the houses and the cars? We would have enough left over to give each family in those six states an annual cash allowance of $5,000— not just for one year, but for forever.[7]

The cost of one Stealth bomber would give pre-natal care to 950,000 mothers. Not operating one aircraft carrier for one year would pay for cleaning up 28 major toxic waste sites. Two attack submarines would pay for college grants to 500,000 low income students. Deactivating two World War II battleships would subsidize housing for 238,000 families. The money spent on 4 nuclear weapons tests would be enough to inoculate all of the 140 million children born each year across the world against the six major childhood diseases, from which 3 million children die each year. Two and one-half Trident submarines would subsidize mass transit in nine cities.

For too many Americans, human rights is a spectator sport, a kind of NBA in which all the players are black and the spectators white. But in this true to life game, the players are of every color and condition, the fate of all fans tied to points scored on the floor. When either team wins, the spectators win too. When four little girls died in a Birmingham church bombing, Sally Ride won the right to shoot the moon. Because black students faced arrest at Southern lunch counters almost 30 years ago, the law their bodies wrote now protects older Americans from age discrimination, Jews and Moslems and Christians from religious bigotry, and the disabled from exclusion because of their condition.

When the struggle for civil rights began to intensify three decades ago, we knew it would be hard fought and never cost free. But we hoped the American people would bear the burden and pay the price. And for a while, Americans answered, "We will." But when it began to pinch and squeeze, their commitment began to fade. The 1960s movement and the ferment which preceded it grew from the willingness of ordinary people—housewives, students, a seamstress, teachers, a railroad porter—to seize control of their lives. They did not wait for mythic charismatic leaders to organize a march or boycott; they organized themselves. They did not wait for mass approval—they faced rejection, knowing they were right.

Today, we wait for others to certify our politics, to give sanction to our protests.

It took one woman's courage to start a movement in Montgomery, the bravery of only four young men in Greensboro to set the South on fire. Surely there are men and women, young and old, here today who can do the same. If there are hungry minds or hungry bodies starving near these wealthy walls, someone here can feed them. If there are precincts of the powerless poor nearby, someone here can organize them. If there is racial injustice on the campus or in the town, someone here can conquer it. If America still spends more on

guns than butter, someone here can reverse that ancient trend. Now is the time in the third century of our republic to make the promise of the founding fathers come true—one nation, with liberty and justice for us all.

When I entered the labor force more than 30 years ago, 5 workers paid into the Social Security system to support every retiree. Their names were probably Carl, Ralph, Bob, Steve and Bill. When I retire, there will only be 3 workers for every retiree. Their names will probably be Kwanza, Maria, and Jose. I want them to have the best future they possibly can. Again, DuBois speaks to us from the past. He said, at the turn of the twentieth century:

I believe in God who made of one blood all the nations that dwell on the earth. I believe that all men—black, brown and white—are brothers, varying through time and opportunity, in form and gift and feature, but differing in no essential particular, and alike in soul and in the possibility of infinite development.

Especially do I believe in the Negro race; in the beauty of its genius, the sweetness of its soul, and its strength in that meekness which shall inherit this turbulent earth.

I believe in pride of race and lineage itself; in pride of self so deep as to scorn injustice to other selves; in pride of lineage so great as to despise no man's father; in pride of race so chivalrous as neither to offer bastardy to the weak nor beg wedlock of the strong, knowing that men may be brothers in Christ even though they be not brothers-in-law.

I believe in service—humble, reverent service, from the blackening of boots to the whitening of souls, for work is heaven, idleness hell, and wages the well done of the master who summoned all them that labor and are heavy-laden, making no distinction between the Black sweating cotton hands of Georgia, and the first families of Virginia, since all distinction not based on deed is devilish and not divine.

I believe in the devil and his angels, who wantonly work to narrow the opportunity of all human beings, especially if they be Black; who spit in the faces of the fallen, strike them that cannot strike again, believe the worst and work to prove it, hating the image which their maker stamped on a brother's soul.

I believe in the Prince of Peace. I believe that war is murder. I believe that armies and navies are at bottom the tinsel and braggadocio of oppression and wrong, and I believe that the wicked conquest of weaker and darker nations by nations white and stronger but foreshadows the death of their strength.

I believe in liberty for all men; the space to stretch their arms and their souls; the right to breathe and the right to vote, the freedom to choose their friends, enjoy the sunshine and ride on the railroads, uncursed by color, thinking, dreaming, working as they will in a kingdom of god and love.

I believe in the training of children Black even as white, the leading of little souls into the green pastures and beside the still waters, not for self or peace, but for life lit by some large vision of beauty and goodness and truth; lest we forget, and the sons of the fathers, like Esau, for mere meat barter their birthright in a mighty nation.

"Finally, I believe in patience—patience with the weakness of the weak and the strength of the strong, the prejudice of the ignorant and the ignorance of the blind, patience with the tardy triumph of joy and the mad chastening of sorrow ƒ patience with God."[8]

Endnotes

1. *San Antonio Express,* (September 12, 1963) as quoted in Jefferson Maley, "Bush and the Blacks: An Unknown Story," New York Review of Books 39 (January 16, 1992): 19-26.

2. *Austin America,* (September 25, 1964) as quoted Jefferson Maley, "Bush and the Blacks: An Unknown Story," New York Review of Books 39 (January 16, 1992): 19-26.

3. *The Dallas Morning News,* (October 28, 1964) as quoted in Jefferson Maley, "Bush and the Blacks: An Unknown Story," New York Review of Books 39 (January 16, 1992): 19-26.

4. W. E. B. Dubois, *The Voice of the Negro,* (Atlanta: voice Publishing Company, 1905) as reprinted in a *Documentary History of the Negro People in the United States,* edited by Herbert Aptheker, (New York: Citadel Press, 1966), p. 906.

5. Tom W. Smith, "Ethnic Images, (Chicago: National Opinion Research Center, 1990). GSS topical Report No. 19.

6.. Martin Luther King, Address before the 4th Consitutional Convention, AFL-CIO, Dal Harbour, Florida, December 11, 1961.

7. Harry G. Shaffer. *Republic Ailine Magazine,* May, 1986.

8. W. E. B. DuBois, "Credo," *Independent,* (New York) 62 (October 6, 1904): 787.

The Electronic Piñata: Information Technologies and the Future of the Library

Paul Saffo
Institute for the Future
Menlow Park, California

It is hardly news that we live in a time beset by paradox and uncertainty in the knowledge business. The most extraordinary events come to pass with barely a mention that a record amount of information is being stored electronically, while at the same time, we are consuming record amounts of paper. We fret over growing illiteracy in the face of record book and magazine sales. We have become a TV culture that nonetheless sends record amount of text back and forth via courier and fax machine.

Change is no longer the news when it comes to information technology. It is the norm. Moreover, change is clustering at the extremes, a sure sign that yet more fundamental change lies ahead. And the agent of change has been the micro-processor—the chips hidden inside our PCs—and a host of appliances from copiers to automobiles. But the sheer ubiquity of the micro-processor and our preconceptions about it obscure its impact on our culture and your profession.

But a curious paradox hints at what lies ahead. Paper consumption in the United States until recently has increased at a rate greater than growth in gross national product for every year since World War II. Meanwhile the electronic sector has grown even more quickly. In short, the information industry has become like a huge electronic piñata, a thin paper crust surrounding an essentially electronic core. Recall that as a sphere increases in size, its surface area increases more slowly than the volume of the interior. Paper is the skin, and electronics its core, growing more quickly yet.

Specific technologies can be arrayed as a series of concentric rings in the piñata, from interface technologies close to the surface, to advanced computing and communications technologies at the core. Thus, a copier represents a shallow dive into the piñata to turn an image into electrons only long enough to make an identical paper copy. Desktop publishing goes slightly deeper, adding processing to create entirely new images. If copiers increased paper volume, but desktop publishing changed the nature of paper as a medium, sometime around 1985, the nature of paper as a medium changed profoundly, from storage to interface. We think of paper as a communications medium, but above all it has been storage. Think about how little time your favorite book spends being read, and how much time it gathers dust on a shelf.

Paper became interface when it became cheaper to store information electronically than on paper. Increasingly, we will print information on demand to be read, and dispose of it when we are done—that is paper as interface. Thus paper is far from obsolete, but its role will change dramatically, creating plenty of surprises in the next two decades.

This is a small indicator of a larger revolution. We live on the cusp between two revolutions: one of print, four centuries old and not yet spent, and another of electronics, twenty years old and yet not really under way. The problem is the shape of the new knowledge order to come remains uncertain and undefined. Everything, absolutely everything, in the knowledge industry is up for grabs.

Of course, this shift is not unique. It is just the latest episode in the coevolution of our technologies and information media. In particular, today's revolution very closely resembles the period from Gutenberg's invention of the printing press around 1450 to Aldus' definition of modern publishing in 1501. Before Gutenberg, books were lovely, but hard to reproduce, and comparatively low in the volume of information per page. Gutenberg's device upped information densities tremendously, but of course the product was hardly modern. For the most part, it was a copy of what scriveners did by hand, down to typeface and even word contractions adopted by the writers to avoid medieval carpal tunnel syndrome from too many hours wielding a stylus. Just as plastics' inventors struggled to make the stuff look like wood and tortise shell, print's pioneers worked to conceal the novelty of their new books.

What ensued in the years before 1501 was a period of Silicon Valley-style entrepreneurship, where entrepreneurs pursuing wild ideas on shoestring budgets collectively refined the technology and defined the elements of the modern book. The result was the shift from the technology of movable type and infant print technologies to the medium of publishing. The period is defined by a word, "incunabula"—books from the cradle of publishing. Today, we live in an age of electronic incunabula, a moment between two revolutions where everything is up for grabs, nothing makes any sense, and incredible opportunity surrounds us all. The forces that shaped change then are not so different than the forces that are shaping change today.

In fact, especially in the high-tech world, the slowness of change is the rule rather than the exception. For example, the patents had almost expired by the time the first Xerox machine had arrived in the early sixties. And the computer itself followed a long and tortuous path from those monster calculators of WW II to the mainframe of the sixties and eventually the personal computer. The mouse was invented in 1963 by Doug Englebart, but it didn't catch on with users until the mid-1980s.

Things seem to change quickly because we confuse surprise for speed. Even in the high-tech world of information technologies, things take much longer than any of us are prepared to admit and no amount of effort can speed it up. In Zen monastaries, the koan, "what is the sound of one hand clapping" is the proper subject for a lifetime of contemplation. In Silicon Valley though, the answer is quite simple: it is the sound of an entrepreneur patting her or himself on the back, convinced he or she just invented a product that is so obviously useful that the whole world will instantly beat a path to her or his door.

The lesson from the history of information technology is to never mistake a clear view for a short distance. It is that sense of standing on a ridgetop, looking across a great forest at a distant mountain goal. The mountain seems so close until, of course you are down in the forest. But the examples I have mentioned also illustrate a second wrinkle: change is not just slow, it is also slow in getting stared. At moments, it seems, like the mouse and the copier, that most ideas take about 20 years to become an overnight success. The notion of hypertext is an especially recent example, having become popular only in the last few years. But Ted Nelson coined the term in 1963, Vannevar Bush de-

scribed it in the *Atlantic Monthly* in 1945, and Roget conceived of it in the 1800s in the form of the thesaurus.

The consequence of this tendency is "macromyopia", a peculiar form of forecasting double vision that leads us to simultaneously over- and under-estimate the impacts of a threatened change. Our overheated expectations lead us to overestimate the short-term impacts of a threatened change, and when reality fails to conform, our disappointment causes us to underestimate its long-term implications. Home computing is a familiar example. By 1980, every PC maker was certain that soon every home would have a personal computer. When it didn't happen by the mid-80s, everyone concluded that it would *never* happen, and abandoned the home market entirely. Then, just a few years later, one company built a special purpose home computer which performs one task only—entertainment. The company was Nintendo and their computers are now in nearly 40% of American households.

It turns out that it takes about 30 years for any truly new idea to fully seep into our culture. There is a cadence to change that we can ignore only at our peril. And this is so because technology does not drive change at all. Technology merely enables change. It is our collective cultural response to technology that drives change. Change occurs at the speed of thought and of habit, not at the speed of electrons tunneling down circuits. And in a world of stubborn people, change can be slow indeed. At moments I suspect that we don't change at all—we just age and die. Perhaps we form our ideas in our teenage years and, carry them with us into the work force. We nurse them along until we become managers, and then have twenty years to implement our ideas before we are shoved off the stage by the next generation, coming along with ideas of their own. Thus, 30 years is no coincidence—it equals a generation and a half.

Change is also slow because inventors are generally utterly clueless about the uses of their technology. Graham Bell, suspected that the phone might be a means of sending audio entertainment to towns too small to have their own theatres. Similarly, there is evidence that Gutenberg was an unwitting inventor who was merely seeking to lighten the load of the copyists. His machine would print the black and white portions, leaving the copyists free to spend more time on color capitals and the like. Aldus was driven to open his press in part because he was obsessed with reviving overlooked Greek and Roman classics in what he perceived to be a dangerously modern time.

And it isn't just inventors who are wrong-headed. Our collective misimpressions as users also slow things up, as we pin our hopes on the nearest new information technology to come along. For example, around the turn of the century, many imagined the newfangled phonograph to be the successor to written letters, and even newspapers. Instead of writing and reading, we would speak and listen. Recall that even though newspapers have been around since about 70 B.C., they were rather new fangled at the time, having been reinvented by the telegraph and wire services to carry breaking news and short stories rather than local information and long essays of the Dickens type. Readers loved the new papers, but they complained that the ink rubbed off on their fingers. The 19th century propellerheads said, "Don't worry, the newsprint is just temporary—we'll replace it all with phonograph wax cylinders and the like." I'm sure the librarians of the time were contacted about phonograph preservation and disposing of the soon to be obsolete books.

Our expectations as users add an intrinsic cultural perversity to technological change. Most future visions never come to pass as expected. For example, we flew in our minds before the first airplane ever left the ground, and the vision was one of personal aircraft, not the huge airliners of today. Remarkably, this vision of personal transport persisted all the way into the 1940s, despite steady evidence of an airliner future. Our hopes for personal aircraft blinded us to what was really happening.

How are our expectations leading us to misinterpret the future of libraries and information technology today? How are we getting fuzzy ideas like multimedia information appliances and virtual reality wrong now? Eventually though, it is users who make collective sense of the use to which new information technologies will be put. And it turns out that it takes about a decade for this implementation to begin in earnest. Radio offers an excellent example. It was originally called wireless because everyone assumed that it would be a substitute for telegraph and telephone. And so, every radio was built with both a transmitter and a receiver. The result was big, awkward bulky devices that took money and training to use.

But as the wireless operators were talking to each other, a handful of hobbyist experimenters began to eavesdrop—and a few entrepreneurs noticed. One

wondered what might happen if he had one powerful transmitter and a whole bunch of cheap receivers. The result by the early 1920s was the maturing of the technology of wireless into the medium of broadcast. Ultimately, it grew into an infant media industry— radio.

There are actually three distinct periods within the thirty year cycle, which I will illustrate with the example of the movie industry. First is the "cowpath" decade, when the new technology is put to old uses; using the technology to do an old thing in a slightly new way. With film in the 1890s, kinetoscope parlors offered silent shorts of prosaic events like a horse jumping a fence, a man sneezing and the like. It was so incredible we could do it at all, it took us about 10 years to realize just how dull what we were doing really was.

The second decade is the decade of the skunkworks. For movies, this began around 1903, with D.W. Griffith and Angus Porter, who shot "The Great Train Robbery. It was one of the first films shot out of doors, and it incorporated revolutionary concepts like panning the camera and cutting between scenes. Audiences were electrified, and entrepreneurs were inspired into a new round of innovation. Just like the age of incunabula four centuries ago, or Silicon Valley in the 1970s, everyone with a crazy idea was pursuing their dreams on a shoestring budget, and without a lot of adult supervision. A favorite skunkworks film for me is Selig's re-enactment of Columbus' discovery of America, shot around 1906. If you look carefully at the print, there are no waves in the background, because the film was shot on a lake in Chicago. The boats had been bobbing out there since 1893, a gift from Spain. Selig dressed up his actor friends in what he thought Spaniards would wear, and they dragged a bunch of potted palms from the hotel across the street unto the beach.

Eventually the creative skunkworks chaos grows and complexifies into young industry. Specialization occurs, and the price of entry rises as everyone figures out the winning formula. This sets the stage for the third and final decade, the age of the moguls, financiers and lawyers, whose job it is to fully integrate the maturing technology into society. Film's third decade can be measured from opening night of "The Jazz Singer." This film was the endpoint of years of development of talking technology, and it was shown in specialized theaters, to which marketeers with big budgets enticed audiences.

Today we are just ten years into the microcomputer revolution. We have paved all the cow paths we are going to pave, and it is no coincidence that interesting things are happening. But the main event in the information revolution is yet to come. I can say with certainty that the '90s will be full of overdue events coming to pass in utterly unexpected ways. In the short run, we are certain to see more paper than ever, for the technologies intended to replace paper are continuing to generate more of it than ever.

Meanwhile, the amount of electronically mediated information is growing even more quickly. Without question, the dominant form of storage will be electronic, but we won't look at on our PCs, for the PC itself is already obsolete, the horseless carriage of the first decade of this particular revolution. The 80s were really the decade of the micro-processor, during which we explored the implications of processing power cheap enough to install on everyone's desk in the form of a PC.

In contrast, the 90s are being shaped not by the micro-processor, but by the communications laser. Lasers lurk in our compact disk players, CD-Rom drives, fax machines, and of course, laser printers. The 80s were a processing revolution, but the 90s will be an access revolution. The PC is a processing-driven device, and thus will disappear, replaced by new access-driven workstations on our desks and information appliances everywhere else. Our new desktop devices will be defined above all by what they connect us to, not by what they process. In the long run, they will be like telephones. A single phone sitting on a desk unconnected to any other telephone isn't a phone at all. It is a paperweight. Similarly, an unconnected workstation will be the ultimate in office oxymorons by the end of this decade.

The other half of the PC revolution will be supplanted by information appliances, devices that are information-rich like PCs, but inexpensive, special-purpose and ultra-portable. We're going to carry these devices in our pockets, briefcases and cars. We will hang them on our walls and stuff them into our notebooks. We will even wear them as "information exoskeletons"—ultra-portable and powerful information tools supporting us with information wherever we are.

Other surprises are in the works as well. For example, paper is going to become a two-way control medium. Two-way fax is already a growing publishing medium for custom newsletters and the like, and Xerox is hard at work on new ways to encode information on paper in a format readable by a whole new generation of digital copiers. Of course, two-way paper in the form of the original Hollerith punch-card was a cornerstone of the early computer revolution, proving once again that nothing is ever truly new. I note with interest that the Hollerith card was derived from the index card, invented by librarians in the late 1800s.

Of course, as the electronic piñata expands, holes and thin spots begin to appear in it's skin. So far, those holes and thin spots have been exceptions and modest successes, like Minitel, which is popular in France, but did not replace paper directories as everyone expected. Email networks used by researchers in lieu of traditional research paper offprints are another example. Still these instances are the first halting signs of a new paperless world—controversial and special circumstance, but truly paperless. Typically, the first two tasks a new medium is put to is to reproduce the Bible—and also to produce pornography. both have already happened in electronics. The first Bibles were done several years ago, both as software, and as hand-held information appliances. Of course, these devices don't replace paper bibles. Instead, they supplement the paper version as reference engines, convenient tools for finding specific passages. Thus new media rarely replace old technologies directly. Instead they perform some task that the old technology could never do, and gradually displace the old activity. Only after the new technology is mature does it ever actually replace the older medium.

We have multiple instances of electronic pornography, and we also have "electronic books" as well. One company, Voyager is offering electronic versions of titles like Jurassic Park designed to be read on Apple's PowerBook portables. Elsewhere, Broderbund has published a clever children's "book" titled Just Grandma and Me. IBM has announced a series of "illustrated books" on optical disk, and Sony is demonstrating its "BookMan" CD-Rom reader.

Of course, these shifts will profoundly change the library profession, even as it reinvents the entire information environment, to say nothing of libraries. Already, it is unthinkable that a single library could hold all the information available today. Will the library of the future cease to be a place at all, becoming instead a space within a new electronic environment? Long before that happens though, technology will profoundly change the researcher-librarian relationship.

Online information systems have already transformed this relationship. When a reader goes into an online information system themselves, they are assuming the role of both editor and reader, dynamically choosing what to pursue and to ignore. This model has not had a greater impact only because our current on-line conventions are dreadful. Most are built on the "Conan the librarian" model of access. It is as if the systems were run by some maniac reference librarian, loaded with lots of arbitrary rules and absolutely no mercy. But other models are emerging, some on utterly different transactional models where the system dials the user and not vice-versa. DowJones' DowVision system is one example, providing a constant real-time information feed into customer computer systems that extract crucial bits of news and automatically resend it on to the ultimate user.

To conclude, there is much more in the wind than anyone of us can possibly imagine. But because technology merely enables, it can be any future we want, for we are the ones who will shape it. The trick is to keep a larger perspective so you don't end up being surprised. Zen monk Dogen once wrote that the crane does not know the sky it flies in, the shark does not know the sea it swims in. Marshall McLuhan was more blunt yet, observing that "I don't know who discovered water, but it was not a fish."

As librarians though, you are in a position to do more. You work in the middle of the current information revolution, which also positions you to be among the first to discover the new options and opportunities and surprises that it will present, both for your institutions and yourself as individuals. Whether you want to be or not, you are infonauts on the edge of a new, unexplored information world. By all means, explore, but as you do so, recall the motto of the Aldine press—festina lente, make haste slowly. Make haste where the opportunities are ripe and ready to be seized, but do so slowly, lest you get in too early and spend forever waiting for the future to arrive. As we might observe in Silicon Valley, never mistake a clear view for a short distance—or a straight line.

Women, the Information Society, and Freedom[1]

Catherine R. Stimpson
Rutgers University
New Brunswick, New Jersey

Perhaps my subject, "Women, the Information Society, and Freedom," is complex, but my argument is simple. Today, women in all their diversity are seeking full citizenship in an information society that ought to value freedom. Their strength is historically unique. Yet, full citizenship is still as much dream as reality. We in "the information game" need to close the space between dream and reality.

I will jumpstart my argument with a recent memory. In 1991, the United States celebrated the 200th anniversary of the Bill of Rights and the 1st Amendment. In late November of that year, I had to travel from my home on Staten Island to Manhattan in order to attend a meeting of librarians and discuss the 1st Amendment. To my regret, I was downcast and gloomy. I prefer to be upbeat and cheerful. I also knew that librarians were staunch in their devotion to the 1st Amendment and freedom of information. Yet, wherever I looked in our public life, I saw assaults on intellectual freedom. To be sure, intellectual freedom is always in danger. Galileo was in danger. John Milton was in danger. W.E.B. DuBois was in danger. Margaret Sanger was in danger. However, the smell of the up-to-date fire and brimstone of the battalions of the orthodox—be the orthodoxy religious, political, or moral—was lacerating.

In the Staten Island ferry terminal, I had bought the borough newspaper. It headlined a victory in appellate court that permitted the paper, at last, to report on events in a mundane murder trial. In my satchel was a copy of the *Columbia Journalism Review* (November/December 1991). It mapped international violations of freedom of the press. A few days earlier, on November 19, the House of Representatives had failed to override a presidential veto of legislation that would undo the "gag rules" that keep health workers from talking to women, most of them poor, about abortion.[2] A few months earlier, in July, two scholars, one Italian, one Japanese, had been stabbed, to death. They had the temerity to translate *The Satanic Verses* of Salman Rushdie.

As the big, squat ferry crossed New York Bay, I brooded about still other assaults. Marring the screen my mind's eye was watching was Senator Jesse Helms, laying his siege to the National Endowment for the Arts; his compatriots, setting off false alarms about "P.C." on campus; and, on the other side, academics claiming that rigid regulations on speech will control hate speech. Then, the ferry passed the Statue of Liberty. There she loomed, that great, greenish statue, with her torch and spiky crown and tourists. Intellectual liberty, I thought, intellectual liberty is a battered woman.

Immediately, I regretted my spontaneous, crude metaphor. For it exploited real battered women. Then, I began to wonder, as the ferry maneuvered into the Manhattan terminal, if men and women did not have different relations to intellectual freedom and to information. In part, my question seems ridiculous. Surely, freedom is a principle that both men and women of all races cherish and defend; surely, freedom is a good to which both men and women aspire; surely, freedom is a condition that both men and women enjoy. Surely, we all thrive on information and messages, even if we sometimes want to erase the messenger.

All this is true, but this truth does not make my question wholly ridiculous. For men and women do have different relations to intellectual freedom as well; different relations to information and, in the broadest sense, education. Exactly what this difference is depends on who a particular man is; who a particular woman is; what their time, place, and circumstances are. Even in the midst of these crucial variables, gender helps to shape our education; our ability to learn and process information; our ability to express ourselves and give information; our ability to use information and make "informed choices." In brief, the battered woman and her batterer have different needs. She must learn how to escape the fist; he must learn how to keep his hand from balling into the battering fist.[3]

Because I cannot speak about women, information,

and freedom everywhere, I will focus on women and higher education, especially in the United States. Although I have this focus,[4] I realize that higher education is a part of a larger system of formal education and that this larger system is the partner of still other systems: the family, that most powerful of faculties; the peer group, that most irresistible of faculties; the economy that toughest of faculties; the media, that most insidious of faculties; and our discourse, the master faculty that instructs the others. Little will change in higher education unless all else changes. Little will change elsewhere unless higher education changes.

The condition of women and higher education is now mixed. After long and painful struggles, the education of women has made amazing gains. Much, though, is left to do. As a recent headline states glumly, "Old Issues Unresolved: Environment Still Hostile to Women in Academe, New Evidence Indicates."[5] Women are at once inside and outside of the precincts of higher education and information; at once comfortable and bruised, confident and anxious, cheerful and angry, on edge. Moreover, the backlash against women is also whipping through our culture. Susan Faludi writes pungently of "The backlash brain trust: from neocons to neofems."[6] Assassins of the dreams of education for us all oil and cock their weapons. Of course, the assassins would have nothing to do if the dreams were not moving closer to reality. A blow abhors a vacuum.

To offer another metaphor: imagine women and higher education as a hurly-burly of a kitchen. Beyond the kitchen is a dining room. Here, a well-fed group mingles around a table. Some of its members are eagerly anticipating a new dish from the kitchen. Others, however, are muttering that only bad food can come from these cooks. They are looking in the yellow pages for a restaurant specializing in more traditional home-cooking. In the kitchen itself, on the stove top, some pots—a rich stew, a soup, water for vegetables—are simmering nicely. The burners under other pots refuse to ignite. In one oven, an angelfood cake rises delicately. In another oven, a sullen roast of pork stays cold. Many women and men are working hard, peeling and scrubbing, sweeping and stirring. Some sit at a wooden table, wondering how to pay the bills. In one highchair, a child claps its hands and sings; in another highchair, a child throws porridge on the floor. A cat sits in a corner, waiting for mice and rats. The outer door of the kitchen is partly open. There, in the yard, women and hungry children wait, I fear, for food and shelter.

Let me begin my cook's tour of women and higher education. I will first crack open the past, then sift through the present, and end by offering a recipe for a home-brewed future.

Like men, women have always been taught. If baby girls survive, they are educated, formally and informally, in the customs of their culture. My female ancestors, in the damp peasant cottages of the English Midlands and the wet fields of Wales, learned how to speak, stitch, plant, cook, give birth, and pray. I am grateful for their genes. I am equally grateful that I do not have to imitate their lives.

Like men, women have always wanted to learn. However, the processes of modernization manufactured a particularly sturdy, and once very radical, framework of ideas about women and education. These ideas proposed that women were capable of self-definition and of "the life of the mind." The cultivation of the life of the mind was indispensable to self-definition. If rational thought characterized the highest life of the mind, as it did for Mary Wollstonecraft in *A Vindication of The Rights of Woman* in 1792, women were strong enough to lift the barbells and weights of reason.

Modernization, then, pumped up the phrase "knowing women," a triple pun. "Knowing women" means, first, women who know, women of active and assertive consciousness, women who are a lively part of the give-and-take of information. For them, knowing, no matter how painful it might be, is freeing. An example: a recent study asked female students in India if they had any information about menstruation before their menarche. 63.01% did; 36.99% did not. Of those with some knowledge, the majority found menarche a normal physiological function. All those with no knowledge were "appalled and horrified."[7]

Second, knowing women means knowing about women, the information and ideas that men, women, and children carry with them about gender. One such idea is the symbolic association of women and liberty, even when women lack political liberties, as women of all races and black men did in the 19th century when France gave the United States the Statue of Liberty. Third and finally, the phrase means the woman who says "No," the woman capable of refusals, grand and small. Modernization wrote a new chapter in the history of "no-ing" women, who answer "No" to ideologies that lobotomize their intelligence; "No" to institutions that would deny them admittance or treat them rawly; "No" to false and demeaning stories about them. "No-ing women" have made "knowing women" possible.

If the modern proposition about women's consciousness and capacities for information is powerful, so, too, is the resistance-secular and theological—to it. Remember that hot-tempered Englishwoman, Sarah Fyge Field Egerton. Born in the late 17th century, she was one of six daughters of an apothecary and sometime poet. Her rebelliousness and creativity enraged her father. Expelled from home, she married—first a lawyer and then a clergyman. Neither alliance seems to have been a tribute to wedded bliss. More happily, we hope, she wrote. In an early 18th-century poem, "The Emulation," she declares:

And shall we Women now sit tamely by, Make no excursions in Philosophy,

Or grace our Thoughts in tuneful Poetry? We will our Rights in Learning's World maintain, Wits empire, now, shall know a Female Reign . . .[8]

Logically, then, women belong to the institutions, like the library and university, that organize the life of the mind. To exclude women harms them as individuals. It is also unjust, unfair, and wasteful. As Carolyn G. Heilbrun writes, "Where the university must change is in allowing the energy of women to be exercised fully and to its own ends. Nothing is perhaps so wasted in our culture as the energies of women."[9] Women and men—of all classes, races, and nationalities—were willing to translate these modern beliefs into actions. Some efforts were subtle, others less so. In the late 19th-century, a woman's gift of a great deal of money to The Johns Hopkins University in Baltimore was the key that opened medical school doors to women. When some institutions persisted in excluding women, women's colleges came into being. By the end of the 19th century, the family of higher education had three siblings: the all-male institutions, the big brother; the all-female institutions, the spunky sister; and the co-educational institutions, the androgyne, who tolerated sister but preferred the company of older brother.

In co-educational and women's institutions, some women sought to reform research and the curriculum to reflect experiences of women. In the United States, in the last part of the 19th-century and first part of the 20th, women explicitly studied sex and gender. They "launched the modern study of sex differences."[10] Perhaps their most famous daughter was Margaret Mead. These prophets of women's studies also offered courses about women, sex, and gender at such diverse places as the University of Chicago, Wellesley College, Goucher College, and the University of Washington.[11] Sadly, their innovations were to be forgotten until women's history, systematically developed after the 1960s, recalled them.

Valiant though these struggles for and by the knowing woman were, they had their sapping difficulties. Extirpating the blindnesses of others, leaders retained the privileges of their own. The first woman president of my own women's college, the formidable M. Carey Thomas (1857-1935), argued fearlessly for the most rigorous possible education for women and for their social and professional opportunities. "Our failures," she announced sternly, "only marry." She told President Eliot of Harvard University that he had a "dark spot of medievalism" in his "otherwise luminous intelligence" because he stupidly declared that "the great tradition of learning . . .existed only for men."[12] Yet, she had awful, awful prejudices.

Many difficulties for the knowing women have been the consequence of the jagged, asymmetrical development of modernizing societies. These societies have, eventually, been prepared to contemplate a policy of educating all men and women to some degree. They have been prepared to educate some women to a high degree. They have not yet been prepared to abolish the structures and ideologies of gender that usually give men more public power and cultural authority than the women of their class. In the United States, the imbibers of the theories of Jean Jacques Rousseau and/or of "Republican Motherhood" have been as forceful as the imbibers of the theories of Mary Wollstonecraft. A recent account of a consultant's visit to two women's colleges in Saudi Arabia is a poignant example of the jaggedness and asymmetries of development.[13] Because of a movement for the education of girls and women that began in the 1950s, these colleges exist. Women now teach and learn in them. Yet, the colleges face "immense" problems. Women cannot move freely from the library of one institution to the other. Each library is inadequately stocked and staffed. Controlling and ratifying every library decision is a General Directorate for Girls' Education, all-male.

Inevitably, many supporters of the knowing woman

have accepted this contradictory message, this double bind. The purpose of a woman's education, they state benevolently, is to prepare women to cement the family and to serve god and society (or only society in a secular country). They next commonly muse, "If this is the purpose of a woman's education, what best fulfills it?" Should a woman get the same education and information as her brother and potential husband, even though her post-graduate role will differ from theirs? Or, should she get a different education and information from her brother and potential husband, because her post-graduate role will differ from theirs?

For a number of reasons, the struggle for and by the knowing women subsided during the middle part of the 20th-century, certainly in the United States. In the 1960s, it re-emerged. The reasons for this included a push for general educational reform; a commitment to social justice and racial equality that generated a renewed commitment to gender equality; some worry about the dissipation of the talents of educated women; the entrance of women of all races and classes into the public labor force, which provoked fresh questions about their education; new technologies of reproduction, such as birth control, which helped to re-define women's sexuality; and the rebirth of feminism in the 1960's, a rebirth inseparable from the changes I have outlined in truncated form.

Not coincidentally, the struggle by and for the knowing woman re-emerged at exactly the same time as the Information Society. In 1962, Fritz Machlup published *The Production and Distribution of Knowledge in the United States,* analyzing the production of knowledge as an economic activity and industry with its own occupational categories: education, research and development, the communications media, information machines (such as computers), and information services. In 1963, Betty Friedan published *The Feminine Mystique.* In 1972, the Japanese issued a white paper, *The Plan for Information Society, a National Goal Toward Year 2000.* In 1972, *Ms. Magazine* began publication. In 1977, the American Library Association, after its own careful planning, took up the question of libraries in a post-industrial, information society. In 1977, Elaine Showalter published *A Literature of Their Own* and Barbara K. Smith "Toward a Black Feminist Criticism." In 1982, John Naisbitt, in *Megatrends: Ten New Directions Transforming Our Lives,* told Americans that the most explosive shift in their lives was that from an industrial to an information society. In 1982, Carol Gilligan authored *In A Differ-*

ent Voice, her greatly influential study of women and moral reasoning.

In the Information Society, education matters for survival and success. As one commentator writes bluntly, "Upward access through the social-economic strata of this society is assumed to depend upon advanced education even more than at present."[14] Supporters of the struggle for the knowing woman want her to be a full citizen of the Information Society; opponents of the struggle do not. Not everyone who cares about women's citizenship in the Information Society is a feminist. Significantly, the necessity of educating women, at least narrowly, is a theme on which feminists and many non-feminists agree. Few people today believe that women are best barefoot, pregnant, and illiterate. However, feminists care passionately about the knowing woman. For us, education is a necessary means to the ends of autonomy, dignity, equality, mobility, self-sufficiency, power, and even, with luck, pleasure. Misogynists and the blindest of gender traditionalists have been right to fear the consequences of the education of women. "I think," reads a feminist button, "Therefore I am dangerous."

Self-consciously and imaginatively, contemporary feminism structured itself as an educational reform movement with five goals.

First, feminism would improve child-rearing and socialization practices. Next, it would organize small "consciousness-raising" groups. In them women would learn from each other about their lives in order to change these lives. Next, feminism would attack the media, the studios that market lessons and images, often trumped up, for a mass culture. Next, feminism would create cultural alternatives, a splendidly new art, literature, film, music, journalism and religion. Finally, feminism would "transform," or at least alter, the sites of formal education from child-care to research centers.

The explicit alliance between contemporary feminism and higher education, which began in the mid-1960s, has had its triumphs, so many that some now conclude that feminism has given way to postfeminism. A wry United States academic woman writes, " . . . feminists are beset by the fear that academe will declare premature victory for women in higher education . . . the students themselves may believe that the crisis has passed." To such students, feminists are now "feminine Dead Heads, congregating periodically around a few aging leaders so as to hear a tired repetition of a few standard tunes left over from the late 1960s."[15]

These triumphs are genuine. They include: [16]

— Most overt discrimination, which official policies and practices had formalized, has disappeared.

— Educators are aware of sex discrimination as an issue. On-campus rape, date rape, and sexual harassment are more visible.

— Women have organized themselves to end this discrimination. Some of their organizations are a part of institutional infrastructures, for example, as a Committee on the Status of Women or as a women's center.

— There are laws on the books against discrimination. Indeed, in 1992, on the 20th anniversary of Title IX, which prohibited schools that receive federal funds from discriminating against women, the Supreme Court ruled unanimously in *Franklin v. Gwinett County Public Schools* that students can sue schools that discriminate.

— There are, as well, institutional policies against discrimination, which are, at least partly effective.[17]

—We are aware of differences among women, especially racial differences, and of their importance.

— More women are entering colleges and universities. Between 1980 and 1990, the number of Native American women attending college increased 30%; of Asian American women 99%; of African-American women 16%; of Hispanic women 73%; of white women 15%.[18]

— Hiring is more equitable. Between 1972 and 1989, the proportion of women who were assistant professors grew from 24% to over 38%.

— Women and gender, as subjects, have entered our public consciousness and the curriculum. This has, in turn, pushed the gatekeepers of our information systems to change; to ask, for example, if the vocabulary of a catalogue is racist or sexist.[19] Dressed in a variety of names, "women's studies"

has leapt into being.

Quantitatively, the growth in research and teaching about women is impressive. If it were a stock, it would be booming. In 1969, in the United States, there were 16 or so courses devoted to the subject of women and gender. Today, there are women's studies courses in over 2/3rds of our universities; nearly 1/2 of our 4 year colleges; about 1/4 of our 2-year institutions. Altogether, about 2000 colleges and universities have some sort of a women's studies curriculum.[20] About 621 of these institutions have organized departments and programs. In 1970, at the American Philosophical Association's convention, none of the 100 papers was on race or gender. In 1990, 21 of 224 papers took up these issues.[21] A 1990 survey of English departments showed that 92.8% of them still wanted students to learn the intellectual, historical, and biographical backgrounds needed to understand the literature of a period; 88.6% still wanted students to derive pleasure from the wisdom and artistry of literary works. In addition, 61.7% hoped students would grasp the influence of race, class, and gender on literature and its interpretations.[22] In 1991, the Schlesinger Library at Radcliffe College had about 50 items on its list of current periodicals, from *Affilia: Journal of Women and Social Work;* through four journals with "gender" in their title; through *Sage: A Scholarly Journal on Black Women,* edited at Spelman College since 1984; to *Women's Studies Quarterly.*[23]

The three meetings that the United Nations Decade for Women sponsored helped to strengthen the global perception of the importance of the knowing woman.[24] By 1990, there were at least 164 free-standing and university-based research centers that focused on women: 66 in the United States and Canada; 29 in Asia, 10 in India alone; 25 in Europe and England; 23 in Mexico, Central America, and Latin America; 8 in Northern and Sub-Saharan Africa; 5 in Australia and New Zealand; 4 in the Middle East; 4 in the Caribbean.[25] One center is now being formed in Russia.

No matter how marginal, no matter how thinely financed, these achievements are in place. Books and articles are in print. Teachers and students are in classrooms. Students get diplomas and certificates. Following a miserable tradition, the presence of success has even provoked a family wrangle. For we thought of ourselves, not as settled and sedate, but as transgressive. We have resisted being the good girls of the conference room, library, and lab. We have upset apple carts and criticized epics about Eva as Apple Eater. Writing of the feminist art history she has done so much to establish, Linda Nochlin warns : " . . . feminist art history is there to make trouble . . . to ruffle feathers in the patriarchal dovecotes . . . At its strongest, a feminist art history is . . . (an) anti-establishment practice, meant to call many of the major precepts of the discipline into question . . . "[26] Linking transgression and renewal, Barbara K. Smith introduces the anthology, *Home Girls.* "I sincerely hope that Home Girls is upsetting, because being upset is often the first step toward change."[27] How does one maintain an anti-establishment practice when one gets tenure at a major university? What should a movement for change do when change occurs? What should a rebellious graduate student do when she becomes a graduate dean?

Ironically, the resistance to women's studies helps to keep it on its toes. Some people are appalled by an educational reform movement that has debts to feminism and speaks cheerfully of ruffling feathers and being upsetting. For them, feminism is a fright wig of a word, or, to shift the metaphor, a disease that infects higher education with the plague of politics and polemic, the bacteria of bias, the germ of ideology. One ostensibly nonpartisan observer warns sternly, "Although the subject (Women's Studies) is formally nonpartisan, in practice such courses are dominated, disproportionately, by feminist—often radical feminist-perspectives. In practice, lesbian and socialist ideologies are heavily emphasized."[28] In some countries, feminism is also the synonym for lesbianism; in others, a destructive Western import.

It is not surprising that women's studies has stimulated opposition. This reflects the resistance to any change in our bibliographies and lecture notes. It also reflects two gender specific fears. First, that women of all races, like minorities of both genders, are irrational, castrators of reason, by nature nonacademic,[29] and second, even more broadly, that changes in our thinking about women will order up changes in their social and subject positions. Cynthia Fuchs Epstein writes:

> First, it is difficult for members of any social order to question their own order and not regard it as necessary for the continued functioning of social life. Second, social structure makes some kind of thinking and knowing easier than others. Third, because gender distinctions are a basic element in the creation of the social order—and because those distinctions are typically stratified, with

men at higher ranks, men have a stake in justifying and continuing the status quo. Challenges to a social order do not typically come form those who benefit from its arrangements.[30]

Unfortunately, women's studies has given its opponents plenty of tasteless, and even tainted, food to spit at. In its urge to change higher education, women's studies has sometimes spoken as if there were nothing good about the quad and ivory tower. Some feminists have refused to see any hope in higher education, believing it to be impossibly entangled with the ideological and methodological net of domineering "male thought." For them, only hobnailed boots do footnotes. Intellectually, women's studies has also often been far too reductive and prone to labelling. In the late 1960s and early 1970s, it spoke most sweepingly about "The Patriarchy" and about "woman" — as if "The Patriarchy" were the equivalent of original sin and "woman" the equivalent of redemption. In the 1970s, women's studies turned from "The Patriarchy" as a description of the workings and fixings of history and turned to an iron triangle, "race/class/gender," a three-fold set of historical categories that was meant to characterize all societies, at all times, at all places. Of course, race, class, and gender are profoundly important historical categories, but so are tribe, nation, religion, and age.

Simultaneously, women's studies has indulged in vulgar games of identity politics, "the assumption that a person's racial or ethnic (or sexual) identity and views are one and the same."[31] Such labelling, of self or others, has often been as self-righteous as it has been an oversimplification of both identity and politics. "Did we as feminists," asks one woman, "in our zeal to delineate the pervasiveness of racism and sexism in our society stretch our concepts to such an extent that one must now use the same label to talk about a Ku Klux Klan lynching and the failure of a women's music festival to provide a sliding scale of entry fees?"[32] Emotionally, women's studies was also to provide a perfect haven of principle and a nurturing sanctuary. If women's studies lapsed for a moment, it was to be condemned as if it contained salmonella or as if it were the unforgivably never good-enough mother.

Yet, even these blunders cannot account for the hysteria and hyperbole of the opposition to knowing women. Like a shadow, the opposition has mutated as women's studies has evolved and as large forces have gathered and stormed over the sociopolitical landscape. In the past decade, some social conservatives and neoconservatives have organized campaigns that have targeted women's studies and announced that this phenomenon, often labelled "academic feminism," represents the ills of the postmodern world. In this campaign, women's studies/academic feminism is a symptom of a vast degeneration. It betrays the free market, the free world, free and objective inquiry, the family, and heterosexuality without tears. Religious fundamentalists chime in that women's studies/academic feminism is ungodly, too. In sum, we "are accused of being intolerant, close-minded, parochial idealogues. Like the witches of the fifteenth century, we are seen as a dangerous and wicked bunch, operating as a cult to threaten all that is sacred and good . . . we are threatening democracy, closing the American mind, and undermining the very concept of academic standards . . . we have fostered a climate of intolerance on university campuses, where feminism rules, where gays and lesbians define the dominant sexual discourse, and where racist, sexist, and homophobic speech and behavior are no longer allowed."[33]

Recently, a small group of women, who call themselves feminists of one variety or another, have joined in the search for red women's studies. Perhaps one of the triumphs of women's studies is that it has provided such a nice career opportunity to these ladies. They are reconstituting the dreary binary opposition between Good Women and Bad Girls, here between themselves, the Good Women of Responsible Feminism and Academic Tradition, and the others, the Bad Girls of Irresponsible Feminism and Academic Defilement, witchy creatures who prefer peaked hats and broomsticks to caps and gowns. Interestingly, in this picture, all the Bad Girls of Irresponsible Feminism seem to be white, a contemptible erasure of the contributions to women's studies of women of color.[34] The most highly publicized, and self-publicizing, of these opposing women is Camille Paglia. Paglia, of course, likes to project herself as the baddest of girls and academic feminists as the dreariest of good girls. Often, in this self-romanticizing mode, she seems like Vanilla Ice, the white male rapper, with a Ph.D. However, Paglia advances, not an avant-garde position, but the yawniest and most atavistic of theories. For her, man is culture (art, politics, athletics, philosophy, science). Woman is nature. Paglia yelps, "Woman's body is a sea acted upon by the month's lunar wave-motion. Sluggish and dormant, her fatty tissues are gorged with water, then suddenly cleansed at hormonal high tide."[35] As a spokeswoman for the anti-feminist backlash, Paglia also repeats history and the messages of female anti-

feminists of 1890-1920, another period of agitation over the "Woman Question." Toughly and smartly, Naomi Wolf pins her "recycled Darwinism" and "goggling and shameless untruths."[36] Poor Paglia—she wants to be an international voice, more powerful than CNN, but she is a revved-up canned echo.

Today, women's studies offers the Information Society several goods. One is a moral vision of a just and equitable educational community. This community guarantees freedom of inquiry, although freedom notoriously permits cultural iniquities. I loathe violent pornography; it is hate speech written on women's bodies. Nevertheless, even the sleazy producers and consumers of pornography have their rights under my freedom of information act. More happily, in women's studies, the moral vision of community pictures access to learning for rich and middling and poor alike, mutual respect among all learners, and policies that serve all learners. Among these policies are child-care; freedom from racial and sexual harassment; democratic self-governance; and equitable hiring of all races and both genders. Despite affirmative action, equitable hiring is an ideal, not a commonplace. In 1992, in the United States, only about 12% of the chief executive officers of our 3,500 or so institutions of higher education were women. Tenure is still more elusive for women than for men. In part, hiring and promoting women is hard because of deep, persistent tensions between our expectations of what a woman ought to be like and our expectations of what a professional ought to be doing.[37] How can one be "a woman," self-sacrificing and domestic, and "a professional," selffulfilling and public?

A second good that women's studies offers the Information Society is a rich, gusty, cross-disciplinary menu of ideas about sex and gender; sexuality; sexual difference; differences among women; and difference itself. The initial recipe after World War II was Simone deBeauvoir, *The Second Sex.* Under the influence of deBeauvoir, women's studies has distinguished between sex, a biological condition, subject to some of the rules of nature, and gender, a social construction subject to the rules of culture. These rules of culture govern much of what we believe to be natural--our bodies, for example, or our sexuality. Joan Scott explains, " . . . gender is the social organization of sexual difference. But this does not mean that gender reflects or implements fixed and natural physical differences between women and men; rather gender is the knowledge that establishes meanings for bodily differences."[38] Historians are now demonstrating how cultures have drawn their particular geographies of sex and the body. For example, modern heterosexuality and homosexuality did not spring from an eternal matrix of Mother Nature. Instead, they were made in the foundries of nineteenth-century culture. Crucially, societies vary from each other. All have biological women, but the meaning of being a woman differs radically from one to another. All have biological men, but the meaning of being a man differs as radically from one to another. All have gender systems, but the meaning of each system differs as radically from one to another. Under the pressure of these perceptions, women's studies has taught itself not to speak of a universal woman, of an "essential femaleness." To do so is to commit the intellectual sin of "essentialism."

Much of the energy of women's studies has been spent showing how often a gender system is hierarchical; how often sexual difference is synonomous with sexual discrimination. Economists document economic inequalities; political scientists the denial of citizenship to women; psychologists the reasons why men batter and women submit; media critics the demeaning or silly representations of women and sexuality; educationalists the drastic short-changing of girls in primary and secondary school[39] and the "chilly climate" for women in higher education.[40]

However, in the 1970s and early 1980s, many feminists began to distrust this distrust of difference when difference meant only discrimination. These feminists prized "the female" as weak and deplored the dangerous differences between "the female" and "the male." In the humanities, scholars began to search for a women's culture, a women's literary and artistic tradition, and a new, free women's writing that would be the poetics of a newly-freed body and psyche. In philosophy, Sara Ruddick began to elaborate the theory of "maternal thinking," a picture of the cognitive and ethical behavior that arises from the practice of mothering.[41] Among the best-known figures who arose during this period are the French writer Helene Cixous, a creator of "ecriture feminine," and Carol Gilligan.

In the 1970s, several other developments also emerged, in part in reaction to the elaboration of "the female" or "women's culture." Among them were men's studies, an elaboration, often despairing, even woeful, of "the male" or "men's culture" or "the construction of masculinity." Much more than the evocation of Iron John, men's studies has intellectual potential. A second development was the creation of

"gender studies," sometimes defended as an intellectual alliance between women's studies and men's studies that would show how "femininity" and "masculinity" fit together, like two huge Lego blocks, to form a gender structure. As often, the brief for gender studies states that expanding our focus from a sex, i.e. women or men, to a structure, i.e. gender, will permit greater intellectual range.

Superficially, it might seem contradictory to conceptualize sexual difference as both destructive and constructive. However, seen as a whole, women's experiences have been contradictory, full of conflicting conditions and clashing forces. To note but four: First, if the family is the home plate of patriarchy, the family may nevertheless be the place in which men and women are companions against a hostile world. Second, if many societies devalue women, they may nevertheless generate a special set of values, "female values," that have their own meaning and worth. Third, if many societies scorn women as creators and guardians of public organizations and culture, women have resisted in two ways. They have created and guarded their own organizations (the women's movement, for example) and cultural spaces (e. g., the women's colleges, West African wall paintings, Greek mourning songs). Women have also demanded access to public organizations and cultural domains that would exclude them. Fourth, most painfully, if many societies deprive women of power over themselves, women still have powers to exercise. Women, though Other to men, have their Others, too. In the United States, white women did own black slaves—of both sexes. In Nazi Germany, Nazi women did brutalize and kill Jews—of both sexes. Colonizers both lorded and ladied it over the colonized. Affluent women hire servants—of both sexes.

In brief, the picture of Woman as Total Victim is as false as the picture of Woman as Total Woman. The study of women and power shows what common sense alone should have: the historical and contemporary differences among women that race, class, sexuality, tribe, nationality, age, religion, and a host of other conditions cut. In the 1970s, women's studies fissured into a number of groups, each of which fused the study of sex and gender with that of another powerful element of identity: class for Marxist Feminist or Socialist Feminist Studies; sexual preference for Lesbian Studies; colonization for post-colonial studies; region for student of rural or urban women; nationality for Australian Women's Studies or Canadian Women's Studies; race and ethnicity for Black Feminist Studies, Chicana Studies, or Asian-American Women's Studies. Deborah McDowell, a black feminist critic and African-American literature scholar, suggests: "Black feminist critics ought . . . to consider the specific language of Black women's literature . . . describe the ways Black women writers employ literary devices . . . compare the way Black women writers create their won mythic structures."[42]

Each of these groups has now three, intersecting tasks. First, each has to explore its own history, culture, social structure, and gender relations. These explorations are labyrinthian, demanding, and intricate. Each group will have its own information needs.[43] Each group will have its own complexities. So will every individual member of it. Cherrie Moraga, talking about her birthright of Chicana mother and Anglo father, writes of questioning "my right to even work on an anthology which is to be written 'exclusively by Third World women.' I have had to look critically at my claim to color, at a time when, among white feminist ranks, it is a 'politically correct' (and sometimes peripherally advantageous) assertion to make."[44] Such materials must then become available for "mainstreaming" into women's studies and the larger curriculum.

Second, each group must confront its relations with other groups. It must ask how deeply relations of domination and dependence affect and infect these relations. It must excavate the errors it is prone to make about other groups—in part because of relations of domination and dependence. Like many white professional women, I am guilty of blunders about race and class. Slowly, I have begun to dig out the beliefs and assumptions of my own benevolence that remain about Native Americans because I grew up in a town a few miles from a despised "Indian reservation." Fortunately, one of the gifts of the education I received in my primary school and family was a serious regard for Native American cultures.

Third and finally, each group can and should enter into coalitions with others. So can individuals of various groups. For it is now time for us—as women and as men and women—to dwell with both our good differences and our unities. We must not table our differences. On the contrary, we must continue to struggle against the bad differences and to celebrate the good. Simultaneously, we must realize that we sit at the same table. Because we have begun to measure our differences honestly, we can now begin to put our oils and vinegars together, dress up our common interests. Together, despite our suspicions and difficulties, we can compose big, renewing historical, social, and philosophical narratives. "Dialogue and principled coalition," writes Patricia Hill Collins, "create possibilities for new versions of truth."[45] Together, across and through and beyond our differences, we must construct and reconstruct our classrooms. One source of unity is a moral vision of education, like that I sketched before.

If women's studies can fulfill this third task, the living with our good differences and unities at once, it will deepen its experiment with educational democracy. Women's studies will continue its role as our seasoned pioneer in multi-cultural, multimethodological research, teaching, and governance. If we are to survive well into the 21st-century, we, this harming species, have much to do. We must educate a literate populace; feed, heal, and shelter us all; establish human rights; respect the ecology of earth and space. Women's studies speaks to these desperate issues. We must also learn to live equitably in a multi-cultural, multiracial, multi- specied world. Yes, women's studies affirms, we will respond to this moral, political and intellectual imperative as well.

As I regard the future of women, the Information Society, and freedom, I have my market share of dread. My dread has two sources. One source is that we will not grant the knowing woman full citizenship in the Information Society; that the knowing woman will continue to be too dangerous; that we will not give her the tools that she needs. If we do not, we will be guilty of an enormous historical blunder and scandal. Even today, women do not have guaranteed access to basic literacy. Table 1.3 of the *1989 UNESCO Statistical Yearbook* gives the percentage of men and women over the age of 15 who are illiterate in 129 countries and territories. The percentage of illiterate men is alarming, the percentage of illiterate women, especially rural women, more so. The sexes are equally literate in fewer than twenty countries. Women are more literate than men in eleven places, all small, a high proportion of them in the Caribbean. Men are more literate than women in all the rest.[46]

Nor, crucially, do women have equal access to the science and technology that is the foundation of the Information Society. One study found that 49% of the boys in the 11th grade in American high schools had used an electricity meter, but only 17% of the girls.[47] In

1989, men took 91.8% of the doctorates in engineering in American graduate schools; women 8.2%. Men took 81.2% of the doctorates in the physical sciences; women took 18.8%).[48]

Nor, I fear, will we give the knowing woman the information that she needs about herself—about her own history; about her capacities for work and love in the Information Society; about her body, health, and sexuality. The story of silicone-gel implants seems, in part, a story about women being both misinformed and uninformed about their health.[49] This story also seems, in part, a story about some women who obey still-powerful cultural norms that reduce their identity to their flesh, their beauty and sexual allure. Ironically, the Information Society tells us that our minds, not our bodies, are our power generators.

The second source of my dread is the uncertainty about the future of the Information Society itself. Cyberspace is still new territory, though familiar territory to readers of speculative fiction and hackers. The laws that will govern it are up for grabs.[50] So is the nature of the freedoms it will enjoy. It is unclear what men and women will compose the Constitution and Bill of Rights of Cyberspace. As Mitchell Kapor, the founder of the Lotus Development Corporation, writes, "Our society has made a commitment to openness and to free communication. But if our legal and social institutions fail to adapt to new technology, basic access to the global electronic media could be seen as a privilege, granted to those who play by the strictest rules, rather than as a right held by anyone who needs to communicate."[51] A test, I suggest, of the authentic freeness of cyberspace will be the freedom of the knowing woman.

Though anxious, I have a stubborn muscle in my optimism. This muscle flexes and insists that history can be its Nautilus machine as well as rack and Catherine wheel. My optimism reminds me that men and women have worked throughout history for the knowing woman; that women's studies has invented itself in the last thirty years. And, my optimism whistles, the gender changes that have been inseparable from both the rebirth of feminism and the birth of the Information Society seem irrevocable. So encouraged, I was, on December 12, 1991, sitting in Staten Island and reading *The New York Times*, my home town newspaper. This experience often throws acid on optimism, but on this day, I saw a story, "Brooklyn College Firsts: Marshall and Rhodes."[52] For the first time in its 61-year old

history, Brooklyn College had won a Marshall Scholarship and a Rhodes Scholarship, both prestigious, both for study in England. Both the winners were women: Lisette Nieves, who had won the Rhodes, and Toba Friedman, who had won the Marshall. Friedman said that she had never planned to go to college, but, working as a secretary, she found her "mind going to mush." A friend said, "Try college." She did and took a course in English history taught by Bonnie Sour Anderson, a vital figure in women's history. "She blew me away," Friedman said. Here, I thought, is a sign, a sign that we are building a democratic wits empire. This wits empire will know neither a male reign, nor a female reign, nor a reign of terror. Instead, we will be a company of equals, some smarter than others no doubt, but all of us cooking up an educational and intellectual storm, processing our words in an open kitchen of plenty, and pleasure, and freedom.

Endnotes

1. A version of this paper was given on March 31, 1992 as the Bella Abzug Lecture at Hunter College in New York City. It builds on, alludes to, and refines my earlier work, including but not limited to Catharine R. Stimpson, *Where The Meanings Are: Feminism and Cultural Spaces* (New York and London: Methuen, Inc., 1988); a paper, "On Feminist Scholarship," given at the Radcliffe Conference, "Defining the Challenge: Emerging Needs and Constraints," Radcliffe College, December, 1988; an article, "What Am I Doing When i Do Women's Studies in 1990?" in *Left Politics and the Literary Profession,* edited by Lennard J. Davis and Bella Mirabella (New York: Columbia University Press, 1990); a paper, "Mind Changes," read at the American Library Association, annual meeting, Chicago, Illinois, June 1990; "Knowing Women, The 1990 Marjorie Smart Memorial Lecture," given at the University of Melbourne, published in *Women in Higher Education: An Agenda for the Decade,* ed. David R. Jones and Susan L. Davies, p. 11-45 (University of New England, Australia, Department of Administrative, Higher and Adult Education Services, 1990).

2. In 1988, the Executive Branch issued such "gag rules" for federally financed family planning clinics. The Supreme Court upheld these rules in Rust v. Sullivan. Congress then passed legislation to revoke the Court's ruling, which President Bush vetoed, the veto that could not be overridden on November 19, 1991. On March 20, 1992, the Executive

Branch said that doctors in federally financed family clinics, but not nurses or counsellors, could give limited advice about abortions. However, doctors could not actually refer women to abortion clinics. Philip J. Hilts. "White House Allows Some Advice At Public Clinics About Abortion." *New York Times* 1 (March 21, 1992), 41 A-l, 10.

3. Roma M. Harris. "The Information Needs of Battered Women." *RQ* 28 (Fall, 1888): 62–70.

4. Judith G. Touchton and Lynne Davis. *Fact Book on Women in Higher Education.* (New York: American Council on Education and Macmillan Publishing Co., 1991). Touchton and Davis is a useful factbook about women in higher education in the United States.

5. Debra E. Blum. "Old Issues Unresolved: Environment Still Hostile to Women in Academe, New Evidence Indicates." *Chronicle of Higher Education* 38 (October 9, 1991): A-l, 20.

6. Susan Faludi. *Backlash: The Undeclared War Against American Women.* (New York: Crown Publishers, 1991).

7. K. P. Skandhan, Amita K. Pandya, Sumangala Skandhan, and Yagnesh B. Mehta. "Menarche: Prior Knowledge and Experience." *Adolescence* 23 (Spring, 1988): 149-154.

8. Sarah Fyge Field Egerton. The Emulation, in *First Feminists: British Women Writers 1587-1799,* ed. Moira Ferguson, p. 170 (Bloomington, Indiana: Indiana University Press and Feminist Press, 1985).

9. Carolyn G. Heilbrun. "The Politics of Mind: Women, Tradition, and the University." *Papers on Language and Literature* 24 (Summer, 1988): 231-244.

10. Rosalind Rosenberg. *Beyond Separate Spheres: Intellectual Roots of Modern Feminism* (New Haven and London: Yale University Press, 1982).

11. Barbara Miller Solomon. *In the Company of Educated Women: A History of Women and Higher Education in American.* (New Haven: Yale University Press, 1985), p. 87.

12. Barbara M. Cross. *The Educated Woman in America: Selected Writings of Catharine Beecher, Margaret Fuller, and M. Carey Thomas.* (New York: Teachers College Press, 1965).

13. Elizabeth J. King. "Libraries of Two Women's Colleges in Saudi Arabia." *International Library Review* 19 (July, 1987): 243-248.

14. Rollin Marquis. "Prologue: Post-Industrial Society and the Growth of Information: The Impact on Libraries," in *The Information Society: Issues and*

Answers. ed. E.J.Josey. (Phoenix, Arizona: Oryx Press, 1978), p. 1–3.

15. Mary Burgan. "Women in Academe in the '90s: *Back to the Future* Part II," *Change* (March-April, 1990): 74-76.

16. I derive this list from my observations, from a conversation with Bernice W. Sandler, March 23, 1992, and from Mirian K. Chamberlain, *Women in Academe: Progress and Prospects* (New York: Russell Sage Foundation, 1988).

17. Elizabeth A. Williams, Julie A. Lam and Michael Shively. "The Impact of a University Policy on the Sexual Harassment of Female Students." *Journal of Higher Education* 63 (January/February, 1992): 50-64. A survey of sexual harassment studies, shows that a good sexual harassment policy and grievance procedure can reduce faculty and staff harassment. Michele A. Paludi and Richard B. Barickman. *Academic and Workplace Sexual Harassment: A Resource Manual.* (Albany: State University of New York Press, 1991).

18. "College Enrollment by Race, Selected Years." *Chronicle of Higher Education* 38 (March 18, 1992): A-35.

19. Susan Searing. "Institutions of Memory: Libraries and Women's Work(s)." *Michigan Quarterly Review* 26 (Winter, 1987): 228-241.

20. Mariam K. Chamberlain and Alison Bernstein. "Philanthropy and the Emergence of Women's Studies." *Teachers College Record* 93 (Spring, 1992): 556-568.

21. Johnella Butler and Betty Schmitz. "Ethnic Studies, Women's Studies, and Multiculturalism." *Change* 24 (January/ February, 1992): 36-41.

22. Phyllis Franklin, Bettina J. Huber, and David Laurence. "Continuity and Change in the Study of Literature." *Change* 24 (January/February, 1992): 42-52.

23. Schlesinger Library on the History of Women in America, Radcliffe College. Schlesinger Library's Current Periodicals (October, 1991).

24. The meetings were in Mexico City, 1975; Copenhagen, 1980; and Nairobi, 1985. Janice J. Monk, "Feminist Scholarship: An International Perspective," *Journal of Population Studies* 11 (June, 1988): 197-218, is a sensible overview of international feminist scholarship. *Les Cahiers des Grif* has issued an undated report about a research project done in 1987-88 and presented at a 1989 conference about women's studies in Europe, Women's Studies: Concept and Reality: A Research Project Being Part of EEC Action Program for Opportunities in

Education.

25. Mariam K. Chamberlain. "International Centers for Research on Women." (New York: National Council for Research on Women, 1989). Also personal observations.

26. Linda Nochlin. *Women, Art, and Power and Other Essays.* (New York: Harper and Row, 1988), p. xii.

27. Barbara Smith, ed. *Home Girls: A Black Feminist Anthology* (New York: Kitchen Table, Women of Color Press, 1983), p. iii.

28. David P. Bryden. "It ain't what they teach, it's the way that they teach it." *The Public Interest* 103 (Spring, 1991): 38-53.

29. An armory of defenses emerged vividly in a "mainstreaming" project that involved 45 faculty members, 42 male, all tenured, at the University of Arizona. Several men were unable to relinquish ideas and feelings about gender. The myth of the castrating woman and the association of women with disorder and irrationality died particularly hard. Susan Hardy Aiken, Karen Anderson, Myra Dinnerstein, Judy Nolte Lensink, and Patricia MacCorquodale, *Changing Our Minds: Feminist Transformations of Knowledge* (Albany: State University of New York Press, 1988).

30. Cynthia Fuchs Epstein. *Deceptive Distinctions: Sex, Gender, and The Social Order,* (New Haven and London: Yale University Press and Russell Sage Foundation, 1988), p. 9.

31. Daphne Patai. "The Struggle for Feminist Purity Threatens the Goals of Feminism." *Chronicle of Higher Education* 38 (February 5, 1992): B-1, 2.

32. Noretta Koertge. "P.C.: A Feminist Response," *Women's Studies in Indiana* 17 (September/October, 1991): 1.

33. Margaret L. Andersen. "From the Editor." *Gender and Society* 5 (December 1991): 453-458.

34. Margaret L. Anderser, Ibid.

35. Feminist philosophy offers a case study of conflict about feminist scholarship. In 1987, Christina Hoff Sommers, a self described moral philosopher and "equity feminist," at Clark University gave a paper at the 1987 meetings of the Eastern Division of the American Philosophical Association. Alison Jagger was a respondent. Margarita Levin, "Challenge to Feminist Philosophy," *Academic Questions.* 1 (Fall, 1988): 48-53, writes up the event dramatically, casting Sommers as a philosopher capable of good questions, academic feminists as incapable of handling them. Signing herself Christina Sommers, Sommers published a paper, "Should The Academy Support Academic Feminism?" *Public Affairs Quarterly* 2 (July, 1988): 97-120, which overlaps with the talk Levin describes and which thanks Levin, among others, for her help. Scrutinizing "academic feminists" unfavorably, she compares them to the more intellectually responsible "liberal academic feminism." Over a year later, she published a version in "Feminist Philosophers Are Oddly Unsympathetic to the Women They Claim to Represent," *Chronicle of Higher Education* 36 (October 11, 1989): B 23. This provokes a number of letters, from Jagger among others, in the *Chronicle,* November 1, 1989, B 3-4; November 15, 1989, B 3-4; November 22, 1989, B-4. The row in *The Chronicle* resumes with Scott Jaschik, "Philosophy Professor Portrays Her Feminist Colleagues as Out of Touch and 'Relentlessly Hostile to the Family'," *Chronicle of Higher Education* 38 (January 15, 1992): A-1, 16, 18, "The Acrimonious Debate Over Feminist Philosophy," "Letters to the Editor," *Chronicle of Higher Education* 38 (February 12, 1992): B-4,5; "Philosopher answers anti-feminism charges," *Chronicle of Higher Education* 38 (February 26, 1992): A–38

36. Naomi Wolf. "Feminist Fatale." *New Republic* 206 (March 16, 1992): 23-25.

37. An example of the career differences between a man and a woman because one was a man and the other a woman: In 1988, Gertrude B. Elion won the Nobel Prize for Physiology or Medicine. She said that she chose her career because she wanted to help people, that her family was supportive. However, she had to struggle against "preconceived notions of what careers were suitable for women." Graduating from college in 1937 with a degree in biochemistry, she taught high school because no laboratory would hire a woman, a practice that the hiring necessities of World War II finally broke. In 1944, she got a job in private industry. She worked for a Ph.D. at night, until the school insisted she become a full-time student, a status she could not afford. Convinced that marriage and a career were incompatible, she never married. In contrast, her coworker and co-winner of the Nobel, George H. Hitchings, got a Ph.D. in biochemistry at Harvard, married, had two children, and hired Gertrude Elion. Gina Kolata. "A Research Collaboration Spanning Four Decades," *New York Times* (October 17, 1988): C-16. The literature about that tension between women's domestic role and a scholar's public role is depressingly extensive. A recent, major addition is Nadya Aisenberg and Mona

Harrington. *Women of Academe: Outsiders in the Sacred Grove.* (Amherst: University of Massachusetts Press, 1988). See also Katherine S. Mangan. "Women Seek Time Off to Bear Children Without Jeopardizing Academic Careers," *The Chronicle of Higher Education* 34 (February 3, 1988): A-1, A-16. Personal reports from a single discipline are in Women's Classical Caucus 1988. I might add that my use of the adverb "depressingly" is a mark of the feminism in my scholarship.

38. Nadya Aisenberg, op. cit.; Joan Wallach Scott. *Gender and the Politics of History* (New York: Columbia University Press, 1988), p. 2.

39. American Association of University Women Educational Foundation, Wellesley College, Center for Research on Women. The *AAUW Report: How Schools Shortchange Girls.* (Washington, D.C.: AAUW Educational Foundation, 1992).

40. For example, Bernice Resnick Sandlen, *The Campus Climate Revistied: Chilly For Women Faculty, Administrators, and Graduate Students,* (Washington, D.D.: Project on the Status and Education of Women, Association of American Colleges, 1986).

41. Sara Ruddick. *Maternal Thinking: Toward a Politics of Peace.* (New York: Ballantine Books, 1990).

42. Deborah E. McDowell. New Directions for Black Feminist Criticism in *The New Feminist Criticism,* ed. Elaine Showalter. (New York: Pantheon Books, 1985), p. 186-199.

43. Betty J. Glass. "Information Needs of Minority Women and Serial Resources: A Selected Bibliography." *The Reference Librarian* 27/28 (1990): 289-303.

44. Cherrie Moraga. "La Guera." in *Race. Class. and Gender: An Anthology,* edited by Margaret L. Andersen and Patricia Hill Collins. (Belmont, CA: Wadsworth Publishing Co., 1992), p. 27.

45. Patricia Hill Collins. *Black Feminist Thought: Knowledge, Consciousness. and the Politics of Empowerment.* (New York and London: Routledge, 1991).

46. *The World's Women 1970-1990* (New York: United Nations, 1991), Social Statistics and Indicators Series K, No. 8 is a statistical handbook about women globally. Pages 45-53 focus on literacy, education, and training.

47. American Association of University Women Educational Foundation, op. cite, p. 28.

48. "Almanac." *Chronicle of Higher Education* 38 (August 28, 1991): A–27.

49. Joan E. Ridgon. "Women Find It Difficult to Get Breast Implants Removed." *Wall Street Journal* 73 (March 20, 1992): B-1, 10. 50. Anne W. Branscomb. "Common Law for the Electronic Frontier." *Scientific American* 265 (September, 1991): 154-158.

51. Mitchell Kaporl. "Civil Liberties in Cyberspace." *Scientific American* 265 (September, 1991): 158.

52. "Brooklyn College Firsts: Marshall and Rhodes." *New York Times* 141 (December 12, 1991): B-3.

Why We Stopped Eating Bicycles: New Measures of Success in College and Research Libraries

W. David Penniman
Council of Library Resources
Washington, D. C.

I'm pleased to speak to ACRL, the largest division of ALA, today and to address some issues that I believe are crucial to the mission of your organization. Your mission is in part to enhance the ability of academic and research libraries to serve effectively the library and information needs of current and potential library users. The Council on Library Resources' mission is to conduct or foster research to address the problems of libraries in general and research libraries in particular. So our missions have much in common. Over the years the Council has had a distinguished record of significant work in a variety of library areas. Just as you are dealing with a changing environment, so is the Council. Not surprisingly, then, the research agenda for the Council is evolving. As the new president of the Council it is my responsibility to shape that agenda to serve our constituency well. During the past year, I have travelled extensively to campuses across the country and listened to library directors and staff, to faculty and deans, to graduate students and administrators. I have also met with funding sources and critical suppliers of services and materials crucial to library operations. From these discussions come many of the ideas I will present to you today as a research agenda for you and for the Council.

Now, what does all this have to do with eating bicycles? Well, it is a catchy title that I thought might get a little more attention than the official version, "Research Agenda for Academic Libraries." But there is more. I will tell you why we can learn something from the bicycle-eating and other such escapades, but I won't tell you yet—that would be much too early in my talk. First I want to give you some insight into my biases and overall philosophy about libraries.

I've had some fun in previous talks with various fictional descriptions of libraries. One of my favorites appears early in *The Name of the Rose*,[1] and it is as follows:

The library was laid out on a plan which has re-

mained obscure to all over the centuries, and which none of the monks is called upon to know. (Should we read that as faculty?) Only the librarian has received the secret, from the librarian who preceded him, and he communicates it while still alive, to the assistant librarian, so that death will not take him by surprise and rob the community of that knowledge. Only the librarian has, in addition to that knowledge, the right to move through the labyrinth of the books, he alone knows where to find them and where to replace them. He alone is responsible for their safekeeping.

We are well past the era described in this fictional piece, but we still have libraries that are labyrinths, users for whom the "plan" of the library is obscure, and librarians who must devote much of their time to the "safekeeping" of books. As Billy Frye, provost at Emory University and a member of the Council's board described in a recent talk,[2] librarians in academic institutions are struggling with the costs of three libraries:

1) The library of the past, focused on building comprehensive collections and providing direct physical access to printed materials.
2) The library of the present, with extraordinary added costs of inflation, automation, and preservation of decaying print.
3) And the library of the future for which they must plan, which includes not only the development of new ideas, but the implementation of new prototypes for publishing, acquiring, storing, and providing access to information through new technology and new attitudes about such fundamental things as ownership and access.

This future library is not predestined or assured, but as I will argue later, it is essential if our users are to be served well in our changing world.

I do not now and have never believed in a future that

"unfolds before our eyes" as we sit passively by or make tentative guesses at what lies ahead. Such an approach assumes a predestination that I find difficult to swallow. I believe we must shape the future, not let it shape us. I believe that, despite the tremendous changes in information technology we have seen in our own lifetime. We have seen storage technology advance from paper to microfilm to magnetic and optical technology. Where we once could store only a few hundred characters per cubic inch, we can now store billions of characters per cubic inch. Transmission capabilities have made similar startling advances. We've jumped from the 50 words per minute of telegraphy to billions of words per minute via glass fibers, and 100 trillion words per minute is within reach. Processing has gone from hundreds to billions of instructions per second, and parallel processing makes the rate practically limitless.

Yet our ability to process all this information is virtually unchanged from the time our ancestors emerged from their caves where they had scrawled primitive symbols on the walls. They could process symbols at about 300 units per minute—and so do we. This limit, and our inability to speed up our own processing capacity, is symbolic, I believe, of our greatest challenge. That challenge is to assure that all this information (which in the future may be stored, processed, and transmitted as bits) can and will be delivered as *knowledge* that is of use to humans.

Our ability to use technology to address this last barrier (the barrier to understanding) is sorely limited—not because we lack technological know-how, but because we lack strategic know-how. We have not developed a clear view of what we want to achieve and what goals we seek. Yet strategic goal seeking is the key to preparing for—and surviving in—the future. And strategic goal seeking has never been more crucial for libraries than it is today, because libraries have the potential for delivering knowledge, not just bitstreams. Libraries can focus on content as well as channels. That is what sets them apart from most other information delivery systems. Yet we see library budgets being cut or contained while operating costs continue to rise.

Of all the information delivery systems that exist in our society, none is so pivotal as the library. For the library can be, first and foremost, a people-oriented information delivery system. Libraries can deliver information across time (their archival function) and space (their lending and resource sharing function), but

they fail to—if they do not focus on *delivery*. We lose sight of that when we focus our energies on elaborate buildings that emphasize form over function or the size of collections housed in such structures. But we must not lose sight for long, because I believe that libraries are strategic to the fabric of any society as well as strategic to the institutions in which they reside. I also believe we are in danger of damaging that fabric, not because of technological change nor because of financial crises—though both are forces to be reckoned with. I believe libraries are in jeopardy because we do not have a clear vision to guide us into the future; where such visions have been created we have been unable to muster the "followership" and alliances necessary to support a radical departure from the status quo.

On the flight out here I saw the latest Star Trek film—*The Undiscovered Country*. We learn, partway into the film, that the future is the undiscovered country and that even thousands of years from now people are still talking about the fear of change. Granted that is fiction, written and acted by today's humans, but I believe the paradox of change is likely to be timeless. There is always fear that some "empire" will be lost due to change. I argue that *without* change, the empire (if we must call it that) will certainly be lost. This paradox of change is deceptively simple: If we do nothing, we *will* change, but not as we wish, for we are in a changing environment and without adjustment our institutions degrade. To survive we must adapt. To state the paradox another way: To remain as we are—that is, vital—we must change; if we don't change, we won't remain vital.

And what of the current environment in which we all reside? How is it changing? Carla Stoffle summarized the results of a session of the American Society for Information Science (ASIS) in which global societal factors were evaluated.[3] These factors, as they relate to the U.S., included:

   o   A switch from a manufacturing-based to an information-based society. I would modify that to say that we are seeing a switch to a service-based society where companies are focusing on customer service even though they may still manufacture goods—often in other countries. Other institutions, including universities, are beginning to view themselves in this service based environment from a *business* viewpoint.
   o   Second, we see an increased em-

phasis on "accountability." Institutions are being challenged to their very core. Their worth is no longer accepted on the basis of anecdotal evidence. Characteristic of this trend, I see a new level of accountability emerging. Institutions are being asked to measure their performance and to have their leaders accept responsibility for this performance. If they don't achieve their goals, new leaders are brought in. Institutions that were previously funded routinely are being asked to demonstrate their worth. My recent visits to a variety of institutions tell me that this trend is increasing, and it is not limited to industry or a few exceptional universities; it is pervasive.

o The final factor identified in the ASIS session is the changing demographic makeup of the United States. This move towards more cultural diversity is more adequately described in a report titled *Workforce 2000*, issued in 1987,[4] which was given personal meaning on Sunday when Julian Bond referred to the workers who would contribute to his "social security" in coming years.

I would add two other factors to the three, which I have just listed.

o First is the increasing globalization of our industries and institutions. We can no longer operate in isolation for both competitive and moral reasons. Countries, industries, and vital social institutions are no longer isolated. East and West are meeting in the market place as well as in political forums. And all institutions must learn how to work across global boundaries.

o Second, a trend we can no longer deny: a shrinking economy in the United States in which even some of our most vital institutions are having to rethink their levels of spending. At the same time global economics is playing an increasing role, we see the fragmentation of Eastern Europe, the unification of Western Europe, and the continuing emergence of the Pacific Rim as a major economic force.

And what of our universities in particular? Again I turn to Billy Frye, who characterized change as the hallmark of the 1990s for our universities. He foresaw:

o Shrinkage in size as resources become limited;
o Revisions in curriculum;
o New approaches to and greater emphasis on teaching;
o More focus and selectivity in academic programs; and
o New ways of publishing and evaluating scholarly work.

The driving factors for these changes will be:

o A decline in college-age population;
o An impending shortage of Ph.D.-trained faculty; and
o An urgent need for cost control and program redesign due to limited resources.

If these are the forces acting upon the world in general and our parent institutions in particular, what about libraries themselves? Certainly technology has played a major role in the evolution of libraries and will continue to do so even in (or especially in) tight economic times. But my position is that we must look at our libraries as social systems, not merely technical systems. We must act in social and behavioral terms when we look to the changes ahead for libraries.

Now it is time to answer the question "Why did people stop eating bicycles?" There is a management adage that you get what you measure. For years we have measured our success by reporting the *size* of our libraries. Like us, the *Guinness Book of World Records* reports all manner of feats. Included in their records were feats of gluttony including one for a world's record for consuming bicycles (it seems someone ground them up and ate them). By 1982 the editors of this book began to worry about what their measures might be encouraging and they began to step away from records based on volume of consumption and only reported on speed of consumption.

While referring to the consumption of bicycles (or other non-edible objects) as the "height of stupidity," they continued to report the world's record in this area. By 1991 the editors concluded they had best change their measures entirely and announced that henceforth they would cease to report any new records in the area of gluttony. They recognized that you *do*, in fact, get what you measure.

Now it is time that we do the same. We must change our motivation for the operation of the information

33

delivery systems we call libraries, and the problem of motivation rests with how we measure our success. If we continue to measure success on the basis of the *size* of our collections and subscriptions, the number of staff reporting to us, the number of computers we control, or the number of databases we own, we will have static, nonresponsive organizations that fail to serve their users as fully as they could. We will talk technology, but will be thinking about control of assets. We will be skeptical of some of our latest information technology or radical changes in underlying information handling processes because we have not, in the past, been rewarded for increased productivity—especially if it led to a decrease in assets, against which our value has been judged. So I would argue that initially we must *change* the way we measure our libraries. With the correct measures, we will begin to consider the drastic redesign that must occur and we will begin to rethink how our current dollars are spent.

ALA, ARL, and ACRL are investing considerable effort in the area of measurement and measurement redesign. This is not a simple issue, and letting go of old measures is not as easy for us as it is for the editors of the *Guinness Book of World Records*. But *let go* we must, for our future is at stake. We must embark on a radical change process.

Where will the funds come from for this change process? I am convinced that the funding for the significant changes that must occur will come from resources in current budgets, not from new sources of funds. That means that we must rethink some of our most basic assumptions about what a library is and what it does.

Where will the new measures of performance come from that help to drive the change process? Who will give them to us? Again, as in the case of funding, I believe we must look within. I believe we must develop these new measures, and we must make a decision. We must work with our professional organizations, certainly, but we must make a personal commitment to develop and use new measures and we must choose a new philosophy of information service leadership.

The traditional view is that libraries are institutions providing service of immeasurable value. Most libraries function under this philosophy. Many of the academic institutions in which they reside also operate with this philosophy. This "immeasurable value"

philosophy has lulled institutional leaders into a false sense of unvulnerability. As the overhead costs of information services in all institutions come under the magnifying glass, this philosophy, I am convinced, will cease to be viable.

The *alternative* philosophy is that every information service (or product) *has a measurable value*.. The value of a service may be its cost versus the cost of a competing service when the unit costs of both are well understood. However value is computed, it needs to be *made explicit,* or the value will end up being *realized too late* as the lost opportunity cost once the service is eliminated or seriously curtailed.

This approach of measuring value (as well as cost) has serious implications for the infrastructure of a library. It moves the library and its services into the mainstream of the broader community in which it resides. It positions the library as a *delivery mechanism* rather than a *warehouse*, with an emphasis on output, not assets. It also implies that the mission and goals of the library should be aligned with the broader mission and goals of the institution in which it resides, and this is crucial. Each library must become more tightly coupled in its planning and execution with the larger institution it serves.

This approach consequently moves library leaders closer to key decision makers who understand this type of quantification, and closer to other information providers on campus who are more likely to use such quantitative approaches.

The Council has committed major funds to bridge the gap between library leaders and the key decision makers in their parent institutions. The Council has done so by funding projects at the following institutions:

o Columbia University
o A consortium of SUNY universities (Albany, Binghamton, Buffalo, and Stony Brook)
o Harvard University
o A consortium of North Carolina universities (University of North Carolina at Chapel Hill, Duke University, and North Carolina State University)

Each project is quite different, but each will address in a significant way, the essential elements for integrating the planning processes of the libraries and the broader planning processes of their universities. We have already seen one of the first products of these studies—a strategic plan for the Harvard College Library. In the future I believe these studies will be viewed as strategic activities in elevating the issues of library planning and operation across many academic institutions.

I believe that changing the measures of success for information services and service leaders, when accomplished, will be equally strategic. Changing the philosophy of management will also be necessary. But we need to go beyond that. We need to learn how to create "learning organizations" i.e. organizations that treat every effort, every group, every program as an opportunity to share experience and to learn from that experience. And that is the challenge for all of us. I believe we must all be change agents in the library community. We must create these "learning organizations." And we must help to address issues that are of concern to everyone in this room. These issues, in concise terms, are:

o How to live with constant or declining funding; and yet
o Continue to maintain the information flow that is essential to a free society, effective institutions, and an increasingly global perspective.

A Framework for Research and Some Research Questions

In the total scheme of things, foundations such as the Council provide a very small amount of the total funding used by libraries. The future will not go to those of you who, through prospecting, find a new pocket of foundation funding to stretch your budgets while continuing in the same direction as in the past. The future will belong to those of you who take the bold steps necessary to redesign your institutions and methods of operating, and the Council on Library Resources intends to help those interested in taking such steps. The areas of interest to the Council in the future will be based on the strong belief on my part that we cannot continue as we are. We must be prepared to be held accountable for the benefits as well as the costs of the services that we provide. That is true for the Council, for libraries, for colleges and universities, and for all of our societal institutions.

Many of the issues I've addressed today will be reflected in the research projects that the Council will fund or encourage in the future. I have already said that libraries must be viewed, first and foremost, as information delivery systems, not warehouses. The dilemma is that, as delivery systems, libraries still have many facets: that of warehouse, gateway, intermediary, a channel in the scholarly communication process, and a preserver of "what we know." The major challenge must come in what we see as the *driving force* or motivation for libraries. For what will we be held accountable? When we have our backs to the wall (as many now do), what will be the essential vision and force that motivates our decisions? Will it be risk averse or bold? How will the success of the institutions we lead be measured? I believe the Council can help bring about necessary changes and I believe we can help bring about those changes with an immediacy that is essential for the future of libraries in our society.

It is clear that the Council intends to continue to be a vital force for change in the library arena. But to do that, the Council must also be concerned with the issues faced by related organizations, including campus computer centers; university bookstores; bibliographic utilities; university, commercial, and professional presses that provide input to library collections; and other facilities and services that are emerging as the information resources important to libraries of the future. The Council is uniquely positioned as a fulcrum for change at the national and international levels. It does not have a single constituency to serve, nor does it have a vested interest in one area—only a commitment to assure that libraries, as they evolve, will serve society well.

And that leads me to identify four general areas that I believe need significant attention and that I believe form a research agenda for the Council and for you, the representatives of the institutions it serves.

First is the area of *human resources*. We need to look at the end-to-end issues of attracting, educating, maintaining, and advancing individuals in the information services profession. While it is easy to focus on the dilemma of failing library schools, I believe the more urgent question centers on how to assure a steady stream of talented people into leadership roles in libraries and related information service organizations. Some specific questions I would pose for research in this area include:

o What can be done as far upstream as possible to attract bright young people into the information profession?

o How and when should these people receive their basic education and their first professional degree in the information services area?

o How can we assure that professionals in this arena will be able to serve the culturally diverse audiences that will make up their user population? And how do we assure that our workforce has that same diversity?

o What mechanisms are needed to assure that continuing education becomes a normal part of the professional's life and that the people already in the profession receive the training necessary to continue to serve their users well?

o How can mentors as well as other developmental mechanisms be used to assist in creating strong leaders? And as leaders reach the end of their careers, what can be done to assure that their skills and experience are used to "prime the pump" and create more leaders in the information profession?

Second is the area of *economics of information services*. Over time, we need to address the full range of economic issues associated with libraries and related information services, including both micro- and macroeconomic issues. At the outset, however, I believe we should focus on microeconomic issues and, more specifically, on those questions that will lead to a deeper understanding of information service operations in libraries. We need to be able to answer questions such as:

o How much do we really know about the specific functions that a library performs in terms of being able to measure these activities?

o What are the unit costs of these functions and how/why do these costs vary across libraries?

o How do these functions fit together to form information services (e.g., document delivery), and what is the overall cost of these services?

o What are the ways in which we can measure benefits of these resulting services in order to perform cost/benefit analyses from the user's viewpoint as well as from the viewpoint of the institution in which the library or service provider resides?

o I am convinced that the cost and value of information services must be understood and that quantitative analyses are essential to the responsible management of libraries now and in the future. In addition, I believe that many of the tools and techniques used in the "total quality management" programs currently receiving major attention in U.S. industry and academic institutions are appropriate for the redesign of our information services. We need to understand more fully how these tools can be applied in the information service arena.

Third is the broad concept of *infrastructure*. This umbrella term includes the systems, services, and facilities that are drawn upon to help libraries and other information services operate more efficiently and effectively. Included in infrastructure are communication networks, bibliographic utilities, software and hardware vendor communities, publishers, and legal and regulatory systems. Also included as a major component of infrastructure is the current array of physical structures that are viewed as essential to information service operation—e.g., the buildings that house libraries as we now conceive of them. Questions that should be addressed in this category include:

o How will emerging, as well as in-place, electronic networks modify the balance of power as well as the allocation of resources among different information service segments (including the public library segment)?

o How can publishers and libraries work together via experiments that demonstrate processes of change that are beneficial to both segments as well as to the end users?

o What changes are necessary in our intellectual property laws to encourage, not inhibit, the use of our knowledge base?

o What alternative designs for library facilities can demonstrate a focus on service rather than structure and illustrate that form can follow function when the function is clearly understood and articulated? We need to stop using 50-year-old design parameters for our libraries.

o How can system vendors and bibliographic utilities work together when large central operations and local systems seem to be on a competitive collision course? Is there a long-term strategy that makes sense for both and serves libraries and their users well?

While the concept of "infrastructure" is extremely broad, I believe that a few well-chosen projects can begin to move us toward a more rational environment in which both information producers and information consumers are served well by libraries.

Fourth, and finally, is the dynamic duo—*access and processing. All* processing undertaken by a library should be for the purpose of access. The two should not be separated (just as the Commission on Preservation and Access has made the point with regard to preservation). If we look carefully at today's libraries, we find that much of the resource is consumed to support internal processes. It is often unclear how these processes directly (or indirectly) benefit the user. There are many research questions that can be addressed on both the processing and access sides that could significantly influence the cost and/or benefit of library processes. Examples of questions I believe should be addressed include:

o What steps are necessary to reduce the cost/ time of internal processing significantly from where they are today, and how radically can our processes be revised to not only maintain, but enhance access for our users? (Total Quality Management can help here.)

o If the users were to design their ideal information access mechanism, what would it be and how would it vary across different user segments? How would it vary from what we now have (our imbedded base)?

o How would such a design change the current internal processes in libraries necessary to sustain an access system?

o What actually occurs when users "browse" a physical collection, and how could the processes be transferred to electronic access systems?

o What mechanisms create the "serendipity" that is one justification for our large, costly central collections, which are organized to allow users to discover ideas in unusual ways? How can those mechanisms be enhanced-especially where physical resources may be curtailed?

o These four areas—human resources, economics, infrastructure, and access/processing represent the broad umbrellas under which specific research projects must be undertaken if we are to prepare for and create the libraries of the future.

Thank you.

Endnotes

1. Umberto Eco, *The Name of the Rose* (New York: Harcourt, Brace and Jovanovich, 1985).
2. Billy E. Frye, "The University Context" (paper delivered at the Institute of Technology Library Seminar, The Kanazawa Institute, Kanazawa, Japan, June 1991), 24-25.
3. Carla Stoffle, "Libraries, Funding and Creativity, Part 1: Funding," *Bulletin of the American Society for Information Science* 17, (December/January, 1991): 1618.
4. William Johnston and Arnold Packer, *Workforce 2000* (Washington: U.S. Department of Labor, 1987).

CONTRIBUTED PAPERS

I.
ACADEMIC LIBRARIANSHIP

The Benefits of the "Invisible College" for Academic Librarians

Stephen Atkins
Texas A & M University
College Station, Texas

Abstract

Suggests how librarians might improve library research.

A persistent theme among academic librarians has been the need to improve the quality of library research. Benefits of research for both the academic library and individual careers of the librarians has been acknowledged in various sources. Among these benefits have been job advancement, personal recognition, improved relationship with teaching faculty, increased responsiveness to change and innovation, and better library service.[1] Another benefit is an improvement in the status of the library profession within the university environment. Research has been characterized as "one of the traditional measures of faculty competence—indeed, the only tangible evidence of originality, continuing scholarly interest, and professional dedication."[2] Academic librarians have little choice but to participate in the scholarly process or be left out of the mainstream of the institution.

Critics of library research have been eager to point out its deficiencies. Among these criticisms are the lack of a theoretical methodological framework for to handle library research problems.[3] A vague type of social science methodology, and the how-my-library-did-it-good studies have been given as obvious examples of this failure to establish a methodology. Another is the perceived lack of quality control. These critics always point out the amount of substandard research, but the level of criticism has reached the point that it has been characterized as "literature bashing."[4] Part of the problem is that the academic library profession is dependent upon a too limited number of researchers. While some academic professions depend on as few as twenty percent of its members for scholarship, the academic librarianship has only been able to attract researchers at a rate 15 percent of academic librarians at Association of Research Libraries (ARL) institutions.[5] Another factor is the inordinate number of scholars from other disciplines publishing in library and information science. A personal survey of the most influential and prestigious journals in the field of library and information science in the period from 1975 to 1990 showed that academic librarians comprised less than sixty percent of the total number of authors. If not for the influence of a number of faculty status libraries, the research pool would be even smaller. Some type of effort has to be made to both improve the quality of library research and to recruit more talented researchers.

Other disciplines in the past have needed to build their pool of research talent. Studies of scientific researchers in the 1960s showed that the growth of scientific knowledge was promoted by scholarly interaction among scientists. The resulting diffusion of ideas increased productivity and quality of research. These scholars belonged to what was characterized as the "Invisible College." Those disciplines with low level of interpersonal communication and influence found that research stagnated rather than advanced.[7] In those disciplines where the researchers were active participants in the "Invisible College," scientists were recruited to work on large-scale research problems. Senior scholars would search out and identify promising junior faculty to start research on advanced problems. After an interval of sustained and productive research, another theme would be developed and the process would take over again. The common thread was to examine concepts and solve research problems in the most informal manner possible without campus or department restrains. This philosophy acknowledged that scholars engaged in serious research have a greater loyalty to the discipline than the institution.[8]

A key ingredient of the invisible college environment is the informal structure of communications. Colleagues gather together frequently and discuss research strategy and preliminary findings. Drafts, preprints, and final versions of articles are circulated for constructive criticism before they are submitted for publication. Key conclusions are studied before deciding on the future directions of research. Suggestions are entertained to select specific individuals with methodological skills to direct the next components of the research project. Once the research has reached the end of a cycle, the scholars convene again to study other approaches. The result is a continuous stream of high quality research with new colleagues under recruitment at all times.

Academic librarians have research agendas in the same way as scientists, but the scholarly interaction necessary for the development of the invisible college concept is lacking among librarians at present. While a number of research topics cry out for treatment, the current research effort is erratic depending too much on the competency of individual authors and the whims of journal editors. Research without direction has produced a few promising lines of research inquiry, but it has not promoted the sustained levels of production. Sometimes the scholarship on a topic takes several decades before an end is in sight. Academic librarians need to develop the same kind of interaction as scientists have done and the sooner the better. Instead of criticizing the efforts of the current crop of researchers in academic librarianship, special attention should be directed toward cultivating the environment to promote the "Invisible College."

The goal for the academic librarians is for library literature to match the exponential growth experienced by scientific literature in the past decades and at the same time improve the quality of research. A student of the sociology of literature production maintains that research areas are capable of being expanded rapidly if researchers with other commitments decide to shift their research priorities.[9] A key point is for librarians to decide the areas of research within librarianship which are of highest priority. Various individuals and organizations, journal editors, and ALA units, have made worthwhile suggestions for an ongoing research agenda units but a more concentrated effort is necessary. Perhaps the Association of College and Research Libraries (ACRL) could sponsor an organizational meeting where a research priority agenda could be discussed. Once a research agenda is established then the next steps toward implementation can be undertaken.

The responsibility for deciding and implementing the research agenda will have to come from those already active in research. These individuals should take a leadership role in subsequent discussions. They also need to recruit new researchers. This will mean closer interaction between academic librarians and library and information science school faculty. Academic librarians need to improve their methodological skills for research, because most academic librarians leave library science schools with only a rudimentary understanding of research methodologies. Consequently, closer interaction between academic librarians and library school faculty is a requirement for improving research standards. Both have something to provide for the other; academic librarians provide the research agenda and the statistical data, and the library school faculty offer research methodology and research expertise. Library school faculty could also identify promising researchers and provide them with specialized training before introducing them into the new research environment.

A positive manifestation of the invisible college concept will be an atmosphere that is conducive to research. Evidence from other disciplines shows that scholars who perceive colleagues to be supportive were more likely to seek the advice of and collaborate with colleagues on research projects of common interest.[10] Collaborative research projects provide both a supportive environment and the potential for a higher quality product. In the physical and life sciences authors collaborate on research projects from 67 to 83 percent of the time.[11] At present academic librarians average in the low twenties. Collaboration also allows for mentoring of young researchers.

Developing a sponsor-mentor relationship is one of the positive benefits of the invisible college environment. Most disciplines use the doctoral program for senior researchers to mentor young researchers, but sometimes a sponsor-mentor relationship is acquired in the work environment.[12] Except in the rare case of a faculty status library, mentoring in academic librarianship comes from outside both the library science school and the work environment, if at all. This system permits mentoring of novice researchers and allows them an opportunity to gain worthwhile research experience.

The ultimate goal of the invisible college for academic librarians is to improve the quantity and quality of research, but most of the effort would have to be in the pre-publication phases. Once a theme was picked and the research team organized, topics on the research theme would be assigned to researchers with the interest and abilities to complete the tasks. Tentative deadlines for first drafts would be agreed upon and these first drafts could be either sent to other team members by mail or placed on electronic mail for comment. An essential part of each research team would be the recruitment of individuals with editorial skills. These individuals would suggest changes in form, while other commentators would add suggestions for alterations in content. These comments would remain suggestions since the authors would always have the final authority on the content of their research. The next stage would be a meeting where members of the research team would submit their final drafts for review. Again suggestions would be made to improve the contents of the draft. Finally, authors would make the necessary alterations and the final version would be sent to a journal for publication, or in the case of more in-depth research to a book publisher. Once a project was completed, the members of the team would discuss other related topics in order to start the process over again.

A component of this system is for individuals to have the freedom to come and go during the research process. Each research team should have a mix of editors, specialists on methodology, researchers, and proofreaders, because it is this assortment of talent that will make a quality product. Each participant, however, needs to receive proper credit for their contributions to the final product.

The invisible college concept has worked well for the sciences and some of the social sciences in the past. While academic librarianship has fit closer to the social science type of research than the sciences, the adoption of the interactive communication mode of scientific research provides an avenue for academic librarians to improve the quality and quantity of library research. Many librarians will opt out of this system, because they are more comfortable in the traditional go-it-alone way of library research. This is to be expected, but for those librarians who want to participate in an invisible college environment the challenge is there for them. It most be remembered, however, that the strength of a profession is reflected in the quality of its professional literature.

Endnotes

1. Dale S. Montanelli and Patricia F. Stenstrom, "The Benefits of Research for Academic Librarians and the Institutions Which They Serve," in *Energies for Transition,* (Baltimore, MD: ACRL, 1986), p.18-20.

2. Arthur M. McAnally, "Status of the University Librarian in the Academic Community," in *Research Librarianship: Essays in Honor of Robert B. Downs*. Edited by Jerrold Orne. (New York: Bowker, 1971), p. 44.

3. Danny P. Wallace, "The Use of Statistical Methods in Library and Information Science," *Journal of the American Society for Information Science* 36 (November, 1985): 408.

4. John Budd, "Publication in Library and Information Science: The State of the Literature," *Library Journal* 113 (September 1, 1988): 125.

5. Ronald Rayman, and Frank Wm. Goudy, "Research and Publication Requirements in University Libraries," *College and Research Libraries* 41(January, 1980): 47.

6. Diana Crane, *Invisible Colleges: Diffusion of Knowledge in Scientific Communities*, p. 22-25. (Chicago: University of Chicago Press, 1972).

7. Ibid., p. 25-26.

8. John D. Millet, *The Academic Community: An Essay on Organization* (New York: McGraw-Hill, 1962), p. 70-71.

9. Crane, op. cit., p. 24.

10. Deborah E. Hunter, and George D. Kuh, "The 'Write Wing:' Characteristics of Prolific Contributors to the Higher Education Literature," *The Journal of Higher Education* 58 (July-August 1987): 451.

11. R. T. Bottle, and E. N. Efthimiadis, "Library and Information Science Literature: Authorship and Growth Patterns," *Journal of Information Science: Principles and Practice* 9 (1984) : 107.

12. Deborah E. Hunter, op. cit., p. 453.

Librarian's Occupational Stereotype: Will It Ever Change?

Indra M. David
Oakland University
Rochester, Michigan

Abstract

The primary purpose of the study was to investigate whether there are any personality differences between acadamic librarians and the members of the general occupation of librarianship, often stereotyped by society as conventional and conservative. All librarians tested were dominant on Holland's Artistic type and not on the Conventional type, as depicted in several earlier studies. Nor were there statistically significant differences in vocational interests or personality patterns between academic librarians and those who word in technological environments, such as database and systems librarians from all types of libraries.

For more than a century, librarians have struggled to overcome the unpopular image of the occupational stereotype of the librarian, created by society and further augmented by the mass media. In 1971 an American Motors Company ad, depicting a negative stereotypical image of the female librarian, so incensed the profession that its action made representatives from the automobile company publish a public apology to the profession. Currently, *American Libraries* features a regular column, "IMAGE: How They're Seeing Us," in which readers send in references from the media. Sometimes the references are actually complimentary but often they reflect society's stereotypical image of the librarian.

Yesterday's Librarian: The Stereotype!

During the eighteenth and nineteenth centuries the librarian was caricatured as a bibliophile, a pale and undernourished man who lived only for his books. In the post-war era, especially during the Depression, the profession began to be dominated by the single professional female, partially because of the war but also because men could no longer afford to raise a family on a librarian's wages. The twentieth century stereotype of the librarian has not changed over the decades:

. . . unfailingly and eternally middle-aged, unmarried, and most uncommunicative. She exists to put a damper on all spontaneity, silencing the exuberance of the young with a harsh look or hiss. Her only task seems to be checking out books and collecting fines. Books to her are best left upon the library shelves where they do not become dirtied or worn . . . There at the desk she will stay, stamping out her books, until her retirement.[1]

This unflattering, stereotypical image of the librarian held by the public has prompted serious research by librarians during the last few decades. Is it our personality type and our behavior that causes society and the media to think of us in those terms, or are those attracted to librarianship befitting of the stereotypical image?

A review of the literature on the personality patterns and vocational interests of librarians, and library school students clearly suggests that in general, librarians (academic librarians included) have been indeed conventional, conservative, rigid types, not dissimilar to the image associated with the stereotype. Librarians as well as those preparing to enter the profession (library school students) tended to have similar personality traits. Many of the results of such studies were "consistent with normal personality profiles and congruent with the stereotypical image of librarians."[2]

Today's Librarian: Has the Stereotype Changed?

With the advance into the Information Age and the focus on information literacy, changing roles have been emerging for academic librarians. Librarians must deal with information literacy as well as information technologies. Information literacy, "the ability to find, evaluate, and use information effectively in personal and professional lives,"[3] goes hand in hand with techno-literacy. This implies that academic librarians must be challenged rather than frustrated by the technological environment. As professionals, librarians must enjoy being educators and researchers and as information providers must continuously be a step ahead of those that need or seek that information. To be effective, librarians must constantly keep up with the changing technologies. The challenges brought about by the information revolution, coupled with the responsibilities inherent with faculty status, have changed the role of the academic librarian. Today the profession must attract and retain a new breed of academic librarians. They must have a somewhat different pattern of interests than those depicted by the stereotypical image of the occupation.

As electronic publishing gradually complements the printed media and electronic communication becomes the norm rather than the exception, librarians can no longer be protective of the information processes and sources, interpreting their jobs as keepers and protectors rather than suppliers and communicators. The ability to access information from around the world through computers and telecommunication systems, as and when the need arises, is changing the whole idea of what constitutes a library. Some question the profession's readiness and ability to accept advanced technology, which suggests that the occupational stereotype still exists: conventional, conservative and not very innovative.

The Problem

The primary purpose of this study is to find out whether the vocational interests and personality patterns of today's academic librarians are indeed more like the traditional stereotype or are beginning to see a change, because of the changing nature of the profession and its work environment. The research questions postulated are as follows:

Is there a significant difference in personality patterns and vocational interests:

(1)	Between today's general population of librarians (i. e., the professional norm) and those surveyed to form the occupational norm for the Strong Interest Inventory (SII) a few decades ago? (The SII measures vocational interests and relates it to occupational choices. It is based on the theory that "like" personality patterns and vocational interests are attracted to "like" occupations.)

(2)	Between today's academic librarians and a typical member of the library profession (the current occupational norm, consisting of all types of librarians)?

(3)	Between today's academic librarians and those librarians working in a technological environments from any type of library (project managers of integrated online systems and librarians doing online database searches in public, college, school and special libraries?

The study also compares today's librarians with men and women in general, on three variables: College Professor Occupational Scale, Academic Comfort Scale and Introversion-Extroversion Scale. The College Professor scale provides a comparison to the vocational interests and personality patterns of this occupational group. The Academic Comfort Scale measures the degree of comfort in being in an academic setting. The Introversion-Extroversion Scale reflects a person's interest in working with things or ideas versus working with people.

The theoretical underpinnings for this study are based on John Holland's theory of vocational choice. Holland's theory uses the Strong Interest Inventory to measure occupational interests and personality styles. According to Holland, people behave in accordance with the dominant characteristics of one of six major personality styles which influenced their choice of vocation. His six categories of vocational interests with their related occupational themes are: Realistic, Investigative, Artistic, Social, Enterprising and Conventional. He explicitly recognizes the role of personality to be influenced largely by the "fit" between personality and work environment.

Research has indicated that Holland's theory can predict the kinds of vocational choices that people in the six personality categories will make. Based on this theory and measured by the Strong Vocational Interest Inventory (SVII), there was a time when Holland's Conventional Type used to be illustrated by librarians, accountants and secretaries. However the up-dated 1985 edition of the Strong Interest Inventory, categorizes librarians as an occupational group, in the Artistic category. Clearly, the personality pattern of today's librarians has changed from that of yesteryear, despite the occupational stereotype that still exists! This study was undertaken to confirm that librarians belonged to Holland's Artistic category (and not the Conventional category as depicted in the stereotype), and to find out whether academic librarians were different from the professional norm.

The Study

According to many psychologists and career and vocational choice experts, there appears to be evidence that personality traits (often measured by vocational interests) have a bearing on occupational behavior affecting choice of occupation and success. Several of these studies match people's psychological, including vocational needs, values, attitudes, personality traits and styles with their choice of career and job satisfaction. For John Holland, "The choice of a vocation is an expression of personality" and "Interest inventories are personality inventories." He believed that "Vocational stereotypes have reliable and important psychological and sociological meanings." Since members of an occupation hold similar self-concepts, they theoretically share personality characteristics and traits.

Based on this conceptual framework, an attempt was made to determine if academic librarians differed in personality patterns and vocational interests from those librarians working in technological environments or from the occupational norm. Is the academic library beginning to attract a different type of professional now that the computer has become an everyday tool of the occupation?

Methodology

The vocational interests and personality patterns of three groups of librarians, Academic, Database and Systems librarians, were compared to those who comprise the professional norm. The norm consisted of a sample group of public, school, special and college librarians in the same proportion as in the general population of Michigan librarians.

Three hundred and eighty (380) Michigan librarians were mailed the Strong Interest Inventory (SII) Form T325 and a fact sheet for demographic data. Two hundred and thirty two (61%) responded of which two hundred and thirteen (56%) were valid and usable. The average age was 44 and the average years of experience was 14. Those who did not have the graduate library degree of MLS or equivalent, returned incomplete or blank questionnaires which were eliminated from the study. The data on the individual surveys were computer scored and analyzed by the Strong Interest Inventory professionals. Analysis of variance and T-tests were then performed to test for differences between the professional norm and the three samples of different types of librarians on the Strong Interest Inventory scales, including the academic librarian sample.

Discussion of Results

Unlike those earlier studies on the personality of librarians, or as most frequently depicted in stereotypical portrayals of the profession, the study indicated that none of the librarian groups tested were dominant on the Conventional type, Instead, results of the study confirmed the SII findings and showed the following:

(1)   Today's librarians are dominant on the Strong Interest Inventory's Artistic category indicating that most likely a typical member of the profession "prefers artistic . . . situations . . . uses artistic competencies to solve problems . . . perceives self as expressive, original, intuitive, nonconforming, introspective, independent, disorderly . . . values aesthetic qualities." Occupations in this category include authors, reporters, art teachers, artists, and art museum directors among others. Typical work activities include composing, writing, creating art work and working independently. Potential competencies include creativity, verbal-linguistic skills, artistic aptitudes and musical abilities. People in this category prefer work environments that are unstructured, flexible organizations that allow self-expression, institutions that teach artistic skills such as universities, music and dance schools and art institute. People in this category enjoy working in museums, libraries and galleries. Their hobbies include reading, going to theaters and museums, and writing.

Neither academic librarians nor the librarians in the general occupational sample were inclined to be the Convential type even though this is how librarians were depicted in earlier studies and are freqently portrayed in the stereotype.

(2)   There were no statistically significant differences in vocational interests or personality patterns between today's academic librarians and the occupational norm for librarians in general.

(3)   There were no statistically significant differences in vocational interests or personality patterns between academic librarians and those working in technological environments in any type of library.

(4) Librarians in the study were significantly different from "Men and Women in General" (i.e., the average person) when compared on the College Professor occupational scale. Academic librarians as well as the librarians in the Norm group were more like College professors than the average person on the street, even though, as a profession, librarians were dominant on the Artistic theme whereas the professorate was dominant on the Investigative theme. When the librarian sample groups in the study were compared with each other on this scale, the Database librarians' scores were closer to the professorial occupation than any of the other librarian groups.

(5) When librarians were compared to people in general on the Academic Comfort scale there was no significant difference between the two, indicating that librarians, as a professional group, had an average comfort score for working in an academic environment. They were not like college professors, who scored very high on this scale. Surprisingly, academic librarians did not score significantly higher than any of the other sample librarian groups on this scale!

(6) Academic librarians as well as the Norm group were compared with people in general on the Introversion-Extroversion scale. The data showed that male and female academic librarians as well as typical female librarians (as represented in the Norm group) tended to be more introverted than the average person, confirming findings from some earlier studies. The typical male librarian in the Norm group, however, was more like the average male, on this scale.

(7) Another test of significance that was performed was to see if there were differences in vocational interests and personality types between academic librarians with less than 14 years professional experience and those with 14 or more. Though there were no significant differences between the less experienced and the more experienced librarians in the Realistic, Investigative, and Artistic scales, there were indeed differences at the .05 level of confidence both on the Enterprising and Conventional scales. The less experienced college and university librarians were observed to be less "Enterprising" than their more experienced counterparts. However, they also tended to be less "Conventional" than their more experienced colleagues. It is interesting to note that no significant differences were observed on any of the scales, between the less experienced and more experienced librarians in the other three samples (Database, Systems

and Norm librarians). In short, "Years of Experience" was a somewhat significant variable only for academic librarians and even that only on two of the six scales.

Conclusions of the Study

The findings of this study indicated that (1) those who work in academic library environments have the same vocational interests as those who work in technological environments, such as systems and database librarians and that (2) librarians as an occupational group are dominant on the Artistic theme.

Librarians of the Future: Will the Stereotype Change?

Changing technologies have become so much an integral part of academic and research libraries that the tools of the trade for academic librarians are more likely to be computers and databases than printed bibliographies and indexes. However, the intellectual work of creating information-based applications, including learning tools, structuring and organizing information and even knowledge, is what must become the primary focus of the information professional of the future.

The occupational score for librarians, although dominant on the Artistic category, was by no means very high. This suggests that as the profession continues to evolve, academic librarians in particular may become, like their teaching colleagues, dominant on the Investigative theme, as more and more people are attracted to academic librarianship because of their "investigative" vocational interests.

Faculty librarians who intend to become partners with the teaching faculty in pursuit of excellence in higher education may have to change from being caretakers and providers of a support service within the educational process, to that of direct participants in that process. To achieve this it is likely that they must be attracted to the profession because of their interest in working in an intellectual environment while also having vocational interests that are creative, investigative and research oriented. As early users of the information technology, librarians in higher education, in particular, will have to be "part technician, part explorer, and part futurist."

Academic librarianship, can no longer afford to attract the conventional, the conservative and the rigid.

Research indicates that the profession is still evolving and that today's librarians are "artistic". Perhaps tomorrow's academic librarians will find themselves categorized as "investigative" and flexible, enjoying ambigous tasks, comfortable in the intellectual and technological environment of the profession, and confident of their own scholarly and intellectual abilities. Occupational stereotypes are slow to change but the emerging breed of academic librarians may indeed eventually change society's perception of the stereotype associated with the occupation!

Endnotes

1. Edith M. McCormick, "Confession of an Error," *Publisher's Weekly* 199 (January 18, 1971): 28.
2. "Images: How They're Seeing Us," *American Libraries* 20 (February, 1989): 106.
3. Arnold P. Sable. "The Sexuality of the Library Profession: The Male and Female Librarian," *Wilson Library Bulletin* 43 (April, 1969): 748-751.
4. Ibid., p. 748.
5. Indra M. David, *A Study of the Occupational Interests and Personality Types of Librarians* (Ph.D. diss., Wayne State University, 1990).
6. John Agada, "Studies of the Personality of Librarians," *Drexel Library Quarterly* 2 (Spring 1984): 22-45.
7. ALA Presidential Committee on Information Literacy, "Final Report," (Chicago: American Library Association, 1990).
8. M. Freedman Carlin, "Librarian's Agreement," *Library Journal* 111 (January, 1986): 48-49.
9. F. W. Lancaster, "The Electronic Librarian," *Journal of Library and Information Science* 10 (1984): 11.
10. Allen Kent, "Let the Chips Fall Where They May," in *Libraries and Information Science in the Electronic Age,* ed. Hendrik Edelman, (New York: ISI Press, 1986), p. 86-99.
11. John Holland, *Making Vocation Choices: A Theory of Vocational Personalities and Work Environments* (New York: Prentice Hall, 1985). Provides detailed information on his theory that like people are attracted to like occupations beause of the "fit" between personality patterns and work environments.
12. S. H. Osipow, Jefferson D. Ashby, and Harvey W. Wall, "Personality types and vocational choice," *Personnel and Guidance Journal* 45 (September, 1966): 38. The authors' observations were based on studies on vocational interests done by Edward Strong, the original creator of the Strong Interest Inventory, as indicated in his seminal work, *Vocational Interests of Men and Women* (Sanford, CA: Stanford University Press, 1945).
13. Ibid., p. 38.
14. Jo-Ida Hansen and David P. Campbell, *Manual for the Strong Interest Inventory,* 4 (Stanford, CA.: Stanford University Press, 1985). This latest edition of the *Strong Interest Inventory* continues to place library clerical staff in the conventional category, but librarians are listed with the artistic types.
15. See the "Review of the Literature" section of Indra David's doctoral dissertation, *The Occupational Interests and Personality Types of Librarians,* Wayne State University, 1990.
16. John Holland, *Making Vocational Choices: A Theory of Vocational Personalities and Work Environments* (New York: Prentice Hall, 1985), p. 7.
17. Ibid., p. 8.
18. Ibid., p. 9.
19. Melvyn Hollander and Harry J. Parker, "Occupational Stereotypes and Self Descriptions: Their Relationship to Vocational Choice," *Journal of Vocational Choice* 2 (January, 1972): 57-65.
20. See John Holland's *Making Vocational Choices,* for a more detailed description of each of the six categories and p. 7 for a fuller description of the vocational interests of Artistic types.
21. Pat Molholt, "Libraries and the New Technology: Courting the Cheshire Cat," *Library Journal* 201 (January 1988): 37.
22. Ibid., p. 37.

Before the Waters Parted: Minority Leadership in Academic and Research Libraries

Donald G. Davis, Jr.
University of Texas
Austin, Texas 78712

and

John Mark Tucker
Purdue University
West Lafayette, Indiana

Abstract

Academic Librarians have become increasingly concerned about racial and cultural diversity, as they are concerned about recruiting a more diverse professional staff. Past achievements of minority librarians illustrate the problems and potentials of developing a strong corps of minority professionals for the 21st century. The study of African-Americans is one source of practical insight into the issues that affect our attempts to incorporate multicultural elements into a principally Caucasian, middle-class profession. Arthur Schomburg, Monroe Work, and Dorothy Porter merit special attention. The achievements of these leaders indicate how a racial or cultural group seeks to establish both a sense of uniqueness and of common agreement with the majority membership of a profession. Differences explored in an environment of mutual respect can serve educational functions that stimulate effective action and increase accountability within the library community.

Major trends influencing academic libraries as they approach the 21st Century include (1) a renewed sensitivity to affirmative action, (2) rising numbers of Hispanics in search of economic opportunity, (3) an influx of technological expertise from Asiatic nations, and (4) growing demands for international connections throughout society. Academic librarians increasingly concerned about cultural and racial diversity, can sharpen their vision of the future and further develop their understanding of the past by re-examining those in the profession who overcame racial and social barriers to professional achievement. As library patrons become more diverse, so, too, must the labor force that meets the information needs of those patrons.

The library profession attempts to recruit and train racial minorities reflect efforts spread widely throughout higher education. The tools needed for this work include the best political, managerial, and personnel abilities. In addition, librarians can use reports of recent research such as *Librarians for the New Millennium,* issued by the ALA Office for Library Personnel Resources.[1] Indeed, an array of resources (human, economic, and technological) will be tested. Amidst these efforts the authors propose the value of reflecting on what minority leaders have accomplished in the library and information field and, since it isn't feasible to examine all minorities, one group is examined, African-Americans, whose example offers insight into how librarianship could prepare for a more diverse future.

African-Americans in the United States

Among American minorities, peoples of African descent have the most peculiar history. Black presence in the United States owes primarily, though not exclusively, to the institution of slavery. Following the Civil War and emancipation, the nation entered a transition period characterized, ironically for blacks, by political opportunity and economic unrest. These culminated in 1896 when the United States Supreme Court sanctioned separate travel accommodations for African-Americans.[2] Thus began a pattern of federal, state, and local statutes designed to separate blacks from the dominant population and to exclude them systematically from political, economic, and educational opportunity. The reversal of this pattern did not achieve significant legal sanction until 1954 when the Supreme Court unanimously overturned the "separate but equal" concept in public education and required that racial integration become the norm in the nation's schools.[3] In the period 1896-1954, then, blacks existed in a twilight zone of second-class citizenship, racial bigotry, cultural deprivation, and inconsistently applied ordinances and customs.

Although bigotry did not begin in 1896 or end in

1954, these dates mark convenient lines of demarcation between which those blacks who contributed substantially to our profession merit scholarly attention. While many others made important contributions during these six decades, three have been selected whose influence spans generations, cultures, and nations. Capable and visionary, these leaders overcame barriers common to the human condition, but they also provided leadership in an extra dimension by refusing to accept the limitations imposed by second-class citizenship. The remaining comments focus on their achievements; an analysis of the potential of minority viewpoints for a service-conscious, information profession; and an agenda for biographical research in African-American librarianship.

The Legacies of Schomburg, Work, and Porter

Arthur A. Schomburg was born in Puerto Rico in 1874 and served in that nation's revolutionary efforts to free Cuba and Puerto Rico from Spanish dominion. He migrated to New York in 1891 and, following Cuban independence in 1898, toured Central America and the Caribbean. He worked in the law offices of Pryor, Mellis, and Harris and, later, on Wall Street in the mailing room of the Bankers Trust Company.

Schomburg began collecting photographs and books about African-Americans during his student days at St. Thomas College in the Virgin Islands. By 1926 his collection numbered 5,000 books, 3,000 manuscripts, 2,000 etchings, and several hundred pamphlets. Grants from the Carnegie Corporation and the Urban League facilitated the New York Public Library's acquisition of Schomburg's materials which became central attractions in the new division of Negro Literature, History, and Prints at the Library's 135th Street Branch, currently the Schomburg Center for Research in Black Culture.

Although Schomburg published several pamphlets and small books, his legacy to scholarship is most apparent in the research center that bears his name but it is also perpetuated through the dictionary catalog of the collection that has provided essential bibliographical information to students of Afro-Americana throughout the world.[4] Schomburg retired in 1929 and served as Curator of the Negro Collection at the Fisk University Library from 1930 to 1932 when another Carnegie grant enabled him to return to the New York Public Library in the same capacity, a post he held until his death in 1938.[5]

Monroe Nathan Work was born in 1866 in North Carolina and grew up in Cairo, Illinois and Ashton, Kansas, migrations intended to provide stability and opportunity for a family of thirteen. Work studied theology and sociology at the University of Chicago and taught at Georgia State Industrial College from 1903 to 1908 when he was appointed Head of Records and Research at Tuskegee Institute.

In this capacity, he established an information bureau that responded to hundreds of requests each year about black American life principally in education, economics, sociology, anthropology, history, and political science. He supplied data for the speeches and writings of nationally-recognized leader Booker T. Washington and prominent sociologist Robert E. Park.[6]

By the time of his retirement in 1938, Work had built a collection of 350,000 books, pamphlets, statistical surveys, articles, news clippings, and reports from governmental bureaus and private boards. Out of this rich collection he produced the annual *Tuskegee Lynching Record* which was reported in more than 300 daily newspapers. He edited nine editions of the *Negro Year Book: An Annual Encyclopedia of the Negro*.[7] His best known compilation, *A Bibliography of the Negro in Africa and America*, identified more than 15,000 items, drew a favorable response from the scholarly community, and served as the principal bibliographical resource on African-Americans for nearly four decades.[8]

Dorothy Burnett Porter (more recently, Dorothy Porter Wesley) is sometimes referred to as the "Dean of Black Research Bibliographers." She was born in 1905 in Warrenton, Virginia; she attended the Miner Normal School in Washington, D.C. and Howard University where she earned a B.A. in 1928. The first African-American to study in the library school at Columbia University, she earned a B.L.S. (1931), an M.S. (1932), and a Certificate for the Conservation and Administration of Archives (1957).

From 1930 to 1973 Porter served as Librarian at Howard University where she established the Moorland-Spingarn Research Center, a special collection of materials about "Blacks of any continent or any country."[9] This collection dated from 1914 when Howard University Trustee Jesse Edward Moorland gave the library his collection of 6,000 books, photographs, brochures, manuscripts, and artifacts about blacks in the United States and Africa. Porter's genius involved the ability to conceive of the research potential of a special collection and to begin the process of collecting, organizing, and promoting that would make it a reality. In 1946, at Porter's instigation, the University acquired the 5,000 volume library of Arthur B. Spingarn, then President of the NAACP (National Association for the Advancement of Colored People). Like the Schomburg Collection, the Moorland-Spingarn Collection has aided scholars throughout the world with the publication of its dictionary catalogs.[10]

Porter deserves scholarly attention for a second reason, her work as a skilled and prolific bibliographer. She compiled more than ten books, the earliest dating from 1939 when the Howard University Library published the *Catalogue of Books in the Moorland Foundation Collection*.[11] She was still productive thirty years later when one of her most extensive works appeared, *The Negro in the United States: A Selected Bibliography*.[12]

The accomplishments of Schomburg and Work grew out of an exciting period of intellectual and creative ferment, a period of ground-breaking interest in African-American history, literature, and culture in general. The years preceding and including the Harlem Renaissance of the 1920s were years of rising self-consciousness and organizational maturity in fields essential to black scholarship. These impulses became apparent in 1896 in the field of sociology with the inauguration of the Atlanta University Studies by W.E.B. Du Bois, the establishment in 1897 of the American Negro Academy designed to promote African-American research and writing, the formation of the Negro Society for Historical Research in 1911 and, four years later, the Association for the Study of Negro Life and History. Major African-American anthologies appeared soon thereafter: in 1925 Alain Locke's *The New Negro*, devoted to fiction, drama, poetry, music, art, history, biography, and education; and in 1934 Nancy Cunard's *Negro Anthology,* a massive collection of poetry, folklore, ethnology, history, music, and art, as well as writings devoted to education and politics in North America, South America, the West Indies, Europe, and Africa.[13]

These and scores of related developments constituted the intellectual environment in which the achievements of Schomburg, Work, and Porter, a generation later, germinated and eventually evolved into lasting contributions to librarianship. The powerful legacy of the Harlem Renaissance and the years immediately following it continue to be felt in disciplines related to black consciousness and is nurtured by the libraries accumulated by collectors and the sources created by bibliographical scholars.[14] It must never be forgotten, however, that, during the 1896-1954 period, the intellectual ferment that facilitated major library-related achievements was not mirrored in society at large where factors endemic to American life actively opposed those achievements.

Lessons for a Profession

In considering these examples of minority leadership, we may find lessons that would suggest paths to professional achievement for other ethnic and cultural minorities. Schomburg, Work, and Porter demonstrated patience in building research resources and services that would meet the needs of future users and contribute to the building of self-esteem in the African-American community. These were not flash-in-the-pan activists, although each held deeply-felt commitments to racial progress. Rather, they took a longer view, working consistently to produce something of lasting value. The size and quality of the collections they built depended not on large infusions of funds but rather on a broad understanding of retrospective scholarship in a wide range of disciplines, keen insight into the book trade on the three major continents that produced black materials, the compulsive and sometimes dismaying habits of committed bibliophiles, and finally, an unswerving faith that accurate race knowledge constituted an essential cornerstone of the foundations of racial equality and opportunity. Scholarly research and publication became critical issues in the lives of these three, with the result that they influenced the majority culture in a manner potentially available to any minority.

Applied specifically to academic and research librarianship, members of minority groups can perform the following functions that strengthen the professional community as a whole. First, they bring perspective to what eventually may become a genuine consensus. Establishing agreement means that if and when minority views can be incorporated into an accepted understanding, a common position can emerge.

Second, they stimulate response by holding majority groups accountable for their research and scholarship. This is the educative task that, while not always pleasant, is necessary for the evolution of broad truth that takes into account as many facts and perspectives as possible.

Third, they demonstrate the value of active patience that acknowledges the reality of a situation even in the face of constant challenges. Total agreement is seldom possible, and advocates of minority views must monitor changing situations in search of more opportune moments.

Fourth, they enter into a continuing intellectual dialogue with the larger culture. They can demonstrate lessons, particularly useful to younger professionals, that influence is frequently earned by convincing one's academic and professional peers over a period of time and in a variety of venues.

Finally, advocates of minority views enhance through their human graces the collegiality of the entire community. Despite the complexity of the task, one can acquire the ability to promote one's views with tenacity, while at the same time trust and respect as persons from those colleagues who hold differing views.[15] To serve the profession in this manner is to model the intellectual integrity that should characterize all viewpoints in a productive dialogue.

Representatives of minority views and perspectives enrich society—and the library profession—through their enduring contributions. The profession continues to need academic librarians from diverse racial and cultural backgrounds who will find and retain rewarding careers in higher education and assume leadership in academic and research libraries. Librarians and those who use the collections and services, will benefit.

Agenda for Research

At the Fifth National ACRL Conference in Cincinnati, the authors called for "a fuller retrospective view of libraries in historically black colleges and universities that pays especially close attention to personnel and the social barriers they encountered as well as services and collections."[16] This need remains as acute as ever.

Major collected works seem to appear at the rate of about one every ten years. E. J. Josey's *The Black Librarian in America,* appearing in 1970, consisted almost entirely of poignant, incisive autobiographical essays describing the challenges of minority professionals. A new revised and expanded edition is in preparation. Logan and Wilson's *Dictionary of American Negro Biography* (DANB), published in 1982, included scholarly essays on nineteen important book collectors, bibliographers, and librarians. One

hopes that a second edition will include as many librarians as it does bibliophiles. Individuals such as Schomburg and Work have become the subject of book-length studies, and others deserve comprehensive treatment. *Black Bibliophiles and Collectors,* compiled by Sinnette, Coates, and Battle, appeared in 1990. Like the DANB, it focused primarily on collectors and on the research collections honoring their benefactors. *Notable Black American Women* (NBAW), edited by Jessie Carney Smith and published in 1992, included sixteen entries devoted to librarians.[17] These sources enhance substantially the scholarship of library-related biography and are richly suggestive of the potential for further research. To these should be added the nine essays published about African-Americans in the *Dictionary of American Library Biography* and its supplement.[18] For African-Americans, the profession needs something comparable to Wayne Wiegand's *Leaders in American Academic Librarianship, 1925-1975*[19] which could recount the lives not only of important research librarians like Dorothy Porter Wesley but also library directors of liberal arts colleges and other historically black institutions.

Two recent essays on library biographical research remind us that biography as art and method suffers from second-class treatment in humanities research in much the same way that history suffers in library and information science research. A veteran biographer, responding to a survey by James V. Carmichael, complained about the "ahistoricity" of the library profession.[20] Boyd Rayward recently discussed the artistic, psychic, and intellectual rewards of scholarly biography, reminding us of the "emotional and dramatic" potential of life-writing and encouraging the would-be biographer to aim for "sympathetic detachment."[21] He concluded by arguing that biography offers perspective on the principal issues of our profession—how best to improve access to the knowledge and information on which our civilization depends, and how best to relate the success and failures of the past to the challenges that lie ahead.

Endnotes

1. William E. Moen and Kathleen Heim, eds., *Librarians for the New Millennium* (Chicago: American Library Association, Office for Library Personnel Resources, 1988).
2. *Plessy v. Ferguson* 163 U.S. 537 (1896).
3. *Brown v. Board of Education* 347 U.S. 483 (1954).

The year 1954 also marks the beginning of the period treated by Taylor Branch in his prize-winning history, *Parting the Waters: America in the King Years, 1954-1963* (New York: Simon & Schuster, 1988). The title of the present paper is a variation on the title of Branch's book.

4. New York Public Library. Schomburg Collection of Negro Literature and History, *Dictionary Catalog* (Boston: G.K. Hall, 1962), nine volumes; seven supplements (1967-76).

5. See Elinor Des Verney Sinnette, *Arthur Alfonso Schomburg, Black Bibliophile & Collector: A Biography* (New York: New York Public Library, distributed by Wayne State University Press, 1989); and "Arthur Alfonso Schomburg (1874-1938), Black Bibliophile and Collector," in *Black Bibliophiles and Collectors: Preservers of Black History,* ed. E.D.V. Sinnette, W.P. Coates, and T.C. Battle (Washington, D.C.: Howard University Press, 1990), 35-45; Jean Blackwell Huston, "The Schomburg Center for Research in Black Culture," in *Black Bibliophiles,* 69-80; and Rayford W. Logan and Michael R. Winston, eds., *Dictionary of American Negro Biography* (New York: Norton, 1982), s.v. "Schomburg, Arthur Alfonso (1874-1938)."

6. John Mark Tucker, "'You Can't Argue with Facts;' Monroe Nathan Work as Information Officer, Editor, and Bibliographer," *Libraries & Culture* 26 (1991): 151-168; and Linda O. McMurry, *Recorder of the Black Experience: A Biography of Monroe Nathan Work.* (Baton Rouge: Louisiana State University Press, 1985).

7. (Tuskegee, Alabama: Negro Year Book Company, 1912-37).

8. Monroe Nathan Work, *A Bibliography of the Negro in Africa and America* (New York: H.W. Wilson, 1928); Crisis 35 (1928): 301; *Journal of Negro History* 13 (1928): 539-540; *Annals of the American Academy of Political and Social Science* 140 (1928): 348; *American Journal of Sociology* 35 (1929): 126-27; *Sociology and Social Research* 13 (1928): 182. *A Bibliography of the Negro* was reprinted by Argosy-Antiquarian in 1965 and Octagon Books in 1965 and 1970.

9. Maurice A. Lubin, "An Important Figure in Black Studies: Dr. Dorothy B. Porter," *CLA Journal* 16 (1973): 154-58. See also Jessie Carney Smith, *Black Academic Libraries and Research Collections: An Historical Survey* (Westport, Connecticut: Greenwood Press, 1977); and Lelia Gaston Rhodes, "A Critical Analysis of the Career Backgrounds of Selected Black Female Librarians" (Ph.D. diss., Florida State University, 1975).

10. Howard University. Jesse E. Moorland Collection of Negro Life and History, *Dictionary Catalog* (Boston: G.K. Hall, 1971), nine volumes; and Howard University. Arthur B. Spingarn Collection of Negro Authors, *Dictionary Catalog* (Boston: G.K. Hall, 1970), two volumes.

11. *Catalogue of Books in the Moorland Foundation Collection* (Washington D.C.: Howard University Press, 1939).

12. *The Negro in the United States: A Selected Bibliography* (Washington, D.C.: The Library of Congress, 1970).

13. See "Schomburg, Arthur Alfonso (1874-1938)," p. 547; Alain Locke, ed. *The New Negro* (New York: Albert & Charles Boni, 1925); and Nancy Cunard, ed. *Negro Anthology* (London: Nancy Cunard, 1934). *The New Negro* was reprinted by Boni in 1927 and Atheneum in 1968, 1970, and 1992. *The Negro Anthology* was reprinted by the International Microfilm Press and the Negro Universities Press in 1969 and by Frederick Ungar in 1970.

14. Scholarship devoted to the Harlem Renaissance is growing to such an extent that it ought to become the subject of a comprehensive bibliography. Recent reference works devoted to the topic include Lorraine E. Roses, *Harlem Renaissance and Beyond: Literary Biographies of 100 Black Women Writers, 1900-1945* (Boston: G.K. Hall, 1990); and Bruce Kellner, ed. *The Harlem Renaissance: A Historical Dictionary for the Era* (Westport, Connecticut: Greenwood Press, 1984).

15. Jessie Carney Smith, "The Four Cultures," in *The Black Librarian in America,* ed. E.J. Josey (Metchen, New Jersey: Scarecrow Press, 1970), 191-204.

16. Donald G. Davis, Jr. and John Mark Tucker, "The Past Before Us: The Historiography of Academic Librarianship, Past and Future," in *Building on the First Century: Proceedings of the Fifth National Conference of the Association of College and Research Libraries,* ed. Janice C. Fennell (Chicago: ACRL, 1989), 66-70.

17. Jessie Carney Smith, ed. *Notable Black American Women* (Detroit: Gale Research, 1992).

18. George S. Bobinski, Jesse Hauk Shera, and Bohdan S. Wynar, eds. *Dictionary of American Library Biography* (Littleton, Colorado: Libraries Unlimited, 1978); and Wayne A. Wiegand, ed. *Supplement to the Dictionary of American Library Biography* (Englewood, Colorado: Libraries Unlimited, 1990). See also Edward A. Goedeken, "A Prosopography

of Library Leaders Based on the DALB and Its Supplement," in process.

19. Wayne A. Wiegand, *Leaders in American Academic Librarianship, 1925-1975* (Pittsburgh: Beta Phi Mu, 1983).

20. James V. Carmichael, Jr., "Ahistoricity and the Library Profession: Perceptions of Biographical Researchers in LIS Concerning Research Problems, Practices, and Barriers," *Journal of Education for Library and Information Science* 31 (1991): 342.

21. W. Boyd Rayward, "The Case of Paul Otlet, Pioneer of Information Science, Internationalist, Visionary: Reflections on Biography." *Journal of Librarianship and Information Science* 23 (1991): 135-145.

Collegial Leadership and Management: An Example in a Cataloging Department

Nancy Deyoe, Margaret Fast, and Sue Weiland
Wichita State University
Wichita, Kansas

Abstract

Since 1989, the Cataloging Department at Wichita State University has operated under a collegial leadership and management system, where the four catalogers collectively bear complete responsibility for all departmental activities. To put this new form of management in perspective, past organizational structures are outlined, followed by the factors which led to the decision to implement collegial management. The strengths and weaknesses of this system are then discussed from the perspectives of both the catalogers and other staff from throughout the library (obtained anonymously through a survey), and collegial management is affirmed as an effective management style.

Introduction

In June 1989, the Cataloging Department at Wichita State University (WSU) implemented a new organizational structure. The traditional structure of a department head supervising catalogers and paraprofessional staff was replaced by collegial leadership and management. Under the new form of management, decisions are reached by a consensus of the catalogers and a few high-level paraprofessionals. This article will briefly summarize the literature and discuss the past and present organizational structures at WSU, the effectiveness of WSU's collegial structure to date, and the reaction of the library administration, librarians, and staff in the Cataloging Department to the collegial system.

The human relations school of management began exploring participative management in the 1920s and 1930s, and participative organizational structures have become widely accepted over the past twenty years. Librarians began to adapt participative management to their environment in the 1970s. In general, library literature has been supportive of this style and several case studies have been published. For example, Joan Bechtel describes the organization at Dickinson College where librarians divide their time between two library departments, such as reference and cataloging; are involved in library planning, decision making, and administration; and rotate as chairperson of the library.[1] Ellen Gerry and Susan Klingberg report the results of a survey of participative management at California State University libraries. They state that participative management can increase morale and communication, and allow rank and file librarians to be involved in the administration of their libraries.[2] There are numerous other examples; a selective list of references is appended to this paper as Appendix A.

By contrast, very little has been written on how participative management might work within a cataloging or technical services department. One case study by Gerald Lowell and Maureen Sullivan discusses self-management teams at Yale University. In preparation for implementation of an online catalog, technical services staff were reorganized into teams; each team was given responsibility for acquisitions, cataloging, and preservation functions for a specific type of material.[3] Lowell and Sullivan comment that Yale's early experience has been very positive.

The Cataloging Department at WSU has taken the participative management model one step further and instituted a collegial system, where all catalogers and a few paraprofessionals have responsibility for leading and managing the personnel and operations of the department. What has evolved is partly a new organizational structure and partly a new set of methods, or system of management. A brief history of the Cataloging Department's evolving organizational structures may provide some insight into the development of collegial management.

Past Organizational Structures

For many years, the Cataloging Department at WSU experienced great stability in terms of its catalogers. Turnover was low; some stayed for a decade or more.

By the early 1980s, however, this period of stability had ended. Catalogers arrived, worked in the department for two to three years, then left; thus, the continuity enjoyed in previous years was lost. By 1984 the Cataloging Department had developed an organizational structure that reflected the frequent turnover of professional staff. It featured a strong traditional department head who supervised three catalogers and ten paraprofessional staff members (Figure 1). Catalogers were assigned subject specialties and within their subject areas they performed all original and complex copy cataloging for books, serials, and nonbook media. The nature of their work did not mandate much interaction with paraprofessional staff nor with OCLC and NOTIS. Instead, three high-level paraprofessional staff members known as "lead people" supervised, trained, and assisted the Head of Cataloging in evaluating lower-level staff. These "lead people" also coordinated day-to-day departmental workflow and were responsible for all input and database maintenance in OCLC and NOTIS.

In June 1987, WSU hired a Head of Cataloging who believed that all catalogers in the department should have leadership roles. Two new catalogers were hired shortly thereafter. It seemed an opportune time to change the structure of the department, and a thorough reorganization was undertaken. Three units, called "sections," were established—Monographs, Serials, and Music & Media—based on the format rather than the subject of library materials. A cataloger was put in charge of each section and all paraprofessional staff members were assigned to one of the sections (Figure 2).

The new structure enhanced and expanded the role of the catalogers. While the department head had previously been the final authority on cataloging issues, catalogers now filled the role of expert in the particular formats of material for which they were responsible. In their role as Section Heads, the catalogers set priority levels for cataloging and database maintenance within their sections. They also supervised, trained, and evaluated the section's paraprofessional staff.

The reorganization also changed the roles of the paraprofessionals. Three experienced staff members were assigned leadership positions as Assistant Section Heads, and they aided the catalogers in training, supervision, and in coordinating workflow. The seven other paraprofessionals in the department were also trained to take on more complex duties, giving them a better understanding of cataloging principles and processes.

Both the Section Heads and Assistant Section Heads participate in weekly meetings with the Head of Cataloging to assist in departmental planning and policy making. These meetings also functioned as a forum to discuss day-to-day operations and procedures, and to develop more streamlined workflow in the department.

Factors Influencing the Move
to a Collegial System

The Head of Cataloging who had reorganized the department in 1987 left the library in April 1989 and the Cataloging Department was again faced with the search for a new department head. An acting Head of Cataloging was appointed and a search committee, which included the three catalogers, was formed to try to fill the vacant position. Before beginning the search, however, the committee undertook a review of the priorities and needs of the Cataloging Department to determine what characteristics and qualities would be most important in a new department head. In several meetings during a two-week period, the committee considered the issues facing the Cataloging Department, including productivity, automation, organization, communication, leadership, and planning.

The search committee agreed that the number one priority in the Cataloging Department was continued high productivity. Better-trained staff and streamlined workflow had increased productivity during the past two years. The department had kept up with current acquisitions, and had eliminated some specialized backlogs. This increased productivity had raised morale within the department and improved Cataloging's image throughout the library. Second priority was assigned to a few large retroconversion project. Beyond that, major enhancements to OCLC and NOTIS were anticipated.

The committee next discussed departmental organization and communication. They agreed that the increased responsibilities of the catalogers had led to a department which was both efficient and effective. The catalogers were comfortable in their roles as the final authority in their sections, both in cataloging and in staff supervision, and there was no obvious reason to return those responsibilities to a department head. When asked to comment, paraprofessional staff in Cataloging concurred that the present organizational

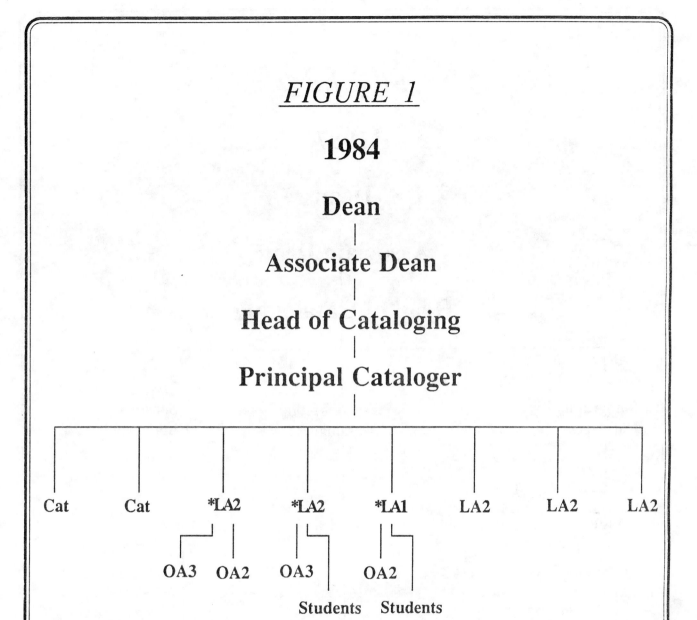

FIGURE 1

1984

Dean

Associate Dean

Head of Cataloging

Principal Cataloger

| Cat | Cat | *LA2 | *LA2 | *LA1 | LA2 | LA2 | LA2 |

OA3 OA2   OA3   OA2

Students   Students

Cat   = Cataloger
LA   = Library Assistant
OA   = Office Assistant
*   = "Lead people"

Head of Cataloging & Principal Cataloger evaluated two other catalogers. Principal Cataloger and LAs were evaluated by Head of Cataloging. "Lead people" trained and supervised OAs, but the Head of Cataloging was responsible for their evaluations.

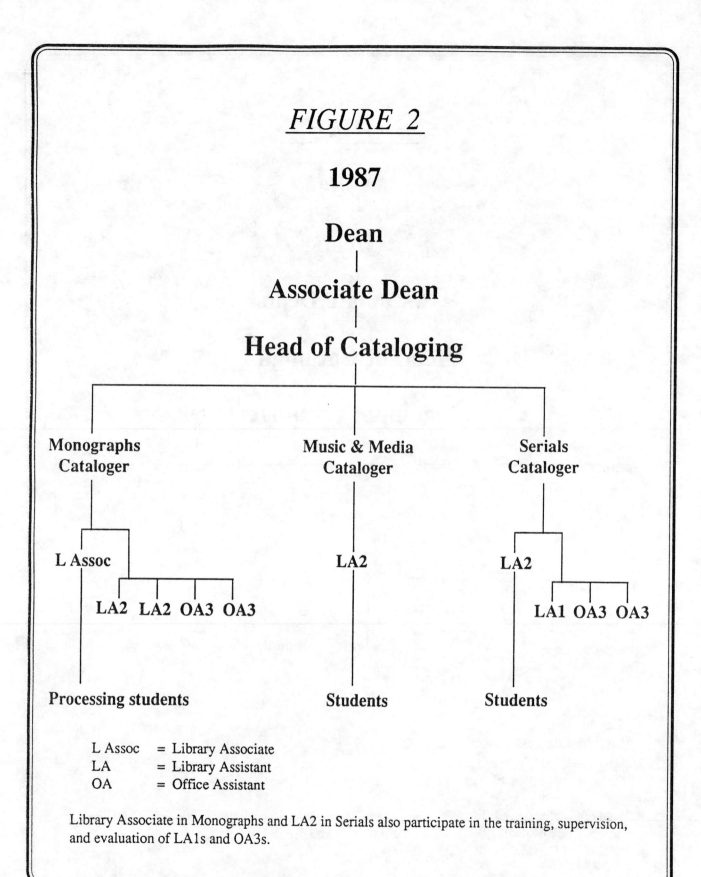

FIGURE 2

1987

Dean

Associate Dean

Head of Cataloging

Monographs Cataloger | Music & Media Cataloger | Serials Cataloger

L Assoc

LA2 LA2 OA3 OA3

LA2

LA2

LA1 OA3 OA3

Processing students | Students | Students

L Assoc   = Library Associate
LA   = Library Assistant
OA   = Office Assistant

Library Associate in Monographs and LA2 in Serials also participate in the training, supervision, and evaluation of LA1s and OA3s.

structure worked well. Several staff commented that yet another reorganization would be disruptive and accomplish little. The committee also recognized that the current structure provided for improved communication within the department via the meetings of the Section Heads.

Finally, the committee discussed leadership, goal setting, and planning for the Cataloging Department. It was noted that these needs were already provided to some degree by the Section Heads and Assistant Section Heads, who, within their sections, set cataloging standards and priorities, adjusted workflow patterns, and planned other activities and projects. As mentioned above, the weekly meetings with the Head of Cataloging provided a means for section activities to be explained and reviewed, for departmental planning and workflow to be addressed, and for policies and procedures to be discussed and developed.

It became evident to the search committee that hiring a traditional department head was not the only option for filling the vacant position in the Cataloging Department. The past few heads of Cataloging at WSU had been primarily responsible for administrative and managerial functions and had limited cataloging responsibilities. Supervision of staff and responsibility for many departmental functions were now assigned to the three catalogers. The functions that had not been reassigned no longer constituted a full-time position. In order to create a full-time department head position, catalogers would have to relinquish responsibilities which had allowed for closer staff supervision and improved workflow routines. The committee also considered the project needs of the department. Each cataloger already bore responsibility for several related forms of material, and no one cataloger could be assigned to full-time project management. Temporary project assignments did not allow catalogers to become familiar with the nuances of cataloging older materials in unique formats or subjects; but a full-time project assignment would allow for satisfactory cataloging quality for project materials. Organizational change in the department had already accommodated many managerial needs, but the "project" cataloging needs of the department had not been met. After careful consideration, the committee suggested that the remaining administrative needs of the Cataloging Department could be absorbed by the catalogers, while the retroconversion and recataloging projects were of such magnitude that only full-time staff could make significant progress. Therefore, the committee recom-

mended that a "project" cataloger be hired rather than a department head.

Since the department did not require a full-time department head, the committee also recommended that Cataloging implement a collegial leadership and management structure. Rather than have one person lead and set the direction for three others, the catalogers would share the leadership role in the department. Working together, they would develop the department's mission, plan for its future needs, prioritize its current activities, and oversee its day-to-day operations. However, the department still needed a single representative to attend various library meetings, to handle administrative tasks, and to act as a final authority in any disagreements. The committee recommended that these duties be assumed by a departmental coordinator, who would be chosen from among the catalogers. Based on the committee's recommendation, the library appointed a Coordinator and hired a project cataloger in the summer of 1989 (Figure 3).

The Collegial System in Practice

Collegial leadership and management is new to the library at WSU, and will require some time to develop and mature. Since the collegial structure has now been in place for two years, however, an initial analysis is possible. The rest of this paper will discuss the effectiveness of the collegial system to date. Each issue will be described first from the perspective of the catalogers, followed by the reactions of other staff in the library. These reactions were collected by means of a staff survey conducted in February 1991. Responses were received from the two administrators, twelve of seventeen full-time librarians, and nine of ten Cataloging Department paraprofessional staff. (A copy of the survey is provided at the end of this paper as Appendix B.) Issues important to the catalogers and the library staff include the general impact of collegial management, its strengths and weaknesses, suggestions for improvement, and whether the collegial structure should continue.

Collegial management has most significantly impacted the catalogers. They have experienced substantial changes in their responsibilities, as all are now more involved in providing leadership and in managing the department. Catalogers have learned to develop initiatives and plan projects on their own, without waiting for a department head to provide the impetus. Writing departmental policies and procedures is shared;

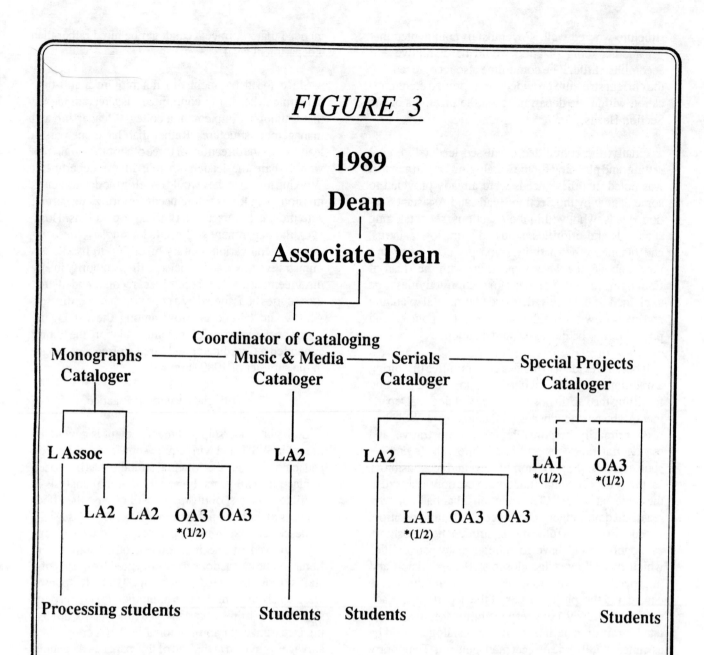

FIGURE 3

1989
Dean

Associate Dean

Coordinator of Cataloging

Monographs Cataloger — Music & Media Cataloger — Serials Cataloger — Special Projects Cataloger

L Assoc

LA2

LA2

LA1 *(1/2)   OA3 *(1/2)

LA2 LA2 OA3 *(1/2) OA3

LA1 *(1/2) OA3 OA3

Processing students

Students

Students

Students

L Assoc	= Library Associate
LA	= Library Assistant
OA	= Office Assistant

* The LA I and the OA3 are assigned on a half-time basis to both the Serials and the Special Projects Sections, and the Monographs and Special Projects Sections respectively. These are temporary assignments and will be reevaluated as projects are completed.

Library Associate in Monographs and LA2 in Serials also participate in the training, supervision, and evaluation of LA1s and OA3s.

the development of a given policy is either assigned to the cataloger with the most expertise on the issue, or one of the catalogers volunteers to investigate the issue and prepare a policy. Responsibilities for learning about and implementing enhancements to OCLC and NOTIS are distributed among the catalogers. The Assistant Section Heads often aid in policy development and workflow coordination, and other staff in the department may have specific tasks delegated to them, especially if they have a special skill or interest. Ultimate responsibility and accountability for all departmental activities, however, rest with the catalogers. They have expanded their focus, to include not only the activities of their sections, but also issues which affect the Cataloging Department and the library.

The person serving as Coordinator has additional responsibilities. The Coordinator represents the Cataloging Department at meetings of the library administration and department heads and to the rest of the library in general. This person also writes annual evaluations for the other catalogers, makes tenure recommendations, if needed, and ensures that vacancies in the department are filled. The Coordinator prepares agendas for and runs the weekly Section Heads and the monthly Cataloging Department meetings. Finally, the Coordinator handles all other routine administrative tasks, and has the final say in any issue that cannot be otherwise resolved. So far, there have been two Coordinators, each serving a one-year term.

Aside from the four catalogers, the impact of the change to collegial management has been minimal. Cataloging staff members continued their work and reported as usual to their respective Section Heads. Survey results showed that the Cataloging Department staff appreciated both the lack of disruption when the collegial structure was implemented, and the lessening of tension as a result of the catalogers all working together. They also liked having as Coordinator someone who had already spent some time in the department. Librarians in other departments were also minimally affected, reporting that what impact there was, generally was positive: Cataloging was more responsive and operated more as a unit. The catalogers carefully planned for the change from one Coordinator to another in July 1990, and the survey showed that the transition was remarkably smooth. The one person who is somewhat adversely affected is the Associate Dean, to whom the Coordinator reports (as do all department heads). It is especially important for that person to establish a good working relationship with

each new Coordinator. As a "trained" pool of catalogers develops, however, this may become less of a problem.

Two years under the collegial system have proven that it appears to have many strengths. Primary among them is that the Cataloging Department has retained a sense of its purpose and can determine appropriate directions to pursue. Several months after the collegial system was implemented, the catalogers engaged in a planning session. This brainstorming session explored current and future issues facing the department. This process resulted in a mission statement, an overall departmental plan, and a work plan for accomplishing the most important objectives. One year later, the plan was reviewed and updated as some objectives had been completed and new issues appeared. The flexibility of collegial planning allows for necessary changes in departmental priorities. The survey revealed that Cataloging staff believed the department knows what it is trying to accomplish; the rest of the library generally agreed, but suggested that Cataloging could do better at articulating and disseminating its vision throughout the library.

Good communication is essential to the success of a collegial system. Regular meetings within the department, which had lapsed prior to the implementation of the collegial system, were immediately reinstated and have become the primary venue for the exchange of information. The Coordinator, who attends library-wide meetings of the department heads, prepares summaries of the meetings for the Section Heads. Minutes of the Section Heads meetings are routed throughout the department. Decisions reached within Cataloging are channeled to the library administration through the Coordinator. Information thus flows freely both horizontally and vertically. On the survey, several librarians commented that the greatest strength of collegial management was the increased communication by the catalogers. Paraprofessionals in the department expressed support for the regular meetings, the increased opportunity to discuss departmental issues, and the effort to keep staff at all levels informed.

The collegial structure mandates that decisions be reached by consensus and compromise. Consensus decision making takes more time and on occasion has required more frequent and longer meetings. This was true during the first year of collegial management, but the length of meetings has now decreased, as the catalogers have gained experience and become proficient at the art of building a consensus. The catalogers believe that decisions reached by consensus can be stronger than those made by one person. Since input from several people is automatic, the knowledge and expertise of all are tapped, thus minimizing the possibility of decisions being based on false assumptions or having unforeseen consequences. Consensus decision making also ensures that once an agreement is reached, all those involved will have a stake in seeing that the decision is successfully carried out. Two responses to the survey mentioned the seeming increase in the number of meetings, but these comments were balanced by others which indicated that the catalogers seem to be more aware of and felt more responsibility toward Cataloging's activities.

Consensus decision making has also manifested its strength in unanticipated ways. During the summer of 1990, the catalogers worked together to draw up a set of specific criteria by which they would be evaluated. This was an important step, as no comparable document existed under either of the two previous department heads. A second strength is the input given to the Coordinator by catalogers and Cataloging Department staff; it enables the Coordinator to be fully informed when representing the Cataloging Department. Many library department heads reacted very favorably when the survey asked if the Coordinator was effective in representing the Cataloging Department.

Despite the increased responsibilities of the catalogers, survey responses from throughout the library agreed that neither the quantity nor the quality of the department's cataloging and database maintenance has suffered under the collegial system. This is partly due to the efforts of the Special Projects Cataloger, who began to convert the non-current serials. A stable, better-trained staff also contributed to continued high productivity. Morale in Cataloging has also improved significantly. Paraprofessionals reported increased confidence in the expertise of the catalogers, and stated that the "team spirit" had improved the overall work environment. Librarians outside Cataloging also noticed that Cataloging staff morale has improved under collegial management, primarily because staff now feel more valued. Finally, the collegial system encourages the professional growth of the catalogers. All have gained administrative experience and a wider perspective; this is particularly true while serving as Coordinator.

The past two years have also revealed a few weak-

nesses the collegial system. The most obvious is that the Coordinator serves for only one year. Though the short length of the term has so far caused no major problems, many of the survey respondents stated that the term should be lengthened. The discontinuity inherent in a one-year term would be eliminated. The catalogers share this concern, and in the future, Coordinators will serve a two-year term.

Some respondents pointed out that the success of the collegial system might be due not only to the structure but also to the people involved. The three catalogers who initiated the system were experienced and worked well together. Respondents were concerned that when a vacancy occurs, it might be filled by someone who is unwilling or unable to fulfill the increased responsibilities now expected of all catalogers. Potential for leadership and the ability to function in a collegial role have been added to all position descriptions and are considered in the hiring process. A vacancy did occur in mid-1991, but the new criteria did not seem to affect the size of the applicant pool, and a qualified candidate was hired. Future search committees must continue to place a high value on an applicant's ability to succeed in a collegial system.

A final concern among survey respondents was the extra responsibilities assigned to the Coordinator. Since this role is added on to a full-time position it constitutes a heavy workload. Cataloging of items with low priority can be slowed and some small projects postponed, but both Coordinators have had to put in overtime during their terms. Perhaps as catalogers become comfortable in the Coordinator role, overtime will be reduced; if not, the two-year term will need to be carefully reviewed.

The Future of Collegial Management

The survey question which asked whether the collegial structure should continue or if a more traditional structure should be reinstated provided the most telling response to people's views on collegial management. Of the twenty-one responses to the survey, sixteen believed that the collegial structure should be continued. Support for the collegial structure was expressed by both faculty and staff. The responses of the library administration acknowledged that traditional and collegial structures have differing strengths. They recognize that the collegial system has worked well to date, but should be reviewed periodically as the library environment changes. For the immediate future, however, they expressed no desire for the Cataloging Department to return to its former organizational structure.

In conclusion, collegial leadership and management has proven to be an effective management style in the Cataloging Department at Wichita State University. During the first two years, its strengths appear to have outweighed its weaknesses. The positive experience of both the catalogers and other staff in the library suggests that collegial management can be a viable management style for the foreseeable future. Collegial management might be considered as an option for other departments who wish to explore non-traditional means of leadership and management in libraries.

Endnotes

1. Joan Bechtel, "Collegial Management Breeds Success," *American Libraries* 12 (November, 1981): 605-607.
2. Ellen Gerry and Susan Klingberg, "A Survey of Participative Management in California State University Libraries," *College and Research Libraries* 49 (January, 1988): 47-56.
3. Gerald R. Lowell and Maureen Sullivan, "Self-Management in Technical Services: The Yale Experience," *Library Administration and Management* 4 (Winter, 1990): 20-23.

Appendix A
Selected Bibliography

Joan Bechtel. "Collegial Management Breeds Success." *American Libraries* 12 (November, 1981): 605-607.

Dale Susan Bengstson, and Dorothy Shields. "A Test of Marchant's Predictive Formulas Involving Job Satisfaction." *Journal of Academic Librarianship* 11 (May, 1985): 88-92.

Nancy Brown. "Academic Libraries an Operational Model for Participation." *Canadian Library Journal* 36 (August, 1979): 201-207.

Nichols C. Burckel. "Participatory Management in Academic Libraries: A Review." *College & Research Libraries* 45 (January, 1984): 25-34.

Robert Burgin, and Patsy Hansel. "Library Management: A Dialogue." *Wilson Library Bulletin* 65 (March 1991): 77-79.

Ann De Klerk, and Joanne R. Euster. "Technology and Organizational Metamorphoses." *Library Trends* 37 (Spring, 1989): 457-467.

Marva L. Deloach. "Human Resource Management in Technical Services." *Illinois Libraries* 69 (February, 1987): 112-116.

Ellen Gerry, and Susan Klingberg. "A Survey of Participative Management in California State University Libraries." *College & Research Libraries* 49 (January, 1988): 47-56.

Katherine Hawkins. "Implementing Team Management in the Modern Library." *Library Administration and Management* 4 (Winter, 1990): 11-15.

Martin, Jaffe. "The Road Less Traveled: An Alternative to the Bureaucratic Model for Librarianship." *Wilson Library Bulletin* 65 (December, 1990): 49-51.

Peggy Johnson. "Matrix Management: An Organizational Alternative for Libraries." *Journal of Academic Librarianship* 16 (September, 1990): 222-229.

Louis Kaplan. "The Literature of Participation: From Optimism to Realism." *College & Research Libraries* 36 (November, 1975): 473-479.

Louis Kaplan. "On Decision Sharing in Libraries: How Much Do We Know?" *College & Research Libraries* 38 (January, 1977): 25-31.

Louis Kaplan. "On the Road to Participative Management: The American Academic Library, 1934-1970." *Libri* 38 (December, 1988): 314-320.

Louis Kaplan. "Participation: Some Basic Considerations on the Theme of Academe." *College & Research Libraries* 34 (September, 1973): 235-241.

Rensis Likert. *The Human Organization.* (New York: McGraw-Hill, 1967).

Rensis Likert. *New Patterns of Management.* (New York: McGraw-Hill, 1961).

Gerald R. Lowell and Maureen Sullivan. "Self-Management in Technical Services: The Yale Experience." *Library Administration & Management* 4 (Winter, 1990): 20-23.

Douglas McGregor. *The Human Side of Enterprise.* (New York: McGraw-Hill, 1960).

Maurice P. Marchant. *Participative Management in Academic Libraries.* Contributions in Librarianship and Information Science, no. 16. (Westport, Conn.: Greenwood Press, 1976).

Maurice P. Marchant and Mark M. England. "Changing Management Techniques as Libraries Automate." *Library Trends* 37 (Spring, 1989): 469-483.

Charles Martell. "The Nature of Authority and Employee Participation in the Management of Academic Libraries." *College & Research Libraries* 48 (March, 1987): 110-122.

Charles Martell, and John Tyson. "OWL Strategies: Quality Circles." *Journal of Academic Librarianship* 9 (November, 1983): 285-287.

Deborah A. Mourey, and Jerry W. Mansfield. "Quality Circle for Management Decisions: What's in It for Libraries?" *Special Libraries* 75 (April, 1984): 87-94.

Bob Perdue, and Chris Piotrowski. "Supervisory Rotation: Impact on an Academic Library Reference Staff." *RQ* 25 (Spring, 1986): 361-365.

Robert S. Runyon. "Some Principles of Effective Decision Making in Academic Libraries." *Journal of Academic Librarianship* 8 (July, 1982): 144-150.

Joan S. Segal, and Tamiye Trejo-Meehan. "Quality Circles: Some Theory and Two Experiences." *Library Administration and Management* 4 (Winter, 1990): 16-19.

Susan Swords Steffen. "Living With and Managing Change: A Case Study of the Schnaffner Library." *Illinois Libraries* 69 (February, 1987): 126-129.

Giesla, Webb. "Preparing Staff for Participative Management." *Wilson Library Bulletin* 62 (May, 1988): 50-52.

Appendix B
Collegial Management Survey

1. Has the change from a typical organization with a department head to the collegial structure with a Coordinator had an impact on you? If so, please specify.

2. Would you prefer a return to the typical structure with a department head for the Cataloging Department? If so, why? If not, why not?

3. Have the classified staff in your department been impacted by the collegial structure? If so, please specify.

4. Did the change in Coordinators have an impact on you? If so, how?

5. Do you think the collegial structure could successfully endure for several years? Why or why not?

6. Has the quality and quantity of the Cataloging Department's production and/or database maintenance changed? Please explain.

7 Do you feel that the Cataloging Department lacks direction or a sense of what it is trying to accomplish? Please explain.

8. What are the greatest strengths of Cataloging's collegial structure? Greatest weaknesses?

If you are not a department head, skip to Question 10.

9. Give your estimation of the Coordinators in comparison with other department heads. (For example, have they appeared knowledgeable in meetings of the Executive Council and Department Heads?)

10. What would you like to see addressed or changed with regard to the Cataloging Department and/or the leadership of the department?

Any other comments

[Note: Questions 3 and 9 were omitted from the survey sent to the paraprofessional staff in the Cataloging Department.]

Do The Faces of Librarians Reflect Cultural Diversity

Tami Echavarria
University of California, San Diego
La Jolla, California

Abstract

Response to changing demographics in the United States means that more minority librarians are needed in the profession. But despite recruitment efforts, libraries seem to be drawing from the same numbers of minority librarians in candidate pools. Aggressive and proactive efforts such as mentoring programs need to be supported to attract more minorities to select careers in library science. The Undergraduate Student Internship Program (USIP) at the University of California, San Diego, is one such program. It is funnelling minority students into library schools and it's success is encouraging.

A lack of cultural diversity among librarians has been an area of concern well-documented in the professional literature. There are relatively few librarians, 11% nationwide, who are members of underrepresented minority groups.[1] Among academic librarians it is even lower. Libraries are traditionally institutions frequented by the middle and upper middle class white sector of the American population and this is reflected in the ethnic composition of librarians. However, changing demographics reflect larger minority populations who are becoming the more numerous groups in the American workforce as we approach the year 2000.[2] As agencies which reflect the intellectual and social values of our society, universities and libraries must be responsive to these demographic shifts.

Despite proactive affirmative action hiring policies, scholarship programs, and postgraduate internships, libraries continue to exchange the few minority academic librarians with other academic libraries in searches to fill position vacancies. Libraries are recruiting from the same small pool of minority librarians already in the profession as well as the few minority library school graduates. To attract more minority librarians to candidate pools, the numbers of available minority librarians must increase. Library schools throughout the nation are making concerted efforts to recruit minority library school students and are meeting with some degree of success. Academic librarians can contribute by attracting more minority individuals to career choices in library science.

Why people choose their careers gives insight as to what librarianship can offer potential career seekers. A student's gender, socioeconomic status, abilities, and the expectations of the significant people in his/her life are related to job preference.[3,4,5] Knowing a role model in the profession, having worked in a library environment, the appeal of the high-tech nature of the field, intellectual opportunities, and management opportunities are the most influential factors for librarianship career choices among minorities.[6,7] Student populations are becoming more culturally diverse with each year of new entering freshmen. Yet few select library science as their chosen profession.

In responding to changing demographics, academic librarians need to consider patrons from the culturally diverse emerging majority. Libraries, service-oriented by nature, must meet the needs of the patrons who use them. Do patrons see themselves mirrored in the faces of librarians when they use libraries? Do we look like role models to them when choosing their own professions? To meet the needs of this changing population, the professionals with whom the patrons come in contact must look as familiar to them as the faces they see in their own mirrors. For libraries to be hospitable environments to non-traditional user populations, those users must see people with whom they can identify who are part of the libraries. Librarians must be role models to these users as well as resources for information needs.

Efforts that are more proactive and aggressive need to be adopted to attract potential career seekers to library schools. These efforts must reach not only those who already are considering library science careers, but must also reach those who otherwise would never have considered the library profession. At each successive higher level of academic achievement, fewer minorities remain in school,[8] and few professional minority role models exist for them. By appealing to students' needs, an effective strategy for recruitment emerges. To reach those individuals requires a proactive approach.

Mentoring is a proactive method that can succeed in reaching students who would not have thought of library science as a career, who are undecided about their career plans and who might have interest in librarianship if they had mentoring available. Using a combination of teaching and mentoring, the University of California, San Diego, Library has developed a program called the Undergraduate Student Internship Program (USIP), whose results are very encouraging.

The target group for recruitment is aspiring minority undergraduates who are working in the University Library and enjoy this work atmosphere. These students are already succeeding in attaining their bachelor's degrees and are goal oriented and career oriented. It is reasonable to assume that they like working in a library environment as they continue to remain in their jobs. This is an important factor in career satisfaction.

Each Spring, as Coordinator of USIP, the author puts out a call to colleagues in the library, asking them to identify students working in their departments who are minority, seem to like their jobs, may not have definite career plans or may be interested in librarianship as a potential career choice. Many minority students have not had professional role models in their families and they and their parents may dream that they will get a college education, but have no idea beyond that. When surrounded by fellow students in the university who have definite career goals, these students are often confused. It is these students who can often be the best candidates for USIP. Most often when asked if they have considered the possibility of becoming a librarian, the students answer that they have never thought of it. This is significant because it points out the necessity of bringing this career alternative to their attention in a deliberate way. It is insufficient to assume that they will think of it themselves. Librarians must initiate a proactive approach by talking to students. After speaking with these students about the Undergraduate Student Internship Program, colleagues refer them to the USIP coordinator.

The following year four to eight students begin an academic year-long relationship with the Coordinator of USIP. The object is to convince these students that there are viable career opportunities for them as librarians, and to then guide them to library schools where they can complete the requisite graduate work for a Masters in Library and Information Science. The program is in part instructive in the different specializations possible in librarianship and different types of libraries. And in part it is a mentoring program in which each student is given individualized attention in making the decisions that he/she is comfortable with for his/her own future. The students spend 2 hours a week with an academic librarian observing that librarian's job. Some colleagues assist the coordinator by presenting a session or more in their areas of expertise. Some of the areas covered are: preservation, bibliographic instruction, technical services, and reference. The MLS degree, opportunities for minorities, library schools, and financial aid are covered in detail. (Appendix A.) Individual guidance is given to the students as they begin selecting schools and progress through the application process. The coordinator writes letters of recommendation. When students submit their applications, the coordinator contacts the recruitment officer in those library schools to ensure that applications and financial aids applications are given careful consideration. The coordinator remains available to each student as a resource and advisor.

The incentive for these students to attend the program is to pay them for their attendance time at the same rate which they receive when working at their library jobs. This costs the library:

$5.00/hr. X 2 hrs./wk. X 9 wks./quarter X 3 quarters/yr. = $270/student

In addition to this, approximately $50.00 per year in library career recruitment materials, available from the American Library Association and the California Library Association is used. Assuming that eight students per year are an optimum number, the cost per year is $2,210 and impacts one librarian's time for 120 hours per year, 60 hrs. of class time plus 60 hours of preparation time. The funding comes from Library Administration funds which have been set aside for Cultural Diversity/Affirmative Action purposes.

The results are encouraging. Out of eighteen students who have gone through USIP in its first three years, two are now in library school. Five are currently applying for admission. Five intend to apply in their senior year or after a year out of school. Two have decided not to pursue a career in library science. Four are still undecided. And the University of California, San Diego, Library is committed to the continuance of the program.

Few programs like this exist in universities.[9] It is one solution which makes a contribution toward adding more minority candidates to the ranks of librarians because the students that are being reached are often not those who would have selected library science as a career without the mentoring of such a program. If replicated in more universities, proactive programs like this will have a cumulative effect that will increase the number of minority candidates in recruitment pools as these students graduate from library schools. Mentoring makes the difference in the career choice of these students. That translates for the profession into a larger number of minority librarians that will be available to be hired by universities. To encourage the participation of minorities in library and information science careers, librarians can help students to see librarianship as a positive and socially valuable career choice.

Endnotes

1. African American, Asian American, Hispanic American, Native American.
2. U.S. Department of Labor, *Opportunity 2000: Creative Affirmative Action Strategies for a Changing Workforce.* (Washington, D.C.: GPO, September, 1988).
3. John Saltiel, "The Wisconsin Model of Status Attainment and Occupational Choice Process: Applying a Continuous-Choice Model to a Discrete-Choice Situation." *Work and Occupations* 15 (August, 1988): 352.
4. N. T. Feather and John A. Said, "Prefernce for Occupations in Relation to Masculinity, Feminity, and Gender." *British Journal of Social Psychology* 22 (June, 1983): 123.
5. Bruce W. Hartman, et al., "An Analysis of Gender Differences in the Factor Structure of the Career Decision Scale." *Educational and Psychological Measurement* 47 (Winter, 1987): 1105.
6. William E. Moen and Kathleen M. Heim, The Class of 1988: Librarians for the New Millennium." *American Libraries* 19 (November, 1988): 858-860.
7. William E. Moen, "Ethnicity" In *Occupational Entry: Library and Information Science students' Attitudes, Demographics and Aspirations Survey.* (Chicago: American Library Association, Office of Personal Resources, 1989).
8. *Chronicle of Higher Education Almanac* 38 (August 28, 1991): 13.
9. Kendrick, Curtis, et al., "Minority Internship/ Scholarship in Library and Inforamtion Science." *College and Research Library News* 51 (November, 1990): 965-972.

Appendix A

Undergraduate Student Internship Program

Fall Quarter

Week 1	Introduction
Week 2	History of Libraries
	Place of Libraries in Society
Week 3	Preservation
	Film - "Slow Fires"
Week 4	Bibliographic Instruction
Week 5	Types of Libraries
	Professional Positions
	Opportunities for Minorities
Week 6	MLS
	Library Education
Week 7	Issues in Librarianship
Week 8	Resumes
	Jobs in Libraries
Week 9	Non-traditional Settings

Winter Quarter

Week 1	Biomedical Librarianship
Week 2	Collection Development
Week 3	Special Library - Tour
Week 4	Cataloging Introduction
	Acquisitions Overview
Week 5	Acquisitions
Week 6	Cataloging Overview
Week 7	Original Cataloging
Week 8	Authority Work
Week 9	Management of Technical Services

Spring Quarter

Week 1	Professional Concerns in Technical Services
Week 2	User/Public Services
Week 3	Public Library - Tour
Week 4	Reference Services
	Answering Simple Questions
	Reference Interview
	Film - "6 Ways to Ask A Reference Question"
Week 5	Reference Observation (2 hrs.)
Week 6	Reference Observation & Answer Simple Questions (2 hrs.)
Week 7	Reference Evaluation and USIP Evaluation
Week 8	Conclusion

Modern Racism and Academic Librarianship in a Period of Diversity

Edith Maureen Fisher
President Tenge Enterprises
Encinitas, California

Abstract

In an evolving period of multiracial and multicultural diversity and modern racism this paper discusses (1) a growing concern in librarianship about the impact of racial attitude and behavior among contemporary librarians; (2) interpretations of recent shifts in racial attitude and behavior, and evidence of a widespread attitude of racism; (3) the theory of modern racism distinguished from old-fashioned racism and descriptive characteristics of the aversive form of racism; (4) the theory of racialism, prejudice developed along racial or color lines, differentiated from other forms of social prejudice; and (5) findings of a study exploring racial attitude and racialistic awareness conducted among 250 academic librarians in California. It provides a framework for stimulating discussion and further race relations research in librarianship.

The largest public health and mental health problem in the United States is racism.[1]

Racism—institutionalized, subtle, taught and absorbed from birth in conscious and unconscious ways—is still a problem prevailing among libraries and librarians.[2]

In an evolving period of multiracial and multicultural diversity where racism is often covert, subtle and seemingly intangible; and on the other hand clusters of white supremacy groups openly engage in overt racists hate crimes, racism warrants seriousconcern and attention. A growing concern about the impact of racial attitude and behavior among contemporary librarians has resulted in a number of consciousness-raising conferences and workshops aimed at heightening librarians' racial sensitivity, thereby attempting to effect a change in racial attitude and behavior. During "Librarians As Colleagues Across Racial Lines: Strategies for Change," a national program held at the 1988 American Library Association annual conference, speaker and well known California librarian Elizabeth Martinez Smith was subsequently quoted for noting that racism is still a powerful and complex social force affecting every institution today and that institutional racism is fueled by a reluctance to change what permeates an organization. She says it well with her article title in *Library Journal* "Racism: It Is Always There."[3] It has been noted by Jennings in American Libraries[4] that librarians tend to shy away from discussions of racism, because of their reluctance to acknowledge that there are some librarians who still hold prejudicial attitudes. Jennings also noted that although discussions may make librarians uncomfortable, it is good to identify the types of racist behaviors which might negatively influence the quality of service they provide their patrons or the manner in which they interact with co-workers who are of a race different from their own.

Shifts and theories in racial attitude and behavior.

Three broad types of interpretations of recent shifts in racial attitude and behavior in the United States are presented by Jaynes and Williams in their 1989 landmark study.[5] For some these shifts created new expectations for race relations and perpetuated the notion that racism would somehow vanish. On the contrary as renowned author Haki Madhubuti notes "Racism is not only alive and well in America, it is a growth industry. We need to understand that white world supremacy (racism) is a given fact of life in the world and is not vanishing."[6] Regardless of the interpretation one accepts of the recent shifts in racial attitude and behavior Jaynes and Williams' findings of survey data lead to four general conclusions. The foremost conclusion is that race still matters greatly in the United States. Much of the evidence reviewed in their report indicates a widespread attitude of racism. The second major conclusion regarding racial attitude is that there has been a record of genuine progress, from the once widespread acceptance of segregation and negative discrimination as the guiding principles of black-white relations to acceptance of the principles of desegregation and equal treatment. The third major conclusion is that in the midst of progress there remain significant forms of resistance to a variety of proposals for racial change. Their fourth major conclusion is that the observed patterns of racial progress and resistance are affected by a number of value-based concerns.[7]

Accounting for the shift over time in racial attitude and behavior, theorists have distinguish old-fashioned racism from modern racism. The theory of modern racism conceptualized by McConahay,[8] which provides a basis for this paper, attempts to account for the intensity of new contemporary conflicts in race relations and to measure the attitude that has both supported and emerged from it. McConahay notes[9] that some white people endorse the ideology of modern racism, some do not, and some white people believe in some of its characteristics and not in others. Those white people endorsing the ideology of modern racism do not define their own beliefs and attitude as racist because racism, as they define it, is consistent only with the characteristics of old-fashioned racism: beliefs about black people's intelligence, ambition, honesty and other stereotyped characteristics, as well as support for acts of open negative discrimination.

The fundamental nature of white people's current racial attitude is complex and in conflict. A nationwide survey in 1991 found negative racial stereotypes still persist among white people.[10] In their analysis of historical trends Gaertner and Dovidio note that the process of abandoning racist traditions and prejudiced beliefs may be especially difficult because of their deep-seated ingrained nature in American culture.[11] In their work[12] they discuss aversive racists who regard themselves as non-prejudiced and non-discriminatory but who almost unavoidably possess negative feelings and beliefs about black people, and, I would add possibly other nonwhite people. Aversive racists sympathize with the victims of past injustice and support public policies that, in principle, promote racial equality and ameliorate the consequences of racism. They also identify more generally with a liberal political agenda. Because of the importance of their egalitarian value system to aversive racists' self-concept their negative feelings and associated beliefs about black people, and I would add possibly other nonwhite people, are typically not always a part of their awareness. Their inability to acknowledge their negative racial feelings and their apparent rejection of negative racial stereo-

types, together with their sympathetic feelings toward victims of injustice, convince them that their racial attitude is largely positive, and certainly not prejudiced.

Allowing for a more refined diagnosis of the problem of racism research, Taylor[13, 14] established the theory and taxonomy or classification system of racialism, prejudice developed along racial or color lines, which provides a basis for this paper. Racialism is differentiated from other forms of social prejudice. It is used as a generic term to refer to the several varieties of prejudice, each organized around different assumptions and having a different ontogenesis, i.e. life history or development. The term racialism encompasses (1) racism, the practice of white supremacy, a specific form of prejudice and negative discrimination directed toward a nonwhite racial group(s) and (2) racial prejudice that may exist between nonwhite racial groups. As Taylor points out all examples of racialism are not necessarily cases of racism where as all examples of racism are also instances of racialism.

Exploring racial attitude and racialistic awareness.

To provide some initial insights into the complex climate of modern racism in librarianship a study[15] was designed to explore (1) racial attitude and racialistic awareness, (2) the relationship between racial consciousness and awareness of racialism and (3) the factors that may be associated with racial tolerance and sensitivity. The study used the survey research method to gather data on a three-part R.A.A.P. Questionnaire (Racial Attitude and Awareness of Prejudice). A Pearson's correlation was used to analyze the questionnaire scores to determine the relationship between variables of racial attitude and racialistic awareness. To determine if the relationship of the variables differed based on demographics of level of responsibility, years of experience, age, gender and racial/ethnic group, the Test for Parallelism (also know as Differences in Slope, Equivalencies of Slope, and the Test of Assured Homogeneity of Regression) was used. An ANOVA (analysis of variance) was conducted of the demographic variables to determine whether or not they differed according to racial attitude or racialistic awareness. Because of the small number of nonwhite respondents no comparative data by race/ethnic group could be provided from the study.

Conducted among 250 academic librarians in California this study found the majority (86 percent) of the total respondents fell into the category of low to borderline racialistic awareness. Most (84 percent) of the respondents, however, also achieved a positive racial attitude. For the most part these findings for racialistic awareness alone and racial attitude alone were not significantly affected by level of library responsibility, years of library experience, age or gender. The five conclusions from this study are as follows:

First, this study confirmed that racialistic awareness and racial attitude are relatively independent. It corroborates Taylor's assumption that racialistic awareness is an independent dimension and Allen's assessment that racialism, prejudice developed along racial or color lines, is so deeply rooted in this society that individuals have little or no awareness of racialistic behavior and attitudes.[16] This independent relationship between the two dimensions suggests that a person may be (1) positive in racial attitude and evidence low awareness of racialistic incidents; (2) positive in racial attitude and yet very aware of racialistic incidents; (3) negative or low in racial attitude and show little awareness of racialistic incidents or (4) negative or low in racial attitude and yet sensitive to racialistic incidents. For example, in this study a more positive racial attitude was associated with a lower level of racialistic awareness among 66 department head respondents and 48 respondents in the 55 and over age subgroup. A more positive racial attitude was also associated with a higher level of racialistic awareness among 89 respondents in the 35-44 age subgroup.

Second, this study revealed a low to borderline awareness of racialism, prejudice developed along racial or color lines. Ninety-six percent (214) of the respondents replying in this study had a low to borderline awareness of racialism. This low to borderline awareness of racialism may lead to denial that race has any impact and thereby impede racial understanding and communication, foster environments where individuals and their institutions are prone to act in negative discriminatory ways, and contribute to maintaining racism by being unable to acknowledge its existence. Therefore, as Taylor pointed out nearly two decades ago, "The challenge is to seek out strategies for increasing the level of cognitive racialistic awareness as well as reducing the presence of racialistic attitudes."

Third, the findings of this study suggest that racialistic awareness alone and racial attitude alone were not affected by factors of level of library responsibility, years of experience, age or gender for the most part.

Therefore, to affect change, efforts are necessary to determine what factor(s) influence racialistic awareness and racial attitude. Change strategies need to take into account the influence of value systems and the importance of needs motivated behavior, as well as the social/psychological processes through which racial attitude is formed. According to Taylor these processes are (1) social effect, (2) internalization, (3) identification, (4) utilitarian or instrumental, (5) frustration-aggression-displacement and (6) ego-defensive; and several of them may be operating simultaneously.[18] Appropriate environments for change implementation also need to be identified.

Fourth, this study found that there may be a difference by age where there is an association between racialistic awareness and racial attitude. For example, in this study, the 89 respondents in the 35-44 age subgroup had a higher level of racialistic awareness associated with a more positive racial attitude. This group grew up during the 1960s civil rights era in American society. During that period there was a heightened degree of awareness of social injustice which may have increased individuals' sensitivity to prejudice and negative discrimination toward black Americans. Therefore, it is not surprising that this age subgroup should have a more positive racial attitude and a higher level of racialistic awareness. Their heightened awareness occurred in the context of an acute awareness of social injustice and may have affected this age group in enduring ways that may still be influential and detectable today. In comparison, the 48 respondents in the 55 and over age subgroup had a lower level of racialistic awareness associated with a more positive racial attitude. This group grew up during the pre-1960s civil rights period when negative discrimination was not only customary but legal. They may also have been affected by the shift during the twentieth century from old-fashioned racism to modern racism. Therefore it is not surprising that this age subgroup have a lower level of racialistic awareness associated with a more positive racial attitude. Although in the results of this study the magnitude of the correlations were in the weak to moderate range the differences that may occur between age generations in racialistic awareness and racial attitude merits further study.

Fifth, the results of this study suggest that there may be a difference by gender in racialistic awareness. For example, although the difference was minimal, 88 male respondents were slightly more able to recognize the existence of racialism than 162 females. However, overall racialistic awareness was low to borderline for both males and females. In part, this difference that occurred may be related to a finding in Carter's 1990 study[19] of a difference in racial identity attitudes among white males and white females. According to Carter the difference occurring between genders may reflect the dominant role men have played in creating and maintaining a racially divided society. In this study although the magnitude of the difference was less than one-half of a standard deviation and only about two percent of the variance could be explained by gender, the differences that may occur by gender in racialistic awareness merits further study.

Summary

In summary, awareness of prejudice is not influenced by simply having a positive racial attitude. Lack of awareness of prejudice may contribute to denial that race has any impact and thereby impede racial understanding and communication, foster environments where individuals and their institutions are prone to act in negative discriminatory ways, and contribute to maintaining racism by being unable to acknowledge its existence. For the most part, level of responsibility, years of experience, age or gender do not affect racial attitude or awareness of prejudice alone. Age may be a factor where there is a difference in racial attitude and awareness of prejudice. Gender may be a factor in awareness of prejudice.

This paper provides a framework for stimulating discussion and further race relations research in librarianship. Awareness of prejudice and racial attitude impact librarianship in its efforts to (1) create environments in libraries, schools of library and information science and library associations that ameliorate the consequences of racism; (2) consciously target black and other nonwhite people to attract them to the profession and ensure their advancement and retention; (3) provide relevant library services to black Americans and other nonwhite populations; (4) implement human relations training and continuing education sensitive to race relations issues and (5) develop new public policies for change in an evolving period of multiracial and multicultural diversity and modern racism.

Definitions of Terms

Racial attitude: apparently manifested in three atti-

tude components of prejudice, discrimination, and stereotype.

Prejudice: the affective component of racial attitude, the subjective feelings, states or moods, and the psychological responses that accompany an attitude; an unjustified, negative attitude toward an individual, based solely on that individual's membership in a group.

Discrimination: the behavioral component of racial attitude, the physical and mental processes that prepare the individual to act in a certain manner; negative, often aggressive behaviors aimed at a person and based on that person's membership in a group.

Stereotype: the cognitive component of racial attitude, the beliefs and opinions through which the attitude is expressed, although these are not always conscious; oversimplified mental images of some category of person or event which are shared by a large number of people. In other words, stereotypes are generalizations people assign to other groups of people. A stereotype can be negative, e.g., dirty, cheap, or it can be positive, e.g. intelligent, strong, moral.

Racism: the practice of white supremacy; a specific form of prejudice and negative discrimination, directed toward a nonwhite racial group(s). It may exist at either the individual or the institutional level, and is both overt and covert. It is a term that can be misused to account for racial prejudice that may exist between nonwhite racial groups.

Old-fashioned racism: characterized by open bigotry and beliefs in pre-Civil War racial stereotypes of the innate inferiority of black people as a race. It supports restrictions on interracial social contacts, such as segregated formal negative discriminatory treatment in education, employment, housing and other areas of life. It is in opposition to equal access or equal opportunity for people of all races, and in support of racial discrimination. It is distinguished from modern racism.

Modern racism: characterized by beliefs that (1) negative discrimination is a thing of the past because black people now have the freedom to compete in the marketplace and to enjoy those things they can afford; (2) black people are pushing too hard, too fast and into places where they are not wanted, and that their tactics and demands are unfair; (3) recent gains are undeserved and the prestige-granting institutions of society are giving black people more attention and concomitant status than they deserve; (4) racism is wrong and (5) these beliefs do not constitute racism because these beliefs are perceived to be empirical facts. It is more subtle, more indirect, less overtly negative; distinguished from old-fashioned racism and based on the theory of modern racism.

Theory of modern racism: attempts to account for the intensity of new contemporary conflicts in race relations and to measure the attitudes that have both supported and emerged from it. Distinguishing old-fashioned racism from modern racism, it proposes the following: (1) Anti-black prejudice has not declined at the same rate as the measures of racism reported in most opinion polls; (2) Prejudice, the affective component of racial attitude, acquired early in socialization, mostly verbally without direct contact with black people, is very resistant to change by later experiences. This lingering feeling influences the cognitive and affective components of white peoples' racial attitude when they are called on to interpret new events or to engage in such activities as voting, giving opinions to survey interviewers, serving on juries, or interacting with black people on a day-to-day basis; (3) Racial prejudice is regarded as a socially undesirable trait or behavior in the present social and racial climate and, as a result of this, a negative racial attitude cannot be exhibited except in a manner that will defend the person from a self- or other-generated attribution of prejudice; (4) The specific contexts necessary for the expression of a negative racial attitude and behavior are those characterized by racial ambiguity, where there is a plausible, non-prejudiced explanation available for what might be considered prejudiced behavior or intended behavior.

Aversive racism: assumes that racist feelings and beliefs among white people are generally the rule rather than the exception, given (1) the historically racist American culture and (2) human cognitive mechanisms for processing categorical information.

Aversive racists: characteristically regard themselves as non-prejudiced and non-discriminatory but almost unavoidably possess negative feelings and beliefs about black people. They sympathize with the victims of past injustice and support public policies that, in principle, promote racial equality and ameliorate the consequences of racism. They also identify more generally with a liberal political agenda. Because

of the importance of their egalitarian value system to aversive racists' self-concept, their negative feelings and associated beliefs about black people are typically not always a part of their awareness.

White racism: practicing white supremacy; old-fashioned and modern racism perpetuated by a Caucasian or white person(s) toward a nonwhite person(s). A misleading term that implies some other form of racism exists.

Racialism: prejudice developed along racial or color lines. It is differentiated from other forms of social prejudice. Racialism is used as a generic term to refer to the several varieties of prejudice, each organized around different assumptions and having a different ontogenesis, i.e. life history or development. All examples of racialism are not necessarily cases of racism although all examples of racism are also instances of racialism.

Racialistic incidents: types of incidents where racialism occurs. Their descriptive factors include (1) mode of expression, (2) setting of occurrence and (3) manifestation of racialism.

Racialistic awareness: sensitivity to incidents indicating racialism.

Endnotes

1. C. V. Pierce, "Violence and Counterviolence," *American Journal of Orthopsychiatry* 39 (1969): 555.
2. C. Starr, "White Women Working Together on Personal and Institutional Racism," *American Libraries* 19 (March, 1988): 184.
3. E. M. Smith, "Racism: It is Always There." Presentation delivered at the Program ALA New Orleans, July 1988, *Library Journal* 113 (November 1, 1988): 35-39.
4. K. A. Jennings, "Applauds ALA's Focus on Racism, *American Libraries* 19 (March, 1988): 166.
5. Gerald D. Jaynes and Robin M. Williams, Jr., *A Common Destiny: Blacks and American Society* (Washington, D.C.: National Academy Press, 1989).
6. Hski R.Madhubuti, *Black Men: Obsolete, Single, and Dangerous? Afrikan American Families in Transition: Essays in Discover, Solution and Hope* (Chicago: Third World Press, 1990), p. vi.
7. Gerald D. Jayne, op. cit., p. 155.

8. John B. McConahya. "Modern Racism, Ambivalence, and the Modern Racism Scale" in *Prejudice, Discrimiantion, and Racism,* edited by John F. Dovidio and Samuel L. Gaertner, (Orlando: Academic Press, 1986), p. 93.

9. John B. McConahay, op. cit.

10. L. Duke. "Whites' Racial Sterotypes Persist," *Washington Post* (January 9, 1991), p. A1.

11. John F. Dovidio and Samuel L. Gaerthner, "Prejudice, Discrimination, and Racism: Historical Trends and Contemporary Approaches" in *Prejudice , Discrimination and Racism,* edited by John F. Dividio and Samuel L. Gaertner, eds.) (Orlando: Academic Press, 1986), p. 1.

12. John F. Dovidio and Samuel L. Gaertner, "The Aversive Form of Racism" in *Prejudice, Discrimination, and Racism,* edited by John F. Dovidio and Samuel L. Gaertner, (Orlando: Academic Press, 1986), p. 61-62.

13. J. Taylor, "Proposal for a Taxonomy of Racialism," *Bulletin of the Menninger Cllinic* 35 (1971): 421-428.

14. J. Taylor. "Dimensionalizations of Racialism and the Black Experience: The Pittsburgh Project," in *Black Psychology,* edited by Reginald J. Jones, (New York: Harper and Row, 1980), p. 384-440.

15. E. M. Fisher. *Modern Racism in Academic Librarianship Towards Black Americans: A California Study* (Ph. D. dissertation, University of Pittsburgh, 1991), p. 10.

16. J. G. Allen, *The Development of a Racialistic Incidents Inventory* (Ph. D. dissertation, University of Pittsburgh, 1975), p. 2, 80.

17. Ibid.

18. Ibid.

19. R. T. Carter. "The Relationship Between Racism and Racial Identity Among White Americans: An Exploratory Investigation," *Journal of Counseling and Development* 69 (September/October, 1990): 46-50.

The Role of Librarians in a University Seeking to Internationalize: A Position Paper

Peggy Johnson
University of Minnesota, St. Paul Campus
St. Paul, Minnesota

Abstract

Internationalization is becoming one of the higher priorities in U.S. higher education. This concept refers to a compelling need to make the university more relevant in an increasingly interdependent world. Academic institutions are becoming sensitive to needs articulated by the U.S. business community to become more competitive in the global marketplace. They are seeking to guild a cadre of young professional who can work effectively in international settings. At the same time, foreign countries and businesses are increasing the number of students they send to study and conduct research in the United States. Area studies programs are proliferating on U.S. campuses. There is a trend to send more American students, faculty, and researchers abroad both to study and conduct research and to assist in development projects. Emphasis on sensitivity to cultural diversity, while evidence of concerns at the national level, is also a manifestation of the importance being placed on international issues in universities. Internationalization is seen as a cooperative, collaborative partnership between U.S. institutions and foreign governments, agencies, institutions, and individuals. The academic library and its librarians have an important role to play in supporting this partnership.

This paper will explore four areas in which libraries and librarians can assist with the internationalization of the university. These are:

1. Becoming more globally aware in collection building.
2. Becoming active participants and stakeholders in institutional internationalization efforts.
3. Becoming partners in cooperative development projects.
4. Providing opportunities and support for librarians to contribute individually to international education and development.

Becoming More Globally Aware in Collection Building

Libraries need to develop local and cooperative mechanisms to ensure that they are meeting the growing international information needs of both institutional faculty, students, and researchers and visiting students and scholars. As scientific and technological research becomes increasingly cooperative on an international scale, developments occur in laboratories around the world. Researchers in the United States depend on these developments for progress in their own work, yet the results are increasingly being printed outside the U.S. For example western European and Japanese authors wrote 40% of the papers indexed in the BIOSIS database in 1988.[1]

Foreign language instruction is increasingly stressed in colleges and universities as part of the preparation for careers in the international marketplace.[2] Many libraries face expanding collection needs as U.S. students become more knowledgeable in foreign languages and the curriculum develops in these languages. At the same time, librarians should become more sensitive to the needs of visiting students and scholars to have access to materials in the vernacular, relevant to their native countries. The internationalization of the collection must recognize both types of needs.

Decisions about acquiring more foreign publications are problematic because of continuing increases in materials prices, particularly foreign materials, coupled with shrinking library budgets. Despite a compelling need, libraries are being forced to change purchasing patterns. An Association of Research Libraries report on trends in library acquisitions suggests that research libraries in the United States are reducing the number of foreign publications they acquire.[3] Not only is the number of publications added annually declining, libraries are losing ground as the volume of foreign publications continues to increase.

Librarians will find no easy answer to the opposing forces of constricting budgets and expanding demands. Some forums are developing for coordinating national efforts to collect globally, such as the RLG effort to coordinate the collection of representative sub-national documents among several research libraries. The best decisions will grow out of increased sensitivity to institutional priorities and considered responses to articulated need.

Becoming Active Participants and Stakeholders in Institutional Internationalization Efforts

Libraries historically have directed their collections and services to the support of particular disciplines, programs, colleges, and departments. One of the more common organizational structure in academic libraries is client-based, i.e., the medical library, the agriculture library, the humanities library, and, more common in the past, the undergraduate library. Librarians have been less successful in supporting initiatives that do not neatly parallel existing organizational lines. Subject areas (such as environmental studies) and user groups (foreign students) which cut across disciplines and across client-based service units often receive less attention. Frequently libraries have created new positions in order to focus on emerging institutional concerns and priorities. An example of this is the proliferation of library positions specifically assigned responsibilities for addressing cultural diversity in services and collections.

One way that libraries can focus attention and energy on internationalization is by creating a new position or specifically assigning a librarian to monitor and support international programs. With increasing emphasis both nationally and locally, librarians have an important role to fill as active participants in the move toward the "international campus." A first step is to learn the demographic profile of foreign students and visiting scholars on their campuses, the countries, and languages they represent and their fields of study. In addition, librarians should learn about current overseas development programs in which their institution is involved. This information is available from the institutional program or programs charged with supporting and coordinating international activities. There may be one or more offices, often called office of international programs, international education, or international development.

Once the library learns more about its parent institution's international activities and visitors, librarians can begin to develop programs in their support. Promoting existing library services (general reference service, document delivery, interlibrary loan, tours, database searching) can be meaningful in acclimating foreign students to the library. Beyond this, seminars and tours can be designed to meet the specific needs of foreign students, visiting international faculty, administrators, and dignitaries. Leaflets, handouts, and other publications about the library can be tailored to visitors' needs and made available in the library and in the international program office.

Librarians can also provide information and service that directly support staff members in the international programs offices. By working closely with these staff, librarians can identify what will be most useful. As in many other administrative offices in the university, the staff members in international program offices don't always realize the information and services that libraries can provide. They may feel they are imposing when they ask for advice on CD-ROM hardware and software as part of supporting a development project. Librarians need to stress that they provide services and information to all members of the university community, not just teaching faculty and students.

Librarians can support international activities by providing information to members of the local university community who are going abroad. Directories of study abroad, student exchange, and faculty grant programs should be in the library. Once the traveler knows where he or she is going, the library must be prepared to satisfy more detailed information needs. These will range from materials on cross-cultural sensitivity to maps to local publications to general overviews of the country to be visited. The U.S. Department of State Bureau of Public Affairs Background Notes provides very current reports on individual countries in just a few pages and are an excellent introduction to social and economic conditions in those countries.

Becoming Partners in Cooperative Development Projects

Universities have been involved in overseas development projects for some time. These projects have been supported by such agencies as the World Bank, W.H.O. (World Health Organization), and U.S.A.I.D.

(Agency for International Development) and focus on education, training, and technical assistance with an emphasis on sustainability. Cooperative development projects bring foreign students and scholars to the U.S. as well as send American faculty abroad as technical assistants and visiting scholars.

Development projects vary from institution to institution, depending on the awarding of project contracts and funding. In order to become partners in cooperative development projects, librarians should be familiar with local priorities and commitments. Many projects now explicitly state that there is "no development without information." Librarians can assist in articulating and supporting this concept. In addition, they can provide valuable assistance through collection of information for and participation in project proposal writing, contract negotiations, project planning, monitoring, and evaluation.

Some university libraries have developed new professional positions specifically charged with backstopping the institution's international development office and its programs. A librarian can develop a support and liaison role through participating in international program office meetings on a regular basis. This will help to work together to identify ways in which existing projects and programs can benefit from library support and to position the librarian to assist in planning for new initiatives. The international programs librarian can work with development project directors to identify, implement, and coordinate appropriate mechanisms for the delivery of information to and library support for project participants overseas.

There are several associations that provide a way for librarians to network with others, outside the local institution, who are interested and involved in international development. Librarians are members of the Association for International Agricultural and Extension Education (AIAEE), a professional association and network for agricultural educators who share the goal of improving agricultural education and institutions, especially in developing countries. An informal group of librarians with shared interests meet every two years for a Conference on Librarians and International Development. The next conference will be at Florida State University in 1993.

Providing Opportunities and Support for
Librarians to Contribute Individually to
International Education and Development

International programs provide resources to internationalize the education of the current and next generation of students, faculty, and professionals. They enable and strengthen faculty and graduate student participation in international research. They offer counseling and advice to foreign nationals for academic, immigration, and other concerns. As librarians become more aware of internalization activities at their university, they can identify ways in which librarians can contribute individually to institutional initiatives.

The library can design new supportive roles for librarians as designated links between the library and international program offices. This approach stresses the library's commitment and creates defined channels for communication between the library and the departments, programs, offices, and individuals involved in international activities. Librarians can act as consultants for proposal writing and overseas development projects and become participants in projects. An international programs librarian can serve as a resource for overseas opportunities for local librarians in overseas teaching and research activities. He or she can facilitate the selection of appropriate candidates for short and long term librarian/information specialist positions with projects. With library and institutional support, librarians can participate in opportunities for personal development and contribution, for example, the Library/Book Fellows Program (funded by the U.S. Information Agency and administered by the American Library Association), Fulbrights, and other grants for travel and research. Most important, librarians committed to the international campus can work to raise the awareness of local library staff members and to help these colleagues to become more responsive to the needs of international programs and activities.

Summary

Libraries and their librarians need to recognize the increasingly important international mission of their parent institutions. As universities seek to bridge to a successful future in a complex and interdependent world, librarians can provide important information and services in support of this mission. In order to do so, librarians must seek to integrate their institution's international activities as a coherent perspective within the activities of the library.

Four key areas present opportunities for librarians to support the international dimensions of their parent institution. They can build collections that match the international needs of their library users. They can craft roles for themselves that are actively involved in institutional internationalization efforts. They can assist in the design of and participate in cooperative overseas development projects. Finally, librarians can contribute individually to international education and development. Librarians have important information and service roles to fill as the United States moves forward with internationalizing higher education.

Endnotes

1. Francis Narin and J. Davidson Frame, "The Growth of Japanese Science and Technology," *Science* 245 (August 1989): 603.
2. Charles J. Andersen, *International Studies for Undergraduates, 1987, Operations and Opinions,* (Washington, D.C.: American Council on Education, 1988), Higher Education Panel Report Number 76.
3. Association of Research Libraries "Research Libraries in a Global Context, (Washington, D.C.: Association of Research Libraries, 1989).

Curriculum Reform: Catalyst for Building Strong Faculty/Librarian Partnerships

Natalie Pelster
Betsy Baker
Northwestern University Library
Evanston, Illinois

Abstract

Curriculum reform has opened many doors for librarians and faculty to work together to actively engage students in the learning process.

True education ... is at once a fulfillment and a spur; always at the goal and never stopping to rest, it is a journey in the infinite, a participation in the movement of the universe, a living in timelessness. Its purpose is not to enhance particular abilities; rather, it helps us to give meaning to our lives, to interpret the past, to be fearless and open toward the future. (Hermann Hesse Reflections 1974)

In *College: The Undergraduate Experience in America,* Ernest L. Boyer stated that one of the most important traits of effective colleges and universities is "a clear and vital mission."[1] The search for this sense of purpose, however, has been an ongoing one in most of our institutions of higher education. Under the rubric of "curriculum reform" both theorists and practitioners have carried on a long standing debate about what constitutes a good undergraduate education and what should be included in the curriculum. On numerous college campuses today, discussions surrounding the quality and substance of undergraduate education are taking place. This is attested to by a recent publication of the Committee on Institutional Cooperation which states:

One of the constant features of our universities is the continual process of reviewing and revising what we offer our undergraduate students and how we do it. At any given time each of our institutions is almost certain to be engaged in one or another of the many phases of the cycle— examining current practices and programs, proposing changes, implementing approved changes, and evaluating the effects of the changes. It is probably true that no other single topic receives as much faculty attention at our universities today as does undergraduate education.[2]

Northwestern University, too, has been participating in the national discussion of how to provide an excellent undergraduate experience. In the late 1980s, the University undertook its first comprehensive review of undergraduate life in two decades, resulting in the publication of the *Report of the Task Force on the Undergraduate Experience,* 1988. The Task Force was comprised of faculty members, students, and administrators, including the University Librarian. The campus is now engaged in a multitude of actions to implement the recommendations made by the Task Force, recommendations that contain many interesting distinctions from those made by a faculty planning committee twenty years earlier.

In this paper we will use the recent experience at Northwestern University as a springboard for a discussion of general trends surrounding the undergraduate curriculum. Specifically, we will highlight ways that curriculum planning efforts, either explicitly or implicitly, invite libraries and librarians to participate in the curriculum. Finally, we will offer suggestions for furthering a role toward which librarians have been moving for some time via their involvement in user education, a role that we are calling co-creator of the curriculum.[3]

The Evolving Curriculum

Curriculum reform is, of course, not a new phenomenon. The twentieth century has witnessed many cycles of curriculum reform as attested in W. H. Schubert's *Curriculum Books: The First Eighty Years.*[4] In the 1920s John Dewey became well known for his efforts to bring society "out of the educational confusion" that he believed was caused by the "segregation of the subjects" in the schools. He stressed that a more project-based learning atmosphere would naturally draw upon all areas of knowledge, as they are interrelated.[5] Several decades later, the launching of Sputnik prompted educational reformers in the 1960s to upgrade scientific knowledge for all American students. Some propelling forces behind the most recent reform movement are the growing awareness of the dimensions of illiteracy in society and the difficulties of handling increasingly large quantities of information in all areas of life.

In an article on curriculum history in the fifth edition of the *Encyclopedia of Educational Research,* Daniel Tanner identifies three major sources and influences for curriculum development: the body of organized scholarship, the needs of the learner, and the demands of society and adult life. He also notes that reform movements throughout the twentieth century, rather than moving in a "progressive spiral," have often tended to emphasize one of these influences at the expense of the others.[6] In recent years, there have been numerous publications in both the professional and popular press about the "search for academic excellence" and any number of various "literacies." These writings stress the need to improve education in order to improve the quality of our society and to keep the nation competitive. At the same time, an increased importance is placed on the individual's right to access information that can enhance his or her life. The needs of society and the needs of the individual are interwoven in this reform movement.

The *Final Report* of the American Library Association Presidential Committee on Information Literacy acknowledged that educational institutions of all types have a responsibility to prepare individuals for roles in an increasingly information-oriented society. To ensure a climate conducive to students becoming "information literate," the Report stresses that "there must be a move from textbook and lecture-style learning to resource-based learning." The Report continues:

Inherent in the concepts of information literacy and resource-based learning is the complementary concept of the teacher as a facilitator of student learning rather than as presenter of ready-made information.[7]

The Educational Role of the Library

The struggle to make the library an integral part of the educational process is a long-standing one. Through

their involvement with course instructors in library instruction efforts and now with their leadership in the area of information technologies, librarians have emerged as a more visible and apparent part of the academic experience of students on our campuses. At Northwestern, this was strikingly underscored by the recognition given to the educational role of the library and of librarians in the University's recent report on the Undergraduate Experience. For example, in its discussion of campus resources, the Report urged that library and information technology programs be integrated into course work at various levels.[8] One of the programs specifically mentioned was our Freshman Seminar program, a program which provides small-class settings in which students work on writing and discussion skills while studying a topic of special interest. For example, the history department offers "America in the Sixties" and the physics department offers "Transportation Systems of the 21st Century." The report states:

In the development of Freshman Seminars, the instructors should draw on the Library for assistance and guidance in the most effective use of [information] resources. This should include bibliographic instruction, training in theuse of LUIS [the online catalog] and database systems . . . . Students should become acquainted with members of the Library staff . . . . Since commitment to learning as a lifelong process is a central goal of Northwestern education, then the Library and its use must be instituted as a lifelong habit at the undergraduate level.[9]

In contrast, the report on undergraduate education completed at Northwestern in 1968 stated no such links between the Library and the classroom.

But, more importantly, explicit mention of the Library is not the only significant difference between the recent report and the one issued in 1968. In the expression of educational goals, the backbone of any reform effort, the two also varied greatly. In its mission statement, the recent task force stressed that beyond providing students with a depth of knowledge in their fields,

Northwestern fosters in its students a broad understanding of the world in which we live, as well as excellence in the competencies that transcend any particular field of study: writing and oral communication, natural science, and quantitative analysis.[10]

Also especially significant is the fact that the report's Mission Statement closes with the following line:

Northwestern expects its graduates, by their experiences in the classroom and in their lives on campus, to have developed the attributes of an educated person: responsibility, both personal and social; critical ability; reflectiveness; creativity; and commitment to learning as a lifelong process.[11]

The aims of undergraduate education expressed in the 1968 report were strikingly different. Rather than developing a mission statement per se, the authors of this report summarized the aims of undergraduate education in three sweeping categories: 1) the achievement of competence in one or two established academic disciplines, 2) the perception of the relations between the undergraduate competence and other disciplines, life and society, and practical applications, and 3) the development of civility.[12]

What we see through the examination of these strikingly different goal statements is a clear endorsement in the late 1980s of the role of libraries in the educational process. The commitment to lifelong learning and research abilities expressed in the report are in unison with library user education goals. Moreover, it is important to note that while we are citing goals expressed in a Northwestern report, they are certainly not unique to Northwestern. These are the same goals that have been articulated on numerous campuses across the country.

Window of Opportunity for Librarians

The issue of whether curriculum reform documents have noted the role of libraries has been of concern to librarians. Patricia Breivik and Gordon Gee have noted that many curriculum reform documents have largely ignored libraries.[13] Although unfortunate, we do not believe this is a reason for discouragement. Had we merely been looking for mention of the library, even Northwestern's Report on the Undergraduate Experience, which, as we have shown, is very conducive to library goals, would have been disappointing upon first perusal. The library was not highlighted in the sections of the report dealing with the academic life of the university. Rather, it was included in Chapter 16,

"Campus Resources," (the last chapter) right after the section on the student union. When we looked at this report however, we were not necessarily looking for prominence placed on the library. Instead we were looking for prominence given to goals such as independent research experiences for undergraduates, written and oral communication skills, and critical ability: goals to which library and information use skills are central. Our mission as librarians is to show other educators on campus how we and the library can facilitate attainment of these goals.

The latest wave of curriculum reform clearly represents an unprecedented window of opportunity for librarians. Not only are its goals conducive to librarian involvement, but the profession is now in a much stronger position than ever before to know what it has to offer to the curriculum. Library instruction efforts over the past twenty years have given librarians a basis for seeing more clearly where they fit into the overall educational arena. Faculty and others outside the library are also more aware of what librarians can offer to the research process. Patrick Hill, former provost at the Evergreen State College, has gone so far as to state that librarians, with their ability to make connections between disciplines, are in a position to lead in curriculum reform.[14]

Strategies for Library Involvement in Curriculum Planning

By taking a pro-active approach, librarians can move library and information handling skills into the institutions's broader educational goals. Ideally, the library's involvement in any large-scale review should be from the outset, as it was at Northwestern with our University Librarian serving on the President's Task Force on the Undergraduate Experience. We realize, though, that in many cases this does not happen. However, even if the library is not involved from the outset, connections can be made later—and to good purpose.

There are many strategies for becoming involved in curriculum reform efforts. First, when the Provost or other senior administrator issues a call for departments to prepare action plans detailing how they will respond to the challenges and recommendations enumerated in such a report, librarians should be ready to articulate where the library can facilitate the goals of the curriculum reform. The library may indeed not be asked explicitly to provide such documentation, although other departments will certainly be expected to do so. It is important that the library not wait for an explicit mandate but be alert to campus wide calls for action. As soon as such a call was issued at Northwestern University, the Library established an Undergraduate User Education Planning Task Force for the express purpose of preparing such documentation. Betsy Baker chaired this task force and Natalie Pelster was a member. With such a task force in place, the Library was able to respond to any requests from university administrators for information regarding educational activities in the Library. For example, when schools and departments were asked to draft mission statements showing how their units' goals meshed with the university's mission statement on undergraduate education, the Library Task Force created a specific mission statement for undergraduate library user education. (See Appendix.) This mission statement was an appendix to the Final Report of the task force.[15] Such a statement serves as visible evidence, both within and beyond the library, of the library's commitment to facilitating undergraduate study and research. Furthermore, it establishes a framework librarians can use to articulate how the library can work in tandem with departments and programs of the institution.

Second, librarians need to be aware of activities and discussions taking place in various schools and academic departments as they, too, respond. To insure that the library's programs are not overlooked in the educational plans of academic departments, librarians should attend faculty meetings and planning discussions prepared to speak out and comment on the library's programs and to discuss ways that the library can support and facilitate new initiatives being proposed. Libraries that have established liaison responsibilities for librarians to academic departments should use these connections for this purpose.

Third, curriculum reform reports can be used to identify new or proposed academic programs with the objective of becoming involved with them from their inception. Early involvement is often the best way to have impact on curriculum planning. For instance, at Northwestern, the Undergraduate Experience Task Force recommended that the University institute a program of junior tutorials and senior research projects that would provide undergraduates with more exposure to self-directed and independent research. The Library did not wait for the program to take shape before approaching the chair of the junior tutorial planning committee. We are now regularly in touch with faculty who are teaching these junior tutorials and often take part in the teaching of these tutorials.

Finally, librarians should use the goals of campus curriculum reform initiatives as a point of reference in ongoing discussions and communications with campus administrators and deans. One of the most important responsibilities of librarians is to keep campus decision makers aware of the relevance and importance of the library in the curriculum. By presenting library services in a way that complements and reinforces the educational themes that campus leaders themselves are discussing and espousing, librarians can bring the library into a more central and vital position in the curriculum. Deans and administrators will know that the library has an expertise to offer in the university's educational programming and planning.

Librarians as Co-creators of the Curriculum

The end goal of all of these efforts on the part of librarians is not simply the scheduling of more library instruction sessions, more online training sessions, and so forth, but rather a true partnership between teaching faculty and teaching librarians in the development of the curriculum. Librarians have been involved in the curriculum for some time, but for the most part, their involvement has consisted of planning and providing instruction within a previously determined course. As such, questions surrounding the context of the course or the relationship of one course to another in the undergraduate curriculum have not been within their purview. This level of involvement could be called curriculum with a small c. Even those librarians who plan complete courses often experience curriculum with a small c.

To be involved in curriculum with a big c is to be involved with the very purpose of education. It is to ask the underlying questions "what is most worth knowing and why?" and "how can this knowledge best be attained?" It is to provide links between what is being studied in a particular course to that which is known and to that which will be further studied. Determining how these linkages can be provided is central to providing an integrated undergraduate experience. Providing these linkages, however, is one of the most difficult challenges facing educators. In Learning Communities Professor Faith Gabelnick states:

One of the oddest things about the university it that it calls itself a community of scholars yet it organizes itself in a way that conceals the intellectual links of that community from those who don't already see them .... This results in a dependency on individual teachers to make sense of the parts of the curriculum for students.[16]

The library is one place on campus where the disciplines come together and many intellectual links are found. Librarians not only bring an interdisciplinary perspective to education but also bring a knowledge of information systems and structures that are of benefit throughout the curriculum. As we approach curriculum with a big c, our efforts will focus more on advocacy and liaison than on the one hour library instruction session. Greater emphasis will be given to working with faculty on a one-on-one basis or in small group settings to develop strong educational experiences for our undergraduates. This role, while not as clearly delineated as planner of library instruction sessions" is, will entail greater outreach and resource activities.

Conclusion

Curriculum reform is a continual process. This particular wave of curriculum reform, growing as it has out of the demands of the information age, is very conducive to library involvement. With the strong emphases placed on lifelong learning, the ability to cope with a vast number of resources, and ability to make independent, critical judgements, the importance of the library is fairly self-evident. But this is not the last wave of curriculum reform. In any reform effort, librarians must find and point out the connections between the goals of undergraduate education and the library. By looking for underlying goals and seeing where the library has a logical and implicit role to play, librarians can find opportunities to contribute to and collaborate in the development of an enriched and strengthened undergraduate curriculum. In so doing, librarians can truly attain the role of co-creator in the educational process.

Endnotes

1. Ernest L. Boyer, *College: The Undergraduate Experience in America* (New York: Harper & Row, 1987)
2. Committee on Institutional Cooperation, *Values Added: Undergraduate Education at the University of the CIC* (Urbana, IL: Office of Public Affairs/Office of Publications of the University of Illinois, December 1989).
3. Norm Weston, librarian for Northwestern University Library's Curriculum Innovation Project, coined the phrase "co-creator of the curriculum" to describe the role librarians can and should play in shaping the curriculum.
4. W. H. Schubert, *Curriculum Books: The First Eighty years* Lanham, MD: University Press of America, 1931.
5. John Dewey, *The Way Out of Educational Confusion* (Cambridge, MA: Harvard University Press, 1931).
6. Daniel Tanner, "Curriculum History." In *The Encyclopedia of Educational Research,* Fifth edition, (New York: Macmillan, 1982), p. 417-418.
7. American Library Association Presidential Commission on Information Literacy, *Final Report* (1989), p. 2.
8. Northwestern University. *Report: Task Force on the Undergraduate Experience* (Evanston, IL, 1988), p. 84.
9. Ibid., *Report,* p. 84.
10. Ibid., *Report,* p. 4.
11. Ibid, *Report,* p. 4.
12. Northwestern University, *A Community of Scholars: New Programs for Undergraduate Education* (Evanston, IL, 1968), p. 5-6.
13. Patricia Senn Breivik and E. Gordon Gee, *Information Literacy: Revolution in the Library* (New York: Macmillan,1989), p. 2.
14. Patrick Hill, "Who Will Lead the Reform of Higher Education? Librarians, of Course!" *Washington Center News* (Winter, 1991): 3-8.
15. User Education Task Force Final Report. (Evanston, IL: Northwestern University, University Libraries, 1989) ERIC Ed 333 893.
16. F. Gabelnick, *Learning Communities: Creating Connections Among Students, Faculty, and Disciplines,* New Directions for Teaching and Learning (San Francisco: Jossey-Bass, 1990), 18.

Appendix

Mission Statement for User Education

The purpose of Northwestern University Library's user education program is to provide members of the Northwestern University community with information-handling abilities appropriate for their individual levels of scholarship and for ongoing research interests. Information-handling skills range from a basic awareness of the value of information to knowledge of communication networks and complex systems for information retrieval.

Central to the goals of both liberal and professional education is the ability to make sound decisions about the appropriate use of information. To fulfill its role in the educational process, the Library must actively strive to enable individuals to: 1) recognize the role, power, and value of information; 2) understand standard systems of organization for information within disciplines; 3) retrieve information from many systems and in various formats; 4) evaluate and synthesize information; and 5) manage their own information collections.

While students, faculty, and administrators of Northwestern University are of primary concern, the service responsibilities of a research library extend beyond the immediate university community to other scholars and, to some degree, the general public. As with all other services, some level of assistance should be provided to these non-affiliated user groups.

Mission Statement for Undergraduate User Education

The purpose of Northwestern University Library's undergraduate user education program is to promote students' use of information resources available in and beyond the Library as they pursue course work and independent projects. Through these endeavors, they will become acclimated to the process of information seeking and become discerning in their use of information—in essence, information literate. Information literate individuals can: 1) recognize the role, power, and value of information; 2) understand standard systems of organization for information within disciplines; 3) retrieve information from many systems and in various formats; and 4) evaluate and synthesize information.

To be successful, a program that fosters information literacy must actively strive to enhance students' awareness of information sources, change their perceptions about the accessibility of information, develop their information access and retrieval skills, and challenge them to think critically about information they find.

Through its user education program, the Library supports the University's mission to enable its undergraduate students to gain a broad understanding of the world and excellence in competencies that transcend any particular field of study.

Extending Library Services to Remote Sites: Regis University as Case Study

Susan Potter and Sandra Hughes Boyd
Regis University
Denver, Colorado

Abstract

A major challenge faces traditional libraries which serve institutions where exponential growth of extension programs is taking place. How do libraries adapt library services to provide extended campus patrons with access equivalent to that offered students at the main campus? Regis University has utilized a number of methods to achieve this goal. Working together, the extended campus and main campus public services librarians have assessed needs, developed programs, adapted existing operations, and initiated unique cooperative agreements with on-site libraries. Following ACRL Guidelines for Extended Campus Library Services, this paper describes how on institution has met these programs needs.

Introduction

In the last decade, Regis University has multiplied its student body eight-fold by creating an adult education program geared specifically to the needs of working adults in the Rocky Mountain region. Rather than incorporating these students into the existing campus programs, new programs under separate administration were instituted which offer courses taught by faculty who are practitioners in their subject fields at ten campus locations in the region.[1] Similar programs are offered at fifteen prison sites throughout the state, at a number of corporations, and through an independent study program. Together these developments have offered a significant challenge to the traditional college library. The library's responsibility, formerly to provide services for a homogenous community of on-campus users, now must in addition provide services for a heterogenous community of users at a variety of distant campuses. The services for these users must, in the words of the "ACRL Guidelines for Extended Campus Library Services," be "equitable with [those] provided to the on-campus community.[2]

This challenge has been addressed in many different ways at Regis. The library recognized the importance of these new responsibilities by creating a new position for extended library services. This full-time professional librarian has devoted her time to developing services for the more than two dozen programs or sites. The main campus public services librarian has sought to adapt the services of the library to meet the requirements of these new programs. The cooperation be-tween these two librarians has been key to the success of the expanded duties brought about by the new programs. Following the ACRL Guidelines for Extended Campus Library Services, the ways sought to meet the program needs in these areas are discussed: (1) reference assistance; (2) computer-based bibliographical and informational services; (3) consultation services; (4) library user instruction; (5) assistance with non-print media and equipment; (6) reciprocal and contractual borrowing and interlibrary loan services; (7) prompt document delivery; (8) access to reserve materials; and (9) promotion of library services.

Services

Reference assistance and other services are considerably enhanced by the creation of a number of cooperative agreements between Regis University Library and a half dozen junior college and public libraries in extended campus locations. Many of Regis' extended programs are located on junior college campuses where we offer a continuation of programs to the bachelor's and master's degree levels. The services and collections of junior college and public libraries must be enhanced to match the requirements of students in these programs. In accepting this responsibility, Regis purchases and places books and serials at junior college and public libraries in exchange for a commitment to providing reference services to Regis students.

Regis University's philosophy with respect to these cooperative agreements is unusual in that the cooperating libraries are given ownership of the books and serials rather than ownership being retained by Regis. This divergence from the standard contract binding two cooperating libraries helps to enrich Regis' relationship with cooperating libraries and enhance services to our students.

An important factor in the development of cooperative library agreements is the establishment of a written contract between the two participating institutions. Such a formal document has several advantages: it formalizes the libraries' plans, forcing the two institutions to put into writing the goals and objectives of the partnership and reduces the chance of changes in priority by future administrators; it establishes the boundaries of mutual responsibility, eliminating the hazard of mismatched expectations between the two institutions; it provides a contract which will hold up during budget-cutting because a contract simply must be honored; and finally, when two institutions make this kind of commitment, it says something very powerful about the agreement's priority in the hierarchy of institutional missions.[3]

Cooperative agreements are fiscally beneficial to both institutions. The cost of working cooperatively with a public or junior college library is about one tenth that of operating a branch library. In the case of Regis, our agreement with the Loveland Public Library provides our students with access to a collection numbering 100,000+ volumes, staffed by 23.4 FTE (5.5 of whom have M.L.S. degrees) and a facility that is open 62 hours per week. In Colorado Springs, where we have over 750 students, a branch library was justified. The staff, collection, and services of the branch are geared specifically to our constituency with the collection numbering 20,000 volumes, the staff numbering 2.5 FTE (1.5 with M.L.S. degrees) and the facility being open 53 hours per week. The Loveland Public Library also benefits by providing to all of its patrons additional resources such as online computer services, business, religion and philosophy serials and books.

Reference services are also available from the main campus library by telephone, E-mail, and FAX during a nearly 80-hour reference service week. A major adjustment has been that the main campus library hours can no longer vary according to a traditional campus seasonal schedule but must remain open 95 hours per week year round.

Computer-based bibliographical and informational

services are provided largely through the existing online catalog system CARL (Colorado Alliance for Research Libraries). This system includes the library holdings of most of the major college and university libraries in the state of Colorado, a number of junior college libraries, several public library systems, the state library collection, as well as selected collections from institutions or systems outside of Colorado.

CARL also makes available several indexes to periodical and other literature, some with document delivery capability. Chief among these is CARL's own "UnCover," which provides access to indexing and document delivery of more than 2 million articles in 10,000 journals housed in CARL member libraries. CARL also remains committed to further development of access to such databases. At the few prisons, where CARL is not available directly to patrons due to security issues, print copies of selected indexes have been provided.

CARL's availability has been made possible in several cases through cooperative library agreements. In some instances, CARL service was already available in the cooperating library. In one case, grant funding sought and obtained by Regis provided for the installation of three terminals at a cooperating public library.

Dial-up access to CARL is available to students with personal computers and modems in their homes and is cost-effective within the Denver metropolitan area local calling range. An aggressive program of library instruction for extended campuses ensures that students are aware of this alternative. Beginning July 1, 1992, "access Colorado" will extend this local dial-up access throughout the state. This system was recently approved by the state legislature and funded with donations from number of corporations and private resources.

Extensive consultation services are provided by the extended campus librarian. She has provided assistance in collection development for the libraries with whom Regis has cooperative agreements. In the planning stage are bibliographic instruction for library staffs to enhance the reference assistance they provide for Regis faculty and students. Also underway is a video tape of instruction on CARL use and equipment trouble-shooting.

Library user instruction is made available in several

ways. Reference librarians at the cooperating libraries provide on-site assistance to Regis students. The extended campus and public services librarians at Regis regularly participate in faculty and student representative meetings, acquainting potential users with the availability of instruction. Classroom bibliographic instruction is provided when possible by Regis librarians. This service will be developed and marketed aggressively in the next phase of these programs.

Non-Print media and equipment are provided in several ways. Most equipment requirements are met through cooperative purchasing, either between the library media department and the academic programs or between Regis and the cooperating libraries. For the most part equipment is housed on site, although the main library will lend equipment on request. Transportation is accomplished by the borrower's personal transportation. Media may be borrowed from the main campus and transported by courier or personally for use at the extended campus locations.

Reciprocal and contractual borrowing are made available to users of the ibraries with whom we have cooperative agreements. Regis Libraries extend borrowing privileges to any citizen in the communities in which cooperating libraries are situated. In exchange, the cooperating libraries grant library privileges to all Regis students.

Interlibrary Loan Services at the main campus have been expanded to meet the anticipated increased volume of requests from extended campuses. In a reorganization of the main library public services operation, the intercampus and interlibrary loan operations were separated from the circulation operation and consolidated into one department staffed by a full-time person. This department processes all inter-campus and interlibrary loans for the Regis libraries. Requests are transmitted from branch libraries, cooperating libraries and students' homes to the ICL/ILL department by means of electronic mail and FAX.

Document delivery is provided by means of two daily courier services. The existing interlibrary courier service is supplemented by a contract courier to include locations not otherwise covered by courier. Where courier service is prohibitively expensive or unavailable, U.S. Mail is utilized. Where time is a factor, FAX is used for document delivery. Special efforts are being made by the main library to speed the delivery of articles in its collection.

Access to reserve materials is obtained in several ways. Upon faculty request, the main library provides reserve materials to the cooperating libraries who then take responsibility for making them available to the students and returning them at the conclusion of the course. Several traveling collections have been compiled which meet reserve needs at extended campuses. These are particularly well-suited to the prison programs where collections move amongst libraries staffed by the state at five different facilities dependent on where a particular course is currently being taught. Collections range from twenty to thirty books supporting the course outline.

Promotion of library services is conducted by extensive travel of the extended campus librarian and by regular promotions at faculty and student representative meetings by both librarians. Promotional literature is designed and made available. Future efforts involve more extended outreach to faculty and development of relationships between the librarians and extended campus program administrators.

Conclusion

Regis University has been able to meet the challenge outlined in the ACRL guidelines to a significant degree. In the Regis experience, four factors have been key to that success. The first has been the commitment of the institution to providing the financial means by which the extended campus library needs may be met. The second was the designation of a full-time person whose entire responsibility is to assess the requirements for extended campus programs, set goals, and plan to meet those goals. The third is the flexibility of the main library staff, making possible the adaptation of its operations to meet the increased demands brought about by the new extended campus programs. The fourth is the existence of on-site libraries willing and able to enter into cooperative agreements with the main campus library and to fulfill their end of those agreements.

As Regis University has been engaged in developing new programs to "bring classes to where the people are," the Regis University library has gone a long way toward meeting the challenge of "bringing library resources to where the people are."

Endnotes

1. "Regis in Denver Brings Classes to Where the

People Are." *Wall Street Journal,* (July 17, 1991): p. 1.

2 "ACRL Guidelines for Extended Campus Library Services," *C & RL News* 52 (April 1990): 354.

3. Andrew Scrimgeour, and Susan Potter. "The Tie That Binds: The Role and Evolution of Contracts in Interlibrary Cooperation," in *The Fifth Off Campus Library Services Conference Proceedings* edited by Carol J. Jacob, pp. 241-248 (Mount Pleasant, MI: Central Michigan University, 1991).

Librarians as Academic Advisors

Robert L. Sathrum
Humboldt State University
Arcata, California

Abstract

Academic advising assists students in the clarification of academic/career goals and in the development of educational plans for the realization of those goals. The academic advisor is the key person in assisting students in the exploration of goals and the choosing of appropriate educational offerings consistent with those goals. In most universities academic advising is a responsibiltiy of the instructional faculty. This paper presents background information on the organization and goals of academic advising, qualities of effective academic advisors, and needs of undecided students. It is proposed that librarians can be effective advisors to undecided students and that there are personal and professional benefits to be gained from participation in the advising process.

Introduction

Academic advising has traditionally been a responsibility of the instructional faculty. As a librarian with full faculty status at a four-year university, the author saw academic advising as an opportunity to become involved in an area commonly reserved for instructional faculty, receive university service credit for promotion, become more personally involved with students, and broaden understanding of the university curriculum. After presenting background material on academic advising and undecided students, this paper provides rationale for why librarians are well qualified to serve as academic advisors to undecided students and why librarians may wish to pursue this little-used service opportunity.

Academic advising originally began as a faculty responsibility to help students make appropriate course selections from an increasingly complex university curriculum that evolved at the end of the nineteenth century. Before then academic programs were highly structured, curricular choices were limited, university enrollments were small and there was less diversity in the student body.[1] Unfortunately the quality of advising today is rated by students as one of the weakest areas in their undergraduate experience.[2]

Academic advising has been defined most recently as

   . . . a developmental process which assists students in the clarification of their life/career goals and in the development of educational plans for the realization of these goals. It is a decision-making process by which students realize their maximum educational potential through communication and information exchanges with an advisor; it is ongoing, multifaceted, and the responsibility of both student and advisor. The advisor serves as a facilitator of communication, a coordinator of learning experiences through course and career planning and academic progress review, and an agent of referral to other campus agencies as necessary.[3]

Academic advising is often divided into two focus areas depending upon student level- general education (or premajor) and major. Students can also be subdivided into those who are undecided (or with no declared major) and those who have declared majors.

The Undecided Student

It is estimated that between 20 to 50% of students entering college are undecided (or undeclared, exploratory, open-major, general education major, or special major).[4] At some universities new students are required to declare an academic major as soon as they enter, while at others they are encouraged to delay choosing a major until the end of their first or second year.

While some in the academic community view undecidedness as an unhealthy and worrisome condition, most perceive it to be a natural and temporary state. For the most part undecided students are no different from other students in academic abilities, emotional maturity or social sophistication. Their only distinguishing characteristic is that they are currently undecided about an academic major.[5]

From an advising and developmental perspective undecided students have needs in one or more of the following areas:[6]

1. Informational needs. They may have little realistic information about their own abilities, interests, goals and values; or they may be lacking information about academic or occupational areas.

2. Developmental skills. They may lack appropriate decision-making skills and therefore are unable to formulate academic/career choices.

3. Personal-social conflicts. They may be experiencing conflicts between personal values and goals; interests or abilities and energy needed to attain a desired goal; or personal desires and the pressures from parents or significant others.

New students who are undecided tend to have high attrition rates. Studies have shown a strong correlation between successful academic advising programs and retention of these students.[7]

General Education Curriculum

During the first two years of academic study students are typically involved in fulfilling general education requirements, one of three equally divided components of most university curricula. (The other parts are major and electives.) While the definition, length and implementation of general education varies across the United States, 95% of all universities have general education requirements.

The general education curriculum is typically composed of courses in the following three areas:[8]

1. Advanced learning skills. These are designed to build skills for further study and lifelong learning. Part of these advanced skills include the ability to use the library and other information systems.

2. Breadth or distribution requirements. These are designed to introduce students to the mainstreams of thought and interpretation in the main branches of human understanding (humanities, social sciences, natural sciences).

3. Integrative learning experience. These courses are designed to foster the integration, synthesis, and interconnectedness of knowledge. As a result of coursework in this area, students should be able to visualize large and complex subjects and understand and think about their personal relationship to time and place.

Academic Advising

Academic advising by faculty remains the most common pattern for advising. However, in the last 20 years there has been increased attention given to organizing advising around a central advising office, either as a joint endeavor with faculty or with total advising responsibility. The Third National Survey of Academic Advising conducted in 1987 continued to show that faculty play a large role in advising in 75% of universities. Four organizational models accounted for delivery of most advising services:[9]

1. Faculty-only model (33% of universities). All students are assigned to a faculty member. Undecided students are either assigned to a faculty member in the liberal arts, distributed among faculty who volunteer to advise undecided students, or distributed among faculty who have fewer major advisees assigned to them.

2. Supplementary model (20% of universities). All students are again assigned to a faculty member. In addition there is an advising office which serves both as a clearinghouse for advising information and as a source of referral to other support services on campus.

3. Split model (22% of universities). An advising office advises a specific group of students, e.g., undecided students. All other students are assigned to faculty for advising.

4. Self-contained model (11% of universities). Advising for all students is conducted from a centralized advising office.

Faculty tend to be more heavily involved in academic advising at smaller universities, whereas larger universities typically follow a model having a centralized advising office of some type. The ideal model is a blending of the "faculty-only model" and a centralized advising office.

Academic advisors typically perform the following specific functions which are designed to assist students in gaining their maximum from the college experience:[10]

1. Purpose of a higher education. Students need to understand the goals, value and nature of a liberal education and the university, as well as the rationale for specific curricular requirements.

2. Relationship. Advisors need to create a climate for cultivating one-on-one working relationships with their students. By getting to know each student, advisors become aware of each student's needs, motives, and expectations.

3. Values clarification and goal identification. Students may need assistance in defining and developing realistic educational and career goals which are in consistent with their abilities and interests.

4. Planning. Advisors need to assist their students in making sound decisions on an ongoing basis regarding selection of specific programs and courses in keeping with each student's long-range academic and career goals.

5. Information and referral. Students need to be provided with adequate information on courses being offered, degree programs, educational policies, as well as referral to other university resources and services as necessary.

Academic advising is not something that all faculty can and should do, but unfortunately on many campuses they are required to participate even though they may lack desirable skills and abilities. Some of the qualities that characterize faculty who excel in academic advising include:[11]

1. Communication skills. These include effective interviewing techniques and the ability to focus attention and interest on the student through active listening.

2. Knowledgeable. Advisors should be the most informed faculty members on campus regarding university curricula, resources, policies and practices.

3. Available. Advisors should have regular office hours and be willing to work around busy and demanding schedules to meet with students.

4. Concerned and empathic. Advisors should have the ability to put themselves in a student's place, recalling previous academic and career experiences.

5. Organized. Recordkeeping and notetaking are a necessary part of advising.

6. Ability to use information and referral resources. These resources may be printed materials or other campus services.

More than half of all universities offer training and resources for advisors in the form of workshops and printed materials.[12] Ideally these workshops should include an overall philosophical perspective on advising; specific training and information concerning admission, registration, transfer policies, degree requirements, and financial aid; a general orientation to the university; and advising simulation exercises. In addition to formal workshops there should be an ongoing in-service program for maintaining and upgrading advising information and skills. Unfortunately, many faculty feel that their training has been inadequate.[13]

One of the major advantages of having faculty involved in advising is the opportunity for student-faculty contact and development of a relationship that is an important part of a student's college experience. For the student who has declared a major this normally works out for the best. Instructional faculty are experts in their discipline, knowledgeable about specific courses in their department and familiar with educational and career opportunities in their area of concentration.

On the other hand, the discipline orientation of instructional faculty may create a distinct disadvantage for the undecided student wishing to explore several unrelated academic areas. In addition a frequent complaint of undecided students is that their faculty advisor knows little about general education requirements and curricular options.[14] The librarian advisor may be well equipped to fill this generalist need. For undecided students advisors need to be generalists in academic information, knowledgeable about student development theory, and able to understand career development as well as career/academic relationships.

Librarians as Academic Advisors

Librarians are highly qualified to serve as academic advisors to undecided students who are exploring academic and career options as well as completing general education requirements. Many of the qualities and skills which are needed for effective academic advising to these students are characteristic of librarians, including:

1. Communication skills. Many librarians, especially those in reference service, have well developed communication skills acquired through education and experience in conducting the reference interview where there is a "dialogue between someone in need of information and someone—the librarian—able to give assistance in finding it."[15]

2. Generalists. Many librarians have a more global view of academic life and human knowledge rather than the more narrow focus sometimes found in instructional faculty. The author recalls one of his advisees saying the advisor was specifically chosen because the advisee felt that librarians would have a broad perspective.

3. Referral techniques. Librarians are usually knowledgeable about other campus resources and are practiced in the art of making referral to other sources of information. They are masters in understanding and making use of reference and other information resources.

4. Individualized instruction. In one sense academic advising is individualized instruction, something that reference librarians do on a frequent basis. There may even be opportunities for individualized library instruction with advisees.

5. Long term perspective. Librarians are concerned about skills necessary to prepare students for lifelong learning; in the same way they can take a long term perspective on the advising and developmental needs of students.

6. Accessibility. Librarians may be more flexible than instructional faculty members in finding time to spend with their advisees.

Service—professional, community and university—is one of the three criteria commonly used in librarian evaluation for tenure and promotion. University service is a vague category covering almost any university activity, including university governance and committee work which is outside the librarian's library responsibilities. While advising has been mentioned as a miscellaneous university service in several recent surveys on evaluation criteria for librarians, there has been no presentation in the literature on librarian participation in academic advising.[16]

Based upon the author's experience these are a number of benefits which can be gained through participation in academic advising. Besides the obvious credit for university service and participation in a traditional instructional faculty responsibility, there are several intangible benefits. One is the opportunity to gain a greater awareness of the educational mission and curricula of the university and the resulting ability to apply that within the library. Another is the opportunity to develop more extensive and longer-term relationships with students, something which is more difficult to do for librarians who do not have the same level of exposure to students as instructional faculty nor participate as much in student activities outside the library.[17]

This paper would not be complete without discussing some of the problems faced by participation in academic advising. The most obvious is time commitment. Unless one is able to get release time for this activity, which is unlikely, academic advising comes as another workload on top of library, university and professional responsibilities. This time commitment will vary depending upon the number of advisees and extent of relationships developed. Another problem at some universities may be the extent and quality of advisor training as well as lack of printed resource materials such as an advisor's handbook. A third problem at many universities is the lack of an award system for academic advising. Unfortunately, universities continue to place a low priority on recognition or reward for this activity. It plays a minor consideration in the tenure and promotion process,[18] although for librarians it has the potential to be a stronger element in university service.

Conclusion

This paper has presented background material on undecided students, academic advising, and academic advisors before making a case for librarian participation in academic advising. Based upon a review of the literature and the author's experience as an academic advisor, the article shows that librarians are as equally (or better) qualified as instructional faculty to serve as advisors to undecided students. It may be that the opportunity does not exist on every campus to participate in advising because of the organizational model used. Librarians are encouraged to consider the possibilities and become involved. There are personal and professional rewards to be gained through service as an academic advisor.

Endnotes

1. Judith J. Goetz, "Academic Advising," in Audrey L. Rentz and Gerald L. Saddlemire, *Student Affairs Functions in Higher Education* (Springfield, IL: Charles C. Thomas, 1988), p. 21.
2. Ernest L. Boyer, *College: the Undergraduate Experience in America* (New York: Harper and Row, 1987), p. 52.
3. David S. Crockett, *Advising Skills, Techniques and Resources; a Compilation of Materials Related to the Organization and Delivery of Advising Services* (Iowa City, Iowa: American College Testing Service, 1988), p.3.
4. Virginia N. Gordon, *The Undecided College Student: an Academic and Career Advising Challenge* (Springfield, IL: Charles C. Thomas, 1984), p. x.
5. Thomas J. Grites, *Academic Advising: Getting Us through the Eighties* (Washington,D.C.: American Association for Higher Education, 1979) (ERIC Document Reproduction Service No. ED 178 023), p. 37.
6. Virginia N. Gordon, op. cit., p. 43-45.
7. David S. Crockett, "Academic Advising: a Strategy for Improving Student Persistence," in David S. Crockett, *Advising Skills, Techniques and Resources,* (Iowa City, Iowa: American College Testing Service, 1988), p. 167-191.
8. Carnegie Foundation for the Advancement of Teaching, *Missions of the College Curricula* (San Francisco: Jossey-Bass, 1977), p. 164-179.
9. Virginia N. Gordon, op. cit., p. 26-32; Wesley R. Habley and David S. Crockett, "The Third ACT National Survey of Academic Advising," in Wesley R. Habley, *The Status and Future of Academic Advising: Problems and Promise* (Iowa City, Iowa: National Center for the Advancement of Educational Practices, 1988), p.19-21; Wesley R. Habley and Michael E. McCauley, "The Relationship Between Institutional Characteristics and the Organization of Advising Services," *NACADA Journal* 7 (Spring, 1987): 27-39.
10. Judith Goetz, op. cit., p. 23.; Charles Bostaph and Marti Moore, "Training Academic Advisors: a Developmental Strategy," *Journal of College Student Personnel* 21 (January, 1980): 45.
11. Virginia N. Gordon, op. cit., p. 94-95.; Jerry R. Wilder, "A Successful Academic Advising Program: Essential Ingredients," *Journal of College Student Personnel* 22 (November, 1981): 489 .
12. Wesley R. Habley and David S.Crockett, op. cit., p. 71.
13. Charles Bostaph and Marti Moore, op. cit., p. 48.
14. Arther Levine, Handbook *on Undergraduate Curriculum* (San Francisco: Josey-Bass, 1978), p. 145.
15. William A. Katz, *Introduction to Reference Work,* Vol. 2: *Reference Services and Reference Processes,* 4th ed. (New York: McGraw-Hill, 1982), p. 41.
16. Betsy Park and Robert Riggs, "Status of the Profession: a 1989 National Survey of Tenure *College and Research Libraries* 52:283 (May 1991); Lynne E. Gamble, "University Service: New Implications for Academic Librarians," Journal *of Academic Librarianship* 14 (January 1989): 347 .
17. Kathleen Dunn, "Psychological Needs and Source Linkages in Undergraduate Information-Seeking Behavior," in *Energies for Transition: Proceedings of the Fourth National Conference of the Association of College and Research Libraries,* ed., Danuta Nitecki (Chicago: ACRL), p. 177.
18. Wesley R. Habley and David S. Crockett, op. cit., p. 71.

Promoting Research in Special Collections Librarianship: The Role of a Professional Journal

Alice Schreyer
University of Chicago
Chicago, Illinois

Abstract

This position paper examines research and the current state of publishing in the field of special collections librarianship, based on the first five years of the ACRL journal, *Rare Books & Manuscripts Librarianship*. The paper also examines the role of a professional journal in fostering professional research. Following a summary of the background to the journal's founding in 1985, the author surveys manuscripts submitted for publication in *RBML*, reviews strategies employed to stimulate the submission of manuscripts to the journal, and enumerates research needs that have been identified.

It is widely acknowledged that establishing a specialized journal is an important milestone in the development of a scholarly discipline or profession. A journal creates a regular vehicle for communication within the field, a mechanism for the publication of research results, and a stimulus to expanding the knowledge base by encouraging further research.[1] This paper will examine these assumptions from the perspective of *Rare Books & Manuscripts Librarianship*, a relatively new ACRL journal. My experience as *RBML* editor suggests that a new journal provides an excellent opportunity for strengthening the literature of a field. Through a review of strategies developed over the first five years of *RBML's* existence, I hope to demonstrate that a professional journal can play a vital role in fostering the articulation and pursuit of research needs and opportunities.

Rare Books & Manuscripts Librarianship was founded in 1986, in response to efforts on the part of leaders of the Rare Books and Manuscripts Section (*RBMS*) of ACRL. Interest in a journal devoted to theory and practice of special collections librarianship reflected change within the profession. By the early 1980s, the administrative focus in most special collections had shifted from the expansive collection-building of the previous decades to funding, bibliographic control, fostering collection use, security, and other issues similar to, yet distinct from, those in the rest of the library.[2] The acceptance of these responsibilities by a new generation of special collections librarians resulted in a perceived need for specialized communication and professional development opportunities. The Rare Books and Manuscripts Section provided the structure for developing standards, guidelines, brochures and other professional publications through a growing number of committees charged to accomplish specific tasks.[3] Other responses to increased communication needs include the founding of the *RBMS Newsletter* in 1984 and the establishment of an information exchange to meet at ALA conference and midwinter meetings.

Also at this time, ACRL was reviewing its own efforts to foster the professional growth of members through its publishing program. At the same time ACRL president, David Weber proposed an expanded publications program that would include a journal directed at rare book and manuscript librarians. This suggestion was enthusiastically embraced and pursued by RBMS members.

Under the auspices of the ACRL Publications Committee, an ad hoc subcommittee investigated the feasibility of an ACRL journal for rare book and manuscript librarians. The committee compiled a questionnaire which was mailed in the fall of 1984 to a sample of 415 individuals, drawn from a combined membership list of 2,220 members of the Rare Books and Manuscripts Section, the Bibliographical Society of America, and the Society of American Archivists.[4] Of the 47% who responded, 80% agreed that there was a need for the new journal, and the potential subscription pool was estimated at over 1,000. The purpose of the questionnaire was to gauge potential copy as well as estimated audience. Here, the results were not as encouraging: 77% responded "no" to the question of whether they were "PRESENTLY researching a topic which would be appropriate for such a journal." Since 24% responded that it was "likely" they would "submit a manuscript to this journal for possible publication within the next two years," 8% said "definitely" and 3% said "very likely," there was at least some indication that if the journal were established, a small number of the 77% intended to undertake research with a view toward publication in the journal.

ACRL established *RBML* on a provisional basis, as a subscription journal to appear twice a year; volume 1, number 1 appeared in April 1986. Ann Gwyn, the founding editor, called for "articles that will contribute to the profession by communicating new knowledge, by summing up the state-of-the-art, by evaluating contemporary theory and practice, or by exploring the implications of new methods made possible by modern technology, with the hope that RBML will become in time the accepted professional journal for all who are concerned with any aspect of special collections."[5] Following a trial period of three issues, during which the journal achieved the ACRL subscription target of 500 and advertising revenues reached a satisfactory level, ACRL made the journal a permanent part of its publishing program in 1987.

In the first five years after the founding of *Rare Books & Manuscripts Librarianship*, 75 papers were submitted for publication, of which 31 were accepted. The topics on which the highest number of papers were submitted include bibliographical access and histories and descriptions of particular collections, with 10 each. The acceptance rate for each category was quite low, however, with only three papers on bibliographical access and two on historical aspects published during that period.

On subjects relating to the administration of modern manuscripts collections, 8 papers were submitted, of which 6 have been published, including one on congressional archives. This is an interesting figure in light of a misperception that *RBML* focuses primarily on rare book matters, with archival and manuscript topics covered principally by the Society of American Archivists' journal, *American Archivist*. The same point of view is sometimes heard with respect to *RBMS* itself, although recent ACRL Rare Books and Manscripts Section leadership patterns and committee activity indicate a vigorous responsiveness to the needs of manuscript curators, similar to the editorial policy of *RBML*.

Of the submissions to *RBML* between 1986 and 1990, 29 were originally presented as talks at an RBMS Preconference, an RBMS program at ALA, or at other professional meetings. The high percentage of RBMS Preconference talks submitted and published is consistent with an original impetus for the journal's founding, namely a regular outlet for the publication of papers that were of consistently high interest to special collections librarians.[6]

The low number of papers submitted that did not derive from talks, and the extremely high rejection rate for "original" manuscripts that were not directly solicited from a particular author, reveal that at the time of *RBML's* founding there was no body of research waiting for a suitable outlet. This is a clear confirmation of the responses to the ACRL survey question regarding current research.[7] The challenge faced by the RBML editor and board was to exploit the journal's existence to promote research and writing leading to publication.

One effective strategy has been to utilize the existing structure of ACRL's Rare Books and Manuscripts Section. Shortly after becoming editor, I invited all RBMS committee chairs to place the subject of research needs on committee meeting agendas and report back on the results of the discussions. In some instances, I received suggestions of topics to pursue; in others, committee members volunteered to take on the writing of specific articles. Among the published results of this activity are a series devoted to various aspects of exhibition catalogs emerging from the Exhibition Catalogue Awards Committee; and an article on the revised *Bibliographic Description of Rare Books*, coauthored by the present and past chair of the Bibliographic Standards Committee. Other topics suggested in committee discussions and currently being pursued are the implementation of thesauri for rare book cataloging and projects for reducing large cataloging arrearages.

Another strategy employed by the *RBML* board and editor is the direct solicitation of articles on topics of identified need from appropriate authors. For example, two published articles, one on buying trips and one on curator/conservator relations, were solicited in response to two topics listed among the highest priorities on the ACRL survey—acquisition/collection development and preservation/conservation—on which few articles have been submitted. An obvious explanation for the low number of preservation and conservation manuscripts is that this field has a flourishing, specialized literature of its own, and most authors choose to write for their peers. Although we seek to stimulate use of the journal as an arena for interaction, where specialists from other areas of librarianship and researchers give voice to matters that relate to, or should interrelate with, special collections librarianship, so far this effort has had only limited success.

We also pursue standard editorial tactics, soliciting papers and cajoling colleagues in writing and in person, attending lectures and conferences in search of talks or topics that can be developed. RBMS Preconference organizers are encouraged to invite speakers to consider publication in RBML at an early stage of correspondence, and this too has had good results. It is by now evident that electronic bulletin boards constitute a vital source of information on current issues and possible authors, but I have not as yet exploited this potential. Along with many of my colleagues, I am still unsure of the niche in the communication circuit occupied by discussions on bulletin boards. The more lively interchanges offer useful insights into what people are dealing with on a daily basis, and there is a fair amount of impromptu brainstorming, but I am not yet convinced that there is a direct correlation between these activities and subjects suitable for in-depth treatment.

Several recent developments seem especially promising. *RBML* volume 5, number 2, contained the first "Review Essay," on the subject of "Mass Deacidification in the 1990s." This feature represents both an expanded scope for the book review section and our interest in covering issues on which special collections and general library concerns intersect.

RBML volume 6, number 1, was the first special issue of the journal, devoted to the subject of "MARC Cataloging for Medieval Manuscripts." The guest editor had organized a seminar session on this subject for an RBMS Preconference, and the presentations were later expanded into a set of papers under her guidance. RBMS Preconference seminars (as opposed to plenary sessions) typically focus on practical concerns; over the past few years there has been a marked increase in the number that rise beyond merely local application. Many of these have the potential to be developed into fuller presentations of publishable quality.

Also quite recently, Sam Streit, the chair of the RBMS Publications Committee, a member of the RBMS editorial board, and a strong supporter of the journal in both of these capacities, has taken the initiative to raise funds and establish an ACRL Award for the best article published over a 2-year period in Rare Books & Manuscripts Librarianship. The award has just been approved by ALA, and we hope to present the first award at the 1993 RBMS Program Meeting at Annual Conference. We anticipate that the combination of recognition, publicity, and a cash prize, will encourage potential authors to become active contributors.

Since becoming *RBML's* editor in 1988, the authors moved from a state of perpetual anxiety over insufficient copy to the relative luxury of concern over how to stimulate research on particular topics. In fact, the opportunity to engage in analysis of communication and research needs for special collections librarianship with colleagues on the editorial board has been the principal intellectual satisfaction of my tenure. I would like to conclude with a very brief survey of these desiderata.

Although one article based on a survey pertaining to collection use has been published, much more work needs to be done in this area.[8] We yearn to know more about what and how materials in special collections are used, who our users are, and how they find their way to our departments. We need to assess current collecting strategies in light of research trends, drawing faculty into the process, in order to determine directions for the future. How are online catalogs and retrospective conversion projects affecting use? As technologies for creating documents become more sophisticated, how can we work with faculty and library colleagues to identify criteria for artifactual values that justify conservation of items in original format? Professional education for special collections librarianship is a topic of immediate concern, in light of the closing of Columbia's library school, with its specialized training program. Other areas include strategies for cooperative collecting programs, the impact of library-wide budget cuts on staffing and acquisitions in special collections, and integrating MARC AMC records and local access files for printed materials into an online environment. What is the impact of the increasingly sophisticated exhibition and publications programs that developed over the past decade—with encouragement from the ACRL Katharine Kyes Leab and Daniel J. Leab *American Book Prices Current* Exhibition Catalogue Awards—and are they commensurate with the resources we are allocating to them?

Recent thefts of library materials have focused attention on collection security issues and on professional ethics. An RBMS committee is working to revise the current ethical standards, and the literature of special collections librarianship should provide a forum for the exploration of the issues raised by these events. To date, I have not identified or provoked research on these and other similarly complex matters.

Hovering over all of these topics is the central concern of how special collections librarians can best articulate their role in the research process and the academic library of the present and future. Although one might like to dismiss the "Faculty Bill of Rights for Library Services," published in the March 1992 issue of the American Historical Association Newsletter, *Perspectives,* with its erroneous accusation that rare book purchases compete for allocated funds with textbook acquisitions, this flagrant attack is a reminder to special collections librarians that old stereotypes of elitism are still very much with us. Our voices must be heard in library and campus-wide discussions about new technology and humanistic research; access and ownership; academic library priorities, programs, and funding. A professional journal should assist in formulating concepts and strategies for this dialogue.

RBML board members and I recognize that a central problem in stimulating professional writing and publishing is the lack of a broad academic base for special collections librarianship, which means that the core of researchers—faculty and graduate students—simply does not exist for rare books and manuscripts librarianship. We are realistic in understanding that our colleagues write when they can and about what they do, which may not be what the profession needs most to know about. Most special collections librarians at major repositories are not in faculty status situations and do not have a career-advancement impetus to publish, let alone in a professional journal. Indeed, many of our most prolific special collections colleagues choose to remain active in their academic discipline, or to focus their research and writing energies on topics reflecting institutional collection strengths. A good deal of research by special collections librarians is devoted to scholarly rather than professional topics, a pattern that is both appropriate and healthy.

There are, then, many sound reasons why the ex-

istence of a specialized journal may not either result from or automatically produce research in special collections librarianship. However, the first five years of *Rare Books & Manuscripts Librarianship* indicate that the journal provides an opportunity to strengthen the literature of special collections librarianship by aggressive work on the part of editor and board. We believe that this activity in turn contributes to the vitality of the field through focusing attention on important issues.[9] Over the coming year, the journal will undergo an editorial transition. It will also face its first major budget deficit, the result of declining advertising revenues afflicting every sector of publishing including other ACRL journals. These two factors will prompt assessment and evaluation of *RBML's* role, a healthy activity with respect to the journal, as it is for special collections librarianship itself. I am confident that the journal's first five years provide ample evidence that *RBML* is fulfilling the important goals with which it was founded and will continue to do so.

Endnotes

1. See Margaret F. Stieg, *The Origin and Development of Scholarly Historical Periodicals* (University, Alabama: University of Alabama Press, 1986) for a thorough study of this subject based on the historical profession.
2. See Daniel Traister, "A Caucus-Race and a Long Tale: The profession of Rare Book Librarianship in the 1980s," *Library Trends* 36 (Summer, 1987): 141-156, for an overview of recent changes within the profession.
3. See John B. Thomas, III, "Standards and Guidelines Prepared by the Rare Books and Manuscripts Section of the Association of College and Research Libraries," *RBML* 2 (Fall, 1987): 109-112.
4. The questionnaire results were summarized and analyzed in a memorandum of January 3, 1985, from Nicholas C. Burckel to the ACRL Publications Committee.
5. *RBML* 1 (April, 1986):3.
6. See Stephen Ferguson, "ACRL/RBMS Preconference Institutes and Preconferences, 1959-1988: Record of Published Lectures and Papers," in Alice Schreyer in "RDMS at 30: Growing Along with the Profession," *RBML* 3 (Spring, 1988): 10-16.
7. During the early to mid-1980s, the following publications relating to special collections librarianship appeared: *Rare Books 1983-'84,* edited by. Alice Schreyer (New York: Bowker, 1984); "Recent Trends in Rare Book Librarianship," *Library*

Trends, 36 (Summer, 1987); and a special issue of *Wilson Library Bulletin* 58 (October, 1983). The frequency with which the articles in these three collections is cited confirms the lack of breadth to the literature.

8. William Matheson, "Institutional Collecting of Twentieth-Century Literature," *RBML* 4, no. 1 (Spring, 1989): 7-43.

9. A model for this approach is provided by *Academic Libraries: Research Perspectives,* edited by Mary Jo Lynch; ACRL Publications in Librarianship no. 47 (Chicago: American Library Association, 1990).

Table 1. Papers Submitted to RBML, 1985-90

Topic	Submitted	Accepted
Access (bibliographical)	10	3
Access	3	1
Administration	5	3
Book collecting	1	
Book trade	2	1
Collection development & Acquisitions	3	1
Conservation/preservation	5	1
Deaccessioning	2	
Education & training	3	1
Exhibitions[excluding catalog awards list]	4	3
General overview	6	1
Historical/Collection descriptions	10	2
Legal aspects	2	1
Modern manuscripts	8	6
PR/fundraising/development	4	2
RBMS committee work	4	3
Security	3	2
TOTAL:	75	31

Table 2. Papers Submitted to RBML, 1985-90
Originally Delivered as Talks

Topic	Accepted	Rejected	Total
Access (bibliographical)	1	1	2
Access	1		1
Administration	3	2	5
Book collecting		1	1
Book trade			
Collection development &			
Acquisitions		1	1
Conservation/preservation			
Deaccessioningaining		1	1
Exhibitions		1	1
[excluding catalog awards list]			
General overview		3	3
Historical/Collection descriptions	2	4	6
Legal aspects	1		1
Modern manuscripts	4	1	5
PR/fundraising/development		1	1
RBMS committee work			
Security			
TOTAL:	13	15	29

Table 3. Papers Submitted to RBML, 1985-90
Not Originally Delivered as Talks

Topic	Accepted	Rejected	Total
Access (bibliographical)	2	6	8
Access		2	2
Administration			
Book collecting			
Book trade		1	1
Collection development &			
Acquisitions	1	1	2
Conservation/preservation	1	4	5
Deaccessioningaining		1	1
Education	1	2	3
Exhibitions			
[excluding catalog awards list]	3		3
General overview	1	2	3
Historical/Collection descriptions		4	4
Legal aspects		1	1
Modern manuscripts	2	1	3
PR/fundraising/development	2	1	3
RBMS committee work	3	1	4
Security	2	1	3
TOTAL:	18	28	46

Library Ethics: An Aspirational and Culturally Sensitive Alternative to Its Commandments

Mark A. Spivey
University of Utah
Salt Lake City, Utah

Abstract

Cultural diversity raises dilemmas for the library profession, some of which are difficult to resolve on the basis of its absolutist ethical prescriptions. Psychological studies of class, cultural, and gender differences in moral reasoning support a professional ethics based upon care and cultural sensitivity, instead of universal and obligatory principles. Librarians can change their professional codes of conduct, in order to express more realistically their aspirations and community responsiblities, while accommodating social differences.

The Dilemma of Mr. Broadview and Ms. Caring-Tu

Mr. Broadview, a well-traveled librarian at a liberal arts college, explained his decision to add culturally varied materials to the library's collection with some biographical remarks. He talked about his background in the Peace Corps in Third World countries, and he referred to an upcoming meeting of Amnesty International.

Ms. Caring-Tu, an Asian-American librarian at the same college, decided that the library should use its remaining collection development funds to replace tattered classics of Western civilization and to add other great books of the tradition. In defense of her decision, she told the campus press about her nephew, who participated in the Tiananmen Square demonstrations. He had written recently and asked for a copy of John Stuart Mills's essay, "On Liberty." She found that it, and other important documents, were not represented in her library's collection.

The two mature and professional librarians defended their opposing choices in interviews, which were not examples of fine critical thinking. They used no logical arguments. The librarians appealed to no universal principles, and to no profession's code of ethics. Instead their narrative and biographical explanations were stories with the kind of wisdom some of us get from grandmothers and grandfathers.

Moral Reasoning with Cultural & Gender Sensitivity

The dilemmas of public service in libraries are aggravated by the library profession's obligatory and absolutist principles, such as those in the *Intellectual Freedom Manual* and in the "Statement on Professional Ethics 1981."[1] Library professionals need to examine their absolutist stance on censorship and confidentiality, and their naivete in demanding that professionals distinguish clearly between their own opinions and those of their clientele. If librarianship is typical of professions, it has some ideological and elitist components.[2] We are understandably suspicious that "neutrality is just following the crowd."[3]

The decision of reference librarians who supply suspicious patrons with information, which could jeopardize property or persons, can be questioned. Yet, as one popular study found, these librarians act deliberately upon the basis of the principle of freedom of access to information. We may ask, "Does the social responsibility of librarians ever take precedence over information dispensing?"[4] The ALA stand on intellectual freedom assumes that such freedom is exercised without the possibility of countervailing obligations. However, the decisions made at a busy reference desk and in collection development are full of implicit countervailing obligations.

Many of us act responsibly without identifying ethical principles. When we are called upon to defend our choices, sometimes we explain them with biographical stories in conversations, such as those of Mr. Broadview and Ms. Caring-Tu. Several kinds of stories are put into dialogue: The stories of our lives, namely our experiences; the stories of our culture, including the ideologies in which we are immersed;

and the stories, which have come from the roots of a faith, that is, our traditions and loyalties.[5]

Persons' everyday interactions can be taken as the basic units of moral analysis. A lived-ethic is decision-making, and it involves communication in order to discover another's position.[6] Dialogue replaces logical inference in the process of a moral discovery.[7]

Objectivity and universality are characteristic of other contexts of reasoning, such as science, philosophical ethics, and legal analysis. In particular, the world of the lawyer is constructed of rights and duties, privileges and powers. The experience of people is viewed under the lens of judicial opinions.[8]

We are not caught in an incomplete phase of moral development, as suggested by Kohlberg's stages of moral development. Nor are we assuming that our colleagues and clientele have "limited good will," and that we need to enforce the profession's code with sanctions.[9] Librarianship does not have to "make virtue pay" for members of the profession.

Psychologists have learned that the moral reasoning of many adults and young people have a conceptual and practical basis in relationships of care and responsibility, rather than in obligation.

Philosophical ethics, with its criteria of generalizability and impartiality, assumes that human beings and situations are similar in morally relevant aspects. Although most philosophers in the Anglo-American tradition march to the beat of Western logic, an increasing number of them fall out-of-step with common-sensical proclamation such as this one from a feminist philosopher:

> . . . the approach that I praise here may be taken to involve a fallacy of relevance . . . an argumentum ad hominem . . . insofar as evaluating does occur or is appropriate, it is by knowing where the author is coming from.[10]

Philosophers and cognitive development psychologists, such as Lawrence Kohlberg, have used socioeconomically advantaged men and their work as the basis for determining the structure of moral reasoning.[11] However, psychological research has found differences in moral reasoning, which are attributed to social class, ethnic, and gender variables.

Kohlberg's stages of moral development do not reflect closely the development of moral reasoning among ethnic groups. One sociologist found that concern over care and responsibility was more common among the Chicanos, blacks, and women in a research sample in which standard dilemmas were presented. However, a white male was similar to the other research subjects, because he explained his decision in terms of "love."[12]

The "moral judgment interview" is a scoring device used to measure moral development along Kohlberg's scale. A Chicano male responded to a psychologist-interrogator:

Question: "Would you steal for your pet?"
Answer: "If the pet were the only friend I had."[13]

Trained scorers have been unable to evaluate some types of interview material, such as the narrative form of moral discourse. A subject may respond in the manner of "Let me tell you a story." With that transition to storytelling, the interviewee becomes the teacher, who is trying to stimulate the interviewer's reasoning.[14]

Women's moral thinking appears to be dominated by life-long considerations of care and connection, and a concern for detachment and abandonment. Their views of the self and others place weight upon interdependence and the need for attention and response.[15] On the other hand, values of justice, autonomy, reciprocity, and equal respect dominate the hierarchial and contractual perspective upon human relationships.[16]

A response consideration is one which the psychologists consider to involve care; a rights consideration involves justice. Both kinds of considerations are found among males and females in real-life conflicts. However, women use considerations of response more frequently than rights, and men use considerations of rights more frequently than response.[17]

An adversarial and critical style of thinking is learned in school. However, studies of girls and women from various ethnic and economic backgrounds, in academic settings and in family agencies, revealed that their subjects exercised a "connected way of knowing." The exceptions among the research subjects were students in an elite liberal arts college, and recent graduates from such an institution. Yet even these students had a proclivity toward responses showing empathy, care, collaborative exploration, and a nonjudgmental stance.[18]

103

Debate continues in regard to whether differences in moral reasoning are attributable more to social class and ethnic variables than to gender differences. We are cautioned about a polaristic and gender-based interpretation of Carol Gilligan's remediation of Kohlberg's research.[19]

The Ethics of Organizational & Human Systems' Development

The relatively new profession of organizational and human systems' development (OD-HSD) is developing an elaborate code of ethics, which takes into account the moral dilemmas arising from cultural diversity, confidentiality, and conscientious objection. Cultural and subcultural differences are recognized in several different ethical guidelines, including this one: "Practice in cultures different from our own only with consultation from people native to or knowledgeable about those specific cultures."[20]

The OD-HSD profession also has a more sophisticated stand on freedom of choice and confidentiality than the library profession. Its code of ethics identifies limits to freedom of choice and confidentiality.[21]

The flexibility, which the OD-HSD professional allows into a code of ethics, acknowledges finally that there are legitimate moral appeals beyond even the most flexible of ethical guidelines: " . . . violation of ethical standards (including morals) may be justified under certain conditions because such violation is required to minimize harm or to serve most fully the ideals represented by our values and ethics as a whole."[22]

With that disclaimer in one of the most flexible of ethical codes, the primacy of something else, such as conscience or care, is admitted. It is acknowledged finally that the good can be served in violation of any prescription. One analyst of professional behavior proposes a second tier of morality beyond that of rules. This level consists of ideals, which can inspire some of us to do more than the rules require.[23]

An Aspirational and Culturally Sensitive Ethics for the Library Profession

In view of the limits acknowledged in the flexible, professional ethics of organizational & human systems' development, and in view of the irrelevant manner in which legalistic models reflect the moral reasoning of many professionals, it would make sense to look for an alternative to the absolutist and obligatory character of the library profession's ethics.

One ethicist believes that professional codes are more meaningful when they are interpreted as an ethics of character or virtue, rather than regulations of behavior—"They tell the professional not only what to do but whom to be." A viable test that we can apply to a contemplated action is whether or not that course fits our life story, that is, does it contribute to our integrity?[24] We can understand how both Mr. Broadview and Ms. Caring-Tu can justify their opposing choices, for each has made a decision which fits well into their biographies.

The alternative proposed, here, is to abandon the absolutist and obligatory language of the library profession's ethical code. Yet we can express our aspirations and responsibilities. Since the focus in this paper has been upon the dilemma posed by cultural diversity for our professional ethics, the paper will close with a recommendation on how to address that dilemma in a professional statement of our ethical responsibility.

The following substitution is recommended for the first and second items in the "Library Bill of Rights":

Original items:

1. Books and other library resources should be provided for the interest, information, and enlightenment of all people of the community the library serves. Materials should not be excluded because of the origin, background, or views of those contributing to their creation.

2. Libraries should provide materials and information presenting all points of view on current and historical issues. Materials should not be proscribed or removed because of partisan or doctrinal disapproval.[25]

Substitution:

Librarians strive to meet the information needs of the primary community, which their mission calls upon them to serve. Material selection is undertaken with an acknowledgment of the filters of different cultures, philosophies, theories, and methodologies, and with the objective of presenting various points of view.

This revision accepts the assertion in the Introduction to the "Statement on Professional Ethics 1981" that librarians influence or control significantly the selection and dissemination of information, *while acknowledging certain implications of that responsibility.*

Librarians do not pretend to be completely impartial and unaffected beings. They have the distinctive limitations of a human being. From a theological perspective, the statement accepts our "fallen" and frail nature. We have constraints imposed by a particular cultural heritage, and yet we have things to contribute and to achieve within our heritage and across cultures.

The statement is aspirational. The library cannot be the ideal of an institution, which meets the needs of everyone perfectly. However, those working in the library have realistic objectives of service, which can be held up to public scrutiny (i. e. librarians try to meet the information needs of a particular community).

The language avoids a judicial and obligatory structure. We are moral beings even when we are not obeying a contract. We are moral by virtue of our intentions, not simply by the degree to which our actual performance is consistent with a prescription. Mr. Broadview and Ms. Caring-Tu do not have to justify their different choices by virtue of citing compliance with a regulation. Their little stories, which are part of their biographies, constitute a full and moral explanation. Their integrity is unquestionable.

In summary, the library profession does not need to jettison codes of ethics, as Samuel Rothstein recommended. Instead, I recommend that we change the legalistic character of the Library Bill of Rights and the Statement on Professional Ethics. Although we need not draw his conclusion, we can ask, along with Rothstein, "Where does it Hurt?"[26] Then we share our stories, and from them we select certain aspirations and service interests, which identify us. These become our ethical statements.

Endnotes

1. Leo N. Flanagan, "Defending the Indefensible: The Limits of Intellectual Freedom," *Library Journal* 100 (October 15, 1975), 1891.
2. John Kultgen, *Ethics and Professionalism* (Philadelphia: University of Pennsylvania Press, 1988), p. 111-112, 128-129.
3. Myles Horton and Paulo Freire, *We Make the Road by Walking: Conversations on Education and Social Change* (Philadelphia: Temple University Press, 1990), p. 72.
4. Robert Hauptman, *Ethical Challenges in Librarianship* (Phoenix: Oryx Press, 1988), p. 72.
5. Eric Mount, Jr., *Professional Ethics in Context: Institutions, Images, and Empathy* (Louisville: Westminster/John Knox Press, 1990), p. 52.
6. The phrase, "lived ethic" or "lived morality," is borrowed from: Paul F. Camenisch, *Grounding Professional Ethics in a Pluralistic Society* (New York: Haven Publishing Corp., 1983). The jargon is similar to "lived time" and "lived space" in much of the literature of existential phenomenology.
7. Kathryn Pyne Addelson, *Impure Thoughts: Essays on Philosophy Feminism and Ethics* (Philadelphia: Temple University Press, 1991), p. 208.
8. Eric Mount, op. cit., p. 40.
9. John Kultgen, *Ethics and Professionalism* (Philadelphia: University of Pennsylvania Press, 1988), p. 34-35.
10. Joyce Trebilcot, "Ethics of Method: Greasing the Machine and Telling Stories," in *Feminist Ethics*, edited by Claudine Card (Lawrence: University of Kansas, 1991), p. 51.
11. Kathryn Payne Addelson, op. cit., p. 191, 201, 206; for a recent discussion of Kantian and Aristotelian dimensions in contemporary moral philosophy debate see: Edmund L. Pincoffs, *Quandaries and Virtues: Against Reductionism in Ethics* (Lawrence: University Press of Kansas, 1986).
12. Anthony Cortesse, *Ethnic Ethics: The Restructuring of Moral Theory* (Albany: State University of New York Press, 1990), p. 103, 125-126.
13. Ibid., p. 91.
14. Ibid., p. 111.
15. Nona Plessner Lyons, "Two Perspectives: On Self, Relationships, and Morality," in *Mapping the Moral Domain: A Contribution of Women's Thinking to Psychological Theory and Education* (Cambridge: Harvard University Press, 1988), p. 42.
16. Carol Gilligan, "Remapping the Moral Domain: New Images of Self in Relationship," in *Mapping the Moral Domain: A Contribution of Women's Thinking to Psychological Theory and Educationn,* p. 8; and Carol Gilligan and Jane Attenucci, "Two

Moral Orientations," in *Mapping the Moral Domain: A Contribution of Women's Thinking to Psychological Theory and Educationn,.* p. 74.

17. Nona Plessner Lyona, op. cit., p. 37-38.

18. Mary Field Belenky et al., *Women's Ways of Knowing: The Development of Self, Voice, and Mind* (New York: Basic Books, Inc., 1986), p. 12, 104, 106-107, 116, 119.

19. Ketayun H. Gould, "Old Wine in New Bottles: A Feminist Perspective on Gilligan's Theory," *Social Work* 33 (September-October, 1988), 411, 414-415.

20. William Gellerman, Mark S. Frankel, and Robert F. Landenson, *Values and Ethics in Organization and Human Systems Development: Responding to Dilemmas in Public Life* (San Francisco: Jossey-Bass Publisher, 1990), p. 114.

21. Ibid., p. 18-169, 174-175.

22. Ibid., p. 151-152.

23. John Kultgen, op. cit., p. 52-53.

24. Karen Lebacqz, *Professional Ethics: Power and Paradox* (Nashville: Abingdon Press, 1985), p. 75, 85.

25. Office for Intellectual Freedom of the American Library Association, *Intellectual Freedom Manual* (Chicago: American Library Association, 1983), p. 14.

26. Samuel Rothestein, "Where Does it Hurt? Identifying the Real Concerns in the Ethics of Reference Service," *The Reference Librarian* 25/26 (1989): 316-317.

The Perceived and Actual Benefits of Contributed Paper Sessions Sponsored by ACRL Chapters

Jay Starratt
Southern Illinois University
Carbondale, Illinois

and

Carroll Varner
Illinois State University
Normal, Illinois

Abstract

This paper describes the expereinces of the Illinois and Nebraska Chapters of the Associations of College and Research Libraries with using the contributed papers format of the ACRL national conference. It explores the assertions made by the proponents of local contributed paper sessions that supportive atmosphere of the sessions, in which non-refereed papers are presented in front of small groups known to the presenter, inspires and fosters research, publication and presentation growth among the presenters, and leads to greater member involvement in the chapter. It presents a short history of each chapter's sessions and analyzes the responses to a participant survey.

Introduction

In 1982, the College and University Section of the Nebraska Library Association inaugurated an annual event, modeled on the contributed papers format of the Association of College and Research Libraries national conferences, in which members of the section presented papers to their Nebraska academic library colleagues. In 1988, the Illinois Association of College and Research Libraries began a similar program. The Illinois sessions were initiated by transplanted Nebraska librarians and were inspired by the librarians' experience with the Nebraska program. Both organizations are ACRL Chapters and each began their programs in order to encourage members' professional growth by providing an opportunity to make presentations to a friendly, non-threatening audience, most of whom are known to the presenter. Other purposes included the desire to promote association participation, especially by new members, and to foster further research, publication and presentation activity.

As part of the effort to foster inclusiveness and to eliminate barriers to participation, the papers have never been subjected to a refereeing process. Proponents of these sessions assert that the lack of refereeing has had a positive effect and that the sessions have done much to stimulate publication activity and professional growth and participation. This paper will examine the history and ongoing activity of the sessions and will include a review of a survey (Appendix 1) employed to assess the opinions of the sessions by the participants.

The paper will also use the reslts of a second survey to examine the extent to which contributed paper sessions have been offered by other ACRL Chapters.

History and Background

As of 1991, the Nebraska chapter had sponsored 9 conferences in which 97 papers were given by 83 different presenters. The Illinois Chapter had sponsored 4 conferences in which 53 papers were given by 52 different presenters. The Nebraska session is normally held as a full day conference the semester opposite the annual Nebraska Library Association meeting and is generally considered the major chapter activity of the year. In Illinois, the session is held in a two hour block during the annual conference of the Illinois Library Association. The Illinois chapter traditionally holds a separate conference in the Fall (at its two-day 1990 Fall meeting, the ILA College and Research Libraries Forum offered refereed contributed papers). There are significantly fewer librarians in Nebraska than in Illinois and the role of academic librarians in the states are different. In the past, some Illinois academic librarians often voiced the opinion that the state association meeting was geared to public and school library interests and that there was little at the state meeting which spoke to academic concerns. The contributed paper session is thus a major part of the academic participation in the annual meeting. However, the session does not play as central a role in the activities of Illinois academic librarians as it does in Nebraska.

Papers and presenters

Judging by the ongoing participation, the sessions appear to be healthy and well-established. Table 1 shows the number of papers given at each conference, as well as the total number of participants. (In 1989 the Nebraska Chapter sponsored a personnel workshop by a national figure in place of the session).

Many factors contribute to the year to year fluctuation in the number of papers. For instance, the more remote the location in Nebraska, the greater the likelihood there will be fewer papers. The 1988 session was held in Kearney. In Illinois, the 1989 session coincided with the ACRL Conference, and the inclusion of refereed contributed papers session at the 1990 Fall ILA College and Research Library Forum Conference probably took a number of the papers away from the spring session. The enthusiasm of each year's organizers also influences the number of papers submitted.

Some people have become mainstays of the conferences. In Nebraska, 16 people have given a paper twice, five have presented three times, three four times and one speaker has given five papers. In Illinois, eight people have given a paper twice, and there has been one three-time presenter and one speaker has given a paper at all four sessions. There have been 42 one-time contributors in Illinois and 58 in Nebraska. Twenty-one percent of both the Nebraska and Illinois papers were co-authored. 37 % of the author credits, however, were attributed to co-authors.

Subjects

The subject matter of the papers has always been diverse and has ranged from global think pieces to treatises on making decisions about claiming late serial issues. Table 2 gives a very broad subject overview of the papers (these categories combine many sub-categories and, obviously, many of the papers had more

Table 1. Number of papers and presenters

	Nebraska		Illinois	
Year	Papers	Presenters	Papers	Presenters
91	8	10	11	15
90	7	12	14	16
89	No Session		10	13
88	5	6	18	23
87	16	19		
86	10	15		
85	14	20		
84	15	18		
83	9	9		
82	14	13		

Table 2. Subject Categories: Number of papers

NEBRASKA	91	90	89	88	87	86	85	84	83
Automation	0	3	2	9	3	6	8	2
BI/Outreach	3	1	0	1	1	0	2	3
Management	1	1	1	2	3	3	0	1
Ref	1	1	0	0	1	1	1	0
Catalog/Serial/Circ	0	0	0	1	0	0	1	1
Resource Sharing	0	0	2	1	0	1	1	0
Collections	1	0	0	2	1	1	0	1
Other	2	0	0	1	1	1	1	1

ILLINOIS	91	90	89	88
Automation	1	1	2	4
BI/Outreach	3	3	4	1
Management	1	0	0	4
Ref	1	0	1	2
Catalog/Serial	1	2	0	1
Resource Sharing	1	2	0	1
Collections	2	3	2	3
Other	1	2	1	2

than one subject, especially the automation papers).

The continuing interest in bibliographic instruction is noteworthy, as is the apparently warming interest in giving papers on automation. Some sessions had themes which occasionally influenced, but never mandated, the selection of topics.

Survey

In order to gauge the perceptions of the participants as to the success of the sessions, a survey was developed and mailed to the 133 participants for which an address could be found. 61 surveys were returned (46%) - 31 from Illinois (60%)and 30 from Nebraska (37%). The uniformly favorable participant opinion of the sessions is seen as almost all (55 of the 56 who answered the question) replied that the paper session was a beneficial experience. Written explanations offered included:

" . . . sharing information with colleagues helpful" (8 similar)

" . . . the presentation before a small supportive group was encouraging" (6 similar)

" . . . helped integrate into state ACRL chapter" (6 similar)

"The commitment to read a paper provides a helpful impetus encouraging the completion of the paper for submission to an editor" (3 similar)

"All public speaking opportunities are beneficial" (3 similar)

"Great confidence builder" (2 similar)

Almost all of the respondents stated that they would recommend to others that they present a paper (Table 3), 82% said they intended to present again (15% thought they might). The speakers were certainly not discouraged by the sessions since 87% said that they thought their paper was a success (5% said their experience was not successful, 8% had mixed feelings).

Table 3. Survey Results: All Respondents

	Nebraska %	Illinois %	Total %
First paper ever	60	33	47
Reasons for participating			
Tenure/promotion	53	45	49
Speaking experience	30	29	29
Persuaded by colleague	23	26	25
Personal development	33	35	34
Professional development	63	64	64
Share information	73	77	75
Published previous to paper session	62	73	68
Subsequent state presentation	54	35	44
Subsequent national presentation	27	43	35
Made contacts because of paper	47	35	41
Gave this paper again	24	31	27
Submitted for publication (not ERIC)	8	19	14
Felt participation was beneficial	100	96	98
Effect of non-refereed format on decision to participate			
positive	21	33	27
negative	14	26	20
no effect	36	33	34
ambiguous	29	7	18
Recommend others participate	90	97	93
Plan to give another paper			
Yes	87	77	82
Maybe	10	19	15
No	3	3	3

44% of the presenters (does not include 1991 presenters) have gone on to give additional papers at state conferences, 35% at national conferences, including ALA, and ACRL (this figure includes 1991 presenters who went on to make presentations at 1991 national conferences).

68% of the speakers had published before. Their publications appeared in a full spectrum of library literature, including *College & Research Libraries*, the *Journal of Academic Librarianship, LRTS* and others.

All of the pre-1991 Nebraska speakers have attended a session again. This speaks to the more central role of the sessions in the Nebraska Chapter. 64 % of the

Illinois speakers have attended subsequent to their presentation. There have been fewer Illinois sessions, of course, but the placement of the paper sessions within the state conference where other events, such as exhibits and programs, compete with the chapters time slot, certainly keeps the attendance down. Also, the notice for the session is often lost amid all the conference publicity.

First time speakers (Table 4)

One of the primary aims of the sessions is to encourage librarians who have never given talks at professional conferences to attempt it for the first time. A substantial 47% of the respondents said that the contributed paper session was their first professional

Table 4. Survey Results: First Time Speakers

	Nebraska %	Illinois %	Total %
Reasons for participating			
Tenure/promotion	61	60	61
Speaking experience	39	60	46
Persuaded by colleague	22	30	25
Personal development	44	40	43
Professional development	78	70	75
Share information	75	60	64
Previously published	61	60	61
Subsequent state presentation	50	50	50
Subsequent national presentation	13	25	17
Made contacts because of paper	39	30	36
Gave this paper again	22	30	25
Submitted for publication (not ERIC)	6	11	8
Felt it was beneficial	100	88	96
Effect of non-refereed format on decision to participate			
positive	35	38	36
negative	12	13	12
no effect	29	38	32
ambiguous	24	13	20
Recommend others participate	100	83	89
Plan to give another paper			
Yes	83	80	82
Maybe	11	20	14
No	6	0	4

presentation. Of these first time presenters, 61% had published before. 17% of these first time speakers (not including the 1991 speakers) have gone on to give papers at national conferences, half have presented at other state conferences. 46% (39% in Nebraska, 60% in Illinois) of these speakers gave "experience in speaking" as a reason for participating. Only 12% of the other speakers gave that as a reason for presenting.

Post paper activity

In Nebraska, the proceedings of the conference are gathered by the chapter and published as photocopied proceedings. The gathered papers are also submitted to ERIC. In Illinois, the presenters are simply given an ERIC release form and encouraged to submit the paper to ERIC. 48% of Illinois presenters (again not including the 1991 speakers) have sent their material to ERIC. Since giving papers, 14% of all the presenters (again excluding 1991 presenters) have submitted their papers to other publishing outlets; 4% have such an intention. One interesting difference between the Nebraska and Illinois presenters surfaces here. 30% of the experienced Illinois speakers submitted their papers, or a version of it, for publication; only 8% of the experienced Nebraska speakers submitted their papers. 27% of all the respondents gave the contributed paper in another session. Another valuable feature desired of the papers is the possibility to engage chapter colleagues and participate further in chapter activities. 41% said someone had contacted them as a result of their presentation.

Reasons for participation

There were a number of reasons given for participation. The primary reason given was the opportunity to share information (Table 3), followed by the chance for professional development. In order, tenure and promotion considerations, personal development, public speaking experience and colleague persuasion were the other motivators.

The participants were asked if refereeing was a factor in their decision to give a paper and it is interesting to note how ambiguous were their responses. One respondent replied that they thought the papers were refereed. 27% thought the lack of refereeing was a positive aspect of the sessions, 20% saw it as a negative condition and 18% had mixed feelings. 34% said it had no effect on their opinion one way or the other. A greater proportion of the first time presenters, 36%, found the lack of refereeing a positive factor. Only 12% of the novices saw it as a negative attribute. Those who tended to point to the low-key atmosphere as a good quality of the sessions were referring more to the audiences than to the absence of prior paper judging. Finally, a few of the respondents' written remarks commented on the uneven quality of the papers, which they attributed to the lack of refereeing, but most of those went on to say that a few bad papers were probably worth the benefit of providing a venue for people to begin presenting.

Conclusions

The Nebraska and Illinois contributed paper sessions are healthy and continue to serve their chapters. The aim of encouraging first time contributors seems to have been met as 47% of the respondents indicated that their paper was their first professional talk. Almost all of the participants rate the experience as beneficial and obviously support the continuance of the sessions by their intentions to participate in the future. A significant number of the presenters have maintained contact with their chapter's offerings and many of them have continued to publish and present, a notable number in national conferences. The amount of post-paper personal contacts, and the continuing attendance and participation in the sessions, indicates that the sessions are useful in encouraging chapter participation. The record of publishing and speaking activity by the participants subsequent to their contributed paper presentation, gives an indication that the sessions are useful prods to the individuals to engage in further research, publication and presentation. Certainly the 30% of the experienced Illinois speakers who went on to submit their papers for publication used the sessions in a manner that would support such a contention.

Since almost two-thirds of the novice speakers were not novice publishers, it would seem that the public presentation opportunity is clearly the most important aspect of the professional development opportunity. The lack of refereeing may not have as great an impact as supposed by the session proponents, although more than a third of the novice presenters saw it as a positive influence.

Other chapters have adopted the paper session format as well. A survey of 41 chapters revealed that 53% of the chapters responding (10 of 19) have held a session at least once. These sessions were likely to be refereed and 40% of them compiled the papers either for ERIC or for a newsletter. A second mailing of the survey should provide more accurate national details.

Information Support for University Decisionmakers

Meredith Whiteley
Kathleen Wolk
Helen Josephine
Arizona State University
Tempe, Arizonz

Abstract

This paper delineates the rationale for a new model of information support for university decisionmakers, outlines the structural issues, and provides specific details of the varied functions the librarian performs in this new model, including environmental scanning, tape and data management, and direct involvement in research design. The discussion concludes with implications this model has for the changing roles of university departments, the new organizational patterns emerging within universities, and the role of the university library.

University administrators are moving increasingly to information-based decisionmaking and planning. Individual decisionmakers, planning and budgeting councils, academic departments, and institutional research offices all require up to the minute information from a broad range of external sources. In addition, universities face mounting pressures to better manage and distribute internal information.

Traditionally, university decisionmakers relied on analyzing, interpreting, and finding relationships in internal data generated on student enrollment, degrees granted, and annual budgets. As an added element, university decisionmakers now are seeking external data from the national, state and local environment. Information files created from these datasets are no longer published in book form for distribution, but made available through electronic networks so that end users have the ability to create cross-file reports and relationships. Both external and internal dataset management involve complex organization, distribution, archival and storage issues.

How can academic librarians meet the challenges offered by the new level of information support required by university decisionmakers? To date, the literature provides two approaches for information support to decisionmakers. Peter Watson and Rebecca Boone, two academic library administrators, describe in a 1989 article the results of a test program to provide information support to academic administrators at California State University, Chico.[1] This program attempted to meet the unique information needs of administrators by designating a librarian to handle research requests from the administration. Other information support needs such as improving access to internal university information, enrollment data, planning information, institutional research reports were not addressed.

A second approach, used in clinical-medical libraries, provides a more integrated and responsive model for library information support. Agnes Roach, a medical library administrator, chronicles the participation of librarians as part of the health care team, a trend which began in the early 1970s. The key to this approach is that the librarian becomes "a member of a patient care team, attends educational conferences, patient rounds, grand rounds, etc. in order to identify needs for information, to find that information, and to deliver it within a very short time (ranging from minutes to hours) .... By being present, the clinical librarian can anticipate questions as well as answer those that might otherwise never have been asked."[2]

The designated librarian approach is inadequate in two ways: 1) The librarian is not solely dedicated to the information needs of the administrative units and does not become part of the problem solving team. 2) The administrative needs for data management are not addressed. While the clinical-medical approach clearly includes a librarian as part of the team, it also does not address the needs of university decisionmakers for environmental scanning, data tape management, or distribution of information.

A few major university libraries address issues of access to machine readable data files by creating positions which include machine-readable data collection and reference support for data retrieval as part of the librarian's duties.[3] These positions, however, are in support of faculty research in the social sciences rather than administrative needs for data management.

What are the specific requirements of an institutional research office that create such unique and challenging information needs?

What is Institutional Research?

Institutional research provides the information and analysis to support decisionmaking in colleges and universities. The office usually reports directly to either the president or the chief academic officer and is linked frequently with budgeting and planning.

Institutional research offices sprang up on campuses during the sixties in response to two developments: 1) the growing ability to generate and analyze data on faculty, students, performance, space, and budgets, and 2) federal and state requirements for this information. The National Science Foundation (NSF), National Institutes of Health (NIH), National Center for Educational Statistics (NCES), and a whole alphabet soup of federal and national agencies developed surveys and data bases to capture and distribute this information to Congress, state legislatures, policy groups, and individual campuses. As internal data became more available, administrators, trustees, and faculty began to use them for decisions on issues ranging from student retention policies to librarians' salaries. Institutional research offices provided both the ability to integrate data from multiple data bases and conduct sophisticated policy analysis.

Figure 1 illustrates the early institutional research process with three key components: 1) Data Gathering/Source, 2) Analysis, and 3) Output/Storage. At this early stage, the information came solely from internal data bases. Institutional research then integrated and analyzed the data, turning out paper printouts or long, often unread, "white papers." All data was stored in its original form on tapes. Frequently, this storage went undocumented, making access and use at a later date almost impossible.

The eighties brought significant changes to higher education, including 1) the power of distributed technology, and 2) the imperative to tear down some of the protective ivy covering and respond directly to the needs and pressures of the external environment. As George Keller, author and editor of *Planning for Higher Education,* noted in 1983, colleges and universities were "shaken from their self-regarding world of internally generated wish-lists and abundance."[4]

The impact of distributed technology on administrations and institutional research offices was to create an exponential increase in the amount of internal data to integrate, distribute, interpret, catalog, and store. The impact of the shift to an external focus was to introduce a host of new issues that require information from new, and often unidentified, sources outside the institution. These changes bring an expansion of institutional research on most campuses into the areas of data administration, futures-based planning, focus groups, total quality management, and environmental scanning. Expansion, of course, brings new "challenges," particularly in the area of information management. Environmental scanning is one good case in point.

Environmental Scanning and Institutional Research

One approach many colleges and universities take to gathering external data is to establish a systematic environmental scanning process. Adapted from industry models, campus-based environmental scanning provides a conceptual framework to guide the search for and ongoing tracking of trends that may impact the institution.

Almost all environmental scanning efforts track key demographic and economic trends. Where the variations come, however, are in the more qualitative areas of technological advances and changing values. Early on, the University of Minnesota's scanning team, for example, picked up on the animal rights issue and began tracking its development nationally and locally. The scanning led to an in-depth policy analysis and significant changes at the university *prior to* a disruptive crisis.[5] Other scanning efforts focus on detecting technological breakthroughs that may provide opportunities for new programs, market niches, or research directions.

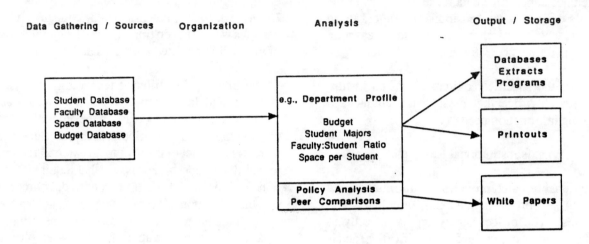

Figure 1
Early Institutional Research Process

Data Gathering / Sources   Organization   Analysis   Output / Storage

Student Database
Faculty Database
Space Database
Budget Database

e.g., Department Profile

Budget
Student Majors
Faculty:Student Ratio
Space per Student

Policy Analysis
Peer Comparisons

Databases
Extracts
Programs

Printouts

White Papers

Environmental scanning is a potentially powerful tool for college and university planning and decision-making. However, as illustrated in Figure 2, adding an external information component, such as environmental scanning, introduces a significant level of complexity to the institutional research function. Data Gathering/Source, expands to include the new subcomponent of External Sources. The problems for many institutions in dealing with external information are in 1) establishing a coherent information gathering and management strategy, and 2) developing information networks to gain access to unclassified information. Added to these are the problems of translating large and disparate data sets into simple formats, easily used on distributed electronic networks. Administrators, faculty, and institutional researchers simply are not trained to do this effectively.

Librarians and Institutional
Research Information Management

Our premise is that librarians are the best people on campuses to deal with the issues of information retrieval and management. Librarians possess the unique information management skills for organization and access, data retrieval from internal and external data files, and acquisition of both traditional and nontraditional information. Our experience, however, taught us that the traditional interface between librar-

ians and college/university administration is inadequate. Even a responsive fee-based library service like Arizona State University's FIRST provides help only with data retrieval, leaving information management needs unattended. Intermittent contact between the librarian and institutional researchers, even when a librarian is designated to provide service from the library, leaves wide communication gaps that are often costly.

Our approach at Arizona State University is to place the librarian directly into the Office of Institutional Analysis as an integral part of the institutional research process and a key member of the administrative research team. What the librarian brings to that team are subject expertise, retrieval skills, networks for obtaining key external information, and, skills and knowledge in information management. The plan is to have the librarian move, over time, into each of the five institutional research process components. The focus at this time, however, is on integrating the librarian into three of the components: Data Gathering/Source, Organization, and Output/Storage. Figure 3 illustrates this integration.

Data Gathering/Sources

Internal Sources. Institutional research offices generally have access to all campus data bases, including the student information system, payroll/personnel,

Figure 2
Institutional Research Process - 1991

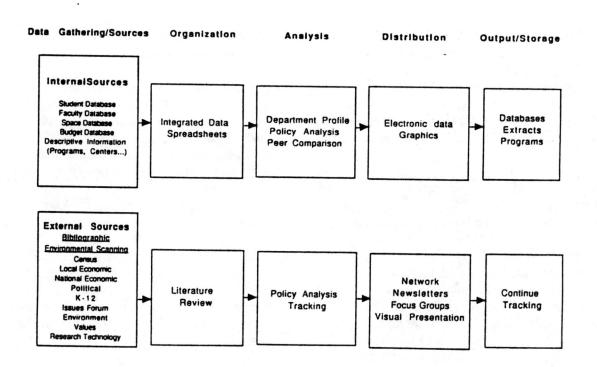

Figure 3
Institutional Research Process - 1991

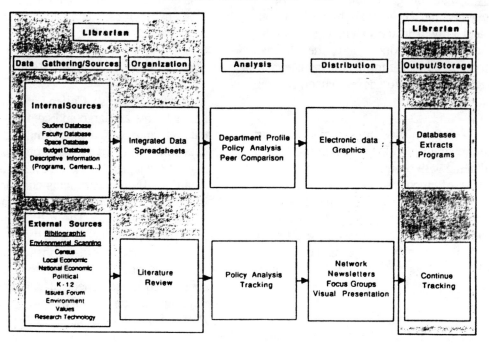

budget, faculty data, and space. This valuable primary source material comprises the history of the university. This information often is integrated with other data on similar (or "peer") institutions to form the broader picture of national higher education trends.

The librarian's involvement at the internal data creation stage is in data element definition. It is critical that the librarian understand each data element in order to operate effectively in the organization/storage components of the process. The librarian's role at this point includes participation in data administration teams at both the campus and system level to determine common data definitions across data bases and systems.

In addition, the librarian participates in the gathering and organization of descriptive materials about the many programs and centers on the campus. This vital qualitative information about the institution frequently is disseminated to legislative committees, economic development task forces, and accreditation review teams. Arizona takes this information dissemination a step further in its newly-created electronic economic information data base, available through all public libraries in the state. Arizona State University's Office of Institutional Analysis is a key player in the design and updating of this system, which includes information on the university's programs and research resources.

External Sources. College and university administrators and planners must benchmark their institutions to changes and growth in the external populations, economics, and other factors. Here, the librarian performs more traditional information management functions, including collection development, control, and resource retrieval.

Institutional research offices must provide support for senior administrators, including the president and trustees, in dealing with complex issues and constituencies. This level of support requires immediate accessibility to the most up to date reports and data available. Frequently, these administrators are confronted in negotiations with data and citations they have not seen. They must be able to pick up the phone, call the campus, and obtain copies of the cited information immediately.

Short time horizons and a sense of urgency carry over into much of institutional research's projects.

Meeting these needs requires that the collection development approach be broad and deep. The librarian establishes and monitors this collection, including monographs, research reports, serials, and extensive non-print information from sources such as the Integrated Postsecondary Education Data System (IPEDS) and the National Science Foundation. In addition, the librarian oversees the operation of an internal online recordkeeping system.

To stay on top of the demand, the librarian must know the issues, be involved in the conceptualization stage of projects, and anticipate the needs of each analyst. Here is where it becomes evident that the librarian must be a member of the institutional research team, located in that research area and not in the library. The librarian conducts searches of commercial online databases, the university's online catalog and databases, government documents, and a broad range of other classified resources. In addition, the librarian must create personal networks throughout the community to uncover new releases and primarily unclassified proprietary information. This includes city planning documents, technical committee minutes for population estimates, and banking or utility internal economic analyses and plans.

The librarian's skills in collection development, control, and retrieval are especially needed to support environmental scanning. The librarian takes the lead in networking and identifying resources in a host of areas outside of the higher education arena, including demographics, political trends, environmental issues, and new research breakthroughs.

Organization

Internal Sources. College and university internal data systems are large and complex. Running these data sets and, particularly, simultaneously integrating data from different systems, creates substantial systemic challenges. Further, the new ability to distribute data directly to departments and faculty adds a new imperative to organize the information into simple and user friendly formats. The institutional research librarian at Arizona State University just recently moved into this component of the institutional research process. The focus of the effort, to date, is on creating a centralized spread sheet of common data elements required for external surveys for publications such as *Peterson's Higher Education Directory*. This task utilizes the librarian's growing knowledge of data element definitions, as well as her organizational training and skill.

External Sources. One of the biggest gaps in the institutional research process is in organizing the large amounts of mostly qualitative information and literature into useable formats that are easily accessed by more than one analyst or user. This is where the indexing and abstracting training of the librarian are particularly useful in developing literature reviews to support research projects and providing abstracts on key new releases for dissemination to a wider audience of university administrators.

One concrete example is the role the institutional researcher played in a meta-analysis project for the Association for Institutional Research, the international professional organization for institutional researchers. Arizona State University's institutional research librarian indexed topic subject areas of papers read at the Association's annual forums over the past ten years. This analysis formed the basis for a detailed decennial study of the direction of international research in this area over the past ten years.

The librarian's role in the office's environmental scanning process is just developing. The first organizational task is disseminating the tide of census data releases, supporting technical notes, and accompanying state and local population projection model updates. The librarian currently is working to develop an iterative spreadsheet of the latest key demographic data, such as county population counts and projections. These, then will be used to support a series of short newsletters for academic departments about the implications of population shifts for university and departmental planning.

Output/Storage

The support a librarian provides in the Data Gathering/Source and Organization components of the model is proving to be integral to the process. However, our initial motivation for including a librarian in the Office of Institutional Analysis was to fix the problems we have with cataloging and storing data. The issue is not a matter of time or interest, but the fact that institutional researchers do not know how to approach the problems effectively. College and university data bases are huge, yet most campuses have not developed effective systems for cataloging and organizing the raw data, the more often used extracts, or the programs. As a result,

institutional researchers often "reinvent the wheel" for each special project instead of drawing upon the work already created.

Internal Sources. The institutional research librarian's tape management tasks involve the storage and maintenance of multiple databases, extracts, and programs. This requires an understanding of the physical properties of magnetic tapes. The first task is to develop a schedule for running tapes so that information is not lost due to "bleeding" or other kinds of tape deterioration. Recent moves to cartridge formats introduce a whole new set of control issues.

In addition, the librarian must organize the documentation for each database. The librarian's knowledge of data definitions is critical at this point. Here the librarian's task is to create accessible catalogs of the programs, file layout, the parameters of the data set, data definitions, and the look-up tables, or "crosswalks," that allow movement from one data element to another. To accomplish this, the librarian works closely with programmers and analysts within the institutional research office, as well as the system designers, other users, and campus technical committees. In this process, the institutional research librarian is the university archivist.

External Sources. The problems institutional researchers have in managing the burgeoning literature and information from external sources are no less complex. Here, the librarian provides a window, matching the ongoing information needs of the university with the appropriate sources. The role of the librarian in this component is to design ongoing tracking mechanisms. These include alerts to identify new literature on topics of ongoing interest as well as new and emerging topics on every aspect of higher education management.

The task is similar but the subject areas broader for environmental scanning. The librarian is responsible for operationalizing the scanning process into the literature and dialogues in areas that often seem far-removed from the educational enterprise. In addition, the librarian establishes systems for adding new data to ongoing trend data on populations, economics, schools, and a variety of other possible topics.

Conclusion

We believe that the model we present here is an

important breakthrough in the professions of both librarians and institutional researchers. While we may seem ignorant of traditional organizational structures and librarians' needs for centralized control, we are not. We just do not believe in them. We believe, instead, that effective management calls for matching the needs with the skills. Librarians have the skills that university administrators increasingly need. However, the traditional compartmentalized university structure impedes the effective team approach necessary to meet the information needs of the university in the nineties. We believe that both librarians and administrators must search for new structural arrangements. The model we present is one working alternative.

Endnotes

1. Peter G. Watson and Rebecca A. Boone, "Information Support for Academic Administrators: A New Role for the Library," *College and Research Libraries* 50 (January, 1989): 65-75.

2. Agnes A. Roach, "The Health Science Librarian: A Member of the Health Care Team Responsive to Emerging Trends," *Library Trends* 28 (Fall, 1979): 253-262.

3. JoAnn Dionne, "Numerical Social Science Databases and the Library," *Choice* 22 (January, 1985): 646-652.

4. George Keller, *Academic Strategy: The Management Revolution in American Higher Education.* (Baltimore, Maryland: Johns Hopkins University Press, 1983).

5. James C. Hearn and Richard B. Heydinger, "Scanning the University's External Environment: Objectives, Constraints, and Possibilities," *Journal of Higher Education* 56 (July-August, 1985): 419-445.

CONTRIBUTED PAPERS

II.
BIBLIOGRAPHIC
CONTROL

Effects on Circulation of Dissertations of Omitting Subject Headings

Michael V. Sullivan, Dorothy McGarry,
Brian Schottlaender, and Barbara A. Miller
University of California
Los Angeles, California

Abstract

A study of levels of circulation of science and engineering dissertations with and without subject headings was conducted. Circulation records for the first two years of shelf life were examined. The dissertations treated with full cataloging were more likely than minimally cataloged dissertations to circulate at least once. The difference was small, though statistically significant. Implications of abbreviated bibliographic access on physical access are discussed.

Introduction

One of the objectives of a library catalog is to assist the user in locating library materials. [1,2] It seems reasonable to assume that improved bibliographic records which comprise the catalog should lead to increased use of the materials referred to in the records. Most recently, this assumption was tested by Gunnar Knutson,[3] who attempted to answer the question Does the catalog record make a difference?" He sought to establish a correlation between the number of access points in catalog records and the amount of circulated use which materials described by the records receive. He found very little correlation. In a later study,[4] he found improved recorded use when previously uncirculated collections of essays and conference papers were augmented with additional subject headings that described their individual parts. Most earlier research on the relationship between circulated use and bibliographic access of which there is little, is compatible with Knutson's findings [5,6] although at least one study contrasts with his results.[7]

It is easy to imagine instances in which multiplying the number of access points would not necessarily reflect a real improvement in bibliographic access, and so should not be expected to be associated with higher use. For example, a cataloger might need to include more subject headings in a bibliographic record because of the lack of a precise match between the subject content of an item and the terms in the subject heading list used. A combination of several subject headings may then be needed, none of them exactly on target. Better bibliographic access, then, might be associated with fewer, more exact access points, rather than numerous, inexact ones. It is, therefore less surprising that insignificant correlations, or even negative correlations, might exist between the number of subject headings and the level of use of library materials.

The relationship between the omission of subject headings from bibliographic records and the circulation use of library materials has received little, if any, study to date. As economic pressures confronting libraries grow, the need to reduce cataloging expenditure while maintaining its yield also grows. Minimal cataloging, which excludes subject analysis and, often, classification, is becoming an increasingly attractive cataloging option to the administrator. This is particularly true in an environment in which online public access catalogs are becoming commonplace, catalogs with powerful free-text and keyword search capabilities which might offset the omission of subject headings from the bibliographic record.

Online catalogs, irrespective of the degree of control exerted over their subject vocabularies, have powerful retrieval capabilities. Bates notes that "online search capabilities themselves constitute a form of indexing,[8] adding that "in online catalogs, title keyword searching can constitute a powerful kind of subject searching."[9] In her 1986 article regarding issues in the design of controlled vocabularies, Svenonius notes that the decision to construct such a vocabulary needs to include some consideration of questions of cost.[10] The same might be said for decisions relative to the application of a controlled vocabulary during the cataloging process. Svenonius then suggests possible avenues for research aimed at clarifying the effectiveness of retrieval using free-text language versus that employing controlled vocabulary.[11] Interestingly, she does not include analysis of circulation use as one approach of such research.

The present study both avoids the disadvantages of the correlation approach, and extends the previous work. Since 1986, as a workload economy, subject analysis has been excluded from the cataloging of UCLA dissertations and theses by the Physical Sciences and Technology Libraries (PSTK). The rationale for choosing dissertations for this brief treatment rather than other library materials was: (1) dissertations in the physical sciences and engineering tend to have informative titles, which could conceivably, in our online environment, substitute for subject heading; (2) library users can resort to *Dissertation Abstracts International* for controlled subject access to dissertations; and (3) it was suspected that library users tend to search for dissertations by known author or title, or by academic discipline rather than by topical subject heading.

Circulation use during the first two years of shelf life of the dissertations was measured for a sample which included Library of Congress subject headings, and some of which did not. It was hypothesized that the omission of subject headings would depress circulated use. The hypothesis assumes that subject headings provide useful bibliographic access, but does not identify effectiveness of that access with an increasing number of headings.

Methods

All 1,462 UCLA dissertations and theses, cataloged between 1982 and 1988, from the School of Engineering and Applied Science, and the departments of Astronomy, Atmospheric Sciences, mathematics, Physics, Chemistry & Biochemistry, and Earth & Space Sciences were identified. Identification was achieved by searching the online catalog for records assigned the form heading: "DISSERTATIONS, ACADEMIC—UCLA-<name of degree program>." Of the 1,462 dissertations identified, 10 were found to be missing, leaving a total of 1,452. Of the dissertations remaining, 976 had been cataloged with topical subject headings, and 476 had received only descriptive cataloging (except that all dissertations had received the form heading just mentioned). All dissertations studied have been represented by records in the UCLA public access online catalog (ORION) since they were first cataloged. UCLA Dissertations are shelved together, with a classification that reflects the degree program, but not the specific topic of study. Therefore, browsing through an area of monographs and journals classified for a given subject would not promote the use of dissertations in our collections. ORION provides access, in separate indexes, to keywords from titles, as well as to subject heading phrases and keywords from subject headings.

Each dissertation, along with the cataloging record was examined, and the following information noted: (1) academic discipline; (2) whether subject headings had been assigned: (3) number of circulation uses during the first two years of shelf life: (4) branch library in which it was housed. Date stamps on slips attached inside the cover of the dissertation comprised the record of circulation use. In 248 cases, slips had been removed. However, since slips were only applied at the time of the first circulation transaction, the visible remains of a removed slip constituted evidence that the dissertation had received at least one use. Hence, results are only reliable with respect to whether a dissertation was used at all, and not with respect to the degree of use. Nevertheless, significant differences in use between dissertations that were cataloged with subject headings, and those that were not were found.

Results and Discussion

Dissertations With Subject Cataloging More Likely To Circulate. The basic finding, shown in Table 1, is that the dissertations with subject headings were more likely to have circulated than those without subject headings. Of the dissertations cataloged with subject headings, 49% circulated, while only 41% of those cataloged without subject headings circulated. The difference in circulation use between the two classes of cataloging treatments is statistically significant (chi-square = 7,700, df = 1, p < .01).

Of course, another obvious difference regarding the two types of cataloging treatment is that the number of dissertations with subject headings is greater than the number without subject headings. This is because the minimal cataloging treatment of the second group has only been in place for 2.5 years when the use study was conducted, while the completely cataloged dissertations span a 4.5 year period. In addition, the number of graduate students enrolled during the periods studied differ, though only slightly (Table 2). For those reasons, the data analysis focuses on the *relative* number

123

of dissertations within each cataloging treatment category that circulated, rather than on their absolute numbers. This focus on relative frequency of circulating versus non-circulating dissertations is reflected in the chi-square test. Moreover, as shown in Table 3, a test of the difference between the proportions of circulated dissertations for the two cataloging groups is also statistically significant.

<u>Breakdown by Discipline</u>. In all disciplines, the dissertations cataloged with subject headings were more likely to have circulated than those cataloged without subject headings (Table 3). The differences were statistically significant according to a test for differences in proportions for the aggregated sample, for the geology dissertations, and for the computer science dissertations.[12]

Table 1. Number of Circulated & Non-Circulated Dissertations

	With Subject Headings	Without Subject Headings
Did Not Circulate	495 (51%)	279 (59%)
Circulated	481 (49%)	197 (41%)
Total	976 (100%)	476 (100%)

Table 2. Graduate Student Enrollment

Discipline	Average Enrollment 1982/85	Average Enrollment 1986/88
Eng.	739.88	717.53
Astro.	18.30	19.00
Atmosphere	32.65	45.43
Chem.	214.50	227.53
C. S.	255.68	227.80
Geol.	97.18	82.23
Math.	111.10	128.03
Physics	182.45	165.53
Total	1651.73	1623.10

Table 3. Percentage: Breakdown by Discipline

Discipline	With Subj. Hdngs	W/Out Subj. Hdngs	# Of Diss. With Subj. Hdngs	# Of Diss. W/Out Subj. Hdngs	Z-Score	Statistical Significance
All	49	41	976	476	2.87	$p < .005$
Engineering	54	49	495	240	1.27	NS
Astronomy	0	0	6	6	N/A	N/A
Atmospheric	27	13	15	8	0.77	NS
Chemistry	34	32	142	50	0.26	NS
Comp. Sci.	60	46	143	79	2.01	$p < .05$
Geology	48	17	65	29	2.85	$p < .005$
Mathematics	25	22	40	27	0.28	NS
Physics	49	41	70	37	0.79	NS

The smallest difference in proportion of dissertations circulated, between subject-analyzed and non-subject-analyzed, was found for chemistry. For this discipline, the proportion of circulating dissertations was almost identical for the two cataloging treatment groups. Might this suggest that the title words for chemistry dissertations were especially informative, so that it did not matter whether subject headings were applied? It might be interesting to study the overlap of information in the subject heading fields compared to the title fields. Moreover, transaction log analysis would be of interest here, to see whether chemists used subject heading indexing less than searchers from other disciplines.

The greatest differences in likelihood of circulation between subject and non-subject cataloged dissertations were found for atmospheric sciences, computer science, and geology. In future research, it might be asked whether the computer scientists, atmospheric scientists, and geologists actually search the subject heading indexes more often than do, for example, chemists. Might it be that subject headings in computer science and atmospheric science are especially up-to-date and precise compared to chemistry? Or that title words in these disciplines are uninformative compared to other science disciplines? Perhaps the belief of many geology librarians that geographic aspects are inadequately represented in geology titles might partly explain why subject headings would be important in this discipline.

Speculations About the Degree of the Effect of Subject headings on Circulation. The data did not allow conclusions about the degree of differences in circulation levels between dissertations cataloged with and without subject headings. As noted in the METHODS sections, however, for 248 of the circulated dissertations, circulation histories were lost because the slips had been removed, and so no information about how *much* those items circulated was available. The only conclusion that could be reached was that they did circulate at least once. Even this point is arguable, since our criterion for whether a dissertation circulated required that the circulation occur during the first two years of shelf life. It is possible that, for some of the dissertations with lost circulation histories, the circulation occurred later than the first two years of shelf life. Based on comprehensive "Pittsburgh study" of library materials use, however, most materials that are used at all are used during the first two years.[13] It can be expected those findings apply to the dissertations in disciplines that are as subject to obsolescence as those in this study. It would nevertheless be useful and interesting to find out more about the specific obsolescence patterns of dissertations in various disciplines.

If the actual levels of circulation, were known some judgments could be made about the trade-offs between the costs to the library for subject analysis versus the costs to the library user for lost access. To acquire the necessary data for such an analysis, it would be necessary to repeat the study, making sure that detailed circulation data are not discarded. Replicating the study would, of course, require that subject analysis of dissertations be resumed.

An additional complication involved in measuring the *amount* of circulation use for dissertations is an inherent one, to be found in almost all circulation studies: that the frequency of circulation is not normally distributed. Note the date in Table 4, which shows the number of dissertations with zero frequency is highest, followed by one circulation, and so on. One consequence of this pattern is that the usual statistical

tests involving the mean, such as the familiar t-test, probably are not valid with these severely skewed data. Such tests assume a normal distribution. Even non-parametric tests of median differences would not tell much, since, with more than half the dissertations showing zero use, the median will hover somewhere below one circulation, no matter what the cataloging treatment. Even if 248 circulation slips had not been lost determination of differences in levels of circulation would not have been straightforward.

Master's Theses Compared to Doctoral Dissertations. Although not the focus of our study, there was interest in whether the doctoral dissertations were more likely to circulate than the master's theses in the study. In the previous data presentations, use tallies are consolidated for the two types of materials. As show in Table 5, theses and dissertations were about

Table 5. Circulations of Master's Theses Compared to Doctoral Dissertations

	Master's Theses	Doctoral Dissertations
Did not Circulate	314 (52%)	460 (54%)
Circulated	293 (48%)	385 (46%)
Total	607 (100%)	845 (100%)

equally likely to circulate. One might have hypothesized that doctoral dissertations would have circulated more than theses because of the bibliographic access to them via *Dissertation Abstracts International*. The marked similarity between master's theses and doctoral dissertations with respect to use patterns casts doubt on the assumption, stated earlier, that the availability of doctoral dissertations through *Dissertations Abstracts International* might influence the use of the dissertations.

This might not be the case if *Dissertations Abstracts International* were more conveniently available to end-users, either through an OPAC or on CD-ROMs. Unlike humanities and social sciences branch libraries at UCLA, the physical sciences libraries do not provide

Table 4. Circulation Frequencies

Number of Circ's	Without Subject Headings	With Subject Headings
0	289	495
1	105	143
2	40	53
3	21	28
4	11	14
5	2	5
6	2	1
7	2	1
8	1	0
9	0	1

on-site copies of *Dissertations Abstracts International* on CD-ROM. It would be interesting to find out whether, for humanities and social sciences disciplines, differences in use patterns for doctoral dissertations and master's theses are more marked.

A further difference between dissertations for physical sciences, in comparison to humanities and social sciences, is the generally held belief that title words in sciences dissertations may be more informative about the topic of the work than they are in humanities or social science disciplines. Perhaps subject headings make more of a difference for non-science dissertations.

Conclusions and Future Research

The study shows that subject headings do make a difference, albeit a small one. In the context of library management, what must still be decided is whether the library should expend the effort required to assign subject headings. Even with subject headings assigned, 51% of the dissertations and theses do not circulate within the first two years of shelf life. It may be justifiable to eliminate assigning subject headings to dissertations even in the expectation that use will be slightly diminished, if it is reasonable to set a higher priority on cataloging other materials more fully or more expeditiously.

Many questions remain unanswered in the study. In addition to questions about the information available in the catalog record, there are other considerations that must be taken into account. For example, in an online database such as ORION, the user must deliberately decide to search title words separately from subject headings, since the two kinds of data are posted to separate indexes. It is suspected that many users do not proceed far enough in their searching behavior, and it seems quite likely that most of them have not learned about the rich variety of indexing and searching techniques available. With more thorough end-user instruction about subject searching, subject headings might make a greater difference. Dissertations might have circulated more frequently had title words and subject headings been searchable in a single index with the same search command. The study results suggest several possible lines of future research. Questions about end-user behavior, and about the organization of databases, can be added to these suggestions. In general, the study of relations between bibliographic access and use of materials can be a useful and interesting direction of investigation.

Endnotes

1. Charles A. Cutter, "Rules for a Dictionary Catalog: Selections," in *Foundations of Cataloging: a Sourcebook,* ed. Michael Carpenter and Elaine Svenonius (Littleton, Colorado: Libraries Unlimited, 1985), p. 67.
2. Seymour Lubetzky, "The Objectives of the Catalog," *Foundations of Cataloging: a Sourcebook,* ed. Michael Carpenter and Elaine Svenonius (Littleton, Colorado: Libraries Unlimited, 1985), p. 189.
3. Gunnar Knutson, "Does the Catalog Record Make a Difference? Access Points and Book Use," *College and Research Libraries* 47 (September, 1986): 462-69.
4. Gunnar Knuston, "Subject Enhancement: Report on an Experiment," *College and Research Libraries* 52 (January, 1991): 65-79.
5. Pal V. Rao, "The Relationship Between Card Catalog Access Points and the Recorded Use of Education Books in a University Library," *College and Research Libraries* 43 (July, 1982): 341-45.
6. Margaret Ann Thomas Taylor, "the Effect of Bibliographic Accessibility Upon Physical Accessibility in a Public Library Setting" (Ph.d. diss., University of Michigan, 1982), p. 241.
7. William Carl Highfill, "The Relationship of Indexing Depth to Subject Cataloging Retrieval Effectiveness" (Ph.D., diss., University of Illinois, 1969).
8. Marcia J. Bates, "Rethinking Subject Cataloging in the Online Environment," *Library Resources & Technical Services* 33 (October, 1989): 400-12.
9. Ibid., p. 403.
10. Elaine Svenonius, "Unanswered Questions in the Design of Controlled Vocabularies," *Journal of the American Society for Information Science* 37 (September, 1986): 331-340.
11. Ibid., p. 338-339.
12. Hubert M. Blalock, *Social Statistics,* Revised 2nd ed. (New York; McGraw-Hill, 1979), p. 232.
13. Allen Kent and others, *Use of Library Materials: The University of Pittsburgh Study* (New York: Dekker, 1979).

Cataloger/Archivist Cooperation, or, Don't Those People Know What a Series Is?

Elaine Yontz
University of Florida
Gainesville, Florida

Abstract

This paper deals with the question: How can catalogers and archivists work together to catalog archival and manuscript materials in a research library setting? Characteristics of archival materials and patrons and the differing perspectives of catalogers and archivists are discussed. Advantages of cataloging teams involving catalogers and archivists are stated and suggestions made as to how to effect a successful working relationship. A cooperative arrangement which is in place at the University of Florida is described.

This presentation opens with a quiz:

Q. Define "series."
A. Answers:
   a. A number of separate works, usually related in subject or form, that are issued successively, usually by the same publisher, distributor, etc., and in uniform style, with a collective title.[1]
   b. File units or documents arranged in accordance with a filing system or maintained as a unit because they relate to a particular subject or function, result from the same activity, have a particular form, or because of some other relationship.[2]
   c. Both of the above.
   d. None of the above.

Those who answered "a," are probably catalogers; "b," archivists. Those who chose "c," the best answer, may be part of a cataloger/archivist team.

First, some definitions. "Archival materials" refer collectively to such materials as: noncurrent records of an organization or institution; private documents accumulated by an individual; handwritten or typed documents. Such material is often arranged in "collections," which are an accumulation of documents devoted to a single theme, person, or event, or having a single source.[3] A typical archival repository will contain several collections. An "archivist" is a professional who works with such materials. Archivists' educational backgrounds may be in history or in graduate programs for archival administration. Some research libraries which employ archivists require that

they also have an MLS. Archivists have their own national organization, the Society of American Archivists.[4] A "cataloger" is a catalog librarian. It may be fairly assumed that in most research libraries, archivists are found in the archives or other special collections departments, where their duties include public service, and catalogers are located in centralized catalog departments which serve many different areas of the library.

Archival materials and practices are so radically different from what goes on in the rest of the library that the perspectives of librarians and archivists can vary dramatically. Archival materials are the intimate record of human activity. They are unpublished and, to a librarian, may appear to be somewhat disorderly. In personal files, everything's not in chronological order nor are LC subject headings used on file tabs. When personal papers are donated to an archives, the curator will attempt to keep them together and to preserve the papers in the owner's arrangement. In archival theory, these ideas are the provenance and registry principles. Provenance means that "... archives of a given records creator must not be intermingled with those of other records creators."[5] The registry principle "... maintains that archives should be retained in their original organizational pattern or structure and in their original filing arrangement in order to preserve all relationships."[6] Historians can learn from observing archival materials in their original organization and arrangement. In other words, apparent disorder may need to be preserved in order to maximize research value. But how many librarians, let alone catalog librarians, are comfortable with the seeming disorder? Here are some ways that librarians have tried to organize archival collections, giving archivists nightmares in the process:

—rearranging personal or agency papers into chronological order;
—combining John Smith's papers on travel in Sweden with Mary Jones' papers on the same subject, such that John's papers are no longer distinguishable from Mary's;
—trying to make archival boxes correspond to units within a collection. One librarian decided that an archival collection should be arranged in one box per calendar year. (To do this, the papers had to be put into chronological order, which is bad enough, but it gets worse.) Some boxes contained very little while one box was stuffed so full that the bulging container had to be sliced apart in order to extricate the hapless papers.

Users of archives have different expectations than do other library users. Finding *some* relevant citations satisfies many library patrons. In contrast, scholars who use primary source material expect an exhaustive listing of relevant collections. In the latter case, success is measured by the ability to retrieve every record relevant to any degree.[7]

These differences in materials and users result in very different cataloging needs. As Hensen points out in his *Archives, Personal Papers, and Manuscripts,* the standard manual used for most archival bibliographic description, "The process of archival cataloging consists predominantly of interpreting, extrapolating, or extracting information from the material and its context. By contrast, a bibliographic approach is characterized by item orientated cataloging to provide a description, usually of a published item, as a physical entity. The cataloging process consists predominantly of transcribing information which appears on or with the item."[8] Hensen's rules provide that the finding aid, a written document created by archives personnel which describes an archival collection and lists the contents, be used as the chief source of information, since information such as title and dates are not usually available for literal transcription. Supplied information is not bracketed, since most of the catalog record must be supplied. Hensen also provides for notes which reflect the nature of archival materials.

Another difference in descriptive cataloging is that archival materials are almost always described at the collective rather than the item level. Most archival items derive their importance from their context within the collection as a whole. Hensen's manual provides the guidance for collection level cataloging that AACR2 lacks. For online cataloging, the MARC format for archives and manuscript control is used. When an individual item within a collection deserves special attention, a bibliographic record for that item is made in addition to the collection-level record. In the AMC MARC format, the 773 field can be used to link such related records.

Because users of archives demand exhaustive searches, archivists want many more subject headings and added entries than are traditionally provided for books. A 1986 survey of cataloging done in manuscript repositories revealed that the average number of index terms assigned to a record was 13, while the average number assigned to books by the Library of Congress is 3.[9] An archivist's ideal online record may contain so many index points that system requirements for number of fields and/or length of record are exceeded.

Two areas which are very familiar to catalogers but which were less relevant to archivists until recently are authority control and strict adherence to nationally-derived standards. Before the era of online catalogs, all aspects of archival cataloging were handled by archives personnel. It was an introspective activity totally controlled by the individual archive. In this setting, a need to catalog the way anyone else does could be less than obvious. Today, if information about archival resources is to be integrated into an online public access catalog or shared with the world through a bibliographic utility, adherence to system standards and to generally-accepted practices of authority control are paramount.

Cooperative cataloging involving archivists and catalogers is clearly advantageous. Each group is skilled in areas which are necessary and beneficial to the other. Archivists, who have specialized knowledge of their materials and users, are the logical people to provide descriptive cataloging and to choose subject access points for these materials. Catalogers are proficient at authority work and at creating records which meet the requirements of online systems. Cooperation between the two groups provides the best use of staff expertise.

The University of Florida has been cooperatively cataloging archival materials for three years. Archives personnel are responsible for descriptive cataloging, choice of index points, preliminary authority checking of names and subject headings, and entering records into RLIN. The catalog department is responsible for additional authority work, proofreading, and entering records into OCLC and the university's NOTIS-based online public access catalog.

Any adjustments made by the cataloger are communicated to an archivist, who updates the RLIN record.

What has made this arrangement work? Two of James Scanlon's ideas for getting librarians to work with computer programmers have been very helpful: work for mutual professional respect, and work for mutual understanding of operational needs of the other organization.[10] Other keys have been to have a well-defined division of labor and to trust the other department in its areas of expertise.

The leaders of both departments have demonstrated the attitude that the staff of each are professionals working together to provide the best possible service. This attitude encourages everyone concerned to practice respect for his or her counterparts in the other department. Inter-departmental contact and workshops have provided the knowledge of the other department's activities and priorities which has made mutual understanding possible. Division of responsibilities has been discussed and documented. Trust that each unit is doing its job has made the arrangement work well. As the cataloger with the most day-to-day involvement, I have learned enough about archival description to realize that I don't know much about it, so I never question the descriptive cataloging the archivists do. Descriptions are altered only in the cases of system problems such as incorrect indicators or exceeding the maximum record length. The archivists' choice of index points are accept without question and the cataloger's attention is confined to insuring that the index points are formulated correctly. Catalogers have learned to distinguish between a heading which is incorrect and a heading which is not her personal choice. In addition to differing to the expertise of colleagues, this approach makes the process efficient. The catalog department serves most of the library system, and involvement in archival cataloging is only one of many responsibilities. By not questioning the work already done by others, archival records can finish in a reasonable amount of time. Thus the department can be contribute to this project without neglecting other responsibilities.

Archival materials are definitely not books. Since archival materials and patrons are so radically different from other library materials and users, the perspectives of librarians and archivists can seem to be worlds apart. But cooperation is possible. Through the development of knowledge about each other's priorities and by developing and exercising mutual respect, archivists and catalogers can work together to produce the best possible access to archival materials.

Endnotes

1. Bohdan S. Wynar, *Introduction to Cataloging and Classification,* 7th ed. by Arlene Taylor (Littleton, Colorado: Libraries Unlimited, 1985), p.612.
2. Frank B. Evans, Donald F. Harrison, Edwin A. Thompson, and William L. Rofes, "A Basic Glossary for Archivists, Manuscript Curators, and Records Managers," *American Archivist* 37 (July, 1974): 430 .
3. Ibid., p. 419.
4. Edward C. Oetting, "Who Are These People and Why Can't We Call Them Librarians?" *Library Administration & Management* 3 (Summer, 1989): 135-38.
5. Frank B. Evans, op. cit., p. 427-28.
6. Ibid., p. 429.
7. Avra Michelson, "Description and Reference in the Age of Automation," *American Archivist* 50 (Spring, 1987): p. 199.
8. Steven L. Hensen, *Archives, Personal Papers, and Manuscripts: A Cataloging Manual for Archival Repositories, Historical Societies, and Manuscript Libraries* , 2nd ed. (Chicago: Society of American Archivists, 1989), p.4.
9. Avra Michelson, op cit., p. 199.
10. James J. Scanlon, "How to Mix Oil and Water: or, Getting Librarians to Work with Programmers," *College & Research Libraries News* 4 (April 1990): 321.

CONTRIBUTED PAPERS

III.
BIBLIOGRAPHIC
INSTRUCTION

Understanding the Freshman Writer: the Pedagogy of Composition and Its Relevance to Bibliographic Instruction

Donald A. Barclay
New Mexico State University
Las Cruces, New Mexico

Abstract

Although librarians frequently provide bibliographic instruction to freshman writing students, the literature of bibliographic instruction suggests that librarians do not concern themselves enough with the pedagogy of freshman writing. This paper argues that knowing more about the dynamic field of freshman composition will help reference librarians provide better instruction to freshman writers. This paper contends that the writing and thinking techniques learned by many freshman writing students can be applied to library research, and that it is up to instruction librarians to show freshman students that there is a continuity between the process of writing and the process of library research.

For over ten years the English department and the library have been co-operating to improve the quality of freshman research papers. Recognizing that the most important part of student research activity takes place in the library, members of the English and library departments took steps . . . to formulate a jointly supervised teaching program, designed to provide students with an appreciation of the objectives and methods of research.[1]

Sound familiar? Innovative? It is from a 1952 article discussing a freshman library-instruction program initiated at Queen's College in 1938. For at least fifty years, it seems, librarians have been working directly with English departments to help freshman writers use academic libraries. What is more, over the years the freshman writer has been the focus of much library-instruction literature, most of which is in agreement with James E. Ford's conclusion that freshman writing courses provide "the best opportunity for librarians to 'relate' to a college course."[2]

Despite this strong interest in the freshman writer, little of the library literature stops to consider an obvious and crucial question: How are college freshman taught to write?[3] The reason librarians have not asked this questions is that most librarians think they already know the answer. After all, isn't writing a basic skill? Can the teaching of writing change? And who should know freshman writing any better than librarians who, semester after semester, help hundreds of freshman research their peas-in-a-pod term papers? In fact, librarians may not know as much about fresh-man writing as they should. The teaching of freshman writing is a challenging and constantly changing field, one which librarians who teach research skills to freshman writers should stay abreast of in the same way subject-specialist librarians stay abreast of more-esoteric academic fields like mechanical engineering, microbiology, or art history.

The History of the Academic Writing Course

The typical freshman writing course offered at an American university has its roots in eighteenth- and nineteenth-century Britain; in particular, American university writing was born in the Dissenting Academies, the Red-Brick Universities, and the Scottish Universities—the first institutions to replace the old Oxbridge curriculum based on Latin and oral examinations with a curriculum based on English texts, written exams, and essays.[4] The strong Scottish influence on American higher education ensured that writing became a part of the American curriculum. Of course the methods of teaching writing to American university students have, over the years, undergone profound changes. The most-traditional method of teaching writing focused on grammatical correctness; however, this pedagogy was largely discredited by Braddock, Lloyd-Jones, and Schoer's publication, in 1963, of their research in written composition.[5] Since the 1960s the traditional "correctness" approach has all but disappeared from the writing curriculum of American universities, replaced by a confusing variety of pedagogies, most of which distance themselves from both the old grammatical-correctness school and from freshman writing's traditional connection to American and British literature. To get an idea of the range of writing pedagogies most likely to be encountered in freshman classrooms today, one can study the three writing pedagogies identified by George Hillocks, Jr. The first of these is what Hillocks calls the "Presentational Mode," an approach which focuses on reading and imitating certain rhetorical modes with feedback from the teacher following the writing.[6] Hillocks calls the second pedagogy the "Natural Process Mode," and this approach is characterized by free writing, peer criticism, and ample opportunities to "revise and re-work writing."[7] Hillocks' third pedagogy, the "Environmental Mode," is similar to the Natural Process Mode but uses more-structured tasks to meet its objectives.[8]

All the changes in the teaching of writing since the 1960s have not managed to eliminate the librarian's old friend (and sometimes bane), the freshman research paper. A survey published in 1961 found that 83% of all colleges and universities required a research paper in freshman writing classes.[9] A survey published in 1982 found that the research paper was offered in 84.09% of all freshman writing programs and that the research paper was required in 78.11% of the programs offering it.[10] However hardy the freshman research paper may currently be, it is today usually administered in a gentler, more-personal form than the once-popular ten-pages-on-any-short-story-in-your-anthology assignment.

Using Freshman Writing to the Librarian's Advantage

There are probably librarians who miss the old grammar-intensive, literature-based ways of teaching freshman to write. In these days of countless research papers on abortion, gun control, and suicide, there is something quaint about the notion of freshmen doing research on *Jane Eyre* or "The Old Man and the Sea." Nostalgia aside, the current methods of teaching freshman how to write offer instruction librarians more and better opportunities for providing course-related instruction than did the traditional freshman English class.

For example, most current freshman writing pedagogy emphasizes writing as a *process* or, more-specifically, as a *learning process*. The fact that many freshman writing students come into a library-instruc-

tion session with some concept of the writing process plays right into the hand of the instruction librarian who has the wits to talk about the *research process* and demonstrate its similarity to the writing process. For another example, most freshman writing students are familiar with such writing strategies as list-making, brain-storming, idea-clustering, and idea-mapping. While these idea- and content-generating strategies are taught as part of the writing process, students can be shown how to apply these strategies to such research processes as mapping broad subject areas that might contain information on a research topic or generating a list of likely subject headings before diving into an index.

Two additional key concepts taught in most freshman writing classes are the concepts of audience and purpose. From the first assignment, freshman writers are taught that writers must know why they are writing and for whom they are writing. They are also taught that different audiences and purposes require different kinds of writing. For example, students might be given an audience-awareness assignment that requires them to write two versions of a single essay—one for their best friend and one for their most formidable college professor. These concepts of audience and purpose apply to library research because any student who can write for different audiences and for different purposes can comprehend that the books, articles, and documents found in libraries are also written for various audiences and purposes and so must be looked at with a critical eye to determine their usefulness. One of the complaints of library instructors is that they never have time to teach critical thinking in a one-hour session. Perhaps librarians don't need to teach critical thinking so much as they need to express the concepts of critical thinking in terms their audience already understands—the terms of the freshman writing class.

Problems and Solutions

There are obvious problems to taking advantage of the pedagogy of freshman writing. For one thing, writing pedagogy is constantly evolving. For example, when freshman writing was first breaking its ties to literature, most writing teachers frowned on anything resembling literature in the writing class; lately, that trend has been reversing.[11] Thus any librarian who wants to keep up with the evolution of freshman writing will need to read such pertinent journals as *Research in the Teaching of English*, *College English*, and *College Composition and Communication*.

Even librarians who keep up with the journal literature, though, won't necessarily know what is actually transpiring in the freshman writing courses of their universities. Just as what is written in library journals differs from what is actually practiced in libraries, so too with writing journals and writing classrooms: a recent survey of writing teachers reported that the pedagogy actually employed by writing teachers is much different from the high ideals expressed in the literature.[12] Another factor which makes it difficult to know exactly what is happening in any freshman writing classroom is the freshman writing teacher. Depending on the situation, a freshman writing teacher might be an under-experienced graduate student, an old departmental work horse who continues to teach writing as it was taught in 1960, a Ph.D. writing specialist who is up on all the latest developments in the field, or an under-paid part-timer— and any one of these types can be the writing instructor who believes freshman writers should not do any research at all.[13]

What all this means is that librarians who want to use freshman writing pedagogy to their advantage must not only read the literature, they must also make contacts with freshman writing faculty, examine course syllabi, and read the texts being used in the freshman writing classroom.[14] This is a lot of work, but, again, it is no more than is expected of subject-specialist librarians who provide instruction for specific disciplines.

The results of coming to understand freshman writing as it is instead of as we think it is may do more than slightly streamline library-instruction sessions. David Bartholomae, a college writing teacher, has written that in every new course a student "has to learn to speak our language, to speak as we do, to try on the peculiar ways of knowing, selecting, evaluating, reporting, concluding, and arguing that define the discourse of our community."[15] This is a lot to ask of students, especially young, inexperienced students. Thus librarians—who frequently come in contact with the youngest, most-inexperienced students in the university— can make the students' task easier by incorporating a language and way of learning already familiar to freshman students. If librarians do this, not only will students feel more comfortable in the library, they may also come to see that what is learned in one academic area has applicability to another, that there is some continuity in the complicated and confusing world of college.

Endnotes

1. Haskel M. Block and Sidney Mattis, "The Research Paper: A Co-operative Approach," *College English* 13 (January, 1952): 212-215.

2. James E. Ford, "The Natural Alliance Between Librarians and English Teachers in Course-Related Library Use Instruction," *College & Research Libraries* 43 (September,1982): 379-384 .

3. Two notable recent exceptions, both published in writing journals, are Carmen B. Schmersahl's "Teaching Library Research: Process, Not Product," *Journal of Teaching Writing* 6 (Fall-Winter, 1987): 231-238 ; and Douglas Birdsall's "Library Skills and Freshman English: A Librarian's Perspective," *College Composition and Communication* 37 (May,1986): 227-233.

4. Winifred Bryan Horner, "The Roots of Modern Writing Instruction: Eighteenth- and Nineteenth-Century Britain," *Rhetoric Review* 8 (Spring, 1990): 322-345.

5. George Hillocks, Jr., Research on Written Composition: New Directions for Teaching (Urbana, IL: Eric Clearinghouse, 1986), p. xv.

6. Ibid., p.117.

7. Ibid., p.119.

8. Ibid., p.122

9. Ambrose Manning, "The Present Status of the Research Paper in Freshman English: A National Survey," *College Composition and Communication* 12 (March, 1961): 73-78.

10. James E. Ford and Dennis R. Perry, "Research Paper Instruction in the Undergraduate Writing Program," *College English* 44 (December, 1982): 825-831.

11. See Christopher Gould's "Literature in the Basic Writing Course: A Bibliographic Survey," *College English* 49 (September, 1987): 558-574.

12. Christopher Gould and John Heyda, "Literacy Education and the, Basic Writer: A Survey of College Composition Courses," *Journal of Basic Writing* 5 (Fall, 1986): 8-27.

13. James E. Ford, Sharla Rees, and David L. Ward, "Selected Bibliography on Research Paper Instruction," *Literary Research Newsletter* 6 (1981): 49-65.

14. For an insight into how librarians are presented in freshman writing texts see Virginia Tiefel's "Libraries and Librarians as Depicted in Freshman English Textbooks," *College English* 44 (September, 1982): 494-505.

15. David Bartholomae, "Inventing The University," *Journal of Basic Writing* 5 (Spring, 1986): 4-23.

Implications of CD-ROM Usage for Bibliographic Instruction

Karen A. Becker and Samuel T. Huang
Northern Illinois University
DeKalb, Illinois

Abstract

In order to determine what type of instructional program is needed by Northern Illinois University library patrons using CD-ROMs, surveys were distributed to users at the CD-ROM terminals during April and May, 1991. The survey results compared users and their needs for two systems: SilverPlatter and Infotrac. Results indicate that users both need and want a formal bibliographic instruction program for searching the more sophisticated and advanced CD-ROM databases. The data collected provides guidance to librarians in decisions about which systems to teach, and assists in development of the bibliographic instruction program.

CD-ROM databases are now common in most academic libraries. As patrons are exposed to searching techniques on various databases from different vendors that use different searching protocols, they often experience much uncertainty. Users also encounter online catalogs in many guises, which adds to their confusion. Searching automated library systems involves sophisticated concepts such as controlled vocabularies, free text, Boolean logic, proximity searching, and limiting parameters. Many reference librarians spend a good part of their time teaching patrons to use these systems in a one-on-one situation, where they are only able to cover the basic mechanics of searching, outline some idiosyncracies of they system, and help with equipment problems.

There is little time for teaching advanced searching techniques or for instruction on database design and function. This situation causes stress for both patrons and librarians. One strategy often proposed to help librarians "take charge" of CD-ROM stress is to provide user 'instruction at a variety of levels.[1,2] In 1990 a questionnaire relating CD-ROM searching to online searching was sent to one hundred college and university libraries. Surprisingly, among the sixty-three questionnaires returned, none of the libraries had a formal bibliographic instruction program devoted to CD-ROM searching, though many such programs are under development.[3] Due to the prevalence of CD-ROM databases in academic libraries, a structural or formal CD-ROM training program designed for end-users is desirable. Northern Illinois University (NIU) is a state supported school serving a population of 18,220 un-

dergraduate and 6,289 graduate students, 1,293 faculty, and 1,249 staff. The University Libraries first became involved with CD-ROMs in 1987 with the acquisition of IAC's Academic Index. The current configuration consists of four terminals with General Periodicals Index and Health Index, and a SilverPlatter network of fourteen terminals, each with Medline, ERIC, Psyclit, Sociofile, and GPO Monthly Catalog. While a few terminals are located throughout the upper floors of the library, the majority (eleven) terminals are located centrally near the General Reference desk. By working with patrons every day and helping them use the CD-ROM workstations, the NIU librarians felt that some type of formal instruction in searching the SilverPlatter (but NOT Infotrac) databases was needed. A program is in place to begin offering specialized demonstration/lecture training workshops in the fall 1991 semester. Our current educational efforts consist of: handouts and signage outlining basic searching procedures; brochures describing the different CD-ROM databases; one-on-one reference assistance; and the incorporation of CD-ROM into current bibliographic instruction sessions (the level of CD-ROM instruction determined by the level and purpose of the class session).

While it was believed that the attitudes and instructional needs of CD-ROM users were understood, it was decided to do a survey and find out if the assumptions were accurate. The aim was to investigate the current state of how users were learning to use the systems, and what users perceived their success rate and instructional needs to be. It was anticipated that

Infotrac and SilverPlatter searchers would have different responses. From observations, upper level patrons were using SilverPlatter, and undergraduates were using Infotrac. The contents of the databases also varied, with SilverPlatter databases retrospectively covering scholarly material and government publications, and Infotrac covering a combination of popular and scholarly current material. Patrons and librarians seemed to feel that the SilverPlatter software, while very powerful, was extremely complicated for users to master, while patrons easily learned to manipulate Infotrac due to its unsophisticated software and user friendly prompts and keyboard. We wanted to find out if users desired formal instruction sessions, and whether they would attend on their own time. The results would also guide decisions on which systems to teach, how many sessions to schedule, and whether users wanted instruction in specific aspects such as using controlled vocabulary or interpreting printouts. The assumption was made that users needed instruction in basic searching, Boolean logic, and use of basic functions such as displaying results and printing, and did not include these topics in the survey.

A literature review of the topic of CD-ROM training revealed two constants: users did indeed want and need some type of instruction;[4,5,6,7] and the preferred method of training (chosen by both CD-ROM trainers and users) was point of use, one-on-one assistance.[8,9] An example of a library choosing to emphasize this method of instruction is Pennsylvania State University, which has concentrated its CD-ROM workstations in one area of the Reference Room, and instituted a special CD-ROM service desk, staffed for at least 40 hours per week.[10] However, this is where the consensus ends. Patrons have indicated many different preferences for other types of instruction, and all methods have been used with some degree of success. In addition to point of use assistance, methods for teaching CD-ROM searching include help screens, demonstration, lecture workshop, hands-on workshop, tutorial/computer aided instruction, handouts, signage, workbooks, incorporation into standard BI programs, and self-directed experimentation. The importance of live demonstration was cited by many studies, including Bostian.[11]

Most libraries, including NIU, are using a combination of these methods. The University of Vermont has an intensive program: in addition to having a specially staffed CD-ROM workstation area, they require students to complete a fairly extensive instructional workbook/CAI package before being allowed to search a SilverPlatter database.[12]

Though the literature suggested important trends and issues, indications were that users' instructional preferences varied so widely that individual libraries should tailor their CD-ROM instructional package to the needs and wants of their patrons. During April and May,1991, a instrument survey was distributed to students using the CD-ROM terminals at Northern Illinois University. The surveys for Infotrac and SilverPlatter were identical, except for one question: the SilverPlatter survey asked whether the user would have preferred to search the print version of the index. (The Infotrac databases have no exact corresponding print index.) Questions fell into five categories: 1) Descriptive—status of the user; which system and which databases were searched; 2) Knowledge of CD-ROM—first time or repeat user; how did the user find out about CD-ROM; did the user plan to use CD-ROM before coming to the library; did the patron use controlled vocabulary; would the user have preferred to search the printed index; 3) Learning to Use the System—how did the user learn to search; should the library offer training workshops; would the patron attend training workshops; does the patron need help understanding printouts; 4) Perceived Success—did the patron find the information needed; and 5) Open-Ended Questions—what helped the user the most; what needs to be explained more clearly.

Surveys were placed at the terminals, but patrons were reluctant to fill these out. Response rate was much better if a librarian handed the patrons a survey and asked for their cooperation. Users of the SilverPlatter databases filled out and returned almost all of the surveys distributed in this manner. In general they spent a significant amount of time searching, and were very interested in helping the librarians investigate CD-ROM training. Since SilverPlatter often has long delays while searching or printing, patrons had "free time" to fill out the survey. Infotrac users, on the other hand, had a much lower response rate. Only about 50% of the surveys were returned. Possible reasons might be that students often had to wait up to forty-five minutes to use the terminals and were not feeling very cooperative by the time they got to use the system. They also seemed to feel that they did not need any training to use Infotrac, so didn't see the need to participate in a survey to measure training needs. Their use of the system was significantly quicker and simpler than the SilverPlatter users. They felt more time pressures and were more rushed both because assignment due dates were coming up and because of the numbers of patrons waiting. Eighty SilverPlatter surveys and 69 Infotrac surveys were collected.

Survey Results and Implications

The results of the survey confirmed some assumptions, while disproving others. The users of the two systems were indeed different: about two-thirds of SilverPlatter users were upper level (senior, graduate, faculty) and about two-thirds of Infotrac users were lower level (freshmen, sophomore, junior). However, the percentage of first-time users was approximately the same for both systems.

The manner in which users found out about CD-ROM was surprisingly different for the two systems. SilverPlatter users were overwhelmingly referred to the databases by their instructors (41%), compared to even the next highest method, reference librarians (19%). Implications for bibliographic instruction might be to target instructors to receive information about SilverPlatter training to pass on to their students, or to encourage instructors to bring their classes to the library for a training session before giving assignments. On the other hand, students found out about Infotrac from the reference librarian (23%), by seeing the computer and trying it (23%), or from a friend (17%). Instructors told them about Infotrac only 7% of the time. Point of use advertising would be the best method to advertise CD-ROM training sessions to these patrons.

About three-fourths of the users of both systems planned on using the CD-ROM system before coming to the library. This is noteworthy in planning of workshops, since if most patrons were impulse users, they would not perceive the need for training in advance of using the system.

The ways in which users learned to search the two systems were very different. SilverPlatter searchers were heavy users of many different types of instruction. Handouts and signs were used by 59%, one-on-one help was given to 56%, help screens and prompts were useful to 50%, and 41% found playing and experimenting with the system helpful. Infotrac users did show a pattern: they preferred independent methods of learning such as help screens and prompts (54%), playing and experimenting (43%), and handouts and

signage (30%). Fewer students had help from a person, with the most common helper being a friend or another patron (20%). A librarian was asked for help by only 7% of the searchers. The differences in the amounts and types of help needed should affect planning for CD-ROM training, and reflect the complexities, sophistication, and user friendliness of the two systems. SilverPlatter users show a much stronger need for instruction.

One disconcerting fact for librarians was that less than half (46%) of SilverPlatter searchers were using a thesaurus. Searchers need to be taught about the function of the thesaurus in searching, and how to use it effectively.

Users generally were able to find at least some information on both systems: 95% on SilverPlatter and 96% on Infotrac. However, unsuccessful searchers might have been less inclined to fill out the survey. Infotrac had a slightly higher percentage of users who found just the right amount of material: 61% compared to 43% on SilverPlatter. Possible reasons might be ease of use of Infotrac, its browsing capability, or the compatibility of its contents with students' needs.

Searchers did perceive a need for training workshops. Not surprisingly, 83% of SilverPlatter users thought that the library should offer training workshops, and 65% said they would attend such a workshop on their own time. Infotrac users saw a lesser need; only 46% thought there should be workshops and 38% said they would attend. While taking into account that the number of students who say they would attend does not reflect the low percentage who actually show up, 38% wanting to attend an Infotrac workshop seems surprisingly high for such a simple system. The need for Infotrac workshops should be more carefully investigated.

In conclusion, the results of the CD-ROM user survey are proving very important in investigating the needs of users for formal CD-ROM training workshops. The information will also be helpful for the front-line reference librarian, since it is always important to know as much as possible about one's patrons, and point-of-use assistance for CD-ROM searchers. Any information which will help lessen the burden at the reference desk and which will allow patrons to search more efficiently, effectively, and independently, will be of benefit to both librarians and library users

Based on this study of SilverPlatter and Infotrac, the status of users was as follows:

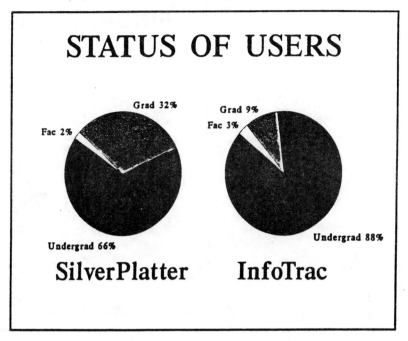

SilverPlatter is used more heavily by upper level patrons. Infotrac is used predominantly by lower level undergraduates.

1. Is this the first time you used the system?

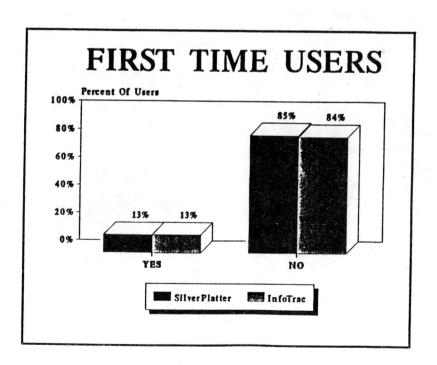

Very similar percentages of first time users.

2. How did you find out about the system?

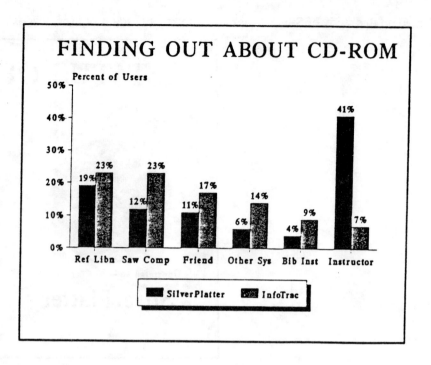

The ranking of these options is very similar between the systems: Reference librarian, Saw computer so I tried it, From a friend, Used a similar system at another library, BI workshop, and Other. The one striking dissimilarity is the number of students who found out about SilverPlatter from their instructor (41.3%) as compared to Infotrac (7.2%). Obviously, instructors are sending their students to use SilverPlatter databases, but are ignoring Infotrac.

3. Before you came to the library, did you plan on using the system?

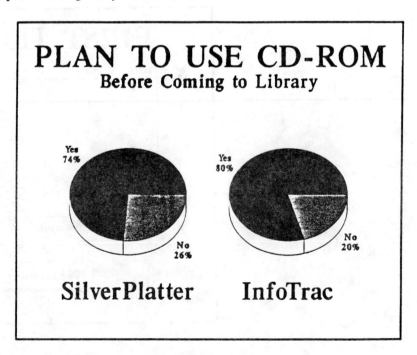

About three-fourths of the students came to the library planning to use a CD-ROM database. Numbers were similar for both systems. Since most patrons were planning ahead, they might be interested in signing up for workshops.

4.How did you learn to search the system?
(Choose as many as apply to you)

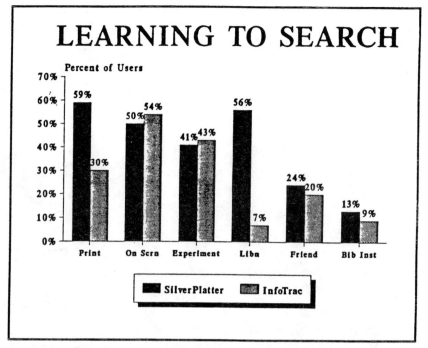

SilverPlatter users showed no significant pattern in their preferences for learning to use the system. Over one half of searchers did ask the librarian for help, showing that one-on-one help is important for these searchers. Infotrac showed that help from the librarian is the least important training tool for searchers (only 7.2% of users asked for help.)

Infotrac does show a pattern in the type of learning taking place. Most users did not ask another person for help. The most significant helpers were friends or other patrons (20.2%), with librarians helping 7.2% of patrons at point-of-use and 8.6% of users in a bibliographic instruction workshop.

5. Did you use a thesaurus (SilverPlatter) or Library of Congress Subject Headings (Infotrac)?

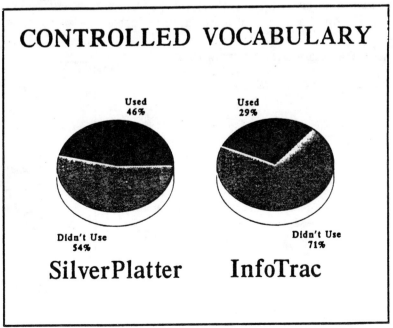

SilverPlatter users were more inclined to use a controlled vocabulary, but still only about half of the searchers used a thesaurus. This is definitely a topic which should be covered in a workshop. The low use of the LCSH for Infotrac might indicate that students don't know about the controlled vocabulary or that they feel it isn't needed since browsing is so easy.

6. Did you find the information you needed?

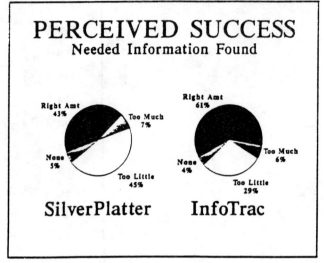

Users generally were able to find at least some information on both systems: 95.0% on SilverPlatter and 95.7% on Infotrac. However, unsuccessful searchers might have been less inclined to fill out the survey.

Infotrac had a significantly higher percentage of users who found just the right amount of material: 60.9% compared to only 42.5% on SilverPlatter. Possible reasons might be ease of use of Infotrac, its browsing capability, or the compatibility of its contents with students' needs.

The main problem faced by searchers was finding too little material (45% SilverPlatter; 29% Infotrac). This indicates that bibliographic instruction sessions should concentrate on broadening or expanding a search. There were considerably fewer patrons who needed assistance in narrowing a search (7.5% SilverPlatter; 5.8% Infotrac), possibly indicating that less time needs to be spent on teaching this process. Alternatively, searchers who retrieve too much information might just be browsing many items and stopping when they have enough citations. While a librarian might consider this "finding too much" information, to a student the actual result of the search is "finding the right amount."

7. Should the library offer training workshops?

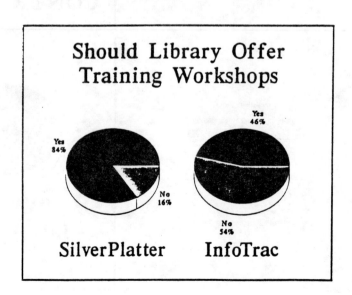

A significantly higher percentage of SilverPlatter users (82.5%) thought that the library should offer training classes than the Infotrac users (46.4%).

8. Would you attend a workshop on your own time?

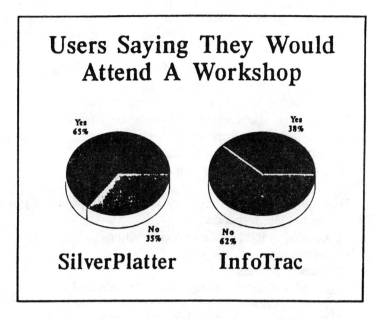

Again, a higher percentage of SilverPlatter users would attend a workshop. However, the percentage of Infotrac users indicating that they would attend a workshop (37.7%) seems surprisingly high for such a simple system. Compare these 37.7% who would attend with the number of unsuccessful or semi-successful searchers (33.3%) (question 6 b); the need for some type of Infotrac training or orientation should be reevaluated.

9. Do you need assistance in reading your printout?

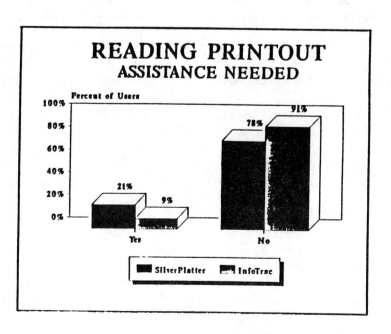

Infotrac users do not seem to need much help in understanding the printout. However, one fifth of SilverPlatter users need assistance, indicating that this topic should be briefly covered in CD-ROM SilverPlatter workshops.

Open-ended questions: These were optional questions which provided an opportunity for patrons to note topics which might not have been covered in the survey, or to expand on any issue that they felt was very important. Most patrons skipped these questions. Responses were read and tallied into broad categories.

10. What helped you the most in understanding how to use the system? SilverPlatter: (39% responded)
    19 A person (instructor, librarian, friend)
    16 Non-person (handouts, help screen, signs)
     4 Previous experience with this or other systems
       Infotrac: (21% responded)
     5 A person (instructor, librarian, friend)
    16 Non-person (handouts, help screens, signs)

11. What do you wish was explained more clearly (what are you still confused about)?
SilverPlatter: (33% responded)
    11 General or total confusion/exasperation
    10 Search strategy
     4 Searching terms
     3 Local periodical holdings should be indicated
     2 Reading printout¡
     1 Need more terminals
     1 Printing
     1 Downloading

Infotrac: (13% responded)
     4 Searching terms
     3 Need more terminals
     3 Location and years of periodicals held should be indicated
     3 Printing

Endnotes

1. Steven D. Zink, "Planning for the Perils of CD-ROM," *Library Journal* 115 (February 1, 1990): 51.
2. Charles A. Bunge, "CD-ROM Stress," *Library Journal* 116 (April 15, 1991): 64.
3. Samuel T. Huang, "CD-ROM Database Searching vs. Traditional Online Database Searching," in *Proceedings of the Twelfth National Online Meeting* edited by Martha E. Williams, (Medford, N.J.: Learned Information, 1991), p. 138–148.
4. Gillian Allen, "CD-ROM Training: What Do the Patrons Want?" *RQ* 30 (Fall, 1990): 90.
5. Patricia Lynn and Karen Bascanyi, "CD-ROMs: Instructional Methods and User Reactions," *RSR* 17 (Summer, 1989): 19-20.
6. Sandra D. Hoffman and Anne-Marie Belanger, "Academic Libraries: The Students' View," *Library Software Review* 9 (July-August, 1990): 233.
7. Alice C. Littlejohn, "End-User Searching in an Academic Library: The Students' View," *RQ* 26 (Summer, 1987): 462-463.
8. Gillian Allen, op. cit., p. 92.
9. Cathy Seitz Whitaker, "Pile-Up at the Reference Desk: Teaching Users to Use CD-ROMs." *Laserdisk Professional* 3 (March, 1990): 32.
10. Bruce Bonta and Sally Kalin, "CD-ROM Implementation: A Reference Staff Takes Charge," *RSR* 17 (Summer, 1989): 10-11.
11. Rebecca Bostian and Anne Robbins, "Effective Instruction for Searching CD-ROM Indexes," *Laserdisk Professional* 3 (January, 1990): 17.
12. Rebecca Bostian, Ibid., p. 14.

Learning Style Theory and Bibliographic Instruction: The Quest for Effective Bibliographic Instruction

Sonia Bodi
North Park College and Theological Seminary
Chicago, Illinois

Abstract

Instructional librarians in academic libraries continue to think critically about their function, methodology and teaching effectiveness as they assist students in their quest for knowledge. While several factors identify effective teaching, one important component is teaching to the diversity of learning styles of the students. This paper examines David A. Kolb's theory of experiential learning. Kolb's theory has been used with success at North Park College in the bibliographic instruction program which focuses both on the process of finding information and on the evaluation of resources.

Those who have been involved with bibliographic instruction for some time have probably tried any number of methods, processes, formats and so forth to improve instruction and teach more effectively. Methods have very likely met with a diversity of responses from students. Some students are delighted with what they've learned, others think it a total waste of time. Furthermore, many librarians are trying to find means to teach effectively the use of CD-ROMs and on-line catalogs to traditional college students, to older adults, to students in newly approved graduate programs and to students from non-Western cultures.

In various studies of the characteristics that produce effective teaching, there is evidence that students value teachers from whom they have learned the most.[1] If one of the important components in education is student learning, then as librarians seek to improve effectiveness, they should study how students learn. "Learning styles" is a broad term that includes the cognitive, affective, and physiological dimensions of learning. Our cognitive style is how we perceive and process information: how we think. Our affective style is how we feel about and value our learning experiences; for example, one of our bibliographic instruction goals is to help students feel less intimidated using the library. Our physiological style involves the environment for effective learning: the time of day we learn best, the lighting and noise level we require, and the position of our bodies. While all components of learning styles are interesting and important to understand, this paper will have as its primary focus cognitive learning style.

Teachers generally teach according to their own style of learning.[2] There is some evidence that the larger the divergence between the student's learning and the teacher's teaching style, the lower the student's gain in achievement and the less positive the student's attitude toward the subject.[3] However, students who are good learners have learned to adapt to a variety of teaching and learning styles. Learning styles have nothing to do with intelligence, nor is any style better than any other; learning style is simply how each one of us learns best.

The goal in all bibliographic instruction programs is student learning. While knowledge of learning styles does not guarantee effectiveness in teaching, it can be a major component in facilitating learning. There are number of theories of learning;[4] however, David A. Kolb's theory of experiential learning[5] with significant success has worked fully in bibliographic instruction programs, primarily with freshman. Kolb's theory is especially attractive because of the emphasis on process rather than on outcome. His theory stresses the role of process in life-long learning, an important goal in bibliographic instruction. Kolb is an organizational psychologist at Case Western Reserve whose theory is specifically used in management, but has significant implications for education. The substance of Kolb's theory is illustrated by this circle. The metaphor of the circle is meaningful because not only is it a practical illustration, but it is a metaphor for the never-ending cycle of new learning.

At the top of the circle is CONCRETE EXPERI-ENCE. This is the first new experience in a learning situation in which students must be able to involve themselves fully, openly, and without bias in new and immediate experiences. An example of a concrete experience could be a literary text, a laboratory, a reading, an example, and an observation. In a bibliographic instruction presentation, this could be the worksheet or instruction booklet, or the terminal. REFLECTIVE OBSERVATION is the stage when students must be able to reflect, observe, and interpret new data. In North Park's freshman bibliographic instruction program, students are required to meet individually for a fifteen minute conference with one of the instructional librarians to give them an opportunity to ask questions and to reflect on what they've done so far. Students are involved with reflective observation in discussion, brainstorming, journaling, and answering thought and rhetorical questions. At this stage, students need to discuss how the CD-ROM and on-line technology are similar to and different from the printed indexes and card catalog. ABSTRACT CONCEPTUALIZATION involves synthesis and analysis, the integration of the concrete experience after reflective observation into new theories. Students are involved with abstract conceptualization in lectures, papers, projects, and analogies. At this stage students plan their search strategy. The fourth and final stage of the circle is ACTIVE EXPERIMENTATION in which students solve problems and make decisions. This is the stage of actually doing the assignment which then leads to another experience to build on the circle of learning. Certain activities can support more than one phase of the circle depending on the instructor's objectives.

There are two dimensions of the learning task. The vertical dimension (Concrete Experience to Abstract Conceptualization) represents the infusion of information either from experience or from abstractions. Those who learn best through concrete experience learn better with the less symbolic such as a prose text rather than poetry, or the Gospels rather than the Book of Revelation. Those who learn best through abstract conceptualization enjoy analyzing concepts and working with theories. They enjoy mathematics, poetry and the Book of Revelation.

The horizontal dimension (Reflective Observation to Active Experimentation) refers to the processing of information by either internally reflecting on the experience or by externally acting upon the conclusions that have been drawn. Those who prefer reflective observation are observers and tend to need time to think about answers to questions. Those who prefer active

experimentation are actors and tend to be the first with their hands up to answer questions, often not caring whether or not they are right. Four action verbs describe the learners at each step. Concrete Experience becomes experiencing; Reflective Observation becomes examining; Abstract Conceptualization becomes explaining; and Active Experimentation becomes applying.[6]

When the ways information is perceived are combined with the ways information is processed, the circle divides into quadrants, each of which is a particular learning style. Those who learn best through a combination of Concrete Experience and Reflective Observation are DIVERGERS. They are imaginative people with one thought stimulating another. They look at alternative ideas and need background information in reaching decisions. They love discussion and brainstorming and are especially interested in people. They tend to be in the Humanities and the Social Sciences. Doing a bibliographic instruction presentation in a class in English, philosophy, religion and so forth, the instruction librarian following Kolb's service would want to be sure to provide opportunities for discussion and for alternate search strategies. Students should chose their topic prior to the bibliographic instruction session so that they have time to reflect on their topic and have time to think of their questions and responses.

The opposite of DIVERGERS is CONVERGERS, those who learn best through a combination of Active Experimentation and Abstract Conceptualization. CONVERGERS learn best through lectures rather than by discussion. They learn through analysis and are swift to make decisions. They look for connections, ways to tie things together rather than looking for divergent ideas. Their greatest strength is their practical application of ideas. They prefer dealing with things rather than people, and like a general analytic detachment. Engineers tend to be in this quadrant. Doing bibliographic instruction with these students would be primarily lecture and showing them the details of a search strategy. They will learn readily the fine points of using CD-ROMs and on-line databases.

ASSIMILATORS are those who learn best through a combination of Reflective Observation and Abstract Conceptualization. These learners can plan and formulate theories, but they are not as interested in the practical application of theory as they are in a theory that is logically sound and precise. In fact, they will change facts to fit the theory. They solve problems through analysis, and learn well as they plan and formulate their search strategies. These students might be in the sciences and mathematics. Presenting bibliographic instruction to science classes needs to involve each student in planning his or her own strategy after the process of a search strategy is explained.

Finally, those who learn best through a combination of Active Experimentation and Concrete Experience are called ACCOMMODATORS and they are the opposite of ASSIMILATORS. These are people who learn best by doing things. They are accomplishment and goal-oriented, but they need frequent feed-back to keep on task. Their strengths are advocating positions and implementing decisions. Unlike the Assimilators, they will change the theory to fit the facts, and they solve problems through intuition rather than through analysis. These students will learn best when they are actually doing the assignment. Accommodators are generally found in social professions such as business, marketing, sales, accounting and politics. The focus of a bibliographic instruction presentation in a business class needs to be on the assignment they will be doing and needs to give them whatever hands-on experience with CD-ROMS and other technology is appropriate. They need to be shown concrete things such as *Business Periodicals Index, Value-Line,* and so forth.

In all bibliographic instruction presentations, the entire circle of learning needs to be presented, but the focus should be on the learning style that seems appropriate for a particular class. However, assumptions should never be made that everyone in a class learns the same way and therefore the differences need to be accommodated.

There are two further divisions in Kolb's circle. Those above the processing line, Accommodators and Divergers, are called LUMPERS. These students need to see the whole picture before they can learn the details and facts. Regardless of the discipline in which the bibliographic instruction is being presented, with an overview of what will be covered during the class, is always used assuming the presence of at least one Lumper. Those who are below the processing line, Convergers and Assimilators, are called SPLITTERS. These students need to analyze the parts before they can learn the concept as a whole. Assuming there is at least one Splitter in any class, I always try to have logically organized details for them.

Bibliographic instruction is a multifaceted process involving a complex relationship between librarian, content, and student. Meeting the various learning modes of students may be the key to improving teaching effectiveness and facilitating learning among students.

Endnotes

1. Peter A. Cohen, "Student Ratings of Instruction and Student Achievement: A Meta-Analysis of Multisection Validity Studies," *Review of Educational Research* 51 (Fall, 1981): 281-309; Wilbert J. McKeachie, "Student Ratings of Faculty: A Reprise," *Academe* 57 (October, 1971): 384-97.

2. For a study of applying David A. Kolb's theory of learning styles of librarians, see Jin M. Choi, "Learning Styles of Academic Libraries," in *College & Research Libraries* 50 (November, 1989): 691-99.

3. George Domino, "Interactive Effects of Achievement Orientation and Teaching Styles on Academic Achievement," *Journal of Educational Psychology* 62 (October, 1971): 427-31 .

4. Several of the major current learning style theories are described in the following sources: H. A. Witkin, "Field-Dependent and Field-Independent Cognitive Styles and Their Educational Implications," *Review of Educational Research* 47 (Winter, 1977): 1-64; Mary Jane Even, "Adapting Cognitive Style Theory in Practice," *Lifelong Learning: The Adult Years* 5 (January, 1982): 14-27; James W. Keefe, ed., *Profiling and Utilizing Learning Style* (Reston, Va.: NASSP, 1988), p.2-37; Pat Burke Guild and Stephen Garger, *Marching to Different Drummers* (Alexandria, Va.: ASCD, 1985); Ronald Hyman and Barbara Rostoff, "Matching Learning and Teaching Styles: The Jug and What's In It," *Theory Into Practice* 23 (Winter, 1984): 35-43; Rita Dunn, "Learning Style Researchers Define Differences Differently," *Educational Leadership* 38 (February, 1981): 372-75; and Charles S. Claxton and Patricia H. Murrell, *Learning Styles: Implications for Improving Educational Practices* (Bethesda, Md.: ERIC Document Reproduction Service, 1987), ED 293 476.

5. David A. Kolb, *Experiential Learning: Experience As the Source of Learning and Development* (Englewood Cliffs, N.J.: Prentice-Hall, 1984); Barbara Carlsson, "R & D Organizations as Learning Systems," in David A. Kolb, *Organizational Psychology: A Book of Readings,* 3rd ed.

(Englewood Cliffs, N.J.: Prentice-Hall, 1979), p. 36-46; Charles S. Claxton, op. cit., Ibid., and Pat Burke Guild, op. cit.

6. Marilla D. Svinick and Nancy M. Dixon, "The Kolb Model Modified for Classroom Activities," *College Teaching* 35 (Fall, 1987): 14-46.

Using a For-Credit Course to Increase Access to a Diverse Collection

Rudolph J. Clay and Clara P. McLeod
Washington University
St. Louis, Missouri

Abstract

Many academic institutions have developed both Afro-American studies programs and library collections. However if the experience of Washington University is indicative these collections are not well used by students in the programs. To address the problem Washington University developed a three-credit course to prepare students to be effective library users. The course involved lecture/discussions and exercises to cover such subjects as library organization, use of reference sources, including online resources, government documents and statistical sources, and the development of search strategy.

Librarians at academic libraries have had to evaluate how their collections represent various cultures and cultural experience within and outside the United States, as our society grapples with the concept of diversity. A number of reports and studies, such as "One Third of the Nation," state that by the year 2000, one third of our citizens will be from what is currently referred to as cultural and racial minority groups: African-Americans, Asian-Americans, Hispanics-Americans and Native-Americans. Academic institutions such as the University of Michigan Library are making efforts to ensure that their library collections broadly represent a variety of cultures and ethnic backgrounds, "beyond the limits of traditional studies of Western civilization . . ."[1] Two important goals are implicit in these initiatives: to prepare students for a more heterogeneous society and to be responsive to the needs of a more culturally diverse student body.

Approximately twenty years ago, institutions of higher education began to include African-American studies in their curricula. The continuing growth of this type of program on academic campuses have influenced directly and indirectly library programs and collections. Librarians have had to evaluate the collection needs as well as modes of access to these materials.

The development of programs designed to promote non-western civilizations studies has been gradual and two typical models evolved: (1) the program model and (2) the traditional department model. The program approach, which views African-American studies as an interdisciplinary pursuit, involves the use of faculty members in traditional academic departments to offer courses in the curriculum in the subject area of African-American studies. The departmental approach involves establishing a new separate discipline in the traditional manner with faculty devoted exclusively to the discipline. Most of these departments are called black studies or Afro-American studies.

In the beginning, many of these programs concentrated their efforts on designing and offering courses at the undergraduate level. A few began offering an undergraduate major. Programs in Afro-American studies currently flourish at many major academic institutions. Today, at least thirty-five states have one or more institutions where undergraduates may pursue a major in black studies.[2] At least twelve institutions offer coursework leading to the Master's degree. Though debate is still occurring on the merit of advanced degree programs, at least one institution (Temple University) has graduated its first PhD in Black Studies, other institutions are now considering the establishment of doctoral programs.[3]

Since 1960 the amount of published material in African and African-American studies has mushroomed. Some libraries have organized special collections; other have simply integrated these materials into the general collection of the library. With the availability of OCLC, RLIN, and other online bibliographic data bases, libraries have access to much of the material though it is not a part of their collection.

While progress has been made on building and maintaining broadly representative collections, one major task remains for academic libraries and librarians which is to use innovative techniques to increase access to those collections for all students. The case study described in this paper utilizes a for-credit course designed to provide greater access to an academic library's informational resources on the various cultures of black people throughout the world.

A number of factors led to the development for a credit course designed to specifically address the needs of students conducting academic library research in the subject area of African, Caribbean, and African-American studies (this subject area would be referred to as ACAS) at Washington University (St. Louis, MO.). This course is thought to be unique as it appears to be the first advanced undergraduate/graduate course specifically designed to address this subject area at an academic library. In their study, Huston and Perry report that a course was developed to increase self-reliance in libraries for 47 predominantly urban black college students in an outreach program at the Evergreen State College in Tacoma Washington.[4] The outreach program had no library collection and the classes and library exercises were conducted in various libraries in the area. The course developed at Washington University differs in two ways: it is designed to address the needs and concerns of any student doing research in ACAS (not only black students, though a significant number of the students who have enrolled in the class thus far have been black) and it has become a regular course of the African and Afro-American studies program, offered each fall semester. During the past few years students at the University have complained to faculty and librarians that they could not locate relevant information on topics concerning ACAS in the library. A few faculty members also complained that their students were unsuccessful in even doing minimal library research such as locating current periodical articles on topics in this area. This was particularly distressing in a library which has had an African and African-American studies bibliographer for some time and a library collection which is one of the strongest in this subject area in the region.

In initial attempts to provide outreach to students enrolled in African and African-American studies courses, bibliographic instruction sessions, pathfinders, and sample bibliographies were presented to students. Students were asked to call upon the African-American studies bibliographer with any questions they might have concerning the library or when preparing for a research project. Few requests for assistance

with library research materialized from these class presentations. Students who did later contact the bibliographer for assistance, usually no longer had the instructional material which had been distributed, or at least did not bring it to the library with them.

Most of the African-American students at Washington University take one or more courses offered by the African and Afro-American studies programs during their undergraduate experience, regardless of their major or vocational goals. Over thirty courses are offered on topics such as contemporary issues in the black community, African history, black women in contempbrary society, African-American and Afro-Hispanic literature, the African-American family, black psychology, and black theater. Bibliographic instruction activities in these courses provide an avenue to introduce students to the role of the library and its collection in their coursework, especially research papers. As in most bibliographic instruction activities students are more interested and receptive when it is presented as an aid for a specific class assignment. Thus more students called upon librarians for assistance when presentations were made to classes in preparation for an upcoming assignment. One other factor that seemed relevant is validation by the instructor. Addressing students in the class room in the presence of the instructor seemed to in some way sanction the notion that what librarians were offering was thought to be important by the instructor and would truly be of value in completing the class assignment.

As the African and Afro-American studies program evolved at Washington University from its inception in the early 1970s, it began to require from students a more analytical approach to the study of African, Caribbean, and African-American people and their culture. The chairperson of the program, concerned that student's research skills are not well-developed, approached the library administration in 1989 concerning the development of a three credit hour course devoted to strengthening the library information seeking skills of students doing work in this area. An advanced undergraduate course open also to graduate students in relevant disciplines, entitled "Research Materials in African and African-American Studies," was developed which focuses on practical and effective strategies for research in ACAS. The goal of the course is to develop practical and effective strategies for research in ACAS. The goal of the course is to develop analytical skills utilizing print and non-print sources such as computerized reference sources.

The course, which has been offered for three semesters, is now a regular part of the curriculum of the African and Afro-American studies program. The thrust of the course is to develop the skills necessary to locate and evaluate sources of information about black people in Africa and the diaspora and their experiences, to gain a working knowledge in the use of libraries, to become skilled in research techniques which will enable the student to use any research institution (archives, museums, historical societies, etc.) effectively, and to develop a systematic method of research which will apply to writing research papers and reports primarily in this subject area. The skills developed will also transfer to research topics in other areas of interest. The format of the 16 week course consists of a lecture/ discussion period followed by practical hands-on-experience in the university library, based on the theory presented in class. A number of guest speakers are utilized throughout the course who are currently involved in research. These include graduate students, faculty members from various departments, and independent researchers involved in civic projects. The purpose of utilizing these researchers is to illustrate the various strategies and research techniques utilized by other users of the collection which build upon the basic techniques presented by the authors in class. The guest speakers also validate for the students that the library collection does support academic research activities of various researchers in ACAS.

The content of the course includes the following major topics:

1) Organization of an academic library
2) Library of Congress Classification System
3) The arrangement and use the card catalog
4) The arrangement and use of the online catalog
5) Reference sources in ACAS
6) Periodical and newspaper indexes
7) Electronic reference sources (CD-ROM indexes, online databases, etc.)
8) U.S. government publications
9) Statistical sources
10) Developing the research strategy
11) Asking for assistance in library

The emphasis in exploring each of these topics is its application to ACAS. The advantages and disadvantages of using the LC classification system to locate information about blacks throughout the world is explored in depth. Students become familiar with the Library of Congress' use of the subject headings Afro-Americans, Blacks, and Negroes. The basic reference sources in ACAS are introduced, including atlases, biographical sources, dictionaries, encyclopedias, and current news sources. One of the major obstacles students have when attempting to do library research in this area is determining where to begin their research. The LC classification system is introduced as the classification system utilized in the card catalog and online catalog. Later in the course, classification systems of other sources such as periodical and newspaper indexes are investigated. It is emphasized that each source uses a different subject classification system and that it is imperative to become familiar with the system used before the source can be used effectively.

A considerable amount of class time is spent exploring the development of research strategies. Students in the subject area often have trouble translating their research interest into questions that can be explored and successfully answered with library resources. The relationship between the development of pertinent questions and the organization of ideas for the paper or project is explored. In many instances, it is these questions about their topic of interest which students must communicate at the reference desk in order to obtain effective assistance. This can become a major issue if the person at the reference desk is unfamiliar with resources in the area. In this case, it is important that the student at least approach the desk with unambiguous research questions. One example which has been used in class to illustrate an ambiguous research question concerns the "changes or effects in the African-American community due to particular presidential policies." It is suggested to the students that since the questions indicates a desire to determine the effects of the president's policies on the African-American community, the initial step would be to determine the indicators in the community that could be explored (employment rates, access to health care, community resources, etc.) and criteria for measuring change. The next step suggested is an attempt to develop a relationship between the indicators and specific presidential policies. This is often not a simple task, but one which a student must address before seeking help at a reference desk. Ideally the student could then proceed to ask for assistance at the reference desk concerning the chosen indicators in the community to be measured, the specific presidential policies, and the relationship between the policies and changes in the community.

The goal of this unit is to have the students develop the kind of questions that have a greater chance of being answered to some degree of satisfaction with library resources.

To demonstrate that information on topics in ACAS are published in a variety of sources, students are asked to take one topic and find at least two citations from a list of fifteen periodical and newspapers indexes. Students are often amazed at the ease with which they could locate information and often how different the same topic was treated in various publications, once they became familiar with the indexing terminology used. Throughout the course it is emphasized that the varying indexing practices of reference sources require topics to be approached either under subject and then subdivision for a specific group or locating the terms used for the group and then a subject division for the particular subject. Thus when searching for information on the topic of adoption of African-American children, one can start with the indexing terms used for "African American children" (i. e. blacks, Afro-American, African-Americans, Negroes, minorities), and then search under those headings for "adoption." The alternative approach, when the approach above does not yield relevant information, is to start with the terms for "adoption" and then search for terms used for "African-American children." In a related exercise which introduces reference sources, students are asked to use biographical sources to obtain information on the authors located above. They discover that biographical sources can often assist users in the process of evaluating the credentials of authors and researchers. One exercise in the course that students seemed to find very interesting is the exploration of primary sources. Many of the students have no previous experience with historical sources that are written by individuals who were living during the event being studied, offering an eyewitness account. Diaries, letters, scrapbooks, institutional records, and taped oral histories are utilized. Students work with letters concerning black Civil War soldiers from the United States National Archives microfilm collection, *The Negro in the Military Service of the United States, 1639-1886*, the *Papers of Bayard Rustin* (civil rights organizer, strategist, orator, and writer), and slavery source material from the local historical society.

Thirty-percent of the class grade for the course results from a bibliographic project due at the end of the semester. The purpose of the project is for each student to compile a bibliography on a topic in the subject area which consists of at least one-hundred citations. The project is designed for students to apply the skills developed during the course and to demonstrate their mastery of those skills. It is expected that students will utilize each of the various tools discussed during the semester: card and online catalogs, periodical and newspaper indexes, CD-ROM indexes, U. S. government publications, statistical sources, and union catalogs of other institutions. Students have prepared bibliographies on the following topics:

African-American Architecture;
Development of Community Resources for
    Black At-Risk Adolescents;
Development of African-American Studies
    Programs on University Campuses;
African-American Women Suffrage;
Experiences of African-American Students on
    Predominately White Campuses;
Blacks and Communism;
Relations between African-American and Native Americans in the 19th Century; and
Black Nationalism.

The remainder of the course grade is determined as follows: midterm examination, 25%; final examination, 25%; class assignments, 10%; and weekly quizzes, 10%.

Students' reasons for taking the course have been fairly similar: to acquire the library skills necessary to find information concerning the African and African-American experiences. The evaluations at the end of the course indicate that students felt they had developed the skills to successfully utilize library and other research institutions to conduct research in this subject area. Students reported that by the end of the course they often found themselves in the position of assisting their peers with their library research needs.

Though this course was designed to increase access to informational sources on various cultures of black people, it could be modified to include the cultures of other area studies. The informational resources to support a course of this type are probably already in place at most academic libraries. What may be absent is a commitment from the area studies program to address the library research skills of its students and a vehicle to demonstrate to students that they can successfully develop the skills to engage in research that is relevant to them. The offering of a formal for-credit course of this type can be that vehicle.

Endnotes

1. Carla J. Stoffle, "A New Library for the New Undergraduate, *Library Journal* 115 (October 1, 1990): 50.

2. *Index of Majors, 1991,* (New York: College Entrance Examination Board, 1990): p. 16-17.

3. Denise K. Magner, "Ph.D. Program Stirs a Debate on the Future of Black Studies," *The Chronicle of Higher Education* 37 (June 10, 1991): A1, A13.

4. Mary M. Huston and Susan L. Perry, "Information Instruction: Considerations for Empowerment," *Research Strategies* 5 (Spring, 1987): 71-77.

Bibliography

Mary A. Ball, and Molly Mahony, "Foreign Students, Libraries, and Culture." *College and Research Libraries* 48 (March, 1987): 160-166.

John N. Berry, "The Michigan Mission: to Serve Diversity; They Demand Education, not Tolerance or Assimilation." *Library Journal* 115 (October 1, 1990) 8 .

Laura S. Kline and Catherine M. Rod, "Library Orientation Programs for Foreign Students: A Survey." *RQ* 24 (Winter, 1984): 210-216.

Boyd Kohler and Kathryn Swanson, "ESL Students and Bibliographic Instruction: Learning Yet Another Language." *Research Strategies* 6 (Fall, 1988): 148-160.

Irene Hoffman and Opritsa Popa, "Library Orientation and Instruction for International Students: The University of California-Davis Experience." *RQ* 25 (Spring, 1986): 357-360.

Barbara MacAdam and Darlene P. Nichols, "Peer Information Counseling: An Academic Library Program for Minority Students." *Journal of Academic Librarianship* 15 (September, 1989): 204-209.

Wendy Moorhead, "Ignorance Was Our Excuse." *College and Research Library News* 47 (October, 1986): 585-587.

Judith Payne, *Public Libraries Face California's Ethnic and Racial Diversity.* (San Monica, CA: Rand Corp, 1988).

Patricia A. Tarin, "Rand Misses the Point: A 'Minority' Report." *Library Journal* 113 (November 1, 1988): 31-34.

University of Michigan Library. *Points of Intersection II: The University Library Moves Toward Diversity.* (Ann Arbor, MI: University of Michigan Library, 1990).

Common Ground: The Composition/Bibliographic Instruction Connection

Barbara Fister
Gustavus Adolphus College
St. Peter, Minnesota

Abstract

Composition, an emerging field born under the same condtions as bibliographic instruction shares much common ground with its library-based cousin, yet in spite of similarities there is remarkbly little dialogue between the two fields. This paper describes three major trends in composition and maps out ways in which they correspond to bibliographic instruction issues. It suggests that collboration between the two fields would be helpful and recommends ways in which that collaboration might be accomplished.

The field of composition is one which we could easily confuse with our own. There is much in common between bibliographic instruction and composition; the surprise is that there isn't more dialogue between the two fields.

Composition—the teaching of writing—has been around a long time, just as has library instruction.[1] However, both fields have emerged as fields in their own right, as legitimate and serious endeavors, only relatively recently. Both fields responded to a new diversity in student populations and expectations in the sixties and seventies, managed to achieve a place in the academic world—if not respectability—by the eighties, and are now exploring a wide range of possible theoretical frameworks in the eighties and nineties. Both fields deal with the teaching of skills rather than content, which makes us stepchildren in the academy while making us innovators in pedagogy. We, more than other fields, attempt to view the academic world from the student's vantage point and try to interpret its peculiar culture in ways that make sense to newcomers. Because of our interdisciplinary nature we teach holistically, attempting to give students a *lingua franca* to gain entry into the bewildering variety of academic discourse communities. Because we want students to learn *how* more than *what,* we are concerned with their grasp of process as much as with product. And, because what we teach must respond to many levels of sophistication, we try to infiltrate the whole curriculum. True, we often have our most organized encounters with first year students, but we use such programs as writing across the curriculum and course-related instruction to make cross-curricular connections.

Given such a similar history and position in the academy, it is surprising how little we have joined forces. Librarians tend to look to other librarians for inspiration. A study conducted in 1989 reported that 75% of literature cited in bibliographic instruction articles came from within library literature.[2] In the author's reading only a small handful of instances can be recalled in which literature from the field of composition was cited by librarians and no doubt, though without figures for this claim, the same applies to composition—library literature is infrequently cited. How curious that two fields that spend so much time and effort on improving student research spend so little time comparing notes.

What follows is a map of the field of composition, which points out some of its chief features and then suggest some areas of common ground. One thing about this landscape that will seem very familiar to bibliographic instruction librarians is that it is a very confusing place. There is a spaghetti junction of intersecting theories and claims and numerous heavily fortified bastions of the "right way" to teach. This sometimes prompts despair. Stephen North wrote a book on composition a few years ago,[3] a "portrait of an emerging field," in which he chided practitioners for racing off in too many directions in search for theory. Others find the diversity enriching, an opportunity to choose pedagogy from a wide variety of options. I think our field is in something of the same situation; while we yearn from time to time for a Grand Unified Theorem, we make good use of a variety of theoretical frameworks available and thereby enrich our teaching.

Focus on the process
• the process is more important than the product
• skills improve with an understanding of process
• the process is recursive and generative

Composition applications:
prewriting
revision
planning
Bibliographic instruction:
search strategies
library anxiety/affective side of research process

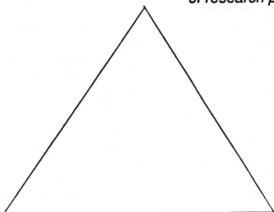

Focus on the writer/researcher
• the object of the enterprise is to discover
• the effect of the enterprise is to empowerment of the writer/researcher
• the skill is not dependent on the context

Composition applications:
freewriting
journals
Bibliographic instruction:
information literacy
lifelong learning
empowerment

Focus on the audience/social context
• knowledge is socially constructed
• the demands of the audience shape the product
• discourse communities make different rhetorical demands on the writer/researcher

Composition applications:
collaborative learning
peer review
writing in the disciplines
Bibliographic instruction:
collaborative learning
examining the publication process
examining the literature of disciplines

An excellent introduction to composition and its literature can be found in a book called *Teaching Composition: Twelve Bibliographic Essays*.[4] George Hillocks provides a survey and meta-analysis of work done since the 60s in his book *Research on Written Composition*.[5] An annual bibliography is being published under the auspices of the discipline's most active organization, the Conference on College Composition and Communication, a lively offshoot of the National Council of Teachers of English.[6] Using these sources to get a quick survey of the field, one can sort out three main trends in composition. They correspond, roughly, to the rhetorical triangle—they tend to focus on the writer, on the audience, or on what transpires in between those two. Early contributors to composition literature were particularly interested in the role of the writer and came up with such pedagogies as freewriting and journal writing to free the writer to use the act of writing for self discovery. Macrorie, Elbow, and Fulwiler are in this camp.[7] Another group of theorists and researchers concern themselves with the process of making meaning. Janet Emig started everyone thinking about process back in 1971[8] and the teaching of writing as process is so entrenched now that it has permeated classrooms from first grade on. A third group—and this seems to be where the action is these days—is concerned with the audience, with the social context of writing. Here the process and the product of writing—and the role of the writer in the text—are all interconnected with the context of the writing, inextricably linked to questions of purpose, audience, evidence, and the social construction of knowledge. Here are found proponents of collaborative learning such as Bruffee[9] and rhetoricians such as Kinneavy[10] and Berthoff.[11]

This landscape has been much simplified. In fact, those divisions blur and subdivide as soon as they are closely examined. For the purposes of perceiving common ground the sketch is sufficient.

A similarity exists between librarians' new emphasis on information literacy and the notion that writing is done for self-discovery and empowerment. Information literacy attempts to remove this act of discovery from a particular institutional context and suggests that the skill is one centered in and empowering for the individual. In this model, bibliographic instruction doesn't serve the agenda of the institution—to train students to better fulfill the institution's expectations—but rather proposes one for the library user—that mastery of information systems will lead to empowerment.

There are obvious connections between the process approach to writing and the librariens' approach of teaching search strategies. When the search behavior of library users or the affective side of research (Carol Kuhlthau[12] and Constance Mellon[13]) are studied librarians exploring the same territory as students of composition. Think how useful it would be to carry on these conversations together—because from the point of view of the student, research and research writing are intertwined activities and it makes little sense to unbraid them and treat them as separate and different processes.

As for the third group, those concerned with the social context point of the rhetorical triangle, there is a rich potential for combining the forces of composition and bibliographic instruction. Collaborative learning, a pedagogy particularly suited for library instruction, is coming into its own just as it has become *de rigueur* in writing classrooms. An examination of the publication process helps students understand the social forces that shape the texts they use for research. And librarians pay a great deal of attention to the literature of disciplines, hoping to give students a key not only to the tools of research, but to the traditions and the values of the disciplines. Deborah Fink has dealt with the social construction of information in her book *Process and Politics in Library Research* in an effort to illuminate the social context of library research.

Having seen some commonalities, what is being proposed? What practical applications arise from recognizing this common ground? There are a couple of ways to answer that question. One is to point out the political advantages of such a collaboration. Some bibliographic instruction programs reach students chiefly through formal ties to a first year composition course. Even when the ties are informal, writing across the curriculum programs have often disseminated composition's innovations throughout the institution and are having an impact on how research writing is taught. Given that fact, and the fact that writing instruction has changed dramatically librarians should do what they can to keep in touch and learn what is going on in the composition classroom so that librarians' teaching will integrate well into the culture of the classroom. Another is to suggest that collaboration will improve both library and writing instruction. Sharing ideas, exchanging teaching tips, teaching together, planning programs together, and learning from one another will enrich the joint understanding of what goes on when people do research.

Here are some specific suggestions for things that can be done to make collaboration work:

—Become familiar with the language and the values of the field of composition. Keeping up with journals such as College Composition and Communication, Writing Instructor, or Pre/Text can be of immense help. This not only aids collaboration, but yields useful ideas for bibliographic instruction.

—Look at the field of composition when doing research in bibliographic instruction. There is a lot published there that deals with the same kind of questions. ERIC is a wonderful tool for cross-fertilization of bibliographic instruction and composition questions.

—Take advantage of every opportunity to share ideas. This may mean going to on-campus pedagogy workshops, serving on writing program or curricular committees, or (if all else fails) inviting English department faculty for coffee. Ask them how they teach a particular concept or handle a particular problem in the classroom. Demonstrate that librarians and composition teachers face common problems and can be useful allies.

—Negotiate encounters with writing classes carefully to make sure that the two agendas mesh with that of the teacher and the students. It is important to clarify the goals of collaboration so that library research can be integrated into the entire research and writing process.

—Share strategies. Make every attempt to plan programs that meet on common ground. Where there are a massive first year composition courses, librarians should attempt to get in on the planning for its curriculum. If there is a writing across the curriculum program on campus, roll up their sleeves and pitch in. When the library is restructuring its bibliographic instruction program, the writing teachers should be invited to join in on the planning. It is certainly possible librarians overtures will be rebuffed, but sometimes the fact is—they didn't know librarians cared.

Finally, making connections is worth the effort. The payoff is valuable for both fields. In joint encounters, librarians should be open minded and prepared to raise questions that don't have answers. Librarians sometimes are overly concerned with image and want to be experts (as do writing instructors!) Conversations should be open-ended and librarians admit that they don't have all the answers. After all, why should they be defensive about turf that is really common ground?

Endnotes

1. For a lively and informative history of the field, consult James Berlin's *Rhetoric and Rality: Writing Instruction in america 1900-1985* (Carbondale: Southern Illinois University Press, 1987).
2. James Bracken and John Turner, "Characteristics of the Journal Literature of Bibliographic Instruction," *College and Research Libraries* 50 (November, 1989): 665-673.
3. Stephen M. North, *the Making of Knowledge in Composition: Portrait of an Emerging Field* (Upper Montclair, New Jersey: Boynton/Cook, 1987).
4. *Teaching Composition: Twelve Bibliographic Essays* (Forth Worth: Texas Christian University, 1987).
5. George Hillocks, *Research on Written Composition: New Directions for Teaching* (Urbana: ERIC and Nastional Council of Teachers of English, 1986).
6. *CCCC Bibliography of Composition and Rhetoric* (Carbondale: Southern Illinois University Press, 1990). This series covers composition literature from 1987 forward and continues the *Longman Bibliography of Composition and Rhtetoric* which covers 1984-1986 in two volumes).
7. Some representative works of these three writers are Peter Elbow's *Embracing Countraries: Explorations in Learning and Teaching* (New York: Oxford University Press, 1980); Ken Macrorie's *Searching Writing: AContext Book* (Upper Montclair, New Jersey: Boynton/Cook, 1984); and Toby Fulwiler's *Teaching With Writing* (Upper Montclair, New Jersey: Boynton/Cook, 1987).
8. Janet Emig, *The Composing Processes of Twelfth Graders* (Urbana: National Council of Teachers of English, 1971).
9. Kenneth Bruffee, "Collaborative Learning and the 'Conversation of Mankind,'" *College English* 46 (1984): 635-652.
10. James L. Kinneavy, *A Theory of Discourse: the Aims of Discourse* (New York: Norton, 1980).
11. Ann Berthoff, *The Sense of Learning* (Portsmouth, New Hampshire: Boynton/Cook, 1981).
12. Carol Kuhlthau, "Developing a Model of the Library Search Process: Cognitive and Affective Aspects," *RQ* 28 (Winter, 1988): 232-242.
13. Constance Mellon, "Process Not Product in Course-Integrated Instruction: A Generic Model of Li-

brary Research," *College and Research Libraries* 45 (November, 1984): 471-478.

14. Deborah Fink, *Process and Politics in Library Research: A Model for Course Design* (Chicago, American Library Association, 1989).

First Things First: Thoughts on Teaching the Concept of Source

Mary W. George
Princeton University
Princeton, New Jersey

Abstract

No concept is more difficult to impress on undergraduates than that of source, and in particular the distinction between primary and secondary sources. This paper suggests a way to teach this crucial but tricky point by defining a source as a tangible container of whatever phenomenon students are investigating. Undergraduates can learn to inspect these containers critically from nine different angles to determine how relatively primary or secondary the sources are and how to select among them. These nine angles are (1) closeness of source to phenomenon, (2) perspective, (3) purpose, (4) audience, (5) content, (6) time, 7) transmission, (8) reliability, and (9) availability. Each is illustrated with an example from the Persian Gulf War.

In twenty years of library instruction experience the concept of source, so central to inquiry in every field, completely mystifies virtually all undergraduates, regardless of their talents or the rigor of their preparation for college. This problem has several causes. First, the term source is used casually by the media to mean anything from an elaborate statement to rumor. Second, students rarely have the opportunity to create sources for themselves. Even in high school science classes, students think of experiments as recipes with only one right outcome. It does not occur to them that the data they recorded in their lab books are primary sources representing the biological or physical process they are studying. That such notations might ever yield a discovery astounds them. Third, in many fields sources have been superseded by textbooks or anthologies that excerpt and interpret the great thoughts of the past. There is no difference in appearance for them, between a novel written a century ago and the *CliffNotes* summary of it, both published last year and both purchased yesterday at the college bookstore. Worse yet, the essential distinction between primary and secondary sources seems too subtle for undergraduates to grasp, no doubt because they are bombarded by both types constantly and because the lines between them are often fuzzy.

The single most important goal for post-secondary library instruction is to clarify the concept of source. Amazingly, the idea is not explicit in the otherwise comprehensive "Model Statement of Objectives for Academic Bibliographic Instruction" first published in College & Research *Libraries News* in May 1987. Here is how an ideal terminal objective might be phrased:

"The user can distinguish between primary and secondary sources pertaining to any information search project and can predict what sources of each type ought to exist." A simple intent, but an extraordinarily complex task on the instruction librarian's part. What follows are suggestions, some tested in a BI setting and some not, on how to achieve this aim.

But first a caution about terminology. The word *source* is terribly ambiguous, so in teaching care is taken to use *tool* when fact, finding (bibliographic), or hybrid (encyclopedic) reference works is meant, and *source* to mean the recorded information actually sought by the user.

An instruction session begins by asking students to define source and to differentiate between primary and secondary ones. There is usually an embarrassed silence, but someone will eventually volunteer what is clearly a memorized response, such as that a primary source is an eyewitness account and a secondary source is hearsay. While not wrong, this response is seldom stated with conviction and students can rarely give solid examples or elaborate. Some more dubious assertions heard over the years from Princeton undergraduates are that a primary source is the most important source for their research, the source they are supposed to use first, the source they list first in their bibliography, and the source that appeared first on their subject. A favorite definition, however, came from a smart aleck who was inadvertently profound, "I know it's a primary source if it makes me sneeze"!

After discussion ends, as it quickly does, a definition

of source as evidence, as the representation of ideas or information or experience which can be perceived by more than one person, either simultaneously or successively is presented. Put another way, a source is the tangible container of a phenomenon. Researchers must first decide what phenomenon they intend to investigate and what questions they wish to ask about it. Then they set about identifying, verifying, locating, and obtaining—in short, finding—one or more sources which record that phenomenon. If they cannot discover any, they design ways of documenting the phenomenon for themselves. They conduct experiments, field studies, surveys, interviews, statistical analyses, or whatever is appropriate to answer the questions they have posed about the phenomenon. The results of their efforts are homemade primary sources which, once disseminated, can also serve as primary sources for others.

To begin a discussion about sources, the focus is on a complex event of current interest. As an example the Persian Gulf War in early 1991, might used. The chart categorizes some of the major sources generated by the event arranged in columns to indicate the nature of each, but with no meaningful order within columns. Just a few items from each side of this list and others are elicited from the group. If, however, time is short, the entire chart is distributed as a handout or projected as a transparency and students are asked to react based on the previous definition of source.

Phenomenon = Persian Gulf War

Primary Sources	Secondary Sources
Conversations	Demonstrations
Diplomatic notes	News analyses
Diaries	Background stories
Memos	Commentaries by experts
Eyewitness accounts	Protest literature
Letters from soldiers	Letters to soldiers
War orders & battle plans	Editorials
Journalists' dispatches	Letters to the editor
Press releases	Speeches
Videotapes & photographs	Essays
News conferences	Satire & cartoons
Interviews	Legislative debates
Briefings & debriefings	Reports of investigations
Intelligence reports	Opinion polls
Peace negotiations	Budget projections
Personnel lists	Charitable donation figures
Target descriptions	Environmental studies
Maps, graphs & charts	Support group newsletters
Casualty & damage statistics	Histories
Materiel inventories	Documentaries
Oral histories	Biographies
Autobiographies & memoirs	Scholarly articles
Films	Conference presentations
Artistic works	Political assessments
New words & phrases	Bumper stickers
Musical & dance compositions	New consumer products
Poetry, drama, fiction	Advertising
War memorials	Yellow ribbons

It is acknowledged to students that this list is incomplete and idiosyncratic, not to mention extremely controversial. But having derived it, the class proceeds to use it to discuss the nine characteristics of any source, those features that determine whether it is primary or secondary or some mixture of the two, and that help investigators decide whether it is well suited to their research. These factors are (1) how close a source is to the phenomenon it contains, (2) the unique perspective of each person who either records or explores it, (3) the purpose of those employing the source, (4) the researcher's audience, (5) the source's actual content, (6) the time elapsed since the source's creation, (7) how the source has been transmitted, (8) source reliability, and (9) source availability. If two reasonable people examine the same physical source in the light of all these criteria, they will often reach different conclusions about its nature. Here are some comments made on each point:

Closeness: This refers to both time and space. Take for instance diaries written during the Persian Gulf War. Those kept by soldiers on either side describing their combat experiences could be considered "more primary" as regards actual maneuvers than those kept by commanders or diplomats far from the scene. In contrast, an interview with a State Department official about why so many Iraq planes landed in Iran is probably a better primary source on that topic than an interview with a radar operator who just observed those flights. The former's broader knowledge and expertise, albeit far removed from the action, would be more authoritative on this question than the latter's temporal and physical proximity to the event.

Perspective: Whether source makers comprehend their act does not affect the nature, primary or secondary, of the sources they beget. What principally establishes the nature of a source, other than its nearness to the phenomenon, is the observer's point of view. In short, a source's character is not absolute but relative. This is easy to grasp when you imagine, say, a newspaper column by Barbara Bush about the Persian Gulf War. Insofar as she is reflecting on the situation to date—based on primary sources she has access to—and offering her analysis and projections of what might occur next, she has authored a standard secondary source. Most people will accept the piece as Mrs. Bush's opinion and file it away mentally as such. But suppose one is doing research for a biography of Barbara Bush and wants to read everything she has ever written: from that perspective her column is a primary source just as interviews with her or her diary would be.

Purpose: At first glance, purpose seems to be the same as perspective. The two are closely related, of course, but they are distinct. Perspective is the researcher's attitude toward a phenomenon. Purpose is his or her reason for seeking information about it. Perspective inspires inquiry; purpose shapes its outcome. For example, suppose the purpose (i. e. the assignment) is to examine newsmagazine coverage of the first week of the Persian Gulf War and to present a ten-minute talk about it, pointing out its strengths and weaknesses. Obviously the phenomenon is "newsmagazine coverage," not the war itself, so that the only primary sources necessary would be issues of *Newsweek, Time,* and *U.S. News & World Report* that appeared during the week of January 20, 1991. If the purpose were different, then clearly the choice of pertinent sources would be as well.

Audience: Audience has a direct bearing on selection, use, and presentation of sources. When researchers intend to reach an expert or sophisticated audience, they will assemble an exhaustive and highly technical group of sources, both primary and secondary. If, on the other hand, they wish to reach a general or special audience, they may decide to limit the number and nature of the sources they rely on. For example, someone preparing a brief talk on the political geography of the Middle East for a class of ninth graders might choose to refer to basic maps of the region, topographic and thematic, rather than strategic maps issued by various governments.

Content: Typically, researchers include chunks of primary sources—quotations, illustrations, or equations, for instance—in the secondary source they produce. Assuming these chunks are accurately presented and labeled (cited), they are not only nice touches for the reader or listener, but often essential to convey ideas and information. An example from the Persian Gulf War would be quotations from interviews with soldiers embedded in a reflective essay. On the other hand, researchers should ordinarily not rely on such aggregate sources, but should track down the full, original version of the evidence.

Time: This has to do with the interval between the recording of a source and its availability to the researcher. In this case, I point to the fact, often overlooked, that events happening in the Middle East one day are not usually made known in the Western Hemisphere until several hours or a day later, by which point they may have been edited and embellished, diluting their role as firsthand evidence.

Transmission: The basic phases in the transmission of a source are capture and publicity. Capture refers to the recognition of a source as such, either by the person who originally records it or by someone else, perhaps centuries later, who encounters it. Publicity refers to making the source known to others by describing it and its whereabouts. Imagine artifacts smuggled home by soldiers serving in the Gulf: as long as such sources remain hidden, they cannot further inquiry.

Reliability: A reliable source should above all be true and concur with other sources reflecting the same phenomenon. It should also be complete whenever possible. This is a very difficult criterion when the object of study is an event as complex as warfare. For instance, students of the Persian Gulf War should ask such questions as how accurate and well corroborated are the accounts of combatants, or whether news releases have been censored.

Availability: This characteristic has two sides, physical accessibility and intellectual accessibility. A source is physically accessible if it already exists, can be identified and located, and can be obtained in the original or a usable facsimile in the time the researcher has for inquiry. A source is intellectually accessible if, once it has been obtained, the researcher can understand it. A good illustration of this distinction from the Persian Gulf War would be published transcripts of subsequent war crimes trials in Kuwait, but if the investigators do not read Arabic, that source is still not readily available to them.

Given the opportunity, the context of the session is reinforced by having students turn in a brief statement about the primary and secondary sources they intend to use for a library research project in any course they are taking, specifying why they wish to use each in terms of the nine factors. This exercise should be completed three to four weeks before the project is due so that there is still time to track down other sources if the student decides to do so. If students do not currently have a library research assignment, then students are asked to analyze the sources in a scholarly book or article they are reading.

Finally, after discussing all these issues, the distinction between sources are the means of inquiry, not its end is emphasized. A BI presentation that can permanently impart that idea and its ramifications will have succeeded.

Comparisons of Graduate and Undergraduate End-Users of ERIC and PsycLit on CD-ROM

Grace Jackson-Brown
Gwen Pershing
Indiana University
Bloomington, Indiana

Abstract

A survey study which examines user satisfaction with search results among 257 PsycLit and ERIC CD-ROM end-users at Indiana University-Bloomington in 1990. The results are used to compare: a) satisfaction levels with search results, and b) differences in time spent conducting searches among graduate and undergraduate students. Comparisons were also made among majors in education, psychology, and others at the graduate and undergraduate levels. The comparisons are summarized in the context of two different library settings—a university education library and a university main reference department.

The Indiana University Libraries system on the Bloomington campus consist of the Main Library, 15 branch libraries, and twelve residence hall libraries. The libraries maintain a collection of over 4.5 million printed volumes, and many computerized resources. CD-ROM databases are becoming an increasingly popular research tool among the students and faculty of Indiana University.

ERIC and PsycLit are two of the most frequently searched CD-ROM databases on the Indiana University - Bloomington (IUB) campus. ERIC, the complete database of educational material from the Education Resources Information Center, corresponds to two print indexes, *Resources in Education* and *Current Index to Journals in Education*. PsycLit is produced by the American Psychological Association and covers over 1,300 journals, technical reports, monographs, dissertations, and unpublished research documents.

At IUB, an introduction to ERIC is taught by a librarian in one class period as part of a required undergraduate computer literacy course in the School of Education. Training workshops on ERIC and PsycLit, one and a half hour in duration, are offered to graduate students and faculty. The workshops are attended on a voluntary basis and include both introductory and advanced searching.

Several substantial CD-ROM end-user studies support the conclusion that formal training is not needed to enable the end-user to search most CD-ROM data-

bases, including ERIC and PsycLit.[1] The experience at the IUB Libraries is that many students and other users of the CD-ROM databases require assistance to conduct their computer searches. The ERIC classroom presentations in the School of Education and the training workshops for ERIC and PsycLIt at the Main Library were established to acquaint users with the particular databases, and introduce various CD-ROM searching techniques. The purpose of the CD-ROM training was to assist end-users in becoming more proficient and self-sufficient searchers, and to ease the demands placed upon a limited reference staff who gave search help.

During spring semester 1990, a survey was designed and administered to a sampling of PsycLit and ERIC on CD-ROM end-users at IUB to determine how training effected end-user satisfaction with search results. Some strong contrasts were found between the satisfaction levels of undergraduate and graduate students who had searched PsycLit and ERIC on CD ROM. The survey, ERIC/PsycLit End-User Satisfaction Survey, was based on previously published CD-ROM end-user surveys, particularly those published in the Association of Research Libraries SPEC Kit #133, "Optical Discs for Storage and Access in ARL Libraries."[2] A procedure of random distribution of the ERIC/PsycLit End-User Satisfaction Survey was adopted at two IUB library sites, the Main Library-Reference Department and the Education Library. This distribution occurred from February, 1990 through May, 1990. In addition, surveys were also distributed to some faculty members in the School of Education after the librarian's classroom presentation on ERIC. The students in the classes were asked to complete the survey along with their ERIC assignment, and the faculty members returned the surveys to the Education Library. Faculty and graduate student workshop participants were given a survey along with a campus mail envelope, and were asked to mail the completed survey to the Reference Department. Two hundred and fifty-seven usable surveys were administered to students during the survey period, 146 undergraduate surveys and 111 graduate surveys. In some instances partially incomplete surveys were counted, thereby resulting in a smaller total than 257 for some survey questions. The composition of survey participants from the two library settings was as follows: 69 undergraduates and 31 graduates at the Education Library, 77 undergraduates and 80 graduates at the Reference Department. There were 99 trained end-users and 158 untrained end-users in the survey.

The results of the survey were tabulated and analyzed using PARADOX, a relational database management program. The basic finding of the survey was that trained ERIC/PsycLit end-users expressed a greater level of satisfaction with their search results than untrained or self-taught end-users. Survey participants were asked if they were satisfied with the results of their searches and were given three possible answers to mark—completely satisfied, partially satisfied, or not satisfied (Table I). Most formally trained end-users marked that they were completely satisfied with their search results. A large majority, 67.7%, of the formally trained users in the survey reported that they were completely satisfied with their search results. In contrast, only 47.4 percent of the self-taught or untrained end-users expressed complete satisfaction with the results of their searches.

The aforementioned finding coincides with the results of a end-user study conducted at Cornell University.[3] The Cornell study found that students using ERIC on SilverPlatter outperformed students searching the same topics in the ERIC printed indices. The students expressed an overwhelming preference for the CD-ROM product over the printed indices. And furthermore, those students who were formally instructed in the use of ERIC on CD-ROM moderately

TABLE I
TRAINING & SATISFACTION LEVEL

n=257 Total Responses	Trained n=99		Untrained n=158	
	Number	Percent	Number	Percent
Completely Satisfied	67	67.7	75	47.4
Partially Satisfied	26	26.2	70	44.3
Not Satisfied	2	2.0	8	3.2
No Response	4	4.0	5	3.2

outperformed students who used the ERIC on CD-ROM without formal instruction.

The trained undergraduate end-user in the IUB study expressed the highest level of "complete satisfaction" among the groups in the IUB survey (Figure I). The trained undergraduate students that indicated complete satisfaction with their search results outnumbered those trained undergraduates that were only partially satisfied by more than a 2 to 1 ratio, or 50 completely satisfied as opposed to 17 partially satisfied. Two trained undergraduate end-users indicated that they were not satisfied with their search results. Similarly, 17 of the trained graduate students were completely satisfied and 9 of the trained graduate students were partially satisfied. None of the trained graduate students stated that they were not satisfied with their search results.

There was a much larger percentage of trained undergraduate students represented in the survey than there were trained graduates. This was probably due to the mandatory nature of the undergraduate ERIC CD-ROM training in the School of Education course (Figure II). Only 25.2% of the graduate students in the survey were formally trained as compared to 48.6% of the undergraduate students in the survey who had received formal training.

Besides the differences in satisfaction and training levels between undergraduate and graduate CD-ROM end-users, the survey also revealed distinct differences in the amount of searching time spent by graduate students and undergraduate students. Survey participants marked their search time on the survey based on the following list of times: <10, 10-20, 21-30, <30 minutes. According to the survey, the majority of the graduate students, trained and untrained, spent more than 30 minutes searching the database per session (Figure III). Regardless of whether or not the undergraduate students had received training, the average time spent searching the database was 10-20 minutes. The larger periods of searching time spent by graduate students probably reflect that their searches were more complex or involved more extensive literature searching than what was required by the undergraduates.

Figure I

164

Status and Training

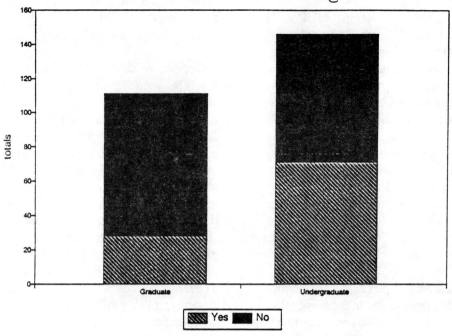

Figure II

Status - Training - Time

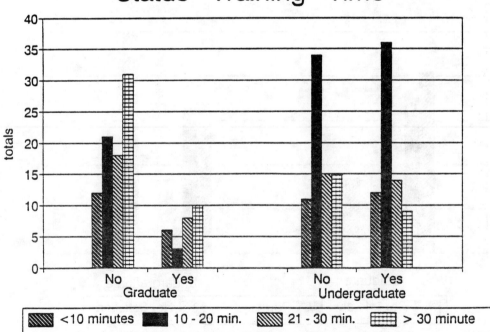

Figure III

The Education Library allows students to reserve 30 minutes per day for searching, and the main library Reference Department allows students to reserve two 30 minute search sessions or an hour per day. However, reserving computer time is not a requirement at either library setting. At both library settings students may search the database as long as they want on a first come basis as long as it doesn't interfere with time that has been reserved. In practice this scheduling scheme works well at both library settings, but it is unknown whether students have conformed to the scheduling structure. The survey seems to indicate that graduate students' average search time is conducive to work in the Reference Department, and the undergraduate students' average search time is more adaptable to the Education Library.

A variety of differences in responses between graduate and undergraduate students appear in the survey results pertaining to end-user satisfaction and student majors. The education major graduate students in the survey gave the "partially satisfied" response for their search results slightly more frequently than the "completely satisfied" response for their search results (Figure IV). Among the graduate psychology majors and other major categories most respondents noted that they were completely satisfied with their search results. A majority of the unknown or unspecified majors among the graduate students also stated that they were completely satisfied with their search results.

The education major undergraduate student response in the survey was quite different from that of education major graduate students with approximately 77% of the undergraduate education majors reporting complete satisfaction with their search results. Psychology major undergraduates who were completely satisfied with their search results only slightly outnumbered those who were partially satisfied. The undergraduates who indicated that they had a major other than education or psychology responded slightly higher in the partially satisfied category. And, the undergraduate unknown or unspecified majors answered slightly more frequently that they were completely satisfied with their search results.

Perhaps the undergraduates education majors in the survey benefited from having a background in the subject discipline of the CD-ROM databases as well as from having formal training for ERIC. The graduate education majors who had not received formal training

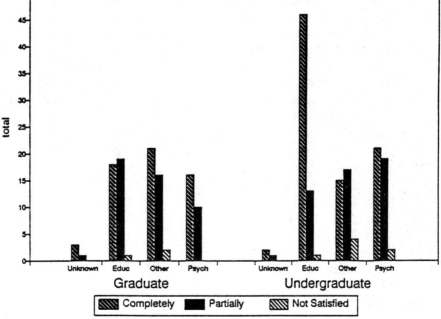

Figure IV

166

in ERIC or PsycLit, but who were faced with the need to conduct complex searches would certainly be at a greater disadvantage than formally trained undergraduate education majors. This frustration is reflected in the survey by about 47% of the graduate respondents who were only partially satisfied with their search results and the one respondent who indicated that he or she was not satisfied with the results of the search which was conducted. In order to improve upon the satisfaction level of graduate students with CD-ROM, the IUB survey points up the need to encourage graduate students to participate in CD-ROM training.

A considerable difference in the level of expressed satisfaction between students at the two library sites was revealed in the survey. Approximately 72% of the students surveyed at the Education Library responded that they were completely satisfied with their search results as opposed to only approximately 45% of the students from the Reference Department who expressed this sentiment.

The authors, who are both reference librarians who work with the CD-ROM end-users on a daily basis, attribute the difference in expressed user satisfaction between the two library settings to a number of factors. Formal training is the primary factor improving CD-ROM end-user satisfaction among the surveyed students, especially among undergraduates. The ability to provide individualized reference assistance to CD-ROM end-users is another factor. Because all undergraduate education majors are required to receive ERIC training in the classroom, and because the Education Library had mainly undergraduate end-users within its surveyed population this increased the potential of accumulating a large segment of completely satisfied patrons at the Education Library.

Many of the surveyed students who had searched either ERIC or PsycLit in the Reference Department had not attended the ERIC and PsycLit training workshops, nor had they received any form of formal CD-ROM database training. Based upon the survey findings, only 29% of the Reference Department CD-ROM end-users were formally trained CD-ROM end-users, as compared to 54% of the end-users at the Education Library who had received formal training. In addition, many of the surveyed students who searched ERIC or PsycLit in the Reference Department may have been undeclared majors or majors outside of the database subject disciplines. In general, the large

numbers of CD-ROM end-user searchers in the Reference Department makes it virtually impossible for a limited staff to give individualized attention to all who may have needed it.

The IUB survey results reinforce what was found by Gillian Allen at the University of Illinois in a survey on what CD-ROM end-users really want in CD-ROM training. According to Allen, "It was the individualized training programs that were wanted: one- to-one instruction, help available, and demonstrations."[4] In conclusion, all but five of the 257 end-users in the IUB survey stated that they would search the CD-ROM database again if the opportunity arose. However, it is important that librarians realize that user satisfaction with CD-ROM database searching among undergraduate and graduate students is influenced by a number of crucial factors within the library including CD-ROM training programs and adequate staffing at the reference desk to provide CD-ROM end-users with individualized assistance.

Endnotes

1. Linda Stewart and Jan Olsen, "Compact Disk Databases: Are They Good for Users?," *Online* 12 (May, 1988): 48-52; Meta Nissley, Peter Anderson, and Phyllis Gaal, "ROMping Through ERIC: Measuring Satisfaction and Effectiveness," *Laserdisk Professional* 2 (January, 1989): 95-100; Mary Gillian Allen, "Patron Response to Bibliographic Databases on CD-ROM," *RQ* 29 (Fall, 1989): 103-110.
2. *Optical Discs for Storage and Access in ARL Libraries,* (Washington, D.C.: Office of Management Studies, Association of Research Libraries, 1987).
3. Linda Stewart , op. cit.
4. Gillian Allen, op. cit.

Bibliographic Instruction in the Electronic Environment: Incorporating Recent Cognitive Theories of Learning

Frances F. Jacobson
Michael J. Jacobson
University of Illinois
Champaign, Illinois

Abstract

While recent advancements in technology have provided many opportunities for library users, there is also increasing complexity associated with this explosion of choice. Current approaches to bibliographic instruction may be limited in their ability to empower users to learn the complexities of the new electronic library environment. Selected recent cognitive theories of learning are examined in terms of their potential for application in bibliographic instruction in this demanding setting. In addition to enhancing the theoretical foundations of the field of bibliographic instruction, it is hoped that application of these new views of learning can better enable novices to surpass the acquisition of inert conceptual knowledge, and to improve their ability to flexibly apply their acquired knowledge in new circumstances that are often highly variable and unpredictable.

Advancements in technology have created an explosion of new options for information storage and retrieval. From CD-ROM products to the emergence of complex supercatalogs, users are presented with a range of choices that only promises to grow larger. But along with its benefits, the availability of choice may also engender feelings of anxiety. Oberman compares this changing scene in libraries to the "cereal syndrome," in which a consumer, faced with an overwhelming selection of cereals in one of today's mega-supermarkets, retreats to the familiar corner grocery store that has a much more limited, but less frustrating, offering.[1] Library users may feel similarly ill-equipped to handle the decisions they must make in seeking information in today's mega-libraries.

Sheer magnitude of choice is only part of what the information consumer must consider. The complexity of accessing these systems and products and making effective use of them cannot be underestimated. Online database search ing, for example, is an information retrieval method that was formerly the sole purview of experts. End user searching of o line systems is now widely available, even as a home consumer product. But intelligent negotiation within such an information-rich environment is neither intuitive nor obvious. Training, accumulated familiarity, and a deep structural understanding of the process distinguish the highly interactive search strategies employed by expert librarian-intermediaries.[2]

How can we best teach users to successfully manage this challenging environment? Certain assumptions characterize the nature of recent approaches to bibliographic instruction (Figure 1). Instruction is most likely to be effective if it is delivered in context, generally manifested as a course-integrated component within the academic setting.[3] Students should also be given a conceptual foundation for information retrieval in this environment, rather than just being instructed in the use of specific tools or protocols. But even as the field of bibliographic instruction has come to embrace the importance of teaching concepts, concept-based teaching in itself is not enough.[4] Students can be tested for the recall of concepts just as they can be tested for the recall of factual informati n, yet not be able to apply the knowledge when it is relevant and appropriate to do so. Their knowledge of the concepts is "inert," often not available for spontaneous adaptation to new or similar situations.[5]

The issue of inert knowledge is not exclusive to the library environment; much educational research has documented the pervasiveness of this general learning problem. We chose to examine some recent cognitively-oriented theories of learning that target this type of problem and which seem to have special potential for teaching information literacy in the electronic environment. Bibliographic instruction based on a synthesis of such theoretical models is intended to teach novices to surpass the acquisition of merely inert conceptual

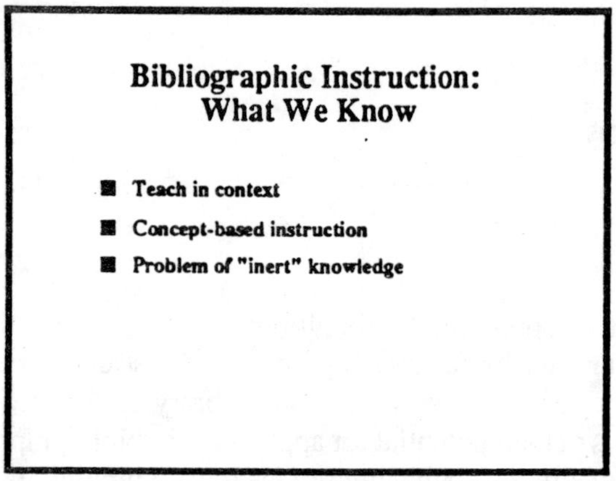

Figure 1

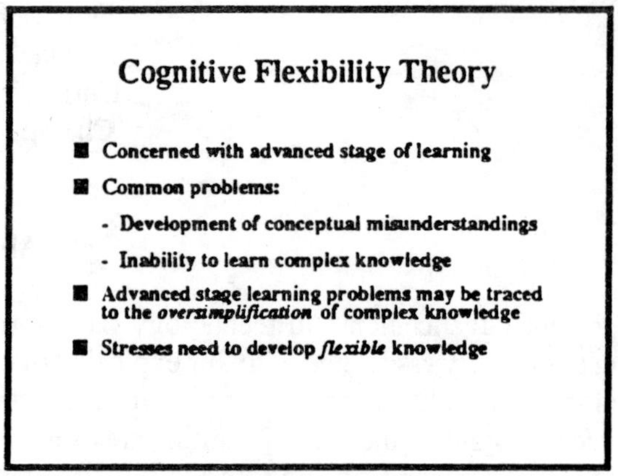

Figure 2

knowledge. In addition, these new theory-based approaches to instruction should better enable students to learn and flexibly apply their acquired knowledge in new circumstances that are highly variable and unpredictable. The next portion of this paper briefly describes two selected current cognitive learning theories (one with two major components) and considers their applicability to bibliographic instruction.[6]

Cognitive Flexibility Theory

Cognitive Flexibility Theory[7] is most directly concerned with the learning that takes place beyond initial exposure to facts and core concepts in a content area, but before the attainment of practiced expertise (Figure 2). In this extensive stage of advanced learning, students must develop a deeper understanding of the material, be able to reason with their acquired knowledge, and be able to flexibly apply this knowledge in contexts that are often quite different than that of the initial learning situation. During this stage, however, there is empirical evidence that learners tend to oversimplify complex knowledge in their attempts to master it.[8] Oversimplification can lead to conceptual misunderstandings and an inability to transfer knowledge to new situations.

To counteract the learning problems of advanced stage learning, Cognitive Flexibility Theory prescribes a number of instructional tactics (Figure 3). The cornerstone of these tactics is in the use of multiple knowledge representations, such as multiple analogies, case examples, or lines of argument. Although teaching commonly involves the use of examples, the tendency is to show only a few of the "cleanest" instances of a concept, rather than the "messy" exceptions that so often occur in context. Cognitive Flexibility Theory, on the other hand, calls for multiple "snapshots" which reveal the richness and complexity of a knowledge domain.

Other instructional tactics include the explicit linking of abstract concepts to case examples (i.e., teaching conceptual knowledge within contexts of knowledge application); the early introduction of manageable complexity (by presenting "bit-sized" chunks or "micro-cases" early on in instructional activity); the stressing of the interrelated and web-like structure of knowledge (instead of isolated and compartmentalized knowledge); and the promotion of knowledge assembly from various previously learned knowledge components (rather than teaching the intact recall of memorized information).

Teaching with the use of cases is especially important in ill-structured content areas in which the application of knowledge is not always prescribed by specific rules or general principles and when there is great conceptual variability from case to case. Presenting knowledge-in-use with case examples helps to avoid the misrepresentation of a complex topic when it is taught in an abstract manner divorced from the contexts or situations in which the knowledge is to be applied, as may be the case with traditional instructional materials and procedures (e.g., textbooks, lectures). In addition, presenting contrasting cases in a classroom situation simulates the way in which experts accumulate their real-world case-based experience.

How does Cognitive Flexibility Theory apply to bibliographic instruction? Searching for information in libraries has always been a complex process in that every search is a unique experience, and frequently previous techniques and strategies may have little relevance in new circumstances. Electronic access enhances availability, but does not diminish complexity. Therefore, teaching rote memorization of a specific search protocol, for example, does not necessarily help users know when or why to apply it in the new situations they are likely to encounter.

Teaching information literacy with the use of many cases which are based on real searches avoids the tendency to oversimplify the instructional material and instead provides multiple exposures to the knowledge that more closely represents the actual searching experience (Figure 4). Conveying abstract conceptual knowledge should also be tightly linked to teaching with different case examples. For example, teaching about the nature of discipline-oriented literatures can be demonstrated by presenting cases showing the same subject search conducted in a variety of CD-ROM or online databases.

It is also important to overlap concepts across search cases in order to reveal the interrelated structure of knowledge and to show that concepts do not occur singly or sequentially. Principles involving search strategy, vocabulary control, or variations in point of view or perspective can all be demonstrated in tandem. In terms of teaching a concept such as point of view, showing the differences between how the biosciences community and the popular press present issues such as euthanasia or animal rights can reveal how the identity of the information producer affects the nature of information content. Finally, cases can be used to elicit appropriate application of knowledge components. By

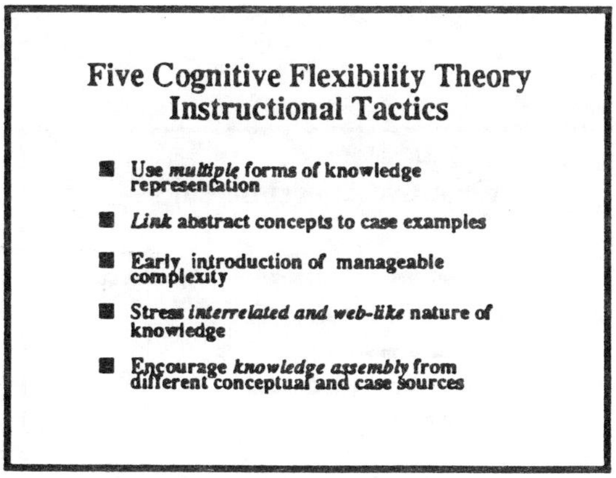

Figure 3

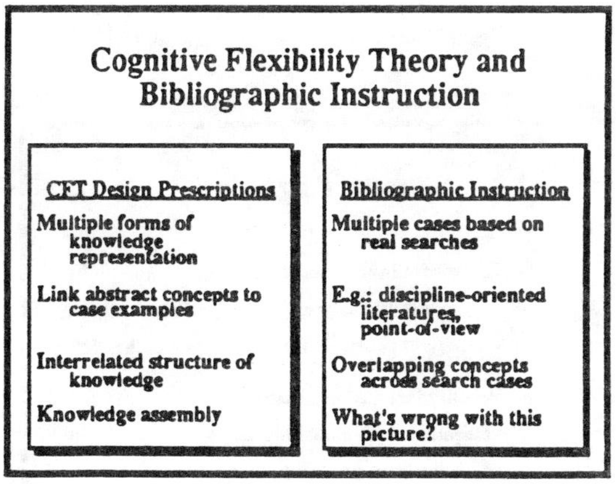

Figure 4

playing a game like "What's Wrong With This Picture?", students can be challenged to identify weaknesses in search strategies or to suggest alternative strategies for achieving different kinds of results.

Situated Cognition

Situated Cognition views knowledge not as an objective artifact, but as an entity that is developed and learned within a social context that itself effects or shapes cognition (Figure 5). The social situation provides a framework for "authentic" activity as practiced by experts or by members of a particular knowledge community.[9] Two primary instructional methods have been articulated from the Situated Cognition framework: cognitive apprenticeship and collaborative learning.

Cognitive Apprenticeship

Apprenticeship has been a widely used educational methodology, one which allows novices to take advantage of the situated nature of knowledge and to model experts in its application. By engaging in an authentic activity under the guidance of an expert, novices learn in an environment that does not abstract conceptual knowledge from the situation in which it is used. The same logic forms the argument for course-integrated bibliographic instruction—that the teaching of information handling skills should be situated within a meaningful context for which information is needed.

The notion of "cognitive apprenticeship," as articulated by Collins, Brown, and Newman,[10] uses the apprenticeship model as it applies to cognitive rather than physical skills or processes (Figure 6). They suggest a paradigm of situated modeling, coaching, scaffolding, and fading. Teachers first model the processes that are used to engage in an authentic activity. After modeling, they coach or provide scaffolding in order to support students' work in the task, and then finally fade or step back and empower students to continue independently. This approach provides a supportive environment in which students can articulate and reflect upon their thoughts, crystalize their understanding of expert behavior, and develop their own problem-solving strategies.

In the library setting, cognitive apprenticeship most likely begins with the librarian modeling searching activities, similar to the cases that characterize Cognitive Flexibility Theory (Figure 7). What happens next,

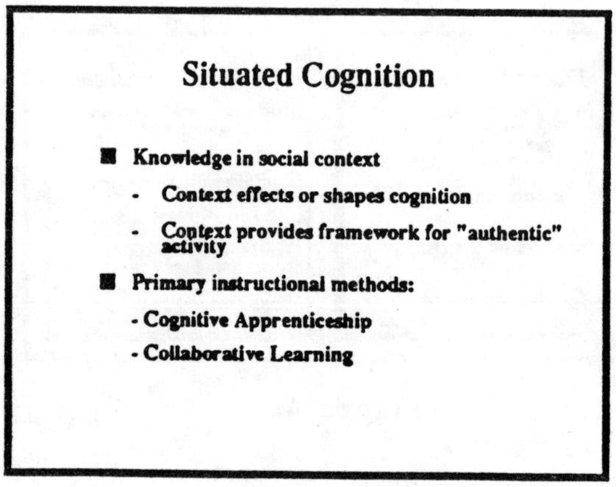

Situated Cognition

- Knowledge in social context
  - Context effects or shapes cognition
  - Context provides framework for "authentic" activity
- Primary instructional methods:
  - Cognitive Apprenticeship
  - Collaborative Learning

Figure 5

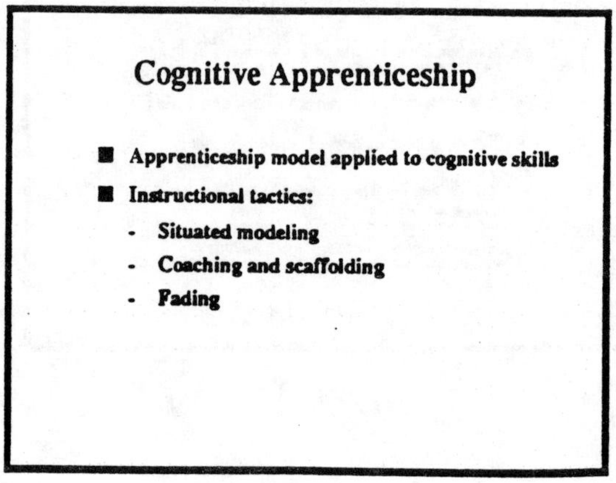

Cognitive Apprenticeship

- Apprenticeship model applied to cognitive skills
- Instructional tactics:
  - Situated modeling
  - Coaching and scaffolding
  - Fading

Figure 6

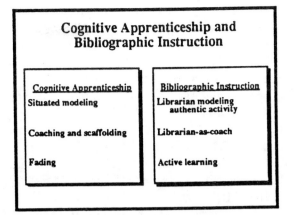

Cognitive Apprenticeship and Bibliographic Instruction

Cognitive Apprenticeship	Bibliographic Instruction
Situated modeling	Librarian modeling authentic activity
Coaching and scaffolding	Librarian-as-coach
Fading	Active learning

Figure 7

Collaborative Learning

■ Collaborative interaction as a catalyst
  - Synthesis: articulation and reflection
  - "Value-added" cognition
■ Culturally-based factors
■ Bibliographic Instruction:
  - Small group work
  - Structured expectations

Figure 8

Theoretical Synthesis

■ Cognitive Apprenticeship and Collaborative Learning (Situated Cognition)
  - Guidance to autonomy
  - Social development of knowledge
■ Cognitive Flexibility Theory and Situated Cognition
  - Active learning
  - Learning in context

Figure 9

however, departs from the format of most traditional bibliographic instruction. The application of cognitive apprenticeship assumes that formal instruction does not cease once content has been initially delivered. Instead, learners engage in actual searching, but under the direct tutelage of the librarian-instructor. Then, as the coaching support begins to fade, students become more independent active learners, but with the availability of expert intervention for more unusual or complicated situations.

Collaborative Learning

Student interactions with one another (and with expert coaches and instructors) serve as a catalyst for learning (Figure 8). Collaborative learning provides an excellent environment for fostering achievement beyond what students might otherwise gain as individuals.[11] By being part of a group, learners tend to speak aloud or declare their thoughts. As in cognitive apprenticeship, this articulation and implicit reflection is intended to enable students to evolve their own problem-solving strategies and to synthesize their knowledge. Collaboration also leads to "value-added" cognition. Learning does not occur in a vacuum; communal or shared thought processes become internalized and emerge as individualized creations.

There are also culturally-based justifications for collaborative learning in the electronic environment. Collective problem solving is a hallmark of cultural groups who have traditionally suffered in learning environments that primarily reward individually generated achievements.[12] For example, Sanders and Stone found that females prefer to use computers in "small friendship groups" rather than individually.[13]

Collaborative learning can be accomplished in the library setting by assigning students to work in small groups for developing their search strategies and for searching at computers. It is important, however, to structure expectations. Directing group activity will elicit the most fruitful and meaningful kind of interaction, and engender desired outcomes of articulation, reflection, and ability to transfer knowledge.

Theoretical Synthesis

There are a number of ways in which these theoretical perspectives overlap and can be combined to form a synergistic model for the development of bibliographic instruction (Figure 9). Within the framework of Situated Cognition, cognitive apprenticeship and collaborative learning are fitting partners. As students progress from the more individually oriented activities associated with apprenticeship and coaching, they often move into a more autonomous stage of collaborative learning. In tandem, cognitive apprenticeship and collaborative learning mimic the real-life social development of knowledge: Group learning promotes collective problem solving, the emergence and confrontation of ineffective strategies and misconceptions, and teaches the collaborative work skills that are increasingly necessary in our society.[14]

Cognitive Flexibility Theory is also an apt theoretical partner to Situated Cognition. Both theories stress the importance of active learning and the avoidance of abstracting or decontextualizing the instructional content. Cognitive Flexibility Theory then provides specific recommendations for how complex knowledge may be organized and presented to students to enhance their understanding of the material and their ability to use it in new situations.

Conclusion

It is hoped that consideration of these new perpectives on learning may enhance the theoretical foundation of instruction in today's technologically-enhanced library environment and strengthen interdisciplinary links to the fields of cognitive science and education. Finally, it is important to note that many of the issues raised by these newer theories of learning directly challenge conventional approaches to classroom and bibliographic instruction. The task of helping students acquire the complex knowledge and skills necessary to appropriate use of an increasing array of library information resources requires a renewed examination of our instructional philosophies. We suggest that new approaches to structuring bibliographic instruction be developed using recent cognitive instructional theories and research. The challenges of educating students for the next millenium are many. It is hoped that with a well-developed theory base, bibliographic instruction will have a prominent future in the support of emerging approaches to learning that aspire to master such challenges.

Endnotes

1. Cerise Oberman, "Avoiding the Cereal Syndrome, or Critical Thinking in the Electronic Environment," *Library Trends* 39 (Winter, 1991): 189-202.

2. See for example, Sara J. Penhale and Nancy Taylor, "Integrating End-User Searching Into a Bibliographic Instruction Program," *RQ* 26 (Winter, 1986): 212-220. and Stephen P. Harter, "Online Searching as a Problem-Solving Process," in *Questions and Andwers—Strategies for Using the Electronic Reference Collection: Proceedings of the Clinic on Library Applications of Data Processing,* ed. Linda Smith (Urbana, Illinois: Graduate School of Library and Information Science, University of Illinois at Urbana-Champaign, 1989), p. 103-120 .

3. See for example, Anne K. Beaubien, Sharon A. Hogan, and Mary George, Learning *the Library: Concepts and Methods for Effective Bibliographic Instruction* (New York: Bowker, 1982) and "Integrating Library Instruction in the College Curriculum," ed. Patricia A. Henning and Mary E. Stillman, *Drexel Library Quarterly* 7 (July and October, 1971): 171-378.

4. Cerise Oberman, op. cit., p. 195-196.

5. John D. Bransford, Jeffery J. Franks, Nancy J. Vye, and Robert D. Sherwood, "New Approaches to Instruction: Because Wisdom Can't Be Told," in Similarity an*d Analogical Reasoning,* ed. Stella Vosniadoua and Andrew Ortony (Cambridge: Cambridge University Press, 1989), p. 470-497.

6. The presentation of these theories is necessarily brief in this forum; for a fuller discussion, which incorporates a broader theory base and is illustrated with an example of teaching end user searching, see Frances F. Jacobsen and Michael J. Jacobson, "Teaching End user Searching of Online Databases: Bibliographic Instruction and the Application of Recent Cognitive Theories of Learning," in submission.

7. Rand Spiro, Richard L. Coulson, Paul J. Feltovich, and Daniel K. Anderson, "Cognitive Flexibility Theory: Advanced Knowledge Acquisition in Ill-Structured Domains," *Tenth Annual Conference of the Cognitive Science Society,* (Hillsdale, N.J.: Lawrence Erlbaum Associates, 1988), p. 375-383.

8. Rand Spiro, Ibid., and Paul J. Feltovich, Rand J. Spiro, and Richard L. Coulson, "The Nature of Conceptual Understanding in Biomedicine: The Deep Structure of Complex Idea and the Development of Misconceptions," in Cognitive Sciences in Medicine, ed. David A. Evans and Vimla L. Patal, (Cambridge: MIT Press, 1989), p. 113-117.

9. John Seely Brown, Allan Collins, and Paul Duguid, "Situated Cognition and the Culture of Learning,"*Educational Researcher* 18 (January-

February, 1989): 32-42.

10. Allan Collins, John Seely Brown, and Susan E. Newman, "Cognitive Apprenticeship Teaching the Crafts of Reading, Writing, and Mathematics," in Know*ing, Learning, and Instruction: Essays in Honor of Robert Glaser,* ed. Lauren B. Resnick (Hillsdale, New Jersey: Lawrence Erlbaum Associates, 1989), p. 453-494.

11. Charles Crook, "Computers in the Classroom: Defining a Social Context," in *Computers, Cognition and Development* ed. Julie C. Rutkowska and Charles Crook (New York: Wiley, 1987), p. 35-53.

12. Ann L. Brown and Annemarie S. Palinscar, "Guided, Cooperative Learning and Individual Knowledge Acquisition," in K*nowing, Learning, and Instruction: Essays in Honor of Robert Glaser,* ed. Lauren B. Resnick 393-451 (Hillsdale, N.J.: Lawrence Erlbaum Associates, 1989).

13. Jo Schucat Sanders and Antonia Stone, T*he Neuter Computer: Computers for Girls and Boys* (New York: Neal-Schuman, 1986).

14. John Seely Brown, op. cit., p. 40.

Assessing the Need for Bibliographic Instruction in Honors Sections of Freshman Composition

Marjorie M. Warmkessel
Millersville University
Millersville, Pennsylvania

Abstract

The bibliographic instruction librarian worked with the professor teaching the honors sections of freshman composition to determine whether or not honors students would benefit from bibliographic instruction. Using methods of qualitative analysis, the librarian evaluated students' attitudes toward the university library by examining writing samples from directed free writes on the topic of the library. Free writes from the beginning of the semester reflect students' fear of the library; those from the end of the semester—after a formal bibliographic instruction session and completion of course assignments—indicate less student apprehension and more willingness to ask for help.

Honors programs at state universities have grown in size and in popularity in recent years. Economic conditions have most likely been responsible for this trend as the relatively low costs of state institutions have attracted bright, academically- motivated, and achievement-oriented students whose families cannot afford to send them to small private colleges. In his 1988 publication *How To Get an Ivy League Education at a State University*, Martin Nemko suggests that "The Honors program is the key to getting an Ivy League education at many state universities."[1]

At Millersville University, a medium-sized (ca. 7000 FTE enrollment), state-owned institution in Pennsylvania, participation in the honors program has grown dramatically since its inception in 1980. In September of 1990 enrollment in the program was 21,393 of whom were newly admitted freshmen or transfer students. General criteria for admission into the honors program include a combined verbal and math SAT score of at least 1100 and ranking in the top 10% of one's high school class. Special exceptions are made on a case by case basis for those students who do not meet these admissions standards and approximately 20% of the students currently participating in the program fall under this category.

In spite of the growth of the honors program at Millersville, nothing has been done to target honors students as a specific audience for bibliographic instruction. The reason for this may be, as Bush and Wells suggest, that " . . . in many instances, professors and librarians presume that honors students have more highly developed research skills than other students."[2] The fallacy of this presumption is borne out in the results of a research project done by Wilson and Mulcahy at Rutgers University. In their study they found no evidence that "intellectually superior undergraduate honors students are also superior in their knowledge of bibliographic skills."[3] In fact, they concluded that honors students have an especially great need for bibliographic instruction because they have "higher research expectations."[4] Sandra Yee also emphasizes the importance of providing bibliographic instruction to honors students, stating that, "If these students are to be challenged and provided opportunities to excel in academic areas, it follows that early in their honors programs they should be provided the opportunity to develop and refine skill in critical thinking and skill in library research."[5]

With these thoughts in mind, in the fall semester of 1990, the author began working with the professor who teaches the honors sections of the required freshman composition course on a research project to evaluate the attitudes of honors students toward libraries, in general, and toward the university library, in particular. Using a method of qualitative research described by Constance Mellon,[6] we examined writing samples from directed free writes on the subject of the library done by 34 students in two honors sections of English composition. The course instructor, who uses both directed and undirected free writes throughout the semester, assigned two free writes on the library: one at the beginning of the semester and one near the end of the semester. To assist the students in the completion of those course assignments that were designed to require use of the library, the instructor also scheduled one class period in the middle of the semester as a formal bibliographic instruction session.

Several dominant themes emerged from the free writes done at the beginning of the semester. Most of the papers expressed the idea that libraries are supposed to be self-explanatory and that one either can or cannot figure them out. The majority of students expressed frustration at not being able to master the university library after their first visit. For those unable to figure it out immediately there seemed to be only two options: either give up completely or go to a smaller, more familiar library. In fact even later on in the semester several students admitted that they had not used the university library at all to complete their course assignments, relying instead on the resources of their hometown public libraries.

There seem to have been four major stumbling blocks to students' understanding of and confidence in using the university library. First, the relatively large size of the building itself emerged as a primary source of fear and intimidation for most of them. Although Millersville's library (the only library on campus) houses approximately 400,000 volumes and is obviously nowhere near the size of a library at a major research institution, it is apparently many times larger than any library our students have ever seen or can imagine. Thirteen of the 34 students used words like "big," "large," "huge," "gigantic," "immense," and "overwhelming" to describe the library. Two typical reactions to the size of the building follow:

Right now when I think of the word library I think of the huge building on campus. I went to a little old high school where the library was about as big as my bedroom. Then I come here and I get an assignment where I have to go to the library to do research to write a paper. Four floors! My god, four floors!

I feel that the library is intimidating, especially to a freshman coming from a small school. It's larger than any of the buildings in my town or any of the towns near where I live.

The second obstacle to students' understanding of the library is its confusing system of organization or, in the case of one student, a perception that the library completely lacks a system of organization. Seventeen students included in their writing such expressions as "confusing," "complicated," "not so simple," and "can't figure it out" in describing the library. The following student's attitudes typify many responses in this regard:

The library can be a very complicated place until you have figured out where everything is and how to use it. Millersville's library left me in a daze for about a half an hour.

The third stumbling block to students' being able to use the library seems to stem from the fact that almost one third of them expressed strong reservations about and even hatred of libraries. Of the eleven students who admitted that they did not like libraries, most explained the reason as a previous "bad experience"— in one case being yelled at by a "spinster librarian." Most students who wrote that they disliked libraries associated them with the pressures of unfinished term papers and other assignments. One student's description was filled with very graphic imagery:

The library. Big, inhibiting. It looms over the campus like a giant. It is a huge reminder of the pressures and seemingly endless responsibilities of a research paper. It is a huge headache that never ends until you have finished your paper. It is a muscle that contracts in your stomach, making you nervous and sick to your stomach.

More than two thirds of the students did not express any particular hatred of libraries and seven, in fact, claimed to love them. Even these students, however, admitted feelings of confusion and fear upon their first encounters with the university library.

The fourth element in students' inability to understand the library was a very strong unwillingness to ask for help. Certainly no one likes to appear ignorant and unwillingness to ask for help is not an attitude unique to honors students. However, some of the students' frustrations and discomfort with the university library seemed to stem from a sense of pride that they, as students of superior intelligence and ability should be able to use all the resources of the library without any assistance from anyone. As stated earlier, the majority of students were obviously discouraged that they could not immediately figure out the university library on their own. Unable to catch on to the library's system the first time through, they envisioned only two alternatives: admit defeat and never set foot in the library again or continue to use their comfortable, albeit small, hometown libraries. Not one person suggested that asking questions of the reference librarians would be a good way to begin figuring out the library. In fact, one student seems to have considered the option of asking for help, but then immediately discounted it as a bad idea.

Sometimes I get a little bit intimidated because I don't know where everything is and I don't like to ask and sound like an idiot.

All of this ties in with one feature that stood out glaringly in the free writes done at the beginning of the semester. Only two students even mentioned librarians when writing about libraries and these were extremely negative comments. Again, these attitudes conform to most students' perceptions of libraries solely as enormous buildings filled with books rather than as places where a variety of services are provided.

In planning for the hour-long bibliographic instruction session, I took into account students' expressed fears, apprehensions, confusion, and downright hatred for the library. Not only was it important to introduce students to the library and its resources in order to help them fulfill their course assignments, but I realized that it was essential to help them overcome their anxiety and, especially, to feel comfortable in asking questions of the reference librarians.

For the most part the free write done near the end of the semester were very encouraging. Only five students still had strong reservations about libraries, down substantially from the eleven who had expressed dislike for them at the beginning of the semester. Having had a formal orientation to the library and instruction in the use of specific resources, as well as having actually used the library to complete course assignments, only a few students used negative terms to describe the library. The majority of students, however, were more positive in their attitudes toward the library; twenty students actually wrote that they now found the library "much easier" to use than they had at the beginning of the semester. Students used such phrases as "helpful," "well-organized," "comfortable," and secure." Nine students actually commented on the helpfulness of the librarians. Typical of these responses is the following:

All in all, I couldn't have made it through this semester without the help of the kind librarians who were willing to help and the many resources Millersville's library has to offer.

Several students reflected on their own progress in overcoming their sense of confusion and intimidation in attempting to use the university library. Recognizing the fact that they were afraid to go near the library as new freshmen, they attributed most of their change in attitude four factors: 1) experience in using the library; 2) having formal instruction in the use of the library; 3) the helpfulness of various library personnel; and, especially, 4) being encouraged to ask questions. Two free writes reflect these views most articulately.

Although the lecture we were given on how to use the library did not clear up in my mind every aspect of the library and its sources, it did increase my knowledge of where to go and what to look for ... At least I am no longer hesitant to ask for help when I need it!

At the begining of this semester I felt really apprehensive about the library because I didn't know how to use everything or where all the materials were located. However, I was encouraged to ask questions if I needed help by the friendly and helpful library personnel, and now I feel that I can utilize a large majority of Ganser Library's resources.

This study confirmed the findings of previous studies[7] that students in honors programs do not necessarily know any more about libraries than other college students. In addition, the data reveal that all honors students do not automatically like libraries and that many of them find the university library to be an insurmountable obstacle in the way of their academic success. Constance Mellon has used free writes and qualitative analysis to determine that library anxiety is a major issue for the typical college freshman.[8] This study has shown that library anxiety may also be a major issue for freshmen in the university honors program.

The information gathered from this study has confirmed the hypothesis that there is definitely a need for bibliographic instruction in the university honors program. Although this conclusion was not unexpected, we did not anticipate the extent to which honors students feared the library and felt uncomfortable using it.

The course instructor was particularly impressed by the attitudes expressed by students about the library both in their first and second sets of free writes. As a result of the findings of this study, he has revised his syllabus, allowing students in his honors sections of English composition to become used to the university library more gradually than he had previously done. Prior to this study he had assigned only two compositions—both near the end of the semester—requiring use of rather complex library resources. Now he assigns three compositions requiring use of library resources. At least one of these writing assignments is due in the first half of the semester and is designed primarily to help students feel comfortable with the university library.

In addition, the course instructor has made a commitment to devote not one but two class periods to formal bibliographic instruction sessions. The first bibliographic instruction session, scheduled early in the semester, will afford the librarians an opportunity to alleviate students' anxiety and confusion about the library, orienting them to the physical structure of the library building and informing them about some of the services provided. Librarians will also use this time to introduce elementary concepts of library research as well as the mechanics of using such basic resources as the online catalog as access to the book collection and InfoTrac as access to the periodicals collection. The second bibliographic instruction session, scheduled after the midpoint of the semester, will allow time to introduce students to more complex library resources, such as the *MLA International Bibliography* and other specialized literary resources required for one of their writing assignments. The second session will also serve as a follow-up session, encouraging students, all of whom will have already had to use the library for at least one writing assignment, to discuss their experiences—both successes and frustrations—in using the university library. In both of these bibliographic instruction sessions students will be able to interact with the librarian and will be encouraged to ask questions.

The course instructor will continue to assign directed free writes about the library to students in honors sections of freshman composition and they will be analyzed to discover whether or not the attitudes expressed in this study continue to be typical of students in the university honors program. In the meantime, the librarians will continue to incorporate bibliographic instruction into the honors sections of freshman composition. The sessions will emphasize the helpfulness of the reference staff, assure students that their feelings of confusion are understood and they are not expected to be able to figure everything out on their own, and, especially, that encourages them to be willing to ask for assistance.

Endnotes

1. Martin Nemko, *How To Get an Ivy League Education at a State* University (New York, Avon Books, 1988).
2. Renee B. Bush and Margaret R. Wells, "Bibliographic Instruction for Honors Students: The University at Buffalo Experience," *Research Strategies* 8 (Summer, 1990): 137-143.
3. Myoung Chung Wilson and Kevin Mulcahy, "To Better the Best and Brightest Undergraduates," *College & Research Libraries News* 48 (December, 1987): 700, 702-703.
4. Myoung Chung Wilson, Ibid.
5. Sandra G. Yee, "The Role of the Academic Library in a University Honors Program," Paper presented at the Annual Meeting of the Michigan Academy of Arts, Science and Letters, Big Rapids, MI, March 23, 1984, p. 2 (ERIC Document ED243 399).
6. Constance A. Mellon, "Library Anxiety: A Grounded Theory and Its Development," *College & Research Libraries* 47 (March, 1986): 160-165.
7. Myoung Chung Wilson, op. cit.
8. Constance Mellon, op. cit.

The Academic Library Trainer and Instructional Design: Opinions and Practice[1]

Pat Weaver-Meyers and Jay C. Smith
University of Oklahoma
Norman, Oklahoma

Abstract

It can be strongly argued that any good library user training program about new technologies must begin with a well-trained library staff. In an effort to discover more about library staff training techniques, a descriptive study was conducted in which academic library department heads and staff development officers were surveyed to determine if they considered instructional design [ID] practices appropriate to academic library training. They were also asked whether they used ID practices when preparing training materials for induction, job or developmental training. Results revealed that respondents generally support the use of ID practices, but actually use them less frequently than they consider them appropriate. Lack of time and resources were cited frequently by respondents as possible reasons for lack of application. ID was considered less appropriate to induction training than the other two types of training. A relationship between gender and the use of ID and between level of research activity and some ID practices were revealed in correlations. The results suggest that more commitment from administrators may be necessary to insure optimal teaching strategies are employed by trainers to train library staff. Further inquiry on the effect of gender and training in libraries may suggest some new strategies for maximizing or equalizing the quality of training among trainers.

Introduction

Academic libraries today are dynamic environments. Rapid technological change and the advance of information science research are forcing libraries to adopt new computer applications and apply new methods of management. Coping with such rapid change requires the regular updating of library staff skills. Such updating places a significant demand on managers for efficient and effective training. Taking advantage of educational theory and practice is one way librarians can maximize their training abilities and insure that training materials they design function as expected. Stuart Glogoff and James Flynn support the use of androgogic learning theory, for example, in the establishment of a systematic training program for an integrated library system.[2] This study sought to determine if instructional design (ID), another such educational theory common to skills training, is being applied to library training. The aim of instructional design is well summarized by Charles Reigeluth and Ruth Curtis

The failure of so many instructional programs and materials has often been the result of an emphasis solely on content, with little regard for principles of instructional design to produce effective, efficient, and appealing instruction. A knowledge of instructional models that adapt to a variety of learning situations provides the foundation for optimizing learning outcomes.[3]

This study surveyed academic library department heads and staff development officers to determine if they consider instructional design practices appropriate to academic library staff development, and whether these middle managers use ID practices when preparing training materials The study also investigated if the use of ID practices differed with the type of training or with certain characteristics of the library trainer.

Design and Methodology

The survey instrument (Appendix) follows general guidelines specified in the literature on survey design and was developed with the assistance of the Research Bureau of the College of Education at the University of Oklahoma.[4] The ID questions in the survey were based primarily on practices forwarded by George Gropper and Paul Ross as currently accepted by instructional designers as well as on concepts supported by others.[5] The division of the questionnaire into three sections on ID was based on Jean Bird's study of library staff development which defines staff development in three ways: induction (orientation to library policies and practices), developmental (training to improve job performance or qualify for more responsibility), and job (training the skills and competencies of basic job function).[6] A scenario describing each type of staff development preceded each twelve-item section. There were two parts to each question, providing the respondent an opportunity to answer on a Likert-type scale, whether he/she believes the practice should be used and how likely he/she is to use the practice. A four point scale was used because during a field trial several academic librarians indicated it was adequate to represent their level of discrimination for the type of question posed.

The questionnaire's validity was examined in a pilot study conducted by administering a trial instrument to a group of academic librarians (n = 26) in an academic library at an institution in the southwest. Participants were asked to comment on any ambiguous, irrevelant or missing information. The survey was revised based on the data from the pilot study. In addition, questions were reviewed by three ID experts to determine that the selection of wording from the sources cited above was common to ID theory. The questionnaire employed a counter-balanced order-of-presentation for the three sections on ID and three different versions of the questionnaire were mailed randomly to participants. The three versions represented 30, 35 and 35 % of the useable respondent group. A one-way analysis of variance for the means of the twelve-item responses to actual use for each type of training was computed (Computations were made using SAS General Linear Models Procedure where means = dependent variables and questionnaire version = independent variable.) No statistically significant difference was found between the different orders-of-presentation represented by the three versions of the questionnaire for these items.

Instrument reliability was determined by calculating the coefficient alpha for responses to the same three sets of items concerning actual use of ID principles (questions B1-D12) using the formula specified by Jum Nunnally.[7] The coefficient alpha for questions B1-B12 (induction training) = .8449, for questions C1-C12 (job training) = .8348 and for questions D1-D12 (development training) = .8552 indicating an acceptable level of reliability.

Sample

The questionnaire was mailed to 210 academic li-

brarians employed as department heads or staff development/personnel officers in member libraries of the Association of Research Libraries with total staff between 250 and 350. The size limitations of the institutions were set because organizational innovation research in libraries indicates that organization size is a factor in the adoption of innovation and because Jean Bird's study of public library authorities in the United Kingdom showed that staff size is a factor in the type and number of staff development programs within institutions.[8] Department heads or staff development/personnel officers were specified because it was deemed likely that they would have some direct experience as trainers and because Ruth Person's study of role concepts in middle managers in academic and public libraries include: monitor, disseminator and technical expert as important components of role involvement.[9] Each of these categories relates, in part, to training.

Data Collection and Analysis

Two mailings of the three randomly distributed versions of the questionnaire produced 109 useable responses for a return rate of 52 %.

Demographics. All department head positions listed in the questionnaire are represented in the pool of respondents. The least represented position is serials department head, which accounted for eight percent. The most frequently represented position is circulation/access services department head, which accounts for 20%. Several other position titles are represented by the "other" category such as library director, assistant director, and acting head. These titles account for 14%.

The mean of responses for number of years as a professional librarian is 13 years, while five years is the average length of time in present position. The responses to gender indicate that 35% are male and 65% female. Sixty percent had ID experience. The most frequent source of experience is a staff development program provided by an employer.

Research activity responses indicated a majority are active. The mean response to number of book reviews published is three. Four articles is the average number published. Most respondents had given a number of presentations, with the average being four. Professional activity responses averaged four meetings for the previous year and two offices held.

These demographics compare favorably with other

research, indicating that although there was a 48% non-response, the pool of respondents is representative of the population. Specifically, Barbara Moran found that ARL department heads were 43.1% male and 56.9% female in 1982 with trends indicating that the percentage of females in department head positions was increasing.[10] General statistics show that 65% of academic librarians were female in 1982.[11] Also, Betty Irvine's study of ARL administrators parallel the publishing activity of this study's respondents.[12]

Results. Tables 1-3 display the means of responses to both the *should be* and *actual* categories of questions about use of ID practices. Table 1 shows the responses to the questions based on the induction training scenario.

Table 2 is a summary of responses to the job training scenario and Table 3 summarizes the developmental training responses. A comparison of the three tables reveals that responses to induction training are the least supportive of ID practices, but that even for induction training, respondents strongly supported the use of ID practices. The overall mean of all twelve responses for *should be* was 3.06 for induction training and 3.28 for both job and developmental training. The overall mean of all twelve responses for *actual* use was 2.34 for induction training and 2.51 for both job and developmental training. Generally, then, respondents indicated that ID practices should be used, but are less convinced that they should be used for induction training. Also, respondents indicate little, if any, difference in their support of the use of ID for job and developmental training.

To determine if there is any relationship between the demographic data and the responses to the questions, a Pearson Product-Moment Correlation matrix was constructed using SAS correlation procedures. The resulting r coefficients are reported in Tables 4-6. Although a total of 125 statistically significant values resulted in the three matrices (induction, job and developmental), only those demographic variables with two or more statistically significant correlations per type of training were deemed practically significant and therefore included in the tables.

Discussion. Although the results displayed in tables 1-6 indicate a myriad of statistically significant relationships, the following general conclusions answer the questions posed by the study or represent the relationships with the strongest correlations. Do academic library trainers support the use of ID and do they actually apply ID in the development of their programs? Respondents generally support the use of ID practices in all three types of training, but do not apply ID as frequently as they indicate it would be appropriate.

Are there differences in the application of these practices to induction, job or developmental training? ID is considered less appropriate to and is actually applied less frequently to induction training than to job or developmental training. Do any demographic characteristics of trainers affect their view or application of ID to library training? Gender consistently correlates with both use of ID and respondents' opinions about ID. Females tend to view ID practices more favorably and use them more frequently. In addition, the respondents' research activity affects their views about and application of ID. Specifically, developmental training differs from induction and job training with respect to respondents' research activity. Research activity negatively correlates with responses to *should be* and *actual* use for several different ID practices concerning developmental training. The same negative correlation was not present in responses to induction or job training.

In analyzing what might be the reasons for respondents support for but limited use of ID, the comment section of the questionnaire was reviewed. The most frequent comment related to why respondents applied practices less frequently than they felt they should be applied. Specifically, lack of time, resources and support were cited more than any other factors.

The suggestion that lack of time and organization support may be a primary factor in lack of application of ID has implications for library administrators. A legitimate explanation may be that adoption of more automation is markedly increasing the need for training by middle managers, as some authors suggest.[13] If so, it appears that academic libraries are not organizationally flexible enough to compensate quickly and reorganize job responsibilities to free middle managers for increased training needs or that administrators have yet to acknowledge and give priority to this development.

Another possible explanation relates to library education. The inability of respondents to recognize less formal application of ID practices as appropriate reflects on their background in ID education. More training in how to train may be necessary at the library

Table 1. Mean of Responses to "Should Be" and "Actual" categories
for Induction Training Scenario

ID Practice	n	Should Be		Actual	
		M	SD	M	SD
Needs Analysis					
1	107	3.11	1.07	2.43	1.07
Task Description					
2	106	2.86	1.03	2.25	1.04
Task Analysis					
3	108	2.92	1.02	2.18	.97
4	108	3.45	.77	2.97	.98
Sequencing					
5	106	3.44	.79	2.99	.99
Objective Writing					
6	107	2.93	.99	2.07	1.01
Test Construction					
7	106	2.39	1.09	1.63	.89
Instructional Strat.					
8	108	3.32	.86	2.63	1.04
Materials Dev.					
9	108	2.97	.97	2.10	1.07
Formative Eval.					
10	108	2.76	1.07	1.97	1.02
11	108	3.27	.89	2.41	.99
Summative Eval.					
12	107	3.38	.79	2.54	.99

Note: Means were determined using the scale: Rarely = 1, Occasionally = 2, Frequently = 3, Almost Always = 4.

Table 2. Mean of Responses to "Should Be" and "Actual" categories
for Job Training Scenario

ID Practice	n	Should be		Actual	
		M	SD	M	SD
Needs Analysis					
1	106	3.57	.69	2.95	.92
Task Description					
2	108	3.06	.95	2.52	1.05
Task Analysis					
3	109	3.31	.81	2.56	1.00
4	107	3.45	.80	2.90	1.00
Sequencing					
5	109	3.63	.64	3.21	.84
Objective Writing					
6	109	3.40	.72	2.56	1.06
Test Construction					
7	107	2.75	1.03	1.74	.88
Instructional Strat.					
8	108	3.41	.78	2.74	1.08
Materials Dev.					
9	107	3.03	.87	2.20	1.05
Formative Eval.					
10	108	2.75	1.04	1.78	.91
11	108	3.46	.72	2.38	.97
Summative Eval.					
12	108	3.54	.67	2.66	.90

Note: Means were determined using the scale: Rarely = 1, Occasionally = 2, Frequently = 3, Almost Always = 4.

Table 3. Mean of Responses to "Should Be" and "Actual" categories
for Developmental Training Scenario

ID Practice	n	Should be		Actual	
		M	SD	M	SD
Needs Analysis					
1	107	3.53	.73	2.83	.96
Task Description					
2	107	3.21	.86	2.68	.95
Task Analysis					
3	107	3.40	.78	2.65	.98
4	108	3.60	.70	3.10	.88
Sequencing					
5	108	3.46	.79	3.01	.92
Objective Writing					
6	108	3.33	.76	2.45	1.01
Test Construction					
7	108	2.68	1.01	1.82	.91
Instructional Strat.					
8	108	3.44	.75	2.70	.99
Materials Dev.					
9	108	3.07	.92	2.10	1.03
Formative Eval.					
10	108	2.75	.97	1.82	.93
11	108	3.39	.79	2.44	.94
Summative Eval.					
12	108	3.49	.69	2.59	.92

Note: Means were determined using the scale: Rarely = 1, Occasionally = 2,
Frequently = 3, Almost Always = 4.

Table 4, Correlation Coefficients for Demographic Variables and "Should Be" "Actual" categories (Induction Training Scenario)

ID Practice present	Master's	Yrs. Exp.	Gender	No ID Dev.	CE	Staff	position
Needs Analysis							
1S		.21008					
1A			.23218				
Task Description							
2S		.20719					
2A						.20809	
Task Analysis							
3S					-.21809		
3A			.20812				
4S				.32645			
4A				.30147			
Sequencing							
5A				.26365			
Test Construction							
7S					-.19359		.24417
7A	-.28262				-.19316	.20053	
Instructional Strat.							
8S	.22894			.22103			
11A						.26642	
Summative Eval.							
12S				.21085			.19082
12A	-.25332						

Note: Only those variables with two or more statistically significant correlations have been deemed practically significant and are included in this table. S = should be, A = actual, $\underline{p} < .05 = \underline{r} > \pm\ .187$

Table 5. Correlation Coefficients for Demographic Variables and "Should Be"
"Actual" categories (Job Training Scenario)

ID Practice	Master's	Gender	CE	"Other" ID Exp	Meetings Attended
Needs Analysis					
1S	.21467				
1A		.21135			
Task Description					
2S	.19143	.23386			
2A		.24138	.23035		.21615
Task Analysis					
3S		.24622			
3A		.31137	.26072		
4S	.33950	.31686			
4A	.23894	.19472			
Sequencing					
5S		.44082			
5A		.40333			
Objective Writing					
6A			.20324		
Test Construction					
7A	-.20701			.27935	
Instructional Strat.					
8S		.23061			.21092
Materials Dev.					
9S					.22384
Formative Eval.					
10A				.21765	
11S		.32586			.19940
11A		.23271	.27785		
Summative Eval.					
12S		.22298			
12A	-.25332			.19225	

Note: Only those variables with two or more statistically significant correlations have been deemed practically significant and are included in this table. S = should be, A = actual, $p < .05 = r > \pm .187$

Table 6. Correlation Coefficients for Demographic Variables and "Should Be" "Actual" categories (Developmental Training Scenario)

ID Practice	Prof. Exp.	Gender	CE	"Other" ID Exp.	Book Reviews	Articles	Mono-graphs	Pre-senta-tions
Needs Analysis								
1S		.22502						
1A		.26235	.26324			-.21340		
Task Description								
2S		.20014					-.26316	
2A			.30637					-.28075
Task Analysis								
3S							-.37221	-.19336
3A	.20230	.22128				-.20878	-.21753	-.25189
4S	-.20082							
Sequencing								
4A		.25874						
5S		.32780		-.23707		-.20457		
5A		.45762				-.22496		
Objective Writing								
6S		.23960		-.30977	-.31337	-.38032		
6A					-.19963	-.29447		-.23533
7S				-.22730		-.20553	-.33358	
Test Construction								
7A								
8S		.29620						
Instructional Strat.								
8A		.21840						
9S		.28189			-.21280			
Materials Dev.								
10A	.22031							
11S		.26033			-.32647		-.24515	
11A		.29642		.26415	-.19574			
Summative Eval.								
12S					-.26037		-.19940	
12A				.24938				

Note: Only those variables with two or more statistically significant correlations have been deemed practically significant and are included in this table. S = should be, A = actual, $p < .05 = r > \pm .187$

school level or at the continuing education level.

The second conclusion, which notes the difference in induction training and the other two types of training may be related to commentary which emphasizes that induction training does not require such formal materials development procedures. Also, several comments on lack of attention to student personnel with high turnover rates suggest that time and emphasis may limit training in areas not directly task - related. Since use of ID in induction training appears to be less important, limited funding may be better spent by administrators on training materials for developmental or job training.

One theory which may explain the gender differentiation is suggested by discussions of Robert Swisher, Rosemary Dumont and Calvin Boyer, i.e. that feminine qualities of nurturing and helpfulness relate to sex differentiation among librarians.[14] Since training intensely employs these qualities, it may be feminine self-concept underscores why males with presumably weaker feminine self-concept are less supportive of ID practices. Swisher, Dumont and Boyer suggest that males strong in feminine qualities may be drawn to librarianship. However, this study tends to suggest that although they may be stronger in feminine qualities than the non-librarian population, they still retain a significantly less nurturing or helpful orientation than females. If further research proves such a relationship, library education will need to stress such qualities in the training sphere, particularly for male trainers.

Another research effort by Charles Skipper suggests that preservice teachers' preference for college lesson plans differed with the gender of the teacher.[15] Females preferred more structured learning activities such as class discussions, workbooks and viewing films. Males preferred independent learning and oral reports. This appears to agree with the findings of this study in that females support more strongly the structured, organized approach represented by ID.

The last conclusion, which relates negative correlations with research activity and developmental training are puzzling. Perhaps research-active librarians see developmental training as a responsibility of the individual, not the supervisor. If so, research-active librarians may unconsciously stymie in-house staff development activities for developmental training and orient subordinates to continuing education provided by professional associations. This may underlie why

some academic libraries provide so little in-house staff development beyond induction and job training.

Overall, comments emphasized the lack of resources available for staff development and the increasing desire and need by staff for more training opportunities. Some respondents felt experienced employees needed more attention, while others believed student assistants and staff did not get the attention professionals were afforded. Respondents also stated that they did not feel adequately trained in staff development methods. A few indicated they were knowlegeable, but found strong resistance from colleagues when attempting to employ ID practices during materials development.

In conclusion, this study found that most middle managers and staff development officers in mid-size ARL libraries supported the use of ID practices, but did not actually use practices as frequently as they indicated would be appropriate. Providing an environment which supports the use of ID and other training techniques, might help librarians cope with the increasing training needs which result from constant change. This study suggests that time and resources are currently insufficient to support the implementation of these and perhaps other learning theories which might improve training efficiency. In addition, some important differences were found in correlations with respondent gender and type of training. In particular, the use of ID techniques by females suggests that male trainers may not be as likely to implement learning theories in their training program planning. Additional research to determine if this disparity between males and females applies to other situations is important to developing the most efficient and effective trainers.

As training needs in libraries continue to expand, the importance of competent trainers will continue to grow. Trainers knowledgeable about learning theory, with sufficient time and resources to apply such theories, will ensure that the quality of training keeps pace with demand.

Endnotes

1. The authors wish to acknowledge the editorial assistance of Jennifer Goodson.
2. Stuart Glogoff and James P. Flynn, "Developing a Systematic In-house Training Program for Integrated Library Systems," *College & Research Libraries* 48 (November, 1987): 528-53.

3. Charles M. Reigeluth and Ruth V. Curtis, "Learning Situations and Instructional Models," in *Instructional Technology: Foundations*, ed. Robert M. Gagne (Hillsdale, NJ: Lawrence Erlbaum Associates, 1987) p. 202.

4. Floyd J. Fowler, *Survey Research Methods* (Beverly Hills, CA: Sage, 1984); Peter H. Rossi, James D. Wright, and Andy B. Anderson, *Handbook of Survey Research* (New York: Academic Press, 1983).

5. George L. Gropper and Paul A. Ross, "Instructional Design," in *Training and Development Handbook: A Guide to Human Resource Development*, 3rd ed., ed. Robert L. Craig, (New York: McGraw-Hill, 1987) p. 195-216; Robert H. Davis, Lawrence T. Alexander, and Stephen L. Yelon, *"Learning System Design: An Approach to the Improvement of Instruction* (New York: McGraw-Hill, 1974); Leslie J. Briggs, "Introduction," in *Instructional Design*, edited by Leslie J. Briggs, (Englewood Cliffs, NJ: Educational Technology Publications, 1977) p. 5-18; Philip M. Turner, "Instructional Design Competencies Taught at Library Schools," *Journal of Education for Librarianship* 22 (Spring, 1982): 275-282; Barbara L. Martin, "Internalizing Instructional Design," *Educational Technology* 24 (May, 1984): 13-18.

6. Jean Bird, *In-service Training in Public Library Authorities*, (London: Library Association, 1986) British Library Research and Development Reports 5898.

7. Jum C. Nunnally, *Psychometric Theory* (New York: McGraw-Hill, 1978), p. 212.

8. Fariborz Damanpour and Thomas Childers, "The Adoption of Innovations in Public Libraries," *Library and Information Science Research* 7 (July, 1985): 231-246; Jean Bird, op. cit. p. 10.

9. Ruth J. Person, "Middle Managers in Academic and Public Libraries: Managerial Role Concepts" (Ph.D. diss., University of Michigan, 1980), p. 118.

10. Barbara B. Moran, "The Impact of Affirmative Action on Academic Libraries," *Library Trends* 34 (Fall, 1985): 199-217.

11. *Library Human Resources: A Study of Supply and Demand* (Chicago: American Library Association, 1983), p. 41.

12. Ibid, p. 44; Betty J. Irvine, *Sex Segregation in Librarianship: Demographic and Career Patterns of Academic Library Administrators*, (Contributions in Librarianship and Information Science (Greenwood Press, 1985).

13. Pat Weaver-Meyers and Nedria Santizo, "The Effect of Automation on the Rate of Change in Procedures," in *Energies for Transition: Proceedings of the Fourth National Conference of the Association of College and Research Libraries*, edited by Danuta A. Nitecki, p. 240-242 (Chicago: Association of College and Research Libraries, 1986); H. J. Hagedorn, "After the Information Revolution: Training as a Way of Life for Line Managers," *Management Review* 73 (July, 1984): 8-13.

14. Robert D. Swisher, Rosemary Ruhig DuMont, and Calvin James Boyer, "The Motivation to Manage: A Study of Academic Librarians and Library Science Students," *Library Trends* 34 (Fall, 1985): 219-234.

15. Charles E. Skipper, "Gender Differences in Preservice Teachers' Preference for College Learning Activities," Paper presented at the annual meeting of the American Educational Research Association, New Orleans, April 1988. ED 299223.

Survey on the Use of Instructional Design
in Academic Library Staff Development Materials

This questionnaire has been designed to investigate the use of instructional design practices in the creation or selection of training materials in academic library staff development. Information you provide will remain completely confidential, so please reply candidly.

1) Your position:

                      _____a. staff development/personnel officer
                      _____b. reference dept. head
                      _____c. circulation/access dept. head
                      _____d. serial dept. head
                      _____e. cataloging dept. head
                      _____f. acquisitions dept. head
                      _____g. collection development dept. head
                      _____h. other (please specify)_____

2) What degrees do you hold? (Check all that apply)

      _____a. Associate   _____b. Bachelor   _____c. Master
  _____d. sixth year certificate   _____e. 2nd Masters   _____f. Doctorate

3) How many years of experience in professional library positions did you have at the end of 1988? _____ How many years in present position? _____

4) Your gender: _____ Male   _____ Female

5) Have you ever attended a course that presented instructional design (i.e. task analysis, performance objectives, formative evaluation, etc.) concepts? (Please check all that apply)

                      _____ have never attended such a course
                      _____ continuing education opportunity provided by
                                a professional association
                      _____ university or college credit course
                      _____ staff development program or seminar organized by your
                                employer
                      _____ other (please specify) _____

6) Please indicate the level of your research activity by listing the number of contributions already made or currently accepted since the beginning of your professional career.

                      Number
                      _____ Book reviews
                      _____ Articles, book chapters or published papers
                      _____ Monographs (edited or authored)
                      _____ Presentations at professional meetings

7) Please indicate the level of your professional activity by listing the number of meetings attended or offices held in 1988.

                      _____ professional meetings attended (state and national only)
                      _____ offices held in professional associations (committee or task
                              force memberships included)

The following questions pertain to staff development/training. There are three sections, which repeat questions concerning instructional design for three different training scenarios. In the first column, please indicate, placing a circle round the letter which indicates the degree to which you believe each practice describes what *should be* part of the design or selection of training materials. In the second column, indicate the degree to which you believe the practice describes what you *actually* do when designing or selecting training materials, considering the limited resources (time, expertise, funding) available.

Please answer this section by assuming that you are faced with the need to prepare or select materials to train experienced employees to improve their performance or broaden their ability to handle more responsibilities. Some examples would be: Stress or time management training, use of new software for a microcomputer or cross-training.

R = Rarely   O = Occasionally   F = Frequently   A = Almost Always
    (0-25%)   (26-50%)   (51-75%)   (76-100%)

Do you: Should be   Actual

B1) Identify the problem by defining the gaps between current and expected skill or knowledge levels?   R O F A   R O F A

B2) Gather data by observing or consulting with experts on tasks required of new or existing jobs?   R O F A   R O F A

B3) Identify learning requirements and forecast potential learning difficulties?   R O F A   R O F A

B4) Analyze the audience, conditions and relevant resources available?   R O F A   R O F A

B5) Identify the relationships between tasks and topics and arrange them in the order they are to be learned?   R O F A   R O F A

B6) Review the task description and formulate descriptions of performance which serve as learning objectives. These should include skills required to begin training and the skills expected as the outcome of training?   R O F A   R O F A

B7) Develop a test to simulate the same performance described in the objectives and decide what is an acceptable level of proficiency?   R O F A   R O F A

B8) Select an approach (lecture, slide/tape, hands-on) that can accommodate the learning requirements imposed by skills and audience characteristics?   R O F A   R O F A

R = Rarely   O = Occasionally   F = Frequently   A = Almost Always
(0-25%)   (26-50%)   (51-75%)   (76-100%)

Should beActual

B9) Construct prototypes of the instructional materials based on decisions made in the previous steps?   R O F A   R O F A

B10) Try out materials on a sample audience?   R O F A   R O F A

B11) Devise a way to evaluate the feedback and
revise the materials accordingly?   R O F A   R O F A

B12) Evaluate the effectiveness of the instructional
materials in your training situation after
implementation?   R O F A   R O F A

Please answer this section by assuming that you are faced with the need to prepare or select materials to train new employees to perform the basic functions of their job such as: using OCLC, answering reference questions, filling interlibrary loans, or preparing book orders.

Do you:

C1) Identify the problem by defining the gaps
between current and expected skill or
knowledge levels?   R O F A   R O F A

C2) Gather data by observing or consulting with
experts on tasks required of new or existing jobs?   R O F A   R O F A

C3) Identify learning requirements for job tasks and
forecast potential learning difficulties?   R O F A   R O F A

C4) Analyze the audience, conditions and relevant
resources available?   R O F A   R O F A

C5) Identify the relationships between tasks and topics
and arrange them in the order they are to be
learned?   R O F A   R O F A

C6) Review the task description and formulate
descriptions of performance which serve as
learning objectives. These should include skills
required to begin training and the skills expected
as the outcome of training?   R O F A   R O F A

R = Rarely (0-25%)	O = Occasionally (26-50%)	F = Frequently (51-75%)	A = Almost Always (76-100%)

	Should be	Actual

C7) Develop a test to simulate the same performance
described in the objectives and decide what is
an acceptable level of proficiency?   R O F A   R O F A

C8) Select an approach (lecture, slide/tape, hands-on)
that can accommodate the learning requirements imposed by the job skills and audience
characteristics?   R O F A   R O F A

C9) Construct prototypes of the instructional materials
based on decisions made in the previous steps?   R O F A   R O F A

C10) Try out materials on a sample audience? R O F A   R O F A

C11) Devise a way to evaluate the feedback and
     revise the materials accordingly? R O F A   R O F A

C12) Evaluate the effectiveness of the instructional
     materials in your training situation after
     implementation? R O F A   R O F A

Please answer this section by assuming that you are faced with the need to prepare or select materials to orient new staff members to the various departments in the library, introduce them to basic library personnel policies and provide them with an overview of the library organization.

Do you:

D1) Identify the problem by defining the gaps
     between current and expected skill or knowledge
     levels? R O F A   R O F A

D2) Gather data by observing or consulting with
     experts on tasks required of new or existing jobs? R O F A   R O F A

D3) Identify learning requirements for job tasks and
     forecast potential learning difficulties? R O F A   R O F A

D4) Analyze the audience, conditions and relevant
     resources available? R O F A   R O F A

R = Rarely (0-25%)	O = Occasionally (26-50%)	F = Frequently (51-75%)	A = Almost Always (76-100%)

                                        Should be   Actual

D5) Identify the relationships between tasks and topics
     and arrange them in the order they are to be
     learned? R O F A   R O F A

D6) Review the task description and formulate
     descriptions of performance which serve as
     learning objectives. These should include skills
     required to begin training and the skills expected
     as the outcome of training? R O F A   R O F A

D7) Develop a test to simulate the same performance
     described in the objectives and decide what is
     an acceptable level of proficiency? R O F A   R O F A

D8) Select an approach (lecture, slide/tape, hands-on)
     that can accommodate the learning require-
     ments imposed by the job skills and audience
     characteristics? R O F A   R O F A

D9) Construct prototypes of the instructional materials based on decisions made in the previous steps?   R O F A   R O F A

D10) Try out materials on a sample audience?   R O F A   R O F A

D11) Devise a way to evaluate the feedback and revise the materials accordingly?   R O F A   R O F A

D12) Evaluate the effectiveness of the instructional materials in your training situation after implementation?   R O F A   R O F A

Do you have any comments about your experiences with staff development and training?

_____

_____

_____

_____

Please return the completed questionnaire by Sept. 15th in the self-addressed, stamped envelope provided. Thank you.

CONTRIBUTED PAPERS

IV.
COLLECTION MANAGEMENT AND DEVELOPMENT

Achieving Academic Excellence in Higher Education Through Improved Research Library Collections: Using OCLC/AMIGOS Collection Analysis CD for Collection Building[1]

Suzanne D. Gyeszly
Gary Allen
Charles R. Smith
Texas A & M University
College Station, Texas

Abstract

Excellence in higher education depends heavily on the quality of academic libraries. As available funds shrink, however, more cost effective and finely tuned collection building must be used to support existing and new academic programs. With this goal in mind, a questionaire was sent to department heads and departmental library representatives a Texas A&M University to gather information related to current and projected curriculum and research directions. The forecasted areas of emphasis for each department were converted to Library of Congress call number ranges to be analyzed by the OCLC/AMIGOS Collection Analysis CD. Once the strengths and weaknesses of the collection were determined, the results of the analysis were used to modify collection development policies and to generate lists of materials to fill gaps. The study provides a model for libraries which plan to evaluate and improve their own collections.

Background

Texas A&M University, a land, sea, and space grant institution was established in 1876 with primary emphasis on agriculture, engineering, and military science. After modest growth fro a century, the university expanded, and a variety of academic specialties were offered. The student enrollment rapidly increased from 14,200 in 1971, to 41,171 by the fall of 1990.

The university currently has 33,204 undergraduate, 7,320 graduate, and 647 professional students (human and veterinary medicine). Growth in enrollment has leveled off, and the university is now aiming for a higher proportion of graduate students. Two thousand, thirty-nine FTE faculty teach in ten colleges: Agriculture and Life Sciences, Architecture, Business Administration and Graduate Schools of Business, Education, Engineering, Geosciences, Liberal Arts, Medicine, Sciences, and Veterinary Medicine. The University has two libraries: the Medical Sciences Library supports the Colleges of Medicine and Veterinary Medicine; the Sterling C. Evans Library supports the curriculum, research, and program needs for the remaining eight colleges. Discussion in this paper refer to the Sterling C. Eavns Library.

The library's strong collections in science, engineering, and agriculture reflect the traditional strengths of Texas A&M University. Holdings in these disciplines, as well as in liberal arts, business, and other programs increased rapidly during the past two decades.

Current holdings of the Sterling C. Evans Library include 1,899,924 volumes, 3,807,197 microforms, and 14,359 serial titles. In addition, maps, special collections, governments documents, and archival materials are important sources for users.

The library funds and expenditures for materials have not kept up with the student enrollment, increased faculty demands, skyrocketing serials prices, escalating monograph expenses, double digit inflation, and declining state support during the past two decades. The total library budget, expenditures for materials, and materials' expenditures per student during the last twenty years are displayed in Table 2.

In 1971 an average of $41.60 was spent for materials per student compared to $89.40 in 1990. However, the buying power of the $41.60 was, of course, much higher in 1971 than the larger figure twenty years later.

STUDENT ENROLLMENT AT TEXAS
A&M UNIVERSITY
1971-1990

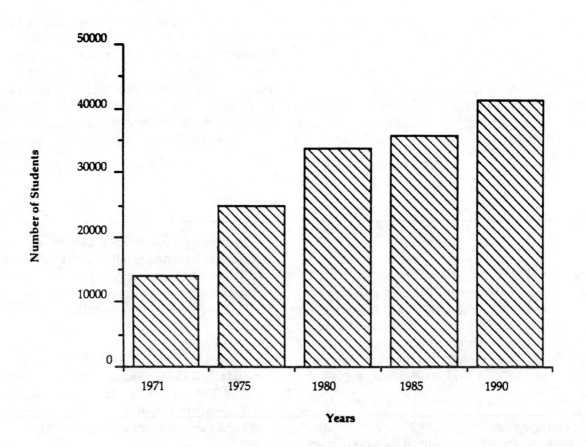

Figure 1

STERLING C. EVANS LIBRARY HOLDINGS
1971-1990

Years	Volumes (Monographs, documents, serials, technical reports)	Microforms (Microfiche, film, prints)	Serials	Maps
1971/72	768,366	524,286	12,922	24,246
1975/76	1,027,458	885,699	15,545	N/A
1980/81	1,358,220	1,815,811	14,438	67,219
1985/86	1,666,368	3,075,667	15,113	116,501
1989/90	1,899,924	3,807,197	14,359	144,075

Table 1

STERLING C. EVANS LIBRARY
FUNDS AND EXPENDITURES
1971-1990

Years	Library Funds (State appropriations, TAMU special appropriation, federal funds, gifts, and others)	Expenditures for Library Materials (Separates, serials, binding)	Materials Expenditures per Student
1971/72	1,605,550	591,556	$41.60
1975/76	3,093,422	1,429,856	57.40
1980/81	4,735,525	1,765,503	52.70
1985/86	8,984,141	3,511,999	98.30
1989/90	8,949,216	3,682,556	89.40

Table 2

Problem Statement

Excellence of the university curriculum and research depends heavily on the quality of the library. Good collections, however, are becoming more effective and finely tuned collection development practices must be used to support existing and new programs.

Texas A&M University has formulated a five year (1990-95) strategic plan for curriculum and research. To be sure the library collection takes a strengths and weaknesses in terms of projected departmental needs was under6aken by the researchers. The strategic plan created several problems related to the library.

— Collection development policies needed revision to reflect projected curriculum and research as well as current "hidden" research.
— Policies required revisions to reflect an increased emphasis on research as the university moves toward more graduate programs and increased graduate enrollments.
— Collection evaluations in new areas of emphasis were required to determine strengths to be built on and weaknesses to be corrected.

Methodology

To solve the problems, the researchers sent out a survey to all academic department heads and to faculty library representatives to learn about each department's current and projected curriculum and research. (Figure 2)Responses were received from 43 departments or 71.7 percent.

The five year strategic plan of the university, because of its breadth, consists of general principles only; thus each department's "interpretation" and method of implementation of these overriding principles was necessary information to the researcher. Once the current and projected curricula and research topics were determined by the survey, they were converted to Library of Congress Subject Headings and appropriate call numbers and/or ranges using CDMARC Subject and NOTIS. These ranges were then compared with the holdings of the peer institutions' libraries using OCLC/AMIGOS Collection Analysis CD.

Analysis of the Data

The OCLC/AMIGOS Collection Analysis CD allowed the researchers to both evaluate the Sterling C. Evans Library collection and prepare for collection development at several levels. Comparing the Evans Library collection with those of a group of ten peer libraries, (Figure 3) one measure of collection adequacy could be made.

In addition, lists of materials to be acquired could be generated for different levels of funding. For example, a list of books found in 80-90 percent of the peer group libraries but not owned by Texas A&M, would likely be the highest priority for acquisition when funding i[s available.

This method provides a mechanism for setting purchase priorities. The generated list of priority acquisitions were checked on NOTIS in order to eliminate a few reprints and older editions of titles already owned. A check on *Books in Print Plus* showed most titles as still available. A self-evident, but nevertheless important aspect of the study was the testing of the Collection Analysis CD as an evaluation and collection development tool.

The next step of the evaluation of the collection using the Collection Analysis CD was a comparison of broad ranges of raw call numbers. It is important to note that the records contained on the Collection Analysis CD cover only titles with 1978-1988 imprints. Collection counts (Table 4) are limited to call number ranges used for the National Shelf List Count.

For each call number range there are three main groups of information: peer group, evaluator, and overlap (Table 4). Under "Peer Group-Titles" within each call number division, the total number of titles held by all peer libraries are listed. For example, in the call number range H-HZ, there are 120,364 titles. In the next category, under "Peer Group-Holdings"- the number of all volumes are counted. Thus, if three libraries hold the same title, it is counted three times. For H-HZ this number is 397,699. This final category lists the "Peer Group-Unique" records, the number of titles which are held by only one of the peer libraries. In H-HZ this number is 48,661. The next group consists of only one category called "Evaluations Titles." This gives the total number of titles held by the home institution; in this case 36,606. A comparison between this number and the peer group number of titles is of very limited value and gives only the roughest impression of how the collection compares with those of other institutions., The next group of statistics—"Overlap"—which shows the overlap of

Projected Departmental Curriculum and Research Survey
based on strategic plan 1990-95

1 Department	2. Name

3. Current curriculum strengths by subject

- -

- -

4 Projected curriculum trends by subject

- -

- -

5. Current research strenghts by subject

- -

- -

6. Projected research trends by subject

- -

- -

7. New courses to be taught 1991-93

8. Preferable format for materials (1, most preferable, to 5, least preferable)

____ Monograph	____ Software	____ Videotape
____ Serial	____ CD-ROM	____ Other:
____ Online data base	____ Micorform	_____

Please attach additional sheets as needed. Your time and effort spent in completing this survey are very much appreciated. Please return by January 28, 1991 to:
Suzanne D. Gyeszly
Collection Development Coordinator
Resource Development Division
Evans Library
Mail stop 5000

Figure 2

Ten Selected Peer Groups of the
Sterling C. Evans Library

University of Arizona
University of Georgia
University of Illinois at Urbana-Champaign
Iowa State University
University of Minnesota-Twin Cities
University of Oklahoma
Pennsylvania State University
Purdue University
Texas A&M University

Figure 3

COLLECTION HOLDINGS DISTRIBUTION

Division		Holdings Range	Evaluator	Peer Group	Average Member	Peer	Average Member
HD1-HD0100		90-100%	279	297	297	0.94	0.94
Economics: Production		80-89%	430	458	412	0.94	1.04
		70-79%	380	428	342	0.89	1.11
Current:		60-69%	301	362	253	0.83	1.19
Peer Holdings	24,302	50-59%	277	405	243	0.68	1.14
Overlap Holdings	16,710	40-49%	248	408	204	0.61	1.22
Evaluator Titles	2,674	30-39%	265	461	184	0.57	1.44
Comparative Size	110%	20-29%	181	485	146	0.37	1.22
		10-19%	143	746	149	0.19	0.96
		1-09%	112	112	11	1.00	10.00
		Unique	58	1,879	188	0.03	0.31
TOTAL		0-100%	2674	6,041	2,430	0.43	1.08

Table 3

COLLECTION COUNTS

Division	Peer Group			Evaluator	Overlap	
	Titles	Holdings	Unique	Titles	Titles	Holdings
A-AZ	3,321	7,272	1,731	398	347	1,902
B-BJ	20,782	77,408	6,891	6,433	6,284	43,656
BL-BX	30,412	76,666	14,500	3,913	3,621	20,840
C-CZ	5,413	13,278	2,820	970	875	5,232
D-DZ	64,372	162,992	31,607	10,161	9,709	60,355
E-FZ	28,158	84,548	12,036	7,374	6,667	43,746
G-GZ	22,121	62,911	9,371	6,945	6,273	33,092
H-HZ	120,364	397,699	48,661	36,606	35,079	226,987
J-JZ	19,680	63,512	8,037	5,259	5,108	35,032
K-KC	7,438	14,319	4,683	855	829	4,412
KD-KDK	1,010	2,480	534	263	251	1,236
KE-KEZ	563	917	370	72	66	202
KF-KFS	11,855	31,581	5,709	3,934	3,375	16,882
L-LZ	19,736	74,448	6,454	6,915	6,593	42,941
M-MZ	11,887	37,887	4,574	1,422	1,374	9,355
N-NZ	37,083	101,419	15,861	7,451	7,041	39,585
P-PA	10,252	38,328	2,997	2,340	2,286	16,569
PB-PH	32,460	71,697	16,907	2,727	2,281	13,161
PJ-PM	29,902	47,746	19,427	847	741	4,201
PN	19,303	64,585	7,245	4,916	4,633	31,176
PQ	40,854	104,319	16,857	3,104	2,944	18,745
PR	18,978	73,847	5,188	7,647	7,137	44,710
PS	23,042	82,856	6,615	10,319	9,050	51,186
PT	14,713	50,605	4,872	2,143	2,098	12,790
PZ	11,633	27,268	4,586	3,212	2,797	10,311
Q-QZ	67,350	278,639	18,838	31,585	29,940	189,681
R-RZ	33,848	96,741	11,445	10,178	9,639	43,949
S-SZ	11,971	39,664	4,178	4,807	4,346	23,735
T-TZ	51,164	170,101	16,810	23,356	21,048	108,145
U-UZ	5,555	18,612	2,127	2,141	1,933	11,752
V-VZ	1,350	3,195	506	766	554	1,895
W-WZ	2,108	3,809	1,240	260	222	651
Z-ZZ	24,670	86,045	7,972	6,069	5,761	39,001
TOTALS	803,354	2,467,394	321,649	215,388	200,893	1,207,113

Table 4

COLLECTION PROPORTIONS

Division	Titles		Comparative Size	Percent of Collection	
	Evaluator	Avg. Mbr		Peer Group	Evaluator
A-AZ	398	727	0.55	0.3	0.2
B-BJ	6,433	7,741	0.83	3.1	3.0
BL-BX	3,913	7,667	0.51	3.1	1.8
C-CZ	970	1,328	0.73	0.5	0.5
D-DZ	10,161	16,299	0.62	6.6	4.7
E-FZ	7,374	8,455	0.87	3.4	3.4
G-GZ	6,945	6,291	1.10	2.6	3.2
H-HZ	36,606	39,770	0.92	16.1	17.0
J-JZ	5,259	6,351	0.83	2.6	2.4
K-KC	855	1,432	0.60	0.6	0.4
KD-KDK	263	248	1.06	0.1	0.1
KE-KEZ	72	92	0.78	0.0	0.0
KF-KFS	3,934	3,158	1.25	1.3	1.8
L-LZ	6,915	7,445	0.93	3.0	3.2
M-MZ	1,422	3,789	0.38	1.5	0.7
N-NZ	7,451	10,142	0.73	4.1	3.5
P-PA	2,340	3,833	0.61	1.6	1.1
PB-PH	2,727	7,170	0.38	2.9	1.3
PJ-PM	847	4,775	0.18	1.9	0.4
PN	4,916	6,459	0.76	2.6	2.3
PQ	3,104	10,432	0.30	4.2	1.4
PR	7,647	7,385	1.04	3.0	3.6
PS	10,319	8,286	1.25	3.4	4.8
PT	2,143	5,061	0.42	2.1	1.0
PZ	3,212	2,727	1.18	1.1	1.5
Q-QZ	31,585	27,864	1.13	11.3	14.7
R-RZ	10,178	9,674	1.05	3.9	4.7
S-SZ	4,807	3,966	1.21	1.6	2.2
T-TZ	23,356	17,010	1.37	6.9	10.8
U-UZ	2,141	1,861	1.15	0.8	1.0
V-VZ	766	320	2.39	0.1	0.4
W-WZ	260	381	0.68	0.2	0.1
Z-ZZ	6,069	8,605	0.71	3.5	2.8
TOTALS	215,388	246,739	0.87	100.0	100.0

Table 5

204

titles between the home institution and the peer institutions, is more useful. A sense of how many of the titles are common or standard can be obtained, assuming that the most basic works will be found in many libraries. In the case of the Evans Library 35,079 of its 48,661 titles were held in common with the peer libraries. Of course these comparisons are meant to give an overall picture rather than detailed information.

Greater detail can be obtained from the subcollections counts which use the same format as the collection counts, but include a more refined breakdown. Instead o fusing the broad range of H-HZ, categories within the H's may also be compared. The categories in the subcollection counts are consistent with those of the National Shelf List. (see Table 5) Collection proportion statistics are more useful in assessing the Library's collection size in any given area because the home institution is compared to average member size (Table 5). For example, within the H-HZ call number range, the average member had 39,770 titles; Evans Library had 36.606 titles, which is 92 percent of this average. The peer group number represents 16.1 percent of the peer group libraries' overall collections. The evaluator number represents 17 percent of the Evans Library collection. So while the A&M collections is slightly smaller in this call number range than the average collection, it is proportionally higher than the average peer library.

The collection analysis CD also can generate "gap" lists at different percentage levels which help researchers prioritize materials for purchase. Titles which are missing from the home institution and which are found in 90 percent of the peer libraries generally will be purchased before materials found in 70 or 80 percent of peer libraries. Such comparisons make possible one method of refining and prioritizing collection needs. In a time of tighter budgets and greater demands, prioritizing becomes indispensable.

Conclusions

As expected, the survey unearthed some areas of projected curricula and research which were unknown to the researchers thereby generating greater Collection Analysis CD worked well in making broad comparisons with peer and other groups of libraries and in generating selective lists of "retrospective classics" for possible acquisition. However, raw data comparisons could not be fine tuned, and only the last ten years of acquisitions were possible for comparison-

making evaluations of the entire library collections impossible.

The increased detail generated by the questionnaire will help researches maintain the highest possible standards of excellence in collections under current budge restrains. The new information provided by the OCLC/AMIGOS Collection Analysis CD will allow collections development librarians to prioritize needs and decide in which areas the library will excel.

Endnotes

1. The authors wish to thank Fay Davis and Sue Meisel-Hater for preparing the manuscript and William L. Wilkin for preparing the tables and figures.

Background Bibliography

Henry C. Dethloff, *A Centennial History of Texas A & M University 1876-1976,* (College Station: Texas A & M University Press, 1975)

Marion Dillon and Kevin Flash, "Design Issure for Microcomputer-based Collection Analysis System." *Microcomputers for Information Management* 5 (December,1988): 263-273.

Jeanne Harrell, "Use of the OCLC/AMIGOS Collection Analysis CD to Determine Comparative Collection Strength in English and American Literature: A Case Study" *Technical Services Quarterly* (Accepted for publication in 1992).

George R. Jaramillo, "Computer Technology and Its Impact on Collection Development"*Collection Management* 10 (1988): 1-13.

Michael Kreyche, "BCL3 and NOTIS: An Automatic Collection Analysis Project." *Library Acquisitions: Practice and Theory* 13 (1989): 323-328.

Steven L. Sowell, "Expanding Horizons in Collection Development with Expert Systems: Development and Testing of a Demonstration Prototype." *Special Libraries* 80 (Winter, 1989): 45-50.

Texas A & M University. Sterling C. Evans Library "Annual Reports, ("College Station: Sterling C. Evans Library, Texas A & M University, 1971-1990).

Texas A & M University. Office of The Registrar. "Summary of Enrollment for the Fall Semesters of 1971-1990," College Station: Office of Registrar, Texas A & M University, n.d.)

Erwin K. Welsch, "Back to the Future: A Personal

Statement of Collection Development in an Information Culture." *Library Resources & Technical
Services* 33(January, 1989): 29-36.

The Price of Progress: Inflationary Effects on Monograph and Serials Purchases

John M. Budd
Louisiana State University
Baton Rouge, Louisiana

Abstract

Much has been written about the rising costs of materials in academic libraries, but much of the writing is anecdotal in nature. The present paper explores actual expenditures on monographs and serial subscriptions over the past few years in ARL and ACRL member libraries. Both monograph and serials prices are escalating, sometimes by a statistically significant amount from one year to the next. The effects of these price increases on total expenditures and on numbers of materials purchased are also examined.

Introduction

Everyone complains about the high prices of library materials. This is a problem for all libraries, but strikes harder at research libraries and the research collections of other academic libraries. At a time when resources available to libraries are not increasing (and in some instances are decreasing) the price increases for both serials and monographs continue. The predicament for libraries is of such magnitude that the word "crisis" is used repeatedly in the report of the Association of Research Libraries project on serials prices. The report states that "The crisis is that the escalating prices of serials are eroding the purchasing power of the research library collections budget, resulting in a loss of information to the scholar and researcher."[1]

Some specific effects of price increases have been reported. For instance, Dougherty and Johnson write that journals produced by three publishers comprise 16.1 percent of the periodicals budget at the University of Michigan and 24 percent of their total cost increase from 1986 to 1987.[2] At another institution with less extensive serials holdings, Louisiana State University, the same three publishers accounted for 25 percent of the total serials expenditures and 43 percent of the increase, according to Hamaker.[3] These findings are supported by the longitudinal study of serials prices conducted by Marks, et al.[4] The effect of serials price increases on materials expenditures has been observed by Budd. He notes that the percentage of total library expenditures at doctoral-granting ,institutions going for periodicals increased from 14.6 percent in 1976, to 18.1 percent in 1985, and the amount earmarked for books fell from 16.7 percent to 11.7 percent during the

same period.[5] The concern over the phenomenon of price increases has not been limited to the library community. Henry Barschall, a retired physicist, has examined the comparative costs of journals in physics.[6]

These various publications point to the increasing complexity of the library market. Basch observes this complexity and further notes that "few scholarly publishers are familiar with the purchasing patterns and procedures of libraries, information that is critical both to reach new subscribers and to retain current subscribers within this important market."[7] One possible conjecture based on the above is that the market is getting more and more competitive and that past purchasing patterns cannot continue. The purpose of this paper is to examine the effect of the inflationary tendencies on actual library expenditures for serials and monographs.

Methodology and Hypotheses

In recent years the annual ARL survey has added questions regarding the numbers of monographs and serials purchased by libraries, as well as libraries' expenditures in these categories. Responses to these questions are used to analyze the purchasing behavior of member libraries from 1985/86 through 1989/90. Only those libraries providing consistently usable data for all five years are examined. Unfortunately, many libraries do not report these data, the assumption is that the reporting libraries are representative of all ARL members. From the available data it is possible to determine the average numbers of titles purchased or subscribed to, the average amounts paid per serial or monograph title, and the average total expenditures for serials and monographs. Further, relative expenditures for serials and monographs can be analyzed.

Some working hypotheses can be formulated regarding the activities of the libraries:

H_1 The average amount paid for a monograph increases by a statistically significant increment from year to year, between 1985/86 aand 1989/1990.

H_2 The average number of monographs purchased per library decreases by a statistically significant increment from year to year, between 1985/86 and 1989/90.

H_3 The average amount paid for a serial subscription increases by a statistically significant increment from year to year, between 1985/86 aand 1989/1990.

H_4 The average amount expended per library on serials increases by a statistically significant increment from year to year, between 1985/86 aand 1989/1990.

These are tested as null hypotheses by employing a t-test to compare means for pairs of years.

In addition to the ARL data, three years of ACRL data (1986, 1987-88, and 1988-89) are available for analysis. While these data are more limited than those for ARL, similar analyses can be applied to them, since the ACRL survey also queries libraries regarding the numbers of monographs and serials purchased. The above stated working hypotheses can apply to the ACRL data as well.

Findings

Using the ARL data, one of the calculations that can be made is the change in the average amount paid by libraries for monographs. Not all libraries report the number of monographs purchased, but 56 of the members responded consistently over the five-year period. One complicating factor is that, for eight of these libraries, the figure for expenditures includes money going for "Other Library Materials." For the purposes of analysis here, all 56 libraries are treated equally and it is assumed that there is no substantive difference between the eight libraries and the others. While less attention is paid in the literature to monographs than to

serials, it is evident that their prices are rising as well. Table 1 illustrates the average amount paid per monograph volume from 1985-86 to 1989-90.

The overall increase in price during the time period is 32.7 percent. The trend establishedfor the time in question can be used to estimate prices in the future. The following linear regression formula can be used for the projection:

$$b = N(‰XY) - X(‰Y)/N(‰X) - (‰X)$$

$$a = Y - b(‰X)/N$$

$$y = a + bx$$

When inserting data into this formula for application in Tables 1 and 2, the X value represents the year (expressed as numbers 1 through 5) and Y value represents the prices for the corresponding year (for instance, monograph prices $30.95 for year 1, $32.31 for year 2, etc.). The value N is 56 for monographs and 46 for serials. The 1994-95 figures, then, are projections based on the data for the years 1985-through 1989-90.

This regression shows that, by 1994-95, the average price paid for a monograph volume will be more than fifty dollars. The first hypothesis can be tested using these data; the only years for which there is a statistically significant increase in price (p<.01) are 1986-87 to 1987-88. The null hypothesis is rejected for that pair of years, but cannot be rejected for the other three pairs. One other analysis that can be applied to the price data is the correlation of the increase as plotted graphically with the ideal regression slope. A correlation of 1.0 would mean a perfect correlation with a linear increase. The actual correlation coefficient is .9908, which implies that the increase is very nearly linear, or that there has been very little deviation from a linear trend upwards. One other conclusion that may be drawn from this is that publishers appear to be employing a linear pricing model, with increases exhibiting a regular upward trend.

The total expenditures for monographs show a fair amount of consistency—only a 14.8 percent increase over the time period. The average amount actually dropped from the first year to the second. The biggest increase (8.8 percent) occurred from the fourth to the fifth year. One thing that this stability signals is a decline in the piece of the materials pie going to monographs. In 1985-86, 42.4 percent of the total was expended on monographs. Over the last three years of the study the percentage has held relatively steady: 35.2 percent in 1987-88, 35.0 percent in 1988-89, and 35.5 percent in 1989-90. The regression model suggests that by 1994-95 the percentage may drop to 30.1. The actions of libraries may alter this trend, though. The correlation coefficient of the plotted data with the ideal slope is .8474. More will be said about this phenomenon later.

The average number of monographs purchased confirms, to a considerable extent, the popular perceptions of librarians—that fewer monographs are purchased each year. As is evident in Table 1, the number declines until the fifth year, when there is a slight increase. That increase corresponds with the rise in expenditures for monographs in the fifth year, as noted above. The second hypothesis can be tested using these data. Although there is a decline form the beginning of the period in question to the end, the yearly decline is in no instance statistically significant. The null hypothesis, then, cannot be rejected for any of the pairs of years. If the trend continues, the average number will fall still further, but, as was previously noted, the trend may not continue as it has manifest itself. The correlation in the instance with the ideal slope is .8764, but the deviation from the trend occurs in the last year.

Similar analysis can be performed on libraries' expenditures on serials. First, the average price paid per subscription by 46 libraries reporting consistently can be calculated; the averages by year are presented in Table 2. The overall increase from 1985-86 to 1989-90 is 54.7 percent, which exceeds the increase for monographs. If the trend continues, libraries will be paying nearly two hundred dollars per subscription by 1994-95. It should be noted that the increase from 1988-89 to 1989-90 is 6.6 percent, which is below the overall publishers price increase for 1990 (excluding Soviet translations) of 9.5 percent.[8] As is true of the increase in monograph prices, the increase in serial prices is very nearly linear; the correlation coefficient of these points and the ideal slope is .9917. The same conclusion regarding publishers' pricing activities pertains here as well. In testing the third hypothesis it

Table 1

ARL Members and Monograph Expenditures (N=56)

Year	Monograph Expenditures	Monograph Prices	Monographs Purchased
1985-86	$1,128,232.63	$30.95	38,199.5
1986-87	1,098,112.07	32.31	36,426.6
1987-88	1,121,220.98	36.30	34,085.2
1988-89	1,190,723.96	38.40	32,495.9
1989-90	1,295,013.46	40.68	33,865.9
1994-95*	1,464,982.11	53.61	26,196.1

* The 1994-95 figures are projections based on linear regression.

is evident that the differences between years are statistically significant for 1985-86 to 1986-87 ($p<.001$) and 1987-88 to 1988-89 ($p<.05$); the differences for the remaining two pairs are not significant. The null hypothesis is rejected for the first two mentioned pairs, but cannot be rejected for the other two.

The overall increase in expenditures on serials per library is near that for average price, 53.2 percent, with increases every year. These data also approach the ideal slope; the correlation coefficient is .9858. The percentage of total materials expenditures devoted to serials is the converse of monographs. This means that the proportion going to serials has been relatively stable over the most recent three years near the 65 percent level. Regression suggests that by 1994-95 nearly 70 percent of the materials budget will go to serials and more than 3.4 million dollars will be spent on these subscriptions. Again, the regression model assumes a continuation of past purchasing habits; this may not be an entirely safe assumption. The fourth hypothesis relates to these data and the only pair of years exhibiting a statistically significant increase is 1985-86 to 1986-87 ($p<.01$). The hypothesis is rejected for this pair but cannot be rejected for the other three.

The average number of subscriptions purchased displays very little consistency or pattern (see Table 2). The number declines in the second year, rises in the third, declines again in the fourth, then declines further in the fifth. Linear regression forecasts virtual stability, or 18,841.3, in 1994-95, but the projection is problematic. Correlation between the plotted data and the ideal slope yields a coefficient of -.3582, or a weak negative correlation. This signifies that activity has not been regular, to which many serials librarians could probably attest. Further, analysis of variance, which measures the means of the groups to determine if they differ significantly from one another, yields no statistically significant difference among the means. The computed value of F is .07; the critical value at $p=.05$ is 2.37. The stability of the percentages of expenditures devoted to serials in the latest three years may be due to the dynamics of serials paid for in these years. Libraries are apparently taking some initiative with regard to the number of serials subscribed to, but the trend in serials expenditures increases has yet to be halted.

The ACRL data are more limited; fewer libraries report consistent information and data for fewer years

Table 2

ARL Members and Serials Expenditures (N=46)

Year	Serials Expenditures	Serials Prices	Serials Purchased
1985-86	$1,534,734.59	$ 87.01	19,107.1
1986-87	1,830,872.83	103.62	18,703.8
1987-88	2,063,777.37	115.54	19,451.8
1988-89	2,213,156.80	126.29	19,025.2
1989-90	2,351,445.94	134.60	18,817.9
1994-95*	3,409,792.18	195.91	18,841.3

* The 1994-95 figures are projections based on linear regression.

are available. Also, the increment from the first set of data to the second is two years, making the inferential analysis as applied to the ARL data much less useful. These data are presented for comparative purposes. For instance, the increase in price for the average monograph from 1985-86 to 1988-89 is 17.9 percent (after a decline in price from 1987-88 to 1988-89). Total expenditures held relatively steady, increasing only 3.1 percent for the period. The number of titles purchased initially declined 15.4 percent, but then climbed 8.3 percent, resulting in a 6.6 percent loss for the period. The piece of the materials pie fell from 43.4 percent in 1985-86 to 33.9 percent in 1988-89.

Serials prices rose 32.1 percent for the period in question, but the average number of subscriptions rose 8.6 percent, after an initial decline. The combination of the two factors resulted in an increase in expenditures of 54.1 percent. As is noted above, these data are too limited to draw conclusions, but some of the patterns exhibited by these libraries appear to be at odds with the ARL set.

Conclusion

The analysis examines the amounts expended by some academic libraries on materials. As is shown, the

Table 3

ARL Members and Monograph Expenditures (N=40)

Year	Monograph Expenditures	Monograph Prices	Monographs Purchased
1985-86	$504,512.03	$29.88	17,176.4
1987-88	506.878.58	36.11	14,888.7
1988-89	520,222.35	35.23	16,119.9

Table 4

ARL Members and Serials Expenditures (N=20)

Year	Serials Expenditures	Serials Prices	Serials Purchased
1985-86	$ 656,998.85	$ 115.18	6,070.7
1987-88	924.962.80	144.47	5,732.9
1988-89	1,012,201.80	152.11	6,591.3

average expenditures for monographic and serials titles have increased in an almost linear fashion. Some libraries may have altered their purchasing habits, but, in the aggregate, the pattern of yearly increases continued throughout the period of examination, indicating that the pricing structure of serials producers has a substantial effect on overall expenditures. This confirms the perception of ever-increasing prices and the shifting of materials budgets away from monographs and towards serials. The question to be asked is: Can any shift in the upward pricing trend and preponderance of funds spent on serials be discerned? There is some evidence from the data that the activity of the earlier years of the data set are not necessarily the status quo for the later ones.

One indication of change is that the increase in the average amount paid per serial subscription declines over the time period studied. This average went up from 1985-86 to 1986-87 by 19.1 percent. The increase dropped to 6.6 percent by the final year and this latter figure is lower than the increase charged by producers for subscriptions. Further, the proportion of funds going for monographs and for serials appears to have stabilized over the last three years of the time period in question. With regard to monograph expenditures, the majority of the increase in total expenditures per library occurred in the last year, after little change in the first four. Also, the number of monographs purchased rose in that year from the previous one.

These phenomena, plus the variance in the number of serials titles subscribed to, indicate that libraries are not necessarily carrying past behavior into the future. These data also suggest that the financial reality of pricing is not going to change of its own accord. For instance, the average price of a serials subscriptions rose by 11.7 percent in 1991.[9] They also suggest that libraries are beginning to look critically at their internal behavior. The indication here is that, while increases in serials expenditures are diminishing, the trend is still upwards. The linear regression presented illustrates what libraries have to look forward to if past trends continue. It remains to be seen if the actions taken by libraries can affect the current pricing patterns. Close examination of financial data for the next few years will provide an indication of any change; tracking of data should continue to test the regression model. Meanwhile, libraries will have to be active players in the economic structure of materials marketing if any trends are to be altered.

One caveat needs to be offered as a postscript to this study. The data used here are the best available but, as is true of much of library research, they may not be entirely accurate. Libraries may well be reporting estimates of purchasing activity rather than complete actual information. Also, local variance in defining and reporting data may present some problems; in the absence of clear distinctions among library practices, it is assumed that there is sufficient consistency for analysis. The problem of non-reporting libraries has already been noted. While these handicaps preclude any pronouncement of conclusions as absolute, the data are sufficient for examination to transcend mere dictum.

Endnotes

1. "Overview and Summary," Re*port of the ARL Serials Prices Project* (Washington, DC: ARL, 1989), unpaged.
2. Richard M. Dougherty and Brenda L. Johnson, "Periodical Price Escalation: A Library Response," *Library Journal* 113 (May 15, 1988): 27.
3. Charles Hamaker, Presentation at the North American Serials Interest Group, Dennison, Ohio, June, 1987, cited in Dougherty and Johnson, p. 27.
4. Kenneth E. Marks, Steven P. Nielsen, H. Craig Peterson and Peter E. Wagner, "Longitudinal Study of Scientific Journal Prices in a Research Library," *College & Research Libraries* 52 (March, 1991): 125-38.
5. Henry H. Barschall, "The Cost of Physics Journals," *Physics Today* 41 (July, 1988): 56-596 John M. Budd, "Academic Libraries: Institutional Support and Internal Expenditures," *Library Administration & Management* 4 (Summer, 1990): 157-58.
7. N. Bernard Basch, "The Scholarly Journal and the Library Market," *Scholarly Publishing* 19 (April, 1988): 157.
8. Kathryn Hammell Carpenter and Adrian W. Alexander, "Price Index for U. S. Periodicals," *Library Journal* 116 (April 15, 1991): 53.
9. Ibid.

African American Reference Sources: No Turning Back and Never Again a Drought

Katherine Dahl
Western Illinois Universitty
Macomb, Illinois

Abstract

African American reference sources have not always been as plentiful as they are today. Except for the last few decades, only a shameful and pathetic amount of African American reference sources has been available, which means that some library users have not been successful in their attempts to gather information, explore a topic, and understand the past. The rise in increased numbers of African American reference sources is tracked. Hopefully, reference sources about all groups and cultures will be produced and published.

Columnist and author George Will recently made fun of those of us who, he said, believe "it is incorrect to feel nostalgic about a decade marred by segregation."[1] The decade in question was the 1950s. Sometime soon, Will may have to write a column making fun of me, too, for as a reference librarian, it is my contention proven by the record of the past and the agreement of bibliographic researchers that most years previous to the late 1960s/early 1970s were indeed 'marred' because reference books about or relating to African Americans were infrequently produced and published. If one believes that in a reference collection it is important to be able to find out about the achievements, progress, and struggles of African Americans, then these are good times far better than some long ago and not so long ago times for it is now possible in reference resources to find out more completely about those achievements and struggles and that progress: those plays, those heroes, that poetry, and those "stars." The "missing pages"[2] that publishers of The American Negro Reference Book referred to in 1966 are being found: reference books have become one of their homes.

As a primary selector for a university library reference collection, it is not uncommon any more for me to become aware in a single month of titles like Directory of African American Religious Bodies and National Black Health Leadership Directory. Which reference librarian did not rejoice in 1990 when Harlem Renaissance and Beyond: Literary Biographies of 100 Black Women Writers, 1990-1945 became available? In 1989 when Black Action Films became available? In 1988 when Blacks in American Films and Television became available?

But how much rejoicing was there to be done by reference librarians—if they hoped to have a core collection of African American reference material—earlier in this century? Only a little—and not often much. W. E. B. Du Bois in 1905 issued Select Bibliography of the Negro American (although reference librarians have always been of two minds as to whether bibliographies should be in reference or in the circulating collection). Some biographical information had been provided in 1887 in William J. Simmons' Men of Mark: Eminent, Progressive and Rising.

The Negro Year Book was begun in 1912. While it was a fine tool, it could not tell everything that, from a reference standpoint, needed telling. In A List of Books for College Libraries the only African American-related reference sources are the just-mentioned yearbook, A Bibliography of the Negro in Africa and America, and the Bureau of the Census' Negro Population, 1790-1915.[3] Slim pickings, to be sure!

The sixth edition of the American Library Association's Guide to Reference Books, published in 1936, included the previously-mentioned titles and the Bureau of Education's Negro Education: A Study of the Private and Higher Schools for Colored People in the United States. By no means did these few titles provide a complete or in-depth picture of African Americans. The ALA and the editor of the sixth edition cannot, of course, be faulted for not listing books that did not exist.

Du Bois was still very active and in 1946, with Guy B. Johnson and through the Phelps-Stokes Fund, issued *Encyclopedia of the Negro, Preparatory Volume with Reference Lists and Reports,* pointing out "the entirely inadequate treatment of the Negro in all existing encyclopedias and other works of general reference."[4] Another positive happening in the 1940s was the birth of the *Guide to Negro Periodical Literature*—now called *Index to Black Periodicals.*

Colonial Press' 1963 publication, *Basic Books for Junior College Libraries: 20,000 Vital Titles,* included nine pages of reference sources, but none were African American-related. In 1965 Erwin K. Welsch in *The Negro in the United States: A Research Guide* centered his remarks around "the Negro protest against discrimination gain[ing] momentum."[5] An outcome of that protest was more and, in some instances, better reference materials about African Americans. Lest we forget that the publishing past has indeed been imperfect as regards African American reference materials, it is worthwhile to consider Ernest Kaiser's 1966 *Freedomways words:* "In the field of reference and guide books on the Negro and Negro collected biographies, we are just beginning to get some volumes, after a mere trickle of these over the past decades."[6]

In her important and helpful 1988 work, *Index to Afro-American Reference Resources,* Rosemary Stevenson asserts that "historical difficulties in getting Black related resources published, exclusionary book reviewing practices, and insufficient bibliographic control of Afro-American publications"[7] for some time prevented us from finding information about African Americans. Reference's William "Bill" Katz, when reviewing *The American Negro Reference Book* in 1966, presaged Stevenson by noting that "until now publishers have assisted in what one librarian has called the 'cultural lobotomy' that has kept the Negro out of many kinds of books."[8] Stevenson suggests that we are now—and have been since the 1960s—in a "period of heightened Black awareness"[9] in which more and more reference works about African Americans continue to be written and published.

Mary Mace Spradling, editor of all three editions of *In Black and White,* reminded us in the first edition of "the frantic inquiries of the Nineteen Sixties," when there was "a deluge of requests for information relating to Black Americans."[10] While that first edition was published in 1971, it is no less true today that patrons are interested in finding reference materials which relate to African Americans: I work with those patrons, I am challenged by their questions, and I want the

reference fount of information to flow—overflow—for them. In the foreword to the third edition of this tool, Albert Marshall is proud to say that the tool includes a "large number of names . . . excluded from such resource tools as the Biographical Index [sic] and determined by the mores of the generation in which they lived."[11]

For this investigation it was necessary to look at literally hundreds and hundreds of issues of library journals—the "main" journals, the journals with a "national" reputation. In the period that corresponded to the heyday of segregation I could find almost no advertisements for the few African American reference sources that were available. *Library Journal* in 1951 did feature a full-page advertisement from the Methodist Church for its *States' Laws on Race and Color* (a publication which would have been considered a reference source by some librarians and not by others). No African American resource was among one publication's "Top Ten Reference Books of 1954."[12] Nor was such a type of resource included in 1954 in that publication's "Reference Books Needed."[13] Nineteen hundred fifty-seven was the year of Little Rock, but a "Reference Checklist" for that year reflected none of the turmoil: two of the academic recommendations were the *Complete Book of Chrysanthemums* and the *Complete Wedding Guide.*[14]

While reviews can be found for the few African American resources of earlier decades, most reviewers were dispassionate and "unKatz-like," seeming not to recognize the dramatic import of the works. Reviewers in some 1980 *Reference and Subscription Books Reviews,* however, used phrases like "neglected area of research"[15] and "neglected area of study"[16] to describe new resources related to African Americans. While articles like "Less Prejudice and Bigotry," "Aspects of Integration," and "For Better Human Relations" did appear in library publications in the 1950s, they never dealt with the fact that only a paltry amount of African American reference material was available.

To its credit, *Wilson Library Bulletin* was one of the first library journals to significantly recognize the need for African American reference resources and the need for information about those resources. In November 1972 it began a four-part series, "Black and Bibliographical." That there was still a dearth of African American reference material was apparent from the columnists' remark that "some titles are included which serve reference functions where the usual reference materials are lacking."[17] In 1977 *American Libraries* reached thousands of librarians with a one-time column, "Keeping Up: A Checklist of Black Reference Books."

Greenwood Publishing has helped many library patrons and librarians through its series, Bibliographies and Indexes in Afro-American and African Studies, but that was a 1980s and now—not a 1950s—happening. Nor was the *Handbook of Black Librarianship* produced during the frustrating and often futile fifties; rather, it was during the more resource-satisfying seventies. The editors of that handbook were certain that their publication "fill[ed] a void for a variety of people needing Afro-American . . . materials and information on the location of those materials."[18]

Examination of editions of and supplements to the *Guide to Reference Books* subsequent to the sixth edition referred to earlier reveals first a drought and then a harvest as regards numbers of African American titles included: 13 in the seventh edition and supplements (1951-1962); 26 in the eighth edition and supplements (1967-1970); 101 in the ninth edition and supplements (1976-1982); and 93 in the tenth edition (1986) (some titles are included in more than one edition and/or supplement).

Gratitude must be extended to all of the authors, editors, and compilers who, through their specialized reference publications, have enabled us to be more informed about African Americans. And the work of those writers is not finished. Bernard L. Peterson, Jr.'s *Early Black American Playwrights and Dramatic Writers: A Biographical Directory and Catalog of Plays, Films, and Broadcasting Scripts* appeared just last year. It was necessary that that book be published, for, as the author says, "Although slightly more than a dozen black playwrights had their plays produced on or off Broadway during the period from 1925 to 1945, only two of them are occasionally mentioned in standard theatrical reference books."[19] A few years before Peterson, Charles D'Aniello's bibliographic study of African Americans involved in cinema was published, in which it was asserted that:

General reference sources . . . have never delved deeply into the uniqueness of the Afro-American experience. These resources have neglected Black publications and ignored potential biographees because they were not deemed important by white

America. Fortunately, for over a decade, there has been a swelling stream of specialized reference sources which identify or provide ready access to appropriate information and material.[20]

Oh, that that "swelling stream" could have flowed earlier: so much information has been unobtainable and so much information has been "missed—information that could have enlightened and inspired. What matters most now, however, is that the stream is not subsiding and the upcoming surge in Black reference books"[21] that Stevenson said heralded the 1980s has continued into this decade.

While my attention in this presentation has not been on Hispanic and some other ethnic reference sources, a surge has begun for some of them too: may it continue for a long time so that all knowledge is uncovered and all information is available for all patrons.

Endnotes

1. George F. Will, "Curdled Politics on Campus," *Newsweek,* 117 (May 6, 1991): 72.
2. John F. Davis, *The American Negro Reference Book.* (Yonkers, NY: Educational Heritage, 1966), p. xi.
3. Charles B. Shaw, *A List of Books for College Libraries* (Chicago: American Library Association, 1931).
4. W. E. B. Du Bois and Guy B. Johnson, *Encyclopedia of the Negro, Preparatory Volume with Reference Lists and Reports,* 2nd ed., rev. and enl. (New York: The Phelps-Stokes Fund, 1946), p. 8.
5. Erwin K. Welsch, *The Negro in the United States: A Research Guide.* (Bloomington, IN: Indiana University Press, 1965), p. xi.
6. Ernest Kaiser, "The Negro Heritage Library and Its Critics," *Freedomways* 7 (Winter, 1967): 64-74.
7. Rosemary M. Stevenson, *Index to Afro-American Reference Resources.* (Westport, CT: Greenwood Press, 1988), p. ix-x.
8. William Katz, "Ignored by Historians," *Saturday Review* 49 (July 16, 1966): 67-68.
9. Rosemary M. Stevenson ,op. cit., p. x.
10. Mary Mace Spradling, ed., *In Black and White: Afro-Americans in Print* (Kalamazoo, MI: Kalamazoo Library System, 1971), p. ix.
11. Mary Mace Spradling, *In Black and White: A Guide to Magazine Articles, Newspaper Articles, and Books Concerning More than 15,000 Black Individuals and Groups,* 3rd ed. (Detroit: Gale Re-

search, 1980), p. ix.

11. Louis Shores, "1954 Reference Checklist," *Library Journal* 80 (January 1, 1955): 28-40.

13. Louis Shores, "1953 Reference Checklist," *Library Journal* 79 (July, 1954): 1266-1271.

14. Louis Shores, "Reference Checklist '57," *Library Journal* 83 (March 1, 1958): 695-702.

15. Review of *The Progress of Afro-American Women: A Selected Bibliography and Resource Guide*, by Janet L. Sims. *Reference and Subscription Books Reviews*, December 15, 1980, p. 591 [within *Booklist* 77 (December 15, 1980): 584-593.

16. Review of B*lack American Playwrights, 1800 to the Present: A Bibliography*, by Esther Spring Arata and Nicholas John Rotoli, and *More Black American Playwrights: A Bibliography*, by Esther Spring Arata, *Reference and Subscription Books Reviews*, February 1, 1980, p. 787 [within Booklist 76 (February 1, 1980): 785-794.

17. James Johnson and Frances O. Churchill, "Black and Bibliographical," *Wilson Library Bulletin* 47 (November, 1972): 248-250.

18. E. J. Josey and Ann Allen Shockley, *Handbook of Black Librarianship* (Littleton, CO: Libraries Unlimited, 1977), p. 11.

19. Bernard L. Peterson, Jr., *Early Black American Playwrights and Dramatic Writers: A Biographical Directory and Catalog of Plays, Films, and Broadcasting Scripts* (Westport, CT: Greenwood Press, 1990), p. xiii.

20. Charles D'Aniello, "Black and White on Film: The Afro-American Experience and the Movies," *Reference Services Review* 12 (Summer, 1984): 41-51.

21. Rosemary M. Stevenson, op. cit., p. xi.

State Pool Funds: An Incentive to Resource Sharing and Collaborative Collection Development among State and Privately-Supported Academic Libraries

Thomas D. Kilton
University of Illinois
Urbana, Illinois

Abstract

An aspect of special state funding to academic libraries which can stimulate resource sharing and collaborative collection development is the allocation of state pool funds for the purchase of expensive research materials. The State of Illinois has administered such funding on annual basis for several years through its Cooperative Collection Management Coordinating Committee. Since libraries must contribute collection assessment data to the statewide conspectus in order receive funding, the project is helping to lay the foundations for substantive statewide collaborative acquisition projects. With a focus on the Illinois plan, this paper examines similar plans underway in other states.

Dwindling library budgets coupled with the mounting prices of library materials have made "outside support" in the form of private gifts as well as federal and state grants to many state-supported as well as private academic libraries a necessity in order for these institutions to have access to certain highly expensive research resources. Within a given state such support is frequently needed to provide a single copy of such materials, especially items considered to be of high quality but which have a low frequency of use. Fortunately the increasing efficiency and speed of interlibrary document delivery systems have made the purchase of a single copy or very few copies of such items for statewide shared-use feasible. Until fairly recently at least one of the larger academic libraries in every state could in general be counted on to purchase a given expensive title, but this is no longer true. Fortunately, however, cooperative purchasing of such titles with a common commitment to interlibrary lending has become one way of helping to eleviate this problem. In the past few years several statewide collaborative collection development projects, some involving the use of conspectuses, have emerged to enable smaller academic libraries not included in the major national research sharing consortia to participate in systematic collaborative purchasing and resource sharing at the state level.

The RLG Conspectus (including the North American Collections Inventory Project), the National Shelflist Count, and the WLN Conspectus (formerly the Pacific Northwest Conspectus), are all familiar tools created within the past decade to map out the collection strengths and collection intensity levels of American research libraries without respect to their locations within specific states. Much has been published on the intent and potential use of these tools, particularly with regard to the assignment of PCRs or "primary collection responsibilities" by participating libraries. Of course the willingness to accept a PCR assignment by a library implies its obligation to collect, usually at a high collection intensity level, materials on a given subject or from a given geographical area of the world. Such a commitment relieves other member libraries from having to purchase the more expensive and/or low-use materials in that same subject or geographical area.

A trend in which individual state libraries and state boards of higher education promote similar resource sharing and collaborative acquisition projects at the state level is emerging. An effective prod to induce libraries to identify and report their strengths and collection intensity levels to statewide conspectuses has been shown in some instances to be the dangling carrot of special state funding, such as pool fund competitions available to only those libraries which have contributed data or have expressed a willingness to contribute data to such collection analysis tools.

I perceive this link between state pool funding and cooperation in systematic resource sharing and collaborative purchasing on the state level to be a sign of enormous potential for enhancing the quality of North American research collections, a process which can encourage the participation of the smaller or lesser-known academic libraries in cooperative ventures. Illinois is an example of a state which for several years has made pool funds available as part of a continued effort to encourage cooperative purchasing and resource sharing and which has limited participation to those libraries which have contributed to its statewide conspectus. I would like to first take a close look at the Illinois model and then compare it with similar programs in a few other states.

Since 1986 there has existed at the state level a Cooperative Collection Management Coordinating Committee which annually administers the awarding of $120,000 for the pool funding of special acquisitions projects. These pool funds are available to academic libraries which are participants in ICAM (Illinois Collection Analysis Matrix), the state conspectus. In order to be eligible for these awards, libraries must be willing to house the materials for which the grants are appropriated, they must agree to provide bibliographic access to them through the statewide online catalog, ILLINET Online and they must be willing to lend the materials to other libraries. Typically, two separate allotments of $60,000 dollars each are designated for the pool funding competitions held each December—one allotment for the purchase of materials within four designated subject areas, and another one for cooperative groups of bibliographers to select and purchase expensive research materials. Each of the 30-40 participating libraries may send one staff member per designated subject area to the competitions. Those areas for the 1990 competitions were: health policy, European studies, nursing, and literary manuscripts in facsimile or microform. Titles may be requested in any format, but serial subscriptions are excluded. A hallmark of the Illinois program is the fact that subject selectors or bibliographers are asked to participate in the application and selection process as opposed to collection management officers or other library administrators.

Because of recurring budgetary crises afflicting book purchasing power, the University of Illinois at Urbana-Champaign Library has benefitted greatly from these pool fund awards, as have several medium-sized university and small college libraries throughout the state. Among the awards granted to the Urbana-Champaign campus in the December 1990 pool fund competition were the *Archives biographiques françaises* (French Biographical Archive) on microfiche by K.G. Saur for $13,500, and a selection of eighty current European monographs on the recent German reunification to-

talling $1,173.00. The *Archives biographiques françaises* award was representative of awards arising out of the $60,000 pot applied for by a cooperative group of bibliographers from three of the state university libraries. In addition to the microfiche set to be located at Urbana, copies of its paper index were awarded to the libraries at Illinois State University and Southern Illinois University, Carbondale. The monographs on German reunification were representative of an award from the designated subject area: European Studies. Before these grants were awarded, not a single library in the state possessed the *Archives biographiques françaises* due to its high cost. And it is doubtful that without the European studies pool fund grant the majority of the monographs on German reunification would have been picked up by libraries within the state.

A new state conspectus entitled the *Illinois Conspectus* is now underway to replace the former *ICAM Conspectus* which served only the 40 or so academic libraries within the statewide circulation system, LCS. The *Illinois Conspectus will* soon involve collection assessment reports of over 200 public and academic libraries, including approximately 40 college and university libraries who are participants in the statewide online catalog, ILLINET Online. The assessment format being used is that of the *WLN Conspectus*. To date no PCRs (primary collection responsibilities) have been established, but a project for the assignment of them is being developed.

Illinois is not the only state to offer annual pool funding grants to its public and private academic libraries and to make the receipt of this funding contingent upon contribution to a statewide conspectus plus a commitment to lending materials received through these grants, but it has been in the lead in this endeavor. And as other statewide conspectuses evolve, the decisions for the awarding of pool funds to institutions in those states can more systematically be based on their collection profiles and the subject areas of primary collection responsibility to which they are committed for sharing. Nevertheless, much work in the way of collection assessment and improved interlibrary loan and document delivery needs to be accomplished in many states before such cooperation can blossom to its fullest potential.

Two other states which have also successfully launched substantial pool funding programs to enable their academic libraries to purchase otherwise unaffordable research titles are Alabama and Washington. In Alabama nineteen academic institutions which are members of its "Network of Alabama Academic Libraries" share in grants in a total amount of approximately $830,000 per year. However, in contrast to the Illinois plan, these participating libraries individually document specific collection deficiencies and apply for funding to shore up these collections. The sizes of awards to individual libraries are based on a formula involving the annual number of volumes added by a library plus the total amount it spends annually on materials. In administering the funds provided by the state legislature through the Alabama Commission on Higher Education, the established strengths and weaknesses of collections documented in statewide collection analysis profiles are closely examined before the grants are awarded. In the state of Washington, $100,000 of federal Library Services and Construction Act Title III money is administered annually by the state to around twelve academic and public libraries for pool funding competitions. There are two qualifications for participation by libraries: 1) performing systematic collection assessments and reporting results to the statewide conspectus; and 2) contributing catalog records of the materials received to a bibliographic utility—OCLC or WLN.

Similar programs are currently in developmental stages in other states. In Ohio a collection management and development system exists within the Ohio Link Project. As yet no statewide grants have been offered to libraries, but a statewide conspectus has been proposed. In states such as New York, successful state funded projects to administer special grants have existed for some time without the existence of any coordinated collection assessment projects at the state level, although in the case of New York a large number of regional conspectuses have emerged. "Coordinated Collection Development Aid" is the name of New York's program for formula-based special funding to academic libraries. Approximately 180 grants per year in a total amount of $1,360,000 are administered through this program.

Some states administer special pool funding to only a special segment of their academic library communities. Under the "Shared Purchase Program" of California, for instance, state funding for special cooperative purchases is provided to the nine campuses of the University of California. This program was begun in 1976 to prevent unnecessary duplication of expensive, low-use materials. Here, however, instead of the state supplying a separate sum of money for shared acqui-

sition projects, approximately three percent of the total materials budget for the nine campuses is skimmed off for pool-fund grants before the regular allocations to the individual campuses are made. Grants for the purchase of materials for the campus libraries are administered by a system-wide Collection Development Committee made up of the collection development officers of each campus. Participants are encouraged to contribute to the RLG Conspectus or the North American Collections Inventory Project.

It is worth noting that in addition to centralized state funding programs which promote collaborative library purchasing through pool fund grants available to all or a select number of academic libraries, there are also urban and regional cooperative purchasing programs in force which are not dependent on state assistance but which internally generate money for collaborative purchasing and which encourage the reporting of holdings statistics and collection intensity levels to regional conspectuses. METRO (the New York Metropolitan Reference and Research Library Agency), a consortium of 245 public and academic libraries in the New York City metropolitan area, is a good example of such a program. Each library within the consortium contributes $5,000 each year to a central pool fund. A single subject, such as music, is chosen annually, and funding for that year is dedicated to special purchases for the collections of those member libraries with significant holdings in that subject. All participating libraries are requested to contribute to the regional conspectus: "The METRO Collection Inventory Project." Several large, prominent research libraries are a part of METRO: Columbia, New York University, New York Public, and Rutgers.

Numerous programs of state funding for libraries exist nationwide under many different guises, but the number of states which offer pool funding to state-supported as well as private academic libraries for the sole purpose of promoting cooperative purchasing is still small. However, those states like Illinois and Alabama which already have such programs in place have been successful in promoting both collaborate acquisitions projects as well as in inducing participating libraries to contribute collection analysis data to conspectuses. After a period of development, these conspectuses will provide bibliographers with precise data on collection strengths, and hopefully their existence will induce participating libraries to establish primary collection responsibilities. Ultimately the conspectus as a tool at the state or regional level could turn out to be more effective in promoting collaborative purchasing and resource sharing than the conspectuses of our present regional and nationwide bibliographic utilities. This is, first of all, because of the greater economy of both money and time which cooperative purchasing and sharing within a limited region assure. Secondly, dwindling income sources to libraries from federal grants to state revenues has been a factor in curtailing some of the progress anticipated for nationwide conspectus work, despite the obvious irony that a library with strapped funds possesses a greater need to share materials. And thirdly, the degree of participation originally anticipated for the North American Collections Inventory Project has simply not been forthcoming.

In order for cooperative collection development and collection analysis projects among libraries to be successful, the receipt of special pool fund or other types of grants from states or other funding sources as an inducement or prod is, of course, not absolutely necessary. Neither is the existence of a refined conspectus outlining subject strenghts and weaknesses of libraries within a state or other regional juristiction paramount for such cooperation. However, based on the experiences outlined above, the awarding of state funding as an incentive for collection development cooperation among libraries of all sizes in a given state or region, and the development of conspectuses to justify more objectively the awarding of grants to institutions within these jurisdictions appear together to constitute a profitable and workable mechanism. It should be examined and contemplated by all coordinators of collection development within the various states.

Output Measures for the Cartographic: Materials Collections of the ARL Libraries: An Exploratory Study

Charles A. Seavey
University of Arizona
Tucson, Arizona

Abstract

Literature measuring and evaluating map collections in this country is briefly reviewed. The measures employed in previous work are identified as simple statistics. The idea of complex statistics is introduced. Output Measures for Public Libraries is identified as the most conceptually advanced, widely used, system for measuring and evaluating libraries in this country. Using available data measures conceptually based on Output Measures are developed for the map collections of the Association of Research Libraries. Descriptive data are produced and evaluated. Rankings of ARL library map collections are developed using two composite index numbers. One measures collection/user interaction, the other measures the facilities devoted to the map collection. Data collection and analysis problems are outlined. Directions for future research are detailed.

Public libraries have done little in the way of measuring of evaluating their collections of cartographic materials (here defined as maps, aerial photography, and remote sensing imagery). Indeed, measurement and evaluation of any part of the academic library is still conceptually limited to simple counts of resources: collections, money, personnel. The Association of Re-search Libraries (ARL) collects data on book, serial, and microform holdings, but does not gather data for the cartographic formats. Hence neither researchers nor library administrators have very much data, let alone agreed upon norms with which to base possible methods of evaluation for map collections.

While the literature includes descriptions of individual map collections, or portions there of, few studies attempt an overall description or analysis of more than one collection. Stanley D. Stevens surveyed 26 predominantly academic map collections in the western United States. His analysis largely dealt with personnel issues, although it did include some general observations on collections.[1] David A. Cobb provided the first attempt to analyze the larger map collections in this country.[2] His analysis was largely descriptive in nature, and limited to the 20 largest map collections in various categories. The second edition of the *Guide to U.S. Map Resources* contains a similar analysis.[3] The present author has measured and ranked the cartographic collections of the ARL institutions, but only on variables related to size and growth of

their collections.[4] These studies are simplistic in that they employ simple counts of individual variables, rather than potentially more information rich complex statistics.

> Complex statistics are defined by Thomas Childers as: " ... more than a simple count; (they) would be calculated from ratios and formulas and would yield a single number that would describe a multifaceted aspect of libraries or library service."[5]

The Public Library Association, in the 1970s, started moving away from standards based on simple counts of resources such as collections and expenditures towards an evaluation system based on complex statistics largely measuring the interaction of the library and its user population.[6] The publication of *A Planning Process for Public Libraries* was the first fruit of this conceptual shift.[7] *Output Measures for Public Libraries* was published as the manual for operational measurement of libraries using the Planning Process. The concepts, and some measures, in Output Measures have been adopted and applied to specific collections within individual libraries, and are starting to have an influence on academic libraries as well.[8]

Output Measures represents a major step towards measures based on complex statistics. The basic goal of Output Measures is to provide measures that reflect both the library and the societal context in which it exists and serves. Twelve library measures are base don 16 variables. All the measures are ratios created by dividing variables by other library variables (i.e: turnover = circulation / holdings), or with potential population being served (i.e.: circulation per capita = circulation /population). The per capita measures are important in that they are measures of the interaction of the library and its public.

This paper is a first attempt to apply the concept of complex statistics, and some of the measures embodied in Output Measures, to map collections in this country. Single numbers are developed to describe multifaceted aspects of cartographic collections. The population selected for study is the map collections of the ARL. The variables developed are those that seem relevant to the peculiar needs of map collections, and that can be constructed from readily available data. It is the first step in a project to study the nature of cartographic collections in this country.

The Data

Data for 89 ARL library map collections located in the United States were collected from the *Guide to U.S. Map Resources*, and the 1988-89 ARL Library Statistics.[9] The variables to be used in this study are presented in figure 1:

Data for *FTE student population* is used to represent the user population in all per capita calculations for this study. Students are not the only users of map collections, and the user population, particularly for ARL collections in large urban areas may be a complex mixture of students, faculty, and off campus users. Students are always the majority of users, and using the FTE count provides the best indicator of overall user population.

Map holdings and *aerial photo holdings* are combined into one figure for calculations involving total holdings.

Square footage refers to the square footage occupied by the map collection.

N. of five drawer map cabinets refers to the number of five drawer, flat file, storage cases used in most map collections. There is some variation in length and width measurements for these units, but the most common are 50" x 38" x 2".[10]

Calculated Variables

Seven variables were calculated from the data collected. All the calculated variables are based conceptually, and in some cases actually, on Output Measures. Because of data collection problems, not all variables can be calculated for all 89 institutions in the population. Hence, they are grouped according to available data. Calculated variables are presented in figure 2:

User related variables were calculated to measure user/collection interaction. *Circulation per capita and turnover rate* are adopted directly from *Output Measures*. Turnover rate is annual circulation divided by holdings. Turnover measures the activity level of the total collection.[11] Turnover, in one sense is a measure of the effectiveness of the collection development policy. Readers per capita is conceptually similar to circulation per capita, and was originally calculated to serve as an interaction variable for measuring institutions that either do not circulate maps, or did not report such data if they do circulate material. Because of the nature of the data it was decided to attempt an overall user interaction measure only for the 46 institutions for which all three variables could be collected.

None of the facilities related variables come from *Output Measures*, and may be regarded as exploratory in nature. *Holdings per square foot* and *square footage per FTE* are both attempts to measure the degree of spaciousness in the facility. Maps are much larger, in length and width measurements than are books, and require more open space for processing, storage, and usage. Reader stations for maps require a much larger square footage than do reader stations for book users. A rule of thumb is that map collections should allow each map user two to three times the space required by a book user. Holdings per square foot, and square footage per FTE are both ways of measuring available user space in the collection. *Maps per five drawer unit* is a way of measuring collection crowding. Three hundred maps in one stack is generally regarded as too many, and most map librarians reckon that 200 per stack, or 1,000 per five drawer unit is an ideal storage situation.[12]

Data Processing

All of the collected variables were entered into the QuattroPro spreadsheet program that was used to derive the calculated variables and all further data manipulation.

Figure 1: Variables Collected

FTE Student Population
Map Holdings
Aerial Photo Holdings
Circulation
Square Footage
N. of Five Drawer Map
Cabinets
Visitors per Month

Figure 2: Calculated Variables

User Related Variables, 58 Institutions
   Circulation per capita
   Annual Readers per capita
   Turnover rate (circulation/holdings)
Facilities Related Variables, 78 institutions
   Holdings per square foot
   Square footage per FTE
   Maps per 5 drawer cabinet

Findings

Findings are divided into two sections: descriptive data, and collection ranking and evaluation. Descriptive data are presented in an attempt to provide some tentative normative data for comparative purposes for non-ARL or non-United States libraries.[13]

Descriptive Data

Figures 3 and 4 present descriptive statistics for user variables and facilities variables, respectively.

The data presented in figure 3 indicate there is a wide variation on these variables among the ARL map collections. While N=58 for all three variables, the data are not from the same 58 institutions. Because of variation in reporting, all three variables are reported by only 45 of the collections. In all cases the coefficient of variation is >1, indicating a scattered distribution.[14] All three distributions are skewed positively. That is, there are more collections on the lower end of the distribution than on the higher. In this situation median, rather than mean, is the more accurate measure of central tendency.

Two of the three variables in figure 4, *holdings per square foot* and *maps per cabinet,* although positively skewed are close to the normal distributions with coefficients of variation <1. *Square footage per FTE* is a more scattered distribution.

Figures 3 and 4 demonstrate that, at least for these variables, there is little consistency among the ARL libraries in usage of the cartographic materials collec-tion. Institutions, or researchers wishing to treat the calculated variables as normative should do so cautiously, except for holdings per square foot, and maps per five-drawer cabinet that are not as widely dispersed as the other variables.

Within the collections a moderate relationship (r=0.64) exists between readers per capita and circulation per 100 FTE.[15] Circulation figures are doubtless more reliable, in most instances, than figures on readers per month. The effect of better data collection on readers might yield a stronger correlation. Circulation per capita and turnover rate are not strongly related (r=0.48), and the relationship of turnover rate and readers per capita approaches entropy (r=0.08).

Ranking the Collections: User Variables

Forty-six institutions collected sufficient data to calculate all three user variables. An overall users index was calculated to rank those 46 institutions. The overall ranking was computed by assigning a rank to each institution for each of the three variables presented above. A score was then assigned based on the reciprocal of that rank using 100 as a base. Thus, if a score ranked first on a given variable it received 99 points (100-1). If a collection ranked 30th it received 70 points (100 30), and so forth. The overall ranking was computed by adding the three variable scores and dividing by 3. A perfect score would have been 99. The numerical scores obtained by this process are statistically meaningless. They serve only to present a rank order of the collections and hence are not reported. Figure 5 shows the 46 institutions ranked by the users index.

Figure 3: Descriptive Statistics, User Variables

	Readers P/C	Circ P/C	Turnover /Rate
Mean	0.23	17.89	0.015
Median	0.17	8.3	0.009
Std	0.31	30.38	0.021
CV	1.3	1.7	1.4
Skew	+	+	+

N≠58
CV+ coefficient of variance

Figure 4: Descriptive Statistics, Facilities Variables.

	Holdings per SqFT	SqFt per FTE	Maps per Cabinet
	N+86	N+86	N=79
Mean	77.1	58.6	1649.8
Med.	58.6	0.14	1267.9
Std.	57.5	0.20	1169.0
CV	0.75	1.2	0.7
Skew	+	+	+

CV= coefficient of variance

Figure 5 represents only those collections that collected sufficient data to calculate all three user variables. Until data collection is improved at the rest of the ARL institutions, such rankings must be regarded as tentative.

Ranking the Collections: Facilities Variables

Seventy-eight institutions collected sufficient data to calculate all three facilities variables. The overall facilities index was calculated in the same fashion as the user index, described above. Figure 6 ranks the institutions according to the facilities index.

In considering figure 6, the reader must remember that these institutions are ranked only because they are the ones that collected data sufficient to calculate all three variables.

There is no way to establish the validity of the facilities index. However, it does tend to confirm the subjective impression of two collections with which this author is familiar. One collection, ranked in the top five by the facility index, is in an area designed to house a map collection in a very recently constructed building. Map cabinet stacks are not more than three high, many drawers are as yet unused, there is a large

Figure 5: Rank, by Overall User Index		Figure 6: Rank by Overall Facilities Index	
N=45		N=45	
1	Texas-Austin	1	SUNY Stony Brook
2	U. Washington	2	Boston University
3	California-Santa Barbara	3	New Mexico
4	Oregon	4	Rice University
5	Florida	5	Stanford
6	Illinois-Urbana	6	North Carolina-Chapel Hill
7	Arizona	7	Northwestern
8	U. of Chicago	8	Syracuse
9	Southern Illinois-Carbondale	9	Columbia
10	Syracuse	10	U. of Washington
11	Utah	11	Arizona State
12	Stanford	12	Miami (Florida)
13	Alabama	13	Oklahoma
14	Penn State	14	Texas Austin
15	Hawaii	15	Michigan
16	Massachusettes	16	U. of Chicago
17	Okalahoma state	17	Alabama
18	Texas A&M	18	Rutgers
19	Arizona State	19	Georgia
20	Indiana	20	Brown
21	Tennessee	21	Calffornia-Irvine
22	North Carolina	22	Nebraska
23	Ohio State	23	Kentucky
24	Minnesota	24	Washington State
25	New Mexico	25	Darmouth
26	California-Berkeley	26	Princeton
27	Missouri	27	Tennessee
28	Iowa	28	Pittsburgh
29	Oklahoma	29	Hawaii
30	Kansas	30	Virginia Polytechnic
31	UCLA	31	California-Santa Barbara
32	Miami (Florida)	32	Texas A&M
33	Kentucky	33	Delaware
34	California State-San Diego	34	Kent State
35	Duke	35	Colorado
36	Vanderbilt	36	Penn State
37	Nebraska	37	California-Berkeley
38	Iowa State	38	Wisconsin
39	Cornell	39	Connecticut
40	Yale	40	Massachusetts-Amherst
41	Brown	41	MIT
42	Michigan	42	Minnesota
43	Rice	43	North Carolina State
44	Notre Dame	44	South Carolina
45	Maryland	45	Ohio State
		46	Iowa
		47	California State-San Diego

amount of space between rows of cabinets, and readers have a lot of space. The other collection, ranked in the bottom third, is in a 1930s era building, in a space not designed for a map collection. The cabinet stacks are at least four high, with little space between stacks, and user space is at a premium. Two bits of anecdotal evidence do not make the facilities index a valid measure, but it does lend it at least some credibility.

Summary and Conclusions

This exploratory research has two goals. First is to create, within the realm of available data, complex statistics measuring multifaceted aspects of academic library map collections in this country and to establish tentatively normative data for other libraries to use for comparative purposes. The second goal was to use the

created variables to measure and rank the ARL library map collections according to complex statistics describing collection/user interaction, and the state of map collection facilities. Goal 1 was accomplished by constructing six ratio level measures based on data from the *Guide to U.S. Map Resources,* and calculating basic descriptive statistics for those variables. Accomplishing goal 2 involved creating composite index numbers out of the individual variables to measure and rank the ARL map collections as to user interaction and facilities.

There are limitations to the study. Based on the descriptive statistics four out of the six calculated variables proved to have very scattered distributions, meaning that their reliability as norms should be viewed with caution. Two of the variables, *holdings per square foot* and *maps per cabinet*, have normal enough distributions that those descriptive statistics can be viewed as having reasonable reliability.

Behind the nature of the distributions displayed, however, lies a larger problem, that of unreliable data collection. It was the author's assumption on starting this study, that the ARL libraries would have reliable data collection methods that would preclude data analysis problems. As shown above, not all libraries collect all variables. It is particularly distressing that only 45 of the collections studied collect sufficient data on their users and usage to be able to construct some very basic output measures. Clearly the ARL collections need to work on establishing standards for collection of data, and sticking to those standards.

Due to data collection and reliability issues, the rankings provided in this study should be viewed as exemplary, rather than authoritative. When data collection and reporting have been refined to the point where we can measure and rank all the ARL collections, then authoritative ranks can be calculated.

While this study has been essentially exploratory in nature, it has demonstrated the possibility of conceptually advancing the state of evaluation of map collections beyond reporting simple counts of sheet maps and aerial photos. Complex statistics, such as those employed here, have been in use in public libraries for almost a decade. It is past time for academic libraries to start doing the same. Maps are almost always used to plot a course into unfamiliar territory, and map collections can plot the course for academic libraries into new territories of evaluation.

Future work in this area involves working with the ARL, and other academic map collections, on improving data collection and reporting procedures, refining and expanding on the measures employed, and developing a holistic evaluation system, conceptually similar to *Output Measures,* for academic cartographic materials collections.

Endnotes

1. Stanley D. Stevens, "Map Librarianship-Today and Tomorrow" *Drexel Library Quarterly* 9: 3-14 (October, 1973).

2. David A. Cobb, "Map Librarianship in the U.S. An Overview" *Wilson Library Bulletin* 60 (October, 1985): 14-156 . The *Wilson Library Bulletin* piece was largely based on Cobb's "Introduction," *Guide to U. S. Map Resources,* 1st ed. (Chicago: American Library Association, 1986).

3. David A. Cobb, "Introduction," *Guide to U. S. Map Resources,* 2nd ed. (Chicago: American Library Association, 1990).

4. Charles A. Seavey, "Ranking and Evaluating the ARL Library Map Collections" *College and Research Libraries* (January, 1992) 31-43.

5. Thomas A. Childers, "Statistics that Describe Libraries" *Advances in Librarianship* 5 (1975): 112.

6. Douglas Zweizig and Elanor Jo Rodger, *Output Measures for Public Libraries: A Manual of Standardized Procedures* (Chicago: American Library Association, 1982).

7. Vernon C. Palmour, Marchia C. Bellassai, and Nancy V. DeWath, *A Planning Process for Public Libraries* (Chicago: American Library Association, 1980). Charles R. McClure, et al., *Planning and Role Setting for Public Libraries* (Chicago: American Library Association, 1987) is the second edition of the *Planning Process..*

8. See Charles A. Bunge, "Factors Related to Output Measures for Reference Services in Public Libraries; Data from Thirty-six Libraries," *Public Libraries* 29 (January-February, 1990): 442-47, and Cynthia M. Wilson "Output Measures Identify Problems and Solutions for Middle Schoolers," *Public Libraries* 29 (January-February, 1990): 19-22. The approach in Nancy Van House, et al., *Measuring Academic Library Performance* (Chicago: American Library Association, 1990), while not strictly the same as that in *Output Measures,* is clearly moving that way. See the discussion on pages 3-9, for instance.

9. David A. Cobb, *Guide* (1990), and Association of Research Libraries, *ARL Statistics, 1988-89.* For a complete description of the data collection process see my "Ranking and Evaluating the ARL Library Map Collections," *C&RL* (forthcoming).

10. Mary L. Larsgaard, *Map Librarianship* 1st ed. (Littleton, Co: Libraries Unlimited, 1978) 165.

11. Douglas Zweizig, op. cit., p. 83

12. This is an essentially undocumented opinion widely held by map librarians. Mary Larsgaard, *Map Librarianship* (1979) uses the figure 300, but implies that the figure is high (p. 163-169).

13. At least one institution not included in early versions of this study has requested such data for comparative purposes. While reliability problems preclude complete acceptance of the data presented here, a start must be made.

14. Hubert M. Blalock, Jr. *Social Statistics* 2nd ed. (New York: McGraw Hill, 1979) p. 84. The coefficient of variation neatly quantifies a statistical rule of thumb which says that if the standard deviation is larger than the mean, the distribution requires careful thought before interpretation.

15. r is used to represent the *Correlation coefficient.* It measures the strength of the relationship between two variables. r can vary from -1 to +1, in either direction, the stronger the relationship between the two variables. See Richard C. Sprinthall, *Basic Statistical Analysis,* 2nd ed. (Englewood Cliffs, NJ: Prentice-Hall, 1982), p. 186-200. Given the nature of the data being analyzed, the figures presented in this paragraph are tentative in nature.

The Impact of ILLINET Online's Development on Resource Sharing

Jay Starratt
Southern Illinois University
Carbondale, Illinois

Carroll Varner
Milner Library
Illinois State University

Pat Cline
Milner Library
Illinois State University

Abstract

ILLINET Online(IO) has a major impact on resource sharing among Illinois academic libraries. The development of IO—first as a circulation system, then as an online catalog, and finally as a statewide union catalog—is reviewed. Use of IO as an interlibrary loan computerized network has generated a wealth of data over the last decade. Interlibrary loan data relevant to resource sharing are identified and used to show one library's resource sharing activity. The data is analyzed to show benefit (borrowing) and liability (lending). A relative benefit of resource sharing to the library is formulated. Two further examples of aggregate data revealing resource sharing patterns are shown. By identifying resource sharing patterns, a case study of one library's resource sharing demonstrates that more equitable arrangements for libraries can be proposed and created.

Introduction

Resource sharing as a concept is supported by nearly every kind and size of library. Nearly twenty years ago, the President of the Inter-university Communications Council (EDUCOM) said, "The rising volume of information and rising level of costs are so great that only through cooperation and the sharing of resources will libraries be able to cope."[1] As resource sharing becomes more important in the library environment and computer technology more powerful, resource sharing systems are being analyzed in an attempt to design and implement more effective resource sharing methods. The source for most data on resource sharing is the interlibrary loan office. As a measure of the importance of its role within academic libraries these days, the interlibrary loan office is frequently overworked, understaffed, and generally struggling to keep up with the demands placed upon it.

In addition to initiating the borrowing and lending of materials, it is usually asked to keep detailed operational statistics. Interlibrary loan is therefore the logical place to start in a bottom-up effort to use existing patterns of lending and borrowing to design new and improved resource sharing systems. In most cases, however, library management uses interlibrary loan data in only a limited fashion, not knowing which data to use or how to apply the data in a meaningful way.

Interlibrary loan among Illinois academic libraries has been greatly aided during the last decade by the Library Computer System (LCS) automated network (now called ILLINET Online or IO). The interlibrary loan requesting mechanism incorporated into IO has resulted in tremendous growth in resource sharing activity. Understanding that growth and recognizing its patterns by analyzing the impact of IO on resource sharing in Illinois is the purpose of this paper.

In describing the future direction of the Illinois experience in library resource sharing, Robert Wallhaus stated in 1985:

First, we will, on a continuing basis, seek to understand the characteristics of our complex, multi-product, multi-echelon, shared inventory. That is, [seek] to analyze the strengths and weaknesses of our statewide library holdings; and to analyze the user demand for our statewide library holdings .... By virtue of [the] LCS data base, I believe, we are well positioned in Illinois to do this.[2]

History of IO

ILLINET Online is a computerized public access library catalog that provides descriptive data for library materials in 800 Illinois libraries. For the 40 libraries that belong to the Illinois Library Computer Systems Organization (ILCSO), ILLINET Online also supports circulation control.

A circulation system was, in fact, the forerunner of ILLINET Online. Developed by IBM for the Ohio State University in the 1960s, the Library Computer System (LCS) came to the University of Illinois with Hugh Atkinson in 1977. The short records of LCS contains holding statements against which transactions can be made for each circulating item. (Full bibliographic records, for the online catalog with circulation data attached, were not created until 1988.)

In 1979, the Illinois Board of Higher Education (IBHE) made funding available via the Higher Education Cooperation Act (HECA) grants for the creation of a statewide network of fourteen academic libraries. The network was planned to enable the use of the LCS system for resource sharing. Fifteen academic libraries and eighteen regional library systems hammered out an agreement for interlibrary borrowing and began exchanging materials in July of 1980. By 1982, the network had grown to twenty academic libraries. Terminals were also placed in each of the eighteen regional library system headquarters and the Illinois State Library for searching and remote borrowing from member libraries. There are presently 40 ILCSO libraries.

In 1980, the Illinois State Library sponsored a project which utilized the software of what was then called the Washington Library Network (WLN) to demonstrate how it might be used as the basis of a statewide automated union catalog. The WLN software was subsequently purchased by the University of Illinois. The River Bend Library System and the University used it to develop a joint catalog of their holdings based on the cataloging data found in their OCLC ILLINET subscription service tapes. This union catalog of full bibliographic records became operational during August of 1984. After receiving LSCA funds in 1985, all of the OCLC ILLINET tapes were included in the weekly update of ILLINET Online. OCLC records processed weekly now total more than twenty thousand.

ILLINET Online can be used to locate a specific item or to do broad subject research. Searches can be done using authors' names, words from titles, subject headings, library call numbers, ISBN numbers, or in several other ways. A search can be done for local holdings or expanded to search the collections of other individual libraries, all libraries in a region of the state (library system), the four Reference & Research Centers, or all 800 ILLINET libraries as a group. After an item is identified and an ILL request is initiated, a document delivery service linking all Illinois libraries transfers the materials between the lending library and the borrowing library.

The document delivery system, Intersystem Library Delivery Service (ILDS), was implemented in 1981 with funding from the Illinois State Library. ILDS makes it possible to offer more efficient and economical delivery services for all libraries within Illinois on six crisscrossing routes run daily.

Today, ILLINET Online contains nearly 5 million unique titles, representing nearly 20 million total holdings, as well as 7 million authority records. The system is available on over 1400 terminals located throughout Illinois. In addition, telephone numbers for dial access users were installed in 1989 for every Illinois area code —six in all. No special authorization is necessary and there are no usage charges. Dial access gives approximately 1500 small libraries the ability to borrow directly from the much larger collections of the ILCSO libraries. ILLINET Online is also available to researchers using the INTERNET as well as some local networks.

Each year, over half a million interlibrary loans are transacted among ILCSO libraries. This level of resource sharing has the potential to save Illinois libraries and taxpayers money by giving people access to items that no single library could hope to provide. As book and journal prices continue to rise, ILCSO libraries share the costs of library materials and the automated service that enables access to them.

Overview of the Data for ARL and ACRL Libraries

The twenty Illinois academic libraries which have been using the LCS system since 1982 may be divided into three categories: two are Association of Research Libraries (ARL) members (a third became an ARL library in 1989); three are members of the Association of College and Research Libraries (ACRL) statistics program (one became an ARL library); fifteen are smaller academic libraries. For purposes of this study, only the ARL and ACRL libraries' statistics are examined. The most recent five year cumulation of those libraries' interlibrary loan data, as submitted to ARL and ACRL, comprises Table 1.

It is readily apparent that all the libraries experienced rapid growth in interlibrary loan activity of all types during the five years. What is not apparent are the internal factors which have contributed to this growth,

TABLE 1

Total Borrowing

Library	FY85	Chg	FY86	Chg	FY87	Chg	FY88	Chg	FY89	5 yr Chg
Illinois State Univ.	6774	28%	8696	19%	10,342	(3%)	9981	4%	10,382	53%
Northern Illinois Univ.	26,520	(3%)	25,618	20%	30,751	3%	31,691	10%	34,755	31%
Southern Illinois Univ.	4692	12%	5265	22%	6429	29%	8311	(1%)	8240	76%
Univ of Illinois Chicago	32,018	(53%)	15,139	294%	59,628	(73%)	16,031	203%	48,639	52%
Univ of Illinois Urbana	132,383	9%	144,760	9%	157,645	5%	164,950	7%	176,750	34%

Source: *ARL Statistics; ACRL University Library Statistics*

Total Lending (Table 1 continued)

Library	FY85	Chg	FY86	Chg	FY87	Chg	FY88	Chg	FY89	5 yr Chg
Illinois State Univ.	15,276	7%	16,415	3%	16,935	14%	19,350	22%	23,579	54%
Northern Illinois Univ.	25,747	32%	34,082	19%	40,522	23%	49,903	(4%)	47,818	86%
Southern Illinois Univ.	46,791	6%	49,570	19%	59,181	(10)%	53,429	4%	55,594	19%
Univ of Illinois Chicago	34,541	(15%)	29,415	187%	84,411	(62%)	31,799	283%	121,899	253%
Univ of Illinois Urbana	119,420	3%	122,803	7%	131,498	4%	136,745	(6%)	128,988	8%

Source: *ARL Statistics; ACRL University Library Statistics*

nor are there external perspectives on the libraries resource sharing relationships. The benefits of this data are the ability to rank each library using the raw numbers and to compare a library's total borrowing to its total lending to determine whether it is a net borrower or net lender.

Taken as a group, we see that rankings change year to year, except for the University of Illinois at Urbana (UIU), which has a huge volume total in both categories every year. (Both of the University of Illinois campuses have recently reported major data irregularities for the 1985-1989 period.) Four of the libraries are consistently net lenders while UIU is consistently a net borrower. From this much data we can see a large commitment to resource sharing (in real numbers, even by UIU, which has a small percentage increase), although internal factors and external perspectives are not clear.

It is not the purpose of this paper to explore the internal factors contributing to interlibrary loan activity. Rather, we attempt to establish a list of data elements which can be used to shed light on the resource sharing activity of these libraries so that upon examination, the benefits and liabilities of that activity can be more clearly seen.

The information in Table 2 is a preliminary list of the interlibrary loan data elements which would be most useful when attempting to show resource sharing patterns. Since the data for resource sharing are not presently being gathered by many interlibrary loan departments, and since traditional operational statistics, e.g. fill rate, response time, are not a concern here, the data must be derived from existing records and recodified. However, the next generation of data can be collected and displayed with the intent of showing resource sharing patterns.

Relative Benefit

As Table 3 demonstrates, a relatively few libraries can account for a high percentage of the interlibrary loans between one library and all other IO participants. From the data supplied by the network, it can be seen that the amount of lending and borrowing between the major participants and a library can be used to generate a "relative benefit" number. Deriving the relative benefit between libraries shows whether a library has a net liability or net benefit from resource sharing with any other library.

After the "borrowed" (benefit) number and the "loaned" (liability) figures are converted into a per-

Table 2

Resource Sharing Data Checklist FOR Interlibrary Loan

I. Number of Items BORROWED from and LOANED to:

    A. Each library in an automated network to which the library belongs.
    B. Each library in a system and other formal arrangement (including a state) in which the library participates.
    C. All other libraries deemed important internally or by agreement.

II. Number of Items by Type of Material

    A. Books
    B. Articles
    C. Microforms
    D. Theses
    E. All other types deemed important internally or by agreement

Table 3

Total Charges and Renewals

Illinois State University, FY89

	Borrowed	% of Total	Loaned	% of Total	B/L Ratio
SIU	524	4.4	329	.8	5.5
UIC	571	4.8	577	1.5	3.2
UIU	5,119	43.3	20,328	53.7	.81
NIU	604	5.1	2,468	6.5	.78
WES	1,077	9.1	6,467	17.1	.53
Subtotal	7,895	66.9	30,169	79.7	1.06
TOTAL	11,806	100.0	37,834	100.0	1.0

Source: LCS Stat 20

centage of totals for an institution, a ratio is created by dividing the borrowed percentage by the loaned percentage. The resulting ratio is the relative benefit. A figure less than one represents a liability and greater than one, a benefit.

The table shows that after calculating the relative benefit between ISU and the other four major libraries in the network, the ISU library has a liability in transaction activity with UIU and NIU. Note that the ratios cannot be compared to one another, but only used for an indication by the ISU library of the relative benefit. Among the libraries remaining, only one (WES; in the same metropolitan area as ISU) has a greater liability.

Using the relative benefit ratio, both internal and external relative benefit for a library can be mapped for any one year or over time. A resource sharing case study for any of the libraries produces significant patterns.

One Library's Interlibrary Loan Patterns Over Time

For this paper, the authors have chosen to show the aggregate use of the IO network by a single library over the last five years. This will reflect the cumulative benefits and liabilities for a library to see if interlibrary loan via the IO system has fulfilled its projected role of enhancing resource sharing. In Table 4, Illinois State University's borrowing has been separated into the two material types which account for over 99% of its activity, books and photocopies. In addition, photocopies acts as something of a control due to the fact that IO has no capability for borrowing photocopies. We are able to judge by the percentage of book borrowing in the state of Illinois and on the IO system what the level of photocopy activity will likely be when the ILL subsystem in development is activated.

Table 4
Illinois State University
Milner Library
Interlibrary Borrowing Statistics

Borrowing -- Books

FROM	FY86	%	FY87	%	FY88	%	FY89	%	FY90	%
Illinois	269	7%	377	7%	464	10%	459	10%	564	10%
Illinois LCS	3085	78%	4223	76%	3441	75%	3347	71%	3612	69%
U.S.	576	15%	937	17%	710	15%	884	19%	1088	21%
TOTAL	3930		5537		4615		4690		5264	

Borrowing -- Photocopies

FROM	FY86	%	FY87	%	FY88	%	FY89	%	FY90	%
Illinois	2969	68%	3529	71%	3867	76%	4154	80%	4604	81%
Illinois LCS	0	-	0	-	0	-	0	-	0	-
U.S.	1399	32%	1467	29%	1198	24%	1047	20%	1061	19%
TOTAL	4368		4996		5065		5203		5665	

Table 5
Illinois State University
Milner Library
Interlibrary Lending Statistics

Lending -- Books

TO	FY86	%	FY87	%	FY88	%	FY89	%	FY90	%
IL Systems	2450	13%	1427	10%	1557	9%	1897	10%	1990	9%
IL LCS	13,826	76%	12,080	82%	13,434	75%	14,680	79%	18,137	82%
U.S.	2010	11%	1119	8%	2837	16%	2125	11%	2076	9%
Total	18,286		14,626		17,828		18,702		22,203	

Lending -- Photocopies

TO	FY86	%	FY87	%	FY88	%	FY89	%	FY90	%
IL Systems	1229	68%	1527	69%	2067	70%	3463	74%	8248	77%
Illinois LCS	0	-	0	-	0	-	0	-	0	-
U.S.	566	32%	687	31%	866	30%	1196	26%	2512	23%
Total	1795		2214		2933		4659		10,760	

The amount of book borrowing within Illinois by the Illinois State University Library has ranged between 79 and 85 percent of its total borrowing and within the IO network between 78 and 71 percent, decreasing over that time. The activity on the IO network can be viewed as internal resource sharing benefit and the remainder within Illinois as external resource sharing benefit. Including photocopies, the amount of borrowing within Illinois has ranged between 68 and 81 percent of the total (increasing). This represents a five year growth rate of 55 percent for intrastate borrowing. The percentage of total photocopies being borrowed from outside of Illinois during this time declined from 32 percent of the total to 19 percent, which demonstrates a substantial benefit from IO.

Table 5 is divided in the same manner as Table 4 and shows startlingly similar results. While the totals in real numbers are much larger for lending (roughly 3 to 1 lending to borrowing), the percentage of books loaned to non-IO libraries has decreased from 13 to 9 percent of the total over five years. (Recall that the borrowing total from IO libraries had increased from 7 to 10 percent of the total borrowing.) The photocopy lending within Illinois ranged between 68 and 77 percent (increasing), while photocopy borrowing ranged between 68 and 81 percent (increasing).

Summary

Without question, interlibrary loan activity in Illinois academic libraries has increased markedly during the last decade. By examining data collected by the libraries, their relative borrowing and lending characteristics over time can be shown. Not only can it be shown, but to some extent it can be predicted; net borrowers tend to remain net borrowers and net lenders tend to remain net lenders. To be useful for resource sharing, however, the libraries' collected data must continually be re-examined and data which lends itself to resource sharing analysis must be collected.

Such data could be analyzed in several profitable ways: by a library to determine its resource sharing activity each year and over time; by a network to model resource sharing benefits and liabilities among its members; by a state to arrive at a picture of its library resource sharing patterns. Numerous operational and planning questions can be posed and answered using resource sharing data.

Examination of one library's data over time yields worthwhile information pertaining to the benefits and liabilities derived from resource sharing. In the case examined briefly here, it can be seen that while the total number of borrowed and loaned items increased, the relative benefit within the academic library network decreased somewhat for books, but increased somewhat for photocopies. The relative liability then increased somewhat for books and even more for photocopies. However, neither in the case of books, nor of photocopies, was the relative liability significantly greater over time than the relative benefit.

Much work remains to be completed before a comprehensive picture of resource sharing by a single library or group of libraries can be drawn. By identifying these patterns, however, we believe that a better understanding of resource sharing's effects will be reached, so that a way for a more equitable arrangement for all libraries can be proposed and created.

Endnotes

1. Henry Chauncey, "Regional and National Computer Networks for Resource Sharing by Colleges and Universities," in Resource Sharing in Libraries , Allen Kent, ed. (New York: Marcel Dekker, Inc., 1974), p. 268.
2. Robert Wallhaus, "Library Resource Sharing: The Illinois Experience," in Coordinating Cooperative Library Development, Wilson Luquire, ed. (New York: Haworth Press, 1986), p. 18.

Psychology Collection Development in the Academic Library: Issues and Local Strategies

Ellen D. Sutton
University of Illinois
Urbana-Champaign, Illinois

Abstract

Psychology bibliographers need to make use of available information and work within their own institutions and across institutions to establish adequate support for the discipline today

A number of issues have emerged in the past several decades relevant to collection development of psychology materials for the academic library. The nature of the discipline has been changing toward an increasingly scientific definition, and the configuration of psychology departments and their coverage of the various subdisciplines of psychology have changed as well. Additionally, the responsibility for training clinical psychologists and the presence of a medical library in a university library system can have a decided impact on collection development issues for the psychology bibliographer, requiring cooperative decision making with the psychiatry/ mental health bibliographer of the medical library. Psychology publishing is changing as well, and reflects the maturation of psychology as a science. Journals in psychology are proliferating, and the inflation rate for psychology journals is one of the highest of all disciplines over the past several years. Their titles reflect the increasing specialization within the discipline. Books continue to be important in the field of psychology, so concentrating collection funds on serial publications is not feasible for this discipline.

The total allocation for psychology in large research libraries is often inadequate for the support of the campus' research and instructional activities, and is a matter of growing concern among heads of graduate departments of psychology in this country. This paper will examine both internal and external issues surrounding psychology collection development in academic libraries, as well as a means of acquiring both published and local information necessary for making difficult decisions.

Nature of the Discipline

Psychology emerged as a discipline akin to philosophy, as both were loosely associated with the nature of the human mind and its motivating concepts or principles. This early association of psychology with philosophy is evidenced by the fact that both disciplines share the BF classification of the Library of Congress classification system and the 100 category of the Dewey Decimal System, which is entitled "Philosophy, parapsychology and occultism, psychology". The current practice of academic psychology is less mentalistic than previously, and is soundly based in scientific inquiry and method, such as the experimental replication of human behavior and the examination of the physiological phenomena of perceptual processes.

Internal Factors: Local Academic Psychology Programs and Library Support of the Subdisciplines of Psychology

As resources for library materials have become more scarce, it has become increasingly important to learn the aspects of psychology supported in the curriculum and research activities of the department of psychology at individual institution's. One problem faced at the University of Illinois is the lack of adequate financial support to accompany the continuous assignment of responsibility for the subfields for which there is no principal or alternative home. In a given psychology department at a major university, various schools of psychological thought, such as Jungian, Freudian, Adlerian, or Gestalt, may have no representation in terms of instruction or research. The influence of psychoanalysis as theory remains particularly influential in humanistic disciplines such as literature and philosophy, but psychoanalysis has become increasingly disassociated with academic psychology in the United States. However, the library has been charged to represent these schools of thought for the purposes of other departments, other members of its clientele, cooperative collection development agreements with other academic libraries, or its own sense of responsibility as a research library. It is difficult to rationalize continuing to spend psychology money on the journal *Psychoanalysis and Contemporary Thought* at the expense of *Developmental Neuropsychology* when faculty request the latter title. The library should definitely have both titles, but the responsibility for purchasing may be difficult to determine or justify. The problem of support of psychology can be mitigated or compounded by the presence or absence of a medical school on campus which trains psychiatrists and practicing psychoanalysts, whose library supports these clinical areas. In institutions which have no local training program for medical practitioners, the main library has to support these areas as best it can and work on improvement of document delivery services from outside institutions.

Local psychology collection development policies are guides to definitions of appropriate subfields and relative levels of support of those areas within a particular institution. Determining the needs of the local academic community has become increasingly important now that bibliographers are faced with difficult choices among appropriate scholarly materials. Locally obtained data from faculty and student clientele can contribute to better informed decisions. For example, examination of local library circulation data can furnish information on amount of use of certain journals or categories of monographs. A user survey can elicit information on foreign languages read by faculty or student members of the psychology department. While external data, such as a journal's citation impact factor or coverage in *Psychological Abstracts* will contribute to a decision to keep a foreign language journal, data on whether local users are likely to read the journal may be helpful for a borderline title.

Economic Factors and Publication Output
in Psychology

Journals in psychology are proliferating, although at a slower rate than other scientific disciplines. Psychology journals in the Faxon database increased by 23% between 1977 and 1989; during that same time period, science and technology titles increased by 103%. It should be noted that the Faxon category for psychology includes general psychology titles, whose call numbers are in the BF category, and not clinical psychology titles, whose call numbers are in the R category, the category which represents medicine. Several major

new psychology journals per year are emerging from major U.S. publishers such as Erlbaum, Wiley, Plenum, and Pergamon. Adding new titles may require cancelling a title the Library has held for seventy or more years. However, the new journals are more likely to reflect current trends and concerns in the field, and have recruited prominent psychologists for their editorships and editorial boards. The fact that libraries are finding it more difficult to add new titles seems to have had little impact on the will of a publisher or a professional organization to establish a new journal. Additionally, publishers seem no more inclined to reduce the gap between individual and institutional subscription rates.

Inflation of serial prices in psychology has been a serious factor for the past several years. Unpublished Faxon estimates from Spring 1991 indicated that inflation for psychology journals would be among the highest of all disciplines in 1992: approximately 16%. *Library Journal's* annual survey of U.S. periodical prices has ranked psychology 7th in average subscription price for the years 1985 to 1991. The average price for a psychology journal subscription in 1991 was $135.40. The average 1991 subscription price for engineering periodicals, ranked 6th, was $160.13; and for sociology and anthropology, ranked 8th, the average subscription price was $88.69.[1] Book prices are also increasing, although their rate of increase is more representative of the general inflation rate, with the exception of certain publishers.

Erosion of the psychology monographic budget to accommodate serials price inflation is not a viable option for the research library, because serial publications do not dominate psychology to the extent that they do in fields such as chemistry and physics. The American Psychological Association's Office of Nonserials Operations has estimated that 2,187-2,343 professional level books of interest to researchers and academicians are published per year, based on the years 1987-1989, and that an estimated one-third of books published in this category are edited books.

The publishing industry has developed various mechanisms for accumulating and reporting data on publishing output and price indexes. The companies compiling this sort of data for publication have been associated with the field of library science for quite some time. Most of the published data on publishing are produced by the R.R. Bowker Company and are summarized in the *Bowker Annual of Library and Book*

Trade Information.[2] It is important to distinguish figures for all publications or for trade publications from figures on scholarly or professional publications when interpreting the available data. There are certain problems with these standard sources of publication data with respect to psychology. For example, *Publisher's Weekly's* annual figures for book production lump psychology and philosophy in one category.[3] Other measures, such as *Library Journal's* "Price Index for U.S. Periodicals," mentioned above, are more refined with respect to subject and are therefore more useful.

Publication data for a specific discipline is sometimes available on request by distributors such as Faxon and agencies involved in indexing journals, such as the American Psychological Association. For example, the APA's Nonserials Operations office furnished on request the previously mentioned findings, on the number of psychology books being published. Such data is extremely useful in determining the proportion of the budget to be spent on books versus periodicals. Information on publishing output is available through published research as well, by persons who have already synthesized data from various other sources. For example, a recent study traced indexing by various databases, including PsycINFO, for over twelve years, and reported figures for numbers of total records and records of various languages added to the databases.

Assembling Your Argument: Gathering Data on Peer Institutions

Information collected from other institutions about their allocations and expenditures for psychology and the existing strengths of their collections can be extremely useful in determining appropriate local support and marshalling an argument for an increased level of support for psychology. The relative level of support of psychology with respect to other disciplines has never been reconciled to the satisfaction for psychologists and psychology bibliographers at a number of research libraries. Now, in times of greater fiscal constraints, efforts to increase the percentage of a library's budget to accommodate an appropriate level of support of psychology is likely to require reallocation of internal resources rather than assignment of new resources.

In determining levels of support needed for psychology materials in a research library, it is useful to have comparative data from peer institutions. For example,

if most research libraries with approximately equivalent collections budgets supporting relatively similar psychology programs spend 3% of their annual collection budget on psychology and another library spends 2%, an argument can be made to increase the latter's budget. Gathering comparative statistics from multiple libraries requires great care in ensuring that comparable things are being counted and that the most knowledgeable person or persons are being contacted.

In cross-institutional comparisons, specific subdisciplines covered in the academic program of all institutions being compared must be delineated, and factors such as size and reputation of the respective departments considered. Comparative data on institutions is somewhat scarce, and not entirely satisfactory. The most thorough assessment of graduate departments of psychology was done in 1982, and is entitled *Assessment of Research-Doctorate Programs in the United States: Social and Behavioral Sciences*,[4] part of a series of such assessments sponsored by the Conference Board of Associated Research Councils. It offers little synthesis by institution of the various categories of information provided, but is extremely thorough and useful for comparative data by specific categories, such as program size, amount of research support, library size, and reputation of faculty.

Once peer institutions are identified, data on library support of psychology materials must be collected from the person or persons responsible for collection development in psychology at those institutions. The number and nature of all of the funds supporting psychology materials within each institution must be identified. Once all of the applicable funds are identified, non-psychology funds need to be analyzed to determine amount of allocation or expenditure for psychology titles. For instance, the expenditure on the education materials fund for educational psychology materials needs to be assessed.

A problem in assembling comparable data is local variation in accounting and distribution of materials funds. Serials funds and monographs funds may be combined in one library and not in another, and approval plan funds may be separate from subject funds. Some libraries may not break down data on their materials funds into finer categories than, for example, "social sciences" or "life sciences."

Data on relative collection strengths among peer institutions is useful in assembling an argument for collection support locally, but may be equally difficult to obtain. Measures of collection strengths in particular subject areas across libraries have been problematic. Two major projects involved in evaluating relative collection strength are The National Shelflist Count (NSC)[5] and the North American Collections Inventory Project (NCIP).[6] Both projects include counts of call number ranges in shelflists, with all of the inherent pitfalls in counting psychology materials, which are spread over many LC classifications and branch libraries. Both have methodological problems related to indefinite application guidelines and local practices in recording holdings.

The National Shelflist Project is more mature than the NCIP and has produced data every several years on the holdings in psychology for participating institutions since 1973. The major flaws of the National Shelflist Count are 1) that it is a simple count of total holdings, and represents size rather than quality of the collection, and 2) that participation by various libraries has been inconsistent.

The North American Collections Inventory Project, which was introduced by the Association of Research Libraries in association with the Research Libraries Group, Inc. (RLG), and has been refined in recent years, is a more complex, flexible and ambitious undertaking which provides a framework for analyzing the quality as well as the quantity of various subject collections within and across institutions. The project makes use of the Conspectus, a tool created by the RLG, which is used to create an "overview of existing collection strengths and future collecting intensities at specific institutions."[7] It allows for the assessment of specific subjects by subject specialists as well as more quantitative measures of collection strength.

Problems in using the NCIP process as a source of comparative data include the fact that the process allows varying degrees of thoroughness in application of its evaluation process and local flexibility in defining the subject areas, collection strengths, and collecting levels. Thus, the very strength of the NCIP process, which recognizes both the complexity of collection evaluation (including the institutional context in which the collection is used) and the reality of local factors related to participation in the project (such as subject expertise and available staff hours for conducting the evaluation), makes it less valuable as a source of comparison across institutions than as a source of information about one's own collection.

A more recent tool for comparative analysis of collections among peer institutions is the AMIGOS Collection Analysis Service and the preconfigured OCLC/AMIGOS Collection Analysis CDs. Both of these systems make use of machine-readable bibliographic records, in this case MARC records from the OCLC database, to provide computerized quantitative analyses of individual library collections or the mutual holdings of a prescribed set of peer institutions. The Collection Analysis Service can utilize a variety of subject indicators, including RLG Conspectus subject categories or Library of Congress classification numbers. While the Service offers more opportunity for customized analysis employing a larger segment of the OCLC database, the CD products may be used repeatedly for a variety of local applications and operate on equipment ordinarily available in OCLC member libraries. The savings in labor from new systems such as AMIGOS over manual efforts required to collect statistical data from a shelflist or even local automated systems will make collection assessment a more feasible undertaking for libraries.

Conclusion

Emerging trends, such as electronic publishing, document delivery services, cooperative collection development among research libraries, and decreasing support for higher education will have a great impact on collection development in academic libraries. In the meantime, psychology bibliographers need to work within their own institutions and across institutions to ensure that academic psychology is adequately supported in the nation's major research libraries.

Endnotes

1. Kathryn Hammell Carpenter and Adrian W. Alexander, "Price Index for U.S. Periodicals 1991," *Library Journal* 116 (April 15, 1991): 53.
2. *Bowker Annual of Library and Book Trade Information,* 1955/56. (New York: Bowker.)
3. *Publisher's Weekly* collects general statistics on book production in the U.S. These are no limited to scholarly book production, and are summarized each March in *Publisher's Weekly*.
4. *An Assessment of Research-Doctorate Programs in the United States: Social and Behavior Sciences.* (Washington, D.C.: National Academy Press, 1982).
5. The most recent count is *National Shelflist Count: Titles Classified by Library of Congress and Na-*

tional Library of Medicine Classifications 1989. prepared for the Association of Library Collections & Technical Services, American Library Association, by the Library Research Center of the Graduate School of Library & Information Science, Univeristy of Illinois at Urbana-Champaign, 1990.

6. The primary source of information on the NCIP process is *Manual for North American Inventory of Research Library Collections.* Revised ed. Prepared by Jutta Reed-Scott. (Washington, D.C.: Association of Research Libraries, Office of Management Services, 1988). For further information on the NCIP, see, for example, Jeffrey J. Gardner, "National Collections Inventory Project: A Brief Description," in *Encyclopedia of Library and Information Science,* Vol. 31, Supplement 6, p. 229-230, (New York: Marcel Dekker, 1986); or Paul H. Mosher, "A Natural Scheme for Collaboration in Collection Development: The RLG-NCIP Effort," *Resource Sharing and Information Networks* 2 (Spring/Suimmer, 1985): 21-35.

7. Nancy E. Gwinn and Paul H. Mosher, "Coordinating Collection Development: The RLG Conspectus," *College & Research Libraries* 44 (March, 1983): 128-140.

8. Ann Armbrister, "Library MARC Tapes as a Resource for Collection Analysis: The Amigos Service," *Advances in Library Automation and Networking* 2 (1986): 119-135.

The Leopoldo Cicognara Project: Access to Primary Literary Sources in the History of Art and Archaeology

Lizabeth (Betsy) Wilson
University of Illinois
Urbana, Illinois

Abstract

In 1824, the Vatican Library acquired the entire library of approximately 5,000 books on art and archaelogy assembled by Leopoldo Cicognara (1767-834). This was the largest and most judiciously selected art library ever brought together. The majority of Cicognara's books are presently unavailable outside the Vatican where, at most, five may be viewed on a typical day. Through a major collaborative, international, not-for-profit initiative, the collection is now available on microfiche to libraries world-wide. By employing available technologies, physical and bibliographic access has been enhanced, so that the literary sources in art history have become widely available in a fascinating diversity and can be surveyed as a whole in libraries everywhere.

In the world's great libraries are unique collections to which scholars travel at significant personal sacrifice in order to further their research. The Leopoldo Cicognara Collection in the Vatican Library has been beckoning scholars over the past century and one-half. Those who can not journey to Rome have come to appreciate its riches through Cicognara's annotated catalog, if a copy of the now long-exhausted edition is locally available. Through a major, international, not-for-profit initiative involving the Vatican Library, the University of Illinois at Urbana-Champaign Library, the Samuel H. Kress Foundation, and Chadwyck-Healey, Ltd., scholars no longer are required to travel to Rome to consult the most significant collection of books on art and antiquity. Through the creative use of available information and microphotographic technology, Cicognara's books are now available to an expanding circle of scholars, students, and librarians world-wide.

Cicognara's Life[1]

Leopoldo Cicognara (1767-1834) was a member of the nobility of Ferrara. The foundation of his interest in art was that of an aristocratic dilettante. He welcomed the French Revolution as an Italian patriot and a lover of liberty. The glory of art and the dignity of society under a rule of freedom were intimately connected for Cicognara. He supported the progress of the French armies into Italy as a commander of Italian forces and later distinguished himself as an able administrator in the recently freed Italian territories.

Napoleon appreciated his bravery and his circumspection and loyalty as a civil servant. A great political career lay ahead of Cicognara, but he was alienated from French policy by the decrees which forced the transfer of many of the finest works of art from Italy to Paris.

Cicognara decided to put all his energies into the defense of the arts. Works of art continued to be dispersed or suffered destruction in consequence of the enormous social changes all over Europe by the Revolution. Their protection and the study of their history gained a new urgency. In 1808, Napoleon appointed Cicognara president of the newly re-established Accademia delle Belle Arti in Venice. Cicognara reformed the Academy, enlarged its museum, and defended the artistic patrimony of Venice. After the fall of Napoleon, the Austrians reconfirmed Cicognara's appointment acknowledging that his expertise and commitment to art were above politics.

Cicognara's working library of over 5,000 books on art remains the largest and most judiciously selected collection ever assembled from the point of view of a humanist. His *Catalogo* is a veritable guide to the history of the arts from antiquity to his own time.[2] It was this library that provided the foundation for Cicognara's magisterial survey of the history of modern sculpture, the first illustrated book that gives an account of the history of an art.[3] Cicognara's library is his legacy to the study of the literary sources of art and kindred subjects.

The Cicognara Library

In 1824 the Vatican Library acquired the Cicognara Library. Its possession established the Vatican Library as a generously equipped center for studies in the history of art and classical archaeology as well as of art criticism, taste, and aesthetics. The Cicognara Library allows one to enter into discussion, from book to book, on the purposes, the dignity, as well as the practice of art from antiquity to Cicognara's own time. Next to a central hoard of treatises, books, pamphlets, poems, orations, and programs regarding the arts of painting, sculpture, and architecture and their history and relation to literature, music, rhetoric, theology, philosophy and other branches of knowledge, the Library contains everything in print that Cicognara could assemble on the practice of the arts.

Included among these books are many bound volumes of engravings with texts that show how to draw and paint, how perspective works, and how to build houses, bridges, fountains, and machines. In addition, there is a large stock of books on museums and private collections, travel to historic and artistic sites, and guides to illustrated books. Other bound volumes of engravings illustrate works of art and architecture, feasts, funerary rites and solemn entries, costume and dress, and emblems and hieroglyphs. A perusal of the library offers an enlightening view of how artists worked and how collectors of art made their choices.

Challenge of Physical and Bibliographic Access

Limitations on physical and bibliographic access to the Cicognara Library had until the current initiative restricted the exploration of the sources to a small, persistent number of historians. The majority of Cicognara's books are presently unavailable outside the Vatican, where at most five may be seen together on a typical day. In order to discover the full range of material in the collection, a scholar would have to remain in Vatican City for extended periods, a luxury few researchers can afford. Additionally, the physical condition of these rare and old books is a significant preservation concern.

Cicognara's *Catalogo* is one of the earliest and most important bibliographies in the field of art, although not consulted without some difficulty. While scholars, librarians, and students of art have long acknowledged the importance of Cicognara's collection to the study of artistic traditions, it is rarely examined as a total entity because Cicognara's catalog does not provide the researcher ease of access to the collection. Cicognara's system of classification reflects his historical framework and education, making the catalog awkward for those who have been schooled in 20th century art historiography and indexing conventions.

Enhancing Access

Anyone who works with the *Catalogo,* even if he or she is in a well appointed library, can only wish to be in the Vatican, not only because Cicognara owned works are not found anywhere else, but because handling the *Catalogo* fills one with a desire to browse among Cicognara's books. It is almost impossible to satisfy this kind of longing, which is, a chief source of true scholarship, anywhere that rare books are only made accessible in a reading room. The very thought of sitting in the reading room for months on end, with the aim of digging one's way through five thousand books that have to be called up to be looked at is daunting indeed.

The University of Illinois Library and the Vatican Library joined together almost four years ago to render the entire Fondo Cicognara on microfiche. The Vatican Librarian, Father Leonard Boyle, conducted a survey of the condition of the books, reviewed the capability of the photographic services of the Vatican to cope with such a vast assignment, and after consultations with his photographers, determined that the Bibliotheca Apostolica Vaticana would be able to undertake the filming.

The preparation of a new enlarged and critical edition of Cicognara's *Catalogo,* which will be published by the Vatican press, proceeds hand-in-hand with the filming of the Library. The new edition is a cooperative effort of a librarian, an art historian, and a classicist.

In the new edition, all entries in Cicognara's *Catalogo* will be verified and, after each of his entries, all earlier and later editions or translations of a work will be added. Cicognara did not always list his titles accurately but offered approximations or, particularly in the case of German titles, only his own loose translations.

The new catalog will preserve the integrity of Cicognara's original work but at the same time enlarge its usefulness. Anyone concerned with the study of a work of art or a particular subject, will be able to tell, more or less at a glance, what may have been available in print that pertained to the making or the judging of a work of art or to the debate concerning a particular subject. Furthermore, the new edition should be of help to readers not only in establishing their bibliographies but also in tracing the books they need such as those which can be found in libraries other than the Vatican.

International Collaboration

Without the generosity of the Vatican Library and the active support and engagement of Father Boyle, the project could not exist. The University of Illinois at Urbana-Champaign Library has supported the project wholeheartedly from its beginning. The Samuel H. Kress Foundation has rovided material resources and continues to encourage the progress of the Project. The Foundation is particularly interested in the distribution of the microfiche to institutions of learning in the former East Bloc whose libraries suffered calamitous losses due to the wars and other disasters of our times. Sir Charles Chadwyck-Healey, whose firm Chadwyck-Healey, Ltd. of Cambridge, England, produces the microfiche and distributes them to subscribers, accords break-even rates in the interest of the service the Project performs. The Vatican Library is, of course, the chief agent in the creation of the microfiche collection. The delicate task of photographing these rare books, page by page, is performed by the Vatican Library's Department of Photographic Services.

The enterprise is undertaken entirely as a service to scholarship and that not-for-profit status is taken very seriously. The Project is unique in its scope, in the opportunity it offers to students in a variety of fields to explore on their own the history of the visual arts as humanistic discipline, and in its remarkably low cost to subscribers. The intent has been to offer the Cicognara Library at a price that will assure its relatively wide distribution. Only in this way can it produce its chief benefit: to let the sources speak for themselves in fascinating diversity and harmonies.

From Shelves to Fiche

The filming of the books is done in the photographic laboratory of the Vatican Library with a camera equipped with specifications provided by Chadwyck-Healey. The film is then sent to Chadwyck-Healey in Cambridge, where diazo copies are produced. Proof copies are sent to the University of Illinois Library

where, sheet by sheet, assistants check for legibility and for accuracy in the sequence of photographed pages. Project editors establish the abbreviated author-title entries that are found running across the top of each fiche. This information is keyed at Illinois using labeling software and forwarded on computer disc to Cambridge. Chadwyck-Healey then proceeds with the final printing of the microfiche and its delivery to subscribers.

At any given time, project staff is working simultaneously in three locations: Vatican City, Cambridge, and Urbana-Champaign. Communication, trouble-shooting, and establishment of operating procedures are sustained through telephone, FAX, data file transfer, and express mail. Given the range of time zones involved, fax has become the mode of choice.

As of March 1992, almost one-third of the Cicognara Library has been photographed and close to two thousand books and pamphlets on microfiche have been distributed to subscribers. Deliveries to subscribers are made as sets of books are photographed and transformed onto microfiche. As a rule, subscribers receive a delivery of five to eight hundred fiche every three months. It is anticipated that this phase of the filming will be completed within the year.

Conclusion

The advantages which the realization of this project offer to the study of the history of art and to research libraries are self-evident. For a sum within the reach of most institutions, libraries can become the owners, by proxy, of the world's finest library of the literary sources of the history of Western art. Through international cooperation and application of available technology, a unique collection is accessible at every moment of the daily work of the scholar, librarian, or student. Just as art historians cannot imagine doing their work without the help of slides, so perhaps, the day may come when, like Cicognara himself, scholars, students, and librarians too cannot think of doing research without a steady contact with the books that mattered to him so much that he impoverished himself in order to acquire them.

Endnotes

1. This narrative on Cicognara's life is based on an essay delivered by Philipp P. Fehl at the College Art Association Conference in Washington, D.C.,

on February 21, 1991.

2. The full title of the catalog is *Catalogo ragionato dei libri d'arte e d'antichita posseduti dal Conte Cicognara* (Pisa, 1821).

3. *Storia della scultura dal risogimento su in Italia sino al secolo do Napoleone* (Venice, 1813-81). The second, revised, and enlarged edition was more wisely entitled *Storia della scultura dal risorgimento su in Italia fino al secolo di Canova* (Prato, 1823-24).

4. *Die Kunstliteratur* (Vienna, 1924). Translated into Italian as *La Letteratura artistica* (Florence, 1956), with additions by Otto Kunz.

CONTRIBUTED PAPERS

V.
GENERAL
ADMINISTRATION

The Question of Paperbacks for Academic Libraries: Selection, Treatment Options, and Durability

Stanley P. Hodge
Ball State University
Muncie, Indiana

Abstract

Many criteria are considered by collection management librarians when selecting monographs for an academic library. Of increasing relevance is the availability of simultaneous editions of paperback and hard cover editions. This paper examines two important budgetary considerations and the results of a durability study testing three conservation alternatives for quality paperbacks. First, comparative cost data for paperback vs. hard back editions are presented based on books reviewed by CHOICE. Second, cost factors, including in-house labor, are examined for three options of treating paperbacks. Third, results are provided for a 21/2 year durability study of 368 paperbacks added to an academic library collection. Significant materials and binding budget savings may accrue to academi libraries when sound judgement is exercised in selecting paperback editions and choosing cost-effective conservation treatments.

The concept of collection management encompasses many facets, which include: sound use of the materials budget; judicious selection based on multiple variables; and, cost-effective conservation decisions. The question of selecting paperback books for an academic library embraces all three of these concerns. As an acquisitions or collection development librarian for many years, this writer has been intrigued by the price differentials between quality paperback books and their hardbound equivalents. "Intrigued" is perhaps too mild a term. In many cases, "surprised," or "shocked" is more appropriate; for it is not unusual to find a difference of twenty-five or more dollars between the two versions of the same title. Thus, an initial question confronting the collection management librarian regarding paperbacks is a budgetary one. To illustrate the potential magnitude of this issue, some findings using *Choice*, a popular selection tool used by most academic library book selectors, are provided in Figure 1.

Retail Price Considerations: Paper vs Bound

The May, 1991 issue of *Choice* reviews 92 books offering the selector an option to choose either a paperback or hardbound version of the same title. The mean list price for the 92 paperback editions is $17.15, while that of their corresponding hardbound versions is $43.21. This mean difference of $26.06 is more than enough, on average, to purchase an additional paperback at the same price for each title and still have funds remaining for conservation treatment.

Some of the more glaring examples of the wide price differentials in this issue of *Choice* are:

Nonlinear Waves, Solitons and Chaos, Cambridge U.P., $29.95 pap., $85.00 bound.

Teaching, Schools, and Society, Falmer, $33.00 paper, $88.00 bound.

A Hemisphere To Itself: A History of U.S. -Latin American Relations, Zed Books, $15.95 paper, $55.00 bound.

Despite these extreme examples and the overall average price differential in this survey, many "traditionalist" collection managers may object to selecting paperbacks for strictly economic reasons. Typical reactions may be:

* "We collect for *posterity* and want the best edition available; the paper and other physical characteristics of paperbacks are inferior."

* "We would buy the hardback even if there were an option since paperbacks won't hold up under circulation. When forced to select a

FIGURE 1

MEAN AVG. RETAIL PRICE OF 92 SIMULTANEOUS
EDITIONS REVIEWED IN MAY 1991 ISSUE OF CHOICE

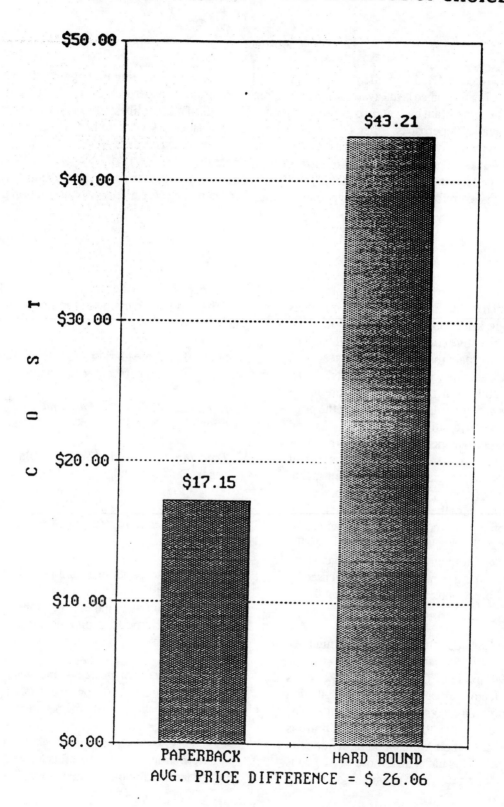

paperback we would proceed with our automatic policy of having it commercially bound."

Two examples from collection development policies of academic libraries imply this:

The library will purchase single copies of hardback books whenever possible. Paperback books will be acquired only when there is no choice in the format of binding . . ." (Wilkes College Library Collection Development Policy)

The (Library) adds permanently bound volumes to the collection, except in those cases where paper bound titles are originals." (University of Wisconsin-Stout Library Collection Development Policy)

There are circumstances when it is judicious to select the hardbound version for a library collection, despite a difference of $15.00 to $20.00, or more. And, the two objections above are addressed later in this paper.

Conservation Treatment Options

First, let's look at another paperback question confronting collection managers—conservation treatment. During November, 1988, 389 newly acquired paperbacks awaiting conservation treatment in Ball State University library's processing unit were randomly assigned to three groups for a test of treatment options. (Table 1)

Option One consisted of no conservation treatment. The paperback book was placed on the shelf with only

TABLE 1

TREATMENT OPTIONS AND COST/TITLE

		SAMPLE SIZE
OPTION 1 -- NO TREATMENT		122
Materials	$ 0 00	
In-house Labor	$ 0.00	
OPTION 2 -- KAPCO "EASY COVER"		137
Materials	$ 0.90	
In-house Labor	$ 1.06	
TOTAL	$ 1.96	
OPTION 3 -- HECKMAN "HPB" COMMERCIAL BINDING		130
Bindery's Charge	$ 3.25	
In-house Record Keeping	$ 0.36	
TOTAL	$ 3.61	
Total Sample Size		389

its call number, book pocket, and the usual property stamps, with no reinforcement or cover protection whatsoever.

Option Two was the "Easy Cover" solution, performed in-house. This consisted of affixing to the paperback's cardboard covers and spine, a clear .5 mm plastic coating with a self-adhesive glue applied by Kapco, Easy Cover's manufacturer. The material and in-house labor associated with this option averaged $1.96 per title.

Option Three, called "HPB," consisted of sending the paperback book to the Library's commercial binder, Heckman, where cloth-covered boards and end papers were "perfect bound," or glued to the spine. The book's original front cover was also fastened to the front, and the author, title, and call number printed on the spine. The binder's average charge for "HPB" was $3.25 per title, and in-house costs for record keeping associated with these bindery shipments averaged $0.36, for a total conservation cost of $3.61 per book.

This division of randomly selected paperbacks for three treatment options was preparatory to the next phase of the paperback survey—a test of the durability after they were subjected to the rigors of handling by university faculty, students, and library shelvers. A log sheet (Table 2) for each title was prepared indicating call number, bibliographic information, type of treatment, and a record of condition and circulation data at periodic time periods.

Durability Study

The 389 randomly assigned titles covered the full range of the LC classification schedule, and included 10 titles assigned to a juvenile collection and two oversize books as well. Every six months, each title was examined as to its condition and the number of circulations to date. Over two and one half years, five data gathering checks were completed and recorded on log sheets. At the survey's conclusion, 21 books had been reported either lost, missing, or circulating, and were deleted from the study's final results. Some findings for the 368 surviving titles, along with circulation data are portrayed in Figures 2-4.

Seventy percent of the 368 remaining books had circulated at least once. The mean for circulating titles ranges from 4.5 for the "HPB" books, to 5.2 for "Easy Cover" titles. Noteworthy was the fact that 13 books

circulated at least 15 times, the most being 23 over the life of the test. In contrast, 110 titles (30%) in the sample did not circulate at all. Collection managers are always interested in what titles or classification categories circulate the most, and which just sit on the shelves. (The winner of the popularity contest in this study was *No more fear: sexual assault and the option of rape prevention*, followed closely by *The truth about Dracula*, with 22 circulations. These popular books should not be construed as reflecting poorly on Ball State's reputation. Even in academia we occasionally nod our heads in the direction of the "Give 'Em What They Want" philosophy!)

However, what is more important in our examination here is the durability of the conservation treatments. Of the 368 titles available for examination at the conclusion of the test period, 68 had sustained minor damage not requiring immediate repair; five books had been rebound; and one had been repaired. Table 3 categorizes, by treatment option, the amount and types of minor damage encountered. Figure 5 graphically portrays the percentage of books in each treatment option that: (1) sustained no problems; (2) incurred minor cover damage; (3) required rebinding; and, (4) were repaired. The contents of all books, i.e., the pages themselves, were all intact, though some pages were bent, marked, or slightly loose.

It is interesting to compare results found for Option 1, (no treatment), with those found by Presley and Landram at Georgia State University Library a few years ago. Their study tracked life expectancy of unbound paperback titles in initial and follow-up articles published in *Technical Services Quarterly*.[1,2] About the same percentage (72%) of paperbacks circulated after four years at G.S.U. as did untreated paperbacks at Ball State after two and one half years. They found that after four years, 38% were damaged, with only eight (3%) of the 188 unbound paperbacks requiring binding. In comparison, 41% of the untreated books in the Ball State study were slightly damaged after two and one half years, with one rebinding. Presley and Landram also concluded that "whether a paperback book is glued or sewn appears to make little difference as to its durability ..."[3]

Conclusions

In conclusion, let me restate the two previous hypothetical objections to the purchase of quality paperbacks in lieu of hardbound editions, despite significant

TABLE 2

LOG SHEET

Type: __No Treatment__

Call No: DS 559.8 .S3 B37 1988

Author/Title: Berry, F. Clifton
Gadget warfare

Glued:____   Date Selected:_____
Sewed:____   Cost:_____

Date Checked	Not on Shelf	Charged Out	No. X Circ	Condition*	Rebind	Replace	Remarks
5/11/89	✓	No					
6/7/89			2	Good			
12/13/89			3	Front pages starting to come loose			
6/20/90			5	good, front pgs. loose			
12/19/20			5	front pages loose cover slightly frayed at edges			
7/1/91			6	front pgs very loose cover fraying			

*Use the following phrases as appropriate:

   Broken spine
   Bent cover
   Torn cover
   Loose cover
   Missing cover
   Loose pages
   Bent pages

Indicate the extent of the above conditions: slight, moderate, severe

FIGURE 2

NO TREATMENT

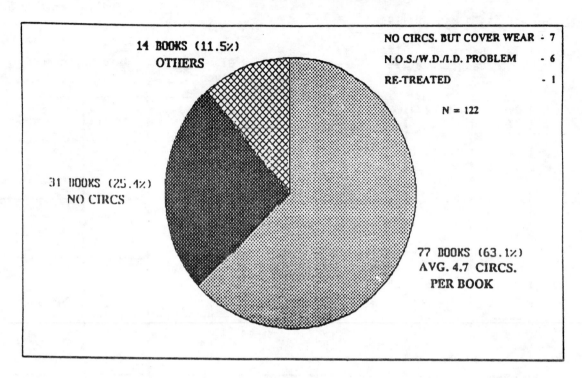

14 BOOKS (11.5%)
OTHERS

NO CIRCS. BUT COVER WEAR - 7

N.O.S./W.D./I.D. PROBLEM - 6

RE-TREATED - 1

N = 122

31 BOOKS (25.4%)
NO CIRCS

77 BOOKS (63.1%)
AVG. 4.7 CIRCS.
PER BOOK

FIGURE 3

EASY COVER

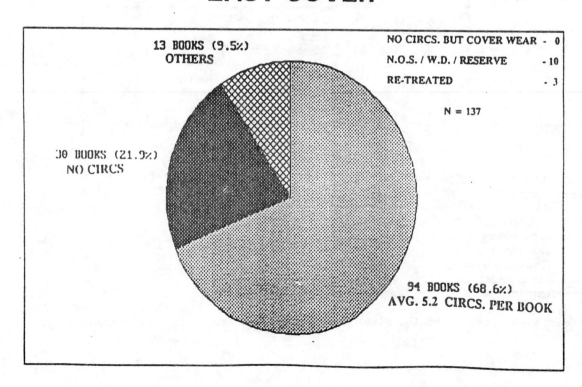

13 BOOKS (9.5%)
OTHERS

NO CIRCS. BUT COVER WEAR - 0

N.O.S. / W.D. / RESERVE - 10

RE-TREATED - 3

N = 137

30 BOOKS (21.9%)
NO CIRCS

94 BOOKS (68.6%)
AVG. 5.2 CIRCS. PER BOOK

FIGURE 4

HPB BINDING

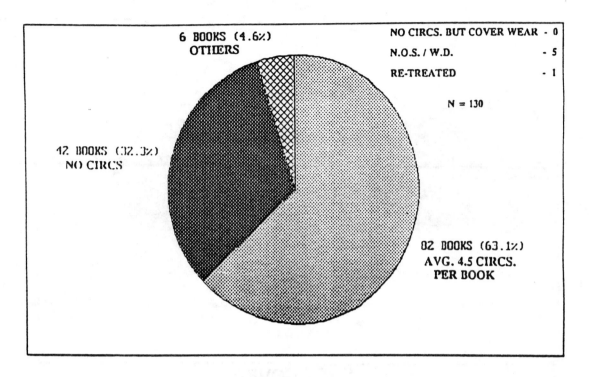

TABLE 3

TYPE OF MINOR DAMAGE BY TREATMENT OPTION

DAMAGE	NO TREATMENT N = 116	EASY COVER N = 127	HPB N = 125
1. BENT COVER	20	6	0
2. WORN COVER	12	1	1
3. BENT & WORN	7	3	0
4. LOOSE COVERS	3	5	0
5. LOOSE PAGES	1	3	0
6. BENT & TORN	2	0	0
7. LOOSE & TORN	.1	1	0
8. LOOSE & WORN	1	1	0
REPAIRED	0	1	0
REBOUND	1	3	1
T O T A L	48	24	2

FIGURE 5

NO TREATMENT   HPB BINDING

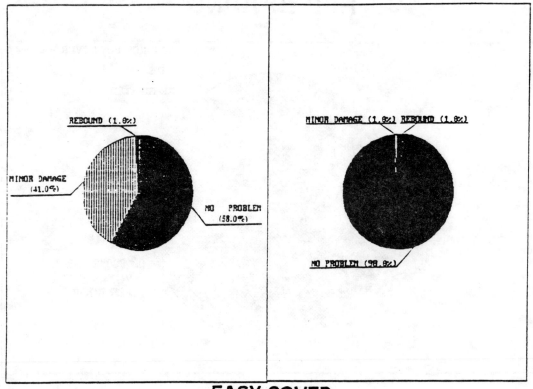

EASY COVER

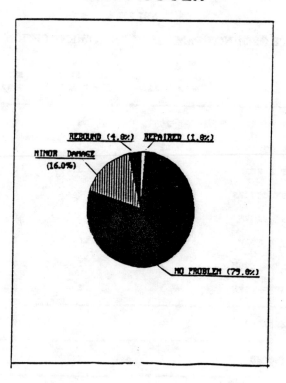

price differences:

* "We collect for posterity and want the best edition available; the paper and other physical characteristics of paperbacks are inferior."

Have you checked the quality of publisher's hard cover bindings recently? Loose and broken spines abound after minimal use. It has been my sense that more books in their original bindings may need preservation treatment after use than do treated paperbacks but that's another study. As to paper quality, trade paperback publishers now use higher quality paper, often acid-free and on heavier stock, than they did five or ten years ago.[4] As part of an informal survey, several comparisons of paper and hard bound editions of the same titles were made, with no difference in paper quality or typography detected. For titles with perceived long-term value in the collection, opting for the paperback edition and expending about $4.00 for a durable binding is still a cost-effective measure.

* "We would buy the hardback even if there were an option since paperbacks won't hold up under circulation. When forced to select a paperback we would proceed with our automatic policy of having it commercially bound."

Results of this and the Georgia State University Library surveys show that even untreated paperbacks fare well under use in academic environments. For those books that do not circulate frequently, or receive no use at all, any conservation treatment is probably a waste of money. Though this durability study reveals that damage, minor though it was, significantly declines as conservation treatment is enhanced by more costly measures, a policy of having all paperbacks commercially bound is not cost-effective use of the preservation budget.

There is another potential advantage that paperbacks have over hardback editions. Some librarians have found that retaining illustrated covers on books increases circulation. This is possible with all three treatment options used on paperbacks for this study. Observers have also noted that paperbacks with their original covers circulate more frequently than their "plain-covered" hardback equivalents.[5]

How much money may be saved by opting for a paperback edition? That depends on the size of an institution's materials budget for books; how many

selections are published with a hard/soft option; and how books are obtained. If a large proportion of acquisitions are through approval plans, options will be limited. One approval plan representative explained that specifying paperbacks would drastically affect overall discount, since book jobbers obviously won't make the same profit on paperbacks that they would with hardback editions. In terms of practical applications, sound library selection and treatment policies may be formulated in response to the availability of simultaneous editions, on findings of durability of treatment options, and on the characteristics of specific libraries. For example, titles with perceived high use may still be purchased in hard bound editions when the price difference over paperbacks is within reason. Or, paperbacks may be selected as a rule and treated with appropriate in-house or commercial binding methods. Likewise, paperbacks that are very thin, very tall, or have very flimsy covers to begin with should probably be reinforced to better withstand the strains of use or life on the shelf. Even Class A binding might be considered for reference books that are not expected to be superseded in the near future. As the trend toward publishing more books in the hard/soft option continues, and as academic library purchasing power for books diminishes, we need to periodically study the issues of paperback vs. hard bound and perhaps rethink some of our old biases and policies regarding the paperback question.

Endnotes

1. Roger L. Presley, and Christina Landram, "The Life Expectancy of Paperback Books in Academic Libraries," *Technical Services Quarterly* 4 (Spring, 1987): 21-31.
2. Roger L. Presley, and Christina Landram, "The Life Expectancy of Paperback Books in Academic Libraries: A Follow-up Study," *Technical Services Quarterly* 7 (No. 4, 1990): 1-10 .
3. Ibid., p.7.
4. Barbara Hoffert, "The Paperback Bind," *Library Journal* 116 (July, 1991): 51-55.
5. Ron Hayden, "If It Circulates, Keep It." *Library Journal* 112 (June 1, 1987): 80-82.

Diversifying the Academic Library to Meet the Challenges of Economic Development

Ada D. Jarred and Fleming A. Thomas
Northwestern State University of Louisiana
Natchitoches, Louisiana

Abstract

This paper relates the case study of a small university library's positive response to financial exigency and economic recession. It suggests alternative strategies to the commonly accepted truism that decreased budgets mean reduced services.

In mid-1991 the United States finds itself struggling with an economic recession that resists solution. A national debt of almost 3 1/2 trillion dollars and an economy in transition from heavy manufacturing to service industries are burdens that weigh heavily on the economic conditions of the nation.[1] State after state is experiencing budgetary crisis. The April 22, 1991, issue of *Business Week* projects state budget deficits of $12.6 billion for California, $1.7 billion for Connecticut, $1.2 billion for Florida, $850 million for Massachusetts, $800 million for Michigan, $6 billion for New York, and $4.7 billion for Texas.[2]

Do academic librarians as information specialists have a role to play in addressing the economic woes that surround them? The librarians of Northwestern State University of Louisiana (NSU) believe they do and that the experiences in a state and region that are not Johnny-come-latelies to economic distress are worth sharing. The model being developed at NSU may well be of benefit to librarians elsewhere.

Louisiana is a state in the direst need of economic remediation. It has yet to recover from the loss of tax revenues received from crude oil production before OPEC took over the world market and virtually eliminated Louisiana's oil producers from competition. The state's per capita income for 1991 is projected at $11,086, a mere $55 more than the per capita income for Mississippi, traditionally the lowest wage-earning state in the South.[3] The public school system is only marginally adequate, and it is estimated that one of every six adult Louisianians is illiterate.[4] Fully one-third of Louisiana motorists are uninsured, and at least twenty-five percent of the state's families have no health insurance. To compensate for the latter, Loui-siana is the only state in the U.S. to continue a charity hospital system, part of the state's current $9 billion dollar budget.

Louisiana, of course, is part of the "Sunbelt," a region that saw its impoverished per capita income, only 50% of that of the nation as a whole in 1930, rise to 85% of the U.S. per capita income in 1975.5 The policies that industrialized the South during that dramatic forty-five year period, however, are no longer relevant in the new economy. "Our future . . . ," as David Osborne has said, "depends upon our ability to innovate and our ability to use our minds, which means our most valuable resources are no longer things such as raw materials and cheap land and cheap labor. Our most valuable resources are people who can innovate and the information they need to do so."[6]

In 1988, the Southern Growth Policies Board—an agency financed and governed by thirteen states and territorial governments—published its ten-point agenda for regional economic action. Among its recommendations were: "mobilize resources to eliminate adult functional illiteracy; increase the economic development role of higher education; increase the South's capacity to generate and use technology; implement new economic development strategies aimed at homegrown industry; and enhance the South's natural and cultural resources."[7]

How could an academic library, especially one of a university newly recovered from financial exigency, respond to these initiatives? The library in question had experienced cuts in faculty and staff along with the rest of the campus. The remaining public service librarians were swamped with demands for information from new and reorganized academic programs; the residual technical service personnel were inundated with the results of the of the publishing explosion; and both were hard pressed to keep up with rapidly changing technology, new formats of information, and improved information delivery systems.

Reallocating our meager financial resources to increase the use of computer technology in the library was the key. This began with the introduction of computerized serial indexes on compact disks (CDs). The resulting reduction in staff time required to assist users with printed indexes soon became obvious.

In general, librarians have been pleased to use computers for sharing resources, as the growth in interlibrary borrowing via the OCLC system clearly illustrates—as well as for cataloging, acquisitions, and serials records management. On the other hand, many librarians are increasingly concerned about the use of computers in public services, the traditional domain of reference librarians and readers' advisory specialists. They are alarmed by the closing of some library schools, the incorporation of certain library science programs into other departments, and the shared identity of still others with "information science." These librarians see the strength of the profession resting with individuals who desire to continue the tradition of humanism that has characterized librarians for most of this century.

Their concern may be an over-reaction to a new and different discipline, but there does appear to be some genuine cause for concern. For example, one need only to observe a reference room in which several CD-ROM periodical indexes have been installed. Students use these machines with enthusiasm, albeit not always too productively, because they feel comfortable with them. What one notes in particular is that these students do not consult a reference librarian, as they might have done in the past when confronted with table after table of printed indexes. Other configurations, of course, offer students access not merely to a variety of data bases but to both text and illustrations as well.

The easiest solution is for librarians to become computer specialists, an answer that could engender a caretaking role for the librarian that would be injurious to the profession. A more reasonable approach seems to be one that continues the diversity of skills and knowledge held by librarians while simultaneously developing a new or modified role for the library and

its professionals. Such an approach in no way undermines the importance of the individual or the institution.

The reference services staff of Watson Library took advantage of the time released by advanced technology to write two successful grant proposals, both of which have resulted in contributions to the community beyond the confines of the university campus. The first, to the regional Job Training Partnership Act (JTPA) office, suggested evaluating the vocational aptitudes of JTPA trainees, as a means of encouraging them to remain in their respective training programs. The proposal resulted in the creation of a Career Evaluation and Information Center, housed in the library and staffed by three full-time psychologists. The program is supported by an extensive collection of occupational literature; approximately $18,000 in grant funds has been invested in this collection of print and non-print materials. The special collection is available to all students of the university and to any walk-in client seeking information about a potential career. Assistance with preparation of resumes is also provided. In 1989 the center was given responsibility for the evaluation of JTPA trainees in ten parishes of northwest Louisiana, and a satellite office was opened on the campus of another university.

Recently, the university began requiring all freshmen without declared majors to take the center's diagnostic evaluation as part of an experiment in student retention. The library faculty volunteered to serve as student advisors, and they now counsel these freshmen without declared majors. Each librarian has approximately thirty students to advise. This new responsibility is a significant step towards the placement of library faculty on full parity with classroom faculty.

The second successful application was to the U.S. Dept. of Education for establishing one of the first Student Literacy Corps programs in the state. Under this two-year project, the library recruits and places tutors in four elementary schools, two vocational-technical institutes, and two social service agencies. During the first two semesters, each of forty-seven students, recruited from the university's Division of Education, tutored at one of these eight sites for an entire semester and earned three semester hours of credit for his or her work. The gratitude of overburdened staff members at these locations has been overwhelming, and all of the tutors have declared a strong interest in continuing this kind of community service whenever the opportunity exists. Generating such enthusiasm is, of course, one of the goals of the Student Literacy Corps. Apart from its intrinsic merit, the project produces sufficient credit hours to pay for itself. Moreover, since the program is presently funded by a grant, the credit hours provide a welcome margin of additional revenue for the university.

Meanwhile, the administrative arm of the library, in cooperation with humanities scholars, was addressing economic growth through the development of local cultural resources. The celebrated American author Kate Chopin devoted much of her writing to the people and life of Natchitoches Parish, where NSU is located. An application to the Louisiana Endowment for the Humanities (LEH) was approved, and "Kate Chopin and the Cane River Region," a 2 1/2 day conference met in April, 1989. Several hundred people attended, coming from sixteen states, the District of Columbia, France, and Austria. Most of the sessions were held on the university campus, but participants also visited the Bayou Folk Museum housed in Chopin's former home in nearby Cloutierville, as well as Melrose Plantation—another local site of literary interest. Thus, this grant became an investment in the development of the regional tourist trade. The second Kate Chopin conference, funded by the International Paper Company and the LEH, was held in April, 1991.

A successful proposition to the National Endowment for the Humanities (NEH) to develop a reading and discussion project also focused on Kate Chopin. This award funded the preliminary work and research in preparation for a series of six programs in twelve parish libraries. In 1990 the NEH funded the implementation phase of the project, and humanities scholars led presentations of "Kate Chopin: A Woman of Yesterday, Today, and Tomorrow" in the fall of 1990 and the spring of 1991. Public response was resoundingly positive.

In 1986, the Constitution of the State of Louisiana was amended to establish two funds, the Louisiana Education Quality Trust Fund and the Louisiana Education Quality Support Fund. Grants from the Support Fund are made available annually to higher education based on the following criteria: "1. the potential for the award to enhance the overall quality of higher education in Louisiana, and 2. the potential for the award to enhance the economic development of the state."[8]

Watson Library received a grant from the Louisiana Education Quality Support Fund in 1990 for the improvement of library operations. Seven areas of the library were enhanced: archives; cataloging; collection development; government documents; interlibrarloan; serials; and the administrative office. With funds from this source the library acquired five microcomputers, six printers, five compact disk drives, one microcomputer hard drive, and three FAX machines. Here are some specific examples of how this modest investment in equipment has been used to foster economic development:

—Clients of the university's Small Business Development Center are accessing government documents in CD format—such as County and City Data Book, County Business Patterns, Census of Agriculture, Economic Census, Census of Population and Housing, State Energy Data Report, Consumption Estimates, and State Energy Price and Expenditures Data System Report—to establish, market, and manage their own businesses.

—A faculty member in biology obtained and used numerous journal articles in developing a biological insecticide for cotton that is environmentally safe. The product is being manufactured in north Louisiana.

—Another faculty member accessed library materials in preparing a revision of the safety codes for the state's vocational-technical institutes. Better safety procedures for students will result in graduates who are prepared to implement similar measures in future workplaces.

—A local person has been studying patents to reclaim used oil; he is using information obtained from the library.

—A faculty member is developing a plan for agricultural development along the Red River waterway, using library materials.

—A nearby plantation is obtaining grants to restore brick slave cabins that remain from the 19th century. The original plans for the dwellings were located in the library's archives. Tour guides were trained for the local

Chamber of Commerce using other historical materials from the archives.

By addressing five of the Southern Growth Policies Board's regional objectives, the librarians of NSU have had a significant impact on northwest Louisiana over the past few years. More JTPA trainees in the region complete their vocational programs, thus increasing the availability of skilled workers. University students, unsure of their career preferences, are helped to make those determinations and find encouragement, thereby reducing student attrition. The collection of career information encourages others to seek professional training and a better education. Student tutors contribute to the elimination of adult illiteracy and assist in better preparation of younger students in basic skills. Education majors are trained for tutoring in other communities after graduation from the university. Literary conferences draw participants to the area. Thought-provoking cultural programming is provided to small, rural communities. Information services to patrons of Watson Library are improved.

Obviously, our efforts have created new jobs, infused grant funds directly into the economy of our small city, and earned badly needed revenue for the university through indirect cost rebates and credit hours produced. At the same time, our innovative projects have raised the visibility of librarians both on campus and in the community. We are now perceived as activists, rather than just information providers, and we enjoy the higher esteem which accompanies this perception, as well as the new responsibilities. In brief, Watson Library has become an effective agency for change in our region of Louisiana.

During the past decade most American libraries suffered some form of budget reduction, ranging from the extreme of financial exigency to the postponement of minor building repairs. This experience is likely to remain with us as the U.S. economy continues to struggle with the national debt and encounters the painful realities of global competition.

The librarians of small NSU have proven that severe budget cutbacks do not necessarily demand concomitant service reductions. Over the past few years we have expanded library services by obtaining well over half a million dollars in grant funds which improve—both directly and indirectly—the economic conditions of our rural community. We challenge other academic

libraries in areas of economic hardship to benefit from our experience.

Endnotes

1. U.S. Council of Economic Advisers, *Economic Indicators* (May, 1991):32.
2. *Business Week* (April 22, 1991): 24-26.
3. Editor & Publisher, *1991 Market Guide* (New York: 1991): IV[i].
4. Louisiana Literacy Task Force, A *Literate Louisiana: The Key to Economic Recovery and Future Growth* (Baton Rouge: Louisiana Literacy Task Force, 1989).
5. Jesse L. White, "The Future of Economic Development in the Region," The S*outheastern Librarian* 40 (Summer, 1990): 61-63.
6. David Osborne, "The Role of Information in the Economy of the Southeast," *The Southeastern Librarian* 40 (Summer, 1990): 57-59.
7. 1986 Commission on the Future of the South, *Halfway Home & A Long Way To Go* (Research Triangle Park, N.C.: Southern Growth Policies Board, 1988), p. 8.
8. Louisiana Board of Regents, *Policies and Procedures* (Baton Rouge: Louisiana Board of Regents, 1977-   ), Section II, 5.01.02.

The Age of Re- . . . Rethinking, Redefining, Redesigning Library Organizational Structures

Patricia M. Larsen
University of Northern Iowa
Cedar Falls, Iowa

Abstract

Libraries are in the "Age of Re-" in that technological and societal changes increasingly require rethinking, redefining, and redesigning our organizations to more adequately meet the needs of today, as well as to anticipate the needs of an uncertain future. Few guidelines exist to help librarians lead their staff members through a trauma-less change process to achieve new organizational structures. Implementation of a full scale job redesign project is proposed as a logical starting point for initiating library-wide reorganization. The principles and approaches for successful job redesign efforts which are supported by research are described, and a practical methodology for applying the theory in libraries is outlined.

The pressures on contemporary library organizational structures continue to build as the world moves towards the 21st century mark. Nowhere is this more true than in the higher education arena, which has been shaken simultaneously by demands for increasing excellence and accountability, by threats of deteriorating economic resources, and by the necessity for keeping up with an incredible rate of technological change. Librarians in this context are being challenged to examine their library's mission and role, and to recreate an organization designed to meet more adequately the needs of today, while at the same time anticipating the needs of an uncertain future. As librarians, we clearly are in the "Age of Re-" in that we need to rethink, redefine, redesign, reorganize, and re-engineer nearly every aspect of our organizations.

Library leaders prophesy that library organizational structures must become more participatory, innovative, adaptable, and capable of responding quickly to change.[1] Hierarchical structures are "out". "Flat" structures, as epitomized by matrix management principles, are "in". Key words being used today to describe library operations and services are "collaborative," "flexible," and "fluid." Whether or not librarians generally accept such concepts as conventional wisdom remains to be seen. What does appear to be accepted is that new organizational structures are desirable, particularly when online systems are implemented. Even so, libraries have been slow to change. They are still largely hierarchical, departmentalized organizations, despite the fact that the automation of many library processes has removed the underlying rationality for compartmentalization along functional lines. The reasons for why the pace has been so slow are numerous, but surely a contributing factor is the scarcity of models and guidelines which might help librarians initiate and successfully achieve major organizational change. The purpose of this paper is to outline one approach to initiating such change. The basic premise of the proposed methodology is that the logical starting point for initiating library reorganization begins with the analysis and redesign of jobs. Re-examination of the work which needs to be done to accomplish the library's mission, may provide insight into possibilities for new organizational alignments of both individual staff members and groups. By basing such changes on recognized job design theory, the human resource contribution to the work of the library may be increased. The purpose for redesigning jobs in the context proposed is that of analyzing at a very basic level the work which needs to be accomplished and of starting from ground zero to regroup tasks into meaningful jobs.

A systematic approach for redesigning jobs ensures that job changes extend beyond the tinkering stage, that workloads are balanced, and that the library's goals and objectives are serviced to the greatest extent possible. The first requirement then must be that library jobs meet the needs of the organization. Materials have to be ordered and processed; clients must be served. In fact, it is likely that one of the organizing principles for realigning tasks will be to increase the centrality of the library's users. Staying "close to the customer"[2] and becoming more "client-centered"[3] are old ideas which have gained new life in recent years. As a matter of fact, librarians are not at all alone among service professionals in revisiting this concern. The nursing profession has recently issued revised standards which make the patient the center of care! (As potential patients, could we hope for anything more? or, had we expected anything less?) Nursing managers are using the new standards to redesign jobs around direct service to patients, shifting non patient tasks as much as possible to other job categories.[4]

The second requirement in designing jobs must be to give adequate consideration to what constitutes a "good" job from the point of view of the person in the job. The most clearly articulated statement of the characteristics of a good job is that described in the Job Characteristics model developed by Richard Hackman and Greg Oldham.[5] (Figure 1) Their model focuses on the work to be accomplished and aids in shaping jobs in such a way that conditions are created which enhance those psychological states identified through research as being strongly related to producing high internal motivation. In their model, jobs are designed ideally around the core dimensions of autonomy, feedback, task significance, task identify, and variety of skills and tasks used. Job Characteristics support the individual's need to experience responsibility for the work performed, to experience work as meaningful, and to have knowledge of the results of work. The model also recognizes the need to gain an understanding of the worker's individual differences in the areas of growth need strengths, context satisfaction, knowledge, and skills. Jobs designed according to these principles are considered to be more likely to result in higher productivity rates, and a motivated, satisfied work force.

The process of job design can be approached in a variety of ways and can produce quite different outcomes depending on the approach selected. Michael Campion and Paul Thayer have identified four approaches commonly used in job design: mechanistic, motivational, biological, and perceptual/motor.[6]

The *mechanistic* job design approach is closest to the principles of scientific management, characterized by job specialization, specialization of tools and procedures, task simplification, repetition, and degree of automation. Many jobs in library technical services divisions are still designed according to this approach.

Motivational job design derives from the work of organizational psychologists and addresses the major theories of work motivation and organizational behavior. Motivational job design is concerned with such things as degrees of autonomy within the job, job feedback, and social interaction. Other factors affecting motivational job design include (1) task variety, identify, and significance; (2) ability/skill level requirements and variety; and (3) the operative reward system (promotion, pay adequacy, recognition, and job security). Library jobs associated with this approach tend to be public service jobs, particularly branch or departmental library positions.

Biological job design has to do with the study of body movements and is concerned with such things as requirements for strength, lifting, endurance, wrist movement, noise, climate, work breaks, and shift work. This approach seeks to minimize the physical costs and biological risks of work. Recently librarians have become more concerned with this kind of job design, because of the increased use of video display terminals and health concerns associated with their use (e.g., carpal tunnel syndrome and eye strain.)

The *perceptual/motor* job design approach takes into account not only the individual physical requirements of the job but considers also the required skills and the mental capabilities. It pays attention to work condition factors such as lighting, ease of learning and of using equipment, printed job materials, work place layout, information input and output requirements, information processing and memory requirements, stress, and boredom. The goals of designing jobs around the individual's perceptual/motor limitations are to decrease the likelihood of errors and accidents, and to reduce the general mental demands of a job. Library jobs which might fall into that category are those related to sorting and re-shelving books, shelf reading, and photocopy services.

Campion and Thayer list a number of questions which can be used as a quick checklist to measure the quality of jobs designed in terms of the four approaches. Positive and negative outcomes for each type of approach are summarized in Figure 2. While ideally all jobs would be highly motivating, and ergonomic considerations accounted for thoroughly, in practical terms, trade-offs between individual and organizational outcomes may be required. Initial attention given to identifying the most appropriate approach for job design, based on desired outcomes, will help to produce a better fit between individual jobs and organizational needs.

Figure 1.

JOB CHARACTERISTICS MODEL

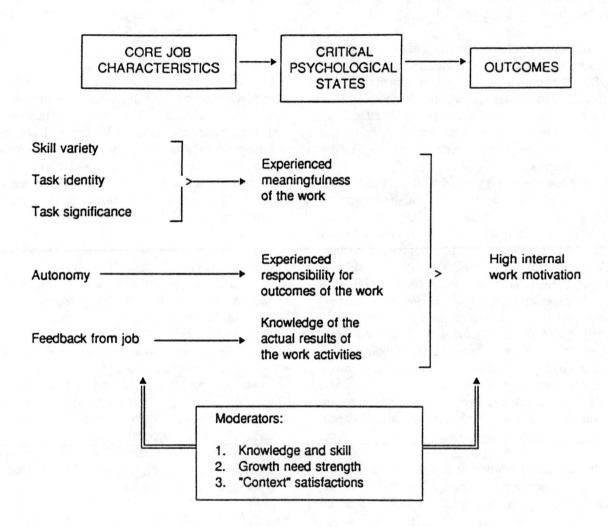

Moderators of the relationship between the job characteristics and internal motivation.

From: J. Richard Hackman and Greg R. Oldham, <u>Work Redesign</u>. Reading, Mass.:
        Addison–Wesley, 1980, p. 83.

FIGURE 2.

SUMMARY OF OUTCOMES
FROM THE JOB–DESIGN APPROACHES

Job–Design Approach	Positive Outcomes	Negative Outcomes
Mechanistic	Decreased training time Higher utilization levels Lower likelihood of error Less chance of mental overload and stress	Lower job satisfaction Lower motivation Higher absenteeism
Motivational	Higher job satisfaction Higher motivation Greater job involvement Higher job performance Lower absenteeism	Increased training time Lower utilization levels Greater likelihood of error Greater chance of mental overload and stress
Biological	Less physical effort Less physical fatigue Fewer health complaints Fewer medical incidents Lower absenteeism Higher job satisfaction	Higher financial costs because of changes in equipment or job environment
Perceptual/motor	Lower likelihood of error Lower likelihood of accidents Less chance of mental overload and stress Lower training time Higher utilization levels	Lower job satisfaction Lower motivation

From: Michael A. Campion and Paul W. Thayer, "Job Design: Approaches, Outcomes, and Trade-Off's", Organizational Dynamics. 15 (3) 1987, p. 76.

Given that jobs are the building blocks of organizational performance, and that they can often be designed to include motivating potential and to minimize dissatisfying aspects of work, and that there are various approaches which may be used in analyzing and designing jobs, how can a library proceed with a redesign project?

The first step must be to determine the limits of the change effort and to obtain administrative support for the process. It is critical that the boundaries of the effort be clearly established and supported by the administration. Hackman and Oldham warn against the "small change" response, when less change is brought about than was originally intended, and "chipping away" at the design effort commences.[7] Such responses may begin to occur when changes in one part of the organization create stress in other parts not involved in the change effort. Upper level administration must provide adequate insulation for the organizational units engaged in the change process to guard against lessening the change results. The recommendations which follow assume a library-wide change process as opposed to that confined to a department or division, but the principles are the same for either.

The second critical step is to obtain the support and participation of key players by establishing a job design task force which includes representation from every staff category in the library: management, librarians, paraprofessionals, and clerical. Other sub-groups may be appointed as needed, with the number of groups dependent upon the size and complexity of the library. The task force will be responsible for guiding the total process through its various stages: data collection and analysis, problem solving, and implementation and evaluation.

Data Collection and analysis. A significant part of the task will be the analysis of the existing work system. This includes the examination of all existing jobs, determination of staff concerns and interests, and the examination of structural relationships, workflows and task groupings. One of the more important aspects of this analysis should be the identification of work system constraints and facilitators impacting the performance of the tasks central to the library's mission.

A staff needs assessment survey may be conducted. The purpose of such a survey is to identify the intrinsic characteristics of existing jobs and staff member job satisfaction levels. The Job Characteristics Survey developed by Hackman and Oldham is a widely-tested instrument and is considered easy to administer and interpret. (For a copy of the instrument and instructions on its use, consult *Work Design* by Richard Hackman and Greg Oldham.[8])

Consciousness raising sessions should be conducted for all persons who may possibly be affected by the redesign effort. The goal of such sessions should be to communicate clearly and to provide ample time to discuss such things as the library's mission, the characteristics of a good job, and the factors considered to be conducive to supporting high levels of motivation and supportive of job satisfaction.

Opportunities for individual input should be created through conducting group brainstorming sessions for all affected staff. Such sessions should focus on generating ideas for improving present jobs, task alignments, working conditions, and irrational lines of communication or workflows. Posing questions such as the following may serve to stimulate discussion: "If I could change three things about my job, I would . . ." "What's wrong with the way I am required to perform my work?" "What needs to be improved in order for the library to provide better service to its clientele?"

Upon completion of the data collection stage, the processing and evaluation of data received from all sources commences. Problem solving skills must be used to identify irrationalities of the current system and to evaluate the feasibility and applicability of suggestions received through the small group sessions. At this stage, the objective should be to produce a job redesign inventory, listing every job to be changed and detailing the particular changes to be made. Job design evaluative criteria, such as those described by Campion and Thayer, Hackman and Oldham, should be employed to weigh the relative merits of the proposed redesigned jobs. It is at this point that trade-offs will most likely have to be made, to reconcile organizational and individual needs.

Implementation and support for on-going change. The final stage of the process requires the development of a thorough implementation plan which addresses the questions of who, what, and when. A clear timeline with target dates identified for each major step should be created. Provisions should be made for facilitating a post-processing period. This period includes the means for evaluating changes and establishes a process for continuing modifications and adaptations as they seem needed.

Nurturing and maintaining open communication channels should receive the highest priority throughout the process. Research results indicate that staff members accept change—and also the rejection of some of their suggestions for change—much more readily when they are provided with information regarding the reasons that specific changes were, or were not, made.[9]

An issue which should be resolved early in the process is that of securing outside help. Is a consultant needed? The answer hinges largely on the existing organizational climate and individual skills available within each library. If communication is good, leadership skills adequate and reasonably dispersed throughout the library, and the climate generally considered to be healthy, then it is possible that a library can manage the change effort with a minimum of outside help. However, if conditions are not generally healthy, then a library may do well to consider securing help for at least the key points in the process. Such points might include the introduction of the change effort and training task force members to improve their group facilitating and problem solving skills.

While the methodology described here does not guarantee success, it does offer an approach which is rooted in solid research. It offers a means to re-group the functions which form the basis of library service and to remove the blinders which make it so difficult for us to visualize a new organization. Change processes grounded in a firm theoretical base can increase immeasurably the likelihood for successfully rethinking, redesigning, and renewing library organizational structures, thus enabling them to meet both present and future challenges.

Endnotes

1. Anne Woodworth et al., "The Model Research Library: Planning for the Future," *Journal of Academic Librarianship* 15 (July, 1989): 132-138.
2. Tom Peters, *In Search of Excellence,* (New York: Harper & Row, 1982).
3. Charles R. Martell, *The Client-Centered Library: An Organizational Model* (Westport, CT: Greenwood Press, 1983).
4. Paul Eubanks, "Nursing Restructuring Renews Focus on Patient-Centered Care," *Hospital* 64 (April 20, 1990): 60, 62.
5. J. Richard Hackman and Greg R. Oldham, *Work Redesign* (Reading, MA: Addison-Wesley, 1980).
6. Michael A. Campion and Pual W. thayer, "Job Design: Approaches, Outcomes, and Trade-Off's," *Organization Dynamics* 15 (Winter, 1987): 66-79.
7. J. Richard Hackman, op. cit., p. 248.
8 J. Richard Hackman, Ibid.
9. William E. Rosenbach and Robert A. Zawacki, "Participative Work Redesign: A Field Study in the Public Secor," *Public Administration Quarterly* 13 (Spring, 1989): 112-121.

Prior Consent: Not-So-Strange Bedfellows Plan Library/Computing Partnerships

Kristin McDonough
Baruch College
New York, New York

Abstract

The universal access to computing has blurred distinctions between libraries and computing centers, causing administrators to rethink traditional separate organizational structures. So far only 16% of these reorganizations include the library but if the trend continues information providers should start now to forge crucial alliances. A one year planning effort at a medium size college in the City University of New York stystem has not yet been completed. Despite some resistance to reorganization, staffs from the units have moved beyond the discussion stage into project teams work, setting the stage for collaboration and leading to enhanced understanding of and respect for each other's fucntions and expertise.

The increasing sophistication of information technologies and the nearly universal access to computing have blurred distinctions among campus information delivery units, in particular the computing centers and the library. This phenomenon is forcing higher education institutions to rethink the administrative structures that evolved when computing in academe was more localized, isolated, and minimal.

According to the EDUCOM/USC National Survey of Desktop Computing in Higher Education,[1] over 36% of colleges and universities have reorganized computing and related activities in the last two years, with another 29% anticipating similar restructuring in the near future. At present only an estimated 16% of these reorganizations include the library.[2] Rutgers and Cal State (Chico) follow the model where a librarian oversees comprehensive information and computing services while at Bradley and Stanford Universities, the information czar has come the other route, i. e., computing or media services. There is every indication that this trend toward the close collaboration and joint reporting, if not convergence, of libraries and computing centers under a vice-president for information or a chief information officer will continue.

For the remaining 80% of academic libraries facing the probable prospect of some sort of administrative consolidation, it is imperative to begin now to forge crucial alliances. I am a library director who for the past year has been engaged in intensive discussions with computing and media services colleagues at my medium-sized library, one of the 18 units of the City University of New York. After months of talk, the proposal has been virtually stalled, leaving me more convinced than ever that relationships established among staffs during the formative planning process are crucial to realizing the vision shaped by directors.

Clearly, among the daunting challenges that lie before campus information providers, the human issue of cooperation is as important—and as thorny—as the technological ones of connectivity and networking. The negotiations that precede the integration of technology-based units on campus are delicate and require strong leadership, interpersonal skills, and even empathy on the part of directors. The planning process is best entered into with the realization that the desired end product, the formal planning or reorganization document, "may well be far less important than the process of discussion with all involved constituencies."[3]

At my institution, our close to two years' efforts failed to produce a consensus on our proposal for a new information systems and services unit. The envisioned ISS was comprised of the library, media services, and the two reorganized computing centers, educational (ECC) and asministrative (ACC). The library would report with these units to a chief information officer (CIO), as well as to an academic dean for curricular and faculty matters.) The reasons for the delay are many, ranging from an interim college administration, to tensions between the academic and administrative sides of the house and a budget crisis. But at least some of the foot dragging is clearly due to the fact that early on we did not encourage full staff participation and feedback—with the result that extra effort and time has been spent more recently in bringing our reluctant staffs along.

We clearly did not act on what we knew: the information revolution has impacted on organizations by creating a more flattened management environment than the hierarchical one that has heretofore existed in higher education.[4] With information flowing, or perhaps leaking, informally across divisions and units rather than in a more formal vertical reporting structure, it is important, especially in a reorganization in a rapidly changing environment, that the official, occasionally confidential, sometimes tentative, and often cautious deliberations at the directors' level are fueled with input from fully informed and invested staff members in each of the principal units. We realized this a bit late.

Our initial, and I think misguided, effort had the chief administrators of the two computer centers and the library working with the associate provost on a joint exercise. We characterized information-provision functions requisite to the institution and grouped these under umbrellas like "operations management," "applications systems delivery," "training and instruction," "information retrieval.") We aimed to identify duplicative activity that might be funneled into one unit (e.g. maintenance) or administered centrally by CIO staff (e. g. purchasing). After several iterations, this list of streamlined functions was presented to our respective units's senior managers, in my case the members of the library's administrative committee, who were quick to point out those responsibilities—most minor, though a few major—that the directors had not clearly delineated. They questioned as well, rather defensively, the assignment to another unit or the chief administrator's office of functions that they felt were "theirs." Clearly, we had not anticipated how for some staff members in each unit our proposal presaged the loss of something: prestige, power, autonomy, or authority.

Initally, some librarians felt that by accommodating to a new organizational paradigm they were sacrificing needed autonomy in important areas such as designing library software applications. Other librarians feared that our materials allocation might suffer. Many librarians felt that closer identification with technical experts would compromise our hard-won faculty sta-

tus. Budget crisis talk of paring down "support staff" did not do much to ease anxiety here.

Our computing counterparts were also uneasy. The academic computing managers felt that their unique role as liaison to the university's mainframe computer center was being minimized. The administrative computing staff felt vulnerable when we proposed that software installation in microcomputer labs be assigned to personnel used to working primarily in a mainframe environment.

At this point, months into the process, the directors knew that it would have been bettter to adopt the approach used at Bradley University where each unit in that institution's new Information Technologies and Resources division had brought to the planning process a mission statement, and a set of goals and objectives, as well as a description and evaluation of both present and future functions and services.[5] Syracuse University used a similar planning approach when their academic and administrative computing functions were merged. [6] We went back to the drawing boards.

With each unit thus engaged in internal self study—and avid self-justification—it was perhaps not surprising to discover just as we were about to circulate the draft document to administrators and the faculty senate, that our proposal's "rationale for change" was singularly unsuccessful in communicating to our consumers how the proposed reorganization would make life easier for *them*. Fixated on turf and ownership issues, we had never developed the *catchiest* aspect of our "sell, " and the very concept about which we had, early on, been so enthused: a central point of inquiry and referral for all technology-related issues, an IT "hot line," if you will. We forgot, as Quinlan so aptly puts it, that "regardless of how or why computer centers and libraries cooperate, it is imperative that the needs and expectations of the campus user community become the focus of activity."[7]

At this point we opted for democratic input by holding a series of open meetings to which all staff from the three units were invited. Attendees asked a lot of hard questions, aired grievances, vented frustrations; after this, some shifts to more positive attitudes were apparent. Increased input and participation within and across units had the added advantage of making the players feel invested in the outcome of the reorganization. Involved staff seemed less apt to feel their positions threatened by concepts such as "reduction of duplication", and "elimination of overlap." These are clearly cogent elements in any argument for greater integration. It was important that the combined staffs hear the associate provost acknowledge that for the reorganization to work there was need for more, not less, staff.

These staff meetings helped to break down barriers, exacerbated by language. Just by talking with their computing colleagues librarians became more aware of, and sensitive to, the different meanings of terms in respective fields. Librarians who initially took umbrage when the term "tape librarian" appeared on the computing systems organization chart, came to understand why their colleagues balked at the librarians claim that the library is the "chief academic information center" engaged in " information resources management." We each had appropriated terms that had a special cache in our colleagues' field. It was fascinating to me, and instructive, I think, that after several discussions about the fact that the traditional terms "computing," "library," and "audio-visual" were too limiting, we ended up with "computing services," "computing systems," "library," and "media services" on our organization chart, largely because the newer and more au courant "information services," "information systems," and "information resources" might confuse our users. After all, they had succeeded in confusing our staffs.

Ultimately, though, the element of the planning process that has most successfully engendered a healthy respect for each other's complementary skills and strengths turned out to be the establishment of project teams in the matrix management mode. Although our library has an integrated online system, its implementation was a joint project of the university's computing center (UCC) and the CUNY offices of academic computing and library automation. Representatives from the two computing centers had served on the library's NOTIS implementation committee in the past, but, incredibly, administrative and academic computing personnel had not collaborated on their own projects. Now they, the systems librarians, and a media specialist are responsible for creating a campus-wide information network. The initial projects have expanded to a half dozen, with some unexpected dividends. Catalogers met with media personnel to plan for the inclusion of video holdings on our OPAC and in the process media services agreed to promote the library's costly but little used "Video Encyclopedia of the 20th Century" through the video production classes. A

librarian working with an ECC programmer to develop an application to generate circulation statistics by LC classification on NOTIS was able to present the center, gratis, with a copy of the expensive software for putting Paradox on a LAN. Librarians and administrative com- puting personnel are working with a vendor to design and test our new ID card with a digitized barcode replacing our current paper strips. Stealing an idea from an ALA Atlanta poster session, the library and computing centers hope to co-sponsor an INFO-EXPO, as well as several sessions to bring the INTERNET to faculty at their departmental and school meetings. Most gratifying of all, because it has resulted in an immediate and much appreciated improvement of service to students, a librarian is now teaching, and writing the documentation for the seminars run by computing services on accessing COMPUSTAT, CRSP, and CITIBASE data files. In the future, the library has agreed to purchase these from our materials budget. Even though we have fallen short of completing and approving a collective vision statement for the new division, library and computing colleagues have managed to break through barriers, exploit each other's expertise and skills, and improve information and computing services. The key may be that there is no longer the sense that in calling for help across units one is asking for a favor.

As the RLG document *Preferred Futures for Libraries*[8] underscores, libraries and computing centers have no choice but mutual exploitation. Today's library is expected to support traditional needs as well as new kinds of research involving simulation, modeling, visualization; to instruct and consult in the use of print and online sources as well as in communications and personal information management software; to manage local as well as access distant and increasingly complex catalogs and databases; and to provide individuals at a distance with the ability to query and order materials from them directly. Often the expectation is that we will do all this with the same or even reduced resources as we have in the past. Clearly, this is a time for partnerships with technical professionals faced with similar demands, branded with the same "bottomless pit" label, saddled with the same expectations of being able to do more (and value-added!) with less. Together we need to orchestrate the concerted pitch that we can increasingly meet expectations, but that it will cost.

To counteract the continued emphasis in the literature on the irreconcilable cultures of librarianship and computing, today's effective library administrator might want to test her powers of persuasion in two directions. When the librarians she manages are quick to note yet another instance of computing's failure to meet promises, understand the end-user's needs, or appreciate the complexities of the bibliographic record, she might remind them that there used to be talk of separate "cultures" in our own profession, as exemplified by public services and technical services librarians. Today, technological advances have forced a cross-over, with catalogers serving at reference desks and as OPAC consultants, and reference librarians becoming conversant with the intricacies of the MARC record. As a result, catalogers have a more immediate grasp of the retrieval habits of the end user, and reference librarians are more aware of cataloging protocols. Another salient point is the competition that has existed on many campuses between administrative and academic computing. Rather than "cultures," might not the issue be the pull between vested interests? Ultimately, of course, most library faculty will rightly insist on remaining under the academic vice-president, which is the only place to be when faculty senates suggest that "the administration" should absorb budget cuts.

It may take less persuasion to make computing personnel appreciate the advantages of closer identification with the library than one might think. Certainly, closer association with librarians won't have a positive effect upon their salaries. On the other hand, librarians, though we sometimes don't seem to realize it, are well respected for their bibliographic and retrieval skills and ability to write comprehensible documentation. With the burgeoning interest in artificial intelligence and expert systems, computing specialists are having to deal with structured databases which have for so long been the librarians' stock-in-trade.

To our computing colleagues with a short history indeed, librarians have an enviable history of managing increasingly complex units and may be perceived as being taken more seriously on campus. Librarians are generally recognized as being far more conversant with the informational content that is to be transported on the electronic superhighway of the INTERNET. We know how to retrieve, evaluate and apply the "stuff" after we have pushed the buttons. Librarians, with their history of cooperative resource sharing have, with computing's help, created integrated library systems which in many cases—such as City University's CUNY+—is the most successful cooperative automation project within a university system. Hawkins

draws computing specialists' attention to the example of interlibrary loan and suggests that the library model of centrally funded services offered free to users might be the model that computing centers follow.[9]

Dollars may be a factor, too. Our colleagues' sense that libraries are better funded is illusory, given our chronic underfunding. I have discovered though, that the sheer size of our operations may make our allocation for materials, equipment, and temporary workers seem comparatively large to computing staffs. When powerful faculty interests protest the necessary diversion of funds from teaching to IT, the computing specialists, for this reason, may recognize librarians as allies in making computing as central as the library to the mission of the college.

A quarter of a century ago, the information options included print, audio-visual, microforms, and processing done on remote mainframes. In today's microcomputer environment, the options include e-mail, text editing, spreadsheets, databases, graphics, desktop publishing, word processing, AI, expert systems, multimedia, online catalogs, integrated online systems, videodiscs, laser printing, bibliographic searching, and a variety of software applications. Clearly, the possibilities are greater but it will take more money, more consistency in planning, a more unified approach. The sum of it is that we need each other and each other's attention which, in the words of Richard Dougherty, "should not be focused on the rhetoric of mergers and takeovers but on the roles the respective organization can play as the principal providers of information to campus communities."[10] Through better communication, we must start now to create and nurture partnerships to meet the challenges ahead.

Endnotes

1. Kenneth C. Green and Skip Eastman, "National Survey of Desktop Computing in Higher Education," (Los Angeles: Center for Scholary Technology, University of Southern Caolifornia, 1991), p. 30.
2. James Penrod, Michael Dolence and Judith Douglas, *The Chief Inforamtion Officer in Higher Education,* CAUSE Professional Paper Series #4, 1990, p. 2.
3. Brian Hawkins, "Administrative and Organizational Issues in Campus Computing," in *New Directions for Higher Education: Making Computers Work for Administrators, no. 62* (San Francisco:

Jossey-Bass, 1988), p. 20

4. Anne Woodsworth. *Managing Information Technology on Campus* (Chicago, ALA, 1991), p. 72.

5. Telephone Conversation with Ellen Watson, Library Director, Bradley University, August 2, 1991.

6. Carole Barone, "Planning and Changing the Role of the CIO in Higher Education," *Information Management Review* 5 (1989): 23-31.

7. Catherine A. Quinlan, "Libraries and Computing Centers," in T*he Evolution of Library Automation: Management Issues and Future Perspecitves.* Ed. Gary M. Pitkin. (Westport: Meckler, 1991), p. 104.

8. Richard M. Dougherty and Carol Hughes. *Preferred Futures for Libraries: A Summary of Six Workshops with University Provost and Library Directors.* (Mountain View, California: Research Libraries Group, 1991).

9. Brian Hawkins, op. cit., 24-25.

10. Richard M. Dougherty, "Libraries and Computing Centers: A Blueprint for Collaboration," *College and Research Libraries* 48 (July, 1987): 289.

Systematic Planning in Small Academic Libraries: Does It Make a Difference?

Judith Jamison Senkevitch
University of Wisconsin-Milwaukee
Milwaukee, Wisconsin

Abstract

Selected findings with implications for management and planning practice are reported from an exploratory study of the consequences of implementing the Planning Program for Small Academic Libraries (PPSAL) at twenty-six small colleges and universities. Data collection methodology included content analysis of library planning reports and sixty-eight structured telephone interviews with library directors, chief academic officers, and faculty. Three consequences most frequently described were major library improvements, more favorable attention for the library from the college community, and improved quality and effectiveness of library services and programs. In a majority of cases, however, PPSAL did not appear to instigate continuing systematic library assessment and planning.

Over the past two decades there has been continuing interest in the library field in developing systematic planning and evaluation processes to enhance academic library management. Key efforts in this area include the programs developed by the Office of Management Studies of the Association of Research Libraries such as the Management Review and Analysis Program[1] and the Academic Library Development Program,[2] as well as the recent publication by the Association of College and Research Libraries of a manual to facilitate assessment of library performance.[3] These programs or tools were evaluated as part of their development, and a number of articles describing individual experiences implementing these programs have been published. However, with the exception of a study undertaken in 1976-77 by Johnson and Mann[4] to evaluate the impact of the *Management Review and Analysis Program* (MRAP), little research has been published on the longer-term consequences or effects of implementing such programs. Further, at the time the Johnson and Mann study was conducted, a number of the participating libraries were still in the early stages of implementing the MRAP program. The researchers noted that "evaluating the impact of MRAP on organizational change by further studying implementation should be the focus of another study."[5] A review of the relevant literature confirms the need to examine the longer-term consequences of the implementation of systematic organization-wide planning and assessment processes in libraries.[6]

In order to contribute to the understanding of the potential longer term consequences of implementing a systematic planning and assessment program in small academic libraries, a study was conducted of all twenty-six colleges and universities that undertook the *Planning Program for Small Academic Libraries*[7] prior to 1988. The *Planning Program for Small Academic Libraries* (PPSAL), developed by the Association of Research Libraries' Office of Management Studies, is an assisted self-study program intended for use by small colleges with a library staff of fewer than twenty people. The study yielded potentially useful findings on several levels, with implications for both theory and practice. This paper highlights selected findings from the study with direct implications for library management and planning practice.

Research Question and Methodology

The key research question posed by the study was: does the introduction of a systematic planning and assessment program appear to make a difference in small academic libraries, and if so, to what constituencies and for what purposes? Using a qualitative, theory-building approach guided by the work of Glaser and Strauss[8] on the discovery of theory from data, the study explored the following factors:

1. Perceptions of change within the library and its parent institution. This was based on informant perceptions and on existing documentation.
2. Apparent degree of change, based on the extent to which objectives specified in the individual library's written planning report had been acted upon.

3. Evidence that the planning and assessment process had continued in the user library, as specified in PPSAL, as an ongoing cycle.

The data collection methodology included content analysis of existing documentation such as the planning reports prepared by the libraries using PPSAL; structured telephone interviews with chief academic officers, library directors, and faculty at the participating institutions; and supplemental interviews with individuals knowledgeable about PPSAL projects. Twenty-three of the twenty-six libraries which embarked upon the planning program prepared written documentation describing the process, assessing the state of their libraries and parent institutions, identifying user and system needs, and detailing recommendations and action strategies. Two of the libraries did not complete the PPSAL process; one did not prepare a written report. Of the sixty-eight structured interviews, twenty-six were with library directors, and twenty-one each with chief academic officers and teaching faculty currently knowledgeable about library planning. In four cases, for varying reasons only the library directors were interviewed.

The structured interview instrument had two parts. The primary instrument used with all three groups of interviewees included both open- and close-ended questions derived from the research interests underlying the study, the goals articulated in the PPSAL manual, and information contained in the library final reports. This interview guide was designed to take into account a range of respondent knowledge about both the PPSAL self-study and current library planning activities. In addition, a second part of the interview guide included a unique set of questions tailored to each institution designed to determine the outcomes of specific recommendations set forth in each library's final report. This secondary set of questions was asked of the twenty-three directors of libraries where PPSAL projects had resulted in a report or draft document. Interview questions are included as Appendix A and B.

Selected factors suggested by existing theory and research were also examined for their potential relationship to outcomes of the PPSAL self-studies. These factors included organizational size, location, the library director's length of tenure, the chairmanship and nature of the PPSAL planning committee, and the state of institutional planning efforts.

The study was theory-building, rather than hypoth-

esis-testing in nature, and as such, did not seek to quantify the impacts of the PPSAL program. Available documentation in the form of the individual library PPSAL planning reports offered some balance to the limitations inherent in the study's "post hoc" design. Also, because the colleges which undertook the PPSAL are predominantly located in the north central United States, this places further restrictions on the extent to which findings may be relevant to other small academic libraries.

Institutional Characteristics. The schools studied are predominantly private, religiously-affiliated, co-educational four-year liberal arts colleges.[9] They are established institutions, with a large majority (73%) at least a century old. They are located in seven states in the northern and central portions of the United States, predominantly in small communities in rural settings. The schools all had small undergraduate enrollments ranging from approximately 160 to 3,000 full-time students.[10]

The twenty-six schools are listed in Appendix C. It should be noted that while the names of PPSAL institutions were publicized by the Association of Research Libraries, in this study in order to maintain the privacy of participants, no individual or institution is cited by name.

Findings

There was a range of perceived outcomes from the PPSAL projects, including outcomes that were described as highly positive, major, and long-term, as well as those that were seen as minimal or initially disruptive. However, in virtually all institutions where the assessment and planning program was fully implemented, library directors, college administrators, and faculty members familiar with the program perceived at least some positive changes as a result. These changes included readily observable or documentable improvements for the library, such as an online catalog or a new building, as well as less easily observable improvements perceived, such as greater awareness of the library on campus. The extent of perceived outcomes from the PPSAL appear to distinguish it from other library planning and assessment programs studied previously where few results were noted. Casserly,[11] for example, in a study of four academic libraries, found that self-studies conducted for accreditation had little perceived impact. Similarly, Harris,[12] in a survey of 31 public libraries that had implemented the *Plan-*

ning Process for Public Libraries ,[13] found relatively little identifiable effect of the program.

Respondents familiar with their library's PPSAL self-study were queried on their perceptions of the effects of library participation in PPSAL on ten specific areas, such as the library's relationship with the college administration, overall quality of library services, and the library's share of institutional funds. Because this set of questions was not posed to library directors at two colleges that did not complete self-studies nor to other interviewees who were unfamiliar with the PPSAL, the number of respondents for this section is fifty-seven. Of those interviewees most familiar with their library's PPSAL study, a large majority (74%) saw the overall quality of their library's services as having been improved by the library's participation in the assessment and planning program. Table 1 summarizes interviewee perceptions of ten selected PPSAL effects. Table 2 compares the positive responses of the three interviewee groups, ranking the areas from one to ten (with one as the area receiving the most positive responses, and ten, the fewest.).

Library Directors' Perceptions. Most of the twenty-two library directors addressing these questions believed that their library self-study had a positive impact on the quality of the library's services (74%), on the college administration's (73%) and the faculty's (73%) awareness of the library's capacity to contribute to instructional and service programs, and on the faculty's perception of library effectiveness (68%). In several areas where a number of directors perceived the PPSAL study as having had little or no effect—such as the library's relationship with the college administration (32%), physical facilities (36%), and staff attitudes toward change (32%)—the responses reflect varying rationales. In some cases library directors expressed discouragement that little progress had been made on specific objectives in these areas, such as physical facilities. In contrast, however, in other instances directors described the self-study as having had no effect in a particular area because that area was already quite strong or positive prior to the study. For example, the library may already have had a new building, or there may already have existed a very positive relationship between the library and the administration. Similarly, a number of library directors indicated that PPSAL had not affected library staff attitudes toward change, because these were already very positive and indeed enabled them to undertake the self-study.

The area where the largest number of directors (45%) saw no effect from PPSAL was the library's general budget. This appears to reflect genuine discouragement on the part of library directors on this issue. Grants and other outside funds have in many cases enabled them to move forward on automation, building, and other special projects, including collection development. Nonetheless, a large number of directors expressed consternation over the lack of an increased level of funding for the library.

The one area where several library directors (14%) saw a negative impact from having undertaken a self-study was library staff morale. These directors generally described discouragement and frustration that anticipated changes had not come about. Table 3 summarizes the responses of library directors for ten selected areas.

Administrators' Perceptions. A large majority (74%) of the fifteen administrators describing PPSAL effects saw four of the ten areas as having been equally positively affected by their self-study. These areas included the quality of library services, the administration's awareness of and relationship with the library, and the library's physical facilities. In contrast to library directors, a majority (67%) of the administrators thought that their self-study had had a positive impact on the library's share of institutional funds.

In questions regarding the impact of their self-study on other groups such as faculty or library staff, the administrators were somewhat more likely than the library directors to respond that they did not know. For questions on the library staff's morale, attitudes toward change, and knowledge of institutional development, for example, 40% of these administrators responded that they did not know what effect the PPSAL study may have had. Similarly, 27% indicated they were unaware of its impact on faculty perception or awareness of the library. None of the administrator respondents perceived negative effects in these ten areas. Table 4 summarizes the responses of fifteen administrators.

Faculty Perceptions. Like administrators and library directors addressing this set of questions, a majority (70%) of the twenty faculty respondents viewed their self-study as having had a positive effect on library services. Faculty interviewed were more likely than administrators and less likely than library direc-

Table 1. Interviewees' Perceptions of Self-Study Effects in Ten Areas

(N=57)	Nature of Perceived Effect:			
	Positive	None	Negative	Other
Quality of library services	74%	12%	2%	12%
Administration's awareness of library capacity to contribute to college .	63%	19%	0	18%
Library's relationship with college administration	61%	19%	4%	16%
Faculty awareness of library's capacity to contribute to college .	61%	21%	0	18%
Faculty perception of library effectiveness	59%	16%	2%	23%
Library physical facilities	56%	28%	0	16%
Library staff morale	56%	7%	7%	30%
Library share of institutional funds .	53%	26%	0	21%
Library staff knowledge of current institutional developments	51%	18%	0	31%
Library staff attitudes toward change	44%	23%	0	33%

Note: These questions were answered by fifty-seven of the sixty-eight individuals interviewed; this set of questions was not posed to library directors at two colleges that did not complete PPSAL nor to other interviewees unfamiliar with the process. Response of "Other" above includes "Don't Know" and "Unsure."

Table 2. Comparison of Interviewee Group Perceptions of Positive PPSAL Effects in Ten Areas

(1 = Highest Number of Positive Responses Received, 10 = Lowest)

(N=57)	Ranking by Interview Group: Lib. Dir.	Admin.	Faculty	Overall
Quality of library services	1	1	1	1
Administration's awareness of library capacity to contribute to college .	2	1	7	2
Library's relationship with college administration	5	1	3	3
Faculty awareness of library's capacity to contribute to college .	2	6	3	3
Faculty perception of library effectiveness	4	7	2	5
Library physical facilities	7	1	7	6
Library staff morale	5	7	3	6
Library share of institutional funds .	10	5	3	8
Library staff knowledge of current institutional developments	7	7	9	9
Library staff attitudes toward change	7	10	10	10

Note: Each area with the same number of positive responses has been assigned the same rank number. Subsequent areas have then been assigned rank numbers which reflect sequential numbering of preceding items (e.g., if three areas were equally ranked as 1, the next area would be assigned a rank of 4).

Table 3. Library Directors' Perceptions of Self-Study Effects

(N=22)	Nature of Perceived Effect: Positive	None	Negative	Other
Quality of library services	77%	237%	0	0
Administration's awareness of library capacity to contribute to college .	73%	23%	0	4%
Faculty awareness of library's capacity to contribute to college .	73%	23%	0	4%
Faculty perception of library effectiveness	68%	14%	4%	14%
Library's relationship with college administration	64%	32%	4%	0
Library staff morale	64%	9%	14%	14%
Library physical facilities	55%	36%	0	9%
Library staff attitudes toward change	55%	32%	0	14%
Library staff knowledge of current institutional developments . . .	55%	32%	0	14%
Library share of institutional funds . .	45%	45%	0	9%

Note: This reflects responses from twenty-two of the twenty-six library directors interviewed; it includes only individuals familiar with completed studies. "Other" above includes responses of "Don't Know" and "Unsure."

Table 4. Administrators' Perceptions of Self-Study Effects

		Nature of Perceived Effect:			
	(N=15)	Positive	None	Negative	Other
Quality of library services		74%	13%	0	13%
Administration's awareness of library capacity to contribute to college .		74%	13%	0	13%
Library's relationship with college administration		74%	13%	0	13%
Library physical facilities		74%	13%	0	13%
Library share of institutional funds . .		67%	13%	0	20%
Faculty awareness of library's capacity to contribute to college .		60%	13%	0	27%
Faculty perception of library effectiveness		53%	20%	0	27%
Library staff morale		53%	7%	0	40%
Library staff knowledge of current institutional developments . . .		53%	7%	0	40%
Library staff attitudes toward change .		47%	13%	0	40%

Note: This reflects responses from fifteen of the twenty-one administrators interviewed; it includes only individuals familiar with completed studies. "Other" above includes responses of "Don't Know" and "Unsure."

tors to report that they viewed their self-study as having had no effect. In general, for most of the ten areas, a smaller percentage (50% or fewer) of faculty reported positive effects than either library directors or administrators. Similarly, faculty were more likely than the other two groups to respond that they did not know about the impact of PPSAL on a particular area.

Interestingly, faculty perceptions of the impact of PPSAL on library facilities are similar to those of the library directors; fewer respondents in both groups saw this as positive than did administrators. In terms of library funding, the area where 45% of library directors saw no effect from their self-study, faculty members were more likely than the directors to regard the impact as positive (50%) and more likely than both other groups to state that they didn't know (35%) what the impact had been. Table 5 provides an overview of the responses of faculty.

In addition, open-ended questions were posed to the respondents familiar with their library's self-study in order to elicit further perceptions of changes resulting from or relating to PPSAL. The data from the open-ended questions is rich, and unfortunately can only be touched on here. The three consequences of the PPSAL studies most frequently described by interviewees were: the implementation of major improvements relating to the library, noticeably increased awareness of and favorable attention for the library from the larger college community, and again, improved quality and effectiveness of library services and programs.

Recommendations Undertaken. The libraries' final reports from their self-studies included specific recommendations for future actions. Library directors were asked specifically whether or not selected key recommendations from their reports had been completed, partially completed, were still in progress, or had been systematically reviewed and revised. All of these alternatives were considered for purposes of the study as positive, systematic actions taken on the recommendations.

In order to gain additional understanding about the nature of the colleges' key PPSAL recommendations and their outcomes, the recommendations were grouped into general categories. Those types of objectives entailing significant dollar expenditures include library building and renovation programs, general budgetary increases, staffing increases, and automation projects. Other types of recommendations include

desired changes in institutional and library policies, in library programs or services, and in library organization or management practices. Table 6 summarizes the types of recommendations and their rates of implementation.

Because the recommendations included in the study in some cases were selected by the researcher in lieu of using all recommendations for a given institution, this summary can only suggest the overall distribution of the types of recommendations. Based on this selective data, the recommendations most frequently proposed were those involving changes in library programs or services and in institutional policy regarding the library and those specifying automated library services. Types of recommendations with the highest completion rates were those involving library (as opposed to institutional) policies, library programs, and automation. The areas of least success were recommendations for library budget increases and for changes in institutional policy regarding the library.

The PPSAL and Planning Practices. A key goal of the PPSAL approach was to initiate systematic library assessment and planning as a continuing library management practice. The study examined whether this was perceived to be an outcome of the self-studies. Interviewees at fewer than half (40%) of the colleges that undertook the PPSAL believed that systematic assessment and planning had continued in their library after the PPSAL self-study. Of these colleges, interviewees at only six (24% of the total) attributed this continuing library planning either directly or indirectly to the library's participation in the self-study. In sum, based on interviewee perceptions, the *Planning Program for Small Academic Libraries* was less successful at instigating continuing systematic library assessment and planning than at initiating other positive library changes.

Interviewees were also asked about the presence of institutional planning at their school and their perceptions of the library's role in the process. At 58% of the institutions studied, all or a majority of respondents described a college-wide systematic planning program. However, there was no relationship observed between PPSAL self-study outcomes and the perceived current presence or absence of institutional planning.

An unexpected feature of the data on current library and college-wide systematic planning was the extent of

Table 5. Faculty Perceptions of Self-Study Effects

| (N=20) | Nature of Perceived Effect: | | | |
	Positive	None	Negative	Other
Quality of library services	70%	0	5%	25%
Faculty perception of library effectiveness	55%	15%	0	30%
Faculty awareness of library's capacity to contribute to college .	50%	25%	0	25%
Library's relationship with college administration	50%	10%	5%	35%
Library share of institutional funds	50%	15%	0	35%
Library staff morale	50%	5%	5%	40%
Administration's awareness of library capacity to contribute to college .	45%	20%	0	35%
Library physical facilities	45%	30%	0	25%
Library staff knowledge of current institutional developments . . .	40%	15%	0	45%
Library staff attitudes toward change	30%	20%	0	50%

Note: This reflects responses from twenty of the twenty-one faculty interviewed; it includes only individuals familiar with completed studies. "Other" above includes responses of "Don't Know" and "Unsure."

Table 6. Types of Recommendations and Rates of Completion

	(N)	Percent Undertaken	Percent Not Done
Automation	(30)	90%	10%
Staff	(14)	86%	14%
Building	(22)	77%	23%
Budget	(15)	67%	33%
Sub-total of Monetary	(81)	81%	19%
Library Policy	(24)	96%	4%
Programs/Services	(42)	93%	7%
Management and Organization	(20)	75%	25%
Institutional Policy	(32)	69%	31%
Total of Key Recommendations	(199)	83%	17%

Note: The types of recommendations were summarized from the libraries' written PPSAL planning reports.

disparity of views among respondents, particularly between library directors and college administrators, at the same institution. This disparity may be a reflection of several factors, such as individual respondent interpretation of what constitutes systematic assessment and planning or the lack of a well-defined and clearly communicated planning program. In those cases in otherwise positive settings where the library directors were more negative than their administrators about the presence of library planning, this may reflect a sense of pressure or strain on limited human resources in a very small organization.

Suggestions for Further Development

In order to gain further from the insights of those who had undertaken the *Planning Program for Small Academic Libraries,* interviewees were asked what improvements they would recommend in a systematic planning and assessment program for small libraries. In response to this query, interviewees at a majority (69%) of the twenty-six colleges stated that they had found the PPSAL a worthwhile program.

While overall the existing program was viewed quite favorably, there were concerns expressed about the following areas: the constitution and dynamics of the self-study committee; the selection of consultants; and the amount of resources required for the PPSAL self-study. These concerns were as likely to be expressed at a college that perceived its project outcomes as very positive, as at an institution with minimal PPSAL results.

The Self-study Committee. At a large majority of the colleges (77%), respondents described problems or offered suggestions for improvements relating to the nature and functioning of the self-study committee. These include the following aspects.

1. Broad-based representation. A number of respondents stressed that the self-study committee should be broadly representative of campus interests. This was viewed as critical both to gain support for the study results and to ensure that the study recommendations are reflective of and aligned with the larger college community's best interests. Interviewees at nearly half the colleges specifically stressed the need to have the college administration fully involved in the self-study process from the outset, as well. Clearly, as one library director stated, "one of the most important components of any kind of planning or assessment

program is a mechanism to inform the administration."

The PPSAL manual suggests a committee of five to seven people, three of whom are to be library staff.[14] This size and constitution would seem unlikely to ensure the type of broad representation just described. Based on the final planning reports, in fact, a number of the colleges apparently had somewhat larger committees, perhaps with a small working core group, and/ or they had numerous task forces that drew in additional people from the academic community.

2. Selection and Dynamics. A number of respondents expressed dissatisfaction with the functioning of their self-study committees, and suggested that more attention be given at the outset both to the process of selecting the committee and to facilitating the group dynamics. One library director suggested: "We needed some type of training in interpersonal relationships."

Interviewee comments suggest that at least some colleges would be aided by additional consultant help at the beginning of the study, specifically in designing the individual self-study process and in preparing the committee to work as a team. Particular attention should be given to ensuring that the "plan for planning" clearly articulates a viable program both for explaining or promoting the project to the college community on a continuing basis and for continually channeling input from that community on its needs and perceptions.

Consultant Selection. The use of consultants to help begin and monitor the self-study process is fundamental to the PPSAL approach, and it was generally seen as desirable and beneficial by interviewees. As one library director observed, "The consultant[s] . . . were useful because they could form questions in an integrated way that insiders could not."

Problems or areas of dissatisfaction that occurred involving consultants generally related to the fortuitousness of the match between the individual consultant and the college. As an administrator noted, "Picking the right outside consultants for the kind of institution you are dealing with is very important." For project facilitator or monitor, interviewees wanted a consultant who was aware of the kind of problems faced by their institution and who was compatible with or could adapt to the style or dynamics of their particular organization.

Extent of Resources Required. Interviewees also expressed concern about the amount of time and level of effort required for the PPSAL program. Some interviewees suggested that release time for a committee chairman or key participant would ease the burden on limited human resources. At one-third of the colleges, respondents believed that the process—and the manual—should be abridged. They wanted less emphasis and time given to the preliminary sections on institutional history and on trends in higher education and the library field, with a more immediate focus on issues affecting the library. As one interviewee summarized: "We spent too much time on background material. Most of it has already been written; we should have just borrowed and shared. By the time we got to issues, we ran out of gas." Similarly, another respondent suggested: "You need to redesign it in such a way that the temptation or pitfall of over involvement in the first part is lessened."

Respondents at 42% of the colleges also believed that access to shared information, including standards and comparative data on other institutions, would facilitate the self-study process. One respondent observed, for example, "we spent a lot of time seeking standards. . . . It would be helpful to have these gathered ahead of time and made available as part of the PPSAL program." Another noted, "The opportunity to compare data from libraries of similar institutions is an essential ingredient."

Ready access to systematically prepared synopses of key library and higher education trends and comparative overviews of library statistics might indeed facilitate the PPSAL process. This is especially the case at small institutions with very limited resources and perhaps limited access to other resources, such as online or even major printed indexes and extensive collections of professional journals.

Conclusion and Recommendations for Further Research

In response to the key research question, whether the introduction of a systematic planning and assessment program appeared to make a difference in small academic libraries, perhaps the most succinct response is one given by an administrator interviewed in the study: "Yes, it did make a difference. . . . You just can't tamper with a key part of an institution without some effect." However, additional research is needed both to explore the generalizability of the findings discussed here to other groups of libraries and other planning processes, as well as to enhance further our understanding of the consequences of implementing library planning and assessment programs or tools.

Endnotes

1. Duane E. Webster, *Library Management Review and Analysis Program: A Handbook for Guiding Change and Improvement in Research Library Management* (Washington, DC: Association of Research Libraries, Office of University Library Management Studies, 1973).

2. Association of Research Libraries, Office of Management Studies, *The Academic Library Development Program: A Self-Improvement Process for Libraries* (Washingtion, DC: Association of Research Libraries, 1978).

3. Nancy A. VanHouse, Beth T. Weil, and Charles R. McClure, *Measuring Academic Library Performance: A Practical Approach* (Chicago: American Library Association, 1990).

4. Edward R. Johnson and Stuart H. Mann, *Organization Development for Academic Libraries: An Evaluation of the Management Review and Analysis Program* (Westport, CT: Greenwood Press, 1980).

5. Ibid, p. 151.

6. See for example: Stanton F. Biddle, "The Planning Function in the Management of University Libraries: Survey, Analysis, Conclusions, and Recommendations," (D.L.S. diss., Univ. of California, Berkley, 1988); Judith J. Senkevitch, "Consequences of Innovation: Perceptions and Correlates of Change After Systematic Assessment and Planning in Small Academic Libraries," (Ph.D. diss., Rutgers Univ., 1989); and Mary F. Casserly, "Accreditation-related Self-study as a Planned Change Process: Factors Relating to Its Success in Academic Libraries," *Journal of Library Administration* 8 (Spring, 1987): 87–88.

7. P. Grady Morein, Maxine K. Sitts, and Duane E. Webster, *Planning Program for Small Academic Libraries: An Assisted Self-Study Manual* (Washington, DC: Association for Research Libraries, Office of Management Studies, 1980).

8. Barney G. Glaser and Anselm L. Strauss, *The Discovery of Grounded Theory: Strategies for Qualitative Research* (New York: Aldine, 1967).

9. College Entrance Examination Board, *The College Handbook, 1987-88,* 25th ed. (New York: College Board, 1987).

10. Ibid.

11. Mary F. Casserly, "Self-study and Planned Change

in Academic Libraries: A Case Study Analysis of Regional Accreditation Self-Study Experiences" (Ph.D. diss., Rutgers Univ., 1984).

12. Rebecca B. Harris, "Survey of the Use Being Made of the Planning Process," *Public Libraries* 22 (Winter, 1983): 144-147 .

13. Vernon E. Palmour, Marcia C. Bellassai, and Nancy DeWath, *A Planning Process for Public Libraries* (Chicago: American Library Association, Public Library Association, 1980).

14. P. Grady Morein, op. cit., p. III-1

Appendix A

Structured Interview Questions

Interviewee Name: _____

Title: _____

                                                          Interview Appt.:

College: _____   Date: _____

Telephone: _____   Time:_____

(Time Started:_____ Time ended:_____) On Site:_____   Telephone_____

Interviewer Notes Taken from Initial Call:

    Participated in original study? YES_____ NO____

    Had been aware of original study? YES___ NO___

    Did study have a final written report? YES___ NO___ Draft___

    Written follow-up study? YES____ NO____

    (*Faculty:* Serves on Faculty Library Committee? YES_____ NO____)

NOTES:

_____

1. a) To your knowledge, is there an ongoing college-wide planning effort, as a matter of institutional policy at (your college)?   YES_____ NO_____

    b) *(If YES,)* Does the library regularly participate in that effort?

                                                           YES___ NO_____

2.   In one or two words, how would you characterize the library's current planning and assessment activities?

    <u>Comments:</u>

3.   One of the original aims of the PPSAL approach was that systematic planning and assessment activities would become a regularly occurring, formalized process— ie., that at least every several years on a continuing basis, there would be a systematic review and reassessment of the library's overall objectives and programs, with new recommendations and objectives established.

    In your perception, has this happened in your library since your original PPSAL program in 198__?
YES____ * NO__   <u>(If NO, WHY NOT?)</u>
(If no, go to 4.)

(*If YES:) a)Is this, in your opinion, a result, either direct or indirect, of your library's having participated in PPSAL? YES_____ NO_____

    b) Roughly, how often (at what intervals) is the planning process or cycle occurring?

(Suggestions: yearly, every 2 or 3 yrs., 4 or 5 years, no particular interval,)

c) Does it result in written memos or reports?   YES___ NO__

d) Does it involve only library staff or include input from faculty and administration?

Lib. Staff only_____   Outside input also_____

e) Do you see this as a continuing process (ie. ,one that will continue in the future)?

YES_____   NO_____

f) Is this part of a larger college-wide, institutional planning program?

YES_____   NO_____

Comments:

4)   Your library's 198__ report from the initial PPSAL effort outlined specific recommendations and objectives; some of these had targeted completion dates. I'd like to very quickly mention several of these key objectives and ask you to comment on their present status. **(Question 4 for Library Director Interviews Only. See Appendix C for Sample Questions.)**

5)   Have you used or referred to the written report (if no report, any study summaries or papers) from your (original) PPSAL effort, in the years since the project?

YES_____   NO_____

6)   So, if you were to characterize the report (material) as a planning aid or reference, would you describe it as: ?

currently useful_____   used in the past____   not useful__   non-existent__

7)   Can you recall (do you know) why the library undertook the PPSAL?

NO____   YES_____   *   Explain briefly:

(If YES:) What in your recollection was the single most important motivational factor in participating in the PPSAL? _____

8)   From your present vantage point, with several years having passed since the library's PPSAL project, what impacts (results) or consequences do you see of the library's having undertaken that program? None___ Explain other:

9)   What about lingering intangible (less tangible) effects, such as improved communication between faculty and library staff; greater responsive or awareness; etc?   None_____ Explain:_____

10)   Is the library currently involved in any systematic planning and assessment effort?
NO__ YES_____* Explain_____

(IF YES:) Did this in your opinion come about directly or indirectly as a result of the library's participation in PPSAL? No___ YES_____

11)   Again, from the vantage point of your current position and given what you know about your library's involvement in the PPSAL, what is your perception of the effects of participation in PPSAL on the following?:

a) library's relationship with administration?

b) faculty's perception of the library's effectiveness?

c) the overall quality of the library's services?

d) library's physical facilities?

e) library's share of institutional funds?

f) library staff morale?

g) library staff's general attitude towards change?

h) the faculty's awareness of the library's capacity to contribute to instructional & service programs:

i) the college administration's awareness of the library's capacity for contributing to instructional & service programs:

j) the library staff's knowledge of current institutional developments & emerging opportunities:

Comments:

12)   If someone were to redesign PPSAL or were to design a new systematic planning and assessment program for a group of small libraries, is there any particular advice you would want to share with them — or anything in particular that you would want to see included or deleted?

13)   Are there any questions about the impact of PPSAL on your library that I should have asked you but did not?_____

14)   Are there any questions that you have for me?

Appendix B

Sample Questions on Recommendation Outcomes

Your library's 198__ report from the initial PPSAL effort outlined specific recommendations and objectives; some of these had targeted completion dates. I'd like to very quickly mention several of these key objectives and ask you to comment on their present status.

	Attained?			Still in	Reviewed &
List of objectives	YES	NO	Partially	process	altered or deleted

(Recommendations include:)

1. Form a separate faculty library committee.

2. Involve faculty routinely in the book selection process.

3. Write a description of collecting practices and strengths in each discipline and distribute to all faculty and key administrative personnel (by librarian).

4. Expand library space in lower level of Hall.

5. Reduce noise level — this is a priority in building renovation.

6. Update inventory of A-V equipment on campus and gather use statistics to pinpoint demand.

7. Conduct internal staff performance reviews 3 or 4 times a year.

Appendix C

Participants in the Study on
The Planning Progam for Small Academic Libraries

Organization Name	Address
Anderson University	Anderson, IN
Butler University	Indianapolis, IN
Carleton College	Northfield, MN
Centre College	Danville, KY
DePauw University	Greencastle, IN
Earlham College	Richmond, IN
Franklin College	Franklin, IN
Gannon University	Erie, PA
Goshen College	Goshen, IN
Hanover College	Hanover, IN
Hope College	Holland, MI
Huntington College	Huntington, IN
Illinois Wesleyan University	Bloomington, IL
Lake Forest College	Lake Forest, IL
Manchester College	North Manchester, IN
North Park College	Chicago, IL
St. Joseph's College	Rensselaer, IN
St. Mary's College	Notre Dame, IN
St. Meinrad College	St. Meinrad, IN
St. Olaf College	Northfield, MN
St. Xavier College	Chicago, IL
Taylor University	Upland, IN
Transylvania University	Lexington, KY
University of Evansville	Evansville, IN
Valparaiso University	Valparaiso, IN
Wittenberg University	Springfield, OH

Towards a Theory of Organizational Change in Libraries

Judith Jamison Senkevitch
University of Wisconsin-Milwaukee
Milwaukee, Wisconsin

Abstract

Using a qualitative, grounded theory approach, the perceived consequences of implementing a systematic library planning and assessment program in twenty-six small academic institutions were explored. The data collection methodology included document content analysis and structured interviews with sixty-eight institutional participants. Based on the perceived outcomes from the planning programs, the population of organizations studied clustered into groups with distinct characteristics. Findings suggest that the outcome of an assisted planning and assessment program in small academic libraries is positively related to the state of organizational readiness for change at the time of the program and to the presence of certain key organizational properties.

The need for additional research on the impact of planning and assessment efforts in libraries[1] and on the consequences of adopting programmatic innovations in organizations[2] has already been well documented in the literature. In response to that identified need, a study was undertaken to explore the perceived consequences of implementing a systematic planning and assessment program in small academic libraries. The purpose of the study, in seeking systematicall to derive theory from data, was to contribute both to the understanding of the potential longer term consequences of implementing a systematic planning and assessment innovation in libraries, as well as to the understanding of the larger area of organizational change.

Description of the Study

Using a qualitative case-study design guided by the approach to the systematic discovery of theory from data elucidated by Glaser and Strauss in their *Discovery of Grounded Theory*,[3] the study explored the perceived longer term consequences of implementing the 1980 *Planning Program for Small Academic Libraries* [4] (PPSAL) at all twenty-six colleges that had used the program prior to 1989. The PPSAL, developed by the Association of Research Libraries' Office of Management Studies, is an assisted self-study planning and assessment program intended for use by colleges with a library staff of fewer than twenty people.

The key research question posed by the study was whether or not the introduction of an innovative planning and assessment program appeared to make a difference in small academic libraries. The data collec-

tion methodology included: (1) content analysis of the written library planning reports that resulted from implementing PPSAL; (2) sixty-eight structured telephone interviews with chief academic officers, library directors, and teaching faculty at the subject institutions; and (3) supplemental interviews with additional individuals especially knowledgeable about the PPSAL projects and their aftermaths. The structured interviews had two parts: the principal set of questions, both open- and close-ended, posed to all interviewee groups, and an additional set of individualized questions posed only to library directors to assess specific outcomes recommended in each library's planning report. The interviews explored perceptions both of relatively tangible changes, such as the extent to which specific objectives were acted upon, and intangible outcomes, such as expressed changes in status, morale, or flexibility.

The study had several major methodological limitations. It was theory-building rather than hypothesis-testing in nature; as such, it did not propose to quantify the impacts of the innovation under study or to demonstrate cause and effect relationships. It was a "post hoc" study, with all the limitations inherent in such designs. The available documentation, in the form of the library planning reports, provided data with which to balance the "post hoc" informant perceptions.

Of the twenty-six PPSAL projects, eight were completed in 1980; ten in 1981; five in 1982; and one in 1985. Two of the projects were not completed. In four of the twenty-six cases studied, for varying reasons, only the library director was interviewed. The interview guide was designed to take into account a range of re-spondent knowledge about both the PPSAL planning self-study and current library planning activities.

Although the names of institutions undertaking the PPSAL were publicized by the Association of Research Libraries, in order to maintain the privacy of participants in this study all interview responses and institutional references are generic, with no individual or institution cited by name.

Interviewee Characteristics. A majority of the sixty-eight respondents interviewed had been present at their institutions at the time of the PPSAL projects. At the twenty-six schools studied, twenty of the library directors interviewed (77%) had been present either as director or as staff during their library's initial PPSAL self-study. Of the six library directors new since the time of the PPSAL project, only two (8%) were unaware of the PPSAL self-study or of any final report produced. However, in both of these cases the institutional administrators interviewed were familiar with the self-studies.

The twenty-one institutional administrators interviewed were predominantly chief academic officers with oversight responsibility for the library—vice president for academic affairs or provost. Nearly all, nineteen, were either present during the study or stated that they were aware of it; two indicated they had been unaware of the PPSAL self-study prior to being contacted.

The twenty-one faculty members interviewed included four current department heads, and represented a range of disciplines. Ten of these individuals, or slightly fewer than half, were currently serving on faculty library committees or otherwise saw themselves as actively involved in library planning activities. As with the other two groups interviewed, a large majority (86%) had been present at the time of their library's PPSAL study; fourteen had served on the PPSAL self-study committees. Two of the faculty were not aware of the self-studies.

Findings

Data collected from the population of institutions which implemented the PPSAL revealed a range of perceived outcomes from the self-studies. This range included cases where the impact of the projects on both the library and the institution as a whole was seen by interviewees as highly positive, significant, and long-term, and instances where the self-study was viewed as having had virtually no long-term effect or as having been initially disruptive. The differences in these perceived outcomes were not explained by differences in any of several factors examined in the study, including organizational size, location, the presence of a recently hired director, or the chairmanship of the PPSAL self-study committee.

Based on these perceived outcomes, the organizations studied clustered into categories or groups with distinct properties and characteristics. The findings relating to these conceptual categories and their implications for a theory of organizational change are the focus of this paper.

Conceptual Categories and Their Properties. These groups or conceptual categories appear to represent, in effect, similar organizations clustered at various points along a continuum of organizational change. The clusters are somewhat reminiscent of—and indeed may be partially explained by—the various stages and forces in group change described by Kurt Lewin in his early theory of quasi-stationary equilibria and social change. Lewin, in discussing the creation of permanent changes, not only describes potential stages in the process of implementing change, such as "unfreezing," moving, and freezing at a new level, but also characterizes settings and circumstances in which change may most likely occur.[5]

Table 1 lists the conceptual or outcome categories and summarizes their key properties. The six categories are described briefly below.

Group I: Highly Positive, Long-term Results

You won't find many programs that, when undertaken, will produce the cosmic results that this has for us. It's been the most germinal ten years in the existence of this institution.

—Group I Administrator

In this cluster, interviewees referred to the impact of their library's having undertaken the PPSAL as very important, with decade-long effects. The seven institutions in this group, at the time they undertook the study, were already committed or receptive to change. With one exception, they were either already committed to a new building program or were aware of the need for renovated facilities, and all but one have indeed undertaken major building programs since the PPSAL projects.

The libraries either had a new director with a strong mandate from the administration for change, or they were led by an established director who was well-respected in the campus community and who was in the forefront of managing change. At all of the colleges with established library directors and at most of those with new directors, interviewees described a historically positive, constructive relationship between the library and other sectors of the college community. In most cases, the institutional administration appears to have strongly supported the library and the expansion of its role in the academic community and to have been consistently interested in the library's progress.

TABLE 1

OUTCOME CATEGORIES AND THEIR PROPERTIES

	Key Characteristics
I. Highly Positive (N=7)	a. Major long-term results from PPSAL b. Institutional readiness for change c. Positive library/college relationship d. Politically sensitive library director e. Library staff openness to change
II. Moderate (N=4)	a. Positive results, but less perceived effect than in Group I b. Displays two or more other Group I characteristics
III. Short-term Negative (N=5)	a. Institutional discontent with library b. Conflicting forces for change c. Subsequent turmoil d. Gradual progress after PPSAL
IV. Frustrating (N=3)	a. Institutional discontent with library b. Lack of progress after PPSAL c. Insularity of library d. Continuing frustration over lack of library change
V. Minimal (N=3)	a. Little or no impact from PPSAL b. No strong impetus for change c. Long-term administrative stability d. Insularity of library
VI. Problematic (N=3)	a. Institutional distress b. High administrative turnover c. Library retrenchment

Note: The categories reflect data from twenty-five of the twenty-six institutions studied.

Virtually all these libraries had directors who appeared to possess a quality referred to here as the "political sensitivity factor." This includes not only political savvy, but the following traits as well: ability to articulate the library's needs to the larger academic community; ability to build up support and channels of communication for the library with both faculty and administration; desire and ability to promote faculty involvement in the library; and an orientation towards viewing inclusive planning and assessment as a viable means both of coping constructively with change and of enabling the library to have some control over its destiny

At schools in this cluster there appears to have been, at the time of the PPSAL study and since, a fortuitous combination of institutional receptiveness to change, administrative vision and support for the library, and a library director who possessed a number of the qualities described above. These library directors, however, were not necessarily initially enthusiastic about undertaking the PPSAL project.

Finally, interviewees in this group, when asked about their perceptions of the library staff's attitude towards change, were likely to describe the library staff as being in the forefront of change.

Key shared properties of group I organizations are: (1) major long-term impact of PPSAL; (2) institutional readiness/impetus for change; (3) a positive relationship between the library and the academic community; (4) "political sensitivity" of the library director; and (5) library staff openness towards change. These characteristics are also supported by earlier findings on organizational change and innovation. This is especially the case with the association of positive PPSAL outcomes and the presence of a "politically sensitive" library director,[6] as defined above, and a library staff that is receptive to change.[7]

Group II: Positive, Shorter-term Impact

I felt good about it at the time, . . . [but] one study group two student life-times ago does not make that much of a difference. It's much more the people in the trenches over a long period of time that bring about change, making noises, making waves.

—Group II Faculty Member

The group II organizations are in many ways very similar to those just discussed; however, interviewees in this second group perceived less long-term impact from their PPSAL self-studies. The majority of interviewees at each of these four institutions saw the results of their self-studies as very positive, but most did not attribute to their PPSAL project the same degree of pivotal impact described in group I. To some extent, the four institutions in this cluster represent a sub-group of group I or "exceptions that help prove the rule," and examination of key areas in which these institutions differed from those in Group I provided additional insights into both groups.

While group I and most of the group II colleges seem to have been either already committed to or at the threshold of change, the institutions clustered in group III appear to have been at a different stage of change.

Group III: Short-term Negative,
Long-Term Positive Results

There was a prevailing sense at the time that the study did not benefit the college; but in the long run it did. . . . It made the rest of the college so painfully aware of how central the library was to the campus. Sometimes things have to fall apart in order to refocus.

—Group III Administrator

Institutions in group III, whose title derives from references by several interviewees to this perception of short-term negative but long-term positive consequences, are notable because they generally appear to have been, at the time of undertaking the PPSAL study, at a different, perhaps earlier, stage of readiness for change than schools in groups I and II. Based on interviewee descriptions, there was growing impetus within the institutions for change in the library. However, as suggested by Lewin's[8] theory, there may have been stronger forces opposing change or weaker forces supporting it than in group I. Major changes in the libraries did indeed occur after the PPSAL studies in these institutions, but over a period of years and accompanied in most cases by notable turmoil and dissension. Unlike group I, in all five of these colleges, there was a change in library directorship after the self-study.

According to respondent data, this cluster is most characterized by the following three properties: dissatisfaction with the library on the part of the college community prior to undertaking the PPSAL study; a period of turmoil following the study, usually accompanied by an exodus of library staff; and gradual progress towards what is now perceived as a positive relationship between the library and the academic community.

Interviewees described campus dissatisfaction with the library prior to the PPSAL not only in terms of poor physical facilities or inadequate collections, but also in terms of "personality" and personnel problems. Respondents frequently referred to the library prior to the PPSAL study as having been isolated from the academic community and the director as unable to articulate the library's needs to the campus.

Two other factors that appear related to the nature and level of discontent with the library at the time of the PPSAL study are the following: (1) at four of the colleges the impetus for the self-studies, according to the recollections of interviewees, came from a source other than the library director, usually the administration; and (2) someone other than the library director was likely to chair the self-study committee. In at least several of these cases, the PPSAL study appears to have been used as a tool to force change, rather than primarily to manage it. As such, the self-study processes may have taken on a somewhat punitive aspect. There were also cases described among the group I schools where the administration insisted that the library undertake the self-study. However, in all of these instances there was a new library director who had been hired with a strong mandate for change, and implementing the self-study was seen as a means for facilitating this. In contrast, in the group III colleges, the library directors were all continuing directors of some years tenure.

Invariably in group III, the years immediately after the PPSAL studies are described as a time of continuing, even escalating, discontent. During this period, there was a turnover in library directorship (at least once, sometimes twice) at all five institutions, and at a majority, an almost complete turnover in library staff as well. Although one might reasonably anticipate a period of transition following the end of a library director's long tenure, the circumstances described here by interviewees seem to be of a particularly tumultuous nature.

All the group III college libraries, following the several years of transition and tumult, appeared to have progressed towards a more constructive period. Interviewees at most of these institutions saw the current relationship between the library and the college community in improved, more positive terms; and the libraries have to varying degrees made major accomplishments. As noted earlier, four of the five have undertaken major building programs; three have completed or were in the midst of large-scale automation projects.

Group IV: Frustration as an Outcome

Although the study called for faculty input, there's been no carry thru, no meetings, no committee set up to continue the process. The librarian sees the faculty committee as a threat to the library.

—Group IV: Faculty Member

The three institutions in this cluster are colleges which appear to have resembled—in terms of readiness for change at the time of the PPSAL study—those in group III, but where progress after the study was essentially stalled. As at the group III colleges, the self-studies were undertaken to instigate change. There were continuing library directors at the time of the studies, and the impetus for change appears to have come from a source other than the library director. One administrator recalled, for example, that the study "was mandated by the campus administration because of concern about tension within the library staff and between the staff and director." Unlike group III, however, in these colleges there was no change in library leadership after the study, and virtually no progress has been made on study recommendations.

Key characteristics of this cluster are: (1) existing discontent at the time of the study, (2) a lack of progress towards implementing recommendations after the study, (3) perception by other sectors of the campus of the library and its director as isolated and unresponsive, and (4) continuing frustration with the library on the part of the college community. The libraries were seen as insular; the library directors were consistently described as unable to articulate the library's needs to the college, resistant to change, and unable to delegate even basic tasks. Faculty interviewed saw the library directors as threatened by faculty interest in the library and expressed frustration at the inability to effect library change.

So great, in fact, seemed the frustration of these

faculty and administrators at the lack of change, that their comments about their libraries were the most negative of any group. Remarks ranged from the openly hostile to the plaintive. There is also in these interviewees' statements a sense of waiting for change to occur, of "biding one's time." As one chief academic officer noted, "the pressure for change on the library will continue to grow. Within a year to a year and a half, we will have a new librarian . . . who will be able to implement the desired changes."

Group V: Minimal Impact

Even though, everything considered, the program was helpful, it didn't bring results. That wasn't the fault of the program, just an economic fact.

—Group V: Library Director

Based on interviewee perceptions, this group shares the following properties: (1) little if any impact attributed to the PPSAL study, (2) no strong impetus for library change at the time of the self- study, (3) long-term stability in college administration, but high faculty turnover noted, and (4) insularity of the library. These three institutions all had continuing, rather than new, library directors at the time of their self-studies, with little turnover in the subsequent years. Two of the three libraries did not complete their final study reports. The extent to which they acted on recommendations from the studies varied, but the rate of change tended to be low. One director estimated that no more than 20% of their self-study recommendations had been achieved, and those were internal or policy changes which did not require additional funding. Whatever library accomplishments followed the PPSAL projects were generally not attributed by interviewees to the self-study process.

Although, as at colleges in other groups, interviewee comments cited the need for additional library funding, the frustration so evident in the group IV school interviews with faculty and administrators was not manifest here. However, a strong sense of the library's isolation from the academic community was expressed, in this instance by the library directors rather by faculty or administrators. One director, for example, when asked to suggest as potential interviewees faculty knowledgeable about the library, responded: "I'm not sure any faculty members are knowledgeable about the library." Another stated that "the library is virtually autonomous." Despite the presence of this sense of

library isolation which might suggest that there would be an accompanying sense of frustration on the part of the rest of the academic community, again, there does not seem, based on respondent comments, to be a strong undercurrent of dissatisfaction or impetus for change. Group V colleges, with their apparent lack of impetus for change and isolated libraries, seem the most nearly static of all those institutions studied.

Group VI: Troubled Institutions

There's been a big turnover in library staff, faculty and administration. We had four presidents in four years, and several deans. . . . [There was] a great controversy, an upheaval. Things just fell apart.

—Group VI: Faculty Member

While group VI like group II is essentially a sub-group whose individual institutions can also be represented in other categories, it was useful to examine these schools as a separate cluster because of their unusual circumstances. Key properties of this category are significant institutional distress, high administrative turnover, and library retrenchment. These were colleges where issues or factors external to the library were so dominant or institutional upheaval so great that in the years since the colleges' PPSAL studies these issues appear to have either overshadowed or driven most events relating to the library. These institutional travails included high administrative turnover—two schools had four presidents in four years—which is undoubtedly symptomatic of other difficulties; unusual economic problems such as damaging fiscal mismanagement; or institutional redefinition that becomes an "identity crisis" of almost cataclysmic proportions. This institutional stress is the chief property of this category. The presence of such overreaching issues appears to make the outcomes of the self-studies at these schools distinct from those of similar but less troubled institutions. Like group II institutions, they may be viewed, in effect, as exceptions that help reinforce or clarify other categories.

Regardless of other institutional characteristics described or the perceived state of organizational readiness for change at the time of the self-study, interviewees at each of these three colleges reported little library progress or positive change. In two cases, not only was there a lack of progress noted, but rather a clear sense of serious regression. One library director, for example, in discussing the institution's continuing financial problems, noted that when the self-study was conducted, "the library had a staff of twenty-one, . . . now [there are] only nine people." At another institution, where the self-study occurred simultaneously with (and is credited by one interviewee with precipitating) a wrenching reanalysis of the college's mission and identity, a faculty member observed that subsequently, following the PPSAL project and the ensuing upheaval, "the library went from a high level of professionalism to a lower level of professionalism." Having gone through a period of great trauma or upheaval, these institutions now appear to be in varying stages of recovery. However, retrenchment rather than progress is another key characteristic of this group.

Conclusions

The degree of positive change following the implementation of the systematic planning program appears related to the presence of various factors; chief among these is the institution's state of readiness for change. Organizational receptivity to change was most frequently reflected in interviewee descriptions of an awareness by key sectors of the college community of the need for improvements in library facilities, collections, and/or services. In those cases with the most positive PPSAL outcomes, this awareness was generally coupled with a level of perceived institutional commitment to implementing improvements and an absence of strong resisting forces.

Based on data derived from this study, the following propositions are set forth for further testing as a possible basis for a theory of effects of assisted assessment and planning in small academic libraries.

Propositions for a Theory of Effects of Assisted Assessment and Planning in Small Academic Libraries

It is theorized that: the outcome of an assisted assessment and planning program in small academic libraries is positively related to the state of organizational readiness for change at the time of the study and to the presence of certain key organizational properties. Organizational characteristics that favor positive, long-term planning outcomes are: institutional commitment or receptivity to change, a "politically sensitive" library director, library staff openness towards change, and a positive relationship between the library and the academic community. A "politically sensitive" library director, as described in this study, is one

who demonstrates most of the following qualities: understanding of institutional politics, ability to articulate the library's needs to the larger academic community, ability to build up support and channels of communication for the library with both faculty and administration, desire and ability to promote faculty involvement in the library, and an orientation towards viewing inclusive planning and assessment as a viable means both of coping constructively with change and of enabling the library to have some control over its destiny.

Additionally, it is hypothesized that the emergence of an overriding institution-wide problem, either during or after the self-study, will serve to intervene in this relationship between positive outcomes and the presence of key organizational properties, including readiness for change.

Further elements of this theory are as follows:

1. Just as institutional readiness for change is positively associated with productive assisted self-study outcomes, so a weak impetus for organizational change and/or strong resisting forces are positively correlated with a lack of productive change.

2. Organizations at a similar stage of readiness for change and demonstrating key characteristics to the same extent will have similar levels of outcomes from the assisted assessment and planning program.

3. In organizations where there is strong impetus for change in some sectors coupled with strong resistance in others, it is probable that the self-study process, if undertaken, will have one of the following outcomes: (1) if the forces for change prevail, there will be initial turmoil, followed by gradual progress; or (2) if the resisting forces prevail, frustration will continue until ultimately change occurs.

Recommendations for Further Research

The theory of the effects of systematic assessment and planning in small academic libraries is proposed here as a potential basis for future research in this area. These propositions must be tested and developed further, their generalizability explored, initially through examining other library populations that have undertaken similar planning programs to determine whether the range of outcomes and relationships are similar and can be explained by the theory.

Ideally, this theory should be tested through a longitudinal study that assesses organizations prior to their undertaking a similar planning program in order to determine whether the theory is indeed useful in predicting outcomes.

A model must be developed for assessing both organizational readiness for change and the presence of key factors (described above) that facilitate positive change in libraries. The data described in this research offer one basis for such a model.

Finally, the range of applicability of these propositions should be explored with other types of innovative programs, both assisted and self-initiated, as well as with other information processing organizations, in order to assess whether they offer a basis for contributing to a larger theory of organizational change.

Endnotes

1. See for example: Stanton F. Biddle, "The Planning Function in the Management of University Libraries: Survey, Analysis, Conclusions, and Recommendations" (D.L.S. diss., Univ. of California, Berkeley, 1988); and Judith J. Senkevitch, "Consequences of Innovation: Perceptions and Correlates of Change After Systematic Assessment and Planning in Small Academic Libraries," (Ph.D. diss., Rutgers Univ., 1989).

2. Everett M. Rogers, *Diffusion of Innovation,* 3d ed (New York: Free Press, 1983).

3. Barney G. Glaser and Anselm L. Strauss, *The Discovery of Grounded Theory: Strategies for Qualitative Research* (New York: Aldine, 1967).

4. P. Grady Morein, Maxine K. Sitts, and Duane E. Webster, *Planning Program for Small Academic Libraries* (Washington, DC: Association of Research Libraries, Office of Managment Studies, 1980).

5. Kurt Lewin, "Frontiers in Group Dynamics: Concept Method and Reality in Social Sciences; Social Equilibria and Social Change," *Human Relations* 1 (June, 1947): 5-41.

6. Joanne R. Euster, The *Academic Library Director: Management Activities and Effectiveness* (NY: Greenwood Press, 1987).

7. See for example: James G. March, "Footnotes to Organizational Change," *Administrative Science Quarterly* 26 (December, 1981): 563-577; Mary F. Casserly, "Self-study and Planned Change in Academic Libraries: A Case Study Analysis of Regional Accreditation Self-Study Experiences" (Ph.D. diss., Rutgers Univ., 1984); Mary F. Casserly, "Accreditation-related Self-study as a Planned Change Process: Factors Relating to Its Success in Academic Libraries," *Journal of Library Administration* 8 (Spring, 1987): 85-105; and G. Travis White, "Factors Associated With Successful Adaptation to Environmental Change in College and University Libraries" (Ph.D. diss., Univ. of Denver, 1984).

8. Kurt Lewin, op. cit.

CONTRIBUTED PAPERS

VI.
READERS
SERVICES

Importance of Academic Library Services to Visiting Scholars[1]

Nancy D. Anderson
Lois M. Pausch
University of Illinois at Urbana-Champaign
Urbana, Illinois

Abstract

Scholars visiting libraries at other academic institutions often encounter collection access, services, and facilities quite different from those at their own institutions. A questionnaire was distributed to nearly 900 faculty members at eight large midwestern research universities on their return from sabbatical leave to determine which factors were considered most important to successful research. Results indicate that there are differences in response by field of study to various factors surveyed. The authors make recommendations for changes in library service to visiting scholars.

Academic Library Services to Visiting Scholars

Decreasing budgets and sharply increasing costs of materials over the past decade have forced librarians to face the reality that comprehensive collections can no longer be supported and to turn increasingly to resource sharing as a means of bringing the scholar in touch with the materials needed for research. Some librarians hold the view that scholars will widen use of the collections through better bibliographic access and efficient and affordable document delivery.[2] Alternatively, a few librarians have turned their attention to the needs of scholars, not of their own institutions, for onsite access to their collections. For example, Epp and Segal took issue with the ACLS Survey of Scholars[3] because, as they noted,

> . . . the survey questions scholars on the inadequacy of their institutional holdings and the ease of ILL access to materials not available. However, the survey fails to recognize that scholars must often travel to other institutions in order to gain access to materials in special collections. Whether scholars perceive themselves as impeded in accessing these materials—often located in other cities, states, and nations—is an important concern that the ACLS survey should have considered.[4]

Document delivery may not be the answer if entire issues of journals are needed or if plates and illustrations are important to the researcher. Loaning of some materials may be prohibited and faxing may be too expensive or too low in quality to be worthwhile. Another reason why a visiting scholar may wish to use the library of another institution is because s/he is working with a colleague at that institution, not for any special collection held by the library.

In 1988, the Association of Research Libraries published a list of research questions which they hoped would encourage research activity by librarians. Under the heading, "Impact of Library Procedures on Research", these questions were asked,

> How often and under what circumstances do visiting and independent scholars gain access to research library collections? Are there barriers or inhibitions for visiting scholars gaining full access to the material in the collections of research libraries? Are there additional protocols or procedures through which visiting or independent scholars and others might be given improved access to research library collections?[5]

In response to these questions, Anderson and Stenstrom surveyed the ARL membership on what their policies were with regard to onsite access to library collections by visiting scholars. The documentation in the resulting SPEC kit[6] showed that, in 1989, many research libraries in North America had reached creative solutions to providing this access. Eighty-eight of the more than 100 ARL libraries provided documents defining who is a visiting scholar as well as examples of services, reciprocal agreements, and fees. This offers some documentation of the policies for onsite access by visiting scholars at the largest North American research libraries. There was still very little published on what scholars wanted in access or related library services when they visited other academic institutions.

Over the years, however, the authors had gained some perspective on how library practices affect visiting scholars. Colleagues in teaching departments, upon their return from summer or sabbatical research leaves, reported to them the relative success or failure of research efforts with respect to libraries. It appeared that policies were often idiosyncratic of either the library director or the university's administration. These colleagues also noted that European and Asian libraries often restricted the use of materials while North American academic libraries were commended for their accessibility. The authors decided it might be useful to produce a directory of the kinds of library services a scholar might expect should s/he visit an academic library in western Europe.

What, then, are the services which visiting scholars consider most important? Krieger states that prearrangements or a letter of inquiry, determination if photocopying of specialized materials is permitted, arrangements for billing, hours of opening, collecting and gathering together of scattered holdings, and which, if any, restrictions might apply to materials are important to ascertain in advance.[7] For libraries in the U.S., some of this important information is available to the prospective visiting scholar in the Research Libraries Advisory Committee to OCLC pamphlet.[8] A faculty member who teaches at a participating institution can ask her/his "home" librarian to consult the OCLC Name-Address Directory for information on the library to be visited. This information is usually insufficient to inform the traveler of the facilities awaiting her/him without further inquiry to the institution to be visited.

The authors assumed that visiting scholars would expect and want the same kind of library services and facilities provided by their "home" libraries regardless of whatever institution was visited. However, because little was published about what visiting scholars wanted or expected, the authors decided to send a questionnaire to faculty members at eight large midwestern research universities[9] who had recently returned from sabbatical leave, asking them to answer specific questions on facilities and services which the authors believed could be important to the visitor. This group was

chosen, even though only a small part of a larger group who visits other libraries, because sabbatical leave scholars are more readily identifiable.

The questionnaire used in this study included demographic questions (academic rank, major field of study, length of time in current position) followed by questions which established whether or not the faculty member visited another institution. If so, the visitor was asked whether or not the institution's library was used while there. The information derived from the response was used to determine if there were any measurable differences in the importance of particular collections, services, and facilities for faculty in broad subject fields. Also included were questions on the value of prearrangements for library use.

The next section pertained to the qualities of a library's collection: a special collection (i.e., a specific person's papers, etc.), an outstanding collection in the respondent's field of study, and the overall size of the collection in the library visited. Participants were asked to rate each on a 5-point scale (1 = not important to 5 = very important) as to its importance to the respondent's research.

The bulk of the survey asked faculty to rank various means of access, services, and facilities the authors selected as having some importance to visiting scholars. A 5-point scale was also utilized here. Questions regarding access to materials asked for a rating of open stacks (for browsing purposes, etc.), materials available only by being paged, the ability to charge out materials and take them out of the room/building, availability of interlibrary loan service, cooperative arrangements with other libraries in the area, and computer access to the collection or holdings (i.e., an online catalog). The facilities which were rated included study areas (carrels, offices, or others), photocopying machines and price of photocopies, microform readers, availability of microcomputers for personal use, and handicapped accessibility. The list of services was made up of availability of online search services, reference assistance, library orientation programs, staff with multi-lingual capability, and whether or not a library guide/handbook was available. For each of these categories, respondents were given the opportunity to comment on or to augment the answer choices.

The survey was sent to 891 faculty members who had been granted sabbatical leaves in the 1988-89 academic year. A total of 356 responses (40%) was received. Of these, 242 (68%) had visited another academic institution. Of the 242, 206 or 95% had used the library of the institution visited, and form the basis for all succeeding results. In the 206, there were 59 in the social sciences, 36 in the life sciences (pure and applied), 47 in the physical sciences (pure and applied, including engineering), 61 in the humanities, and 3 in the 'other' category (law, library science, etc.). Because of the small number in the other category, these results were ignored for the rest of this paper.

One collection characteristic, an outstanding collection in the field of study, was rated as 4-5 (important to very important) by 165 of the 197 (83.8%) of those who responded to this question. Responses on the other two facets listed were as follows: of the 187 answers on a special collection, 74 (39.6%) ranked this characteristic as 4-5 while 100 (53.5%) gave rankings of 1-2. The overall size of the collection had 192 responses of which 87 (45.3%) were 4-5 while 53 (27.6%) ranked it as 1-2. Of the three qualities, overall size produced the largest response to the middle value (52 of 192 or 27.1%).

Cross tabulation of these results with field of study show that an outstanding collection in the field of study was considered very important by scholars in all fields (social sciences, life sciences, physical sciences, and humanities). Overall size of collection appears to be essentially neutral in that respondents scored it even across the scale except for the life scientists who found this characteristic to be very important. Table 1 displays the data on responses for these characteristics. It is interesting to note that humanists find a special collection to be much more important than do any of the other respondents.

The most important access characteristic was open stacks access with 78.8% (156 of 198) of the respondents ranking it 4-5 (important to very important) and noting it was available in 82% of the institutions visited. Whether or not materials were allowed out of the room/building was considered important-very important, 4-5, by 72.2% (140 of 194). As shown in Table 2, open stacks was important to scholars in all fields of study. The ability to take materials out of the room/building was important to social scientists, life scientists, and physical scientists while humanists

Importance of Collection Characteristics
Table 1

		Social Sciences 1-2	Social Sciences 4-5	Life Sciences 1-2	Life Sciences 4-5	Physical Sciences 1-2	Physical Sciences 4-5	Humanities 1-2	Humanities 4-5	All Fields 1-2	All Fields 4-5
Outstanding Collection in Field of Study	No.	6/54	41/54	3/34	27/34	1/46	39/46	3/60	55/60	13/199	165/199
	%	11.0	75.9	8.8	79.4	2.2	84.7	5.0	91.6	6.6	83.8
Special Collection	No.	30/52	18/52	23/32	7/32	31/40	6/40	14/60	42/60	100/187	74/189
	%	57.7	34.6	71.9	21.9	77.5	15.0	23.3	70.0	53.5	39.6
Overall Size of Library's Collection	No.	12/51	22/51	8/35	23/35	14/43	16/43	18/60	24/60	53/192	87/192
	%	23.5	43.1	22.9	65.7	32.6	37.2	30.0	40.0	27.6	45.3

were almost equally divided. This may reflect the types of materials with which humanists often work (i.e. rare books, manuscripts) that are seldom, if ever, allowed out of the library. The other aspects of access show various results with scientists finding online catalogs and the use of other libraries more important than humanists and social scientists.

In their comments, many respondents noted that a major source of frustration was that materials could not be checked out and used outside the building and that the most important aspect for users is accessibility. A few commented that, if materials cannot be checked out, then copying services, with overnight delivery, need to be in place. Respondents also commented that cooperative arrangements between nearby libraries made possible the use of more than one library where complementary collections helped to complete their research. Access to home libraries would have been helpful. One repeated comment from a large number

Importance of Access Characteristics
Table 2

		Social Sciences 1-2	Social Sciences 4-5	Life Sciences 1-2	Life Sciences 4-5	Physical Sciences 1-2	Physical Sciences 4-5	Humanities 1-2	Humanities 4-5	All Fields 1-2	All Fields 4-5
Open stacks	No.	7/54	41/54	2/35	30/35	1/47	42/47	7/59	42/59	19/198	156/198
	%	13.0	75.9	5.7	85.7	2.1	89.4	11.9	71.2	9.6	78.8
Materials paged	No.	18/43	9/43	10/25	8/25	10/28	12/28	10/48	31/48	48/146	61/146
	%	41.9	20.9	40.0	32.0	35.7	42.9	20.8	62.5	32.9	41.8
Materials used elsewhere	No.	5/53	46/53	1/34	28/34	2/46	41/46	23/58	24/59	33/194	140/194
	%	9.4	86.8	2.9	82.4	4.3	89.1	39.6	41.4	17.0	72.2
Availibility of interlibrary loan	No.	11/48	24/48	5/31	18/31	11/43	24/43	20/57	26/57	49/182	93/182
	%	22.9	50.0	16.1	58.1	25.6	55.8	35.1	45.6	26.9	51.1
Access to other libraries in the area	No.	17/49	19/49	9/29	14/29	12/41	24/41	23/52	22/52	63/174	80/174
	%	34.7	38.8	31.0	48.3	29.3	58.5	44.2	42.3	36.2	46.0
Computer access to the collection	No.	16/50	24/50	10/33	23/33	11/42	21/42	24/54	20/54	62/182	89/182
	%	32.0	48.0	30.3	69.7	26.2	50.0	44.4	37.0	34.1	48.9

303

of respondents was the need to know about hours/days the library was open, especially during the summer and intersessions. Another concern was for more concrete information about the collection such as where materials are to be found and how to access uncataloged materials.

As shown in Table 3, photocopying is important to all users with 86.9% (173 of 199). Availability of study areas with 55.7% (108 of 194) also ranked highly.

Humanists showed the highest percentages for importance of photo-copiers, price of photocopies, and availability of microform readers.

Reference assistance, from among the services surveyed, received the highest percentage of 4-5 (important to very important) rating, 76.8% (149 of 194) with availability of online search services, 44.6% (79 of 177) and orientation in using the library, 44.5% (85 of 191) nearly matching it. The very lowest rank was

Important Services
Table 4

		Social Sciences 1-2	Social Sciences 4-5	Life Sciences 1-2	Life Sciences 4-5	Physical Sciences 1-2	Physical Sciences 4-5	Humanities 1-2	Humanities 4-5	All Fields 1-2	All Fields 4-5
Multi-lingual staff	No.	33/53	13/53	23/33	6/33	23/44	10/44	32/53	14/53	113/186	47/186
	%	62.3	24.5	69.7	18.2	52.3	29.5	60.4	26.4	60.7	25.3
Online search services	No.	11/49	24/49	10/32	17/32	9/41	18/41	20/52	19/52	52/177	79/177
	%	22.4	49.0	31.3	53.1	22.0	43.9	38.5	36.5	29.4	44.6
Reference assistance	No.	4/54	47/54	3/33	26/33	5/45	28/45	5/59	46/59	18/194	149/194
	%	7.4	87.0	9.1	78.8	11.1	62.2	8.5	78.0	9.3	76.8
Library orientation	No.	13/54	30/54	10/33	15/33	18/44	14/44	18/57	23/57	59/191	85/191
	%	24.1	55.6	30.3	45.5	40.9	31.8	31.6	40.4	30.9	44.5
Library guide or handbook	No.	16/51	22/51	13/31	7/31	20/41	5/41	17/55	19/55	66/181	55/181
	%	31.4	43.1	41.9	22.6	48.8	12.2	30.9	34.5	36.4	30.4
Materials gathered for personal use	No.	27/50	17/50	17/29	9/29	25/38	5/38	15/51	21/51	84/171	54/171
	%	54.0	34.0	58.6	31.0	65.8	13.2	29.4	41.2	49.1	31.6
Help in finding accommodations	No.	35/46	7/46	22/28	5/28	26/33	4/33	38/52	8/52	123/162	25/162
	%	76.1	15.2	78.6	17.9	78.8	12.1	73.1	15.4	75.9	15.5

given to help in finding accommodations with only 15.5% (25 of 162) rating this as 4-5. The full range of responses is shown in Table 4.

Although the question on prior arrangements showed that only 82 of the 197 (41.6%) who responded would have wanted information on what was needed to access collections onsite, this part of the questionnaire provoked a large number of "other" comments. Among the listed prearrangements, the name or position of the person to contact was ranked the highest with 66 respondents checking it. Other arrangements that solicited some response were the need for a letter of introduction (44), the need for sponsorship (36), and the need for prior application (36). Respondents showed least interest in knowing user fees (27). Many comments indicated that prearrangement was essential and helped to expedite short stays. The name of a resource

Importance of Facilities
Table 3

		Social Sciences 1-2	Social Sciences 4-5	Life Sciences 1-2	Life Sciences 4-5	Physical Sciences 1-2	Physical Sciences 4-5	Humanities 1-2	Humanities 4-5	All Fields 1-2	All Fields 4-5
Availibility of study areas	No.	15/52	32/52	8/34	20/34	16/46	20/46	14/59	35/59	55/194	108/194
	%	28.8	61.5	23.5	58.8	34.8	43.5	23.7	59.3	28.4	55.7
Photocopying machines	No.	3/55	46/55	1/35	31/35	4/46	38/46	0/60	56/60	9/199	173/199
	%	5.4	83.6	2.9	88.5	8.7	82.6	0.0	93.3	4.5	86.9
Price of photocopies	No.	11/52	26/52	9/34	10/34	12/40	11/40	6/59	39/59	39/188	88/188
	%	21.2	50.0	26.5	29.4	30.0	28.0	10.2	66.0	20.7	46.8
Billing for photocopies	No.	19/47	20/47	10/33	14/33	17/38	16/38	17/51	21/51	64/172	75/172
	%	40.4	42.6	30.3	42.4	44.7	42.1	33.3	41.2	37.2	43.6
Availibility of microform readers	No.	22/47	12/47	19/30	3/30	25/42	8/42	17/57	26/57	84/179	50/179
	%	46.8	25.5	63.3	10.0	59.5	19.0	29.8	45.6	47.0	28.0
Access to microcomputers	No.	28/50	19/50	12/32	12/32	22/40	15/40	32/53	13/53	96/178	60/178
	%	56.0	38.0	37.5	37.5	55.0	37.5	60.4	26.4	53.9	33.7
Handicapped accessibility	No.	35/44	4/44	20/29	6/29	30/37	2/37	38/46	6/46	126/159	18/159
	%	79.5	9.0	69.0	20.7	81.1	5.4	82.6	13.0	79.2	11.3

person in the subject field was mentioned by several respondents.

The results of this survey indicate that there are measurable differences between scholars in different fields and that there is a real need for additional assistance to be made available to faculty members before they leave to use another institution's library. Librarians at both the home library and the visited library need to be more aware that visiting scholars do not all need the same access, services, and facilities. Those coming to the institution to access a special collection have different expectations than do those who use the library as but one part of their collaborative research with a colleague.

The home library needs to publicize how to obtain information about libraries of the institution(s) to be visited and if prearrangements are necessary. Racine and Harris note that, while reciprocal borrowing programs were excellent public relations tools for libraries, they were not often used.[10, 11] However, while faculty members who do know about them are very pleased, all too often, we noted the following comments: "Some sort of reciprocity arrangement between major universities for faculty use/borrowing while on sabbatical leave (and not necessarily associated with the local university) would be extremely helpful and welcome" and "If a system was in place where I could have easy access to libraries in other cities . . . I would support such a system." One way to alert the faculty to library services to visiting faculty is to supply information to the university unit that processes sabbatical applications so that faculty, before leaving campus, will be steered to their home library for help.

Another area in which libraries can improve services to visiting scholars arises when those libraries are visited. Although both Harris and Racine note that, while onsite access by visiting scholars is not a heavily used service, there is still some workload attached to satisfying the demands of outside users. Much of this load could be met with the designation of a visiting scholar access librarian. As part of this librarian's duties, s/he would be in charge of coordinating arrangements for the use of the collection and would serve as the contact person for those who wish to use it. Several respondents commented on the need for such a person: "Each library should name one staff person who is the contact person before and during the visits, whose job is to assist visiting scholars" and " All that matters is good will. A visiting scholar is disoriented,

tired from travel, uncertain about her/his status. Assign someone with good people skills to handling them and all the other prearrangements is irrelevent."

Both of these programs to the faculty would generate good will, publicity, and support for the library. Neither would need big investments in time or staffing. They would allow research libraries time to develop the reciprocal agreements which offer the best hope for more uniformity of service and greater access to collections by visiting scholars.

Endnotes

1. The authors wish to acknowlege the Research and Publication Committee of the University of Illinois at Urbana-Champaign Library which provided support for the completion of the research reported in this paper.
2. Richard M. Dougherty, "Research Libraries in an International Setting: Requirements for Expanded Resource Sharing." *College and Research Libraries* 46 (September, 1985): 383-389.
3. Herbert C. Morton and Anne Jamieson Price, "The ACLS Survey of Scholars: Views on Publications, Computers, Libraries." *Scholarly Communication* no. 5 (1986): 1-16.
4. Ronald H. Epp and Jo Ann S. Segal, "The American Council of Learned Societies Survey and Academic Library Services." *C&RL News* 48 (February, 1987): 63-69.
5. "Research Questions of Interest to ARL." *College & Research Libraries* 49 (September, 1988): 467-470.
6. Nancy D. Anderson and Patricia F. Stenstrom, *Onsite Access to Library Collections by Visiting Scholars.* SPEC Kit 155. (Washington, D.C.: Association of Research Libraries, Office of Management Services, 1989).
7. Tillie Krieger, "What the Traveling Scholar Needs to Know: an Opinion Piece." *Research Strategies* 3 (Summer,1985): 131-134.
8. Research Libraries Advisory Committee to OCLC. *Reciprocal Faculty Borrowing Program.* Pub. no. 46a. (Dublin, Ohio:OCLC Online Library Computer Center, 1989).
9. Illinois Indiana, Iowa, Michigan, Michigan State, Minnesota, Purdue, Wisconsin.
10. J. Drew Racine, "Survey Provides an Update on the Reciprocal Library Borrowing Program." *Research Libraries in OCLC: A Quarterly* 29

(Winter, 1989): 1-2.

11. Melanie Harris, "External Users of a University Library." *Australian Academic and Research Libraries* 20 (December, 1989): 219-227.

The Campus Health Center as a Model for Reference Service

M. Clare Beck
Eastern Michigan University
Ypsilanti, MI

Abstract

Dissatisfaction with the structure of reference services, particularly the on-demand public reference desk, is widely expressed in the professional literature. This paper offers the campus health service as an example of the alternative models available in business and the nonprofit sector. The health center's delivery of services is described and compared with the library, and its possible advantages as a service mode are discussed.

At ACRL's Fourth National Conference six years ago, Barbara Ford lucidly summarized the considerable literature expressing dissatisfaction with the traditional reference desk service mode in which a librarian at a public desk responds on-demand to inquiries. Ford concluded that "Academic librarians must ask whether their clientele really need a reference desk or whether other services would meet their needs in a more effective manner."[1] Her theoretical model for future service "beyond (and without) the reference desk" relied partly on a computer terminal apparently using an expert system to respond to patron questions, an example of the technological fix that is often proposed but tends to seem grandiose and unrealistic to practicing reference librarians as they deal with the extreme diversity of inquiries from a clientele that may be unskilled and uninformed. The "future of reference" symposia reported in *C&RL News* have provided examples of this conflict between the practical and the visionary.

Meanwhile, still more research, such as that of Joan Durrance,[2] has questioned the effectiveness of the reference desk. Durrance' study of reference interviews in 142 libraries supports the earlier critics of the reference environment "which seems as much to interfere with as to facilitate an effective reference interview."[3] Despite many years of such critical analysis of the reference desk, the understandably conservative response from libraries tends to tinkering at the margins, trying new refinements of past inadequacies, such as tiered information/reference desks or the ever popular and usually unsatisfactory use of student assistants, clerks, or paraprofessionals at the desk. Between the two poles of technological salvation or modest change,

there is a third way, and that is to look at how other organizations in business and the nonprofit sector provide services to see what real-world models might be adaptable to libraries. For example, we have a model available on our campuses in the form of the health center, where professional services are provided one-to-one, partially on-demand, and with greater efficiency, accountability, and clarity than in the library. These services are similar to those of many clinics and HMOs, but with a special orientation to the needs of college students.[4]

The experience of using the health center and comparing it to the library offers a test case of the alternative model. In the hypothetical case a librarian, Mr. X, notices a small growth on his skin and wishes to have it checked by a doctor. The campus health center is conveniently located, and, from the handbook on its services that Mr. X keeps in his office, he knows that a dermatologist is available once a week.[5] Mr. X calls the health center and explains what he wants. He is advised first to see a nurse practitioner who is available every day. Since it it not a busy time for the health center, he is told to stop by anytime. That afternoon, he goes to the reception desk in the health center, explains what he wants, fills out forms identifying himself and his health insurance, and is directed to a comfortable waiting area. After a ten minute wait, during which he reads some of the center's handouts on health matters, its statement of patient rights and reponsibilities, and its patient comment form, he is called into a room by a nurse, who agrees that he should be checked by a dermatologist, and sends him back to the reception desk to make an appointment. A week later, he returns to the the health center and is directed to the dermatology waiting area. After a twenty minute wait, he is called into a room by the doctor, who examines the skin growth, explains what it is and that it can be removed immediately. Mr. X soon goes on his way, satisfied with the service received and pleased that it cost him less time and money than a visit to a private physician.

Now let us look at some of the characteristics of Mr. X's experience, asking ourselves how libraries compare.

1) Mr. X dealt with a receptionist, a position familiar to most Americans but seemingly foreign to libraries. Indeed, in many years of using many libraries, I have only encountered one with a clearly labeled receptionist near the entrance. Since Mr. X understands the duties of the receptionist, he certainly doesn't expect her to provide a diagnosis, nor is he upset at having to deal with her before seeing a doctor or nurse.

2) The health center provides a combination of by-appointment and on-demand service, but the on-demand service is organized to minimize confusion and wasted time. Mr. X understands that he must check-in with the receptionist and wait for the practitioner to be available. He would be shocked if the health center had no receptionist and expected him to mill around with other patients to catch the attention of an unknown person at a desk labelled "health information." It seems reasonable to him that the on-demand service is provided partly by nurse practitioners, while more costly specialists are seen by appointment. The health center's guidebook advises him, "Call for an appointment for greatest convenience or walk over and ask to be seen at the first opening" and assures him that appointments are "generally given the same day you call or the next day."

Mr. X spent more time in the waiting areas than with with either health care professional, but he has had a lifetime of conditioning to expect some waiting period for health services. A Federal Government study showed that the average wait for an ambulatory health care appointment is seven days, longer for various preventive services, and then an average of 31 minutes waiting to see a physician at the health care facility. The public showed little dissatisfaction with waiting times, except when the office wait exceeded one hour.[6]

3) The guidebook lists the types of health professionals on its "team", including physicians, nurse practitioners, registered nurses, nurse educators, counsel-

ors, pharmacists, and technicians. Mr. X understands that they have different roles and different credentials; he would not expect the pharmacist to remove the growth on his skin, nor is he disturbed at having to make two visits, being familiar with the concept of specialization and referral in health care.

4) Mr. X meets with the health professionals in a private room. Though his question does not involve a particularly intimate matter, he would be uncomfortable if he were expected to discuss it in a public area. He prefers to discuss any personal business in the quiet and privacy of an office where he will have the concentrated attention of the professional person he is consulting.

5) The center emphasizes education and the concept of "wellness" rather than just treating illness. Its guidebook states a philosophy that the patient is part of the center's "health care team" and can obtain a statement of rights and responsibilities "to help understand . . . how we can best work together." This statement covers the patient's right to confidentiality, to know the names and titles of staff, and to select a clinician for appointments (but not for walk-in care), and the responsibility to communicate fully, to understand treatments, and to keep and arrive on time for appointments.

A detailed comparison with a hypothetical case involving Dr. Y of the health center attempting to obtain information from the university library is not possible here. It can be suggested that Dr. Y might get superb service but probably would find herself in a more confusing, inefficient, and chancey situation than what Mr. X experienced in the health center.

Of course the library is different from the health center in many respects, but is it really so difficult to envision a library's reference services operating similarly to the health center, with appointments encouraged and on-demand service arranged through the gateway of a receptionist? I cannot imagine doing away with on-demand service for people whose questions develop while using the library or who really do have "just a quick question", but where is it written that on-demand service in libraries cannot have the basic structure of a receptionist, a waiting area, and a private meeting room for the client and professional, as do the medical clinics, storefront law offices, and even hair salons that offer "walk in" service. This is not to suggest that all reference work could be done in the

consultation room; there would be many situations in which, after the intial interview, the librarian and client would go out into the reference room or other areas of the library. As libraries become increasingly electronic, much more can be done in an office, but when it is necessary to leave the office, with a receptionist on duty, the librarians would be freer to move around according to client needs, since they would no longer be leaving an untended reference desk, and they would not themselves be under pressure to watch whether a queue was developing, since monitoring the queue and taking appropriate action would done by the receptionist. Nor does it seem unreasonable to ask users to identify themselves and provide some information, such as the subject of the inquiry, course identification, and class level, but this model does not absolutely require it. Having a form with such information at the beginning of the reference interview would save the librarian time, as well as providing for improved monitoring of
service use.

Adopting this or any new model would require careful analysis and planning, and the details would vary from library to library. Even more than the conventional reference desk, it would require high quality, coordinated bibliographic instruction and public communications, including signs, library guides, and librarian meetings with classes and faculty. In any situation, there would be a number of advantages—and some possible problems to be anticipated.

What are some of the advantages?

1) Librarians would show respect and concern for both clients and the educational goals of the parent institutions. Meeting initially in a private consultation room for uninterrupted (but certainly not unlimited) time, many clients would feel less anxious about asking for help with what they fear is a "dumb" question. In the calm, private atmosphere, it would be easier for the librarian to ask questions and the patron to explain her/his information needs. If there were uncertainty about a class assignment, it would be easier for the librarian to consult the information at hand about the assignment or call the instructor. It also would be easier to consult another librarian or give the student a clear referral to a specialist librarian with whom she/he could schedule an appointment through the receptionist. The client would know whom she/he had met and could arrange follow-up consultations; students might even develop relationships with librarians whom they would consult throughout their college careers. The

librarian could have a record of the client's identity to make follow-up contact if, as often happens, later useful material is discovered. The early birds who start promptly on library work, the conscientious students who want to acquire research skills, and the real learners who want to delve into their subjects would no longer be penalized by a system that is biased towards the quick question, the routine explanation, and the impersonal encounter.

2) Librarian productivity and client use of services could be monitored and analyzed more effectively. The receptionist could be maintaining computerized records of how much time librarians spend with clients, how many clients per librarian, categories of users, course and departmental connections, etc. Providing personal service is costly, even when subsidized by librarians' low salaries, and service use should be monitored as carefully as materials expenditures. At a time when many professionals, including the teaching faculty, and business employees are being rigorously monitored for productivity, our lack of hard information about what reference librarians do is particularly questionable.

3) Accountability for performance could be improved. At the end of each consultation, the librarian would have time to make notes on what was sought and how the inquiry was handled. These records could be reviewed for evaluation of either individual or departmental performance and could be used in training. Surveys of client satisfaction could be done, if those who actually used the service were known.

4) Policies and standards could be clarified. The library might actually decide and articulate what reference services it is able and willing to provide. The library could better cooperate with the wishes of instructors as to what kind of help their students should get and enforce reasonable standards of student responsibilities. This would require assertiveness, but in an environment in which librarians are less likely to expect librarians to support such undesirable behaviors as starting term papers the day before they are due.

This is not a matter of failing to be helpful. All reference librarians aim to be helpful, but real help, especially in education, sometimes requires firmness in upholding standards and discouraging dependency. Nor does it mean a more rigidly bureaucratic system; if no longer obsessed with providing a body at a reference desk, librarians might well become more flexible and creative in providing information services by telephone, e-mail, or other means.

5) Approachability might be improved. A receptionist is by definition approachable, something the public doesn't understand about our current reference desks. Receptionists may appropriately be hired for approachable personal qualities without requiring as many other qualifications as do librarians. The literature of reference service indicates a high level of concern about whether librarians are approachable, often without apparent awareness that the stresses of the reference environment may contribute to approachability problems.

6) Professionalism would be encouraged. Librarians would be operating the way other professionals do and finally would be distinguished from the staff at the circulation desk. This is not just a matter of seeking prestige by aping the style of others, as some have suggested, but a positive assertion of authority over how services are delivered, the quality of those services, and the most effective use of professional and client time.

The intention of this paper is to suggest that there are alternatives in the service economy and this age of information that might be adapted to the reference function. The real issue was posed by Joan Durrance: "Must we assume that the present reference environment, a vestige of the late 19th century, will continue? . . . Are librarians willing to consider altering the environment with the aim of success and creating an environment that better serves the public?"[7]

Endnotes

1. Barbara J. Ford, "Reference Beyond (and Without) the Reference Desk," *"College Research Libraries* 47 (September, 1986): 492 .
2. Joan C. Durrance, "Reference Success: Does the 55 Percent Rule Tell the Whole Story?" *Library Journal* 114 (April 15, 1989): 31-36 .
3. Ibid., p.36
4. I am not suggesting the medical profession or the health care industry in general as a model, since I generally agree with the many critics of their unequal access, high costs, and overemphasis on high-tech hospital treatment.
5. References to health center materials are based primarily on those of Snow Health Center, Eastern Michigan University, Ypsilanti, Michigan.
6. U.S. National Center for Health Services Research. *NCHSR National Health Care Expenditures Study. Waiting Times In Different Medical Settings: Appointment Waits and Office Waits* by Judith A. Kasper and Marc L. Berc. (Washington, U.S. Government Printing Office, 1981) (DHHS Publication No. PHS 81-3296).
7. John C. Durrance, op. cit., p. 36.

Interdependence of Electronic and Printed Bibliographic Information in English Studies

William S. Brockman
University of Illinois
Urbana, Illinois

Abstract

Examines the coexistence of two different means of gathering and providing bibliographic information.

It is all too easy to relegate the bibliographer to the same back room that was inhabited by Samuel Johnson's lexicographer, whom he identified with tongue in cheek as a "harmless drudge."[1] The compiling of enumerative bibliographies can be creative and intellectually rigorous work. This paper will not advocate one form of bibliography over another, but rather will offer a means of analysis—a perspective—that will point the way to more creative and rigorous thinking about bibliographies, whatever their form.

During the 1970s and 1980s, electronic bibliographic databases designed for a scholarly audience became widely available and increasingly sophisticated. At the same time, reference book publishers such as Scarecrow, G.K. Hall, Greenwood, and Garland began publishing an unparalleled number of monographic subject bibliographies. One would have expected online databases and their offspring, CD-ROM products, to eclipse printed bibliographies. But this has not been the case. As databases have become ubiquitous throughout libraries, the publishing of bibliographies on paper in book form continues to thrive.

Inspired by Fredson Bowers' pronouncement that bibliographies are intended to be read as well as consulted, D.W. Krummel has proposed that we distinguish printed bibliographies from online services by identifying these as canonic versus dynamic.[2] Canonic printed bibliographies, fixed on their pages, establish a unity of conception that, influential as it may be, looks backward in time. Dynamic online services, routinely updated and regularly changing, are fluid reflectors of their literature, the qualities of which the researcher determines through use.

A vital coexistence between dynamic and canonic bibliographic forms is particularly evident in the field of English Studies. Both forms have value to the researcher, and consequently, academic and research libraries in the 1990s will have to continue to provide both. Examining specific examples of canonic and dynamic forms can help to focus a comparison. In the field of English Studies, the *MLA International Bibliography*, whether on CD-ROM or through an online vendor, is the principal electronic bibliographic service.[3] For the purposes of the present paper, we shall compare its applicability to research on William Butler Yeats with that of K.P.S. Jochum's well-received *W.B. Yeats: A Classified Bibliography of Criticism*, whose second edition was published in 1990.[4] While my comments regarding the MLA Bibliography apply equally to the online and to the CD-ROM versions, my information regarding the editorial practices of the MLA Bibliography derives from the introductory matter in the latest annual printed edition, since it offers the fullest details regarding compilation of the Bibliography's database.[5]

A useful mechanism for comparing these two forms are the specifications outlined by Patrick Wilson in 1968 for what he calls "bibliographical instruments."[6] Five elements comprise the specifications. First is the domain—in Wilson's terms, "the set of items from which the contents of the work, the items actually listed, are drawn."[7] Second are the principles of selection by which they are drawn. Third is the bibliographical unit to which the instrument descends—does it, for instance, list only monographic titles, or does it detail individual essays within a collective volume? Fourth is the form and content of citation. Fifth is the organization of citations or records within the bibliographical instrument. This paper will examine, in terms of each of the five elements, these two examples of canonic and dynamic forms, the MLA Bibliography in its electronic version and Jochum's Yeats bibliography.

The MLA Bibliography indexes articles from a domain of some three thousand journals in its "Master List of Periodicals."[8] The list is large, but essentially finite: the MLA Bibliography lists few articles in journals not included in the list. The MLA Bibliography's domain is less explicit regarding monographs, separately-authored essays from collected volumes, and items in nonprint media. We can say that it is broad, as the compilation of the MLA Bibliography depends upon a worldwide network of contributors. We cannot know for certain what is not listed, and we cannot easily assess the tool's completeness. We do know that the MLA Bibliography's retrospective domain is limited, at present extending no further back than 1963 online and 1981 on CD-ROM.

Jochum's confident statement in his Preface that "my bibliography aims at completeness, not at critical selection" indicates, referring to Wilson's first principle, that his domain approaches the entire bibliographical universe.[9] Jochum circumscribes slightly his domain by noting areas that he feels he covers insufficiently, such as articles in periodicals from Eastern European countries before 1945, and areas that he does not cover at all, such as items in non-European languages.[10]

The MLA Bibliography is helpfully detailed concerning its scope—in Wilson's terms, its principles of selection, the second element of the specifications. It includes critical works on literature, language, or folklore, and excludes book reviews, literary works, and translations. In terms of level, it includes "works of interest to scholars."[11] It is important to keep in mind that the principles of selection are uniform throughout the MLA Bibliography's domain.

We know from the title of Jochum's bibliography that it lists works of criticism dealing with Yeats. Jochum refines his principles of selection and narrows his broad domain by being, for example, more highly discriminating in his choice of newspaper reviews of books by and about Yeats, of routine articles in encyclopedias, of perfunctory treatments in histories of literature, and of short reviews.[12] It is in areas such as these that a compiler can be indulgently evaluative: which are the most influential newspaper reviews, the most cogent treatments in histories? There is greater opportunity to adapt principles of selection than with the MLA Bibliography's rigid standards.

A necessity for uniformity throughout the hundreds of thousands of records in its database determines the MLA Bibliography's treatment of Wilson's third element, the level of bibliographic unit. It includes "books, book articles, and articles from periodicals."[13] Jochum, on the other hand, in his striving for completeness, can and does vary the level of bibliographic unit, when appropriate, citing single pages within books if they provide significant information or perspective. Wilson recognizes the importance of such flexibility by noting that the bibliographic instrument "with the smaller unit is almost certain to be the more valuable instrument."[14]

The form of citation is Wilson's fourth element. The MLA Bibliography employs a citation format based upon specifications of ANSI, the American National Standards Institute.[15] Individual records note the descriptors through which they can be located, and occasionally note other significant information, such as the availability in a foreign-language work of an abstract in English. The format is clear, except for the occasionally baffling acronyms of periodical titles which drive users to the list of abbreviations.

Jochum uses a hybrid citation format based loosely upon the Chicago and MLA styles. It too is clear, and it too employs MLA periodical abbreviations which similarly drive users to Jochum's index of periodicals. It is the annotations that make a bibliography such as Jochum's such a uniquely incisive tool. Well-informed descriptive and evaluative comments such as Jochum's can extract the essence of an item and set it in context with other Yeats criticism in a way that the MLA Bibliography's standardized descriptors cannot. The reviews cited within Jochum's annotations—up to several dozen, for important books— along with references to first publication of revised works tie together the citations into a critical, canonic web that sharply distinguishes itself from the MLA Bibliography's independent records.

It is in the area of organization, the fifth element of Wilson's specifications, that the two bibliographical instruments differ most significantly. Organization, in the sense of sequence, means little to a user of the electronic versions of the MLA Bibliography, although the accession number corresponding to the sequence could be of limited use in narrowing a search. But in its ability to perform free-text searches and in its opportunities for Boolean combinations, the electronic MLA Bibliography reveals the power of its dynamic nature. A researcher can identify key words in records that might not otherwise appear in more structured indexing and classification schemes and can invent with Boolean combinations his or her own intellectual categories. Within the bounds of domain and principles of selection that have determined the items the MLA Bibliography lists, the researcher can examine overall critical trends or the proportion of the literature devoted to one subject versus another.

A printed bibliography's point of strength is its ability to display through a refined organizational structure the vagaries of a subject. Jochum establishes several broad categories of material, then provides subsections that gather particular approaches. Within major sections devoted to poetry or plays, for instance, Jochum distinguishes between "substantial articles and parts of books" and "less substantial material." A chronological arrangement within the subsection devoted to "Interviews with Yeats" allows a user a purview of the author's intellectual development. Organization by the names of other writers within the subsection entitled "Influences, Parallels, and Contrast Studies" allows instant comparison of the influence of Yeats on Sean O'Casey with his influence on Flann O'Brien. The Yeats bibliography allows one the ineffable experience of holding in one's hand a canonic representation of a hundred years' critical work on the poet.

Citation studies in English and American literature demonstrate that literary scholars cite books more heavily than articles, frequently consult materials published many years previously, and employ a variety of primary sources such as manuscripts.[16] The restrictions of the domain and of the chronological scope, and the rigidity of citation format and of bibliographic level of dynamic sources such as the MLA Bibliography limit research that demands such a diversity of materials. Well-conceived subject bibliographies can address these needs by drawing together in individually adapted formats unusual or tertiary items such as reviews of the books listed, theatrical productions, parodies, or library holdings of manuscripts. Yet dynamic online sources can continually absorb and bibliographically channel a daunting flood of contemporary critical writing, and can provide new opportunities for quantitative research.

It is in the combination of dynamic and canonic forms by electronic means that we can hope to make the best of both. The Modern Language Association is exploring the possibility of producing printed subsets of entries from the MLA Bibliography which would be focussed on interdisciplinary topics such as women's studies.[17] Creative editing of the MLA Bibliography could offer more finely-tuned distinctions in subject than the present descriptors allow. On the other hand, readily-available software such as Pro-Cite could be used to produce microcomputer- oriented subject bibliographies that could be distributed as monographs but easily updated, downloaded, combined with other electronic bibliographies, or further subdivided.[18] In any case, literary researchers in the 1990s will find increased options for their research through a vigorous diversity of bibliographic tools.

Endnotes

1. Samuel Johnson, A Dictionary of the English Language . . . (London: W. Strahan, 1755; reprint: New York: AMS, 1967).
2. D. W. Krummel, "The Dialectics of Enumerative Bibliography: Observations on the Historical Study of the Practices of Citation and Compilation," Library Quarterly 58 (July, 1988): 242-44.
3. MLA International Bibliography, Online. OCLC First Search, Dublin, Ohio and Wilsonline, H.W. Wilson, New York; CD-ROM Wilsondisc, H.W. Wilson, New York.
4. K.P.S. Jochum, W.B. Yeats: A Classified Bibliography of Criticism, 2d ed., rev. and enl. (Urbana: University of Illinois Press, 1990).
5. 1990 MLA International Bibliography of Books and Articles on the Modern Languages and Literatures. (New York: Modern Language Association of America, 1991).
6. Patrick Wilson, Two Kinds of Power: An Essay on Bibliographical Control (Berkeley and Los Angeles: University of California Press, 1968), p. 59-68.
7. Ibid, p. 59.
8. 1990 MLA International Bibliography, op. cit., p. [iv], xi-xxxix.
9. K. P. S. Jochum, op. cit., p. xi.
10. Ibid, p. xii-xiii.
11. 1990 MLA International Bibliography, op. cit., p. [iii].
12. K. P. S. Jochum, op. cit., p. xii.
13. 1990 MLA International Bibliography, op. cit., p. [iii].
14. Patrick Wilson, op. cit., p. 61.
15. 1990 MLA International Bibliography, op. cit., p. [v].
16. Richard Heinzkill, "Characteristics of References

in Selected Scholarly English Literary Journals," *Library Quarterly* 50 (July, 1980): 352-365; Madeline Stern, "Characteristics of the Literature of Literary Scholarship," *College and Research Libraries* 44 (July, 1983): 199-209; John Cullars, "Characteristics of the Monographic Literature of British and American Literary Studies,"*College and Research Libraries* 46 (November, 1985): 511-522 ; John Budd, "Characteristics of Written Scholarship in American Literature: A Citation Study," *Library and Information Science Research* 8 (April, 1986): 189-211.

17. Letter to the author dated 27 March 1991 from Daniel Uchitelle, MLA Director of the Center for Information Services.

18. Pro-Cite, (Ann Arbor, MI: Personal Bibliographic Software).

Using Research Questions in Unobtrusive Evaluation of Reference Service
in a Large Academic Library

Cheryl Asper Elzy
Alan R. Nourie
Illionois State University
Normal, Illinois

and

F. W. Lancaster
University of Illinois
Urbana-Champaign, Illinois

Abstract

Tratitionally unobtrusive evaluations of reference service have employed proxies asking short, factual, ready-reference questions either by phone or in person. In an academic setting, however, this leaves a significant area untested: the research question and the reference question of moderate difficulty which require two or more sources to answer completely and correctly. A large study done recently at Illinois State University used a mix of ready-reference and research questions to examine both accuracy and attitude on nineteen individual and four division levels. Devising and scoring these two types of questions are discussed, as well as advantages of using such questions along with a comparison of study results.

Most reference librarians have heard about or read about half-right reference studies or the 55 percent rule—meaning that most studies of reference quality in libraries have demonstrated that patrons have about a 55 percent chance of getting complete and correct answers to their questions. Many reference librarians are concerned to some degree about those findings and worry even more that the same may be true in their own libraries. Questions about the quality of service at Illinois State University's Milner Library prompted this study.

Milner Library is the central library facility serving Illinois State University's community of over 22,000 students and 1,000 faculty members. Milner Library contains 1.3 million bound volumes, 1.4 million items in microformat, 350,000 U. S. Government Publications, 420,000 cartographic items, 25,000 sound and video recordings, and 10,000 serial subscriptions. The Library is organized into five subject divisions on six floors: Education/Psychology, General Reference and Information, Social Sciences/Business, Science/Government Publications, and Humanities/Special Collections. The five divisions are staffed by twenty library faculty and nineteen classified personnel, plus student assistants.

The study of reference quality at Illinois State University's library was funded, in part, by a grant from the Council on Library Resources. Nineteen librarians were asked ten questions each for a total of 190 cases. Twenty college students were hired and trained to pose the questions in person, record the answer supplied and their impressions of the encounter on an eight-page evaluation form, and attend a follow-up session with the researchers. A pool of fifty-eight questions were used in the project, most of which were asked more than once. Unlike other evaluative studies, however, only about half the questions were short, factual, ready-reference questions. The rest were of a search or research nature. Results of the study were analyzed statistically for accuracy and for attitudinal characteristics. These were further refined to provide the researchers with confidential data for each of the five floors and even by librarian. Aspects affecting success such as time of day, day of the week, minutes spent with patron, by gender of patron and librarian and others were also examined. Based on an elaborate 15-point scale for accuracy and depending on what one considers an acceptable level of response, Milner Library provided an acceptable answer between 58 and 67 percent of the time and had an overall accuracy rate of 10.4251 (Table 1). In measuring attitude a 10-point Likert scale was used for each of 23 different points affecting attitude, such as approachability, eye contact, patience, tenacity, and so on. Milner Library's faculty, as a group, achieved an attitude score of 7.9276 out of 10 (Table 1). For a full description of this project as

Table 1

Accuracy and Attitude
By Floor

Floor	Number of Questions Asked	Accuracy (On a 15 point scale)	Attitude (On a 10 point scale)
A	30(3)*	9.9942	8.2198
B	30(0)	12.8182	8.1012
C	20(2)*	11.5125	8.4459
D	71(2)*	9.6139	7.7275
E	39(1)*	8.1869	7.1437
Mean	190(8)	10.4251	7.9276

* Missing data for accuracy scores. Students failed to provide data.

well as a detailed discussion of the results, please see the September, 1991, issue of *College and Research Libraries* [1] or the Evaluation of Public Services and Public Services Personnel[2] published by the University of Illinois' Graduate School of Library and Information Science.

The ISU study is unique in several respects: most previous studies have taken place in public libraries; most questions used have been posed by telephone rather than in person; most compare libraries rather than study one library in detail; and most are smaller studies while this project involved 190 reference transactions. One other aspect that distinguishes it from other studies is that it used open-ended or research-type questions as part of the pool asked of librarians. The researchers felt it was necessary to use the questions because librarians at reference desks in academic libraries are confronted with a mix of directional, ready reference, research, and extended search questions. To stop at asking only short, factual, ready reference questions would be to construct a study in an even more artificial context than it already was.

There are distinguishing characteristics that can be outlined in describing the two categories of questions used in the ISU study. Basically, ready reference questions require short, straightforward, factual answers generally answerable in a single source—though the answer may be available in many different places. Specific facts or pieces of information are requested.

On the other hand, research questions may exhibit any of a number of characteristics:

- the open-ended question, for example: "I need everything I can get on . . . ," often posed as needed for a research project or paper;
- multiple levels or layers of thought or search activity;
- more than one source had to be consulted in the search—each yielding a necessary component of the complete and correct answer; or
- questions which, while on the surface may look like ready reference types, but aren't because of the difficulty in getting at the answer, for example: "I need the address of Behrends College in Pennsylvania."

317

(All the questions were pretested, so the researchers knew the level of difficulty of the question.)

A good example of a search question which requires multiple levels of responses is: "Where does Andrew Wyeth's landscape with a handicapped girl in it hang?" Here, the first requirement is that the painting be correctly identified; which would entail searching through collections of Wyeth's works if the title ("Christina's World") was not known to the librarian. Next, the location of the painting would have to be determined and finally a source for criticism of the work located. The degree of patron interaction and bibliographic searching involved in a question like this is markedly different from, for example "Where can I get the words to the song "Red Wing"; where the *Popular Song Index* quickly furnishes a source. But even a seemingly direct ready reference question can become more than it appears when the element of timeliness is involved, for example, "Who is the Secretary of Education?" This was asked in April 1989, just after new appointments had been made and the most recent Government Organization Manual, the most logical source, was suddenly out-of-date; and Facts-on-File was more appropriate (as would a variety of other periodically updated sources including newspapers.)

The ISU study incorporated research-type questions because academic librarians usually get as many research as ready reference questions—or more. In order to try to approximate reality and give a fairer assessment of librarians' skills, it was necessary to use the research or multi-level or open-ended questions. From the researchers' point of view, the use of these more extended cases allowed reference interviews and search strategies to be explored more fully. The more elaborate and demanding questions could (and did) give a more accurate picture of the attitudes being presented over the various reference desks. Were Milner's librarians willing to work with students, or were they simply pointing them at areas of the collection? Were the librarians projecting an approachable, friendly demeanor as well? The more automatic ready reference types of questions simply do not furnish as much opportunity to answer these inquiries.

One would hope that the results would furnish an indication of the librarians' responses "under fire", their knowledge of the collection and their ingenuity as well. While not limited to the divisional situation, the researchers could customize questions for subject specialists on the division and even personal levels. This also enhanced the credibility of the questioning situation. In fact, no instances of a student's "cover being blown" were reported, although as mentioned earlier, the librarians were generally aware that an unobtrusive study was going to be conducted during the year.

All of the questions were chosen from a variety of sources—from reference texts, from other studies of reference services, from the researchers' own experience. From a pool of over 500 approximately 150 were chosen for consideration. Many of those were studied and tested and reshaped. Finally, 58 questions were chosen that the researchers had tested and found answerable in ISU's library. Most of those 58 were asked more than once either within one division or in different ones to come to a total of 190 cases. Of the 58 questions, the researchers categorized 29 as ready reference and 29 as research.

Using research questions promised rewards in more reliable results, but posed problems from the beginning. They were obviously more difficult to select and pretest. They took more time and more thought. Then defining exactly what constituted complete and correct was problematic. For example, if someone announced that he was doing a paper on J. R. R. Tolkien and needed all the librarian could find on that author, what could the scorer reasonably consider enough—five sources, the card catalog, the MLA Bibliography? Sometimes this admittedly became a judgment call. Sometimes the librarian being tested found better answers than those originally verified—to be expected, perhaps, since the librarian is the subject expert. Often the student or patron reactions guided the decision on what was complete or correct. If the student felt that he really could have written a paper with what was given him, that reaction tipped the scale toward a higher score. Also factored into the definition of best score were things like whether the librarian asked the patron if the information given was what he was looking for, whether this was enough or too much, whether the kind of material was appropriate. The researchers also considered how much time the librarian spent on the question and how many steps or layers of multilevel questions the librarian completed. Finally, if the librarian told the patron to check back if he needed more help was viewed as a positive indicator that the librarian realized the question asked was open-ended or might require more than basic assistance.

Beyond defining the complete and correct answers for research questions was the problem of verifying the answers supplied on the response forms. As stated previously, the student proxies reported answers on an eight-page form filled out immediately upon completion of the transaction, which the researchers then checked in detail by actually going to the floors and the sources. All this took far more time—actually much more for the search or research questions than for the ready reference questions. There was much more consultation and discussion between the researchers scoring the questions in an effort to ensure as much consistency and fairness as possible. In the end, though, the scoring did have a greater subjective element than the ready reference questions.

The researchers did not set out to compare performance on ready reference and research questions in the original study. It was not an overt goal of the project. As analysis of data continued in more depth, however, it appeared that we had a unique opportunity to isolate information on how librarians dealt with the two types of questions. There were no preconceived notions or hypotheses set forward. One would actually expect that the results should show similar performance -that librarians approach both ready reference and research questions with equal aplomb, efficiency, and success.

As was noted above, the researchers categorized 29 questions as ready reference and 29 as research. Of the 190 cases or reference transactions 101 involved ready reference questions and 89 were of a search or research nature (Table 2).

Table 3 breaks out the accuracy at each of the five reference desks at Milner Library in dealing with the two types of question. Staff at three desks were more successful in answering research questions. Staff at two fared better on ready reference queries. Difference in overall performance was only .7166.

Table 4 provides data on the performance of individual librarians in accurately providing complete and correct answers. The results are almost evenly divided with nine librarians scoring higher on ready reference questions and ten on research. Widely disparate scores are found. Nine scores are over two points different. Five of those vary by five points or more. Yet the overall accuracy, again is only minimally different.

Table 5 takes up the question of attitude by desk. Scores are quite close, but one would expect that the two types of questions should elicit similar responses from librarians used to dealing with a mix of questions. As with the results on accuracy, staff at three desks

Table 2

Types of Questions

	Ready Reference	Search Or Research	Total
Questions	29	29	58
Cases	101	89	190

Table 3

Accuracy
By Floor
(Based on a 15-point Scale)

	Ready Reference	Search Or Research	Total
A	9.7778	10.2105(2)*	9.9942
B	12.6364	13.0000	12.8182
C	13.9000(2)*	9.1250	11.5125
D	10.0278(2)*	9.2000	9.6139
E	7.8500	8.5238(1)*	8.1869

* Missing data

performed better in dealing with ready reference questions. Two handled research better.

Table 6 breaks out attitude scores by individual librarian. Twelve of nineteen were more successful on ready reference questions. Most were within a few tenths of a point of each other. Only five vary one point or more, four of those being more successful in research-oriented questions. The overall difference is less than one hundredth of a point.

Tables 7 and 8 involve particular aspects of attitude as outlined on the Evaluation Form(Appendix). These may prove useful in highlighting isolated points for overall correction or remediation. For example, Aspect 20, "Reminds user to return for more help," scored very low. This leads the researchers to conclude that librarians may not be asking if the answer supplied was what was needed or asking if patrons understand the information given. It is also easily correctable. Some low scores may be attributed to the outcome of the transactions. Aspect 21, "Suggests alternatives outside the library," may not have been a part of the librarian's response if he or she felt the question had been successfully answered.

Table 8 simply compresses the 24 aspects into three manageable groupings to highlight areas of success or need.

Reasons for differences in results are varied. Some academic librarians may respond positively to research questions because they are more interested in challenges or subject areas, or because they feel research is more in line with an academic library's mission. Some prefer the satisfaction of a straightforward, identifiable answer in a ready reference situation. From a patron's perspective—especially from that of a student proxy evaluating a librarian on an eight-page form —research questions, with their potential for more extended contact, offer a better chance to observe and interact with the librarian. In many cases that raises the opinion and scores.

More research is needed. More studies should include research-type questions. Their benefits far outweigh the few negatives. The researchers in the ISU study certainly believe their results present a clearer picture of transactions across the reference desk because of the inclusion of research or search questions.

Table 4

Accuracy
By Librarian
(Based on a 15-point Scale)

Librarian	Ready Reference	Search Or Research	Total
1	10.6667	10.1667(1)*	10.4167
2	7.6000	7.6000	7.6000
3	7.2000	7.8000	7.5000
4	4.7500(1)*	9.5000	7.1250
5	14.0000(1)*	13.7500	13.8750
6	13.7143	11.3333	12.5238
7	10.8571	14.0000	12.4286
8	11.8000	9.8000	10.8000
9	13.8000(1)*	4.5000	9.1500
10	10.5000	5.5000	8.0000
11	10.0000	3.7500(1)*	6.8750
12	11.5000(1)*	12.6666	12.0833
13	10.6667	10.6667(1)*	10.6667
14	10.6000	7.0000	8.8000
15	10.7500	9.0000	9.8750
16	8.5000	10.2857	9.3929
17	13.2500	14.0000	13.6250
18	6.6000	12.1667	9.3834
19	8.0000	9.8571	8.9286
	10.2503	9.6496	9.9500

* Missing data

Table 5

Attitude
By Floor
(Based on a 10-point Scale)

	Ready Reference	Search Or Research	Total
A	8.2444	8.1952	8.2198
B	8.3273	7.8750	8.1012
C	8.8167	8.0750	8.4459

Table 6

Attitude By
Librarian

Librarian	Ready Reference	Search Or Research	Total
1	8.2666	8.1571	8.2119
2	7.6000	6.9000	7.2500
3	7.8000	7.4600	7.6300
4	8.0800	7.0000	7.5400
5	9.0500	8.3000	8.6750
6	8.1142	8.4333	8.2738
7	7.9000	7.3000	7.6000
8	8.5400	7.9200	8.2300
9	8.5833	7.8500	8.2167
10	6.7125	7.7500	7.2313
11	5.1800	6.3000	5.7400
12	5.6857	8.5000	7.0929
13	8.1000	7.6429	7.8715
14	8.0600	7.4750	7.7675
15	7.7000	6.8666	7.2833
16	6.3000	7.5714	6.9357
17	8.8875	7.9000	8.3938
18	7.7600	8.5000	8.1300
19	8.3666	8.7857	8.5762
	-------	-------	--------
	7.7203	7.7164	7.7184

322

Table 7

Attitude by
Individual Aspects

		Ready Reference	Search Or Research	Total
1.	Looks approachable	8.0957	8.4468	8.2713
2.	Acknowledges user's approach to desk	8.8172	8.7204	8.7688
3.	Friendly attitude	8.2979	8.5851	8.4415
4.	Appropriate facial expression - Smiles, shows interest	8.0106	8.1383	8.0745
5.	Appropriate non verbal commication - Eye contact, head nod	8.4787	8.5213	8.5000
6.	Appropriate tone of voice - Volume	8.7128	9.0430	8.8779
7.	Listens attentively	8.7553	9.0430	8.8992
8.	Responses are non-judgemental	8.8261	8.8621	8.8441
9.	Is Tactful, Patient	8.6064	8.4396	8.5230
10.	Responds positively to unusual questions	8.3372	8.1429	8.2401
11.	Keeps trying to answer question, is helpful - doesn't give up too easily	8.0426	7.6333	7.8380
12.	Treats user with courtesy	8.6809	8.8925	8.7867
13.	Puts user at ease - doesn't talk down to user, is not condescending	8.6915	8.5161	8.6038
14.	Determines level of help needed - for own interest, for speech, for paper, in-depth report	6.7033	6.5568	6.6301
15.	Sensitive to user's needs	7.8085	7.8261	7.8173
16.	Is easy to understand - does not use library jargon	9.1398	9.1935	9.1667
17.	Goes to tools with patrons	8.3333	7.2841	7.8087
18.	Explains tools and how to use	6.3889	5.9630	6.1760
19.	Refers users to other subject specialist when appropriate	6.4242	5.3750	5.8996
20.	Reminds user to return for more help	4.9780	5.2442	5.1111
21.	Suggests alternatives outside the library if appropriate	3.7292	2.5000	3.1146
22.	Evidences good knowledge of own collection on the floor - is confident with the resources	8.5909	8.1236	8.3573
23.	Evidences good knowledge of Milner's collection as a whole - knows what tools exist elsewhere in the building	6.4426	6.5231	6.4829
28.	Uses minimum of tools - is efficient	8.5000	8.1452	8.3226

Table 8

Attitude By
Aspect Grouping

Grouping	Ready Reference	Search Or Research	Total
Attitude (X1 - X11)	8.4435	8.5107	8.4771
Interview (X12 - X21)	7.3651	7.1345	7.2498
Search (X22 - 23, X28)	8.1704	7.8074	7.9889

Endnotes

1. Cheryl Asper Elzy, Alan R. Nourie, F.W. Lancaster, and Kurt M. Joseph, "Evaluating Reference Service in a Large Academic Library," *College and Research Libraries* 52 (September, 1991): 454-465.
2. F.W. Lancaster, Cheryl Elzy, and Alan R. Nourie, "The Diagnostic Evaluation of Reference Service in an Academic Library," in Evaluation of Public Services and Public Services Personnel, edited by Bryce Allen, (Urbana-Champaign, IL: University of Illinois Graduate School of Library and Information Science, 1991), p. 43-57, Allerton Park Institute No. 32.

Evaluation Form

Questioner: _____

Librarian/Floor: _____

Question: Number: _____ Short phrase: _____
_____

Time question asked: Date: _____ Hour: _____

Time spent with Librarian in minutes: _____

Answer (actual answer, directions given, Sources or floors provided by
librarian: _____
_____
_____
_____

Source:
   Title: _____
   Date or edition: _____
   Volumes: _____
   Page: _____

Attitude and Demeanor

1. Looks approachable

Not at All		Seldom		Some of the time		Mostly		To a large Extent	
1	2	3	4	5	6	7	8	9	10

   Comments:

   _____
   _____
   _____

2. Acknowledges user's approach to desk

Not at All		Seldom		Some of the time		Mostly		To a large Extent	
1	2	3	4	5	6	7	8	9	10

   Comments:

   _____
   _____
   _____

3. Friendly attitude

Not at All		Seldom		Some of the time		Mostly		To a large Extent	
1	2	3	4	5	6	7	8	9	10

Comments:

_____
_____
_____

4. Appropriate facial expression--Smiles, shows interest

Not at All		Seldom		Some of the time		Mostly		To a large Extent	
1	2	3	4	5	6	7	8	9	10

Comments:

_____
_____
_____

5. Appropriate non-verbal communication--Eye contact, head nod

Not at All		Seldom		Some of the time		Mostly		To a large Extent	
1	2	3	4	5	6	7	8	9	10

Comments:

_____
_____
_____

6. Appropriate tone of voice--Volume

Not at All		Seldom		Some of the time		Mostly		To a large Extent	
1	2	3	4	5	6	7	8	9	10

Comments:

_____
_____
_____

7. Listens attentively

Not at All		Seldom		Some of the time		Mostly		To a large Extent	
1	2	3	4	5	6	7	8	9	10

Comments:

_____

_____

_____

8. Responses are non-judgmental

Not at All		Seldom		Some of the time		Mostly		To a large Extent	
1	2	3	4	5	6	7	8	9	10

Comments:

_____

_____

_____

9. Is Tactful, Patient

Not at All		Seldom		Some of the time		Mostly		To a large Extent	
1	2	3	4	5	6	7	8	9	10

Comments:

_____

_____

_____

10. Responds positively to unusual questions

Not at All		Seldom		Some of the time		Mostly		To a large Extent	
1	2	3	4	5	6	7	8	9	10

Comments:

_____

_____

_____

11. Keeps trying to answer questions, be helpful--doesn't give up too easily

Not at All		Seldom		Some of the time		Mostly		To a large Extent	
1	2	3	4	5	6	7	8	9	10

Comments:

_____
_____
_____

Reference Interview--Librarian--Patron Interaction

12. Treats user with courtesy

Not at All		Seldom		Some of the time		Mostly		To a large Extent	
1	2	3	4	5	6	7	8	9	10

Comments:

_____
_____
_____

13. Puts user at ease --doesn't talk down to user, is not condescending

Not at All		Seldom		Some of the time		Mostly		To a large Extent	
1	2	3	4	5	6	7	8	9	10

Comments:

_____
_____
_____

14. Determines level of help needed

Not at All		Seldom		Some of the time		Mostly		To a large Extent	
1	2	3	4	5	6	7	8	9	10

Comments:

_____
_____
_____

15. Sensitive to user's needs

Not at All		Seldom		Some of the time		Mostly		To a large Extent	
1	2	3	4	5	6	7	8	9	10

Comments:

_____
_____
_____

16. Is easy to understand--does not use library jargon

Not at All		Seldom		Some of the time		Mostly		To a large Extent	
1	2	3	4	5	6	7	8	9	10

Comments:

_____
_____
_____

17. Goes to tools with patrons

Not at All		Seldom		Some of the time		Mostly		To a large Extent	
1	2	3	4	5	6	7	8	9	10

Comments:

_____
_____
_____

18. Explains tools and how to use

Not at All		Seldom		Some of the time		Mostly		To a large Extent	
1	2	3	4	5	6	7	8	9	10

Comments:

_____
_____
_____

19. Refers users to other subject specialist when appropriate

Not at All	Seldom	Some of the time	Mostly	To a large Extent
1 2	3 4	5 6	7 8	9 10

Comments

_____
_____
_____

20. Reminds user to return for more help

Not at All	Seldom	Some of the time	Mostly	To a large Extent
1 2	3 4	5 6	7 8	9 10

Comments

_____
_____
_____

21. Suggests alternatives outside the library if appropriate

Not at All	Seldom	Some of the time	Mostly	To a large Extent
1 2	3 4	5 6	7 8	9 10

Comments

_____
_____
_____

Search Strategy

22. Evidences good knowledge of own collection

Not at All	Seldom	Some of the time	Mostly	To a large Extent
1 2	3 4	5 6	7 8	9 10

Comments

_____
_____
_____

23. Evidences good knowledge of Milner's collection as a whole

Not at All		Seldom		Some of the time		Mostly		To a large Extent	
1	2	3	4	5	6	7	8	9	10

Comments:

_____
_____
_____

24. Finds complete answer

Not at All		Seldom		Some of the time		Mostly		To a large Extent	
1	2	3	4	5	6	7	8	9	10

Comments:

_____
_____
_____

25. Answer accurate

Not at All		Seldom		Some of the time		Mostly		To a large Extent	
1	2	3	4	5	6	7	8	9	10

Comments:

_____
_____
_____

26. Answer appropriate

Not at All		Seldom		Some of the time		Mostly		To a large Extent	
1	2	3	4	5	6	7	8	9	10

Comments:

_____
_____
_____

27. Shows knowledge of Milner's subject specialists

Not at All		Seldom		Some of the time		Mostly		To a large Extent	
1	2	3	4	5	6	7	8	9	10

Comments:

_____
_____
_____

28. Uses minimum of tools--is efficient

Not at All		Seldom		Some of the time		Mostly		To a large Extent	
1	2	3	4	5	6	7	8	9	10

Comments:

_____
_____
_____

General comments and impressions about this librarian and/or the question (or its answer):

Scholarly Use of Academic Reference Services

William G. Jones
University of Illinois at Chicago
Chicago, Illinois

Abstract

Although reference departments in academic libraries are often among the largest in the library and have the greatest concentration of librarians, there is evidence that scholars in the humanities and social sciences make little use of the reference and information services offered by them. Reports of scholarly information-seeking among a group of very productive humanists and their experience in a demonstration project shows that under some circumstances librarians do provide valuable information services to scholars. Analysis of these reports should enable librarians and administrators to begin constructing models of reference service that directly address the needs of scholars, at least for those portions of their research that are conducted in the library. This paper suggest ways in which general library reference services can be organized to address scholarly needs more effectively.

The Context of Reference Services

We know from the literature of librarianship that scholars are not heavy users of general reference services in academic libraries.[1] To be sure, academic reference librarians can report instances where they have provided reference services to scholars, and scholars do interact with library staff in the conduct of inquiry, but more than incidental reliance of scholars upon librarians (and the indexing and abstracting sources upon which librarians rely heavily) is the exception rather than the rule.

Margaret Stieg's survey of the information needs of historians found that on a list of ten methods of discovering relevant published information, librarians ranked 10th in order of "usefulness for research" and 10th in "usefulness for current information.[2] The Bath survey of social scientists ranked librarians 13th on a list of thirteen sources they would consult to locate primary research material, concluding that the "use of librarians was minimal" as a means of locating references for research.[3] Harriet Lonnqvist's study of humanities scholars in five Nordic countries found that mature scholars who had developed broad knowledge of the literature in their fields "derived little help from the librarian or the information specialist in this information-seeking process where information from journals and colleagues is valued highly[4] MaryEllen Sievert's study of the library needs of philosophers concluded that philosophers "are low users of reference materials and other service functions of libraries."[5]

Stephan Stoan assessed the situation well when he dismissed the strategy of information-seeking favored by reference librarians (one emphasizing a patterned use of reference sources) as bearing slight resemblance to the actual behaviors of research scholars. Stone summarized the findings of a number of studies with the statement that these

> ... studies together indicate that footnotes, personal recommendations from other scholars, serendipitous discovery, browsing, personal bibliographic files, and other such techniques that involve no formal use of access tools account of the great majority of citations obtained by scholars.[6]

This point was recently remade by Lanaster in his address "Has Technology Failed Us?" when he said,

> Investigators over many years have consistently shown that seekers of information find much of what they use from specialized bibliographies or bibliographic references in items already known, rather than from databases, library catalogs or consulting librarians. The formal subject access tools are not effective in locating all of the literature on some subject and may not locate much of the literature that subject specialists consider most valuable.[7]

The ongoing research of Stephen E. Wiberley, Jr. and William G. Jones in a study of humanists at the University of Illinois at Chicago has confirmed the findings of many of these earlier studies, most of them survey-based. Jones and Wiberley conducted their research in a context of in-depth interviews with a group of highly productive scholars; these interviews placed information-seeking behavior within a larger framework of scholarly activity.[8,9] At this time, data collected from over thirty library reference services may be summarized as follows.

Through the discipline of their graduate training, scholars begin to identify the important literature in their disciplines and subject specializations. They select what they will read from citations contained in articles and books, from sources noted in scholarly newsletters, book reviews, publishers' flyers, advertisements in reviewing journals, and by scanning specialized bibliographies. They place high value on sources of literature recommended by colleagues. They sometimes scan current bibliographic sources like the PMLA bibliographies, but they do little retrospective searching, having already acquired an extensive knowledge of older literature important to them. They do not use comprehensive indexes of the kind relied upon by librarians, and often have little or no knowledge of the existence of computerized database searching. They usually cannot name librarians who serve at the library's principal reference desk, although they often know and can name the staff at the library's interlibrary loan desk. They report infrequent use of general library reference services, and if they go to reference librarians for assistance, it is very often to verify the correctness of citations or to determine library holdings, whether in their local university library collections or elsewhere. This apparent indifference to formal methods of searching for hitherto unknown secondary literature or for new sources of commentary grows out of practical experience that the bulk of their time is more effectively spent in developing their arguments, analyzing their primary sources, and creating their texts.

Sometimes a scholar's utilization of reference services is incidental An archaeologist who sought information on conversion values for nineteenth century Greek currency was able to find important source data on the value of the English pound when her mentioned his lack of success to a librarian helping him locate a missing journal issue. He told the librarian that he had been unable to find what he needed in British consular reports of the period, and the librarian suggested he use American consular reports, showing him where they were shelved. It was through his chance remark that he eventually located the needed information.

Some humanists acknowledged receiving assistance from librarians in the verifying or unscrambling of citations, those that had been grabled, transcribed incorrectly, or were incomplete. That reference librarians had the means to provide this fundamental service came as a surprise to several humanists who expressed both appreciation and astonishment at the librarian's success.

Although the accuracy of information provided by reference librarians has frequently been called into question,[10] only a few humanists complained about receiving inaccurate information from reference librarians. This is not to imply, however, that humanists attitudes toward librarians were unfailingly positive. In one instance, a reference librarian incorrectly interpreted the collation of a foreign title. The scholar was as much vexed by the librarian's insistence that her interpretation was correct as she was by the librarian's error.

Few humanists have knowledge of database search services, and those who do usually make no use of them. There were exceptions, and some of the use that we know about was associated with utilization of librarians' services growing out of the demonstration project described later in this paper.

Humanities scholars often say that their problem is not a lack of sources and data, but that they have more data than they can use. In the humanities, these data exist to a large degree either as unique sources, or sources that have been reproduced for special purposes. Access to them is frequently confined to specialized archives, research libraries, and centers for humanistic study.

Their use often requires that scholars travel to the locations where these sources are housed, even when the scholar possesses much of what he or she needs in microform or photocopy. It is during trips to archives that scholars talk to special librarians and archivists about other collections that might be of use, identifying clippings files, collections of master's theses, archives, and local history collections that they should visit. The relatively poor systems available for identifying and accessing these collections force scholars to rely or archivists and special collections librarians to a greater degree than is characteristic of their use of general reference services.

Crisis in Reference Services

Those who write about reference services in libraries often refer to them as services in "crisis," and recognition that there might be cause for adopting alternate models of service to research scholars has a long, if not very prominent, history in the United States. Failure to retain experienced people as reference librarians has been variously attributed to the failure of the profession to structure and organize reference services in ways that make them an attractive career path for the most talented and able. The reward system of librarianship favors those who move into administration.[11, 12, 13] There is also a long-standing debate between those that believe reference should be a source of "instruction" (i.e. delivering training on how to find information) and those who believe it should be a source of "information" (i.e. providing answers to questions posed by users).[14,15]

Barbara Ford, in "Reference Beyond (And Without) The Reference Desk," points out that reference desks are expensive to operate and may not work very well.[16] Ford suggests that the time may have come for librarians to explore alternative models for the provision of reference, perhaps even without the reference desk. James Rettig describes an alternative in his history of reference services at the University of Illinois at Chicago.[17] Rettig's alternative was not developed however, for the purpose of supporting scholarly activity through reference services, but was designed to relieve some of the pressure on reference librarians arising from the large numbers of directional questions that librarians received in the department under his management.

What is remarkable about these commentaries on reference services is that so little attention is paid to what academic reference librarians might reasonably be expected to do for the research scholars who constitute such a significant component of the community within which they work.

In 1932, acting on a suggestion of astronomer Harlow Shapley, the Carnegie Commission funded a project at Cornell University and the University of Pennsylvania to support bibliographic specialists who would undertake to provide for the researcher in the humanities and social sciences the same kinds of assistance that the laboratory technician provides for the natural scientist. In the three years during which Carnegie Foundation support was available, project librarians at the two universities each handled about forty assignments from thirty-three different faculty members, some of the assignments requiring a month or more to complete. Summarizing this experiment, Samuel Rothstein wrote,

> When examined closely so as to ascertain precisely wherein the service offered proved of such value, the statements showed a general agreement on two points. As a general and minimum thing, the service provided a worthwhile saving of time and trouble for the research workers. That is to say, the research librarian was doing work which the faculty members might equally well have done for themselves, but of which they were glad to be relieved.
>
> More important, the work of the research librarian represented an important increment, as well as a saving. A number of statements pointed out that the special bibliographical knowledge of the librarian (i.e. his service "qua" librarian rather than "qua" general (assistant) enabled him to bring to light information—such as pertinent material in subject fields outside the scholars' specialties, the resources of other libraries, works in lesser-known foreign languages—which the scholars could not have found for themselves at all![18]

UIC Demonstration Project

A project similar to the Carnegie experiment was undertaken at the University of Illinois at Chicago as part of the university library's involvement with the University's Humanities Institute. This Institute offers a place for humanities scholars to work, meet, and talk while they devote themselves to major research projects, freed from teaching responsibilities for an academic year. For two years the university library supported a demonstration project in which a reference librarian was available to assist fellows in the Humanities Institute with their research projects. At the beginning of each of the project years, the librarian was introduced to that year's fellows. The fellows were told that the librarian would assist them with any information problems that they might encounter in their work, would conduct database searches for them at library expense, and would help them obtain publications and other research materials that they might identify and want. In the course of the academic year fellows are obliged to describe their research in a public lecture to which the campus community is invited. The project librarian attended all lectures given by the fellows in fulfillment

335

of that obligation. Informal receptions followed each event and the project librarian was also present at them. In the two years of the project, thirteen of twenty fellows came to the librarian for help. Several first-year fellows continued working with her into the second year, even though they no longer had formal affiliation with the Institute, nor did they have financial support from the library for the conduct of computer database searches.

The librarian checked local library holdings for the fellows, filled out interlibrary loan request forms on their behalf, and, with library staff assistance, photocopied articles and chapters for them. She verified dozens of incomplete citations and conducted exploratory, multidisciplinary searches of the literature, usually when the fellows were at any early stage in their work. She conducted some searches online, but used print source for others. She performed exhaustive rather than exploratory searches for two fellows. A historian asked what sources the library had that would lead him to primary materials held in a particular geographic region, and another fellow asked for help in obtaining a dissertation. (When the dissertation was identified and a copy produced, the fellow said that he hadn't expected the librarian to be able to able to find it) The services of the librarian were not confined to information-seeking, but included inquiries of non-scholarly content such as locating the most secluded microfilm reader in the library.

The project librarian also received requests to verify citations and to locate copies of obscure regional periodicals; to identify and locate copies of popular nineteenth-century novels by a lesser-known European author; to do exploratory searches on the history of the British civil service, and on the uses of parades and pageantry in the United States; to identify sources of U.S. state and Canadian provincial election return statistics; to facilitate interlibrary borrowing of eighteenth-century pamphlets; to locate reliable information on the history of European weights and measures; and to compile a bibliography of novels about baseball.

No fellow expressed any desire to do his/her own computer searching, even for exploratory research, and few fellows knew of the existence of a librarian-mediated search service offered by the library. Fellows who sought help, even for well defined topics such as "baseball novels," were satisfied to delegate all searching responsibility to the librarian. The fellow who asked for baseball novels assumed the librarian would

generate the bibliography from an electronic database. When she delivered to him two printed bibliographies of baseball literature, each with a section on fiction, he was embarrassed that he hadn't found them for himself. All fellows were eager to delegate the job of citation verification, often appearing surprised when the citations could be quickly found, and they were pleased that the project supported a document delivery service that brought photocopies of needed articles directly to their offices.

Only two fellows communicated with the librarian by electronic mail. Others depended on finding her in her office on their visits to the library or on talking to her when she attended Humanities Institute lectures. Because many fellows worked mainly at home, face-to-face contact was minimal. The librarian estimated that 80 percent of the requests for her services came to her in the five or ten minutes before and after each Humanities Institute lecture. She always came away from a lecture with a new assignment, but no fellow ever said to the librarian, "I have to have this immediately."

About a third of the 160 hours devoted to the project in its second year were for procurment and delivery to the scholar of known-items, that is, providing fellows with material they already knew existed. The librarian gave about five hours of careful attention each week to the fellows' requests. About $500 was spent for online searches of which about $115 was spent on two in-depth searches on very specific topics. Other searches were completed using paper-copy indexes.

In spite of their occasionally expressed disinclination to approach reference librarians or the place themselves in positions where they admitted ignorance, fellows did take advantage of the availability of the project librarian. The project librarian was not introduced to the fellows as an "expert," but as a generalist, someone knowledgeable about libraries who could assist them in the fulfillment of their research goals. (The library had, however, chosen a very skilled reference librarian to participate in the project). The informal intimacy of the institute setting and the frequency of scheduled events, when fellows and librarian were together, made it easy for fellows to approach the reference librarian, away from the formal architecture of the library's reference desk and its assortment of terminals, telephones, and anonymous staff.

The success of the demonstration project (and, by

the reports of humanists who participated in it, it was a success) can be attributed to three elements in the project's organization: 1) The project librarians was introduced to the Institute fellows, her role was described, and the backing of both the Institute director and the university librarian clearly stated; 2) The project librarian attended all publicly scheduled Institute events, including lectures and receptions following these lectures; 3) The librarians' assistance and value was often publicly acknowledged by fellows whenever they met as a group so that fellows who did not initially turn to her for assistance may have been prompted to do so later. The project librarian also believed that another component of her success was that at each meeting with a fellow she provided more information than the fellow asked for, but not more than he/she could be expected to use.

The financial support offered by the project beyond that ordinarily available to faculty was for database searching by the project librarian and for document delivery. Five hours of a librarian's time each week with the added real costs of database searching for a population fewer than a dozen was manageable within the normal range of reference department assignments for special projects, but the service could have strained the resources of the library if it had been offered (and that offer accented) to the entire humanities faculty of the campus. On the other hand, offering the service without the vehicle of the Humanities Institute, with its seminars, discussions, and informal "brown bag" lunches that permitted fellows to interact with the librarian and to share among themselves their evaluation of her work would very likely have had a negligible impact on the library and its librarians.

Alternaative Models of Service

At the conference, Humanitists at Work, Yale sociologist Charles Perrow in his paper "On Not Using Libraries," argued persuasively that one of the major roles of academic libraries is to protect the scholar from too much information, from being overwhelmed by large numbers of documents that are of little value or not relevant to the scholar's current research interests.[18] Perrow says that so little is really new, a scholar will hear of important developments many times over if the developments are important to his or her topic inquiry.

Perrow proposed a form of library information service that would mark a departure from the largely passive information services currently offered by libraries to scholars. In that service (Perrow calls it a library "boutique") librarians, research assistants, and graduate students would pull together information on topics selected by scholars, holding seminars occasionally (with purchasing of library materials part of the process) to learn how different disciplines like to approach problems, sharing their observations with the faculty involved.

I suspect that the current library structure would be in shambles, but if we thought of the library as a collection of semi-automomous units that have to collaborate and cooperate, the structure would appear to be rather straightforward—a large number of units making informal deals with one another, with a few nodes that allocate resources, do long range planning and marketing, andtransmit information about what seems to work throughout the network.

Perrow goes on to suggest.

The professor shares with the library staff, the staff group brings the skills and knowledge from one project to the next, without regard to professorial ownership, other faculty members are seen as key resources, with reciprocal rewards and certainly status, and privileged access to the latest, hottest projects going in related fields. Any small, marginal gains that can be made along these lines will contribute to a community. The present structure of most libraries does little in this regard. The drive to computerize, digitalize, laserize and automate these massive vending machines only serves to privatize the scholarly effort.[20]

The benefits to the scholar are that a scholarship may be advanced and that the librarian may play a direct role in advancing it. The appeal of Perrow's alternative should not, however, prevent us form wondering whether it offers an improvement on the demonstration project. What is of interest about it is that it represents a plausible approach to librarian/research scholar collaboration that research scholars might find more useful than exists under the present system.

Conclusion

The evidence of several decades of studies of scholarly information-seeking reveals that academic library information services, particularly those offered from a general reference desk, have little impact on the work of the scholars themselves. Under some circumstances, scholars may engage in relationships with reference librarians that contribute to scholarly inquiry, but these appear to be exceptions, and they do not occur very often through the mechanisms of reference service that librarians have devised for their libraries. The data collected by the author and the experience of the demonstration project librarian suggest that if reference librarians wish to make themselves of greater use to scholars, they must go to scholars directly. They must be available and prepared (in the broadest sense) to provide information to scholars within the customary pattens of information-seeking that these scholars have developed through many years of practice. Models of reference service that are based on the assumption that scholars are likely to seek out librarians for assistance at reference desks because that is part of the routine information gathering process of scholarship will continue to be of very limited utility.

The creation of new knowledge is one of the most highly valued goals in the modern research university. The contribution of librarians to the creation of this knowledge through their reference services has been less than it might have been, yet little change in the organization of reference services resulting from the well-documented record of this failure has occurred. Academic reference librarians must surely provide useful services to other members of their communities, else libraries would not invest so heavily in them. The success of such initiatives as the UIC demonstration project reveals, however, that even a modest allocation of reference librarians' time toward the support of scholarship can lead to closer and possibly more productive working relationships between scholars and librarian. The idea of an academic community represented both by Perrow and the Humanities Institute implies that dialogue takes place among peers without constraint of desk schedules or the queueing of scholars, one behind another, to have answers to reference questions dispensed from the giant vending machines of Perrow's evocative metaphor.

It should be a matter of the greatest curiosity to our profession why so much effort is expended by librarians on issues of professional standing and so little on analysis of their effectiveness in the communities they serve, and when, in fact, that effectiveness is repeatedly shown to be of limited utility. The fact that scholars appear to function very happily without paying the least attention to librarians other than those in

archives, rare books, manuscripts, and other specialized collections seems to have been sufficient cause for reference librarians to dismiss them as appropriate objects of attention.

Proposals like those advanced by Perrow and projects like the one described in this paper address the possibility that there might be useful consequences resulting from the interaction of librarians and scholars, where librarians' knowledge of a literature or literatures can be placed in the service of those who read those literatures and write about them. But even successful collaborations between scholars and librarians relegate librarians to the role of assistant rather than information expert. Scholars (as they must) validate the sources provided by librarians through their use of those sources. The idea that a librarian might have such an extensive knowledge of a literature that he/she could control its use by a scholar is so far beyond current practice as to appear naive. Instead of moving to secure such indispensability to scholarship, however, librarians have retreated from the challenge. University administrations have correctly assessed the dispensability of librarians and the consequences are being felt throughout the profession.

Library administrators will retain or modify services at their reference desks as they see fit and according to current philosophies of library service, but it is certain that the provision of services to scholars, whatever those services may be, must be based on an understanding of the ways scholars conduct their research if librarians are to play significant roles in supporting and in generating new knowledge.

Endnotes

1. The author gratefully acknowledges the assistance of the Council on Library Resources for its partial support of the research reported in this paper, the unfailing patience and generosity of fellows in the UIC Institute for the Humanities, the advice of James Rettig and Stephen E. Wiberley, Jr., and contributions by E. Paige Weston to the text describing the library demonstration project.
2. Margaret F. Steig, "The Information (of) Needs of Historians," *College & Research Libraries* 42 (November, 1981): 549-560.
3. "Investigation into Information Requirements of the Social Sciences: Research Report," Project Head, Maurice B. Line, (Bath: Bath University Library, 1971), 6v. in 1

4. Harriet Lonnqvist, "Scholars Seek Information: Information-Seeking Behavior and Information Needs of Humanities Scholars." in 56th IFLA General Conference, Stockholm, Sweden, 18-24 August 1990, p. 7-29-8-35. (Stockholm: International Federation of Library Associations, 1980).

5. Mary Ellen C. Sievert, "Scholarly Needs and Library Resources: the Case of Philosophers: Final Report of Research Grant 8011." Presented to the Council on Library Resources. (Columbia, MO.: Department of Information Science, Missouri University, n.d.), p. 84.

6. Stephan K. Stoan, "Research and Library skills: An Analysis and Interpretation," *College and Research Libraries* 45 (March, 1984): 99-109.

7. Frederick W. Lancaster, "Has Technology Failed Us?" in Information Technology and Library Management, 13th International Essen Symposium, October 22-25, 1990, ed. by Ahmed H. Helal and Joachim W. Weiss, (Essen: Universitaets-bibliothek Essen, 1991), p. 2–13

9. Stephan E. Wiberley, Jr., and William G. Jones, "Patterns of Information Seeking in the Humanities," *College & Research Libraries* 50 (November, 1989): 638-645.

8. Stephan E. Wiberley, Jr., "Habits of Humanists: Scholarly Behavior and New Information Technologies," *Library HI TECH* 9(No. 1, 1991): 17-21.

10. Peter Hernon and Charles R. McClure, "Library Reference Service: An Unrecognized Crisis—A Symposium," *Journal of Academic Librarianship* 13 (March,1987): 69-80.

11. Charles Bunge, "Potential and Reality at the Reference Desk: Reflections on a 'Return to the Field,'" *Journal of Academic Librarianship* 10 (July, 1984): 128-132.

12. William Miller, "What's Wrong with Reference: Coping with Success and Failure at the Reference Desk," *American Libraries* 15 (May, 1984): 303-306, 321-322.

13. James R. Rettig, "The Crisis in Academic Reference Work," *Reference Services Review* 12 (Fall, 1984): 13-14.

14. Thelma Freides, "Current Trends in Academic Libraries," *Library Trends* 31 (Winter, 1983): 466-467.

15. Herbert S. White, "The Variability of the Reference Process," *Library Journal* 116 (June 15, 1991): 54-55.

16. Barbara J. Ford, "Reference Beyond (and Without) the Reference Desk," *College & Research Libraries* 47 (September,1986): 491-494.

17. James Rettig, "Users and Services," in *The Academic Library in Transition: Planning for the 1980s,* Beverly P. Lynch, ed. (New York: Neal-Schuman. 1989), p. 97–103.

18. Rothstein, Samuel, "'Research Librarians' in University Libraries," in *The Development of Reference Services through Academic Traditions, Public Library Special Librarianship,* 93-97 Samuel Rothstein (Chicago: Association of College and Reference Libraries, 1955). (ACRL Monographs, no. 14)

19. Charles Perrow, "On Not Using Libraries," in *Humanists at Work,* papers presented at a symposium held at the University of Illinois at Chicago on April 27-28, 1989, p. 29-42 (Chicago:University Library, University of Illinois at Chicago, 1989).

20. Ibid., p. 42.

The Complexity of Science Faculty's Information Seeking Behavior

Mengxiong Liu
San Jose State University
San Jose, California

Abstract

This study focuses on the information seeking behavior of a group of science faculty. Using the survey technique, the researcher investigated the external factors and internal motivators involved in the citing practice of Chinese physics faculty. Findings revealed that the number of reference citations of science faculty's research publications was positively related to the use of their institutional libraries, while the importance of citations was related to their assessment of the value of the original cited publications. Science faculty's information seeking behavior is complex and librarians must understand it to best support faculty's scholarly needs.

Introduction

The university library is an agency of scholarly communication. If it is to fulfill its mission, librarians must understand the scholarly communication process. Communication is a process of information exchange, and it is somewhat under the control of the information user. For any given information need, the choice of which source to employ and which source to cite in the research paper is complex and depends on a mixture of sociological, psychological and cultural factors.

It is important for librarians to understand their users' information seeking behavior and their information needs. How exactly information seekers discover, select, and use the countless information and communication resources available to them when conducting research is a problem often overlooked. Knowing users' information seeking behavior not only helps explain the scholarly communication process, but also aids librarians in developing information systems and services in their libraries.

This study focused on the information seeking behavior of a group of special library users—science faculty. More specifically, this research focused on science faculty's citing practice. It is generally agreed that the citation process is a central aspect of the use of information by scientists in their communications. Although citation analysis has been used quite extensively to study user's citing behavior, critics have questioned both the assumption and methods of many of these studies. There could be numerous reasons why an author cited an earlier work. Cronin conjectured that referencing behavior is the result of the citer's perceptions, attitudes, prejudices or erudition.[1] These are complex mental states, which seem to imply complex citer motives. He pointed out: "Citation is colored by a multitude of factors, not all of which have to do with the conventions and procedures of scholarly publishing. Social and psychological variables play a part, along with subconscious remembering and forgetting."[2]

Therefore, to study the problem of citing, this study developed a new methodology, different from citation analysis. Unlike other citation studies which imposed too much of the researcher's personal judgment, this study utilized a questionnaire survey method by which data were collected from the answers to direct questioning—"the most sensible method of trying to penetrate this private world"[3] of studying citing and information seeking behavior. This study intended to prove that science faculty's citing behavior is related to their internal motivators and external factors.

Data Collection

This study used a subset of data from a larger research effort undertaken by this author. In the large-scale study, questionnaires were distributed to the authors of 725 articles carried in *Chinese Physics* during 1981-87. *Chinese Physics* is a quarterly journal published by the American Institute of Physics as a secondary source. This source journal was selected for its authority and representation of current Chinese physics research. Article selection criteria were based on currency, time extent and citation availability. Since this research required the respondents to answer questions about their motivations while citing particular references, currency became important in enabling them to refresh their memory. Meanwhile, a coverage of 1981-1987 time period reflected a sufficient extent of a seven-year span of physics research development in 1980s. A check of *Chinese Physics* volumes found that, between 1981 and 1987, altogether 973 articles were published. Although one author might publish several papers during that period, only one of his/her most recent article was selected. In the event of joint authorship, only the first author was selected. Papers without cited references were not included. Thus, among 973 articles published in the source journal during 1981-87, 725 articles/authors were identified, constituting 74.5% of the total. A questionnaire packet was sent to each selected article author. Each packet enclosed a copy of cover letter including the instruction for completing the questionnaire, a copy of the questionnaire, and a copy of the title page and reference citation page(s) of the selected article.

Among 725 distributed questionnaires, a total of 415 were returned representing a response rate of 57.2%. In these returned questionnaires, 145 article authors were self-identified as university professors who represented 34.9% of the total responding population. Among the university professors who responded to the questionnaire, the great majority were from large prestigious universities in big cities in China. They engaged in teaching and research in one of the fields of semiconductors, nuclear physics, theoretical physics, laser technology, solid state physics or optics. They knew at least one foreign language such as English and/or Russian and were active in publication during 1981-1987.

By analyzing the data collected from science faculty, this study investigated the external factors and internal motivators involved in the research publications of science faculty. Reference citation characteristics of science faculty were identified and examined in terms of their relationships to internal motivators and external factors.

Reference Citations and Their Importance

Among the 145 surveyed articles, 1494 references were cited with an average of 10.4 citations per each article. The number of references that a science faculty member cited in his/her published paper is, therefore, termed as *citation output*. The proportion of the essential citations was also examined. It shows that a majority of science faculty (65.3%) consider that 21-80% of

their reference citations are essential. The proportion of cited sources which a science faculty member considers to be necessary or important to the development of his/her ideas in the paper is, thereafter, termed *citation essentiality*.

A correlation analysis revealed that there was a negative relationship (r=-.81) between citation output and citation essentiality, which was statistically significant at .05. This negative relationship seems to imply that the more references science faculty cited in their publications, the less proportion of these references were essential. This interesting finding brought about further questions: How did science faculty select references for citing? Where did they locate the cited reference sources? and Why did they decide to use these particular references? There must be a variety of external factors and internal motivators involved in a person's information seeking behavior. Further investigations used *citation output* and *citation essentiality* as the two citation indicators to examine their relationships with information seeking variables.

Utility of Information Sources

Table 1 shows that a great majority of Chinese science faculty (80.8%) confirmed that they used their institution libraries most often when they were doing their research and preparing their research papers. A moderate number of faculty (38.7% and 31.6%) said they used their personal *collections* and *other information services* only a moderate amount of time. However, a fairly large number of respondents (78.3%) said they hardly used *colleagues' collections*. Thus the utility level of the four types of information sources can be ranked as *institution library* the first, *personal collection* and *other information services* the second and *colleagues' collection* the last.

If institution library was the most frequently used information service, how is it related to a researcher's *citation output* and *citation essentiality?* If there is any, what does it imply?

Statistical analyses showed that there was a significant relationship (F=3.14, p<.05) between *citation output* and the use of an institutional library. This relationship indicates that the use of an institution library may have an effect on the number of references that a scientist cites in his/her research paper. However, no relationship was found between *citation essentiality* and the use of institutional library.

Table 1
Utility Level of Information Sources
(Numbers of respondents)

	Least	Little	Moderate	Some	Most	Total
Personal	12	36	48	19	9	124
Collection	9.7%	29.0%	38.7%	15.3%	7.3%	100%
Colleague	72	13	2	5	0	92
Collection	78.3%	4.3%	2.2%	5.4%	0%	100%
Institute	0	2	10	15	113	140
Library	0%	1.4%	7.1%	10.7%	80.8%	100%
Other Info	16	25	36	21	16	114
Service	14.0%	21.9%	31.6%	18.4%	14.1%	100%

(Note: The total number of respondents varies in each category and does not correspond to the total number of returned questionnaires because a few respondents did not complete all the questions.)

Indirect Imperative

In order to find out how social factors, such as those in publishing and academic professions, may affect a scientist's information seeking behavior, faculty were asked two questions: 1) whether or not a publication's editorial policy forced them to search for certain references, and 2) whether or not an individual's power over their career development forced them to select certain references.

Table 2 shows quite a different influential pattern between editorial policy and career influence. A very small proportion of respondents (5%) thought that editorial policy most strongly affected their seeking behavior. On the other hand, more than one third of them (40.6%) believed that editorial policy hardly influenced their referencing behavior. This fact suggests that editorial policy as a force manipulating the scientists' behavior was very weak.

By contrast, almost one-third of respondents (31.7%) admitted that a superior's power over their development in the academic profession somewhat strongly influenced their reference citing behavior and a little less than one-third of them (28.8%) indicated a moderate influence. In contrast to the weak force of editorial policy, an individual's power over one's career development seemed to have some relatively strong impact on one's information seeking behavior.

No relationship was found between the two citation indicators and the two social variables.

Knowledge Claim

Three dimensions were categorized as the *knowledge claim* factor: the degree to which one wants to demonstrate one's familiarity with a certain subject (termed *familiarity*); [4] the degree to which one wants to persuade others (termed *persuasion*); [5] and the degree to which one wants to provide up-to-date information (termed *currency*). [6] Each of these three dimensions represents an author's interest in convincing a reader that he/she possesses the knowledge needed as an authority in the subject of the article.

Table 3 shows the proportions of degree for which each factor is accounted. More than one third of the respondents (44.3% and 43.6%) believed that their referencing practice was influenced by *persuasion* and *currency* factors. However, *familiarity* only receives moderate attention in the citing process.

Table 2
Indirect Imperatives
(Numbers of Respondents)

	Least	Little	Moderate	Some	Most	Total
Editorial	41	17	35	2	5	101
Policy	40.6%	17.8%	34.7%	2.0%	5.0%	100%
Career	17	10	30	33	14	104
Influence	16.3%	9.6%	28.8%	31.7%	13.5%	100%

(Note: The total number of respondents varies in each category and does not correspond to the total number of returned questionnaires because a few respondents did not complete all the questions.)

Table 3
Knowledge Claim Factors
(Numbers of Respondents)

	Least	Little	Moderate	Some	Most	Total
Familiarity	15	12	44	28	15	114
	13.2%	10.5%	38.6%	24.6%	13.2%	100%
Persuasion	5	3	25	40	58	131
	3.8%	2.3%	19.1%	30.5%	44.3%	100%
Currency	7	8	19	32	51	117
	6.0%	6.8%	16.2%	27.4%	43.6%	100%

(Note: The total number of respondents varies in each category and does not correspond to the total number of returned questionnaires because a few respondents did not complete all the questions.)

No relationship was found between the two citation indicators and the knowledge claim factors.

Value Perception

Three dimensions were categorized as value perception factors. They are: the degree to which the number of references is valued; the degree to which the original author is valued (prestige of the cited authors); and the degree to which the journal publication is valued. These categories all display a scientist's assumption that the intrinsic *value* elements of the citation process have a certain degree of utility in his/her acceptance in the scientific community.

Table 4 shows the proportions of degree to which each factor is accounted for. One third of the respondents (33%) thought the number of references was the

Table 4
Value Perception
(Numbers of Respondents)

	Least	Little	Moderate	Some	Most	Total
Number of	33	20	28	11	8	100
References	33.0%	20.0%	28.0%	11.0%	8.0%	100%
Eminent	6	12	42	32	27	119
Author	5.0%	10.1%	35.3%	26.9%	22.7%	100%
Prestigious	16	9	20	35	31	111
Journal	14.4%	8.2%	18.0%	31.5%	27.9%	100%

(Note: The total number of respondents varies in each category and does not correspond to the total number of returned questionnaires because a few respondts did not complete all the questions.)

least important factor when the references were selected. Altogether over half of them (53%) did not think that the number of references would ever influence their citation decisions. On the other hand, over one third of the respondents (35.3%) considered that eminent authors might moderately influence their reference selection. In fact, about half of them positively thought that this factor was "most" or "somewhat" considered in their referencing process. A similar case exists in considering the prestige of certain journal publications. The majority of the faculty (59.4%) believed that, when citing references, they did consider if those references were carried by the prestigious journals.

A positive relationship was found between *citation essentiality* and *prestigious journal* (r=.35, p<.01). The relationship was strong, in which 10% of citation essentiality can be predicted from the use of prestigious journals. In other words, the more the cited journals were valued, the greater proportion of reference citations were considered essential by the science faculty.

Conclusions

It is apparent that the science faculty in China used their own university libraries most frequently when they were conducting their research and preparing their research papers. In addition, their use of the university libraries positively related to the numbers of references they cited in their papers. Academic libraries thus play an indispensible role in the progress of science, in other words, in scholarly communication. However, this study also found that most use of library materials was concentrated in prestigious journals. It suggests that the library should review its selection and weed out journals that lack prestige and/or are never cited.

Compared with university libraries, libraries outside universities are used less frequently, partly because these libraries are located some distance away when special efforts are needed to make the trip. However, more importantly, limited public services and the limited effort to disseminate the information are the major reasons of discouraging the use of these libraries. In addition to their collection development, maximizing the dissemination of existing information becomes the priority task among other services.

It is also obvious that the motives of persuasion and provision of up-to-date information drive the science faculty to cite certain references. Knowing science faculty's strong desire for current and persuasive information, academic librarians must reorient their thinking and practice in acquiring, organizing and disseminating new and existing knowledge to meet the users' needs. On the other hand, science faculty also pay much attention to the journals which they perceive to be important and prestigious in their research areas. This factor directly affects the proportion of essential citations among the total cited references. Collection development librarians need to identify journals valued by science faculty by keeping themselves aware of faculty's journal value perception.

A science faculty member's information seeking behavior is unique, complex and personal. Detailed studies are needed to produce more intricate information. Study of the citation process can provide many important social and cultural insights. A further comparison study of the citing behavior of Chinese and American science faculty could help identify how they differ in choosing materials and citing sources as well as their value perception. Librarians in the United States need to make even greater efforts to understand the increasingly more diversified library users, the various multicultural information sources and channels they employ, and the value of certain types of collections perveceived by different ethnic groups, in order to tailor the library's services and research collections to best support patrons' needs.

Endnotes

1. Blaise Cronin, The Citation Process: The Role and Significance of Citations in Scientific Communication. (London: Taylor Graham, 1984).
2. Ibid., p. 31.
3. Blaise Cronin, "The Need for a Theory of Citing," Journal of Documentation 37 (March, 1981): 21.
4. Janet B. Bavelas, "The Social Psychology of Citation," Canadian Psychological Review 19 (April, 1978): 158-63.
5 G. Nigel Gilbert, "Referencing as Persuasion," Social Studies of Science 7: 113-22 (March, 1977).
6. Terrence A. Brooks, "Private Acts and Public Objects: an Investigation of Citer Motivations," Journal of the American Society for Information Science 36 (July-August, 1985): 223-29.

What Happens When You Eliminate the Reference Desk?

Virginia Massey-Burzio
Johns Hopkins University
Baltimore, Maryland

Abstract

Results of replacing a reference desk with an information desk and consultation service show that the notion of providing an "available body" to answer all types of questions needs to be reevaluated.

Introduction

We know that unobtrusive studies of reference service indicate that only 50 to 62 % of reference questions are answered correctly.[1] We are well-aware of the overwhelming demands made on reference service desks and, in turn, how little hope there is to increase the number of reference librarian positions. We try to prioritize our activities, but we or our bosses can't seem to relinquish anything. Many libraries are offering stress workshops, but, as helpful as these are, they are not a long- term solution to a problem that is getting worse and worse as the years go by. Some solution has to be found.

Some very interesting theoretical pieces have appeared in the literature, including Barbara Ford's in the 1986 ACRL national conference proceedings,[2] Thelma Friedes in *Library Trends*,[3] Mary Biggs in *The Journal of Academic Librarianship* [4] and William Miller in *American Libraries*.[5] In 1990 Jo Bell Whitlatch wrote a book called *The Role of the Academic Reference Librarian* in which she examines the entire process of reference service practice. All of these librarian authors question the effectiveness of the reference desk. Many of us have read these articles and the book with interest, but actually implementing something in practice is rather overwhelming to contemplate. The reference desk was designed 100 years ago and it has remained pretty much the same since the turn of the century. As Barbara Ford has pointed out, "The reference desk appears to be a sacred library tradition that many librarians are unwilling or unable to relinquish or question."

This paper is about what happened when the reference desk was eliminated at the Main Library at Brandeis University. What is interesting about this project is how it changed the behavior of the library patron and the interaction between the librarian and the patron. Hopefully, it brings us nearer to understanding the process of reference service practice and enables us to come closer to an understanding of what constitutes good service.

Background

Brandeis University, as the youngest major research university in the United States, is distinguished by a dual commitment to undergraduate education and the pursuit of advanced research. The student population of four thousand men and women includes about eight hundred graduate students. The University currently offers twenty Ph.D programs. There is one professional school, the Florence Heller Graduate School for Advanced Studies in Social Welfare. The library collections include about 900,000 volumes, 800,000 microforms, 300,000 U.S. government documents and 7,500 serials. There are two libraries, the Main Library (social science and humanities, creative arts and Judaica) and the Science Library (physical and natural sciences, math and computer science).

Description of New Reference Environment

An information desk and a research consultation service office were established in the place of the reference desk. The purpose of the information desk, which is staffed by Brandeis graduate, students, is to provide directional and brief informational assistance that takes no longer than 2-3 minutes to convey. It is also to screen questions and make the proper referrals to the reference librarians. The students have a carefully selected set of ready reference tools behind their desk to assist them in answering appropriate questions. They are given guidelines and samples of questions that are appropriate for them to answer and those appropriate for a referral to a librarian. The overriding guideline is that anything that takes longer than 2-3 minutes to handle or that they cannot quickly find an answer for, even if it seems like a simple question, should be referred to a librarian. They are also encouraged to stay at the information desk because their main function is to be available to handle a high volume of quick questions and to answer the telephone. In order to encourage referrals to the librarian, the statistics sheet includes a referral column, in which they have to note the number of referrals. They are told they should expect to refer about 40% of the questions they receive. This is based on data in the literature that claims about 62.1 % of questions received at a reference desk fall in the quick information/directional area.[6] When a librarian is with a client or not available, the Information Desk student fills out a "Request for Information" sheet to be given to a librarian later. The client is given the option of waiting, returning later or giving a phone number where they can be reached. We found that, contrary to what one might normally expect, library patrons appreciate the opportunity to fill out the sheet and get a callback.

The research consultation service office was designed to provide the optimal environment to enhance the client-professional interaction. Each librarian is assigned office hours in the research consultation office. The office hours are 10 a.m. to 5 p.m. Monday through Friday, 6 p.m. to 9 p.m. Monday through Thursday and noon to 5:30 p.m. on Sundays. Each librarian has office hours 2 hours per day. The office contains appropriate ready-reference tools and a "scholar workstation" that provides the librarians with access to all functions of the library's online system, dial-out access to OCLC, Dialog, and other libraries' catalogs and a network of CD databases. The numerous directional and brief informational questions, as well as the constantly ringing phone, which occur at the traditional reference desk, do not interrupt transactions with clients. Waiting patrons respect the privacy of the consultation and do not hover or try to rush the librarian in any manner. They do not even form a line. The librarian is unaware of how many people may be waiting. The design of the consultation service office, in other words, sends a clear message to the patron, a professional consultation is in progress and should not be disturbed.

Results

This new kind of reference service has been very favorably received by the Brandeis community. Many library patrons have specifically mentioned the value of having the undivided attention of a librarian in a quiet setting. The changed environment has also greatly enhanced the interaction between the librarian and the patron. In a study that Joan Durrance did,[7] she found that the traditional reference desk sends mixed signals to the patron. They are unsure whether they are talking to a librarian, a library assistant or a student. In the author's view this presents a variety of problems for the patron. They fear revealing their ignorance to this unknown person in such a public place and they have no way of knowing whether the person has the capacity or expertise to understand their research problem. As Thelma Friedes has pointed out, the reference desk is more of an impediment than a facilitator because users perceive it as intended for simple questions and quick replies.[8] She thinks that it is just this perception that causes patrons to disguise substantive questions as simple requests for directions. In this new environment, however, the patron fully realizes he or she is talking to a professional librarian. This awareness plus the quiet, private, focused setting has made patrons very verbal in expressing their needs. The librarian is able to fully utilize his or her professional skills and expertise. There appears to be high satisfaction on both sides. The librarians feel more valued by the community and experience greater job satisfaction because of this and being able to utilize the skills they were trained for and the patrons feel they are getting a very special and valuable service. The traditional reference desk is a great source of frustration for everybody. It is based on a fantasy that we can serve everyone all the time. The new service does not profess to serve everyone. It serves those who were left by the wayside at the traditional reference desk—the bewildered novice who needs broad instruction in library use and the advanced researcher who has multiple and complicated questions. These are people that librarians are most especially equipped to help. It is not cost-effective to use librarians to answer directional and quick information questions on the off-chance that a question may be substantive. The priority for librarians should be to answer those questions only they can answer.

The fatal flaw in the design of the traditional reference desk is the philosophy behind it, that is, serving all of the people, all of the time. This philosophy has blinded us to something social scientists who have studied the reference interaction have noted, that is, the reference interaction is a complex, intellectual interaction not unlike that between a lawyer and a client or between a doctor and a patient. Yet the setting is far from conducive to such an interaction. Most social scientists, who have studied the reference interaction, have been amazed by it. Here is one's description.

> Typically, the reference librarian is stationed near or behind a counter or desk in the so-called reference section of the library . . . Her duties require the re-ference librarian to sit or stand at her professional position with an open and inviting but not too daffy look on her face. The pur-pose of this stance is, of course, to invite the library patron to initiate a verbal interchange that is the starting point for the professional service making up the reference librarian's raison d'etre.[9]

He goes on to note that unlike other professionals the librarian must establish the professional relationship with the other person under a severe restriction of time while also being limited to a chance condition of meeting in public. The fact that professional library service succeeds at all is amazing.[10]

In my view the success of this new service model suggests the profession has overstressed user accessibility to the librarian to the detriment of user needs and the most judicious use of professional librarians. User accessibility to the librarian is almost a sacred cow as strongly advocated by 20 year veterans as new library school graduates. Yet there is no convincing evidence in existence to suggest why this should be such an overriding service value. Advocates of user accessibility protest that this model acts as a barrier. This is an interesting argument because they are assuming that the traditional reference desk is not a barrier. I would argue that the people who use the research consultation service were not served at the traditional reference desk. Yet these people have the greatest need of the expertise of a librarian.

I would agree that this model does not provide 100% accessibility. However, there will never be enough librarians to answer all the questions library users may have. This model can at least claim to provide the highest quality service with the most judicious use of staff.

Endnotes

1. Peter Hernon and Charles R. McClure, *Unobtrusive Testing and Library Reference Service* (Norwood, N. J.: Ablex, 1987), p. 3-4.
2. Barbara J. Ford, "Reference Beyond (And Without) the Reference Desk," in *Energies for Transition: Proceedings of the Fourth National Conference of the Association of College and Research Libraries Held in Baltimore, MD, April 9-12, 1986*, ed. Danuta Nitecki (Chicago: Association of College and Research Libraries, 1986), p. 179.
3. Thelma Friedes, "Current Trends in Academic Libraries," *Library Trends* (Winter, 1983): 467.
4. Mary Biggs, "Replacing the Fast Fact Drop-In With Gourmet Information Service: A Symposium," *Journal of Academic Librarianship* 11 (May, 1985): 68-69.
5. William Miller, "What's Wrong With Reference: Coping With Success and Failure at the Reference Desk," *American Libraries* (May, 1984): 321.
6. Jeffrey W. St. Clair and Rao Aluri, "Staffing the Reference Desk: Professionals or Nonprofessionals?" *Journal of Academic Librarianship* 3 (July, 1977): 151.
7. Joan Durrance, "Reference Success: Does the 55 Percent Rule Tell the Whole Story?" *Library Journal* 114 (April 15, 1989): 32-35.
8. Thelma Friedes, op. cit., p. 467.
9. Thomas Lee Eichman, "Speech Action in the Library," in *Linquistics and the Professions,* edited by Robert DiPietro (Norwood, N. J., Ablex, 1982), p. 256.
10. Thomas Lee Eichman, Ibid., p. 256.

Subject Specialists and Library Needs of the Undergraduates: Are They Compatible?

Rebecca Schreiner-Robles
Janet Dagenais Brown
Margaret Fast
Wichita State University
Wichita, Kansas

Abstract

To reflect a university in transition from a teaching to a research institution, the Library at Wichita State University recruits librarians who possess an MLS and a second master's or PhD to fill their subject specialist positions. Over time, this practice of emphasizing credentials and research needs of faculty began to overshadow the needs of the library's traditional teaching programs of reference and bibliographic instruction geared mainly to the undergraduate student. This paper describes how the library made a conscious decision to reaffirm the teaching values of reference and bibliographic instruction by restructuring the reference department to create two new positions dedicated to these two programs. The positive impact these positions have had on the programs of the reference department are presented.

Introduction

In her 1983 article in *Library Trends,* Thelma Freides argued that, among other things,

> ... the earlier trend toward subject specialization has given rise to concern that energy and attention may be drawn away from the mundane activity of answering questions at the reference desk .... This in turn opens some puzzling questions about priorities in reference work and the efficacy of traditional practices.[1]

Nearly a decade after Freides' article was published, Wichita State University library, which has traditionally used subject specialists to serve at a general reference desk, has grappled with some of these same questions about priorities in both its reference and bibliographic instruction programs. Unfortunately, Freides' statement finds little echo within the library field as a whole. A literature review yielded few references on medium-sized academic libraries that are trying to serve both undergradutes and graduates with the same facility, collection, and personnel. For many years at Wichita State University library, subject specialists in the reference department have been responsible for both general reference service and undergraduate bibliographic instruction, as well as subject-specific collection development, faculty liaison, and graduate-level bibliographic instruction. Over time,

the library began to realize that this structure was not placing enough emphasis on the research needs of the undergraduate through the teaching programs of reference and bibliographic instruction. With no new money for positions, the library made some hard choices when positions became vacant and hired a reference specialist and a bibliographic instruction librarian instead of subject specialists. What are the challenges these librarians face? Has the reference department achieved a balance between the teaching programs of reference and bibliographic instruction which primarily target the undergraduate, and the collection development programs which emphasize services to faculty and graduate students? This paper describes the problems that led to the decision to create these new positions, and how they have improved the library's reference and bibliographic instruction programs.

Background

The Wichita State University library is a medium-sized academic library of 900,000 volumes which supports a program of 61 undergraduate degrees, 43 master's degrees, and 8 PhDs in areas of math, chemistry, psychology and engineering. The school enrolls 15,779 students, 13,100 of which were undergraduates in 1991. Non-traditional students are in the majority: one-third of all students are married, 52 percent work full or part-time, and the average student age is 28. In addition, 300 senior citizens are currently enrolled.

The reference department in the library was created and the subject specialist model was adopted in the early 1970s. Currently eight subject specialists are responsible for collections development, faculty liaison, on-line searching and bibliographic instruction for specific subject areas. They also staff a busy general reference desk and participate in a growing bibliographic instruction program for freshman English and speech communication students. In fiscal year 1991, librarians answered 75, 298 questions at the reference desk and gave 368 bibliographic instruction classes and tours.

These subject specialists report to two department heads: the head of reference and the coordinator of collection development. Until recently, the department also had two non-tenure track, part-time, general reference librarians who performed general reference, freshman bibliographic instruction, on-line searching and managed collections in subject areas for which the department had vacant subject specialist positions. The support staff for the reference, bibliographic instruction and on-line searching programs consists of one departmental secretary and about 40 hours of student assistance per week. The department has never had paraprofessionals or library assistants.

The head of reference position turned over in 1980, 1981, 1984, 1988 and became vacant again in 1989. In 1989, three internal candidates from the reference department interviewed for the acting head of reference position. During these interviews, the library administration began to hear concerns about the reference and bibliographic instruction programs.

The Wichita State University

Student Characteristics

Fall 1991

Enrollment

Undergraduate	13,100	Full-time students	7,711
Graduate	2,679	Part-time students	8,068
Total	15,779		

Numbers of Degrees Offered   **Number of Students by Degree**

Bachelor	61	Bachelor	11,993
Masters	43	Masters	3,644
Doctorate	8	Doctorate	142

Age of Students   **Ethnic Origin**

Ages		Afro-american	795
16 - 21	4,808	Hispanic	416
22 - 34	7,589	American Indian	154
35 and above	3,379	Asian	406

| **Residential Students** | 635 | **Single Students** | 10,764 |
| **Commuter Students** | 15,144 | **Married Students** | 5,015 |

Student Employment

10 - 19 hours	2,310
20 - 39 hours	4,785
40 hours or more	4,410

Lack of Support Staff

The effectiveness of the librarians in the head of reference position had always been hampered by a lack of support staff. The head of reference position is largely an administrative position involved in meetings, and responsible for personnel evaluation, budgets, capital equipment, and scheaduling the reference desk. The head of reference was unable to delegate some of these responsibilities since the department had no paraprofessionals and only one secretary who supported all eight of the reference librarians in the department as well as the head of reference. The head of reference was only rarely able to focus on projects which could directly improve the reference or bibliographic instruction programs. One subject specialist in the department described the ongoing problem of lack of management of these programs as "benign neglect."

Effectiveness of Bibliographic Instruction Program Questioned

The library administration also heard concerns about the freshman English and speech bibliographic instruction program which had remained static for several years. The librarians questioned the effectiveness of the one-shot, fifty minute, lectures which they had been delivering for years to freshmen in this program. There was no coordination between the library lectures given to the two different departments and some students heard the same lecture two or three times in their academic careers. Other students didn't receive library orientation at all since it was up to the teaching assistant for that course to request a presentation from a librarian. The bibliographic instruction program did not have goals, objectives, or even a particular philosophy.

In addition, the limited human resources of the reference department were strained by increasing requests from area high schools for library presentations. At a time when the librarians needed to focus on the bibliographic instruction program for the university's students, the department was fragmented by heavy demands from high schools. In fiscal year 1991, high school classes and tours increased by over 150 percent.

Conflict between Teaching Programs and Collection Development/Research

A number of factors contributed to a change in attitude towards reference on the part of the subject specialists. Between 1986 and 1989, the university was under the leadership of a vice-president of academic affairs who had a mandate to guide the university from a teaching university to a research institution. At the same time, the library recruited a new coordinator of collection development with high standards for collection development. In addition, over the years, the department gradually recruited more and more librarians who possessed a second master's degree or PhD in addition to the MLS to fill the subject specialist positions. Research became more important as librarians began to go for promotion in addition to tenure. The qualifications and expertise required of these librarians was a reflection of the university's efforts to empahsize research and specialization. Over time, serving undergraduates at a "general" referenced desk came to be viewed as an activity that did not make the best use of the subject specialists' credentials.

Another factor that exacerbated the problem was of two part-time, non-tenure track, temporary librarians to fill in at the reference desk when positions were vacant. These temporary librarians, who had the MLS and, frequently, more years of experience that the subject specialists, were not required to have the second Masters or PhD degree and were truly "generalists." The temporary librarians traditionally spent the majority of their time at the reference desk, giving the impression to the subject specialists, over the years, that the more hours one had on the desk, the less status one had and the less academic credentials one needed. An attitude developed that reference desk service represented one's position in the departmental hierarchy rather than a valued part of one's job. Where did this leave reference service?

Solutions: A Change in the Organizational Structure

Within a year after the new head of reference was appointed in 1989, the library created the reference specialist position out of the two part-time positions. The requirements for this new position were an ALA-accredited degree and a sound knowledge of reference services and tools. The position description emphasizes reference as this person's "subject specialty." The person in this position is responsible for the administration and evaluation of the reference program. These responsibilities include: development of the general reference collection such as encyclopedias, directories, almanacs and other types of reference sources that cut across the disciplines; supervision of student assistants responsible for shelving and filing looseleafs in the reference area; evaluation of reference service through surveys; development of user aids; and participation in the bibliographic instruction programs.

In 1989, the humanities librarian position became vacant and was replaced by a new "bibliographic instruction librarian" position. Both the head of collection cevelopment and the new head of reference were committed to evaluating and strengthening the freshman bibliographic instruction program and they convinced the library administration to make that change. This decision had a direct impact on the collection development program. The head of collection development decided that the department could afford to take the departments in the humanities and turn them over to the history/political studies librarian and consolidate that position into the humanities/history librarian.

When the library searchead for a Bibliographic instruction librarian in 1990, the requirements were, along with an ALA accredited MLS, a sound knowledge of bibliographic instruction theory and methods through experience in an academic library, or through additional education. The job description refers to the dual role of the bibliographic instruction librarian who is expected to divide time between reference and bibliographic instruction. The bibliographic instruction librarian is responsible for the development, administration, coordination and evaluation of the bibliographic instruction program with primary emphasis on undergraduates and the community.

The new reference specialist and bibliographic instruction librarian positions are now filled. The 1989 and 1991 organizational charts of the reference department illustrate the changes that were made. The reference specialist and bibliographic instruction positions are the only two positions in the department that place primary emphasis on reference and bibliographic instruction.

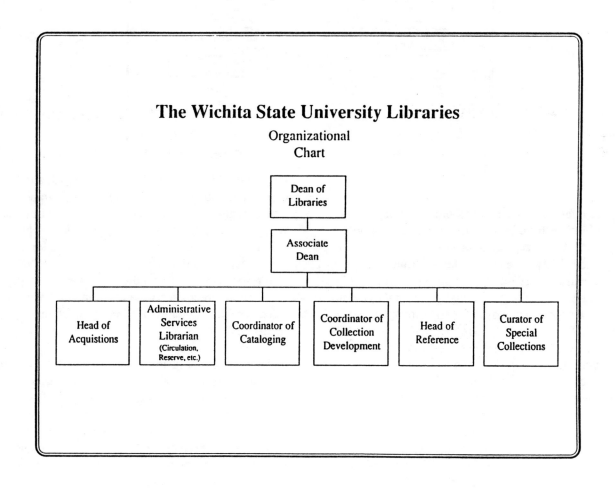

The Wichita State University Libraries

Organizational
Chart

Dean of
Libraries

Associate
Dean

| Head of Acquistions | Administrative Services Librarian (Circulation, Reserve, etc.) | Coordinator of Cataloging | Coordinator of Collection Development | Head of Reference | Curator of Special Collections |

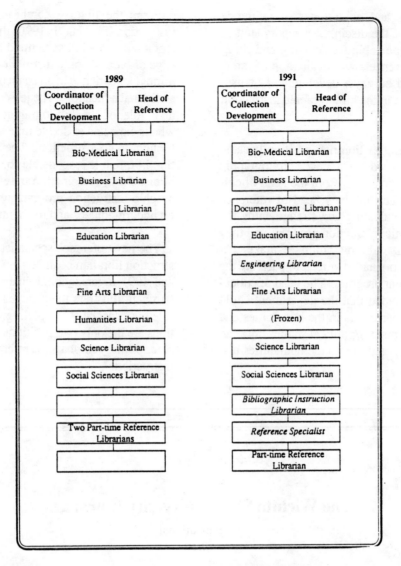

1989	
Coordinator of Collection Development	Head of Reference

- Bio-Medical Librarian
- Business Librarian
- Documents Librarian
- Education Librarian
-
- Fine Arts Librarian
- Humanities Librarian
- Science Librarian
- Social Sciences Librarian
-
- Two Part-time Reference Librarians
-

1991	
Coordinator of Collection Development	Head of Reference

- Bio-Medical Librarian
- Business Librarian
- Documents/Patent Librarian
- Education Librarian
- *Engineering Librarian*
- Fine Arts Librarian
- (Frozen)
- Science Librarian
- Social Sciences Librarian
- *Bibliographic Instruction Librarian*
- *Reference Specialist*
- Part-time Reference Librarian

Implementation

The reference specialist and bibliographic instruction librarians have been in the department for over a year and the success of their positions can now be evaluated. They have been in the department for over a year and the success of their positions can now be evaluated. The reference specialist and bibliographic instruction librarian assumed their responsibilities in June and September of 1990 respectively. The first six months were spent in definition of both these positions. Everyone in the department, including the head of reference was confused about the roles these two librarians were to play in the department. Since, in theory, the head of reference had always been administratively responsible for the reference and bibliographic instruction programs, the roles of these three positions became blurred, especially in regards to personnel evaluations. For example, the bibliographic

instruction librarian is in charge of evaluating the effectiveness of the undergraduate bibliographic instruction program but does not evaluate the librarians who participate in the programs. The head of reference still does the tenure and salary evaluations for all the librarians in the department. The reference specialist is also responsible for recommending ways to improve quality of reference service, but again, it is the head of reference who evaluates the librarians who serve at the reference desk.

Another role confusion came up between the subject specialist and each of the two new positions. For example, the reference specialist was viewed as someone who was to be responsible for anything procedural having to do with reference. If a volume needed to be transferred of of reference, librarians would frequently bring the item to the reference specialist to take to the cataloging department rather than taking it themselves.

353

The job description has recently been revised to delineate which areas of the reference collection are the responsibility of the subject specialists and which are the responsibility of the reference specialist. The subject specialists also had the mistaken notion that the bibliographic instruction librarian would not only administer the bibliographic instruction program, but take on a lion's share of the classes as well.

One benefit of this clarification of roles is that the subject specialist are getting the message that reference and bibliographic instruction are important in the department. They have learned that these positions are not filled by individuals who will simply relieve them of reference and bibliographic instruction duties. Rather, reference and bibliographic instruction are programs which are so important that they each needed a librarian to administer and evaluate them. For example, the bibliographic instruction librarian has developed a program designed to instruct high school teachers and librarians how to teach their own students skills for using the university library. This was not just intended to relieve the subject specialists of high school tours but to allow them time to focus on instruction for the university community. She has also received a university instructional development grant earmarked for the creation of library handouts and a new library workbook. She currently chairs a departmental committee charged by the head of reference to seek ways to improve the bibliographic instruction program.

The reference specialists has made improvements in the library's reference service. For example, a number of years ago, as a way of cutting expenditures, the decision was made to cancel all standing orders, many of which were general reference items. Since no one in the department was directly responsible for collection development of reference materials of a general or interdisciplinary nature, this very vital part of the collection became out-of-date over the years and hampered the librarian' ability to give good reference service. The reference specialist ordered new editions of encyclopedias and put important directories and almanacs back on standing order.

The reference specialist wrote new and detailed job descriptions for the student assistants employed in the reference area, giving them direction and establishing clear expectations. The reference specialist also created signage for the reference area and updated the user aids for the reference collection and computer systems. The reference specialist and bibliographic instruction librarians worked together to develop new user aids for use at the reference desk and in bibliographic instruction classes.

The reference specialist has begun to evaluate reference service through a "problem log" which tracks both patrons" and librarians' problems or complaints about how the reference area is functioning, and she intends to conduct a user survey to better identify what our users need from the reference librarians at the reference desk. The bibliographic instruction librarian conducted an evaluation of instructors and students involved in the freshman bibliographic instruction program. The evaluation data is presently being compiled for an assessment program.

Conclusion: Did it Work

Although the original intent for the positions was that they be devoted solely to reference and bibliographic instruction, due to frozen position in the department and turnover that goal has not realized. The bibliographic instruction librarian performs collection development for the modern languages department and the Reference Specialist was responsible for the women's studies collection. In spite of these added responsibilities to their positions, our conclusion is that they have improved the reference and bibliographic instruction programs. We still have no new support staff and the head of reference is still unable to delegate many of the administrative details of the position. Therefore, without these new positions, many of the improvements in the reference and bibliographic instruction programs described above would not have taken place.

Many questions remain. With these two positions in place, has the department achieved a balance between the teaching programs of reference and bibliographic instruction and collection development? The majority of the people who participate in these programs are still subject specialist who divide their time between general reference and bibliographic instruction, on the one hand, and collection development in specialized areas including working with graduate students and faculty on the other. Each subject specialist must serve two constituencies: the faculty/graduate student and the undergraduate. Is it possible for them to be all things to all people? Are their time and loyalties too fragmented? The reference specialist and bibliographic instruction librarians clearly serves the needs of the undergraduate through the teaching programs of reference and bibliographic instruction which target the undergraduate. with only two librarians out of ten in the department primarily serving the undergraduate, is it enough?

The answer is "No." The fact remains that the majority of students coming to the reference desk are undergraduates. This is not surprising given the fact that there are 13,100 undergraduates who generate 70 percent of the total credit hours at Wichita State University. The head of reference and the coordinator of collection development are beginning to discuss with the library administration taking the reorganization of the department to its logical conclusion: creating a small core of subject bibliographers whose primary function is collection development and faculty liaison, and another core of reference librarians who would be responsible for reference and bibliographic instruction only. Recently, the library administration recommended to a university-wide planning committee line items for an additional general reference librarian in FY 1994, an additional bibliographic instruction librarian in FY 1996, and an increase in clerical and student hours. If this plan is adopted, in the near future, undergraduate students will be served by a group of librarians committed solely to undergraduates reference and instructional needs.

Endnote

1. Thelma Freides, "Current Trends in Academic Libraries," *Library Trends* 31 (Winter, 1983): 457-474.

Selected Bibliography

ACRL Undergraduate Librarians Discussion Group and the ULS Steering Committee, "The Mission of a University Undergraduate Library: Model Statement." *College & Research Libraries News* 48 (October, 1987): 542-44.

Marie Angela Bastiampillai and Peter Havard-Williams, "Subject Specializatio Re-Examined." *Libri* 37 (September, 1987): 196- 210.

Evan Ira Farber, "College Libraries." In *Education for Professional Librarians,* edited by Herbert S. White,. White Plains, N.Y.: Knowledge Industry Publications, 1986, p. 49–65.

Thelma Freides, "Current Trends in Academic Libraries." *Library Trends* 31 (Winter, 1983): 457-74.

Fred J. Hay, "The Subject Specialist in the Academic Library: *A Review Article." Journal of Academic Librarianship* 16 (March, 1990): 11-17.

Thomas J. Michalak, "Library Services to the Graduate Community: The Role of the Subject Specialist Librarian." *College and Research Libraries* 37 (May, 1976): 257-65.

Maurine Pastine and Bill Katz, *Integrating Library Use Skills into the General Education Curriculum.* (New York: Haworth Press, 1989).

Charles D. Patterson and Donna W. Howell. "Library User Education: Assessing the Attitudes of Those Who Teach." *RQ* 29 (Summer, 1990): 513-24.

Malcolm Quinn, "User Education in Academic Libraries: A Review of Recent Developments." *Journal of the Hong Kong Library Association* no. 7 (1983): 35-47.

Anne F. Roberts, "Training Reference Librarians Using Library Instruction Methods." *Reference Librarian* no. 10 (1984): 67-74.

Scott Stebelman, *Characteristics of Public Service Staffing at ARL Libraries.* (Washington, D.C.: National Institute of Education, Educational Resources Information Center, 1981). ERIC ED 220 090.

Carla J. Stoffle, "A New Library for the New Undergraduate." *Library Journal* 115 (October, 1990): 47-51.

David C. Taylor, "Undergraduates' Use of Periodicals—Implications for Library Reference Work." *Reference Librarian* no. 27/28 (1990): 51-65.

Pat Timberlake, et al., *Library Services to Undergraduates. Final Report.* (Washington, D.C.: National Institute of Education, Educational Resources Information Center, 1989.) ERIC ED 322 901.

Relevance Judgments in Computer Searching

Elizabeth S. Smith
Penn State University
Erie, Pennsylvania

Abstract

This study addressed the question of whether relevance judgments are objective. ERIC documents retrieved in full text record format were evaluated for relevancy by three experienced searchers using the binary system of judgment, relevant, irrelevant. The criteria for relevance were presence of correct descriptors or terms in the correct context within the abstracts or titles. Among the statistics obtained were three mean precision scores, one for each judge, and analysis of variance comparing the three means. The results showed that differences in relevance judgments were significant, reinforcing the notion that relevancy is subjective, in spite of objective criteria for judging. The urgency for users to perform and evaluate their own searches is great.

Introduction

Since the inception of online searching in the early 1970s relevance and precision have been of major interest to those in the field. The concept of "relevance" is closely associated with the concept of" precision". Precision is defined as the accuracy of the output and frequently expressed in ratio or percent. Precision is the relationship between the number of relevant documents retrieved and the total number of documents retrieved. It is expressed by the following formula:

$$\text{Precision} = a / (a + b) \times 100$$
(Expressed as percentage)

where a = number of relevant documents retrieved; and b = number of nonrelevant documents retrieved

To calculate precision ratio it is first necessary to determine whether a document is relevant or not. Chamis describes two types of relevance.[1] One type of relevance is objective. Documents are judged relevant if they contain terms or descriptors in the abstracts or titles which are within the correct context of interest, and are meaningful and responsive to the querry.

The second type of relevance is subjective. In addition to having the same criteria as the objective type of relevance, it also involves a value judgment on the part of the user who determines whether or not a document fulfills his/hers information needs. Within this interpretation, a perfectly relevant document in terms of its content's relation to the search strategy, may or may not be pertinent to the user's needs. For example, foreign language documents may be relevant in terms of their contents, however they are useless unless they can be read and understood by the user. Others may have already been seen by the user, or the source of the documents may be unacceptable, or some other reasons may cause documents to be inappropriate and useless. These value judgments are based on tangible or intangible variables specific to the individual.

In the early days of computer searching most searches were delegated. An information seeker submitted a request to a librarian or a professional searcher, who, upon consultation with the user, developed the search strategy, performed the search and provided the user with the finished product. The delegated searcher tries to make relevance judgments objectively, making decisions based on presence or absence of index terms within the context of interest. It is assumed that subjective elements and value judgments which influence relevance decisions are not present in delegated searching.

In the 1980s several factors contributed to end user searching. The growth of microcomputer technology, the outreach to end users by database producers with systems such as KI, BRS After Dark, and STN, as well as the development of CD-ROM technology, all permitted end users to begin doing their own searching.

End users judge their retrieval objectively as well as subjectively. They determine whether a document is relevant or not, based not only on the presence of certain terms within the correct context, but also on value judgments that guide their relevance decisions and determine whether a document is useful or not.

Lancaster states that in a delegated search the precision ratio is a valid measure of the accuracy of the retrieval. In a non-delegated search, where one makes relevant decision along the way, precision ratio becomes less meaningful.[2]

Various precision studies[3] under different conditions have shown the precision range in online searching to be between 42% and 70%. In Lancaster's evaluation of MEDLARS, he found that the average precision for 300 offline searches, which were performed by trained searchers was 50%.[4] Other studies[5] indicate the average precision to be 63% based on 45 searches conducted by biomedical specialists. Half of the biomedical specialists doing the searches had no experience with computer searching, and the other half used it only once or twice. Kiewitt found mean descriptor precision ratio on the ERIC database to be 54.8%, and natural language precision ratio to be 42.0%, attributing the natural language searches to obtaining higher recall and smaller precision.[6] Recall, also expressed as ratio or percentage is the relationship between the number of relevant documents retrieved, and the total number of relevant documents in the collection.

It is important to remember that 100% precision in searching is improbable if not impossible, even with the best searching techniques. This is because neither the indexing of documents nor Boolean approach to searching is perfect. The searcher is dependent on, and restricted by, factors beyond his/her control.

Research Question

The research question in this study is whether relevance judgments of documents by experienced searchers are truly objective when made within strict guidelines of objective criteria. Specifically, will there be differences in relevance judgments of the same documents made by different judges using objective criteria? If so, will the differences be statistically significant, indicating that relevance judgments, in spite of objective criteria are not completely objective, but incorporate value judgments based on variables specific to individuals.

Methodology

Fifteen education majors with no prior knowledge of online searching completed a computer tutorial on basic search strategies for online searching using Boolean. When finished, each student was then given three requests for searches on education topics selected by the researcher in the form that is usually provided by the person seeking the information (Appendix). The students were asked to formulate the appropriate search statement for each request using natural language and Boolean Operators. Each student provided three search statements so that there were 45 search statements in all. The statements were input into the ERIC database by the researcher the way they were received, using the DIALOG Information System. Format 5 which is the full record format that includes the abstract was requested, and the PRINT command was used to obtain citations offline. All searches were limited to 10 citations so that the total would not exceed 450 citations.

The results of each student's three searches were evaluated for relevancy by the researcher and two other experienced searchers using the binary system of judgment—relevant, (yes), irrelevant, (no). Relevancy was determined by objective criteria, that is the presence of correct terms within the context of interest in the abstracts, and/or presence of correct descriptors and identifiers as previously described.

The following statistics were obtained: precision for each search by each student; mean precision for each student; mean precision for each search; mean precision for the group. This was done for each judge. The percent of judgment agreement was calculated which determined how closely the three judges agreed on whether the documents were relevant or irrelevant. This was done for each document retrieved. The percent of judgment agreements was calulated for the number of documents on which three judges agreed, as well as the number of documents on which two judges agreed. This was accomplished by adding the number of documents on which three or two judges agreed (two separate figures) and dividing each number of agreements by the total number of documents, which is the total number of possible agreements. A comparison was also made between the mean precision of the group and acceptable precision scores recorded in the literature.

The analysis of variance (ANOVA) was conducted to compare the three different group precision means obtained by three judges. The obtained F Ratio determined whether significant (true) differences were present among the three different precision means being compared, or whether the differences were due to sampling error. Because the obtained F ratio was larger than the table value at .05 level of confidence, indicating significance, a comparison between the precision means obtained by the three judges was made. Tukey's HSD (honestly significant difference) multiple comparison method was used to determine where the significant differences were.

Results

Altogether there were 404 documents retrieved by the three search statements by 15 students. Individual scores for each search by each student and mean precision for each search as judged by each judge are shown in Tables 1. The three group mean precision scores for the three judges were 55.8%; 49.3%; and 41.5% and shown in Table 2. The anaysis of variance between the three precision means is summarized in Table 3. The obtained F ratio (variation between groups divided by the variation within groups) was 3.23. It was compared to a table value with 2 and 42 degrees of freedom. Table F was 3.22 at .05 level of confidence at df 2/42; and table F was 5.15 at .01 level of confidence at df 2/42. The obtained F ratio of 3.23 was less than the table value of 5.15 at .01 level of confidence, and slightly more than table F of 3.22 at .05 level of confidence at df 2/42.

Tukey's calculated HSD (honestly significant difference) was 13.58 at .05 level of confidence, 40 df, and 3 means and was compared to the precision differences between the means (Table 4.) The precision differences of 14.3 between X1 and X3 was greater than HSD of 13.58, indicating that this mean difference is statistically significant at the .05 level of confidence. The other two precision differences of 7.8 and 6.5 are smaller and are not significant.

The Judgment Agreements yielded data which is shown in Table 5. Out of the 404 documents evaluated by the three judges, 321 (79.5%) were unanimously agreed upon, and the remaining 83 (20.5%) were agreed upon by two judges. Out of the 321 documents, 179 or 55.8% were judged to be relevant, and 142 or 44.2% were judged to be irrelevant. From the 83 documents which two judges agreed upon, 33 or 39.8% were judged relevant, and 50 or 60.2% were judged nonrelevant.

Analysis of Findings

The precision range obtained by people in the field under different conditions has been shown to be between 42% and 70%. In this study the mean precision scores of 55.8%, 49.3% and 41.5% obtained by the three judges compare favorably with precision scores described in the literature.

Analysis of variance compared the three precision means of the group obtained by three judges, to see if the differences in judgments were significant, representing true differences in the population, or whether they were due to error. The F ratio in this study is a comparison between the variation (distance) of the three group means from one another, referred to as "variation between groups", and the distance of precision scores from their group mean, known as "variation within groups". In this F ratio, the numerator represents variation between the three different group precision means obtained by three judges, and the denominator represents the estimate of variation within these groups, that is the distance of any precision score from its group mean. The results show that the variance between groups was larger than the estimate of variance within groups, (numerator = 756; denominator = 233.6), giving a larger F ratio, thus creating greater probability that the differences between the judges are real.

The obtained F ratio of 3.23, when compared to the table value of 3.22 at .05 level of confidence, and the table value of 5.15 at .01 level of confidence, at 2/42 degrees of freedom (Table 3) shows to be slightly larger than the table value of .05 level of confidence, but smaller than .01 level of confidence. These figures indicate that there is a significant difference, between the three means obtained by three different judges at .05 level of confidence but not at .01 level of confidence.

The level of confidence, whether .01 or .05, is a level of probability at which one can accept with confidence the research hypothesis. In this study the research question is whether differences in relevancy judgments between judges are statistically significant and represents real population differences or are they due to sampling error. In other words, .05 level of confidence means that 5 times or less out of 100 (5%) the obtained sample difference will occur by chance, while 95 times our of 100 (95%) the difference will be true, statistically significant, a product of real population differences.

Table 1

Comparison of Individual Precision % for Each Search
by Each Subject by Three Judges

Judge 1 Search			Judge 2 Search			Judge 3 Search		
#1	#2	#3	#1	#2	#3	#1	#2	#3
71	0	90	71	0	80	71	0	60
0	70	100	0	50	100	0	40	100
80	40	0	90	30	0	80	40	0
80	70	90	90	30	80	80	10	60
10	70	90	10	50	90	10	40	60
0	70	0	0	30	0	0	10	10
0	70	50	0	50	50	0	40	50
0	70	100	0	50	100	0	40	100
0	70	90	0	50	70	0	40	60
80	70	90	90	30	90	80	40	60
80	40	90	90	30	90	80	40	60
80	70	0	90	50	0	80	40	0
0	70	90	0	50	90	0	40	60
71	70	90	71.4	50	80	71	40	60
0	40	100	0	30	100	10	10	100

Mean Precision % for Each Search

36.8	59.3	71.3	40.1	40.0	68.0	37.4	31.3	56.0

Table 2

Comparison of Group Mean Precision % for Each Search

by Each Subject by Three Judges

Subject	Judge 1	Judge 2	Judge 3
1	53.6	50.3	43.6
2	56.6	50.0	46.6
3	40.0	40.0	40.0
4	80.0	66.6	50.0
5	56.6	50.0	36.6
6	23.3	10.0	6.6
7	40.0	33.3	30.00
8	56.6	50.0	46.6
9	53.3	40.0	33.3
10	80.0	76.6	60.0
11	70.0	70.0	60.0
12	50.0	46.6	40.0
13	53.3	46.6	33.3
14	77.0	67.1	57.0
15	46.6	43.3	40.0

$\overline{X} = 55.8$ $\overline{X} = 49.3$ $\overline{X} = 41.5$

Table 3

Analysis of Variance of Three Precision Means

Obtained by three Judges

Source of Variation	df	SS	MS	F
Between Groups	2	1512	756	3.23
Within Groups	42	9814.6	233.6	

Table F at .05 level of confidence = 3.22 at df/42

Table F at .01 level of confidence = 5.15 at df/42

****

Table 4

Comparison of Differences Between Means

Against Tukey's HSD

$\overline{X1}$ = 55.8 $\overline{X2}$ = 49.3 $\overline{X3}$ = 41.5

	$\overline{X3}$ = 41.5	$\overline{X2}$ = 49.3	$\overline{X1}$ = 55.8
$\overline{X3}$		7.8	14.3
$\overline{X2}$			6.5
$\overline{X1}$			

HSD (Honestly Significant Difference) = 13.58

Table 5

Three and Two Judge Agreements

(Numbers in parenthesis indicate 2 Judge Agreements)

Subject	Search	Relevant Citations		Non-Relevant Citations		Total/Grand Total Citations		
1	1	5	(0)	2	(0)	7	(0)	7
	2	0	(0)	0	(0)	0	(0)	0
	3	6	(2)	1	(1)	7	(3)	10
2	1	0	(0)	0	(0)	0	(0)	0
	2	4	(1)	2	(3)	6	(4)	10
	3	10	(0)	0	(0)	10	(0)	10
3	1	8	(0)	1	(1)	9	(1)	10
	2	3	(1)	6	(0)	9	(1)	10
	3	0	(0)	10	(0)	10	(0)	10
4	1	8	(0)	1	(1)	9	(1)	10
	2	1	(1)	3	(4)	4	(6)	10
	3	6	(0)	1	(1)	7	(3)	10
5	1	1	(0)	9	(0)	10	(0)	10
	2	4	(1)	2	(3)	6	(4)	10
	3	6	(2)	1	(1)	7	(3)	10

TABLE 5 CONTINUED -- Three and Two Judge Agreements

6	1	0	(0)	10	(0)	10	(0)	10	
	2	1	(2)	3	(4)	4	(6)	10	
	3	0	(0)	10	(0)	10	(0)	10	
7	1	0	(0)	10	(0)	10	(0)	10	
	2	4	(1)	2	(3)	6	(4)	10	
	3	5	(0)	5	(0)	10	(0)	10	
8	1	0	(0)	0	(0)	0	(0)	0	
	2	4	(1)	2	(3)	6	(4)	10	
	3	10	(0)	0	(0)	10	(0)	10	
9	1	0	(0)	10	(0)	10	(0)	10	
	2	4	(1)	2	(3)	6	(4)	10	
	3	6	(2)	1	(1)	7	(3)	10	
10	1	8	(0)	1	(1)	9	(1)	10	
	2	4	(1)	2	(3)	6	(4)	10	
	3	6	(2)	1	(1)	7	(3)	10	
11	1	8	(0)	1	(1)	9	(1)	10	
	2	3	(1)	6	(0)	9	(1)	10	
	3	6	(2)	1	(1)	7	(3)	10	

TABLE 5 CONTINUED -- Three and Two Judge Agreements

12	1	8	(0)	1	(1)	9	(1)	10
	2	4	(1)	2	(3)	6	(4)	10
	3	0	(0)	10	(0)	10	(0)	10
13	1	0	(0)	0	(0)	0	(0)	0
	2	4	(1)	2	(3)	6	(4)	10
	3	6	(2)	1	(1)	7	(3)	10
14	1	5	(0)	2	(0)	7	(0)	7
	2	4	(2)	2	(3)	6	(4)	10
	3	6	(0)	1	(1)	7	(3)	10
15	1	0	(0)	9	(1)	9	(1)	10
	2	1	(2)	6	(1)	7	(3)	10
	3	10	(0)	0	(0)	10	(0)	10

_____

Totals	179	(33)	142	(50)	321	(83)	404
	55.8%	(39.8%)	44.2%	(60.2%)	79.5%	(20.5%)	

The obtained F ratio of 3.23 at .05 level of confidence which is larger than Table F of 3.22 indicates that differences in judgments between the three judges are statistically significant and represents real population differences. The significant F ratio indicates that there are real overall differences among judges who determine whether or not documents are relevant. This is not the case at .01 level of confidence, where the obtained F ratio of 3.23 is smaller than Table F of 5.15.

The comparison of precision mean differences between the judges to the calculated HSD of 13.58 shows that the precision difference of 14.3 between X1 and X3 was greater than HSD of 13.58. (Table 4) This indicates that the difference between the high precision mean of 55.8 by one judge and the low of 41.5 by another judge is statistically significant at the .05 level of confidence. The other two precision differences were smaller and are not significant.

Almost 80% of documents judged were unanimously agreed upon by three judges, of which approximately 56% were judged to be relevant and 44% irrelevant. It shows that the three judges agreed more on documents being relevant than on documents being irrelevant. The opposite was true of two judge agreements, where approximately 40% of agreed documents were judged relevant and 60% were judged irrelevant.

Conclusions

This research focused on the question of relevance of documents as measured by precision. It utilized precision ratios of 45 delegated searches which were evaluated for relevance by three judges using the binary system of judgment. The criteria for relevance were presence of correct descriptors or terms in the correct context within the abstracts or titles of documents.

The difference between two out of the three group mean precision scores (low of 41.5 and high of 55.8) was statistically significant indicating that real population differences in relevancy judgments do exist in spite of guidelines and specific prescriptions for judging. All three judges were experienced searchers, the guidelines for judging were clear and specific, yet the differences in their relevancy judgments were significant. Why? Further research in this area is needed before any conclusions can be reached. However, the study does show that relevance judgments are based not only on objective criteria, but are in part subject to individual attributes and qualities which may or may not be apparent. Also, the fact that three judges agreed more on documents being relevant than irrelevant, which was not the case with two judge agreements, is interesting and worth investigating.

The results of this research reinforce the notion that relevancy judgments are complicated and subjective phenomena, contingent on known and unknown variables which play important roles in the judgment process. The results show that relevance is subjective to some degree, even under the most stringent guidelines of judging. What is relevant to one person may not be relevant to another. Based on these results it is logical to encourage end users to perform and evaluate their own searches whenever possible. When users search and browse the databases themselves, they make relevance judgments based on their knowledge, needs, and other intangible factors specific only to them. There is nobody between them and the stored information to misjudge the results of the search or to misinterpret their information needs. In addtion, there are also the positive feelings of self sufficiency, independence, privacy, convenience, and control. None of these are possible with intermediaries.

It is important to remember that with the availability of end user systems such as KI, STN, BRS After Dark, as well as the growing number of CD-ROMs found in academic libraries, end users must be given the necessary help for searching when needed. It is also essential that end users be taught how to transfer their knowledge of one database to another, or one CD-ROM product to another. This necessitates not only teaching searching skills, but also the principles and the concepts of searching. The teaching function of librarians, thus, is urgent and timely, and the educational functions of librarians are enhanced by end user searching.

Endnotes

1. Alice Yanosko Chamis. Online Database Search Strategies and Thesaural Relationship Models. (Doctoral Dissertation, Case Western Reserve University, Cleveland, Ohio, 1984).
2. Frederick Wilfred Lancaster, *Information Retrieval Systems: Characteristics, Testing and Evaluation.* 2nd ed (New York: John Wiley & Son, 1979).
3. Kiewitt, Eva L. (1979). *Information Storage and Retrieval Systems.* The Probe Program. (Westport, Connecticut: Greenwood Press, 1979); F. W.

Lancaster. "Evaluation of the MEDLARS Demand Search Service; (Bethesda. MD: National Library of Medicine, (1986 ERIC document ED 022494); Frederick Wilfred Lancaster. "Evaluation of Online Searching in MEDLARS (AIM-TWX) by Biomedical Practitioners," (Urbana, IL: Graduate School of Library Science, University of Illinois, 1972). ERIC ED 062989; Katherine W. McCain, Howard, and Belver C. Griffith. "Comparing Retrieval Performance in Online Data Base," *Information Processing and Management* 23 (1987): 539-553.

4. Frederick Wilfred Lancaster, "Evaluation of the MEDLARS . . . ," op. cit.

5. Frederick Wilfred Lancaster, "Evaluation of On-line . . .," op. cit.

6. Eva. L. Kiewitt, op. cit.

Appendix

Search Request

Now that you have gone through the tutorial, please formulate a Search Statement for each request below. You can ask me any questions you wish about the meaning of the search.

Search Request #1: I would like as much information as possible on how I can utilize the business community to help support our school activities.

Search Request #2: I need some articles on group activities for adults, but I don't want to have anything that will include activities for the senior citizens.

Search Request #3: Please find some information on the evaluation of teachers in the State of Florida. I am looking for information published in the 1980s.

Selectivity: A Focus for Excellence

Raghini Suresh, Barbara F. Schloman, and Jeffrey N. Gatten
Kent State University
Kent, Ohio

Abstract

In a period when technology is making new services and new methods of information access a reality, academic libraries must overcome the restrictions of limited fiscal resources and turn to innovative ways of capitalizing on their strengths. Strategic planning focused on selectivity of clientele offers a means for libraries to chart a course with vision, priorities, and maximized fiscal resources. The Kent State University Libraries are implementing a model for excellence in library services designed for such a selected constituency.

The Problem

Growth and stability in higher education are being affected by the current economic downturn. Within academic libraries we are keenly aware of the pressure on materials budgets to maintain collections at adequate levels. Less frequently discussed is the stress being placed on library services as well. Paradoxically at a time when technological developments are making new services and new methods of information access a reality, staffing levels for user services are among those being reduced. Therefore, the problem is that, while there are more opportunities to deliver higher-end services than ever before, it is difficult to capitalize on these capabilities with limited fiscal resources.

Selectivity: The Solution

As in other academic libraries, Kent State University has been involved in a strategic planning process to enable the libraries to better marshal resources toward focused objectives. A major theme of our planning process has been that of "selectivity," which is in keeping with the University's planning. Dr. Carol Cartwright, the University's nw president, stated this spring that Kent must analyze those things it does very well, and invest in the future by focusing on those strengths. This process could be painful because Kent may have to stop doing some things in order to do others better.

One objective of the Libraries' strategic plan is to provide outstanding services and collections to selected academic departments—departments which represent the University's areas of emphases. This, assumes that a basic level of library support will continue to be provided to all students and faculty. Recognizing that selectivity could present a politically sensitive situation, the Libraries have drawn upon a tiered ranking of academic departments provided by the University administration.

The Libraries use this ranking to select top-ranked departments to work with in the design and delivery of specialized information services. It is believed that exceptional information support to these units will demonstrate the role the Libraries can play in enabling the University to achieve excellence in designated areas. The expected outcome is that demonstrated success with selected departments will generate additional funding to expand the services to other academic units.

Selectivity, then, is seen as a means for an academic library to experiment with new services, to determine the costs and benefits, and to garner support to initiate change on a broader scale in its overall programs. This paper presents the experience to date: selecting, planning, administrative commitment, a phased model of implementation, and user response.

Operationalizing Selectivity

Last year the National Science Foundation announced a multi-million dollar award to Kent for the establishment of a Science and Technology Research Center to investigate the optical properties of liquid crystals. The Advanced Liquid Crystalline Optical Materials research center, or ALCOM, is a consortium arrangement with two other universities (Case Western

Reserve University and the University of Akron). Kent, with its Liquid Crystal Institute, serves as the flagship. Private industry interested in the commercial applications of the research will have a strong association with ALCOM through a membership program.

ALCOM, then, provides an ideal opportunity for the Libraries to test selectivity as it applies to offering specialized services. We believe that enhanced information support will significantly contribute to the success of ALCOM and, at the same time, provide high visibility for the Libraries.

Models of Information Management and Networking

A working group was formed to do necessary ground work and to draft a plan of action. It was comprised of the Head of the Chemistry-Physics Library (the primary resource library for the researchers of the Liquid Crystal Institute), the Head of Collection Management, and the Head of Reference and Information Services. The first course of action for the working group was to review the literature and to contact librarians serving other NSF Research Centers. Discussions were also held with researchers from the Liquid Crystal Institute to determine what information needs were most immediate.

From this, an array of services were outlined that, when fully implemented, would establish a Liquid Crystal Information Center. The vision was that researchers will be able to identify and gain access to any book, journal article, patent, proceeding, or report in their specialized areas of interest, regardless of an item's location, format, cost, or language.

INFORMATION MANAGEMENT FOR LIQUID CRYSTAL INSTITUTE

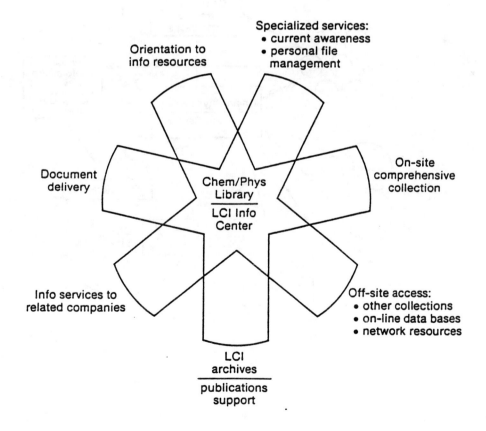

368

In order to meet this model for excellence, a library would need to address all of the following: the delivery of information in a timely fashion with the understanding that traditional interlibrary loan does not adequately meet the critical needs of these particular researchers; individualized orientation to a wide range of information resources and services; provision of current awareness services to keep researchers apprised of new developments in their areas; individualized assistance with managing personal research files; the building of comprehensive collections as well as identifying comprehensive collections at other locations and institutions; ready access to online databases and

INTERNET resources; establishing an archive of the research output from ALCOM; delivering support for publication of research findings; and, finally, furnishing information services to the private industry members of ALCOM.

Next, the working group mapped the relationships that would need to be in place for an information network to function. The Liquid Crystal Information Center would serve as the hub. Included are on-campus constituents, consortium members, and industrial associates, as well as connectivity to information resources in various forms.

INFORMATION NETWORK FOR LIQUID CRYSTAL INSTITUTE

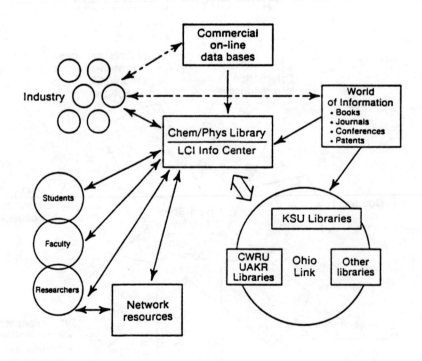

Test Case for Specialized Services

Once these two models were developed, a test was conducted with one researcher from ALCOM. His routine request for information was given priority service. An immediate online search on his topic was followed up with consultation to review and select the articles of primary interest. Sixteen of the twenty-six requested articles were available in our collections. These were photocopied and delivered along with copies of abstracts for those items that could not be obtained the same day. Rush processing was requested for one book that was in the cataloging unit at the Main Library.

Four items held by area libraries were requested by telephone and FAX deliveries were received the very next day. The remaining items included one Japanese and one German patent which were ordered from Chemical Abstracts Document Delivery Service and arrived by Federal Express in less than 24 hours. Thus, within approximately 2 working days, the researcher had copies of all the documents in hand.

Administrative Commitment

Based on the preliminary planning and this one test case, the Dean of Libraries and the working group met with the director of ALCOM and a faculty representative. Presented were three scenarios describing services that could be available as the proposed Information Center developed.

The plan received overwhelming approval and offers of support from the director of ALCOM—not only to help meet the charges incurred for the services and document delivery, but also to assist with any future grant writing in support of the services. The Dean of Libraries was prepared to increase the staffing levels in the Chemistry/Physics Library and to provide some new equipment.

Phased Implementation

Presently, a three-phased implementation is planned. Phase One will focus on providing ALCOM researchers with services such as current awareness, online searching, regular updates, document delivery, and access to translation services—each as efficiently and quickly as possible. Some costs, such as photocopying and a portion of online searching, will be absorbed by the Libraries. Other costs, such as for commercial document delivery services, will be charged to ALCOM.

Researchers will be interviewed to identify specific information needs and individualized research profiles will be established. Regular online searches will keep them alerted to recent articles and patents of interest. Ongoing personal contact will ensure services are provided in a timely manner. The science libraries of the three ALCOM consortium universities will work closely to facilitate resource sharing.

Phase Two will turn to collection building. Both the monograph and serial collections will be evaluated based on faculty research needs and be developed into a comprehensive research collection in the area of liquid crystalline optical materials. The proposed archives will include all faculty publications, annual reports of the Institute and related centers of research. Once appropriate security measures have been established, personal lab notebooks and other proprietary information will be stored on optical disk and be indexed for easy access. An orientation program for LCI's international faculty will be implemented.

Phase Three will establish contact and provide cooperative access to collections located worldwide in academic and industrial institutions engaged in similar research. An annual comprehensive bibliography on liquid crystals will be compiled and made available electronically. The industrial associates affiliated with ALCOM will be offered fee-based information services.

Commitment to Plan Amidst a Fiscal Crisis

Shortly after implementing the initial stages of the demonstration project, an interesting turn of events occurred. Ohio, like many other states during Spring 1991, experienced a serious budgetary crisis. Kent had to return three percent of the current budget to the state, and an immediate hiring freeze was implemented. The hiring freeze hit the Libraries particularly hard, with eight critical positions vacant. However, because of the strategic plan and commitment to the establishment of a Liquid Crystal Information Center, the Libraries stayed the course. Despite severe staffing problems created by the hiring freeze, staffing was increased in the Chemistry-Physics Library by one full-time clerical assistant and ten hours of additional professional time. This was accomplished by reallocating staff from other library departments that were not key to the strategic plan. For example, the archivist was temporarily reassigned to the reference department, in part so that an experienced online searcher from reference could be released to do searching in the Chemistry-Physics Library. Units in the technical services areas were downsized to free a staff member for reassignment to the Chemistry-Physics Library.

Conclusion

In a period when technology is making new services and new methods of information access a reality, academic libraries must overcome the restrictions of limited fiscal resources and turn to innovative ways of capitalizing on their strengths. Strategic planning focused on selectivity of clientele offers a means for libraries to chart a course with vision, priorities, and maximized fiscal resources. Reaching toward the vision will require the Libraries to take responsibility to offer more than is expected and to overcome existing access barriers.

The result of our efforts should be a high profile of the Libraries working in partnership with the premier research center on campus and a demonstration to the University administration of the degree to which librarians can contribute to excellence in higher education. It is hoped that this will, in turn, result in increased recognition and fiscal encouragement to apply these models to other academic departments.

CONTRIBUTED PAPERS

VII.
TECHNOLOGY

Dynamics of Interface Design and Development

Dennis A. Norlin, Elizabeth R. Cardman,
Elisabeth B. Davis, Rae Ann Dossett,
Barbara Henigman, William Mischo, and
Leslie Troutman
University of Illinois
Urbana-Champaign, Illinois

Abstract

Provides reflection upon and analysis of the human dynamics that guided an interface design project.

The Need for an Interface

The University of Illinois at Urbana-Champaign Library (UIUC) purchased the BRS/SEARCH software in June, 1990, in order to provide library users with access to locally mounted periodical index databases. The Library uses IBM microcomputer workstations as public access terminals in the online catalog and BRS/SEARCH environments. This workstation approach provides a convenient platform for the design and development of customized microcomputer interface software for a variety of information resources, including the online catalog, BRS/SEARCH databases, and other information resources on campus and national networks.

Shortcomings in the BRS MENTOR mainframe interface and the desirability of using the workstation capabilities of the PC were factors in the decision to develop and implement a microcomputer-based interface to the BRS software and associated databases. The Interface Design Subcommittee's charge was to design and implement the interface components for the Library Information Workstation, a microcomputer public terminal that provides access to local and remote online catalogs, periodical index databases, campus information resources, and information files stored on the microcomputer. This paper focuses on the design of the interface to the BRS/SEARCH software and ancillary periodical index databases—initially Current Contents, six Wilson databases, and ERIC.

The Process of Design: The Human Factor

Hardware and software alone are not responsible for the outcome of an interface design process; the interplay and exchange among members of the design team is a significant factor in shaping the final results. Most analyses of interface design, however, focus exclusively on the technical results of the process, evaluating the final system's utility, efficiency, and effectiveness.

When the Interface Design Subcommittee met for the first time it quickly became clear that significant differences existed among the participants in their academic backgrounds, professional experience, computer literacy, and perception of typical library users. This group of nine academic librarians soon found themselves embroiled in a whole range of controversial issues.

Over the course of the year that followed Subcommittee members resolved a number of significant issues through reasoned argument and impassioned plea. Participants realized early in the process that the process itself was extremely important. Small groups of two or three gathered to work out agreed-upon language for screens already designed or to experiment with different color combinations that would be eye-catching without producing eye strain; a larger group labeled themselves "non-techies" and began to hold separate meetings at which they wrestled with the use of library jargon or with the complexity of the screens presented to inexperienced users.

By the end of the year the "techies" had rejoined the "non-techies" and the Subcommittee had reached resolution on many of the issues that had initially divided them so sharply a year before. Reflection upon and analysis of the human dynamics that guided the Illinois interface design project may be helpful to libraries and librarians about to embark upon a similar project.

Early Focus on Users and Tasks

From the beginning the librarians' familiarity with their primary users was invaluable in discerning the way patrons could use and respond to the proposed interface. Librarians who served primarily undergraduate students were concerned about library jargon, design complexity, and the kind and amount of online help available; librarians who worked primarily with graduate students were concerned about search strategy and capability, retrieval precision, and efficiency. Librarians who worked primarily with faculty or in a research institute were concerned with providing sophisticated search strategies without overwhelming faculty users and with providing appropriate help without appearing to be condescending.

Designing an interface that would be suitable and useful for these varied groups would require compromise and thoughtful planning. In the course of the discussion certain commonly held assumptions were stated and challenged: "If undergraduates can get their ten sources, they don't care what they are"; "graduate students are going to want to print out every possible reference they can find"; or, "faculty are not going to have the patience to go through three screens of help information before they can enter their search." The presence of librarians representing each of these varied groups was very helpful in challenging and/or reinforcing these assumptions. Because the librarians involved had long-term day-to-day contact with patrons they were able put themselves in the place of their typical user.

Empirical Measurement

Gould and Lewis emphasize "actual behavioral measurements of learnability and usability, and conducting those experimental and empirical studies very early in the development process."[1] It was determined that the only way to measure those qualities was to observe actual users interacting with the system. As soon as there was a working prototype, Subcommittee members installed the interface at their libraries and invited a wide variety of users to try it. Rather than rely on walk-in users exclusively, library support staff and graduate assistants were encouraged to use the system.

Information was obtained by asking users for their response to the interface, by observing them using it, and by helping them when they ran into difficulty with the system. Each time a substantively new version of the prototype was developed, it was installed and reactions to it secured.

Iterative Design

Some Subcommittee members had been involved previously in design projects wherein a design document was carefully developed and then was followed rigidly. Almost inevitably that approach to designing online interfaces is doomed to failure because so many glitches, unforeseen outcomes, and questions evolve during the process that cannot be anticipated even in the most thorough and carefully prepared design document.

From the beginning the approach was iterative. The responses and observations obtained through testing were brought before the Subcommittee and discussed; subsequent changes to the interface were partially based on these debates. Since all members of the design team were faculty at the same institution, it was possible to avoid the contractual and procedural problems that so often frustrate iterative design. Gould and Lewis see those problems as inherent in the employment of an outside contractor:

> When one is an outside contractor (rather than in an internal system development organization), it is often difficult to get a customer to sign a contract that includes the flexibility required in iterative design. There is, typically, insistence, we are told, on a two-stage 'preliminary design' and 'final design' hierarchy, with schedule rigidity that often precludes proper accommodation of usability tests results. Ignoring the need for iterative design is perhaps even more disastrous here since geographic remoteness may further reduce required communication and observations needed to obtain good usability.[2]

Throughout the design process, the UIUC Interface Design Subcommittee relied upon these three principles to analyze, propose, debate, and revise ideas for the new interface. A great deal of time was spent with users studying their responses to the various stages of the interface development; empirical measurement was employed to test our hypotheses about users and use; there is continuing revision of wording, screen design, screen flow, the level of complexity, and countless other aspects of the new interface as it continually grew more usable and powerful.

Level of Search Assistance Desired/Provided

The development of search assistance is an ongoing process, with some issues yet to be resolved. From the start, guided assistance has been an integral part of the overall design of the interface. For example, the committee agreed that, despite an extra window on the screen possibly contributing to a "cluttered" look, the explanation box was an important element of the interface design. This box appears whenever one scrolls through the list of menu options; it clarifies the function of a given menu selection. The design Subcommittee devoted a significant amount of time to editing these boxes to be certain that they contained language free from library jargon and guided users toward the most pertinent selection in their search strategy.

Another feature over which the committee deliberated was the display of a screen that explains how to break down a search request into discrete concepts and then identify synonyms for each concept. This descriptive screen is displayed the first time a keyword or phrase search is selected. Regardless of the searcher's skill, the screen appears and requires depressing the enter key to continue the actual search. Many regular users may become frustrated with this additional keystroke, but the majority of the Subcommittee members believed that most patrons' infrequent use of the system would justify the automatic display of this explanatory box in every session.

A more obvious application of user assistance is the design of help screens. The Subcommittee held a number of animated discussions on the philosophy of help screens. Ideas promulgated ranged from the highly specific context-sensitive help screen to the generic tutorial or an online 'table of contents' to help information.

For the UIUC Interface Design Subcommittee debate over the help facility is on-going. Should help be available for every situation? Should there be an overview of the system, or a tutorial? How many situations require context-specific help? Previous research findings will be combined with empirical testing to answer these fundamental questions.

Conclusion

The UIUC Interface Design Subcommittee sought to create a product that is both utilitarian and graceful in design. Early on, the human factor—the interaction of each members' personality, intelligence, skill, and commitment—was recognized as exerting a significant influence on the deliberations. Following the lead of Gould and Lewis, the Subcommittee placed an early focus on users and tasks; stressed the necessity of empirical measurement, and sought to perfect the product through the principles of iterative design.

The Subcommittee acknowledged the absence of any pat solutions to the problems presented by interface design. The organization of the design-team, following the structured consensual model, enabled the Subcommittee to approach the design problems in an efficient, yet creative and flexible manner.

The Subcommittee's methodology involved the use of rapid prototyping with a user interface management system. A menu-approach was selected for the mode of interface interaction, to be used in conjunction with sophisticated windowing techniques.

A wide variety of issues emerged during the design process. These included questioning each subcommittee members' basic assumptions about the abilities and needs of the user population; the level of search assistance desired and provided by the interface; and, specific issue such as color, printing options, displays, truncation, and system speed versus desirable features.

There will be no final version of this interface; continual and regular updates are anticipated as it adapts to new users, new functions, and new data. However, Subcommittee members are fully cognizant of the fact that these changes must be presented in a way such that the searcher is not faced with a radically new interface each month or that colleagues, struggling with the challenges of bibliographic instruction, are not forced to continually revise instructional materials and teaching methods. It will be a delicate balance.

Endnotes

1. John D. Gould and Clayton Lewis, "Designing for Usability: Key Principles and What Designers Think," *Communications, ACM* 28 (March, 1985): 302.
2. John d. Gould, Ibid., p. 305.

An OPAC for Every Public: Customizing the Catalog for Individual Researchers' Needs

E. Paige Weston
University of Illinois
Chicago, Illinois

Abstract

Historically, online public access catalog interface designs have been compromises, meeting most of the needs—intellectual, pedagogical, æsthetic, and emotional—of most of their users most of the time. Research has shown that individuals differ (by age, gender, discipline, etc.) not only in the way people sort, store, annotate and use the data they retrieve from an OPAC, but in the way they look for it and in the way they prefer it to be displayed on the screen. This paper presents a hypothetical (yet practicable) model for an easily personalizable interface to an online public access catalog.

Years ago, a few months after the University of Illinois at Chicago's online catalog became available on the academic network, university librarians were approached by an established, productive, and technically savvy member of the teaching faculty who wanted to download every single record he might ever someday want (everything under certain subject headings, everything by certain authors, everything from certain presses, and everything in certain LC classifications) in order to create, *and own,* his own personalized catalog. We talked him out of it. Our arguments had to do with the data (what would he do about updates?) and with the storage (why should he pay to store data the library was already committed to storing?). He acquiesced, but he was disappointed. His disappointment had to do with the interface, and with a thwarted desire—a basic, human, emotional need—to control his own environment. I've been feeling guilty, ever since.

A comfortable human-machine interface is, in fact, a very personal thing. In 1989 Darrell Jenkins published a report on the struggle, in Illinois, to design a generally acceptable, mainframe interface to the statewide bibliographic resource-sharing system. He called his article, "Everyone Wants One . . . a Slightly Different One."[1] The interface to an online public access catalog is one of the most important human-machine interfaces in the life of an academic, more important in the long run than, say, the interface to an automatic teller machine, even though the academic may use the ATM much more frequently. The fact that many library system vendors are now providing "customizable"

OPAC interfaces, and that many more individuals across the country are, nevertheless, hard at work on microcomputer front ends to these customized mainframe OPAC interfaces, illustrates how strong the urge is, now that the technology is available, to seize control of our own information retrieval environments.

In recent months Public Access Computer Systems Forum (PACS-L) has been the marketplace for a lively debate on what characteristics make the best OPAC interfaces. "It might be better to show a 'normal' catalog record first and ask users if they want to see contents etc., or perhaps show record and contents and ask if they want to see a description,"[2] says one participant. "Ranganathan could have been convinced: for each OPAC its own display, for each display its own OPAC,"[3] says another. Both contributors' remarks must be read in the context of the discussion's underlying assumption: one database has one OPAC interface.[4] But compelling research findings[5] in recent years confirm what we have known all along and have not dared to admit: different people prosper with different kinds of interfaces, so one single interface, no matter how customized for the local population of users, will never be as successful as many personalized, or personalizable, interfaces, for individual users.

Of course, for the foreseeable future libraries will still need to design a single, standard, best-possible-compromise interface to their OPACs, because I would argue that one standard look for the OPAC is desirable on all public in-house terminals. Moreover, segments of the local population may not have the mainframe account or the microcomputer equipment they would need to support a personal interface. Remote users dialing in from the suburbs or TELNETing from across the country may not have enough invested in using the database to bother with profiling, or personalizing, their access. (This argument cuts both ways, however: users with only a short-term need for a database are less likely to want to spend time learning the peculiarities of a remote host's standard, and may prefer using the personal interface they use locally to using a Command Command Language. Z39.50 and projects like the NOTIS PACLINK are a ray of hope for those who think this way.) The chief reason, though, for not abandoning our efforts to design a best-possible-compromise interface is that novice users will still need a starting point: a suggested, or default interface. Options that second-time users choose among, when personalizing their interface, should be options designed by those who know the database, and information retrieval, the best: librarians informed by the iterative process of giving users options, and seeing which options users take. Kristina Hooper offers an extended analogy between interface design and architectural design. She writes,

> ... the architectural example shows us that flexibility in personalization may not necessarily provide adaptable systems. One may want to rely on expert judgments of a best system as a first approximation, making changes available from this base level. One might want to prevent the *moving of walls,* for example, but encourage the *rearrangement of furniture.*[6]

How do we support personalizable interfaces? First we remind ourselves of what users have told us they want to control. Then we design models. Mock-ups of a personalizable interface are included below. Set-up must be easy for the user. Products like HyperCard for the Macintosh offer interface building blocks for quasi-programmers. We need to offer OPAC building blocks for non-programmers.

Users want options for:

• Telecommunications. This is obvious. Dial-up users need choices among supported baud rates, terminal types, etc. Support for these options is already fairly well in place across the country.

• Search entry mode. Some users like a menu-driven interface, others like a panel-driven one.

Research has shown that a graphical interface is best for some personality types and learning styles. For more experienced searchers, there's always command mode.

• Controlled vocabulary. Users should be able to maintain an online thesaurus that would complement the library-supported controlled vocabulary. A personal interface would link a user's own cross-references, or her own aliases for, say, Library of Congress terms or combinations of terms, to authority records stored centrally (and inviolate).

• Retrieval display mode. Many different products offer post-processing of search results, to massage and sort them into whatever display format the user requires or is most comfortable reading. Why not build this flexibility into the OPAC itself? We could offer ISBD or catalog-card-style, labeled displays (with pop-up menus of optional/alternative labels?), *Chicago Manual of Style* style, Modern Language Association style, *Science* style, and, of course, a custom style which might be a modification of any of the above, with the option to rearrange or suppress data elements, change labels or punctuation, etc. If users publish articles in journals that follow the *Chicago Manual of Style,* and read books and journals that follow the *Chicago Manual of Style,* then *Chicago* style citations will be most familiar to them. Scanning a familiar, comfortable format, they should be able to pick out needed data elements more readily.

• User-enhanced data. Bibliographic, holdings, and piece data are stored centrally. Evaluative data need to be linked from diverse sources. A user's personal interface could link catalog records to personal annotations, such as, "Worthless," "Remember to put on reserve for course 357," "Good plate on p. 20 for overhead transparency," "Mentions Aristotle's Poetics in chapter 3," etc. The personal interface should be able to search the annotations as readily as the catalog—for instance when the time came to prepare the reserve list for course 357.

• Data export. Users want to send results to local printers, remote printers, to disk, or to somewhere else, via file transfer or electronic mail. Moreover, they want control over what parts of the search results get sent, and in what format.

The following are examples of what screens from a personalizable interface might look like. They are for discussion purposes only. They are not taken from a working model.

A Preferences panel (Illustration 1) might allow the user to select the search and display mode that suits her best. It is likely that once preferences had been recorded, the user would not return to this screen. On the other hand, the user might prefer a panel-driven interface, say, when she is looking for known items, but a graphical interface when she is looking for materials on a faceted subject about which she knows very little.

An OPAC for Every Public: Customizing the Catalog for Individual Researchers' Needs

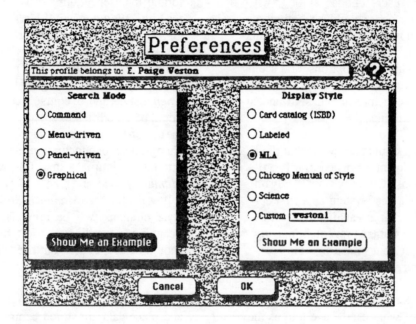

Illus. 1

379

To facilitate the user's choice of search or display mode, the Preferences panel might include some simple examples. Illustration 2 shows what such an example might look like. Text above the diagram would explain briefly how graphical searching works, and what its strengths and weaknesses are. Lengthy explanations should be unnecessary, because, ideally, changing search modes should be easy enough that the user could simply make her selection, connect to a database, and try a few searches to see how search mode functions.

A personal interface might keep track of several custom display modes (illustration 3). To create a new display mode (illustration 4), the user might modify one of the preconfigured modes supported by the local library. The "Suppressed Data Elements" field in the example is a strategy for reminding users of the elements in a MARC record which they will not be seeing if they choose a leaner format. With this in mind, also, OPAC displays might include a prompted command or a button to toggle between a brief (user-defined) and a longer (library-defined) display.

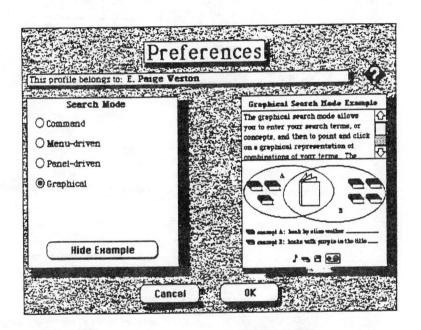

Illus. 2

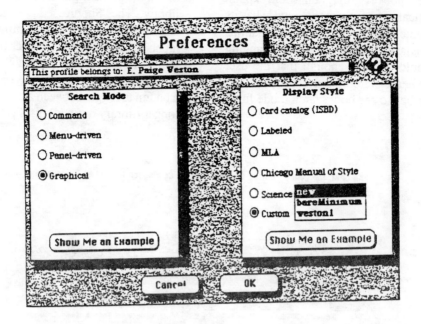

Illus. 3

Custom Display Set-Up

Format name: new   Adapted from: MLA-style for a translation

Dostoyevsky	,	Fyodor	.	*Crime and Punishment*	.	Trans.
Jesse Coulson	.	Ed.	George Gibian	:	New York	:	Norton	,
1964	.

Discussion: Click on a data element or piece of punctuation in the model on the left, to read here what it is, and how it is used

Instructions: use your mouse to alter type styles of data elements, to rearrange them, or to drag them to or from the list of "suppressed data elements." Use your keyboard to alter punctuation, abbreviations, etc.

Suppressed data elements: Format Language Call number

Cancel   OK

Illus. 4

An OPAC-proper search screen (illustration 5) might include a button to return to the Preferences panel. In addition, it might support commands (whether in buttons, pull-down menus, or pop-up menus) to search a thesaurus, or enhance the thesaurus with personally-meaningful cross-references or post-coordinated terms; to select another database; to record or retrace a recorded search strategy; and to annotate a retrieved record or to search for annotations in a "comments" window.

These examples are intended to remind us, now that our years of experience with designing interfaces, and our volumes of data on users' information-seeking behavior have all begun to point, ineluctably, to the need for personalized interfaces, that we do in fact have a solution. The technology is emerging to support personalizable OPAC interfaces. Technical obstacles that examples here have glossed over can be overcome.[7] These examples are intended to remind us that our efforts should be spent bringing our systems a step

An OPAC for Every Public: Customizing the Catalog for Individual Researchers' Needs

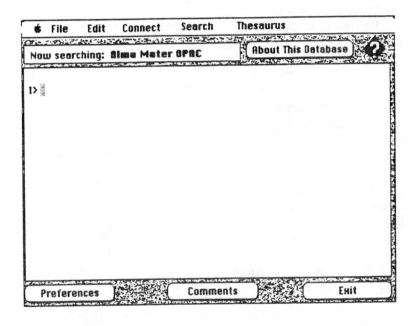

Illus. 5

or two closer to the users, rather than the users a reluctant step closer to our systems.

Endnotes

1. Darrell L. Jenkins, *Everyone Wants One . . . a Slightly Different One: The Process of Introducing a User Interface System into an Online Public Access Catalog Network,* (ERIC ED 324 027).

2. PACS-L posting item # 3563, dated 91/05/26 17:38:46, from STEPHEN@IS.CITY.AC.UK.

3. PACS-L posting item #3466, dated 91/05/09 16:36:47, from PAPAKHI@IUBV.UCS. INDI-ANA. EDU.

4. Since this paper was first submitted the PACS-L discussion has turned specifically to personalizable OPAC interfaces. See especially postings by Thom Gillespie, Jim Hobbs, Jim Morgan, and Sanjay Chadha between 16 July 1991 and 29 August 1991.

5. This is a vast literature. One example with a particularly useful review of previous literature is Christine L. Borgman, "All Users of Information Retrieval Systems Are Not Created Equal: An Exploration into Individual Differences," *Information Processing & Management* 25 (no. 3, 1989): 237-251.

6. Kristina Hooper, "Architectural Design: An Analogy," in Donald A. Norman and Stephen W. Draper, eds. *User Centered System Design: New Perspectives on Human-Computer Interaction* (Hillsdale, NJ: Lawrence Erlbaum Associates, 1986), p. 15.

7. See, for instance, PACS-L posting item #4516, dated 91/10/17 14:44:29, from RGATES@ OREGON.

PROGRAM SESSIONS

VIII.
ADMINISTRATION

Program Sessions

The ACRL Sixth National Conference included six types of programming: contributed papers, theme addresses, exhibits, poster sessions, and program sessions. In the latter case topics and the groups presenting them were selected but the exact nature of the sessions was left to the presenters. Some sessions included panel discussions, in others formal papers were presented with reactor panels, while in still others a large portion of the content was audience participation. Therefore the form of the text for the program sessions varies depending on how the participants wished to report their programs. The variety includes an abstract of the program, a summary of the program content, the text of short presentations by panel members or a single talk which was the subject of discussion. In all cases the program participants are listed with each program session. -Editor's note.

Silence is No Longer a Virtue: Telling the Library Story!

Joseph A. Boisse´, Moderator
University of California-Santa Barbara
Santa Barbara, California

Panelists: Patricia G. Schuman, Neal-Schuman Publishers, Inc., New York, New York; Richard M. Dougherty, University of Michigan, Ann Arbor, Michigan; Ann Symons, Juneau District High School, Juneau, Alaska; Margo Crist, Univeristy of Michigan, Ann Arbor, Michigan

Abstract

A discussion by panelists of the year-long promotional campaign launched with the Rally-On-Wheels project, which travelled from Atlanta to Washington, D.C.

Excellence through Shared Perspectives: Understanding Faculty Perspectives of Academic Libraries

Peter V. Deekle
Susquehanna University
Selinsgrove, Pennsylvania

and

JoAnne Young
Bucknell University
Lewisburg, Pennsylvania

Abstract

A comparative analysis of librarian and faculty perspectives of library roles and functions with suggestions on ways to promote cooperation.

Accentuate the Positive, Eliminate the Negative: Don't Mess Around with Accreditation

Carolyn Robison
Georgia College
Milledgeville, Georgia

and

Janice C. Fennell
Georgia State University
Atlanta, Georgia

Abstract

Speakers from two Georgia institutions provide an overview of the regional accrditation process. Article provides information on how to prepare for a self-study, with emphasis on effectiveness and outcomes.

Accreditation is a process with which all academic institutions are involved. The accreditation process does testify that an institution knows what it wants to do, knows how to go about doing it, is in fact, already doing what it says it is, and can be expected to continue to do so in the foreseeable future. In this day and age of assessment and measurement of effectiveness it is vitally important that the accreditation process be demystified. The goals of this presentation are sixfold: 1) to present an overview of the self-study process focused on institutional effectiveness; 2) to review the steps in measuring institutional effectiveness; 3) to describe the self-study process itself; 4) to share some samples of library assessment documents; 5) to describe what to expect from the visiting team; and 6) to respond to questions and concerns about the accreditation process.

When an institution commences preparation for an accreditation visit, consideration of the planning and evaluation process must be given. The planning process must have broad-based involvement of faculty, administration, and students. Every institution must have established a clearly defined purpose appropriate to collegiate education. The educational goals of the institution must be consistent with the institution's purpose. Procedures for evaluating the extent to which the educational goals are being achieved must be developed. And lastly the results of the evaluations must be used to improve institutional effectiveness.

The theme of the program "Accentuate the Positive, Eliminate the Negative" relates to the idea that in addition to helping institutions do what they do better, an emphasis on assessment of effectiveness should help institutional leaders select what they do best as their special purpose. Self-studies should ask not only "What needs improving?" but also "What do we do easily and best?" In relation to the "Elimination of the Negative," a self-study, with appropriate assessment measures, should identify what an organization is doing poorly. The leaders of the organization must then either take steps to improve those things, if essential to the organization's mission, or consider eliminating the negatives, if they are not essential.

It is vital that an organization/institution/library have a statement of purpose. That purpose declares to the world what the organization values and what it is. Some vital attributes of every statement of purpose are clearness of conception (clarity), scope or comprehensiveness, acceptance by faculty and staff, and relation to the activity of the organization. A statement of purpose must be translated into intended results. The assessment process is used to determine how actual results compare to intended results. There are five steps which can be used in measuring or assessing effectiveness. The steps are:

1) Describe the purpose of the institution and develop goals from the purpose statement;
2) Define (specify) the expected observable results needed to achieve the stated purpose;
3) Describe how these results are assessed;
4) Describe the administrative responsibility for conducting the assessment; and
5) Describe the use made of the assessment findings.

Self-study is one of three major forms of external

reviews gauged to assess and certify academic quality; the others are professional society accreditation and state agency evaluation. Self-study is the centerpiece of the regional accreditation process. Most regional accrediting commissions have made conducting a program of self-study a primary obligation of each institution seeking or continuing affiliation with them. Most of the accrediting agencies require that an institution formally examine itself, assess its strengths and concerns, and plan how to capitalize on the strengths and eliminate or alleviate those concerns. In doing so, an institution documents its present effectiveness and its strategies to continue to improve that effectiveness. The vast majority of academic libraries are regularly involved, albeit to varying degrees, in the voluntary, nongovernmental process known as accreditation.

As the Commission on Colleges of the Southern Association of Colleges and Schools states, "the essential purpose [of a self-study is] to improve the educational effectiveness of institutions of higher learning in the south by helping them reassess their goals, measure their success in attaining these goals and explore ways to increase their educational effectiveness."[1] Self-studies can be used for a number of purposes. First and foremost, a self-study will assist an organization in analyzing its strengths and weaknesses, clarifying its goals, programs, resources, and their effectiveness. A self-study, with its recommendations and suggestions, should assist an organization in improving. A better system of on-going institutional research should be an outcome of the self-study. And lastly, the self-study must serve as a foundation for planning and the resulting plan must include systematic evaluation of all aspects of the organization.

Conducting a self-study provides the campus community with a rare opportunity to take a candid, educational look at itself. Ideally, the self-study process should be on-going and dynamic. The entire institution must be looked at, from the top to the bottom. A point to remember is that the self-study is conducted for the institution itself, not for the accrediting agency; it should be objective, critical, comprehensive, and professional. The preparation of a self-study document can develop a sense of cohesiveness among faculty, administration, staff, and student body. On the other hand a self-study is expensive, time-consuming, and can be used simply as a public relations document. It can be a one-time exercise and mean nothing to anyone. That should not be allowed.

Librarians are becoming more heavily involved in the accreditation and subsequent self-study process. Often librarians are named to chair or serve on the campus-wide steering committee and if not on that committee, librarians often serve on a variety of subcommittees and task forces investigating the programs, administration, purpose, fiscal matters, and other academic issues. Librarians must take advantage of such opportunities. Studies have shown that the most successful self-studies have widespread librarian participation.

Whenever academic administrators and faculty engage in serious discussions or write formally about what constitutes quality and excellence in academic institutions, there is inevitably some reference made to the centrality of libraries in determining quality. An issue with which librarians are struggling is the measurement or assessment of the quality of services. Output measures provide objective data on the extensiveness and effectiveness of library services. They quantify library performance in terms of goals achieved and services delivered.

These data give staff and management feed-back on library performance. Outcomes are difficult, if not impossible, to measure. Output measures are concerned with the results achieved, not the effort or processes that go into producing them, nor their effect on the environment. Inputs are commonly and easily measured. Examples of inputs are staff, equipment, materials; examples of outputs are on-line catalogs, answers to reference materials; and finally, an example of an outcome might well be the degree to which library use affects students' learning. That outcome can be used to help the library improve its processes and outputs and obtain resources. Some library services which should be evaluated are user success, overall satisfaction, ease of use, materials availability and use, facilities and equipment availability and use.

Most of the regional accrediting agencies use four types of committees to visit academic institutions. They are the accreditation committee, which looks at an institution to determine if it is ready for initial accreditation; the substantive change committee, which examines the aspect of an institution which is changing its focus; special committee, and the reaffirmation committee, with which this presentation is primarily concerned. The reaffirmation committee has several specific charges. The committee must determine whether or not the institution is in compliance with all of the Conditions of Eligibility, and it must provide to the accrediting agency a professional judgement as to whether or not the institution is in compliance with all applicable "criteria [or standards] for accreditation," and the quality and acceptability of the institution's self-study.

A reaffirmation committee is made up of faculty and staff from peer institutions. Size of the committee can range from approximately five or six to eighteen or twenty depending on the size of the institution. Faculty members, fiscal officers, student affairs personnel, librarians, vice-presidents and presidents all participate. Prior to the visit the committee members are given assignments relating to their area of responsibility. They become familiar with the specific assignment, as well as all of the written materials and information concerning the institution, which is sent to them. Materials may include the self-study report, current catalog, annual reports, application forms, any public relations documents, financial reports, etc. They also receive a schedule of activities for the visit. During the visit they are to review all records, documents noted in the self-study and interview as many faculty, staff, and students as necessary to evaluate the program.

In order to assess the effectiveness of the library, the visiting librarian must have a thorough understanding of the college's purpose and its programs, must view the library operation in the context of the total institutional program and the purpose of the college, must determine whether the self-study reflects the actual library operations and programs, and must clearly understand the total library/learning resources program. The visiting librarian gains his/her knowledge from a variety of sources, for example, the self-study, interviews, observation of library processes, authenticity of statistics, extent to which the library's collections support the curriculum, support given the library by faculty members, and information provided from library annual report, policy and procedures manual, library hand-outs, statistical reports, etc. Faculty and staff at the institution being visited should keep some points in mind. The visiting librarian is a helpful, professional consultant, dedicated to the task of surveying all library services. He/she is part of a team whose role is supportive rather than critical and destructive, and part of a team whose role is to observe, praise, and note strengths and weaknesses through the format of recommendations and suggestions.

The final report of the visiting committee is written in such a manner as to reaffirm that the institution does meet the standards and/or criteria for accreditation. It normally includes "recommendations" which indicate that, in the committee's professional judgement, the institution does not comply with a requirement of the criteria or standards. Recommendations should not be prescriptive. An institution must respond in writing to each recommendation in the committee report. "Suggestions" offer, for consideration by the institution being evaluated, a course of action that the visiting committee feels would improve the educational quality of the institution, even though such action is not necessary in order to comply with the criteria or standards. Although institutions may respond, they are neither invited nor should they feel compelled to respond to suggestions.

Endnotes

1. Commission on Colleges. Southern Association of Colleges and Schools, *Manual for Accreditation,* (Dectur, Georgia: Southern Association of Colleges and Schools, 1989), p. 7.

Access and Ownership: Issues and Financing

Patricia M. Kelley, moderator
George Washing University
Washington, D. C.

Panel Participants: Dora Biblarz, Arizona State University;
Carolyn Dusenbury, California State University;
Deborah C. Masters, George Washington University;
and Daviess Menefee, OCLC

Abstract

Using as a frame of reference their own institutions' responses to growing demands for resources and expanding options for access to research materials, speakers explore the servcice and collections issues and the financial implications of the choices they are making in collections access.

Deborah C. Masters

Scholars' Express is the name Gelman Library at George Washington University (GW) has given to its document delivery service. This presentation covers the factors underlying the decision to create Scholars' Express, budget allocations for collections and collections access. The context of Gelman Library and GW, the demand experienced for journal articles beyond Gelman's own collections and how that demand was met, are discussed as well as experience with commercial suppliers. The experience of the users of Scholars' Express, and how Scholars' Express is marketed are explained.

Like other libraries, Gelman has a materials budget that has not and will not increase at the rate of inflation for books and serials. In particular, escalation in serials costs due to inflation, postal increases, changes in foreign exchange rates and publishers' pricing policies has meant that Gelman Library could not even maintain current serial subscriptions, let alone order new titles. Two successive rounds of deep cuts in serial subscriptions were made, and there was no end in sight. Currently faculty and librarians are reviewing all of the current serials, and more cuts are anticipated. Another factor, however, was the recognition that the journal article rather than the journal itself is the bibliographic entity of importance to scholarly research. Scholars' Express is Gelman Library's conceptual framework for supporting the need to identify and obtain articles

of interest for scholarly research. It is also an early recognition of the concept of "just in time" rather than "just in case" collections, and an attempt to implement "access" rather than "acquisition" as the basic framework for collecting activity.

Gelman's current collections budget is approximately $1.1 million for serials, $.5 million for monographs, and a budgeted amount of $55,000. for document delivery. Projected expenditures of only $15,000 for our Scholars' Express document delivery services are expected this year. As part of the Scholars' Express service the library defined the accessible serials in three tiers: 1) core collection that is owned; 2) titles that fit the collection development policies, but were canceled or never ordered and can be supplied by document delivery suppliers; and 3) titles outside the library collecting parameters that are obtained through traditional interlibrary loan.

GW is a private, urban university with an enrollment of approximately 19,000 students, with a majority of graduate students, many of whom are part-time working students. Both faculty members and graduate students make active use of other area libraries, and local resources are rich and varied, including many government and special libraries, as well as national libraries. Gelman Library supports all academic fields except medicine and law. GW is a member of the Washington Research Library Consortium which continues longstanding cooperative interlibrary loan and priority service to member libraries, plus direct borrowing privileges among member libraries. Beginning the fall of 1990, Gelman offered shared access to bibliographic data on GW collections through an online union catalog, and periodical article databases were added in the fall of 1991.

Growth in borrowing of journal articles occurred especially as a result of the major serials cut in 1988, which was felt dramatically beginning in 1990 when citations in indexes, footnotes, etc. were leading users to issues unavailable at Gelman. The availability of a shared online catalog providing detailed holdings of other Consortium libraries beginning in the fall of 1990 also increased borrowing requests.

Article suppliers used included UMI and ISI The Genuine Article. Users of Scholars' Express have been 60% graduate students, 25% faculty members, 7% undergraduates and 8% staff. These proportions are in part reflective of GW's high proportion of graduate students in its user population, and also of the fact that undergraduate students typically work in a very short turnaround time and can often use alternative sources, so do not go beyond local collections. Faculty members have a number of options in area specialized libraries, so do not necessarily seek material not owned by Gelman through the Scholars' Express services.

Scholars' Express is marketed through handouts and presentations to such groups as the Faculty Senate Library Committee, and to department chairs and library representatives from academic departments. Individual subject specialists promote the service to and programs. In addition, each article obtained through Scholars' Express is delivered with a buck slip indicating that it was obtained through that service. The name recognition on campus for Scholars' Express is reinforced in that way.

The speakers for this program were asked to address several specific questions. Did we use new money to initiate this service? A choice was made to use $100,000 in "new money" from the university that was added to the library's base budget in 1990/91 to move toward an "access budget." This allocation is reviewed as more a reallocation or leveraging of serials dollars to get more for the same money. The components of that allocation for Scholars' Express at that time included: UnCover access, additional CD-ROM databases and staff time, as well as the actual document delivery costs.

What resources were reallocate? In addition to serials dollars reallocated from ownership to access, a part-time classified position was shifted to the Interlibrary Borrowing Unit. The unit absorbed costs of printing and photocopying materials for publicity, and the use of the fax machine and OCLC costs.

What financial and service risks did we have? The position was taken that not purchasing books will result in permanent "damage" to the collections, while serials subscription cuts allow more alternatives to obtain articles on demand, and to reverse decisions through obtaining backfiles on microform or electronic full text storage. A discrete "collections access" budget line was created which can now be used for such related activities as a monthly charge for LEXIS/NEXIS, another means of obtaining full text articles.

Early user experiences were key to the perception of acceptability of "access" vs. ownership. Turnaround time, quality of copy, availability of sources to provide current awareness, etc. are all integral parts of the package if users are to find "access" as good as "ownership." The decision making process has already been addressed earlier. Internal and external constraints and opportunities include the need for data on in-house use vs. data collected on articles obtained on demand. The ability to decide on subscription vs. ordering articles on demand on the basis of cost effectiveness alone is the desired approach. There is insuffcant data on use of in-house subscriptions to do that. There also is the constraint of not being able to capture data on what users obtain elsewhere, not through Gelman.

The Washington Research Library Consortium and other alternatives for scanning, digitizing and imaging documents will increasingly offer new options for fast access. The process of obtaining material need to be more transparent to users. Right now, there are different procedures depending on whether the item is in Gelman Library, the Consortium or outside the Consortium. Ways for the user to use the same process no matter where the item comes from are need and also capability for the user to enter requests remotely. Only then will "access" and "ownership" be truly transparent. One constraint in achieving that transparency is that costs of photocopying and staff to retrieve materials from local collections are not currently paid by the library.

Experience with Scholars' Express has demonstrated

it to be a cost effective alternative to ownership of all relevant serial literature in the context of Gelman Library and George Washington University.

Looking for Clout: National Statistics and How to Use Them

Richard Meyer, Moderator
Trinity University
San Antonio, Texas

Using IPEDS Data in a Statewide and Network Setting: What Worked, What We Threw Out, and What We Didn't Find, William DeJohn, MINITEX Library Information Network
Libraries, Provosts and Clout, Donald M. Henderson, University of Pittsburgh

National Statistics on Academic Libraries: Who Needs Them and Why

Mary Jo Lynch
American Library Association
Chicago, IL

Introduction

The author's interest in library statistics developed fairly late in her career. As an English major in college, numbers didn't much matter. Now they do, and I often remember how angry I was with a professor who once told a class "If you can't count it, it doesn't count."

Later I came across another quote that does appear in print often and explains why statistics are so important. Lord Kelvin, the famous British scientist, once said:

When you can measure what you are speaking about and express it in numbers you know something about it; but when you cannot measure it, when you cannot express it in numbers, your knowledge is of a meager and unsatisfactory kind.

Anyone who watches CNN or reads USA TODAY knows that Americans love statistics, especially when they are displayed in bar graphs or pie charts or maps with different shades of grey or even better four colors.

Why they are needed

I've never seen academic library statistics in either place but if that ever does happen, the figures will probably come from the major collector and distributor of national statistics on academic libraries, the National Center for Education Statistics. NCES is part of the Office for Educational Research and Improvement in the U.S. Department of Education. Every academic library in the country will get a questionnaire from NCES this fall. There is some small print on the cover that clearly describes why these data are collected and for what purpose. To quote.

Purpose of the Survey. The National Center for Education Statistics (NCES) collects these data periodically to provide . . . a comprehensive picture of the status of collections, transactions, staff, service per typical week, and library operating expenditures in postsecondary institutions. This survey is being conducted in compliance with the Center's mission "to collect, and analyze, and disseminate statistics and other data related to education in the United States . . . "

Uses of Data. Collection of these data over time will enable the nation to plan effectively for the development and use of postsecondary education library resources. Congress uses the data to assess the need for revisions of existing legislation concerning libraries and the allocation of Federal funds. Federal agencies need the data to evaluate and administer library programs. State education agencies and college librarians and administrators use the data for regional and national comparisons of library resources . . . . Finally, library associations and researchers use the survey results to determine the status of library operations and the profession.

In addition to the four groups of users mentioned by NCES, three more can be added:

— Journalists (if there's a story that involves academic libraries the American Library Association gets called for figures about collections and budgets and services).
— People who sell products and services to libraries (sometimes these people have no idea what academic libraries have or do).
— People who give money or products to libraries (these people tend to be more knowlcdgcable but they too have questions).

What's Wrong?

There is data available to satisfy those seven groups of seekers, and I'll talk about specific sources in a minute. But first to mention two big problems with the data: quality (it's not good enough) and timeliness (we don't get it fast enough).

With regards to quality, there is another favorite quote. An English judge, commenting on the data received from India, once said:

The government are very keen on amassing statistics. They collect them, add them, raise them to the nth power, take the cube root, and prepare wonderful diagrams. But you must never forget that every one of these figures comes in the first instance from the village watchman, who just puts down what he damn pleases.

There's no denying that the quality of national data depends on the quality of individual reports and there is much to do as a library community to improve what is reported.

A second problem is timeliness. Historians use data that are several years old but most of the people in the seven groups just mentioned want results much sooner.

For several years now a committee of ACRL members has been working with the ALA office of Research and Statistics and with NCES to improve the quality and timeliness of the biennial survey of academic libraries. The project is described in Appendix A.

Sources

There are a number of statistical sources for aca-

demic library statistics which are described below and listed in Table 1. The first source is NCES. There are two important things to know about how NCES collects data from academic libraries.

The library data is collected as a part of system involving several questionnaires sent to institutions. For years that system was called HEGIS (Higher Education General Information Survey). In the late 80's the universe for those questionnaires was expanded to include not only "higher education" institutions (i.e., accredited to offer degrees) but all institutions offering education beyond high school. HEGIS became IPEDS (Integrated Postsecondary Education Data System). Nine questionnaires are part of IPEDS. Some are sent out every year; some are sent out every 2 years. The Library Survey is in the second group.

The second important thing to know about how NCES operates is that questionnaires are not mailed directly to libraries. Rather, sets of questionnaires are sent from Washington to the state higher education authority (board, council, commission) or authorities (in some states responsibilities are split). In most cases the library questionnaires gets to the librarian but that doesn't always happen promptly.

NCES has been collecting academic library data for a long time but the first item on the handout is the 1985 report. Note that the publisher was ACRL. NCES did publish a brief bulletin with national and state summaries of this data. They ran a printout of the library-by-library data but decided not to publish it. ACRL did, but it was not a best seller.

NCES is now committed to collecting academic library statistics every two years. The 1988 report is the first in that series. Each of the 11 tables in the report is subdivided into 8 parts (A-H):

A = All higher education institutions
B = All four year institutions
C = All with doctoral degrees as highest offered
D = All with master's degrees as highest offered
E = All with bachelor's degrees as highest offered
F = Less than four year institutions
G = Public institutions
H = Private institutions

The 1990 report, due out in May, 1992, will follow the same pattern. NCES will not publish library-by-library data though those data will be available in

Table 1. Bibliography of academic library statistical source.

National Statistics on Academic Libraries: Where to Find Them

I.   National Center for Education Statistics (NCES)

    A.   Fall 1985 HEGIS (Higher Education General Information Survey)

        Library Statistics of Colleges and Universities, 1985: National Summaries, State Summaries, Institutional Tables. Chicago: ALA/ACRL, 1987.

    B.   Fall 1988 IPEDS(Integrated Postsecondary Education Data System)

        1. *Academic Libraries: 1988.* Washington: U.S. Department of Education, Offices of Educational Research and Improvement, 1990.

           Eleven tables of data by state and by sector.

        2. *1988 Academic Library Survey Response.* 2 volumes. Boulder, CO; National Data Service for Higher Education, 1990.

           The 1988 IPEDS data for each responding library. Volume 1 has public institutions and Volume 2 has private institutions. Both volumes organized by state.

        3. *Statistical Norms for College and University Libraries.* Boulder, CO: John Minter Associates, 1990.

           The 1988 IPEDS data are used to show the distribution of statistics and ratios by percentiles (from 10%-90%). Every data element in the 1988 report is displayed that way and ratios are created to show relationships between data elements (e.g., salary expenditures as a percentage of total). Additional variables from other IPEDS surveys are also used to construct ratios(e.g., enrollment, finance). Tables are organized using categories established by the Carnegie Foundation for the Improvement of Teaching and published in (*A Classification of Institution of Higher Education.* Princeton, NJ; Princeton University Press, 1987).

II.   National Associations

    A.   ARL: *ARL Statistics.* Annual (in spring)
    B.   ACRL: *ACRL University Library Statistics.* Biennial (in years IPEDS is not done).

machine readable form. That was true in 1988 as well and ACRL considered using it to produce a paper report of library-by-library data similar to the 1985 report. They didn't, but someone else did.

Item IB2 in Table 1 is the library-by-library listing produced by the National Data Service for Higher Education. Item IB3, produced by the same people under a different name, is more useful for comparative purposes.

In item IB3, the 1988 IPEDS data are used to show the distribution of statistics and ratios by percentiles (from 10%-90%). Every data element in the 1988 report is displayed that way and ratios are created to show relationships between data elements (e.g., salary expenditures as a percentage of total expenditures). Additional variables from other IPEDS surveys are also used to construct ratios (e.g., enrollment, finance). Tables are organized using categories established by the Carnegie Foundation for the Improvement of Teaching and published in *A Classification of Institution of Higher Education*. (Princeton, NJ; Princeton University Press, 1987). Recently, this source was useful when the director of a public two year college wanted to know if he had cause to complain when library expenditures were only 5% of the school's "Education and General" expenditures. The IPEDS data indicated that 90% of public two year schools spent less than 5%. He decided to be happy with what he had.

These reports from Minter are available in machine readable form and a program can be purchased that enables creation of custom peer groups and comparisons. Minter will produce print reports and machine readable files of the 1990 data once it becomes available.

The items in Part II of Table 1 are not comprehensive like the IPEDS reports but they do cover 2 important sets of institutions and have done so long enough and consistently enough that we have time series data for study. As you probably know the questionnaire used to gather the ACRL University Library statistics is the same as the questionnaire used by ARL. The libraries are different, of course. ARL has strict membership criteria. What makes the ACRL University Libraries a group is three things:

— they are not members of ARL
— they are in Carnegie categories Research I and II

or Doctorate Granting I and II (Most are in the latter 2 groups)
— they agreed to participate

With these publications the academic library community has annual data on theseveral hundred largest libraries (largest, in terms of budget, staff, and collections). From time to time ACRL considers collecting from other subsets within the academic library community but the planning stops when the committees becomes aware of the time and cost involved.

FACT SHEET

NCES/IPEDS Academic Library Survey Improvement Project

What is the project?

Statistics on staff, collections, expenditures, and services are collected biennially from academic libraries as one component of the Integrated Postsecondary Education Data System (IPEDS) that obtains data on all aspects of institutionally based postsecondary education (providers, participants, completions, programs, resources). IPEDS replaces HEGIS (Higher Education General Information System) and continues to rely on a network of state IPEDS Coordinators to distribute forms to campuses and ensure their return to the National Center for Education Statistics (NCES).

This Project has identified a librarian in each state to work with the IPEDS Coordinators. For the 1990 data collection some of those Library Representatives took major responsibility for collecting data in the state. Others were available to promote prompt responses from librarians and to assist in problem resolution when anomalies were discovered in completed questionnaires.

The Project also: 1) assists NCES in developing the software package prepared for use by states in reporting library data to NCES; 2) advises NCES on needed changes in the questionnaire and in the way results are reported; 3) promotes analysis of data; and 4) facilitates communication with the academic library community.

Why is it needed?

Data on academic libraries are needed on the local, state, and national level for planning and policy making. The data must be current, however, and the academic library statistics released by NCES in the past have never been less than two years old. The project will shorten the time from data collection to publication and will also improve the quality of the data.

What will change?

The Project speeds the process by adding the following components to the IPEDS system as it relates to academic library statistics:

- a network of library representatives to help the IPEDS Coordinators with the library survey form

- a software package for states to use in reporting to NCES

- aggregation of the data by staff in the NCES Library Statistics Program

March, 1992

Who is involved?

The Director of ALA's Office for Research and Statistics is directing the project. Serving on an Advisory Committee to the project are librarians selected in cooperation with ACRL and the Association of Research Libraries (ARL). Committee members are Susan Brant, Nicolet Area Technical College; Paul DuMont, Dallas County Community College District; Kent Hendrickson, University of Nebraska; Ronald Naylor, University of Miami; Eleanor Pinkham, Kalamazoo College; Sarah Pritchard, Association of Research Libraries; and Kendon Stubbs, University of Virginia. Keith Lance of the Colorado State Library serves as consultant-recorder. John Lorenz coordinates staff support provided by the National Commission on Libraries and Information Science (NCLIS).

When did it start?

The first Advisory Committee meeting was in July, 1990 following several months of preparatory work at ALA and NCES. The Advisory Committee has had six meetings since then and planned the national meeting of IPEDS Coordinators and library representatives that took place in October, 1990.

When was the last survey done?

The last survey was done in the Fall of 1990. A report will be released in May 1992.

When will the next survey be done?

Forms will be mailed to the states in July of 1992.

What is the most recent data available now?

A report of the 1988 survey was published by GPO in September, 1990 as *Academic Libraries: 1988*. Data are also available from NCES on diskette.

How can I get more information?

Contact Mary Jo Lynch at ALA (1-800-545-2433, ext. 4273) or Jeff Williams at NCES (202-219-1362).

March, 1992

The 1986 College Library Standards: An Assessment of Their Use, Strengths, and Weaknesses,
Including Hearings on a Need for Their Revision

David B. Walch
California Polytechnic State University
San Luis Obispo, California

Moderator: Diane Parker
Western Washington University
Bellingham, Washington

Abstract

Reports on a survey of 506 Carnegie Type I and II Comprehensive and Liberal Arts institutions which identifies how and to what degree standards are being implemented and how they can be strengthened.

Beyond the Survey: Using Market Research Techniques to Improve Library Services and Collections

A Panel presentation by:

Paula N. Warnken
Victoria L. Young
Roshan Ahuja
Xavier University
Cincinnati, Ohio

Abstract

Xavier University Libraries have become involved in Total Quality Management. As part of this process they learned about faculty and student library needs by conducting focus groups and administering a quantitative survey instrument. This paper outlines the principles of Total Quality Management and how Xavier University applied them. It discusses how the focus groups were conducted and how the surveys were developed and administered.

Total Quality Management (TQM) is a management approach that assumes long-term success comes through making decisions based on facts, with the goal of ensuring customer satisfaction. The success of a TQM program is based on the participation of all members of an organization in improving processes, products, services and the culture in which they work.

There are five important concepts in Total Quality Management. TQM places responsibility for quality of management on the overall system, and advocates use of a systems approach. The "system" delivers what the customer wants. A systems approach looks at individual departments in the context of the entire library.

TQM emphasizes the need to empower employees. TQM management requires effective delegation, and gives employees the responsibility and authority to solve problems themselves. It requires that staff have adequate resources to do their jobs well and it emphasizes the importance of staff training.

TQM requires organizations to make decisions based on facts, which means collecting and analyzing good data. TQM advocates the use of statistical and graphical tools such as flowcharts, check sheets and cause-and-effect diagrams.

In order to implement Total Quality Management, the library must know its customers and their needs. Although it may not always be possible to satisfy them, the library must make decisions based on a good understanding of who they are and what they need.

Continuous improvement is an important process in Total Quality Management. Policies must be reviewed, questioned and challenged, changing them when necessary. Quality advocates believe "if it ain't broken, improve it."

Quality is defined by the customer. Libraries must find out and understand what customers perceive as quality. There are two kinds of quality: product quality, which is what the library provides, and service quality, which is how what's provided is delivered.

The literature consistently refers to the same companies as examples of good service quality. These companies known for good service quality share several traits: they place a strong emphasis on their employees; they make a connection between employee satisfaction and customer satisfaction; and they place a major emphasis on continuous training. Consequently, employees recognize a difference between "doing the job" and satisfying customers. These companies go beyond meeting customer needs; they try to "delight" customers. Customer delight is defined as products and services that far exceed customer expectation.

Xavier University Libraries became involved in

Total Quality Management as the staff began discussing what they did well and in what areas need improvement. But the library needed to know how it was perceived by its customers (students and faculty) and how those customers identified their library needs. Only then could the library decide what changes to make to improve its products and services. To learn more about their customers, the library implemented a market research strategy.

There are three types of market research: exploratory, descriptive and causal. The type of design chosen depends largely on the current state of knowledge about the topic under investigation. Exploratory research (focus groups, personal interviews or case studies) is used when very little is known. Descriptive research (questionnaires, surveys) is used when there is enough knowledge of the subject to know the questions to be asked. Exploratory research is often followed by descriptive research. Causal research, which is used when a lot is known about the subject, often involves use of experimental and control groups. Xavier University Libraries began researching their customers' needs by using exploratory research in the form of focus groups to gain some initial information. This exploratory research was followed with descriptive research: administration of a quantitative survey instrument to faculty and students.

Focus group research is a technique used to explore people's beliefs, perceptions and attitudes about a certain topic. Focus groups are homogeneous groups of eight to twelve people, with a moderator who focuses the discussion on relevant topics in a non-directive manner. They are called "focus groups" because they start out broad and gradually narrow down to the focus of the research. Xavier library staff attribute the success of their focus groups to the following twelve factors.

1. Choose moderators from outside the library. The success of a focus group depends largely on the moderator and his/her ability to be objective. Employees cannot be objective about their own work situation. Xavier chose two library directors from other institutions and one Xavier administrator with no library affiliation.

2. Select moderators based on skills. Moderators must have good communication skills and experience with group dynamics. Moderators must direct, but not control the discussion. They

must know when to probe and ask for clarification, and at the same time not ask leading questions. If there is a large enough budget, the ideal moderator is someone with professional training; if not, the person must receive training. Although Xavier did not hire professional moderators, the moderators chosen did receive training from professionals.

3. When recruiting, ask for volunteers. Xavier's library recruited volunteers in the four areas that constitute its primary user population: faculty, graduate students, on-campus undergraduates and commuter undergraduates. The library developed brief questionnaires asking for volunteers to participate in a library-wide study that would require approximately an hour.

4. Use stratified groups, separating faculty from students, and undergraduates from graduates. Xavier had separate groups for faculty, undergraduates and graduate students.

5. Plan for groups of eight to twelve, but overschedule, especially with students. Send postcard reminders with a follow-up telephone reminder.

6. Schedule sessions for one-and-one-half hours. The one-hour periods at Xavier didn't always allow enough time, especially in the larger groups.

7. Schedule a minimum of two and a maximum of four sessions per target audience group for the best results.

8. Develop a good discussion guide, based on goals and objectives of the research. Pretest the questions on a test sample, and modify as needed.

9. Hold sessions in a centrally located, easy-to-find room. Ideally the room should have facilities for audiotaping and observation behind a one-way mirror.

10. Reward participants for their time. At the conclusion of each session, all participants were given a candy-filled mug bearing Xavier's library logo.

11. In analyzing data, look for trends or comments that have been repeated in several sessions.

Xavier library staff analyzed the sessions through audiotapes, flip chart paper on which comments were recorded, and notes from those who observed through the one-way mirror.

12. Do not overgeneralize the information gained from focus groups, and do not use information from focus groups to make policy decisions. Because focus groups represent a non-scientific sampling, with no quantification, the information must be used carefully. At Xavier, information from the focus groups gave the staff insight when developing the survey instrument used in the descriptive phase of the research.

The focus groups provided a preliminary picture of the customers and their needs. Information from the focus groups was integrated into the design of the survey.

Writing a survey is a creative process; there is no "perfect" survey. The library developed its survey guided by six steps.

1. Output planning. In this phase analyze what kind of information and data is desired. What is to be learned from the research? At Xavier some of issues were customer satisfaction, usage rates, awareness levels of certain types of collections, and the importance of these collections. The library wanted this information from different groups: faculty from each of the university's three colleges, graduates and undergraduates. For each of the student groups, the library was interested in their college, class standing, whether they were full or part-time students, and whether they lived on campus or commuted.

2. Determine the method of administration. Common methods include mail, telephone and personal interviews. Criteria in making a decision include budget, time and response rate considerations, and what method would provide the necessary types of information.

3. Write each survey question. Number, order and actual wording of questions are primary concerns in writing the survey.

4. Finalize the wording of each question. It is important to use simple words respondents will understand, and to define any terms that may be unfamiliar or ambiguous.

5. Determine the physical characteristics of the survey. Format and layout must be considered. It is important that a cover letter accompany mail surveys and that there is a simple (and free) means for returning the survey.

6. Pretest the survey. This is critical part of the process that cannot be eliminated.

Sampling issues and statistical analysis must be considered. Availability of the sample frame is an important consideration. Can a list of potential respondents be obtained? The type of sample is an issue. Should everyone be canvassed? If not, the sample design is important. There are two primary ways to take a sample, probability and nonprobability. The size of the sample is important. The larger the sample, the better. Consider response rate which will influence the size of the sample.

There are many statistical analysis packages from which to choose. It is important to involve someone who is familiar with the statistical package you use at the begin-ning of the survey to help anticipate data analysis issues.

Xavier University Libraries conducted exploratory research using two six-page questionnaires, one designed for faculty and one for students. All faculty were surveyed with a response rate of forty eight percent. A systematic sample of students was used, sampling every third undergraduate and every other graduate student. Twenty one percent of all students returned the surveys. The information was analyzed using SPSS.

After analyzing the data, library staff summarized the results. A longer, more detailed version was produced for staff, and a shorter summary for faculty and students.

The library has realized many benefits from the survey. The survey demonstrated to faculty and students that the library was interested in them, and it served as an excellent public relations tool. Library staff have begun to get an idea about how the library is perceived and what their customers want.

The library continues to use this information for long-range planning, in prioritizing and in making decisions about collections and services. The implementation of Total Quality Management at Xavier has given all staff members an opportunity to participate in this important process, as the library strives to fulfill its mission based on the needs of the university community.

Self-Censorship in U.S. College and Research Libraries

Charles Willett, Moderator
CRISES Press,
Gainesville, Florida

Abstract

Examines materials, subjects, and ideas which librarians censor, the causes and consequences of self-censorship, and how to recognize and overcome it.

As guardians of the free marketplace of ideas, librarians have a professional and moral responsibility to combat not only external censorship but the more insidious forms that originate in their midst. Self-censorship is rampant, caused by commercial factors of publishing, marketing, and distribution; budget limitations; the dictates of a slavish dependence on technology; policies that favor certain subjects over others, serials over monographs, and core collections over peripheral materials; a mindset that introduces bias under the guise of objectivity; pressure from external censors; prejudice; ignorance; fear; and poor administration. To the extent that librarians tolerate censorship, they are responsible for its consequences.

Each library buys virtually the same core collection as others of its type. Selectors consider only "mainstream" materials which serve the alleged "majority" of students, materials spoonfed by bland corporations and university presses via slick advertising and automated delivery systems. Whatever is "peripheral," or "not high quality," or "one-sided," or "specialized," or "unorthodox," or "distorted," or "inflammatory" is excluded. Vast parts of America—even entire states—do not contain a single subscription to *The Alternative Press Index,* and those libraries that have it subscribe to a mere smattering of its titles.

Are we asleep? Are we mesmerized by the corporate, academic, media, and government disinformation our libraries buy? An intense ideological struggle is going on right now for the hearts and minds of the American people, a struggle much more subtle and frightening than that during the McCarthy era, but librarians seem hardly aware of it.

Outside the great gates of the academy, an extraordinary number of nonpersons—freelance writers, community activists, former government officials, fired journalists, excommunicated scholars, and people of conscience—are attacking established orthodoxy through a rapidly expanding alternative press.

Topics include class; racism; sexism; unorthodox religious and philosophical views; dissident art and culture; nonheterosexual orientations; militant feminism; the men's movement; radical environmentalism; unconventional economics; revolutionary politics; social action; union organizing; civil rights and liberties; ethnic separatism; foreign nationalism; U.S. disinformation and political repression at home; U.S. exploitation, terror, and mass murder abroad; an apocalyptic vision of the future; organizing for peace, non-violence, social justice, and ecological balance; and concern for the millions denied basic human rights here and abroad.

Mainstream books and journals rarely discuss these matters in depth. They don't ask the right questions, and they withhold many of the answers. Coverage by commercial publishers is superficial, while university presses lack passion and compassion. Both shrink from critical analysis that would challenge the dominant American paradigm. Libraries clone each other in sterile conformity, while students wander in the dismal fog before going off blindly to serve the military-industrial complex. With self-censorship, who needs totalitarianism?

Mark Rosenzweig
LaGuardia Community College
New York, New York

It is curious that the subject of self-censorship in

libraries is itself the victim of librarians' self-censorship. In contrast to other fields of information work, where discussion of self- censorship has been an important and relatively wide critical current, in librarianship the discourse has been virtually absent. A search of the literature of the past decade yields so few examples of investigations of this phenomenon, or at least those which call it by its name, that the silence itself becomes eloquent testimony that something is amiss.

One might claim that library self-censorship is a relatively unimportant and marginal phenomenon. I maintain, however, that there is a constant undercurrent of self-censorship at many, if not all levels of library practice and theory, but that it is seldom if ever identified, named, brought to consciousness. Its unacknowledged presence continues to limit and distort the development of library activity in important ways. Indeed, the significance of self-censorship for librarians begins with the fact that it is almost always viewed as an external force acting on libraries. It is predominately considered in its most limited sense, that is strictly in terms of conscious decisions made about selections and acquisitions. The notion of self-censorship itself, widely acknowledged in other fields, is literally repressed in librarianship.

Celeste West, in her 1982 lecture, *The Secret Garden of Censorship,* recognizes that librarians' "putting up with hierarchical working conditions" is the origin of self-censorship: "Obviously, you have to censor yourself if you cannot create a worker self-management situation, and must instead follow the rule of 'higher authority.'"

West's perspective suggests that the unquestioned corporate culture of libraries may be inherently inimical to intellectual freedom and involves censorship of the most fundamental sort. The profoundly undemocratic, institutional arrangement of library work itself imposes limits on library thought and practice, demanding self-censorship of the "library imagination," the critical thinking of librarians about themselves, rendering certain things if not unthinkable, at least unsayable and virtually undoable.

Libraries are a form of organization in which the many subordinates who are allowed to appear to be playing active roles are always participants without power. Their function may be to supply opinions, ideas, and suggestions, but only those which are supportive of the policies of those in command. The retention of such participants is predicated on their ability to keep advice in line with the views of those they advise.

The main point is that there is a sort of continuum between internal censorship and prior censorship, which is an unconscious aspect of the culture of librarianship itself, and those public practices which affect the character and the quality of library services. The key to understanding the role, scope, and significance of self-censorship in librarianship is how libraries as institutions constrain and shape the consciousness of the individuals who play subordinate roles. This constraint occurs in ways which appear consensual and neutral but which in reality are covertly coercive and political.

If we truly abhor censorship, the fight against it begins in our own institutions, begins indeed with ourselves. Challenging self-censorship means first of all articulating the elements of library ideology, especially the unconscious, taken-for-granted ones, and critiquing them thoroughly, ruthlessly. It means democratizing libraries in their internal functioning as well as in their relations to the rest of the world. And it means overcoming the prohibitions against advocacy and activism, against politics, which hobble the library as a potentially powerful agent for social progress.

John Buschman
Rider College
Lawrenceville, New Jersey

I want to take what Charles Willett and Mark Rosenzweig have laid out one step further into self-censorship and information technology, possibly the next generation of what libraries are going to be.

"Censorship," the word, comes from a Latin word meaning to assess, estimate, and judge. In viewing self-censorship and information technology, I think of self-censorship as not assessing, estimating, or judging some of the dimensions of information technology, thereby leaving some aspects unexamined and unchecked.

I will focus on three areas of consequence or possible consequence of information technology in libraries that are widely overlooked, by exploring the sort of power perhaps unwittingly endorsed in choices made by librarians, and how certain forms of communication and privileged through a lack of a critical examination.

The first of these areas is "high status access and the cost and consequences of what is bought." Librarians are opting for high status, electronic access and information resources at the expense of lower status information access and resources. That information technology holds a high status in current culture is a truism. It is the socially preferred medium for access to information and soon the full text of documents. I have argued elsewhere that the library profession is grabbing hold of information technology in an uncritical way as a means of raising a traditionally lowly professional status. The resulting choices of collection building deeply affect our collections, increasing the selectivity that discriminates against the unestablished, the lower status, and controversial materials that Charles Willett has talked about. Information technology is affecting both how and what collections are built.

The second area of consequence of information technology and self-censorship is "the weakening of libraries' historical relationship to print and print literacy." There is little question that the government, business, and technical establishment is pushing librarians in this direction. Librarians are talking about the future as a process of purchasing access to data and texts electronically stored elsewhere. Electronic control and distribution is a necessary foundation of such a system. Distribution can truly be monitored and controlled in terms of the access allowed and the related issue, the cost. Further, in this digital structure the integrity of the historical record is entirely alterable without noticeable traces of change. Digital culture, the culture librarians are adopting, nullifies many of the practical brakes on the censorship of society's cultural and historical record. Has this been examined closely? Purchasing access on a national scale becomes a reality with library support, but the monitoring, control, and cost issues all affecting access are perhaps laying the groundwork for an electronic panopticon.

The third area is "information technology and market censorship." Many scholars have detailed the centralization and privatization of information into very few hands. Librarians are already dealing with the censorship issues of this centralization and privatization. To name a few: fees for services and information, access to U.S. government information, unequal access issues, and the issue of the information rich and poor. Information technology has been much of the driving force in making the centralization possible. Are librarians aware of the source and context of what the profession purchases and sponsors? Has this been a subject of serious study?

This argument should be taken one step further. Corporate centralization of information resources has narrowed the range of the marketplace of ideas. The act of modern censorship is essentially a decision what is to be mass produced and, in addition how it is to be distributed. To adapt Charles Willett's thoughts about self-censorship and politically controversial monographs, librarians, by not examining the contexts and parameters of the information available, are not accepting their professional responsibilities for equality of access and neutrality of collections and information offered. Market centralization and the technology of distribution play a role in what gets produced in the first place and the degree of equality of access. Adapting a quote from Charles Willett, "the manufacture of consent is not a legitimate goal of collection management or the college curriculum," nor the production, distribution, access, and selection of library electronic resources.

Brenda Mitchell-Powell
Editor, *Mulicultural Review*

Paper not submitted.

James McGarth Morris
Public Interest Publications

Paper not submitted.

Front and Center: Library Initiatives for Improvement in Undergraduate Education

Cliff Bishop, Dennis Norlin,
Mary Jane Petrowski, and Lizabeth (Betsy) Wilson
University of Illinois Urbana, Illinois

Abstract

Describes strategies for campus cooperation and proven techniques for further integrating the library into the educational community. Focuses on specific library initiatives to improve undergraduate education.

Introduction

Though often said to be central to the university, the library, in fact, is seldom consulted on proposed curriculum changes, despite the impact such changes may have on collections and services; professors send their students to the library with unreasonable and ill-conceived assignments; policy committees seldom include library representative; and decisions on campus computing are made without library input. At the Undergraduate Library at the University of Illinois at Urbana-Champaign, we have responded to these and similar difficulties by adopting strategies designed to return the library to its proper place at the instructional heart of the university. A recognition of the need to collaborate has been at the core of our efforts, along with an understanding that cooperative enterprises have pitfalls as well as advantages.

Historical Background

Each spring, the Chancellor of the University brings together, at the Allerton Estate, faculty from all across the campus to discuss a specific theme. In 1960, the Allerton Conference focused on "The Undergraduate Climate at the University," and the foundation was set for the extensive curricular reform undertaken at Illinois during the 1960s. As a key component of that reform, the Conference mandated construction of a separate undergraduate library.

At its opening, in 1969, the Undergraduate Library exemplified thetraditional conception of the library as a place. Emphasis was given to the provision of individual study spaces and to shelving for books. There was no reference desk, and no space designated for instruction or for group study. The library was essentially a study hall and a warehouse for books.

Impetus for Change

Today, the library is decidedly more dynamic. Ours is an activeteaching library. Five major factors have prompted thistransformation of the library from its original status as a study hall to its current place front and center in undergraduate education:

Changes in the Curriculum. Of these five factors, changes in the curriculum were perhaps the first to exert an influence. Since 1969 there has been a move away from courses based on textbooks and reserve readings toward courses predicated on case studies, group work, resource-based learning, and independent inquiry. Similarly, the class lecture is increasingly being supplemented by cooperative learning. In 1969, our users competed for individual carrels; the demand now is for group study space. Greater interest in career planning has occurred as well. During the 1980s, too, a myriad of educational white papers stressed the importance of teaching students to become lifelong learners.

Bibliographic Instruction. In 1975, bibliographic instruction was significantly expanded at Illinois. Librarians cooperated with teachers of composition courses to devise a course-integrated bibliographic instruction program. Through such cooperative efforts we realized the extent to which we shared educational goals with the teaching faculty, and that, in practice no less than in theory, our different areas of expertise were indeed neatly complementary. It was from those first experiences that our subsequent cooperative initiatives grew.

Media. In 1977, a "media center" was established. The stress was on slides and audio tapes, collected in direct support of classroom instruction. Since then, media technology has burgeoned, and the current Media Center makes available a full array of non-print formats, each of which has influenced how students learn and how their professors teach.

Structure and Quantity of Information. Changes in information dissemination, coupled with information overload, have changed how students locate and interpret information. Access is often not the problem; excess is. There is simply too much information, in too many unfamiliar forms, for beginning scholars to handle effectively without assistance.

Demographics. Greater numbers of nontraditional students, commitment to cultural diversity, and an influx of international students have dramatically altered the composition of the student population. Today's students enter college with at least some familiarity with microcomputers and other components of Toffler's electronic cottage. Their formative years have been spent in a world in which profound social changes have occurred in the structure of the family, in the base of our economy, as it has shifted from manufacturing toward information, and in the extent to which a new recognition of interdependence, both national and international, has come to color our sense of the world. Taken together, these factors have compelled us to rethink and redesign our libraries. We have responded with novel approaches to familiar tasks and a host of cooperative efforts.

Cooperatives Efforts at the University of Illinois

We have tried to link our initiatives directly to the educational needs of our students. Broadly, these may be categorized as skill needs, information needs, and material needs. The extent of our collaboration with others necessarily varies according to specific needs.

Skill Needs. Mutual cooperation and support have led to the development of a fully course-integrated bibliographic instruction program. We work closely with the teaching faculty in five departments to provide students information seeking skills at their time of need and within the context of their research assignments.

The Writers' Workshop—a free, walk-in tutorial service open to all students—is a case where we provided the necessary space and other units supplied construction funds and appropriate staff. Although the Writer's Workshop didn't open until 1989, its realization was facilitated by the success of our BI program.

Some cooperative ventures involve support for services or programs that already exist in the Library. One example is the intra-library cooperation that has developed between the Undergraduate Library and the Mortenson Center for International Library Programs. In the summer of 1990, the Center became aware that our library was working with the Office of International Student Affairs to provide orientations for new students. After participating in an orientation, the Director of the Center offered immediate financial support, as well as teaching staff, to further develop programs and services for international students in conjunction with the Undergraduate Library.

Information Needs. The Media Center reflects the Library's commitment to providing alternative information formats. Its development depended on our cooperative efforts with the Office of Instructional Resources, which provided equipment, and with the Office of the Vice Chancellor, which provided funds. Ongoing cooperation with development sources, such as the Library Friends and the Mothers Association, has enabled us to keep pace with technological changes. Another cooperative effort, established with the campus Counseling Center, is the Self-Help Information Center (SHIC). The Center opened in 1983, after Undergraduate librarians found a suicide note on the Question Board (an anonymous reference service). The Library provided space and information resources. The Counseling Center offered staff and expertise. As a result, the Counseling Center has enhanced its outreach and gained paraprofessional training opportunities for students. This cooperative effort was recently cited as a model initiative by an accreditation team.

The College and Career Cluster is another instance in which we have been able to expand library services by cooperating with an outside unit. We are now working with the Career Services Office to establish a state-of-the-art, self-service College and Career Cluster within the library; it will provide computers and software, media materials, and print sources on college and career topics, thanks to funds raised on our behalf by the Mothers and Dads Associations at the University.

Material Needs. A number of cooperative efforts have enabled us to meet the material needs of our Microcomputer Lab, the CD-ROM Site, and the Interactive Media Site, as well as special facilities needs. IBM and Apple, the Educational Technologies Board, the Facility Planning and Management Office, Rehabilitation Education Services, the Chancellor's Parents

Fund, and the Senior Class Gift committee are just a few of the organizations with which our library has collaborated in its efforts to improve services.

Strategies for Cooperation

Two broad strategies facilitate cooperative efforts. Librarians must (1) get out of the library; and (2) get others into the library.

Getting Out. Routinely, we participate in the Library School's introductory course on Library and Information Science. We address seniors, in a course for those who plan to teach high school English, on the importance of forming educational partnerships with their teaching colleagues in the school library. We have served as Faculty Fellows (a residence hall program), actively sought places on departmental committees, and worked with student organizations. We have served on Athletic Board committees, and worked with the University Senate. In all of these interactions, we have found that our ability to investigate various literatures gives us instant credibility and a role to play.

Getting Others In. We have space for meetings and parties, and make it available—if such events can take place without disrupting the library. The University Athletic Board has met in the classroom of the Writer's Workshop. Faculty orientations, for those faculty to be involved in our BI program, are now held in the library, where previously they were held at the various departments. We showcase the library whenever possible, as when we held an open house to announce a significant revamping of our Microcomputer Lab. The advantage to such use is that it brings in a wide array of people, from all levels of the university, who otherwise may never set foot in the library. Others are thus better able to see how active our library is, and can be expected to make more informed decisions when considering our requests for equipment or funds.

Skills and Attitudes Needed

Several key skills and attitudes are needed if the library is to be returned to its proper place at the heart of the university. The need for advocacy is constant. A clear sense of mission is crucial. We are willing, and even eager, to take on cooperative projects, but we do make sure we don't involve ourselves in projects that will interfere with our mission as a teaching library or that unduly disrupt library operations.

To ensure the success of cooperative efforts, mutual benefit must be demonstrated. The Writer's Workshop, for example, had been housed in the English Department, where its hours were few and its funding inadequate. One result was that students were asking reference librarians for substantial help with their term papers. Moving the Workshop into the Library allowed the English Department to better share its expertise; librarians were relieved of inappropriate demands; and help was made available at hours better suited to the work habits of undergraduates.

Shared control of space and resources must be tolerated. Negotiation is necessary. Territorial conflicts can arise. The Self Help Information Center (SHIC), for example, is an autonomous entity within our library, run by staff and students from the Counseling Center. Changes in staff have sometimes resulted in misunderstandings as to the nature of the relationship between SHIC and the Library. Renegotiation is sometimes needed to reestablish or to clarify purposes.

Where drawbacks are suitably noted and controlled, however, the advantages of cooperation are significant. Programs and services are enhanced. Additional and different expertise can be acquired. Staff is augmented. Campus services are able to extend their hours and to improve their outreach. And the library, with the success of cooperative efforts, is better integrated into the larger university community in thus assuming its proper place front and center in undergraduate education.

Background Readings
General Discussions

Betsy Baker. "Bibliographic Instruction: Building the Librarian/Faculty Partnership." *Reference Librarian* (No. 24, 1989): 311-328.

Betsy Baker and Mary Ellen Litzinger, *The Evolving Educational Mission of the Library* (Chicago: Association of College and Research Libraries, 1992).

Ernest L. Boyer, *College: The Undergraduate Experience in America* (New York: Harper & Row, 1987).

Patricia S. Brevik and Robert Wedgeworth, *Libraries and the Search for Academic Excellence* (Metuchen, N.J.: Scarecrow Press, 1988).

Evan Ira Farber, "Librarian-Faculty Communication Techniques," in *Proceedings of the Southeastern Conference on Approaches to Bibliographic Instruction* (Charleston, S.C.: College of Charleston, 1978).

Patrick Hill, "Who Will Lead the Reform of Higher Education? Librarians, of Course!" *Washington Center News* 5 (Winter, 1991): 3-8.

Thomas G. Kirk, *Increasing the Teaching Role of Academic Libraries* (New Directions for Teaching and Learning: 18) (San Francisco: Jossey-Bass, 1984).

Barbara B. Moran, *Academic Libraries: The Changing Knowledge Center of Colleges and Universities* (Washington, D.C.: Association for the Study of Higher Education, 1984) (ASHEERIC Higher Education Research Report, No. 8.)

Roland Person, *A New Path: Undergraduate Libraries at United States and Canadian Universities, 1949-1987* (New York: Greenwood, 1988).

Carla J. Stoffle, "A New Library for the New Undergraduate," *Library Journal* (October 1, 1990): 47-50.

Laurene E. Zaporozhetz, "Fifteen Ways to Meet Your User: Public Relations and Outreach Suggestions for Bibliographic Instruction," *Reference Librarian* (No. 24, 1989): 289-296.

Free Service: Term Paper Research Counseling," in *Marketing Instructional Services; Applying Private Sector Techniques to Plan and Promote Bibliographic Instruction,* edited by Carolyn A. Kirkendall (Library Orientation Series: 16) (Ann Arbor: Pierian Press, 1986), p. 94-98.

Lizabeth Wilson and Joyce Wright, "Term Paper Counseling: The Library's Tutorial." *Reference Librarian* 62 (No. 24, 1989): 269-288.

Joyce C. Wright, "The Self-Management Lab: Responding to Personal Needs." *Wilson Library Bulletin* (January, 1988): 12.

Specific to the Undergraduate Library
University of Illinois at Urbana-Champaign

Mary Beth Allen, "Focusing the One-Shot Lecture," *Research Strategies* 7 (Summer, 1989): 100-105.

David N. King and John C. Ory, "Effects of Library Instruction on Student Research: A Case Study," *College & Research Libraries* 42 (January, 1981): 31-41.

David F. Kohl and Lizabeth A. Wilson, "Effectiveness of Course-Integrated Bibliographic Instruction in Improving Coursework," *RQ* 27 (Winter, 1986): 206-211.

David F. Kohl, Lizabeth Wilson, Lori Arp, Stuart Rosselet, and Susan Peck McDonald, "Large-Scale Bibliographic Instruction—The Illinois Experience," *Research Strategies* 2 (Winter, 1984): 4-44.

Dennis Norlin, "Computers at Undergrad: What is Certain in an Uncertain Future," *Illinois Libraries* 72 (November, 1990): 583-586.

Mary Jane Petrowski and Lizabeth Wilson, *Research Guide: An Introduction to Library and Information Skills.* (Champaign: Stipes Publishing, 1991).

Mary Jane Petrowski and Lizabeth Wilson, "Avoiding Horror in the Classroom: In-house Training for Bibliographic Instruction,"*Illinois Libraries* 73 (February, 1991): 180-86.

Donna Pittman, "The Question Board." *College & Research Libraries News* (June, 1987): 327-330.

Virginia Simpson and Lizabeth Wilson, "Selling a

PROGRAM SESSIONS

IX.
BIBLIOGRAPHIC INSTRUCTION

Be a one-Shot BI Hotshot: Applying Instructional Design Principles to Bibliographic Instruction

Jeffrey W. Bauer and Lynne M. Fox
University of Northern Colorado
Greely, Colorado

Abstract

Develop efffective 50-minute bibliographic instruction presentations using the four basic principles of instruction design.

Over View

One-hour, one time introductory bibliographic instruction sessions for groups of students continue to be the staple of most college libraries' instructional offerings despite the recent debate on their effectiveness.[1] Criticisms center on the poor training librarians receive for instructional design and delivery. Improving librarian skills will improve the effectiveness of "one-shot" BI. Many librarians already employ many instructional design ideas because they have acquired their techniques from good role models. This paper builds on that common sense approach by offering principles to follow for design and delivery of effective bibliographic instruction.

May instructional design models have been developed over the past several decades. Some are exceedingly complex and unwieldy for most instructional situations, while others are relatively simple for non-instructional design experts to follow. The information presented in this paper is a generic representation of basic instructional design principles gleaned from several models, including Gagne, Briggs, and Wager, and Dick and Carey.[2] While each instructional design model presents its own unique representation of the design process, most models include four basic steps: (a) front end analysis, (b) developing instructional goals and objectives, (c) designing the instructional package, and (d) evaluating the effectiveness.

Front End Analysis

A major task to perform before the actual instructional design process begins is to gather information about the target learners. This process is often called front end analysis or needs assessment. The basic idea is to identify what skills, abilities, and knowledge the target learners possess relative to library use before bibiliographic instruction begins. This information is compared with the skills, abilities, and knowledge the target learners should possess relative to bibliographic information. The difference between the two represents the instructional need.[3]

There are many ways to conduct front end analyses. Surveys, questionnaires, interviews with students and professors, as well as experiences with prior BI sessions can help the instructional designer identify exactly what students know about bibliographic information. General library skills and student attitudes about using library resources are also helpful in developing bibliographic instruction.

Often a front end analysis will reveal a wide range of skills and abilities among target learners making the design process very difficult. For example, in a typical freshman English class, some students will have used various library resources in high school, including online services and CD-ROMs. Other students will be barley able to navigate their way through a card catalog. This phenomenon may indicate that there are two or more different groups of target learners with different instructional needs. The instructional designer may be faced with developing several different BI sessions aimed at different skill and ability levels. In any case, the next step in the design process is to develop instructional goals and objectives.

Instructional goals and Objectives

In order for instruction to be effective, students must have a clear idea of what they will be able to do after receiving instruction on a given topic. An instructional goal is a clear statement of behaviors that learners will be able to demonstrate as a result of instruction. For example, if bibliographic instruction were being designed for a business writing class, the instructional goal might read as follow:

Student in a business writing class will use the library to find appropriate resources in order to write a business memo on a major corporation.

Once an instructional goal is identified, the instructional designer must determine the major steps involved in reaching this goal. Each of these major steps can be broken down into smaller steps. This process is known as a subordinate skills analysis or a task analysis and can be fairly rigorous. Dick and Carey provide an excellent description of this process in *The Systematic Design of Instruction.*

The next step in the design process is to write objectives for the steps identified in the subordinate skills analysis. Well written objectives typically contain four major components: identification of the learners or audience, the specific behaviors that they are to perform, the conditions under which the behaviors will be performed, and the degree of accuracy needed to indicate mastery of the skill. These components can be remembered as the ABCDs of objectives: A = audience, B = behavior, C = conditions, D = degree.[4]

In the business writing class example, one of the objectives may read as follows:

Students in the business writing class will be able to use the *Business Periodicals Index* to locate at least three appropriate articles in the library pertaining to the corporation that they chose, using handouts and notes taken during the BI presentation.

This objective contains the four necessary ingredients:

Audience = students in the business writing class
Behavior = locate appropriate articles
Conditions = using handouts and notes
Degree = at least three

Objectives serve at least two major purposes. They help the designer develop instructional strategies that are appropriate for the desired behavior, and they

serve as a guide during the evaluation state to determine whether the instruction was effective. Once objectives have been written, attention can be focused on the actual design of the instructional package.

Designing the Instruction

The next step in the instructional design process involves developing the nuts and bolts of the instructional package. There is much to consider in this step. What types of instructional materials will be developed? Which media are appropriate for instructional delivery? Should the instruction be instructor lead or learner guided? Is computer aided instruction appropriate? Should the instruction be delivered to groups or individuals? In bibliographic instruction, logistical constraints often require that instruction be delivered to large groups; consequently, this type of delivery will be featured here.

The instructional goals and objectives will ultimately determine the nature of the actual instruction. However, when preparing instruction, there are some simple steps that can be followed that will improve the likelihood of successful instructional delivery. The nine events of instruction represent a simple, systematic approach to organizing the presentation of information during bibliographic instruction.[5]

1. Gain attention
2. Inform learner of objective
3. Stimulate recall of prior learning
4. Present material to be learned
5. Provide learner guidance
6. Elicit learner performance
7. Provide feedback
8. Assess performance
9. Enhance retention and transfer

In bibliographic instruction, the instructor might ask open-ended questions to gain the attention of the learners, such as, "What would you do if you had an assignment due tomorrow where you were required to use the *Business Periodicals Index* to locate articles about a specific corporation?" The instructor would than inform the class of the instructional goal and the objectives. Recall of prior knowledge could be stimulated by comparing the organization of information in the card catalog with information in the *Business Periodicals Index.* A demonstration of the *Business Periodicals Index* should be followed with guided practice. Eliciting performance by presenting students

415

with the assignment should be followed by careful feedback. Performance can be assessed based on the results of the assignment. Follow-up assignments requiring students to use the *Business Periodicals Index* to find other types of information will help enhance the retention of the skills acquired during the BI session.

Learner characteristics gathered during the front end analysis should be considered when designing the instruction. The instruction should reflect items such as age, cultural background, relative sophistication in terms of library use, and attitudes toward using the library. Once the instructional package has been designed, it must be evaluated and revised if necessary.

Evaluation of Instruction

Formative evaluation involves evaluating and revising the instruction before it is delivered in its final form to the target learners. Again, there are some simple steps to follow that can improve the chances of developing a successful instructional package.

The process should begin with a one-on-one evaluation with a non-librarian who is unfamiliar with the subject, such as a spouse or roommate. The purpose is to uncover large errors in the instruction. The designer should be close at hand to receive feedback on the instruction. Next, a larger group field trial should be conducted. This will give the designer a better picture of problems that need to be corrected in the instructional package. The instruction can then be delivered to a sample of the target learners to get their input. Post surveys and interviews will provide the designer with valuable feedback regarding the details of the instruction. Instruction should be revised after each of the steps in the formative evaluation process. The final result of the formative evaluation should be a quality instructional package.

Summary

Although one-shot bibliographic instructional sessions may not be the best way to teach students necessary information skills, they are a logistical reality in many colleges and universities. If those responsible for designing such sessions follow some basic instructional design principles, the likelihood of learner success can be greatly increased. These principles include conducting a front end analysis, developing instructional

goals and objectives, developing the instructional package, and evaluating the instruction.

Endnotes

1. T. Eadie. "Immodest Proposals." *Library Journal* 15 (October 15, 1990): 42-45.
2. Walter Dick, and Lou Carey. *The Systematic Design of Instruction.* (New York: Harper Collins, 1990); Gagne, Robert, Lesie Briggs, and Walter W. Wager. *Principles of Instructional Design,* 4th ed. (Fort Worth: Harcourt, Brace, Jovanovich, 1992).
3. A. Rossett. *Training Needs Assessment.* (Englewood Cliffs, NJ: Educational Technology Publications, 1987).
4. Robert Heinich, Michael Molenda, James D. Russell. *Instructional Media and the New Technologies of Instruction.* (New York: McMillian, 1989).
5. Robert Mills Gagne, op. cit.

Cooperative Learning and Bibliographic Instruction: Incorporating Small Group Techniques into Teaching Sessions

Mary Jane Petrowski
University of Illinois
Urbana, Illinois

Lori Arp
University of Colorado
Boulder, Colorado

and

Sharon Mader
DePaul University
Chicago, Illinois

Lizabeth (Betsy) Wilson
University of Washington
Seattle, Washington

Abstract:

Cooperative learning techniques provide an effective means of structuring learning in small groups. These cooperative approaches have well-documented positive effects on social development, cognitive skills, motivation, and self-esteem. They are particularly effective for promoting respect for cultural diversity and developing the critical thinking skills requisite for survival in an age of complex information resources and requisite for survival in an age of complex information resources and technologies. The mini-workshop was designed to allow twenty-four participants and opportunity to learn by experiencing a variety of cooperative learning techniques during the two-hour session. The workshop also included mini-lectures on the critical attributes of cooperative learning; a summary of major research findings as well as descriptions of four successful applications of cooperative learning to academic settings (classroom, faculty workshop, library management, and campus committee). Participants received an annotated bibliography and information packet on cooperative learning.

Workshop Goals

The two-hour workshop was designed to facilitate learning by doing. Twenty-four participants working in groups of four were introduced to a variety of cooperative learning techniques which could be applied to a variety of instructional purposes from brainstorming to problem solving. Participants were able to reflect on the nature and value of cooperative learning; identify possible resistance to cooperative learning; and develop solutions to overcoming resistance. Participants also gained an overview of cooperative learning, including its rationale, critical attributes, and research base through a series of mini-lectures. The final part of the workshop allowed participants to focus on ways that cooperative learning has been successfully implemented by academic librarians in bibliographic instruction classes, faculty-librarian workshops, strategic planning, and campus committees.

Cooperative Learning Strategies

The workshop included four classic small-group techniques that work well on the university level, including:

Three-Step Interview. Commonly used as an icebreaker or team-building exercise, this structure can also be used to share information such as hypotheses or reactions to a film or article. Opinion/evaluation questions also work well. Participants interview one another in pairs, alternating roles. They then share in a four-member learning team the information or insights gleaned from the paired interviews. This is an excellent opportunity to practice active listening skills. Workshop participants interviewed each other regarding their experience with cooperative learning and later used their new knowledge to introduce their partner.

Roundtable. Roundtable is a technique that can be used for brainstorming, reviewing, or practicing a skill. The roundtable technique insures that all members of a group are involved. The key to roundtable technique is the question or problem. It must have multiple answers and offer a high probability of success to all participants. Participants all write in turn on a single pad of paper, stating their ideas aloud as they write. As the tablet circulates, more and more information is added until various aspects of a topic are explored. Workshop participants used this technique to identify possible benefits of cooperative learning. Twenty-five benefits were identified n three minutes and all participants were able to contribute and experience working productively as a group.

Group Brainstorming with Recorder. Brainstorming is highly effective method of generating ideas provided that participants defer judgement, strive for unique ideas, aim for quantity rather than quality, and seek to build on or "hitchhike" on ideas of others. Participants used this technique to identify the possible kinds of resistance they might anticipate when implementing cooperative learning. Thirty-nine problems were identified in three minutes.

Pass a Problem. Each group reaches consensus on a real problem the group would like to have solved. In this case, participants chose a particular "resistance problem . After writing the problem on the outside of an envelope, the problems are then sent clockwise to the next group. Each group brainstorms for three minutes on solutions to the problems they receive, and then spends two minutes reaching consensus on their best two or three ideas, All work is put into the envelope and problems are rotated. When the home group receives its original problem, it has several minutes to read all of the previous groups' ideas and develop a prioritized list of possible solutions, which is written on chart paper and presented publicly.

Background on Cooperative Learning

Small group activities alternated with mini-lectures on cooperative learning during the workshop. The first lecture introduced a definition of cooperative learning, discussing the rationale, and outlined the key components of cooperative learning. Although there is not much in the bibliographic instruction literature about cooperative learning, it was been widely embraced by other educators. Reasons include: (1) the realization that cooperation (rather than competition) is funda-

mental to human progress and therefore education should do more to develop social maturity in students; (2) the realization that 70-80% of today's jobs require cooperative interaction abilities rather than rugged individualism, and (3) the realization that learning is a social process.

Cooperative learning has theoretical roots in social psychology research in the early 1900s that focused cooperation versus competition. In 1929 Maller was the first to examine the role of cooperation in the learning process.[1] His work was extended in the 1950s by the British researcher Abercrombie who studied medical school training and theorized that small group learning could be applied to other educational settings.[2] In the 1970s four independent groups of American researchers began to develop and evaluate practical methods and techniques.[3] In to 1980s many teachers looked to cooperative learning as an important alternative to traditional competitive/individualistic classroom environments where students remained isolated from each other.

What Research Shows

Cooperative learning has been shown to benefit students' development in a number of ways, including: 1) helping students develop greater respect for others and greater tolerance for diversity; 2) giving students a sense of confidence in their own powers; 3) improving attitudes toward school and learning; 4) teaching students how to communicate more effectively within groups; 5) generating great trust of people which comes from feel responsible for another's learning. Cooperative learning environments have been shown superior to competitive and individualistic ones Comparative research show s that in structured small groups, students gained increased cognitive skills, experienced more peer support and acceptance, developed group cohesiveness and greater motivation, while learning important communication skills (conflict resolution and decision making.) The overall advantages continue to become clear: cooperative learning promotes active learning, creates a sense of community, insures that knowledge is created, not transferred, and allows teachers to move from being the "sage on the stage" to the "guide on the side". The responsibility for learning and the joy of learning is shifted to the students. Participants also note that cooperative learning gives students the opportunity to learn from each other and to value their peers as sources of assistance and knowledge, provides immediate feedback, allow learners to bring their own ideas and experiences to the learning environment; allows less vocal students an opportunity to participate and creates a comfortable setting in which less confident learners can ask questions.

Attributes

It's not enough to put students into small groups. Cooperative learning must include five essential components to be successful.. First, there must be face-to-face interaction in small groups of 2-6 people. This structure promotes and facilitates important types of verbal exchanges such as oral summarizing, giving and receiving explanations, and elaborating. The second ingredient is mutual interdependence. Students must feet that they need each other in order to complete the group's task, that they "sink or swim" together. Individual accountability must also be assessed. Cooperative learning groups are not successful until every member has learned the material or has helped with and understood the assignment. Since students do not come to school with the social skills they need to collaborate effectively with others, teaches need to teach the appropriate communication, leadership, decision-making, and conflict management skills to students and provide the motivation to use these skills in order for groups to function effectively. The final element is group processing. Students need time to reflect on and to analyze how well their groups are functioning and how well they are using the necessary social skills.

Successful Applications of Cooperative Learning

After discussing why there might be resistance to cooperative learning, four example of successful applications were unveiled. Mary Jane Petrowski explained how the undergraduate library at the University of Illinois recently revamped bibliographic instruction to include group brainstorming with a recorder, mini-lectures, and group processing. Participants watched a brief "before" and "after" video clip designed to show how instruction had changed fro a fifty-minute lecture where sleeping students sat in straight rows to a more engaged classroom where students sit and work in small groups.

Cooperative learning techniques can be used in faculty workshops. Sharon Mader shared her success designing and implementing workshops to promote collaboration between librarians and faculty through small group work at DePaul University. The structured

small group interaction generated many ideas as well as a demand for continuing workshops. Participants were delighted with the opportunity to meet and learn from their peers.

Cooperative learning techniques also have management applications. Lori Arp reported on her use of cooperative learning techniques to do strategic planning in the reference department at the University of Colorado at Boulder. Staff meetings regularly include brainstorming, mini-lectures (in form of position papers delivered by staff members), and roundtable discussions.

Betsy Wilson (formally head of the undergraduate library at the University of Illinois) explained how she was able to introduce cooperative learning techniques to a campus committee in order to improve group dynamics and enhance productivity. Cooperative learning techniques provided the structure necessary to encourage the free generation of ideas and to insure the full participation from all committee members.

Copies of the information packet and annotated bibliography on cooperative learning are available from Mary Jane Petrowski (petrowsk@ux, cso.uiuc.edu), Undergraduate Library, University of Illinois, 1402 West Gregory Street, Urbana, IL 61801.

Endnotes

1. Julius J. Maller, *Cooperation and Competition: An Experimental Study in Motivation.* (New York: Columbia University, 1929).
2. Minnie Lewis Johnson Abercrombie, *Arms and Techniques of Group Teaching.* (London: Society for research into Higher Education, 1974).
3. Annotated references to the work of David W. Johnson, Roger T. Johnson, Shlomo Sharan, and Robert Slavin can be found in Samuel Totten, et al *Cooperative Learning: A Guide to Research.* (New York: Garland, 1991).

Using Op Ed Pieces to Teach B. I.: Running Backwards from the Finish Line, Chapter II

Dal Symes and Raymond McInnis
Western Washington University
Bellingham, Washington

Abstract

Presents ways in which students develop formal scholarly articles from newspaper op ed pieces, and demonstrates how word processing can be used in teaching writing and research.

PROGRAM
SESSIONS

X.
BUILDINGS

Too Much Knowledge, Too Few Dollars: A Library Programming Case Study

Steven M. Foote, Moderator
Perry Dean Rogers & Partners
Boston, Massachusetts

Abstract

A critique of library program written for an undergraduate college of 2,000-5,000 students which includes a statement of philosophy, acquisitions policies, shelving and seating standards, area and technological specifications, and projections for growth.

Using a case study approach seven librarians assembled as a panel to review an all-to-familiar situation. The library staff at a well-known undergraduate college had developed a building program for the future of the library which the college could not afford to complete.

In the context of that problem, the panelists reviewed the program and shared their reactions and suggestions in the hopes of being able to bridge the gap between the requirements and the ability to fund.

The case study was that of the John B. Scholtz Library at the College of La Tourette in rural New England, a prototypical and commonly recognized institution. The college has a population of 1900 full time undergraduates, and its collection presently contains 335,000 monographs with 146,000 publications and government documents, 1,300 periodical titles, 4,200 AV materials and 112,000 microforms. The library is contained in a 35-year-old-building of 70,000 gross square feet, and the program called for an expansion to 106,000 gross square feet; therefore, construction required was 36,000 square feet.

The panel understood that a budget for the work should be $200 per square foot for the project in 1992 dollars.

The panelists addressed the problem as follows:

Sherrie S. Bergman, Wheaton College, Norton, Massachusetts; An Overview of the Programming Process

Joel Clemmer, Macalester College, Saint Paul, Minnesota; The Definition and Commitment to a Library Project

Evan Ira Farber, Earlham College, Richmond, Indiana; Learning from the Earlham Experience

Barbara J. Ford, Virginia Commonwealth University, Richmond, Virginia; Library Programs that Facilitate the Teaching-Learning Process: Efficiencies for La Tourette

John G. Jaffe, Sweet Briar College, Sweet Briar, Virginia; Pitfalls and Politics

Philip D. Leighton, Seating, Stanford University, Stanford, California; Seating, Collections, and the Experience of Building Design

Donald E. Riggs, University of Michigan, Ann Arbor, Michigan; Storage Systems and Retrieval

While in general agreement that the library program presented was a conservative one, the panel was able to present illuminating questions and strategies for the reduction of the program to fit the circumstances. Among the ideas were the following:

1. Libraries should be planned for a maximum of 15 years of projected growth and expansion. Older models of 25 and 30 years no longer appropriate, because requirements for the storage of materials are simply in too much flux given the expansion of electronic acquisitions and information exchange.

2. Libraries, to the extent that they can be, are more efficient operating longer hours than they are with

the provision of unstaffed student reading or study space. The 24-hour study idea is more costly to build and staff, and the alternative of providing longer hours for the library is more efficient.

3. The use of compact shelving, while antithetical to older ideas of browsing was uniformly felt to be a fact of life now and for the future. All journals, government documents and archival material are suitable candidates for storage in compact shelving, and the panel felt that provision for compact shelving should be included in every new building being considered.

4. The 35% ratio of library seats to total population, long considered a minimum, can be reduced to 25% if adequate study space can be found in dormitories or elsewhere on campus.

5. The panel was uniform in its conviction that library needs can only be addressed if the campus community-at-large senses real ownership in the library.

Accordingly, programs should only be prepared with the personal participation of the President, who will lead any institution as it makes major improvements to its physical plant, the "Vice President for Money," whose participation and endorsement is both important and unavoidable, and the conviction of a significant number of the Board of Trustees. There was lively debate on the value of the democratization of the programming process; opinions were held on both sides of the question. The support of the key players was uniformly felt to be essential, and any program prepared in the absence of that support was felt to be at risk.

PROGRAM SESSIONS

XI.
COLLECTION
DEVELOPMENT

Coordinated Collection Development: The Current Impetus

Mary Hong Loe, SUNY College at Oswego, Oswego, New York
Barbara M. Allen, Illinois State, Normal, Illinois
Barbara Doyle, Augustana College, Rock Island, Illinois
Tony Ferguson, Columbia University, New York, New York
Dal Symes, Western Washington University, Bellingham, Washington

Abstract

Highlights several multi-type library, coordinated collection development programs, stressing catalysts and strategies that nurtured their development and funding sources.

A Shared Collections Access Program

Stella Bentley, University of California at Santa Barbara
George Soete,University of California at San Diego,
Karin Wittenberg, University of California at Los Angeles

Abstract

An overview of the collaborative collection development program of the University of California Libraries and its impact on users and public services.

Interpreting the Conspectus Across Disciplines in a Medium Sized Academic Library

Sharon Lee Cann
Rebecca C. Drummond
Mary H. Munroe
Anne Page Mosby
Georgia State University
Atlanta, Georgia

Introduction

In this panel discussion, the Conspectus was defined as a strict methodology which has been created for use either in a consortium or an individual library. It is an overview or summary which includes collection strengths and collecting intensities. The Pacific Northwest Conspectus model was used in these projects.

Assessment is a loose term which refers to an overview of a collection for a particular purpose, and may involve a wide variety of methods. Evaluation refers to a specific set of methods, either in a conspectus or an assessment. Evaluation methods may include list checking, shelf scanning, applying discipline based standards to the collection, checking total resources and document delivery tests, compiling statistics, checking citations of library users, and user opinion surveys.

Although careful and exact statistical methodologies should and can be used, collections are living things, and measurement requires some of the same attention to nuance that apply in opinion research. These methodologies also cannot and should not act as substitutes for informed judgement about the quality of collections.

Interdisciplinary fields are particularly difficult to study because the definition of the fields and the subject classes where they appear in the library may be much less clear than those in traditional subject areas. These fields require interpretation of conspectus methodology for assessment. The four areas covered in the panel discussion were education, African American studies, women's studies, and public administration. Education was included because although it was a traditional conspectus project, education as a discipline exhibits some interdisciplinary characteristics.

Adapting the CONSPECTUS in Education

Among the eight reasons listed for beginning an assessment of the education collection, some of the more important motives included knowing facts about the collection to prepare for the NCATE accreditation team and fostering better relations with book chairs through an informed knowledge base about the professional education collection, including both present strengths and collection needs.

The education librarian, was interested in using conspectus methodologies to accomplish the project. Three methods, shelflist measurement, list checking, and shelf scanning, were used to examine class L (Education) in a triangulation approach. The Georgia State University shelflist was compared with the National Shelflist Count in number of volumes and percentage of total collection. GSU held 26,465 volumes and education represents 2.39 % of the total collections. Lists checked included several suggested by the 1987 Research Libraries Group guidelines for education. Journals were checked in *Current Index to Journals in Education, Education Index,* and *Social Science Citation Index.* For reference materials, Woodbury's *A Guide to Sources of Education Information* (1982) was used, while Mitzel's *Encyclopedia of Education Research* was not used. The new *Books for College Libraries* (1988) was also used because it listed the holdings in Library of Congress classification order and was easily checked by staff in the Collection Development Department. O'Brien's *Core List of Books and Journals in Education* (1991) was also used.

Shelf scanning was done in eight specific subject areas of the subclass LB, Theory and Practice of Education. LB was chosen as it had the largest number of holdings among universities reporting their holdings in the National Shelflist Count, and because it is the most heavily used at Georgia State University. Age, condition, publishers, and usage were examined. The study confirmed that most materials were published in the 1970s, condition was good to excellent, even with high usage, and trade publishers predominated.

The collection was assigned the 3b Intermediate Study Level based on the percentages held in the major lists, the shelflist count, and shelf scanning. Although a traditional conspectus approach was used on the education project, bibliographers must know what is held in other areas to evaluate library collections in education.

Assessing Materials for African American Studies

Georgia State University is in a unique position to develop a program in African American studies because it is a downtown university, located near convenient public transportation, and serves a population which is 26 percent African American. Furthermore, Atlanta has always fostered leadership and activism in the African American community, and Georgia State and other institutions in the area already have on staff several scholars of African American studies with national reputations who are willing to assist in the development of such a program. (Two of the bibliographies used in this assessment were working manuscripts which these scholars have been using in classes.) There has also been a longstanding interest among students and faculty at Georgia State University in developing a viable program in African American studies. Moreover, there are very good library holdings, notably at Clark Atlanta University, the King Center, Emory University, the University of Georgia, and in the new African American Resources Center of the Atlanta Fulton Public Library. Recently a university task force has been working to make recommendations on African American studies and inter-group relations.

Clearly an assessment would be useful, both to present the library's concerns about building this collection at Georgia State, and in developing new opportunities for cooperation with other libraries in the area. Standard evaluation methods were adapted for this interdisciplinary evaluation: bibliography checking, shelf scanning, and shelflist study. Condition of the collection was a particular concern, and measurements included age, use, binding, and degree of brittleness.

Checking some 25 bibliographies produced a finding that on average, GSU holds 50 percent of standard bibliographies, which would suggest a conspectus level of Intermediate Study Level (3b), adequate to support college-level term paper writing. However, shelf scanning revealed facts about the condition of the collections which caused this level to be reduced to Basic Study Level (3a), adequate for curriculum support for basic undergraduate instruction. These findings included heavy use(over 86 percent used, one-third of volumes rebound, nearly one-fourth missing), over half of the titles having 1965-74 publication dates, and one-third of the volumes with brittle paper. These interpretations and statistics will be a valuable aid in fostering cooperative action within the community as well as among library collections in the Atlanta setting.

Evaluating Interdisciplinary Collections: The Women's Studies Conspectus

Tthe Women's Studies conspectus was started in fall 1991. The presentation concerned three areas: 1. methods used to obtain an overview of the collection, 2. problems encountered in the women's studies worksheets, and 3. the methods used to assign levels to the collection.

An overview of the women's studies collection was obtained through sampling a printout of the collection, and shelf scanning to note binding condition, brittleness, use, type of publisher, and language. The results of this shelf scanning indicated that the collection was in good condition, and contained predominantly English language commercial or university press imprints. The collection was also compared to local and national collections. A search strategy similar to that used in the Pullen Library online catalog was used in the online catalogs of Emory University and the University of Georgia and in the online database, LC MARC. The GSU collection was approximately half the size of the local collections and about one fourth the size of the LC MARC collection.

Problems encountered in the worksheets included subjects that were omitted, such as the Medieval/ Anglo-Saxon/Anglo-Norman periods in English Literature (PR), call numbers that were too broad, such as PA for "Women in Greek and Latin literature," and call numbers that were too narrow. These problems were either addressed by adding additional lines to the worksheets or deciding to address the area in later more detailed conspectus projects.

The principal methods used to assign levels included reliance on the Women's Studies Guidelines and results from checking the bibliographies recommended in those guidelines. The guidelines and bibliographies will be used to assign levels at the category level, but the bibliographer's judgement and knowledge of the collection will be used to assign levels at the subject level.

Tailoring Conspectus Methodology: The Public Administration Assessment

One of the goals of a bibliographer is to educate faculty to think about the library when a new program is proposed. Therefore, a proposed Ph.D. program in public administration offered a wonderful opportunity for an assessment of the collection. However, the time frame for the assessment was very short, and the assessment needed to include the cost to upgrade present library resources from master's level to Ph. D. level.

Since no guidelines were available, call number ranges were taken from the Library of Congress Classification Schedules and the Pacific Northwest Conspectus worksheets. These ranges were tested in our online catalog and found to be a good fit for our library.

The methodology included shelflist counts, shelf scanning and checking of lists, and the public administration collection at GSU was compared to major collections in the area to illustrate strengths and weaknesses and to show local resources on which students might draw.

After completion of the shelflist counts and list checking, levels were assigned and a summary of the results went to faculty illustrated by graphs and charts created from the microcomputer software packages used for assessment at GSU.

Finally, the MINIMUM standard for Ph.D. level library support was established. The annual budget for monographs was determined by comparing the present acquisition level with the minimum requirement, established by the Pacific Northwest Conspectus, for Research Level and multiplying by the average cost of a monograph in this field. In journals, the same procedure was followed to bring holdings up to the minimum required. As a result, $9400 would need to be added permanently to the base budget, and an additional $9400 would need to be spent to fill gaps in the collection.

Doing conspectus projects are time-consuming but necessary. The information will be valuable not only for periodic updates on collections, but to support requests for funding both within and outside the base of institutional support. More than a device for making selection more accurate, a conspectus project can help to make the library strategic plan more accurate and realistic—indeed a collection management as well as a collection development tool.

Guidelines and Models of Collection Evaluation

Tina C. Fu, Cynthia Arent, and Susheela Rao,
University of Wisconsin-Oshkosh
Oshkosh, Wisconsin

Abstract

Examines the role that collection evaluation can assume in academic processes (accreditation, academic program reviews, and new degree proposals) and demonstrates efforts in building various evaluation models.

In 1988, the University of Wisconsin Oshkosh campus administration and faculty were engaged in a university-level planning process. The group identified major goals to achieve: among the high priority goals was "Instructional Services and Technology." It was felt by the planning group that in order to achieve this goal, it was necessary to undertake the task of assessing laboratories, library collections, computer facilities, etc. The University Goal Groups were specifically interested in quantitative measures for assessment purposes. As a result, the Collection Development Officer was charged with drafting guidelines so that the library collections could be assessed.

Since it was felt that the entire library collection could not be evaluated in the matter of a few months, the Collection Development Officer examined the types of academic processes on campus in which collection evaluation could be conducted on a regular basis. As a matter of fact, some collection evaluation efforts were undertaken in the past, albeit irregularly and using varying methods. The following academic processes were identified for inclusion in the "Guidelines for Collection Evaluation":

Accreditation and Re-accreditation
New Program Proposals or Degree Entitlements
Regularly Scheduled Academic Program Reviews
As Requested by Departments/Colleges

Research then was conducted to see what kind of evaluation models could be adopted so that collection developers would not have to re-invent the wheel. The "collection-centered measures" found in Blaine H. Hall's book *Collection Assessments Manual for College and University Libraries* were adopted since these measures would meet the quantitative measurement requirement set by the University Goal Groups, and the qualitative measures would help refine collection building efforts. With the availability of OPAC's, a measure to compare our collections with peer institutions (as identified by department/college faculty) was added to Hall's model. Thus, the following collection-centered measures were adopted in the "Guidelines for Collection Evaluation": size, growth, expenditures, checking lists, comparing with peer Institutions, accreditation standards, and interlibrary loan activity.

The "Guidelines" were proposed to the library faculty and the Executive Director of Libraries, and in January, 1989, they were submitted by the Executive Director to the Goal Groups.

Quite a few evaluations have been conducted since 1989, including academic program reviews and several re-accreditation efforts, which were all successful (e.g., College of Business Administration, Journalism, Counseling Education, and Social Work). The models used have also considerably shortened the reaccreditation library self-study reports while meeting all the requirements set by the accreditation agencies. The academic program reviews have drawn a lot of attention from department/college faculty.

The "Guidelines" and models are still evolving, e.g., addition of a section on new access technologies. Technological advances (e.g., document delivery services, telecommunications) can be easily incorporated into the present models, thus moving the evaluation measures from being "collection-centered" to "access-centered." Best of all, the library has managed to turn a negative political situation into a positive one. And in the recent budgetary round, the library is getting more money, as supported by the university administration as well as college/department faculty (over their strong desire to use all dollars to boost their below-the-national-average salaries).

The following two parts will be devoted to examples of new degree entitlements followed by two academic program reviews.

A New Approach and a New Model for Degree Proposals/Entitlements

Granted that the traditional method of checking lists has its uses, it is clearly outdated for modern library collection evaluation purposes in a world of growing sophistication and the new demands of expanding libraries and university departments. Complex problems and new challenges call for new approaches and different devices.

The new model, simply put, is a cumulative approach, which employs the following procedures: doing quantitative and qualitative analysis; checking for currency, adequacy, and completeness; comparing the target institution's collection with the collections of selected outside institutions and again between two periods within itself; and finally, illustrating the collected data statistically and graphically with the aid of computer software.

Perhaps the method can be best explained by describing the procedures followed in the collection evaluation done for the Department of Mathematics, when the faculty wanted to introduce a Statistics Major in 1988, although it had been used for Computer Science Department the year before.

Preliminary to the actual steps of evaluation, the library holdings were divided into four major categories: monographs (books, microforms, etc.), periodicals, reference collection together with indexes and abstracts, and database search services. The actual procedure consisted of the following steps: identify subject headings and correlate them with Library of Congress Subject Headings; identify the names of sister institutions which had successfully introduced the major, then gather statistical data for each subject heading, and compare with UW-O's holdings, followed by a comparison with standard recommended core lists for quality, adequacy, and completeness. Subsequently, a comparison was made between two periods within the target institution for growth rate and also a comparison with chosen sister institutions. Next, a comparison of the periodical holdings between the target institution and sister institutions was made and also with standard core lists. For the reference collection, only standard lists were used for lack of the availability of lists from other institutions. The same procedure was used for indexes and abstracts. The evaluation included information on database services at the target institution together with information on the journals most often used by the faculty at the institution, drawing the information from interlibrary loan request.

In conclusion, it is obvious that this method of collection evaluation with its cumulative approach and its examination of the chosen collection by parts and by comparison provides a more accurate evaluation than the traditional general approach. Because this method contains a check-and-balance feature and a closer examination of the parts of collection, it provides more reliable, more specific, and comprehensive results, and with the use of computers it can only become more effective and valuable.

Models for Academic Program Review

As liaison to ten social sciences departments, the author was requested to perform comparative evaluations of the library collection in the areas of history and psychology. Each department was conducting an academic program review, and had selected "peer institutions"—those with similar programs and resources—for comparison.

Based on the comparison model for program reviews developed by Susheela Rao and Tina Fu, each department identified subject headings to be searched and the names of the peer campuses chosen. The subject headings were translated into Library of Congress subject terminology, and the departments were given the lists of translated headings for their approval. When the departments accepted the LC subjects, the search of online catalogs for this library and the peer campuses was begun.

In order to do a thorough comparison of holdings, plus any requested lists, the library asked for eight weeks to complete the analysis. When the department had less time available, as was the case for psychology, the library worked with the department's representative to determine which parts of the review were most vital for the department's purposes. For the psychology review, the library provided a spreadsheet listing of thirty subject headings, and the holdings under each for the University of Wisconsin-Oshkosh, and two peer institutions: Eau Claire, and Stevens Point. In addition to the comparative search of subject headings, the review included a comparison of periodical holdings to the titles recommended in the William Katz publication *Magazines For Libraries*. The department initially requested journal holdings lists for the peer campuses, which it is still necessary to obtain individually by mail, therefore leaving insufficient time to complete the comparison.

The more extensive history department review included five subject headings from three institutions, plus a comparative list of periodicals and several bibliographies. History was given a spreadsheet list of holdings by subject and campus, as well as a graph of holdings by recent publication date. The department also requested lists of history-related holdings in audiovisual and microform formats. The listing of microforms was difficult because few items had been catalogued. The vast majority were located by a physical search of cabinets.

The discovery of the lack of catalogued microform items, as well as deficits in periodical or subject holdings, actually benefitted the library, as these areas could then be targeted for remedial action. Additional microforms have now been catalogued, and departments will request items for purchase to fill identified gaps in the collection.

Both reports were well received by the departments; however, the faculty had differing expectations regarding the final totals. One department hoped to find this library's holdings to be adequate, current, and comparable to those of peer campuses. The other expected to find the Oshkosh collection inadequate, outdated, and unable to support the department's program of study, and to use the report to gain administrative support for its program. Though the library's review did not give the faculty the expected ammunition, the department did request additional funds, and met with some success from private donors.

These collection evaluation efforts have many advantages besides the ones already mentioned. To name just a few, relationships and communications between librarians and department faculty have greatly improved. The process identified areas of library operations which can be improved, for example, cataloging of microforms. Although the library actually takes some risks in recognizing over-collecting and under-collecting of certain areas, it is felt that because of the benefits, it is worth the risk and the time.

Contemporary Sources for Collection Evaluation and Planning

R. Charles Wittenberg, Blackwell North America
Kathy Teszla, Emory University, Atlanta, Georgia
Joanne Hill, Middlebury College, Middlebury, Vermont
Tricia Vierra Masson, American University, Washington, D.C.

Abstract

Librarians and library vendors explore the use of non-traditional resources, changing attitudes towards use and demand in buying material, and vendor-generted data sources.

PROGRAM SESSIONS

XII.
COMMUNITY COLLEGE LIBRARIES

Project ACCESS: Toward a Curriculum-based Collection in a Library without Walls

Richard Meerdink and James Jandovitz
Milwaukee Area Technical College
Milwaukee, Wisconsin

Abstract

A presentation on the goals and implementation of a federal grant award to enhance access to traditional and electronic materials and information.

Aggressive Teaching for Information Literacy in High-Tech Times

Jimmie Anne Nourse and Rudy Widman
Indian River Community College
Fort Pierce, Florida

Abstract

The development of an effective library teaching program is advocated along with a practical, proactive hands-on approach to establishing the library as an information hub.

Where Are We Now: Ohio Two-Year College Libraries/Learning Resource Centers and the New ACRL/AECT Standards

Marcia Suter
University of Toledo
Toldeo, Ohio

and

Margy Kramer
Hocking Technical College
Nelsonville, Ohio

Abstract

Results of a 1990 survey of Ohio's two-year learning resource centers which compares personnel, facilities, services, and the new ACRL/AECT standards are presented.

Ohio, like only a handful of other states, has a variety of types of two year colleges. These include: technical colleges, community colleges, state community colleges (which differ from community colleges in funding equations and how trustees are appointed rather than in mission), two year branch campuses of four year institutions, community and technical colleges, and an agricultural technical institute. To further complicate matters five branch campuses and five technical colleges share campuses, facilities and sometimes staff to a greater or lesser degree. Two of the community colleges have multiple campuses and a public community college shares facilities with a private university. To outsiders this diversity seems like an administrative nightmare but it has allowed each institution to evolve according to its individual strengths and the strengths of the community it represents. Thus the strengths and weaknesses rest with the institutions and not with the system.

The two year institutions report directly to the Chancellor of the Board of Regents. Though this gives each institution a direct voice to the Chancellor, the unique mission of the two year colleges often gets lost amid the political clout of the universities. Although the four year institutions continue to receive the lion's share of funding, by fall 1991, the two year colleges were serving almost 50% of the student headcount at Ohio institutions of higher education. Administrative units of the colleges have met to share interests and concerns for many years. The Inter-University Library Council was formed in the early 1970s to serve the needs of the libraries of the four year institutions, but two year college LRCs were not included in this group. Two year college Learning Resource Center (LRC) personnel felt the need to meet and share their special problems and concerns. In 1972, the branch campus

librarians began holding an annual mini-conference. In 1975, seven representative from technical college LRCs met during their Instructional Officers' meeting to discuss the desire to hold a meeting of all LRC personnel. The first conference was held at Columbus State Community College, then Columbus Technical Institute, in the spring of 1976. This meeting led to biannual conferences held spring and fall at a different two year college campus. The agenda is chosen by the group to include topics of interest and importance to two year college LRC personnel. The meetings give participants not only the opportunity for professional development, but also allow them to visit different facilities and share unique ideas. The Ohio Two Year College Learning Resource Center Conferences have now taken place for the last fifteen years. Over the years the group has discussed formalizing or affiliating with an organization like ALAO (Academic Library Association of Ohio), but the feeling has always been "if it ain't broke, don't fix it." The loose organization has allowed it the flexibility to meet the needs of the participants as well as enabling them to apply for grants as a group.

From their earliest meetings, the two year college LRC personnel felt that they could assist their institutions by sharing resources as well as ideas. The first resource sharing project involved serials. Members desired to share serials holdings because they are the best resource for up-to-date technical information, the colleges had many unique titles, and their students often could not afford the cost in time or money of traditional inter-library loan. In 1977 the first union list of serials was put together by the librarian at Central Ohio Technical College and included the holdings of eight colleges. Unfortunately, when the librarian left COTC a year later the program for the list went with her. In 1981, the group decided to find a method to produce a union list that could be updated annually and easily allow new members to join. An LSCA grant was written to produce a union list on the OCLC Serials Union List Subsystem. It was the first union list produced in the State of Ohio using the OCLC Subsystem and was the fore runner of SOUL, the State of Ohio Union List. The list is in its ninth printing and the membership has increased from twelve to twenty-two institutions.

In 1988, a second LSCA grant was written to purchase telefacsimile machines to facilitate resource sharing. That year seventeen institutions joined together to apply for a College Library Technology and Cooperation grant to produce a CD-ROM disc of book, periodical, and media software holdings of the participants.

Another need the group met was the ability to share statistical information. The 1972 Guidelines for Two Year College Learning Resource Programs were qualitative rather than quantitative. The *Statistics of Ohio Libraries*, published annually by the State Library of Ohio, provided some basic statistics gathered from the HEGIS (now IPEDS) reports. The variety of types of two year colleges in Ohio often made it difficult to compare them to a community college model. In addition, LRC personnel in Ohio had specific questions about their institutions that they wanted to compare with others of similar size or type. Some of the most interesting and revealing results are:

Standard 1:   Objectives. Directors of the LRCs report to nineteen different administrative titles, from director or dean of the college to director of business services.

Standard 2:   Organization. Nineteen of the forty-two institutions have only one professional librarian.

Standard 3:   Staff. Of the thirty-eight institutions reporting, all but one LRC is administered by a professional with an MLS or a Master's in Educational Technology. Only ten LRCs have professionals who spend more than 50% of their time on reference services.

Standard 4:   Budge. Two small branch campuses are the only ones exceeding the minimum standard for budget as a percentage of their colleges' education and general expenditures. No LRC came close to the standard for expenditures per FTE for learning resources other than salaries.

Standard 5:   User Services. All institutions provide a variety of services. Twenty-five provide CD-ROMS for end-user searching. Half do on-line data base searching.

Standard 6:   Collections. A few LRCs exceed the standards for number of volumes, current serials subscriptions, and audio-visual items. Twenty-four of the surveyed LRCs use some type of automated cataloging system.

Standard 7:   Facilities. The LRCs were open an average of sixty-six hours per week offering traditional library and audio-visual services, teleconferencing, college archives, computer labs and a variety of other functions.

All of Ohio's two year college learning resource centers provide a program of integrated library and media services that is centrally administered. Almost all of them fail to meet the 1990 ACRL/AECT Standards for Two-Year Colleges in regard to staffing requirements, budget expenditures, and collection size; even though all of the colleges are accredited by the North Central Accrediting Agency. The two year colleges now serve almost 50% of the student headcount at Ohio institutions of higher education, yet they receive only 19.8% of the state budget allocated to higher education. The LRCs provide a variety of services and many are integrating new technologies into their programs. To provide these services with limited budgets and staffing the LRCs must have a close connection to the educational process and the needs of the individual campuses. Since budgets have always been limited, spending often reflects the life boat effect—meet the needs of the greatest number of students. The LRCs have been active and willing participants in consortia and have led the state in resource sharing projects. They have become adept at finding creative means to stretch dollars.

The authors have looked at Ohio's learning resource centers very carefully and manipulated the survey data several ways to see if Ohio's two year college learning resource centers met the standards as a group. The standards are based solely on size—FTE enrollment.

Data not only by size, but by type of college—community, technical, branch, or state community college were examined. This helped determine if any type of college—regardless of size—was meeting the standards. None are.

Comments by members in the audience from a variety of states gave a picture very similar to Ohio's—that is, under-budgeted, under-staffed, not meeting the standards, and facing budget cuts.

Questions arose concerning the usefulness of the standards. Are they realistic? Who meets or approaches them? How should they be changed when they are rewritten? If the standards represent an ideal we should strive toward, are they so far from being attainable as to be out of the realm of possibility?

PROGRAM SESSIONS

XIII.
CULTURAL DIVERSITY

Diversity and Pluralism in Staffing: Strategies That Work

Laurita Moore de Diaz
Rio Salado Community College
Phoenix, Arizonia

Abstract

Explores effective recruitment and hiring techniques and employment strategies related to diversity and pluralism.

African-American Studies in Libraries: The Collections Development, Maintenance and Futures

Howard Dodson
New York Public Library
New York, New York

Reactors: Michael C. Walker, Virginia Commonwealth University; Rodney Lee, Roosevelt Public Library; Doris Clack, Florida State University; Stanton F. Biddle, Baruch College, City University of New York

Abstract

The Afro-American collections of major libraries (e. g., Schomburg, Library of Congress, Moorland-Springarn Research Center) grew out of the historical commitment to preserve materials which documents the contributions of Afro-Americans to the development of the United States. Today the rationale for collecting must change to include a full documentation of the life of Afro-American peoples and the Afro-American diaspora throughout the western hemisphere. Libraries can use new collection development strategies and new technologies to collect materials needed to serve Afro-American studies programs and departments.

Seventy-six years ago this December (1916), a group of black bibliophiles gathered at the Washington, D.C. residence of John Wesley Cromwell to explore the feasibility of establishing a Negro Book Collectors Exchange. The occasion was the annual meeting of the American Negro Academy, an association of African American, "men of science, letters and art or those distinguished in other walks of life," founded in the nation's capital in March 1897. Its purposes were to encourage research, writing, and publication of scholarly works dealing with the global African experience. Its members were also encouraged to develop an archive of materials by and about peoples of African descent. Cromwell, a bibliophile and amateur historian, was a founding member of the Academy. The founding meeting of the Academy had also been held in his home.

The Exchange would have a more limited goal—"to centralize all literature written by colored people." In attendance were bibliophiles John Edward Bruce, Henry Proctor Slaughter, the Reverend Charles Douglass Martin, Dr. Jesse F. Moorland, Daniel Alexander Payne Murray, and Arturo Alfonso Schomburg. To achieve the Exchange's objectives, members proposed to establish what we would call a worldwide union list of books by and about people of African descent by asking all the known "Negro book collectors" to register themselves as well as the names of authors and titles of books in their collections with the Exchange.

Equipped with this master database, the Exchange would, in turn, serve as a comprehensive clearinghouse of information on black-related material as well as a vehicle to facilitate trading duplicate copies of books among its members. There is no evidence that the Negro Book Collector Exchange ever met again, much less formally carried out its ambitious agenda. Informally, its members continued to exchange information about their collections and to assist one another in acquiring copies of fugitive titles including duplicates from their respective collections.[1]

Those of us who have inherited these bibliophiles' collections and/or responsibility for continuing to collect and preserve materials documenting the African and African diasporan experience have still not solved the communications problem that was impeding the collection development efforts of our predecessors. Informally, information is shared about recent acquisitions. Occasionally, duplicate copies of rare book materials are made available to sister institutions. The publication and dissemination of respective dictionary catalogues has helped inform each other and the library world of the nature of our holdings. Membership in cooperative bibliographic utilities such as the Research Library Information network (RLIN) and the Online Computer Library Center (OCLC) has extended online access to our most recent acquisitions. Though most participate in these cooperative networks, there still is no organized, systematic collection development and preservation program among the major research libraries and special collections that have primary responsibility for collecting and preserving black-related materials. As a consequence, these libraries are not prepared to respond to the research, information and technological challenges of the last decade of the 20th century. Collection development strategies run the risk of being trapped in a paradigmatic framework that is rapidly losing its centrality if not usefulness in defining the field of African-American studies. Even as the libraries have become parts of cooperative networks, they have continued to function as though each of the collections could, if enough effort was expended, become a self-sufficient repository of publications and information on the black experience, capable in and of themselves of addressing the research and information needs of respective clienteles. Finally, escalating costs and shrinking budget notwithstanding, the libraries have continued to expend scarce revenue duplicating certain holdings or competing for rare and unique items (thereby escalating the costs). A modern version of the Exchange would likely help begin to address the latter problems. The former, however, requires some fundamental rethinking of mission and the scope of collection development responsibilities.

A recent paper by Dr. Ruth Hamilton, director of the African Diaspora Research Project entitled, "Towards a Paradigm for African Diaspora Studies: Research Questions and Strategies"[2] brought me face to face with the realization that most of the material contained in research libraries and other repositories that have been documenting the black experience over the last 50-75 years was collected, managed and preserved to respond to the political and intelligent problems of a different age. Those priorities and strategies require radical rethinking in light of the research questions Dr. Hamilton and the African Diaspora Project have put on our collection documentation and preservation agenda. Stated more bluntly, the proposed paradigm for African diaspora studies requires most comprehensive and collaborative collection development, collection management and documentation strategies than were required for any previous stage of research on the global African experience. What is proposed in this space is a review of the dominant intellectual and political paradigms that have informed our collecting activities. These will then be contrasted with those that are implicit in the African diaspora studies paradigm. Some suggestion of ways the new technologies might facilitate the realignment of the work are provided.

It is likely that the bibliophiles who organized the Exchange shared the collection development philosophy articulated in the Constitution of the "Negro Society for Historical Research." Founded in 1911 by John E. Bruce and Arturo Schomburg, this society sought, "to collect useful historical data relating to the Negro race, books written by or about Negroes, rare pictures of prominent men and women, letters of noted Negroes or white men friendly to the Negro, African curios of native manufacture etc." The Society's purpose was, "to show that the Negro race has a history which antedates that of the proud Anglo-Saxon race." Its founders were committed to collecting books, manuscripts and other historical data to support their claims regarding the antiquity of the Negro race and its contributions to world civilization.[3]

St. Clair Drake, late professor emeritus of emeritus of anthropology at Stanford University and a long term student of the African diaspora, frequently made reference to the development of the "vindicationist school" of black intellectuals that emerged during the late 19th century in the United States. These authors sought, through their research, writing and publications, to defend people of African descent against charges of racial inferiority and historical and cultural insignificance. Selectively drawing evidence of black people's intellectual and social development and their contributions to world civilization from published sources, photographs, art and other documentary resources, these vindicationists scholars helped establish the tradition of black scholarship as a resource in the black struggle for freedom and human dignity.

By the turn of the 20th century, a network of vindicationist collectors had also emerged in the African-American community. The group of bibliophiles who attended the Exchange meeting were active members of this network. Two aspects of their collecting activities are significant for our purposes. First, all of them collected globally though selectively. Their aim was to acquire and preserve the best publications and art produced by black people and the most significant evidence of black achievement worldwide. Second, the collections of several of these individuals became the foundations on which most of today's major black research libraries and special collections in the United States were built. Daniel Alexander Murray's collection became one of the bases for the development of the African holdings at the Library of Congress. Jesse Moorland's collection laid the foundations for today's

Moorland-Springarn Research Center. The black collection at Atlanta University includes the Slaughter collection. And of course, Arturo Schomburg and John E. Bruce's collections provided the foundations for today's Schomburg Center for Research in Black Culture.

Of equal significance, the early development of these collections—primarily of book materials—was guided by a concern for correcting the impression that black people were inferior to whites. Over the years, all the collections have expanded their collection scopes to include a wide array of material (both positive and negative) by and about people of African descent, but the dominant paradigm, a product of late nineteenth and early twentieth century intellectual and political concerns, has not been replaced by an alternative paradigm.

The closest thing to an alternative was established by the field of Afro-American studies as defined and interpreted by Melville J. Herskovits during the 1940s.[4] Herskovits' principle concerns were documenting the presence of Africans in the New World and the processes through which African, European, and native American cultures exerted mutual influence on one another in the hemisphere. Unlike the dominant paradigm, Afro-American studies' disciplinary base was anthropology rather than history. Interdisciplinary and comparative in approach, its method was ethnohistory. As such, unlike the dominant approach, it was concerned (perhaps more so) with black mass-based social groups as it was with black leaders and elite in various fields of human endeavor. Collections developed to support research in this field included published literature. But photographs, artifacts, sound recordings, film, oral history interviews and other forms of documentation were also collected and preserved from both sides of the Atlantic.

Initially concerned with establishing the historical derivation and forms of African diasporan cultures, Afro-American studies introduced such research concepts as retention, reinterpretation and syncretism. In so doing, it pointed up the dynamic quality of African derived cultures in the Americas. Among the principle questions the field placed on the research agenda were the causes of the diversity of African people in the hemisphere. How did Africans accommodate themselves to their new world environments during slavery? How did this process work out in different parts of the Americas where differing ecological settings,

basic industries and cultural orientations prevailed? How did class differentials influence the accommodation process?[5] Herskovits and his colleagues raised these questions in the 30s and 40s and worked on many of them until the 1950s when Herskovits' attention turned to African studies. These kinds of questions would not be taken up again until the late 1960s, with the renewed interest in comparative studies of slave societies in the Americas.

I am a part of the generation of the 1960s and 1970s that raised fundamental questions about the adequacy of what we then called "Negro History" for addressing the intellectual and political needs of the post-civil rights phase of black American's struggle for freedom and human dignity. The development of "Black History" as a critical alternative to "Negro History" paralleled the development of black studies or Afro-American studies programs and departments at American colleges and universities. Rejecting Negro History's liberal, integrationist political outlook, this new black history also posed questions of the black American and American experience that had not been on the vindicationist's agenda. The new black history, we maintained had to be expansive enough to accommodate the experiences of the masses of black people as well as its political and social elite—men and women of achievement. Women, and children as well as men had to be included. Class and ethnic diversity needed to be reflected. Of greatest significance, black people like all human beings, needed to be viewed as history and culture makers in their own right rather than mere participants in or objects of established definitions of American historical and cultural process. The new black American history was seen as a critique of the traditional approaches to the study of both Negro *and* American history. Firmly committed to developing new insights into the processes of historical and cultural transformation that characterized the black American particularity, it was also committed to contributing to the process of redefining and rewriting American history. Its separatist agenda was both a means to an end and an end in itself. Undergirding these formulations was the assumption that black American and American history were part of a broader, dynamic, global process of development and underdevelopment, transformation and change.

What is attractive about the African diaspora studies paradigm is that it applies many of these same principles to the study of African diasporan social formations around the globe. The African diasporan paradigm (ADP) establishes a framework in which both the historical and contemporary dynamics of the diverse African diasporan communities can be studied. It provides a paradigm for comparative studies of these communities as a means of discerning the areas of commonality and difference that exist among people of African descent worldwide. Viewing African peoples living in diasporan settings as actors and subject in history and culture making processes, the ADP establishes criteria for measuring both the processes of change within African diasporan communities as well as the economic, political, cultural, and social impact of African diasporan peoples on the communities and nations in which they reside. Recognizing the diasporan experience of people of African descent as a global phenomenon, the ADP seeks to analyze African diasporan peoples' historical, cultural, social and contemporary thought and behavior in the context of the global political economy.[6]

The ADP then, combines the very best elements of the new black American history with the questions of group formation and change that informed Herskovits' Afro-American studies at the peak of its development. Whereas the earlier research paradigms (and the collections they engendered) were consciously selective and relatively limited in scope because of their explicit or implicit political agenda, the ADP must, of necessity, be more expansive and comprehensive in its approach. Studying the inner dynamics of African diasporan communities requires documentation and analysis of all of the social subgroups that make up these communities. Social and cultural change are viewed as interactive processes in which all elements of the social formation are participants. Whereas the vindicationists focused on the elites and the Afro-Americanists focused on sectors of the masses, ADP requires that both elements as well as their gender, class and color elements be treated as part of the unit of analysis.

Relations between African diasporan communities and their host societies as well as the broader global political economy also require more expansive and comprehensive documentation strategies and conceptual frameworks than was the case in the vindicationist and Afro-Americanist models. This is especially true if we are to come to new understandings of the consequences of African diasporan economic, political, and social action on themselves and their socio-political environment. The points of intersection between African diasporan peoples and their host societies in key areas of political and social action require much more sophisticated documentation strategies than anything we have known in the past. Whereas previously both the vindicationists and Afro-Americansists were content to identify evidence of the "contributions" blacks had made to American and world society, the ADP insists that we go beyond a kind of positivist "contributionism" and seek to understand the consequences of African diasporan people's purposive action—both intended and unintended consequences of same.

Documenting the internal and external dynamics of African diasporan historical and cultural development, then, poses major challenges to our traditional collection development strategies. Focusing on the African diasporan experience in the western hemisphere and its relationship to the development of Afro-American studies programs and research, we will turn to a consideration of some of the short-term implications of these developments for libraries.

Libraries are challenged to develop more comprehensive and more balanced collections on the African diasporan experience. Of special urgency is the need to intensify collecting of retrospective book titles on the African diasporan experiences, especially in Latin America and Caribbean. For those of us involved in supporting and fostering research and scholarship in Afro-American studies, it is necessary we begin to think of Afro-American collections in hemispheric terms. Certainly, high on the acquisitions lists should be any and everything that can be found on the Afro-Brazilian experience. Brazil is the second largest African population in the world (second only to Nigeria). In the context of African American experience in this hemisphere, Brazil was the *first* major importer of African slave labor, the *largest* importer of African slave labor accounting for about 40% of the estimated 10 million and the oldest and longest running slavery system in the hemisphere. It remains to this day one of the most vibrant centers of traditional African culture in the Americas and virtually every aspect of Brazilian culture bears the stamp of the African presence there.

The Caribbean islands, the center of the sugar plantation economy and the second largest importer of enslaved Africans also merits greater attention in collection development and preservation priorities. The French, Spanish, and Dutch colonies established on these islands and along the coasts of the Caribbean sea are virtual laboratories for the comparative study of the processes of cultural transformation that occurred in the hemisphere. Moreover, the migration of these Caribbean islanders (and residents of the Caribbean basin) to Central America, the United States and European metropolises both during and after slavery has had an extraordinary impact on the cultural landscape and economic and social processes of the receiving societies. Works documenting both aspects of this Caribbean diaspora phenomenon should be added to black collections and courses studying these subjects to Afro-American studies curricula.

Finally, the Afro-Hispanic experience should receive greater attention than has been the case in the past. Works documenting the historical and cultural roles of African people in colonial Spanish America are available in greater abundance than in any previous period of African diasporan history. These materials should be collected comprehensively to the extent that budgets and other resources allow. As in the case in Afro-Brazilian studies, works on the Afro-Hispanic experiences in the Americas has, with a few noteworthy exceptions, been sorely neglected by scholars. While the foundations of diasporan African-American culture were laid during the period of slavery, the post emancipation period has been the period of greatest change. Librarians are challenged then, to collect and provide access to as much of this material as is available. It is likely that many of the retrospective materials needed to fill the voids in these areas are out of print and/or not available through existing buying arrangements. Should this prove to be the case, it will be necessary to rethink the relationship of black collections with the collections of research repositories (especially comprehensive research libraries) and the major on-line bibliographic utilities. The Schomburg Center, for instance, is currently involved in a survey project whose goal is to identify African diasporan and African-related materials in the collections of the other research centers of the New York Public Library. Founded before the Schomburg Center, the Research Libraries of the New York Public Library has been collecting black-related materials on other parts of the hemisphere since its inception. In many instances, the general collections on Latin American and Caribbean countries or general subjects related to these areas contain substantial bodies of black-related materials. More often than not, they were not cataloged in such a way as to provide subject access to their black-related content. Most comprehensive research libraries with large retrospective collections do not have plans to initiate large-scale retro-conversion and/or recatalog-

ing projects in the immediate future. In the interim, projects can be organized to identify discrete black-related segments on such retrospective holdings, recatalog, providing better subject access to them, and enter them into the national on-line databases. The overall object of the Schomburg/NYPL project is to do just that.

Collecting, preserving, and providing access to serials on these subjects poses a different set of problems. Newspapers, periodicals, newsletters and other serials, have been published by people of African descent throughout the hemisphere at least since the 19th century. The Historical Society of Wisconsin, which currently houses one of the largest collection of African-American (U.S.) newspapers, recently initiated a project to establish a national union list of holdings in this area. This project should go a long way towards filling the gaps in our knowledge about how many of these kinds of materials have survived and are available for research purposes. A long-term objective of the project appears to be to publish microform editions of the most significant bodies of these materials so they can be distributed more widely.

I am not aware of any comparable project that is focussed on identifying, preserving and providing access to such materials that have been published by blacks in Latin America and the Caribbean. As daily, weekly, or monthly chronicles of black thought and behavior in these parts of the diaspora, such publications are invaluable research resources for the study of African diasporan history and culture. The Schomburg Center recently acquired what is likely the only extant complete run of the *Panama Tribune,* the voice of the West Indian community in Panama during most of this century. No aspect of West Indian life in Panama is not covered by this newspaper. Longer and shorter running publications for all of the Caribbean Islands as well as Brazil and other South and Central American countries need to be identified, collected, preserved, and disseminated as comprehensively as possible.

Nowhere is need for collaborative approaches to collecting, preserving and providing access to African diaspora-related materials more obvious (or possible) then in the area of current serials. The level of duplication of effort in the collection and preservation of these materials is likely enormous. Acquiring and preserving serials has an enormous impact on our budgets. Yet, to date, we have not taken any serious steps toward developing such collaborative initiatives.

The time is right to do just that today. With a minimal level of planning and coordination among the dozen or so research libraries and special collections that systematically acquire serials in this area, we should be able to develop a comprehensive, shared collection development and preservation strategy for these materials. Each participant would assume responsibility for acquiring and preserving materials in its selected or assigned collection areas. Either microform copies could be made available to collaborative members on an at-cost basis or facsimile copies of articles could be made available on an on-demand basis.

At the beginning of the next fiscal year, the Schomburg Center will initiate a project to catalog and re-catalog all of its retrospective serials holdings. At the same time, we will begin the process of reevaluating serials acquisitions and preservation policies. We would welcome the opportunity to meet with sister institutions that collect in these areas to see how best to tackle these nettlesome (and costly) problems.

The biggest problem facing libraries and the field of Afro-American studies in documenting the hemisphere African-American experience lies in the area of identifying, preserving and providing access to the primary research resources that are essential for supporting new scholarship in this field. The preservation and documentation problems are at least hemispheric in scope. However the problems extend beyond the hemisphere because significant bodies of essential primary materials are in the libraries, museums and national, colonial, and religious archives of the major European colonizing powers. This suggests that in addition to a collection development strategy for materials in this hemisphere a comprehensive documentation strategy to identify, preserve and provide access to the massive, but as yet relatively inaccessible corpus of manuscript and archival records on the European continent is also needed. In addition, as in the case of book and book-like materials in existing repositories, records of general collections on countries with significant African diasporan populations will need to be revisited and updated to provide improved subject access to black-related items and or collections in the repository.

The magnitude and complexity of the problem of identifying and preserving an adequate documentary record on the hemisphere African diasporan experience suggests the need to develop a comprehensive documentation strategy. A documentation strategy is generally defined as a local, statewide, regional, na-

tional or international plan to assure the adequate documentation on ongoing multi-institutional issues, activities, functions or subjects.[7] As noted above, primary research materials on the hemispheric African-American experience are likely to be found in provincial, state and national archives throughout the hemisphere. Such records are also found in the libraries, museums, and archival repositories (especially colonial archives) of the major European colonizing powers. Finally, significant documentary materials are to be found in the records of religious and secular organizations. A document strategy on the African diasporan experience in the Americas should include at least four major components: 1) the identification and preservation of relevant research materials located in existing repositories; 2) the dissemination of microform copies of the most significant of these records; 3) the identification of relevant materials that are not currently housed in an archives or other preservation environment; 4) the development of a hemispheric union list of all relevant materials; 5) the establishment of an on-going cooperative program among relevant organizations to insure the continued documentation of this significant hemispheric phenomenon.

Collections Management and Access

Whereas in the past, libraries and archival institutions defined themselves primarily in terms of their collection holdings and saw themselves as relatively self-sufficient entities, the information explosion that has characterized the last two decades and the technological revolution in information science suggests that all libraries and repositories will be forced to rethink their identities, missions and approaches to public service if they are to act responsibly to their respective clienteles. Since no institution can any longer responsibly think of themselves as comprehensive repositories on any subject, the challenge to libraries is to carve out their areas of specialization, refine their collection scopes and levels, and position themselves within a network of complimentary institutions that can provide them and their clients with access to materials that they do not collect. It is likely that libraries of the future will be more defined by the access they can provide to information requested by their clients than by the specific materials they house in their collections. Establishing access to bibliographic records on given subjects and entering into cooperative arrangements with complimentary institutions that can provide access to information is the collection management and access challenge of the moment.

Among the institutions documenting the hemispheric African-American experiences, the Schomburg Center for Research in Black Culture of the New York Public Library and the Moorland-Spingarn Research Center at Howard University have the strongest and most comprehensive collections . Libraries responsible for supporting Afro-American studies programs and departments on college and university campuses are not likely to have the resources to duplicate these collections. Yet, students and scholars working in the field should have on-going access to the collections these two institutions, as well as those the Library of Congress, the National Archives, the Smithsonian Institution and other major collecting entities have amassed over the last century or more.

A small percentage of the collections of these repositories are being disseminated widely in microform formats. The National Archives has pioneered in this area and continues to publish major manuscript collections on microfilm on Afro-American themes. The Schomburg Center has also been aggressively publishing and disseminating microform editions of several aspects of its collections. To date, its Dictionary Catalog, a selection of pre-20th century books, its clipping file and upwards of a dozen of its manuscript collections have been published in microfilm or microfiche editions and made available to historically black college libraries and mainstream libraries serving Afro-Americans studies departments and programs.

It is likely, however, that for the foreseeable future, some other measures of dissemination will have to be put in place if Afro-American studies programs and departments are to have access to the collections of these major repositories on their respective campuses. It appears technologically possible to achieve this objective by relying more heavily on the information available through on-line bibliographic utilities; by taking greater advantage of CD-ROM technology for providing bibliographic access to fugitive materials within the collections; and by using telefacsimile technology to supply copies of documents, published records, photographs and other materials from the major research repositories to Afro-American studies programs and departments.

It is anticipated that by 1994, upwards of 90% of the Schomburg Center's processed collections will be cataloged in the RLIN and OCLC database. A retrospective conversion project is currently converting pre-1972 records to electronic formats. A special

collections access project is cataloging manuscript and archival records, sheet music, playscripts, photographs, prints, art works, sound recordings, motion pictures, videotapes, oral history materials at the collection level in the RLIN database. These records will then be loaded into OCLC. All-member institutions in these bibliographic utilities, will, therefore, have access to records on 90% of the Schomberg holdings.

Two CD-ROM products are being planned. The first, the *Kaiser Index to Black Resources 1948-1986* is a selected bibliographic guide to serials records and ephemera in the Schomburg Center's collections. The Center is currently equipped to provide copies of these materials. The second is a cumulative electronic version of *Black Studies*, the bibliographic guide to the Center's acquisitions from 1973 to 1992. The added advantages of the CD-ROM formats is the rapid subject access they provide.

Finally, the Center is exploring the feasibility of establishing formal relationships either with Afro-American studies programs directly or with their supporting libraries, to provide on-going access to the Center's collections using these and other technologies as they become available and applicable.

Endnotes

1. See Elinor Des Verney Sinnette, *Arthur Alfonso Schomburg: Black Bibliophile and Collector* (Detroit: Wyane State University Press, 1989): 73-74 for a discussion of the origins of the Negro Book Collector Exchange.
2. Ruth Simms Hamilton, "Toward a Paradigm for African Diaspora Studies" in *Creating a Paradigm and Research Agenda for Comparative Studies of the Worldwide Dispersion of African Peoples* edited by Ruth Simms Hamilton, (East Lansing, MI: Michigan State University, 1990): p. 15-26.
3. See Elinor Des Verney Sinnette, op cit., p. 43.
4. See Melville J. herskovits, "Problem, Method and Theory in Afroamerican Studies" *Afroamerica*, I (1945): 5-24 and "The Present /Status and Needs of Aroamerican Research" *Journal of Negro History*, (1951): 123-147 reprinted in *The New World Negro* edited by Frances S. Herskovits, (Bloomington: Indiana University Press, 1966), p. 43-61, 24-41.
5. Ibid.
6. Ruth Simms Hamilton, op. cit.
7. For a discussion of documentation strategies in

libraries and archives see, Helen Willa Samuels, "Who Controls the Past" *American Archivist* 49 (Spring, 1986): 109-124 and Larry J. Hackman and Joan Warnow-blewett, "The Documentation Strategy Process: A Model and a Case Study" *American Archivist* 50 (Winter, 1987): 12-47.

PROGRAM
SESSIONS

XIV.
GENEALOGY

A New Era For Genealogical and Historical Researchers and Libraries

Jay Roberts
Family History Library
Salt Lake City, Utah

Abstract

An orientation to the services and worldwide collections of the Family History Library and its 1,500 branches.

PROGRAM
SESSIONS

XV.
INTERNATIONAL
LIBRARIANSHIP

Book Donations to Third World Academic Libraries: Practical Considerations and a Roundtable Discussion

David L. Easterbrook, Northwestern University, Evanston, Illinois
Margaret Power, DePaul University, Chicago, Illinois

Abstract

Covers the central issues in establishing and managing book donation programs followed by a roundtable discussion on the subject by those present.

Research and the Academic Librarian: A Global View

R. N. Sharma
University of Evansville
Evansville, Indiana

Abstract

The session presented the views of five well known librarians and library educators from Australia, England, India, Kenya and Russia on research activities in the academic libraries of each speaker's country.

Dr. R.N. Sharma, Director of Libraries, University of Evansville was the moderator of the session. Mr. Colin Taylor, Deputy University Librarian, University of South Australia was the first speaker. He discussed the results of a survey of all university libraries in Australia and New Zealand conducted by him in the fall of 1991. In his view, much of the research by librarians in universities is of the developmental "try it and see" type and librarians need to better document and promulgate their achievements to gain re cognition as a legitimate area for research funding. Before discussing his results, Mr. Taylor gave a brief history of universities libraries in Australia and New Zealand.

Ms. Ludmila Kozlova, Chief, Department of International Library Relations, the Russian State Library, Moscow, Russia spoke about the research in her own country. She painted a picture of the past destruction of libraries and the structure which is breaking down but was optimist about the future. In the past, the research was always carried out by the largest libraries including the Moscow State University Library and was financed by the institutions. In the 1970s a complex research program was implemented under the guidance of the Lenin State Library. During the 1990s, the research emphasis is on the social role of libraries in conditions of renovation of the society, book and information cultures of the population, library services for the support of the social rehabilitation, automation of library technologies, and the development of librarianship towards the 21st century. She mentioned the inadequate budget allocation for libraries including poor salaries for librarians which keeps many talented people away from the profession. She was confident that Russia soon will have a place in the library world again.

Professor P. B. Mangla, of the Department of Library and Information Science University of Delhi, India, spoke about the research capabilities of South Asian librarians with emphasis on Indian academic librarians. He presented the history of librarians and research in India and highlighted the role of late Dr. S. R. Raganathan under whose guidance, the libraries and research made progress in India. He emphasized the role of research activities in the professional development of librarians. Professor Mangla is of the view that the quality of research needs to be improved, more dynamic librarians be hired, and more funds be allocated to academic libraries for research purposes.

Mr. James M. Ng'ang'a, Director of Kenyatta University Library, Nairobi, Kenya, spoke on "Research and Academic Librarians in Africa, with an Emphasis on Kenya." He traced the history of academic institutions and the central role of university libraries in Africa. He said librarians are expected to undertake research due to the nature of their academic appointment. West African librarians are more active in research as compared to East and South. Financial support and encouragement is given to all librarians by universities to undertake research and publish. Still the number of librarians engaged in research is very small and the use of technology in research has been minimal. Some of the reasons for lack of success in research include inadequate staff, poor facilities, lack of resources, and current research material, and not enough funds for the academic librarians.

The last speaker of the session was Mr. Stephen W. Massill, Sub Librarian, University of London, England. He spoke about research in Europe with emphasis on the United Kingdom. He traced the history of academic libraries in Britain. Mr. Massill discussed the qualifications of librarians, the role and function of academic librarians, research in librarianship, the scope of scholarship, and the modern scholar librarian. In his view, research and publishing by academic librarians in Europe is voluminous. Trend in academic librarianship have altered the way in which staff carry out their academic role. He said that scholarly work is respected and honored by faculty but still not well rewarded by employers.

Dr. A.L. Carvaho de Miranda, Director of the Institute Brasileiro De Informaco Em Ciencia E. Tecnologia, Braslia, Brazil was unable to attend the Conference due to unavoidable circumstances.

It was clear from all presentations that academic librarians in other parts of the globe, are still not fully engaged in research due to various reasons including lack of interest, encouragement, funds and rewards like their counterparts in the United States. It was the first time in the history of ACRL that speakers from all continents gathered in the United States to speak on the same topic and on the same stage in one conference.

PROGRAM
SESSIONS

XVI.
PERSONNEL

Librarians and Multiple Roles: Assessing Human Resource Needs

Deborah C. Masters
Caroline C. Long
Deborah K. Bezanson
George Washington University
Washington, DC

Abstract

Desribes the Gelman Library approach to organizing librarians in a new administrative structure independent of a traditional departmental configuration.

Dual and multiple roles for librarians have been a topic of discussion within the American Library Association and the professional literature for a number of years. As a part of a major administrative reorganization at Gelman Library, George Washington University, in spring 1991, we specifically addressed issues relating to the organization of librarians in their multiple roles as subject specialists. Through its explanation of our current organizational structure, this program offered one model of how to organize to support and manage dual or multiple roles.

Previous Organizational Structure

Prior to the 1991 reorganization Gelman Library had a traditional organizational structure. Librarians worked in the various library departments which each had a department head to whom librarians reported. In 1985 the subject specialist role was created and overlaid on the existing organizational structure. Each librarian began working as a subject specialist while keeping his or her traditional role of reference librarian, cataloger, administrator, etc. The subject specialist definition hasn't changed substantially since then, but the way a subject specialist accomplishes his/her duties did change with last year's re-structuring.

At Gelman a librarian, or subject specialist, has multiple roles: (1) functional role—reference desk, cataloging, manuscripts work, acquisitions, administration, etc.; (2) liaison with faculty and students in assigned academic departments—an advocate, a troubleshooter, an information source; (3) collection management for assigned subjects—selection, deselection, storage, preservation decisions; (4) ser-

vice management for clientele in assigned academic departments—for instance, assessing the user education needs of the department or the effectiveness of document delivery service for faculty.

In order to fulfill these four functions, a subject specialist needs to understand all library activities and to think about them in terms of serving his/her academic departments.

Rationale for Changing Old Organizastional Structure

The old organizational structure presented a variety of issues that led Gilman librarians to choose a new type of structure that would better support the multiple roles as subject specialists. These were:

o Reporting structure without a functional focus. Previously, librarians reported to department heads responsible for particular functions and operations such as cataloging, reference or acquisitions. Those department heads had a vested interest in the functions they supervised, and there was an implicit priority for individuals reporting to them. In the new structure, they report to someone without an operational responsibility, and whose primary commitment is to the broader mission of the library as a whole.

o Equity in professional reporting. In the old structure, some librarians reported to a department head supervising a large number of professionals; some to department heads with few professionals but a large number of classified staff members.

There was an uneven opportunity for mentoring and learning the subject specialist role.

o Primary identity: subject specialist role. Instead of having a primary identity with a functional area like cataloging or reference, librarians wanted to see the subject specialist role as their primary identity.

o Criteria for performance. Our criteria for performance appraisal and promotion review include effectiveness in librarianship (subject specialist and functional roles, administrative responsibilities, Gelman Library activities, committees, and continuing education), scholarly or creative productivity and service. Librarians wanted to support full professional development and participation in accordance with these criteria without the potential conflict of interest that could arise from reporting to a functional department head.

o Empower individuals. The intent is to empower subject specialists to create individual profiles reflecting their interests and professional development directions.

o Flexibility in use of human resources. Librarians wanted the ability to respond more dynamically to changing demands.

o Create new approaches. The new structure facilitates questioning old assumptions and ways of doing things.

New Organizational Structure

Under the new organizational structure, librarians are still subject specialists. Each continues to fill multiple roles, performing subject specialist duties, duties within specific functional areas, and, for some, administrative duties. The new organizational structure is best seen in two parts: the administrative structure (Illustration 1) and the subject specialist structure (Illustration 2). The administrative structure looks fairly traditional (Illustration 1). Program coordinators for functional areas such as user education report to Assistant University Librarians (AULS) who report to the University

Librarian. Those professionals not in administrative roles do not report in this structure. All professional staff are subject specialists and fall into the subject

specialist structure. In the subject specialist structure (Illustration 2), there is a Subject Specialist Program Coordinator who works with two additional subject specialist team leaders. Each team leader has a team which consists of five front-line subject specialists. These are the primary team members and they report directly to their team leader. The teams also include 4 secondary members who are the AULS and coordinators. Since the secondary members report in the administrative structure, they do not report directly to their team leader. They are, however, part of the team for communication, training, and other activities.

How well does the new organizational structure meet the goals in our rationale for changing the old structure? The new organization allows all primary team members to report to someone without a specific functional focus. The teams are evenly divided so there is an equity in reporting structure. The team leaders do not have functions which they must run so they have time to devote to the mentoring and developmental aspects of their roles. The reporting structure emphasizes the primacy of the subject specialist role as the identity for professionals within Gelman. The annual performance reviews reinforce this emphasis by making the team leaders responsible for the evaluation of all their primary team members. The team leaders base their evaluation on input from functional coordinators and write their final evaluation based on an overall profile including all elements of the subject specialist role, as well as requirements for scholarly and creative productivity and service.

Planning in the New Organizational Structure

In the new organizational structure, professional time available to the organization is defined as hours in a centralized pool. All functional coordinators submit proposals based on needs and their vision for new or enhanced programs. Administrators work with coordinators and department heads to plan, defining human resource needs which anticipate university directions, integrate the library's strategic plan activities, respond to system changes, etc. Each semester the coordinators and department heads define activities that will require subject specialist time. The AULs approve or reject the activities based on their support of the mission and priorities of the library and the university. These requests are reviewed as a group and compared to total professional hours available in the organization, and adjustments are made as necessary to match hours needed to total time available. Subject specialists work

New Organizational Structure

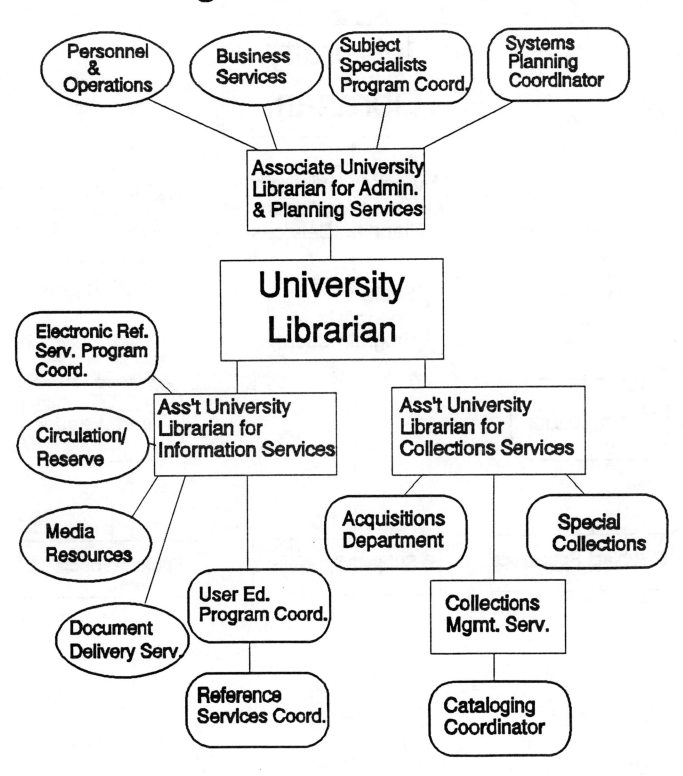

Subject Specialists' Organization

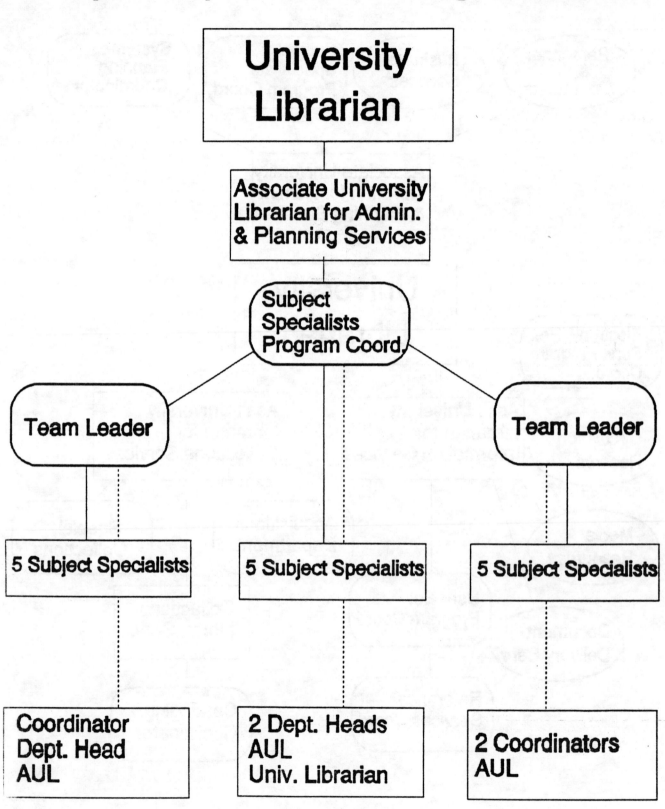

University Librarian

Associate University Librarian for Admin. & Planning Services

Subject Specialists Program Coord.

Team Leader

Team Leader

5 Subject Specialists

5 Subject Specialists

5 Subject Specialists

Coordinator
Dept. Head
AUL

2 Dept. Heads
AUL
Univ. Librarian

2 Coordinators
AUL

with their team leaders to plan how they will spend their time, considering their own interests, expertise and goals for the year. The Subject Specialist Program Coordinator matches the needed hours to the hours offered by subject specialists and initiates negotiations, if necessary. This planning process provides the flexibility to meet changing needs as all the hours available and all the requests for hours are funnelled to a central point. It also provides a mechanism to rearrange individuals' priorities and library priorities when unforeseen circumstances occur in mid-semester. It gives the individual subject specialist the opportunity to create a unique profile of the activities in which he or she participates. The profile negotiation takes place with the senior subject specialists/team leader, not with a department head who would be focused primarily on one functional role.

As with all reorganizations, this one has forced us to examine old assumptions and to explore new avenues since many old avenues no longer exist.

Do Performance Evaluations Help Academic Librarians Achieve Excellence

Mary Reichel, University of Arizona
Rao Aluri, Burr-Brown Corporation Library
Donald E. Riggs, University of Michigan
Carolyn Robison, Georgia State University
Barbara J. Ford, Virginia Commonwealth University

Abstract

A panel discussion on W. Edwards Deming's opinions on performance evaluations and the applicability of Deming's ideas to academic librarianship.

PROGRAM
SESSIONS

XVII.
PRESERVATION

College Libraries Committee, Commission on Preservation and Access—A Progress Report

Kathleen M. Spencer, Franklin and Marshall College, Lancaster, Pennsylvania
Willis E. Bridegam, Amherst College, Amherst, Massachusetts
Joel Clemmer, Macalester College, St. Paul, Minnesota
David Cohen, College of Charleston, Charleston, South Carolina

PROGRAM SESSIONS

XVIII.
PUBLIC SERVICES

Serving Patrons with Disabilities

Katy Lenn
University of Oregon
Eugene, Oregon

Abstract

Covers the practical concerns regarding library services to patrons with disabilities, including legal, architectural, service, and collection development.

PROGRAM
SESSIONS

XIX.
TECHNOLOGY

Electronic Transmission of Order Requests on NOTIS

Pam Cenzer, Carol Walton, and Phek Su
University of Florida
Gainseville, Florida

Abstract

Describes a pilot project at the University of Florida in which collection management staff created bibliographic records in NOTIS. These records were then modified by acquisitions staff to produce purchase orders for vendors.

Total Access to Information: The Impact on Classroom Teaching

Evan Farber
Amy Beth
Sara Penhale
Wil Stratton
Janet Slagter
Earlham College
Richmond, Indiana

and

Timm Thorsen
Alma College,
Alma, Michigan

Anne Caputo
Dialog Information Services, Inc.
Arlington, Virginia

Abstract

Questions have been raised about the impact of information technology on undergraduate education. In a few years all students will have an incredible amount of information instantly at their disposal which presents a new set of problems and possibilities for undergraduate education. Most college faculty and administrators don't understand the power of the new information technology and therefore cannot comprehend this revolution in information or the implications for the classroom teacher. To see what would happen to the teaching/learning process if typical college faculty members did comprehend this revolution, Earlham College persuaded Dialog Information Services to provide its faculty with free online searching for the 1990-92 academic period. With completely free service, access from each office, and a good bit of training, how have faculty members used Dialog in their teaching? Did it make a difference in their classes? What were the resistances, problems, successes and failutes? Some results of the study are presented along with perspectives from two faculty members who participated.

A Chronology of Earlham's Dialog Project: A Joint Project of Dialog Information Services, Inc., Lilly Endowment and Earlham College

February, 1989: Earlham College sponsored a conference attended by college faculty and administrators from across the country called "Teaching and Technology: the Impact of Unlimited Access to Information on Classroom Teaching."(Pierian Press, Ann Arbor, 1991.) It was clear that participants did not understand the full impact of technological developments on access to information or its potential to effect educational change. Earlham librarians speculated that faculty had to use the technology (and use it well) in order to grasp its implications. Earlham's faculty would become the experimental group.

Winter, 1990: Dialog Information Services,Inc. agreed to provide Earlham with an entire year of free and unlimited access to Dialog. Earlham and Dialog would begin a collaborative study of training, usage and potential of an online system in the undergraduate college environment.

Spring, 1990: Anne Caputo, Dialog's manager of academic programs, conducted the first extensive Dialog training of 15 faculty members (purposely varied by age, gender, discipline and number of years teaching).

Fall, 1990: The Fall Faculty Retreat was devoted to Dialog; Roger Summit (then CEO of Dialog), gave the Retreat's main address. Some skepticism was expected, but the faculty greeted the project with great enthusiasm. At the same time the college began providing every faculty member with a computer and modem in each office.

September, 1990: Three open-access Dialog work stations became available to students in Earlham libraries. Reference staff (professionals and student workers) focused on teaching students through hands-on searching. Faculty members, especially those involved in bibliographic instruction, began incorporating the use of Dialog into assignments.

December, 1990: Earlham received a grant from Lilly Endowment's Education Program providing for a detailed analysis of the project's implications for educational change, and to support a full time project administrator.

January, 1991: Training of faculty search skills continued. Three consultants worked with the Earlham library staff to develop questionnaires and methods for the evaluation. Twelve spring semester courses were selected for project focus. Instructors agreed to require use of Dialog for specific assignments and students agreed to have their Dialog use tracked.

Spring, 1991: Faculty and department interviews conducted. Other data continued to be collected. Many faculty appealed for an extension of the project, wanting to use the summer as an opportunity to become more expert with Dialog and to integrate it more creatively into their course work.

Summer, 1991: Dialog and Lilly Endowment both agreed to extend the study for an additional academic year. Several faculty members agreed to write articles relating the impact of Dialog on their teaching. Data and survey results were transferred into machine-readable format. Initial analysis was conducted.

Fall, 1991: Earlham College received a major gift from an alumnus, the income from which is to be used for maintaining and supporting faculty and student use of electronic information systems for the advancement of research and teaching.

Winter, 1992: Librarians, faculty and students began discussions of use of Dialog after project's conclusion: how to limit use yet encourage innovation in teaching and learning. Recommendations were submitted to Dialog for pricing and policies more appropriate for teaching faculty.

The Research Component

Data was collected via : (1) formal survey of the faculty; (2) user invoices from Dialog detailing specific Dialog use; (3) case studies of classes employing Dialog; and (4) interviews of users. Ninety-two surveys were distributed, and of the 88 who returned surveys, 61 had actively participated in the Dialog study. Some of the reasons for not using dialog were Sabbatical, part-time instructors, no office or no Dialog hook-up, and choice. The survey contained 80 items including background information of users, self-estimates of skill and use, areas of difficulty in using Dialog, what users did when they encountered problems, and reasons why Dialog was not used . Results of the survey and the

additional Dialog account data were coded on an Excel spreadsheet, and then viewed from a perspective of Exploratory Data Analysis via a statistics program named Stata. Information from spreadsheets was further viewed to discover relationships among variables via a program named Knowledge Seeker. This program combines artificial intelligence and statistics to discover meaningful relationships normally found only through significant effort and time, and would otherwise be inaccessible to non-statisticians.

Select Findings

During the period of August 1990 to July 1991, the Earlham Dialog study showed that 80% of the faculty used Dialog (used as defined as 3 or more log-ons). Users logged-on to Dialog an average of 31 times, and they "explored" or "investigated" an average of 23 databases. The average total connect-time during the year studied was 8 hours. Averages, however useful for initial description, hide information. Log-ons are not distributed normally, rather, they are much closer to the so-called 80/20 distribution. The 80/20 Rule says that one will get 80% of the results from 20% of the people and that these users will prosper. 80% of the "problems" will come from 20% of the people, and these users will not necessarily produce important results. This leaves 60% somewhere in the middle who have a significant opportunity to be influenced and can increase results. This 80/20 Rule cautions us to be open to the possibility of growth and development with Dialog being a powerful force for faculty development in particular, and thus, a powerful influence on teaching and learning. The humanities and social sciences used Dialog as much as the natural sciences in contrast to our initial hypothesis that the natural sciences would be the heaviest users. This finding cautions us against policies that assume the natural sciences as the heaviest users and sets up a "self-fulfilling prophecy." It is also an important reminder that Dialog may be a significant opportunity in areas that might, at first glance, be overlooked.

Dialog use at Earlham invoved three broad, interrelated areas—teaching, research, and personal interest. The study demonstrated that "personal interest" was a strong factor in promoting Dialog use, comfort, and competence. Policies that narrowly define Dialog use and thus exclude "personal interest use" ironically inhibit successfully employing Dialog. Also, the ability to "browse" and perhaps find serendipidious results is an important factor promoting Dialog use, comfort, and competence. Institutions need to provide adequate support (logistics, time, resources) if Dialog is contribute to mission.

The number of instruction sessions needed to become comfortable with Dialog varied. Faculty in the "middle range" (6-7 years of teaching experience) were the heaviest Dialog users as a group and were the most likely to become comfortable searching in one session. The "low range" (1-5 years teaching experience) split between being comfortable in one session and "still not comfortable" after five sessions. The "high range" (18-43 years teaching experience) was most likely to take more than five sessions to be comfortable. These findings are useful in designing the kinds of instructional sessions that are most appropriate for the user.

Other related findings showed that women used Dialog as much as men despite factors that would discourage women's Dialog use, for example, less time in college teaching and less computing experience. Few faculty reported finding "unexpected databases" for teaching or research, which may point to an opportunity for librarians to help identify new bibliographic tools and materials, especially for interdisciplinary sources or introductory courses. Finally, there is an indication of change in teaching styles among those who became very comfortable with Dialog.

Wil Stratton (Chemistry Professor)

DIALOG has many applications in the planning and teaching of courses in the natural sciences. It gives access to new paths to information and brings the information explosion down to a manageable level. It makes access to information convenient through modems both at home and in the office. It has been used in the design and teaching of a new course which was developed as an introductory chemistry course for non-chemistry/non-science majors. The course was targeted at students who probably dislike science. The course first showed applications, and then science—an unusual non-linear progression. Societal issues were presented, followed by chemical concepts on a "need-to-know" basis. The six assignments were developed specifically with Dialog use in mind. The general goal was to have students find scientific issues and be able to read intelligently. Sample assignments were: Find out about air pollution issues in your (the student's) home city or state; Working with newspapers and wire services—find out about water pollution in a chosen country; Find the latest information about ozone layer

& ozone hole; etc. The use of DIALOG by the faculty resulted in an interesting variety of case studies to be included in the course. The cooperation of the faculty with the librarians gave the students the help they needed in different aspects of the search they were conducting. The students were asked to utilize a number of databases simultaneously in order to look into the issues at hand. We spent time browsing through various databases and came across new information or even new databases that we had not intended to study in the beginning. In some cases where the students had no prior experience in using the vast amount of information accessible through DIALOG, they had problems selecting the right kind of information. Through experience, they were able to select from among databases as well as information.

Jan Slagter (Philosophy Professor)

There is an interesting coincidence in the development of on-line services and the rise in multi-cultural or cross-disciplinary courses and programs and especially new inter-disciplinary programs like critical studies and cultural studies. Writers who write in these fields, and journals that publish writers in these fields, are not widely indexed (e. g., *Differences, Genders, Lesbian Ethics*). The fullness and solidity and the gaps lead to musing and teaching about the process of the production and legitimation of marginalizing or exclusionary practices in academia (*Alternative Press Index, Women's Studies Abstracts*) are some excluded indexes. There are, however, some usef incidences.

For the develpment of a course on the psychology of racism, an anthropologist colleague worked on the concept of authenticity. She compared how this term is used by philosophers, by psychologists, by people in the literary and art worlds. Dialog was used in order to distinguish what she wanted to do from what other people were doing. An anthropology course focusing on Native American peoples made use of Dialog for reading direct quotations of people involved in struggles by accessing regional newspapers, as opposed to merely having to count on summaries from third hand sources like *The Washington Post*. Students found the timely and diverse representation of the regional reporting more credible and drawing than the larger media.

This class would have been tremendously hampered without access to Dialog. The use of Dialog has both encouraged and enabled cooperative learning among those seeking answers to similar questions. It allows many people to share the burden of finding the truth in a certain discipline or even across disciplines. Students and faculty should enjoy what Dialog has provided us with, use it to venture into uncharted territories that we have been kept out of, but we should not be deluded into thinking it is a source to identify all that is important about a topic or everything that has been published on a topic. We should shy away from abandoning print altogether.

The Impact of New Electronic Resources on the Ecology of the Library: Funds, Collections, Service and Staff

Four speakers addressed the title topic. —Editor

Abstract

Examines expectations of users and funding sources for electronic resources, plus the impact of electronic resrouces on library collections, services, staffing patterns, and budgets.

The Changing Ecology of Libraries

Salvatore Meringolo
Pennsylvania State University
University Park, Pennsylvania

Standalone and networked information technologies are today powerful agents for change in the library profession. The profession's success is dependent upon the ability to evolve from where the profession was a decade ago—to where it will be a decade from now—while still preserving and enhancing the professional mission, culture, and ethics. Thus—since this paper is dealing with evolution rather than revolution—the science of ecology was chosen as a metaphor to help illustrate the rather dramatic changes that the profession faces.

Ecology is the study of the structure and function of ecosystems, dealing mainly with the interaction of organisms with one another and with their non-living setting. An ecosystem is a self-regulating community of plants and animals interacting with one another and with their nonliving environment.

There are four fundamental components of all ecosystems:

—producers or foodmakers
—consumers or eaters of plants or animals
—decomposers—a special class of consumers that get food and energy from decaying plants and animals
—nonliving components that have both physical

features such as wind, terrain, and temperature; and chemical features such as water, gases, and minerals.

The defining characteristic of an ecosystem is its balance and each of its components play a vital role in maintaining this balance. Significant changes can occur and do occur when some set of circumstances upsets the natural balance. These changes reverberate through the system until a new balance is struck.

And without a great stretch of the imagination, one can describe libraries in terms of ecosystems. Libraries are essentially the same organization they were 100 years ago. The entire rationale for their existence has been based upon the notion of the ownership of a physical artifact—an artifact containing information largely in the form of the printed book. The preponderance of what is done by the organization has dealt with acquiring, cataloging, lending, and interpreting collections of physical artifacts for users.

The four components of the library's ecosystem might be described as follows:

—The producers are those individuals who organize their thoughts and convert them into literary manuscript, journalistic writing, or scholarly discourse.
—Consumers could be classified into three distinct groups:

1. Primary consumers are the publishers who acquire the output of the producers

483

then package and distribute the product;

2. Secondary consumers are libraries, wholesalers and retailers who purchase the publishers output;

3. Tertiary consumers are library users and the retail marketplace.

—Decomposers in the library's ecosystem can take many forms. For example, many types of scientific and technical information have a limited shelf life— it in a sense decomposes as it helps stimulate new ideas for another generation of producers.

—The nonliving elements in the library's ecosystem include the physical environment, the facilities and the collections themselves.

From the perspective of balance, the library's ecosystem has been remarkably stable over the past one hundred years of "modern day librarianship." Since the acquisition of the physical artifact has been central to the balance in the library's ecosystem, the introduction of electronic information formats has begun to destabilize and redefine each of the components of the library's ecosystem.

Information producers are discovering new methods to communicate ideas and promote scholarly discourse. While electronic scholarly discourse is still in its infancy, a number of professional groups have begun to recognize its potential to radically alter the process of scholarly communication itself. Could the dominance of the journal as a principal means of disseminating new ideas be coming to an end?

If producers begin to discover a new means of scholarly communication, then what becomes of the roles of the three consumer groups. Libraries will need to be busy redefining their roles as information intermediaries.

The decomposers in the electronic environment will expand to include such items as obsolete hardware; system crashes and data loss threats.

The nonliving components are no longer just stacks of books and the buildings designed to house them, but now consist of terminals; servers; desktop, mini, and mainframe computers; networks; and the space needed to provide electronic services.

It is the author's opinion that the changes leading to

the growth in electronically formatted information will necessitate a fundamental change to the way that libraries are organized and the profession is practiced. And this is precisely because all of the components of the library ecosystem—producers, consumers, decomposers, and nonliving elements—have been influenced and changed.

Just as the virtual library describes that amorphous network that extends information resouces to users at home or office—the virtual library organization must consider the challenge of bringing service to a user population that may no longer be active visitors of the library facility itself. This will be a key challenge in the years that lie immediately ahead of us.

User Expectations

Joan L. Clark and Donald Tipka
Cleveland Public Library
Cleveland, Ohio

Electronic access has broadened the kinds of users libraries serve. Traditional users have been augmented by "invisible" dial-up users such as students and faculty from other institutions, "techies," business professionals, and the general public including international users. Each user approaches electronic resources with set expectations. Nonusers such as vendors, administrators, and funding bodies also have the power to meet and shape these users' expectations. Political pressures can also impact on the library's ability to meet user expectations.

The electronic link lets the outside world into the library, and that outside world has the expectations of responsiveness and input. To ascertain user expectations, the following methods can be used: direct questioning, surveys, transaction logs, and market studies.

User expectations are many and varied. There are still some users who distrust the electronic format, some who are "tired of technology," and many who do not use these resources to their full capacity. Users approach electronic resources as a "Universe in a Box," and expect to find completeness in the databases provided on a single terminal. They have poor perceptions of the scope, currency, and accuracy of online sources. They expect free use of databases as well as enough hardware to access and even manipulate information. Users have no perception of the difference between database content and access software. They expect uniform search protocols for diverse sources and are impatient with help screens. No longer satisfied with bibliographic citations, users expect full text of those citations online in the same database.

To meet and shape user expectations the following issues must be addressed: institutional roles and goals and who will be served and how. The following methods can be used to meet and shape user expectations: bibliographic instruction, online tutorials, common gateways, feedback to vendors, participation in users' groups, serving as a test site, and public relations and interaction with colleagues.

Sometimes the process of moving ahead is painful, and it is always a risk, but risks are necessary for innovation. Networking with other libraries can help reduce the risks. Decisions should be grounded in collection development policies and in the library's mission as well as in user expectations.

Quality Services in the New Ecology

Kathleen Gunning
University of Houston
Houston, Texas

Librarians must build new electronic services from disparate components. Librarians provide good service today, plan the next electronic service, and visualize future service configurations. Current efforts should build efficiently toward this goal. The change process is incremental, yet new services produce a cumulative impact. Libraries should prepare a strategic plan encompassing these services.

Librarians can create electronic tools for users, providing basic information about collections and services. Some libraries are developing expert systems designed so that the program's structure and knowledge base are separate. Then they can be used at different libraries. Sharing development projects is important in meeting users' expectations.

As electronic services expand, librarians can:

1) Support efforts to make databases easier to use.

Promising developments include work by database vendors to separate the user interface from the search engine. Libraries can select one interface for multiple databases. Encourage database producers to include and enhance on-line help screens that are sensitive to the search context. Carefully designed online assistance is especially important for remote users.

2) Design convenient instructional programs.

Hands-on computer training is effective for teaching online skills.

Frequently-available, brief classes provide flexibility for users. If networked workstations are in heavy demand, design a space serving alternatively as classroom and user workstations.

3) Explore new reference service configurations. Reference services have been organized by subjects, formats, and user groups in centralized or dispersed arrangements. Every configuration has required proximity to the print reference collection. With multipurpose workstations logical connections will be more important than location. Libraries could have many, few, or even no reference desks. Arrangements for in-person assistance might include: one centralized desk, several service points near workstation clusters offering standardized or specialized services, staff located in academic departments, or service combinations such as basic assistance at service desks and consultations in library or departmental offices. Electronic assistance could be provided via E-mail messages, or on-line assistance using software which enables users at networked workstations to request help. Electronic assistance will help remote users but will also be labor-intensive and require significant staff training.

Selection of electronic databases involves new format choices which relate to use levels. Questions include: How many years of an database to offer in electronic form? Current years of many indexes or more years of fewer indexes? Maintain the print subscription? Selection of interface? Is the interface used with other databases owned by the library, or will new staff training be necessary? Libraries need electronic collection guidelines to clarify the basis for these choices and provide consistency in decision-making.

Systems staff participate in collection decisions such as licensing agreements. Will the database software and the library's hardware provide acceptable response time? Is the operating software installed on a network server, or on individual microcomputers?

INTERNET resources raise additional issues. How

will libraries learn what is available? There are partial listings but no complete index. How do libraries initially connect to databases then set up simple connections for users? How will librarians learn to use new databases?

Libraries traditionally exchanged information regarding collection strengths and developed resource-sharing agreements. Librarians will need comparable information-sharing support for INTERNET resources. Other libraries could replicate support for resources important to their users. For assistance with seldom used INTERNET resources, librarians could refer users to another institution.

Electronic information reshapes the ways people create and obtain information. User expectations challenge the profession's creativity and financial resources. Librarians need to experiment, to participate in shaping the electronic environment. In the new ecology, the profession still faces the core issues of providing services which facilitate and enhance access to information.

IRIS: The Intelligent Reference Information System—Evaluation and Service Impacts of a CD-ROM Network and Expert System

Kathleen Gunning and Kimberly Spyers-Duran
University of Houston
Houston, Texas

Abstract

Key results of the IRIS Research Project and its effects on service provide important information for the ongoing development of end-user computer systems.

The IRIS Project (1989-1991), was partially funded by a $99,852 Research and Demonstration grant from the U.S. Department of Education's College Library and Cooperation Grants Program. IRIS accomplished the goals of: 1) designing and installing a ten-workstation CD-ROM LAN; and 2) designing and developing an expert system called Reference Expert

Between October 1989 and August 1990, project staff implemented the local area network in the Electronic Publication Center [EPC]. This is a service area where all of the CD-ROMs are located along with a service desk. There are eight workstations for public use; one at the reference desk; and another in the systems area, for network administration.

Reference Expert is an easy to use, menu-driven system, containing over 300 reference sources (encyclopedias, statistical sources, dictionaries, and CD-ROM databases). Reference Expert was developed for persons who require assistance when the reference desk is closed, or prefer the assistance of a computer to a reference librarian. It was designed so that the knowledge base was separate from the program, meaning that non-programmer library staff can easily modify or update the knowledge base.

Project staff identified three characteristics to describe a reference resource: 1) content type (e.g. Biographical sources), 2) format (e.g. CD-ROM or printed sources), and 3) subject (e.g. Business, Sciences). In addition the various kinds of information contained in a reference source were described and identified, rather than describing a reference source by type, (e.g. a handbook). This decision provided greater flexibility and precision in identifying the specific kind of information needed.

Reference Expert was made available to users in June 1991, on both networked and stand-alone workstations, and on a dedicated workstation. Reference Expert is available to libraries at no charge.

The three research projects which evaluated IRIS were: 1) response Time Tests of the CD-ROM LAN, 2) user perceptions survey of the CD-ROM LAN and 3) user perceptions survey of Reference Expert. These projects were designed and conducted by the IRIS Research and Evaluation Group .

The response time tests had two components. The first component measured the effects of an increasing number of users on the CD-ROM network, all searching the same database simultaneously. The second component compared the retrieval speed of a networked workstation to a stand-alone workstation. The University's Measurement and Evaluation Office assisted with the design and data analysis for these projects.

To measure response times, four databases were chosen from a variety of vendors based on their searching capabilities and subject matter. Sets of two terms from each database were selected for each workstation, which were used to test the response times to execute the Boolean "AND" command. Two-member teams were assigned to each workstation. On command, inputter(s) pressed the enter key; simultaneously the other member(s) began clocking the search. When the combined postings appeared on the screen, the timer(s) stopped clocking the search. Tests were conducted with 1, 3, 5, 7, and 9 network users. In addition, sets of terms searched on one network workstation were replicated on one stand-alone workstation.

Response times increased for all four CD-ROM databases as the number of network users increased. In addition, the response time was higher for one network workstation than for one stand-alone workstation.

These results indicated that increasing the number of simultaneous users on a network significantly degraded performance. The project team recommends that managers consider this factor when planning CD-ROM networks.

The second research project developed, administered, and analyzed a CD-ROM service questionnaire. This questionnaire focused on user perceptions of: 1) selection of and access to heterogeneous CD-ROM databases; 2) networked delivery of CD-ROM information; and 3) use of the electronic information itself.

A total of 318 usable questionnaires were analyzed. User responses to CD-ROM databases were positive. Almost 90% of users agreed that it was easy to select CD-ROM databases for their research. A wide variety of methods were used to select databases; the most popular being faculty referrals and consultation with library staff. A majority felt that the network menu was helpful in selecting databases.

Most users who had searched databases both on networked and stand-alone workstations reported that it was easier to search more than one database on a networked computer. Sixty percent reported that it was less convenient to check out CD-ROM disks than to select from a menu, but, interestingly, almost 40% disagreed.

A majority felt that CD-ROM databases were easier to use than printed indexes. Most respondents found information faster when using CD-ROM databases. Users also preferred having a similar command structure across the various CD-ROM databases. These results show that networked delivery of information is perceived by users to be an effective means of providing access to CD-ROM databases.

The third research project developed, administered, and analyzed a Reference Expert questionnaire, which focused on user perceptions of the benefits and issues associated with the expert system. To assess the effectiveness of Reference Expert's recommendations,

users were asked to identify the types of sources recommended by the system; to indicate whether they were previously familiar with these sources; and to evaluate the applicability of these sources. Analysis of the 84 usable questionnaires indicated that users believed that Reference Expert was a valuable service, providing another method of identifying appropriate reference sources. Users reported on methods of selecting CD-ROM databases and printed reference sources before and after the availability of Reference Expert.

Use of Reference Expert was chosen more frequently than any other method to select CD-ROM databases and printed sources. Approximately three-quarters of respondents agreed that they would use Reference Expert for research in the library. Respondents liked Reference Expert because it was helpful in selecting CD-ROM databases and printed reference sources; it was easy to use; and it was available whenever the library was open. Responses indicate that expert systems can provide another effective means of assisting library users.

The CD-ROM network and Reference Expert had many effects on library services. Users schedule half-hour appointments for CD-ROM databases. Staffing at the CD-ROM desk tripled between 1989 and 1992. Staffing at the reference desk also increased.

Staff created Quick Reference Cards for each database, which summarize methods for searching, printing and downloading. Samples are available through LOEX. Staff also designed EPC binders containing Quick Reference Cards, instructions for complex searches, and lists of indexed journals. New CD-ROM disks are reviewed for software changes which effect staff training, instruction, and software installation. Staff give many CD-ROM demonstrations. Faculty have developed assignments which use CD-ROM databases. Frequently librarians help prepare these assignments to cope with changes in software and database content. Service is affected when classes complete assignments using the eight network workstations.

Staff who developed Reference Expert continue to enhance the software. Reference staff update the knowledge base including routine changes plus overall review of content.

Electronic services raise management questions.

Should CD-ROM service be within the reference department or separate? How should end-user services be coordinated with the library instruction program? With end-user searching, instruction must be closely linked to electronic services. How should technical support for electronic services be structured? Can the organization afford a technical support unit within public services? Responsibility for network operation may be shared between public services and systems staff.

In January 1992 staff began planning for the following expansion:

I) Expand CD-ROM network

The library will add approximately nineteen workstations, including ones at the CD-ROM desk, the Information Services Office, and library classroom, plus others for users. To create room for workstations, staff are reducing the reference collection. The expansion also involves issues of wiring, furniture selection and layout.

II) Add network servers

The network has two servers that can each accommodate fourteen CD-ROM disks apiece. The library will purchase three servers which can hold twenty-eight disks. Total disk capacity on the network will reach one hundred twelve, a four hundred percent increase.

III) Add CD-ROM subscriptions

Significant factors are: A) Cost; B) Subject coverage; C) User interface. Some databases are available with varying interfaces. Design features of the searching software are very important; D) Available formats: print, stand-alone CD-ROM disks, networked CD-ROM disks, and locally-mounted databases through commercial end-user services; and E) Level of use. The CD-ROM LAN benchmark performance tests showed that response time increases as the number of simultaneous users increases.

Most databases have license agreements structuring costs by maximum simultaneous users. The Library can add workstations without renegotiating licenses. However, the licensed maximum will be smaller than the number of workstations. A user would be prevented from accessing a database when the limit is reached. Increasing licensing limits means a tradeoff between access to more people and slow response times.

Preventing specific workstations from accessing certain databases would contain licensing costs and alleviate response time problems. However, users would have to designate databases before assignment to a workstation. Scheduling could become very complex and segmenting database access could prevent maximum use of network workstations.

Libraries can purchase additional subscriptions for popular databases. This strategy addresses response time and access problems but adds subscription and network server costs.

CD-ROM network expansion is costly. Libraries must decide which subscriptions and how many disks of each to add. The IRIS project offered many different types of databases rather than extensive access to heavily used databases. After the research project, more frequently used databases were placed on the network, including back file disks. Additional network servers provide more flexibility in adding backfiles and new databases.

IV) Add end-user services and electronic journals

Staff will select one service to obtain initial experience, then add others and electronic journals. After this expansion, the EPC desk will be staffed all library hours.

The Library is also acquiring a new integrated library system. There will be a transition from single-purpose to multiple purpose workstations. The new online catalog, a Houston-area CD-ROM union catalog, CD-ROM databases, end-user services and electronic journals will be available from one workstation.

With many multifunctional workstations scheduling can be reduced or eliminated.

As the number of workstations increases proximity to a service desk may no longer be crucial. Staff are investigating software programs which enable users at workstations to receive online assistance from staff in other locations.

With multi-purpose workstations, will there be a functional distinction between the reference desk and

489

the EPC desk? Or will they increasingly provide the same service? Public services managers and staff need to reexamine the most effective ways to provide service in this emerging situation.

With the success of the IRIS Project the public service staff looks forward to the continued expansion of end-user computer systems.

PROGRAM
SESSIONS

XX.
OTHER

Friends Groups in Academic Libraries: Excellence through Diversity

Charlene Clark, Texas A&M, College Station, Texas
Ray English, Oberlin Collge, Oberlin, Ohio

Abstract

Through two case studies and breakout discussion sessions the program will compare successful academic library friends groups and their activities.

Creating a Diverse Workforce: Issues and Concerns

Carla Stoffle, University of Arizona, Tucson, Arizonia
Sharon Hogan, University of Illinois at Chicago, Chicago, Illinois
Detrice Bankhead, University of California, Santa Barbara, California

Strategic Visions for Librarianship: An Open Forum

Don Bosseau, San Diego State University, San Diego, California
Richard Dougherty, University of Michigan, East Lansing, Michigan

Abstract

A forum to discuss the draft Vision Statement and Values document by the Strategic Visions Steering Committee.

Subject Index